MORE PRAISE FOR WESTERN WIND

"This is a unique and marvelous book—there really is nothing else remotely like it."

Burt Kimmelman, New Jersey Institute of Technology

"This is the only anthology I have ever used with enthusiasm. Using it is like having an older and wiser colleague as a teaching partner, a colleague who invites argument and not just agreement."

Walter L. Reed, Emory University

"[*Western Wind*] introduces students to the material at a very sophisticated level, while being clear and entertaining. Students read it, learn from it, respect it, and do not feel condescended to by it."

Andrew Hudgins, Ohio State University

"*Western Wind* is a sophisticated yet accessible introductory text for use in a genre class; probably the best introduction to sound and rhythm I have found. It offers a balanced offering of classic and contemporary, popular and obscure, male and female poets."

Suzanne M. Forster, University of Alaska, Anchorage

"*Western Wind* is an exemplary book, fresh, informative, illuminating. Many introductory texts serve well enough in the classroom, but they hardly strive to become part of the student's library. For the discerning student, however, Mason and Nims's book is a keeper."

James Fowler, University of Central Arkansas

"*Western Wind* is quite simply the best introductory poetry text around. It prepares students for the experiential and technical challenges of reading poems, but more importantly, it also places poetry in the larger context of what it means to be human, and what it means to live in our natural universe. It is the only poetry text I know that not only defines poetic devices and explains how they work, but proceeds to explore the significance of those devices in poems and in our lives."

Jay Rogoff, Skidmore College

"*Western Wind* is simply the best introductory poetry text on the market. I have used it for over twenty years. . . . It is truly a poet's book about poetry, so much so that I have also used it in introductory creative writing classes. It is especially good on the auditory dimension of poetry—perhaps the most difficult aspect of the art to teach—but it's superb on everything, revealing the whole scope of the craft with clarity and simplicity without in any way diminishing it."

B. H. Fairchild, California State University, San Bernardino

"*Western Wind* is as much a love song to poetry as a textbook. It engages both heart and mind. All of us who care about introducing poetry to students in a truly effective way owe a great deal to Nims and Mason."

Jim Moore

"Still exceptionally well organized, still honoring a refreshing diversity of sensibilities, styles, and prosodies, the fifth incarnation of *Western Wind* is a great deal more than a practical introductory teaching tool—it's also an engaging, readable poetry anthology of the highest caliber."

Marilyn Taylor, University of Wisconsin, Milwaukee

"The new *Western Wind* builds on the considerable strengths of the earlier editions. Highly versatile, this is an equally useful text for courses both in literature and in creative writing. The commentary is questing and provocative, and the anthology selections are wide-ranging and unhackneyed. Attentive readers should find their knowledge of poetry deepened and their taste for it enhanced."

Robert B. Shaw, Mount Holyoke College

"*Western Wind* is the classic introduction to the art of poetry, and an indispensable resource for the practicing poet and teacher."

Daniel Tobin, Emerson College

"*Western Wind* always reminds me of how clear, accessible, and engaging the explanation of poetic rhythm can be."

Thomas Cable, University of Texas at Austin

"This new edition of *Western Wind* solidifies its position as one of the best textbooks for introductory poetry. This anthology always had amazing breadth of selection, but the material by David Mason adds both depth and usefulness in creative ways. Still the volume's strength shines through everywhere; this is a book about poetry by members of the craft."

David Roessel, The Richard Stockton College of New Jersey

"*Western Wind* offers a solid foundation in poetry, clear and vital discussions, and provides an exciting and extensive range of classic and contemporary voices."

Diane Thiel, poet, University of New Mexico

"*Western Wind* is an essential poetry anthology that provides students with an interesting mixture of representative historical models, and equally important contemporary verse."

Michael Peich, West Chester University

Western Wind

An Introduction to Poetry

FIFTH EDITION

David Mason
THE COLORADO COLLEGE

John Frederick Nims

Boston   Burr Ridge, IL   Dubuque, IA   Madison, WI   New York
San Francisco   St. Louis   Bangkok   Bogotá   Caracas   Kuala Lumpur
Lisbon   London   Madrid   Mexico City   Milan   Montreal   New Delhi
Santiago   Seoul   Singapore   Sydney   Taipei   Toronto

Higher Education

Published by McGraw-Hill, an imprint of The McGraw-Hill Companies, Inc., 1221 Avenue of the Americas, New York, NY 10020. Copyright © 2006 by David Mason and the Estate of John Frederick Nims. Copyright © 2000, 1992, 1983, 1974 by the McGraw-Hill Companies. All rights reserved. No part of this publication my be reproduced or distributed in any form or by any means, or stored in a database or retrieval system, without the prior written consent of The McGraw-Hill Companies, Inc., including, but not limited to, in any network or other electronic storage or transmission, or broadcast for distance learning.

This book is printed on acid-free paper.

6 7 8 9 0 QFR/QFR 0

ISBN-13: 978-0-07-281959-5
ISBN-10: 0-07-281959-6

Editor in Chief: Emily Barrosse	Interior and Cover Designer: Barbara Jellow
Publisher and Sponsoring Editor: Lisa Moore	Art Editor: Ayelet Arbel
Marketing Manager: Lori DeShazo	Photo Research: Brian J. Peckol
Editorial Coordinator: Betty Chen	Production Supervisor: Tandra Jorgensen
Permissions Editor: Marty Granahan	Media Project Manager: Marc Mattson
Production Editor: Leslie LaDow	Composition: 10/12 Plantin Light by Carlisle Communications, Ltd
Manuscript Editor: Jan Fehler	Printing: 45# New Era Matte by Quebecor, Fairfield
Design Manager: Cassandra Chu	

Cover image: © Alinari/Art Resource, NY

Credits: The credits section for this book begins on page 616 and is considered an extension of the copyright page.

Library of Congress Cataloging-in-Publication Data

Mason, David, 1954–
    Western wind : an introduction to poetry / David Mason, John Frederick Nims.—5th ed.
      p. cm.
    Includes bibliographical references and index.
    ISBN 0–072819596 (alk. paper)
    1. Poetics. 2. Poetry—Collections. I. Nims, Frederick, 1913. II. Title
PN1042.N6 2005
808.1 0151dc22

                                         2004061090

The Internet addresses listed in the text were accurate at the time of publication. The inclusion of a Web site does not indicate an endorsement by the authors or McGraw-Hill, and McGraw-Hill does not guarantee the accuracy of the information presented at these sites.

www.mhhe.com

ABOUT THE AUTHORS

David Mason grew up in Bellingham, Washington, and has lived in Colorado, Alaska, New York, Pennsylvania, and Greece. From 1989 to 1998 he taught at Moorhead State University in Minnesota; he has since joined the faculty of his alma mater, Colorado College. He received his doctorate from the University of Rochester. Mason's books of poems include *The Buried Houses* (co-winner of the Nicholas Roerich Poetry Prize), *The Country I Remember* (winner of the Poetry Society of America's Alice Fay Di Castagnola Award), and *Arrivals*, all from Story Line Press. Chapbooks include *Small Elegies, Land Without Grief*, and *The Collector's Tale*. With Mark Jarman he co-edited *Rebel Angels: 25 Poets of the New Formalism*, and he also co-edited two anthologies for McGraw-Hill with Dana Gioia and Meg Schoerke, *Twentieth Century American Poetry* and *Twentieth Century American Poetics: Poets on the Art of Poetry*. His collection of literary essays, *The Poetry of Life and the Life of Poetry*, appeared in 2000. An advisory editor at both *The Hudson Review* and *The Sewanee Review*, Mason was a Fulbright Fellow to Greece in 1997. He is married to Anne Lennox, a photographer, and lives in the mountains outside Colorado Springs.

Born in Muskegon, Michigan, John Frederick Nims received his M.A. from the University of Notre Dame and his Ph.D. in comparative literature from the University of Chicago. He has taught poetry and given workshops in poetry at Notre Dame, the University of Toronto, the University of Illinois at Urbana, Harvard University, Williams College, the University of Florida, and the University of Illinois at Chicago. He has also been a visiting professor at the universities of Florence and Madrid and has been on the staff of many writers' conferences, including the one at Bread Loaf, Vermont, where he taught for more than ten years. He is the author of eight books of poetry, among them *The Iron Pastoral, Knowledge of the Evening* (a National Book Award nominee), *The Kiss: A Jambalaya, Zany in Denim*, and *The Six-Cornered Snowflake*—books that have brought him awards from The National Foundation of Arts and Humanities, The American Academy of Arts and

Letters, and Brandeis University, which awarded him its Creative Arts Citation in Poetry. He has been the Phi Beta Kappa poet at the College of William and Mary and at Harvard University. He has also published several books of translations, including *Sappho to Valéry: Poems in Translation*, *The Poems of St. John of the Cross*, and *The Complete Poems of Michelangelo*, and edited *The Harper Anthology of Poetry*. Several times on the staff of *Poetry* (Chicago), he was its editor from 1978 to 1984. In 1982, he was awarded the Fellowship of the Academy of American Poets; in 1986, a Guggenheim Fellowship for poetry; and in 1991, the Aiken Taylor Award for Modern American Poetry. He died in 1999.

CONTENTS

APPENDIXES

PREFACE

This fifth edition of *Western Wind* is the first to be done without the book's original author, John Frederick Nims, who died just as we were completing work on the fourth. It was John's freshness and erudition, his playful but rigorous spirit, which made *Western Wind* a leading textbook of its kind. John was a wonderful poet, essayist, and translator as well as a brilliant editor; in this edition, I have added one of his better-known poems, and as before, all the unattributed translations were done by him. My task in this revision has been to make significant additions and clarifications without betraying John's vision. I have composed a new chapter on "Free Verse," subtracted a few poems, and added many new ones—though as usual I regret having had to leave out a number of favorites for reasons of space. I have broadened the two earlier appendixes on "Poetics" and "Writing About Poetry," and compiled a third on "Literary Criticism." These can be found in the back of the book, after the expanded and updated Anthology. Complete poems in the book are now given dates—usually those of their first book publication. In the case of some figures like Emily Dickinson (whose work did not appear in a reliable edition until 1955), I have also given the probable date of composition in square brackets. Every effort has been made to simplify the reader's navigation of the book. The Index of Poetic Terms, for example, can now be found just inside the back cover for easy reference.

The original structure of *Western Wind*, which is based on human nature and the ways of the world we live in, has been retained. The book begins, as our lives do, with sense impressions and the emotions they arouse. It then proceeds to the words with which the poet, like the rest of us, expresses such images and emotions. It goes on to consider the qualities of these words as poets use them: their sounds as well as their meanings, the rhythms they assume, the forms, traditional or "free," in which they find expression.

Individual instructors will have their own "passionate preferences," as Frost called them, about how to approach poetry. Some may prefer to take up the aspects of poetry in an order different from that of the text. That order, like most things human, is flexible: Teachers may move about in it as they choose, dwelling longer on one section, dealing more briefly with another. The flexibility of this design allows for the differences one finds in the aptitudes and interests of individual classes and individual students, and on the length of time available for their approach to poetry.

The exercises are designed not so much to test a student's knowledge as to lure that student into thinking creatively. As many or as few may be used as will suit the levels and interests of the class. Questions more elementary and more general than those given will suggest themselves to instructors, who will have their own favorite ways of formulating basic exercises in such processes as paraphrasing, scanning, analyzing, and comparing poems. For this new edition, I have increased the number of essay and poetry assignments at the end of each chapter to make the book more useful for teachers of both literature and creative writing.

Year after year, wherever writers gather, no piece of advice is heard more often than "Show; don't tell!" Good writers *show* us a world. In critical writing and teaching, this advice also applies. It is more important to show students examples of imagery than to discuss its nature, more important to let them taste ten tangy metaphors than to spoon-feed them the cold gruel of definition. *Western Wind* is richer in examples, many of them contemporary, than other introductions to poetry known to the authors. This feature has been retained, with the addition of many examples new in this edition.

I am grateful first of all to John, who gave me the opportunity to work with him in the last years of his extraordinary life, and indeed gave me the perpetual gift of this very book. All of the editors who have labored on the book's incarnations deserve some credit for its success. For the fifth edition I must especially thank Anne Stameshkin of McGraw-Hill and her Executive Editor, Lisa Moore, as well as Jane Carter, Betty Chen, Leslie LaDow, and Marty Granahan. Two of my colleagues contributed to Appendix C on "Literary Criticism": Jane Hilberry wrote the essay on Feminist Criticism and Regula Evitt composed the one on New Historicism. Derrick Gentry contributed sections on Reader-Response, Psychological, Intertextual, and Postcolonial Criticisms. Also, Paula Pyne was a great help in compiling the indexes.

The following instructors provided valuable comments and advice in their responses to a survey on the third and fourth editions.

Merry Adams, College of Eastern Utah–San Juan Campus
Ruth Anderson, Grossmont Community College
Ray Anschel, Normandale Community College
Karla Armbruster, University of Colorado
Thomas Averill, Washburn University
Thomas Barthel, Herkimer Community College
Geoffrey Becker, The Colorado College
Mary Ellen Bellanca, Muskingum College

Mary Bendel-Simso, Western Maryland College
Emily Berges, Jersey City State College
Toby Bielawski, Chabot College
Jennifer Billingsley, Carl Sandburg College
Harvey Birenbaum, San Jose State University
Daniel Bosch, Harvard University.
E. Jeanne Braham, Clark University
Brenda Jo Brueggemann, Ohio State University
Deborah Burnham, University of Pennsylvania
Anne Calcagno, DePaul University
Michael Cavanagh, Grinnell College
Laurie Champion, Sul Ross State University
Robert Chianese, California State University
Robert Cirasa, Kean College of New Jersey
Molly Cook, University of Southern Maine
Virginia Crawford, Towson University
Martha Crowe, Eastern Tennessee State University
Carmen Cuciontta, Triton College
Lawrence Czer, Martin Luther College
M. Francine Danis, Our Lady of the Lake University
Thomas DeKornfeld, United States Naval Academy
Alice Derry, Peninsula College
Elizabeth Dietz, University of Iowa
Elizabeth Dodd, Kansas State University
Stacey Donahue, Central Oregon Community College
Rita Dove, University of Virginia
M. J. Dunbar, Santa Clara University
D. Dean Dunham, Jr., William Jewell College
Charles Elkins, Florida International University
Lin Enger, Moorhead State University
Deanna Evans, Bemidji State University
B. H. Fairchild, California State University–San Bernardino
Anthony Flinn, Eastern Washington University
Betty Flowers, University of Texas at Austin
Aaron Fogel, Boston University
Suzanne M. Forster, University of Alaska–Anchorage
James Fowler, University of Central Arkansas
Don Foran, Centralia College
Richard Gallagher, University of Michigan
Luis Gamez, Western Michigan University
Maryanne Garbowsky, County College of Morris
Jerome Garger, Lane Community College
Noelle Geiger, Valencia Community College
Diane Glancy, Macalester College
J. Eugene Gloria, Holyoke Community College

Alvin Greenberg, Macalester College
Catherine Halley, University of Iowa
Elaine Handley, Empire State College
William Harmon, University of North Carolina–Chapel Hill
Jerry Harris, Western Oregon University
Mark Hillringhouse, Passaic County College
Janet Holmes, Macalester College
Gregory Horn, Southwest Virginia Community College
Ben Howard, Alfred University
Andrew Hudgins, Ohio State University
John Hughes, Valencia Community College
James Hull, Mount Vernon College
James Irons, College of Southern Idaho
Simon Johnson, Oregon State University
Thomas Johnson, Texas A&M–Galveston
Arnie Johnston, Western Michigan University
Bernard Kaplan, University of Delaware
Maurice Kilwein-Guevara, Indiana University of Pennsylvania
Burt Kimmelman, New Jersey Institute of Technology
Elizabeth Knies, University of Southern Maine
Arm Lauinger, Sarah Lawrence College
Steven Lautermilch, University of North Carolina–Greensboro
Valerie Lester, George Washington University
Robert Lietz, Ohio Northern University
Rick Lott, Arkansas State University
Janet Madden, El Camino College
Jody Malcolm, Augusta State University
Diane Marks, Brooklyn College
Cecilia Martyn, Montclair State University
Charles Matz, Southampton College
Michael McClintock, University of Montana–Missoula
Lorne Mock, University of Cincinnati
Michele Mock, University of Pittsburgh
Margaret Morgan, University of Central Arkansas
Suzanne Morrison, University of Iowa
Manuela Mourao, Old Dominion University
Louise Murdy, Winthrop University
Laurie O'Brien, University of West Florida
James O'Malley, Triton College
Paula Orlando, University at Albany
John Orr, Fullerton College
Ghita Orth, University of Vermont
Gary Pak, Kapi'olani Community College
James Papworth, Ricks College
Rhonda Pettit, Xavier University

Marshall Pipkin, Chapman University
Eileen Pollack, University of Michigan
Elaine Preston, Suffolk County Community College, Western Campus
Shannon Presser, Georgia Institute of Technology
Diane Raptosh, Albertson College
Walter Reed, Emory University
David Richardson, Cleveland State University
John Rietz, Henry Ford Community College
David Ripper, Everett Community College
Michelle Risdon, University of Michigan
Jay Rogoff, Skidmore College
Kenneth Rosen, University of Southern Maine
William Rossiter, Flathead Community College
Kathy Rugoff, University of North Carolina–Wilmington
Michael Ryan, University of California–Irvine
Julie Schmid, University of Iowa
Darrell Semelroth, Triton College
Megan Sexton, Georgia State University
John Skoyles, Emerson College
Grant Smith, Eastern Washington University
James M. Smith, Armstrong Atlantic State University
Nathaniel Smith, Franklin and Marshall College
Adam Sorkin, Pennsylvania State University–Delaware County
Stephen Sossaman, Westfield State College
John A. Stoler, University of Texas–San Antonio
Grant Strickland, Monroe County Community College
Helen Sword, Indiana University
Mark Taylor, Manhattan College
Mary Terchek, University of Maryland
John Terhes, Chemeketa Community College
Richard Terrill, Mankato State University
Randall Tessier, University of Michigan
Karen Themstrup, University of Pittsburgh
Brenda Tooley, Colorado College
Tom Trusky, Boise State University
Jamie Turner, Bob Jones University
Mary Vermillion, Mount Mercy College
Joan Voigt, Our Lady of the Lake University
William Wade, Paducah Community College
Daniel Waterman, University of Alabama
Roger Weaver, Oregon State University
Elizabeth Weber, University of Indianapolis
Terren Wein, Parkland College
Susan Whitmore, University of Missouri–Kansas City
Malcolm Williams, University of Houston

Ken Wolfskill, Chowan College
David Worley, Lincoln Memorial University
Theodore Worozbut, University of Alabama
Elio Zappulla, Dowling College
Ruth Zielke, Concordia College
Clarisse Zimra, Southern Illinois University at Carbondale

I am indebted also to many instructors and students who have written with suggestions, and to the many poets who have made use of *Western Wind* in classes and workshops they have given.

David Mason

BEFORE WE BEGIN

Sometimes we feel like jumping over a fence for the fun of it, or we burst into song for the fun of singing, or we string words together just for the fun of saying them. What we do "for fun" we do for the pleasure of doing it, without having any other purpose in mind. Fun is an expression of the exuberance we feel at being alive, an overflow of the spirit of play that characterizes so much activity, though it may be less evident in adults than in children, less common in our time than in earlier and simpler ages. When we *imagine* anything, we are playing with images, combining them as they have never been combined before, perhaps not even in nature itself. Out of such playing with images came primitive ritual and the mythologies of early religion. Out of our playing with rocks and herbs and the mystery of fire came early science. Out of our playing with hollow reeds or tightened sinews or the beat of bone on deerskin came early music; musicians still "play" on their pianos or guitars. And out of our playing with words, with their sounds and shapes and rhythms and the images they conjured, came early poetry, so wonderful that in all parts of the world it seemed a kind of magic.

To some of us today, poetry may seem an artificial refinement of natural speech. But in the literature of every country, poetry comes before prose does. It is closer than prose to the origins of language. We can even say it is more natural: more primitive, more basic, a more total expression of the muscular, sensuous, emotional, rhythmical nature of the human animal. The ancient Greeks, childlike for all their sophistication, considered the poet an "athlete of the word." In the universities of a truly humane society, they might have felt, poetry would belong at least as much to departments of physical education as to departments of literary criticism.

But what *is* poetry? That is the question this book is setting out to answer. Whatever it is, it is so closely related to the other activities of our lives that we will find ourselves dealing with many curious questions about humans and their world. Some of them are:

If a baby were born with no senses, would it know it exists?
How can we see sounds and hear colors?
Why do cats dislike getting their feet wet?
Why did the thought of a line of poetry make A. E. Housman falter while shaving?
Why do charms against the devil fail to work in translation?
Why do French dogs say "ouâ-ouâ" instead of "bow-wow"?
What kind of rhyme is like a blue note in music?
What American president wrote a treatise on the nature of rhythm in poetry?
Why do metronomes have a poor sense of rhythm?
Why did Picasso say, "Man invented the alarm clock"?

Poetry—like so much we are closest to and know best—is not easy to define. We can begin by saying what it is not. Poetry is not the same as *verse*. Verse is any singsong with rhythm and rhyme, as in

> Thirty days hath September,
> April, June, and November. . . .

The word "verse" refers only to the shape an expression takes, not to its content or quality.

Poetry *may* be in verse, and often does use some kind of verselike structure. Many poets, for example, have been attracted by the shape of the sonnet, which arranges rhythms and rhymes in a definite formation. But the sonnet in itself is only a verse-form; a sonnet may be poetry or it may not. Poetry is not poetry *because* it is in verse; to the shape of verse it has to add qualities of imagination and emotion and of language itself. Such qualities, not easy to describe briefly, are what this book is about.

Much about verse (as opposed to poetry) is arbitrary, just as the rules of a game are arbitrary. The limerick, for instance, has five lines of regulation length, as in Arthur Buller's Einsteinian example:

> There was a young lady named Bright,
> Whose speed was far faster than light;
> > She set out one day
> > In a relative way,
> And returned home the previous night.

The longer lines, 1, 2, and 5, are bound together by one rhyme; the shorter ones, 3 and 4, by another. Nothing in nature says a limerick should have this form, just as nothing in nature says we should have four balls and three strikes in baseball, or four downs to make ten yards in football.

Although verse is arbitrary, poetry is not. Everything in poetry is an expression of what is natural: It is the way it is because we are the way we are.

The whole approach of this book is based upon this certainty: The nature of poetry follows from our own human nature. The main divisions are

organized as we ourselves are. Human experience begins when the senses
give us

(1)

IMAGES of the self or of the world outside. These images arouse

(2)

EMOTIONS, which (with their images) we express in

(3)

WORDS, which are physically produced and have

(4)

SOUND, which comes to our ears riding the air on waves of

(5)

RHYTHM. The whole process, from the beginning, is fostered and overseen by
an organizing

(6)

MIND, acting with the common sense of everyday life, even when dealing with
the uncommon sense of dreams or visions.

In a good poem the elements work together as a unit, just as our own
combinations of body and mind work together. But if we were studying body
and mind as medical students do, we would soon realize that it is impossible
to consider all parts at once. The way to deal with a complicated subject is to
look at it part by part; in medical school we would expect separate lectures
on the heart, the stomach, the lungs, and so forth, even though we realize no
organ can function apart from the others. And so with poetry: We have to talk
separately about the elements that make it up—such as imagery, diction,
rhythm—even though we know they cannot exist in isolation.

Although poetry is not bound by such arbitrary rules as games are, it does
fall under the influence of certain natural laws, like those we call the rules of
health, or like those that govern mountain climbing. Mountain climbers are
not subject to anything as formal as the three-strike rule in baseball, but they
cannot forget that they have only so many arms and legs, that some kinds of
rock crumble and some do not, and that the law of gravitation can exact more
severe penalties than any human rule book. Poetry may not have rules and
regulations, but, as we shall see, it has to make sense in terms of our human
nature.

In such a study as this, specific examples are more persuasive than
definitions. It is helpful to give the definition of a metaphor; it is even more
helpful to give enough examples so that—as in life itself—we can come to our
own conclusions about what it is.

We can also learn about things by observing what they are not. Just as
rudeness can teach us to value courtesy, so a bad line or bad stanza can teach

us to appreciate a good one. Some of our bad examples are so clumsy we may find ourselves laughing at them. Nothing wrong with that: A sense of humor is a sense of proportion. It is also a sense of delight—delight in noting that life has its incongruities and absurdities and that we can live in spite of them. Only a fool, said the French poet Paul Valéry, thinks a man cannot joke and be serious.

Our attitude to poetry—as to any subject—should be a questioning one. We might think of nearly every sentence in this book as ending with a ghostly question mark. Is this statement—we should ask ourselves—really true? We can decide only by considering the evidence we have: the poems we have read, the poems we are reading, and what we know of our own nature.

Although we will have to make some general statements about poetry, we can find exceptions to nearly all of them. A recent cartoon showed a professor of mathematics who had written $2 + 2 = 4$ on the blackboard. He was beginning his lecture with a "However . . ." Readers may come across sentences in this book that they would like to see followed by a "However . . ." They are certainly free to supply their own. *This is a book to live with and be alive with; being alive is often a process of disagreement.*

As individual human beings we differ greatly. In a time of increasing standardization, when more and more things and more and more people are being referred to by number instead of by name, it is important to cherish these differences. It seems to be a part of the general sameness of our culture that we are expected to give indiscriminate approval to accepted values. If we say we like poetry, it is assumed we like all poetry. But why should we? It is only human to have our "passionate preferences." Not all readers are going to like all the poems in this book; nor should they be expected to. Human attention, like everything human, has its rhythms: Now we concentrate, now we relax, pretty much as our interests dictate. Individual teachers and individual classes, as well as individual students, will have their preferences. There is no reason they should read every poem or every chapter with equal interest. Some groups may prefer to skim or skip certain sections so that they can concentrate on others that are more to their liking. Some may prefer to read, here and there, only the poems, which are always more important than what is being said about them. We should not be misled into thinking that the poems are here only to illustrate something about poetry.

Our range of disagreements may be broad—nothing wrong with that. Some of us love the connections that can be made between popular music and the Slam scene, while others are more intrigued by the complexity and precision of "literary" poetry. Some of us respond most readily to contemporary voices, while others have no difficulty taking in poetry of the past or works in translation from other languages. This book is only a place to begin, but it assumes that knowledge is not a danger to your health. The more kinds of poetry we can love—old and new—the richer we are as readers. Learning from old masters of the art helps us put contemporary techniques and visions into perspective.

In discussing such a body of poetry, we can save time by resorting to what look like technical terms. These may put off some readers, who forget that they themselves make extensive use of such terms in speaking of their own interests. Referring to a midline pause in a poem as a "caesura" is no more pedantic than referring to split T's or tight ends or topspin or a chip shot or fuel injection. Such technical terms are nothing but convenient shortcuts.

There are people who think that knowledge destroys their spontaneous reaction to anything beautiful. They are seldom right; generally, the more we know, the more we see to appreciate. There are people who think that to analyze a poem or, as they like to say, to "tear it apart," is to destroy it. But one no more destroys a poem by analysis than one destroys birds or flowers or anything else by means of a diagram.

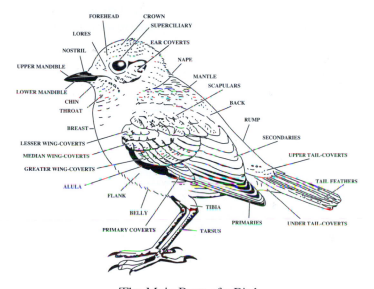

The Main Parts of a Bird

There is no reason to worry about this bird. It has not been injured or "taken apart." If one is interested in birds, one likes to be able to tell one from another—a catbird from a mockingbird, a great rackettail drongo from a blue-faced booby. The diagram shows where points of difference lie. And so with poems. Diagrams and analyses no more substitute for them than our drawing substitutes for a bird. But they may help make a point or two.

If we can talk about the parts of poems without killing them, we can also notice that poems come in different types or genres. The **lyric** or songlike poem can be found in early works like the little four-liner that gave this book its title; it can be found in Edmund Waller's "Go, Lovely Rose" (Anthology, p. 383) or a contemporary work like Joe Bolton's "Adult Situations" (p. 565). **Narrative poetry** is simply that which tells a story. Examples include Robert

Frost's "Out, Out—" (p. 439) and B. H. Fairchild's "Brazil" (p. 533). The **dramatic monologue** is a poem in which a character other than the poet is speaking. Famous examples include Tennyson's "Ulysses" (p. 410) and Browning's "My Last Duchess" (p. 412), but dramatic voice can also be found in such poems as Margaret Benbow's "Crazy Arms: Earlene Remembers" (p. 531). Another genre would be the **ode,** an elaborate and more meditative extension of the lyric. Odes have been written not only by Shelley (p. 401) and Keats (p. 405) but by such contemporaries as Brigit Pegeen Kelly in "Song" (p. 548), her meditation on the origin of tragedy. Knowing the kind of poem you are reading will help not only with analysis but with performance as well. Most poems in this book will be better understood if you read them aloud more than once.

With poetry we have to return to the reading habits of a more primitive age than our own. Poetry has no use for the kind of speed-reading techniques we are encouraged to practice with informational materials. In speed-reading, we are told not to fixate on any one word not to backtrack over what we have already read, and not to subvocalize by half pronouncing the words or by moving our lips. But in reading poetry we have to dwell on the words to savor their implications and relationships; we have to glance back and re-read whenever we have a mind to; and we have to feel the words alive in our mouths, even if we move our lips to do so. We may have to read a poem several times to feel we know it—and then (as with a favorite recording) return to it as many times as we want for further pleasure. In a world increasingly sophisticated, poetry is one of the few ways in which we can still afford to be primitive.

Western wind, when will thou blow,
The small rain down can rain?
Christ! if my love were in my arms,
And I in my bed again!

ONE

The Senses

1

WHERE EXPERIENCE STARTS

The Image

THE ROLE OF THE SENSES

Our first contact with reality begins with what we call an **image**—a piece of news from the world outside or from our own bodies which is brought into the light of consciousness through one of the senses. It may come through the eye as color, through the ear as sound, through the tongue as taste, or through one of the other senses as another kind of physical information. When we remember with any vividness, we remember in images. It is difficult to reason without using them; our dreams are wholly made up of them.

We can think of images as differing from ideas or thoughts in that images are always made up of sense data: They deal in color or sound or taste or smell or temperature or the feeling of physical contact. Ideas and thoughts may suggest images, but they do not necessarily do so. We can think "Charity is a virtue" or "Exercise is good for the health" without having impressions of color, sound, smell, or other sense data—though likely enough, images from church or gymnasium will come trailing.

Poets (like all of us when we dream) naturally think in images. "I no sooner have an idea," said Goethe, "than it turns into an image." But it *was* an image even before it was an idea, because that is how the mind—or the inseparable mind-body combination—naturally works. Juliet, thinking of the family feud that threatens her love for Romeo, wonders, "What's in a name?" Immediately images of color and fragrance well up: "That which we call a rose/By any other name would smell as sweet." Juliet knew the smell and feel and color of a flower long before she speculated about problems of nomenclature. About three-fourths of our brain area is given over to processing data produced by sight and hearing and smell. Poets use imagery because it makes up so much of the human experience. We can hardly imagine anything we value or despise that does not come home to us in terms of physical sensation.

If a child could be born with no senses whatsoever—with no feeling even of warmth—it would have no way of knowing it existed. If we know that we are, and if we know that what we call the outside world seems to exist, from the pages at our fingertips to the farthest reach of the newest telescope, we know it only through the senses. Even imagination is dependent upon them for the elements it rearranges in fantasy, as rearrange them it does: by selecting, by suppressing, by heightening, much as movie directors adapt the scenarios they are presented with. Mere acceptance of whatever the senses give us can be sterile. As the modern Japanese poet Takamura Kotaro has said:

> Because I don't have enough talent,
> I depend on reality.

How the senses work is largely mysterious. The eye gives us information about light rays, but nobody fully understands how the cells of the retina react photochemically to the rays, or how these chemical reactions turn into electrical impulses along the optic nerve, or how these impulses are perceived by sight centers in the brain not as flickers of electricity but as "sundance gold" or "Capri blue" or "apple green." All we know is that some kind of stimulus to the cells in the eye (or in the ear or fingertip or any other part of the body) triggers a reaction, creating a current that travels along the nerve circuits. The current is somehow turned by the brain into perceptions of tulips or tennis courts or another's hand warm in our own as moonlight plays on the lake and night wind stirs in the pine trees. The images of poetry are based on the fantastic realities of body and mind.

An image is anything presented to consciousness as a bodily sensation. We call such images **concrete** (from the Latin word for *solid*), as opposed to ideas that may be **abstract** (Latin, *withdrawn*)—stripped, that is, of physical detail. Such words as "violet," "bread," "sunlight," "surf," and "blond" are concrete; such words as "entity," "nutrition," "meteorology," "recurrence," and "coloration" are abstract.

Poetry is immediately concerned with the concrete, the specific, the particular, with the *bread* and *sunlight* of our life; it has only occasional use for its *nutrition* and *meteorology*. The great English poet William Blake reacted as any poet would when he once read a sentence in praise of abstraction and generality: Against it in the margin he wrote, in indignant capitals, "To Generalize is to be an Idiot. To Particularize is the Alone Distinction of Merit." A few pages later he added another marginal comment: "Singular & Particular detail"—or what we are calling sense imagery—"is the Foundation of the Sublime." The twentieth-century Spanish poet Federico García Lorca put the matter even more directly when he said, "The poet is a professor of the five bodily senses."

The importance of the concrete is not only esthetic. Elias Canetti, the winner of the 1981 Nobel Prize in literature, declared that "Among the most sinister phenomena in intellectual history is the avoidance of the concrete." He meant that in ignoring what is the "closest and most concrete" of realities, we are endangering the future of humanity. When generals and politicians refer to the deaths of innocent civilians in wartime as "collateral damage," they avoid concrete images of mangled bodies, obscuring the truth with abstraction. George Orwell's famous essay, "Politics and the English Language," contains examples of such abuse at all levels of society.

The senses are given us; all creation demands that we use them. Whatever we know of even the divine tends to express itself in matter. As Ralph Waldo Emerson said, "There seems to be a necessity in spirit to manifest itself in material forms; and day and night, river and storm, beast and bird, acid and alkali, preexist in necessary Ideas in the mind of God, and are what they are by virtue of . . . the world of spirit." It is necessary to stress the dignity of physical imagery because there are those who think poets demean themselves in descending to the world of matter instead of taking refuge in the world of spirit. They forget that the poet's word, like the Word of the Evangelist, is not even apparent to us until it is "made flesh."

In "The Same Life" the contemporary American poet Jim Moore (*b.* 1943) relates his awareness of being alive as follows:

> The life that pulses under my wrist
> as blood is the same life
> that sways inside summer weeds.
> The life that is mine day and night
> 5 also belongs to the world.
> It is the same life
> that rocks back and forth in the ocean,
> the same life that opens the gates
> at birth, then closes them at death.   [1995]

Moore's poem is one of a series of imitations or homages inspired by the work of India's Rabindranath Tagore (1861–1941). This act of sympathetic writing suggests that the way we perceive life is at least partly based upon universal human attributes—our circulatory and nervous systems—as much as the cultures we are from.

"We think in generalities," said the mathematician and philosopher Alfred North Whitehead, "but we live in detail." It is these details, these things of this world, that poets choose from to create their own world of poetry. Ezra Pound, one of the great innovators of modern literature, insisted that "The artist seeks out the luminous detail and presents it. He does not comment." There is no piece of advice young writers hear more frequently than "Show, don't tell." *Show* us the world as you see it, they are advised; do not—unless you are an editorial writer—give us your comments on it. So Pound, when he wishes to convince us of the beauty of a Chinese girl named Rafu, does not simply *tell* us she is beautiful; he *shows* us the effect her beauty has on men who see her:

> And when men going by look on Rafu
> 　　They set down their burdens,
> They stand and twirl their moustaches.

So Herman Melville, when he wishes to conclude a poem by reminding us that danger and possibly evil are ever present in life, does not simply *tell* us so; he closes with an image that shows us the danger and possible evil in action:

> 　　　　　　　—The shark
> Glides white through the phosphorus sea.

So Chaucer, long before, did not simply *tell* us that a certain individual was a treacherous hypocrite; he showed us

> The smiler with the knife under the cloak.

　　This is the way of poets; they no sooner have an idea than it turns into an image. This is also the way of scientists. When Einstein tried to describe his scientific work, he had recourse time and again to the concreteness of visual imagery. Instead of saying "Quantum reality is not random," he said, more than once, "God does not play dice with the world." Instead of saying that radiation came only in specific quanta, he said that radiation was like "beer in a keg" that could be dispensed only in pint-size bottles.

　　"Western Wind" is a little poem that was found, with its music, in an early sixteenth-century manuscript:

> Westron wynde when wyll thow blow
> the smalle rayne downe can rayne
> Chryst yf my love wer in my armys
> and I yn my bed agayne

ANONYMOUS (c. 1500)

Or, more comfortably in modern spelling:

> Western wind, when will thou blow,
> The small rain down can rain?
> Christ! if my love were in my arms,
> And I in my bed again!

In this poem, which is so familiar to readers in our century that Hemingway can have his hero quote it in *A Farewell to Arms,* the poet is saying that he misses someone he loves and wishes spring would come so he could see her. The prose meaning of the poem—a **paraphrase** of its ideas—might look like this:

> Characteristic of the coming of spring in Europe is the fact that prevailing winds are from the west; with them comes a marked increase of rainfall, though the spring rains tend to be gentle. I look forward with impatience to its coming, because at that time circumstances will be such that I will be reunited with the person I love and be given an opportunity to express that love in the normal human way.

For the anonymous poet the experience is all *one,* and all sensuous, as in reality. Spring means the wind and the rain on his cheek, so real that he addresses the wind as if it were alive—as it might seem alive to a child or to a simple cave-dweller untouched by the complexities of modern society. He imagines the reunion, too, in its physical reality. The poem does not come just from a mind; it comes from a mind in, and very aware of, a body. Aware of two bodies. Aware of the world. It sounds—though from long ago—like a real voice speaking. If we do not believe the voice in a poem, nothing else matters: The poet has left a credibility gap we will never bridge. Whatever else a poem may be, unless it seems a real voice in a real body in a real world, it is not likely to affect us deeply.

Our preference for sense detail has been embedded in the human psyche for well over a million years. It surfaces most vividly in the free-floating world of dreams and hallucinations, in the poetry of people farthest from the schooling of civilization, and in the thoughts of children before they too, at about the age of thirteen, give up their poetically concrete way of experiencing for the abstractions of adulthood. The child of MacLeish's poem is still living in the richly sensuous "antithink" world of the body.

Eleven

And summer mornings the mute child, rebellious,
Stupid, hating the words, the meanings, hating
The Think now, Think, the Oh but Think! would leave
On tiptoe the three chairs on the verandah
5 And crossing tree by tree the empty lawn
Push back the shed door and upon the sill
Stand pressing out the sunlight from his eyes
And enter and with outstretched fingers feel
The grindstone and behind it the bare wall
10 And turn and in the corner on the cool
Hard earth sit listening. And one by one,
Out of the dazzled shadow in the room,

The shapes would gather, the brown plowshare, spades,
Mattocks, the polished helves of picks, a scythe
15 Hung from the rafters, shovels, slender tines
Glinting across the curve of sickles—shapes
Older than men were, the wise tools, the iron
Friendly with earth. And sit there, quiet, breathing
The harsh dry smell of withered bulbs, the faint
20 Odor of dung, the silence. And outside
Beyond the half-shut door the blind leaves
And the corn moving. And at noon would come,
Up from the garden, his hard crooked hands
Gentle with earth, his knees still earth-stained, smelling
25 Of sun, of summer, the old gardener, like
A priest, like an interpreter, and bend
Over his baskets.
          And they would not speak:
They would say nothing. And the child would sit there
30 Happy as though he had no name, as though
He had been no one: like a leaf, a stem,
Like a root growing—

                                       [1926]
                 ARCHIBALD MACLEISH (1892–1982)

Hardly a line without a physical image.

THE SENSES

Poems rarely limit themselves to one or two senses; most range as our minds do, using whatever sense gives the most relevant information. Nor are the senses limited to five: We can feel what our muscles are doing, can keep our balance, can sense a hot stove in a dark room, can feel pain and other bodily intimations. Scientists have a word ("proprioceptive") for the mechanisms that give us our "body image," or self-awareness; in health they operate so smoothly we are not aware they exist.

One of the most celebrated of body-image poems is by Sappho, who wrote some very modern poems in the sixth century B.C. In it, she tells how it feels to see someone sitting casually next to the person she is in love with. She lets us share the whole force of her passion by detailing, almost without comment, her physical symptoms. The poem, its ending lost centuries ago, begins:

There's a man I really believe's in heaven
—over there, *that* man. To be sitting near you,
knee to knee so close to you, hear your voice, your
      cozy low laughter,
5 close to *you*—enough in the very thought to
put my heart at once in a palpitation.

ABSTRACT/CONCRETE

"I no sooner have an idea," said Goethe, "than it turns into an image." That, typically, is the way the poetic mind works. Here are examples, all from Shakespeare, of how abstract ideas are turned into concrete images—images of *things,* simple and familiar.

ABSTRACT IDEAS	CONCRETE IMAGES

We mean you no harm.

> To you our swords have leaden points, Mark Antony . . .

Just because you're so proper, does that mean other people cannot enjoy themselves?

> Dost thou think, because thou art virtuous, There shall be no more cakes and ale?

Though he is prosperous and secure, you can annoy him in little ways.

> And though he in a fertile climate dwell, Plague him with flies.

Make the best of it.

> Men do their broken weapons rather use Than their bare hands.

We cannot trust anyone.

> Where we are, There's daggers in men's smiles . . .

Ungrateful children are a source of suffering to their parents.

> How sharper than a serpent's tooth it is To have a thankless child.

I have much to worry about.

> O, full of scorpions is my mind, dear wife!

People who fail lose many friends.

> Men shut their doors against a setting sun.

I often change my mind.

> I am a feather for each wind that blows.

I, come face to face with you on a sudden,
    stand in a stupor:
tongue a lump, unable to lift; elusive
10 little flames play over the skin and smolder
under. Eyes go blind in a flash; and ears hear
    only their own din.
Head to toe I'm cold with a sudden moisture;
knees are faint; my cheeks, in an instant, drain to
15 pale as grass. I think to myself, the end? I'm
    really going under? . . .

SAPPHO (*fl. c.* 600 B.C.E.)

In an early poem T. S. Eliot wants to tell us that life in a big crowded modern city can be lonely, depressing, sordid, hurried, anonymous, that it can leave human beings nervous, dissatisfied, frustrated. These are abstract ideas, which Eliot never states directly in his poem. As poet, his problem is to find the images that will embody these ideas; in the poem that results, there is hardly a line not made up of sense imagery.

Preludes

I

The winter evening settles down
With smell of steaks in passageways.
Six o'clock.
The burnt-out ends of smoky days.
5 And now a gusty shower wraps
The grimy scraps
Of withered leaves about your feet
And newspapers from vacant lots;
The showers beat
10 On broken blinds and chimney-pots,
And at the corner of the street
A lonely cab-horse steams and stamps.
And then the lighting of the lamps.

II

The morning comes to consciousness
15 Of faint stale smells of beer
From the sawdust-trampled street
With all its muddy feet that press
To early coffee-stands.
With the other masquerades
20 That time resumes,
One thinks of all the hands
That are raising dingy shades
In a thousand furnished rooms.

III

You tossed a blanket from the bed,
25 You lay upon your back, and waited;
You dozed, and watched the night revealing
The thousand sordid images
Of which your soul was constituted;
They flickered against the ceiling.
30 And when all the world came back
And the light crept up between the shutters
And you heard the sparrows in the gutters,
You had such a vision of the street
As the street hardly understands;
35 Sitting along the bed's edge, where
You curled the papers from your hair,
Or clasped the yellow soles of feet
In the palms of both soiled hands.

IV

His soul stretched tight across the skies
40 That fade behind a city block,
Or trampled by insistent feet
At four and five and six o'clock;
And short square fingers stuffing pipes,
And evening newspapers, and eyes
45 Assured of certain certainties,
The conscience of a blackened street
Impatient to assume the world.
      I am moved by fancies that are curled
Around these images; and cling:
50 The notion of some infinitely gentle
Infinitely suffering thing.

      Wipe your hand across your mouth, and laugh;
The worlds revolve like ancient women
Gathering fuel in vacant lots.   [1917]
                                          T. S. ELIOT (1888–1965)

Operating with imagery is more than a preference of the mind; it is an actual necessity. When people are sense-deprived, left alone in darkness and silence, they begin to hallucinate. We find something like this hallucination in the poetry of John Keats, who said, "O for a life of Sensations rather than of Thoughts!" His "Ode to a Nightingale" (see Anthology, p. 405), which begins with proprioceptive sensations, whirls away on images of sight, sound, touch, taste, and smell, escaping into pure imagination in spite of the interference of "the dull brain." The fifth stanza is an example of compensatory dreaming: Unable to see what flowers—imaginary flowers—are around him, Keats proceeds to identify them by their imaginary smells.

Poets in all ages have turned ideas into images, as the ancient Greek poet did when he lamented that a lady who had rejected him in youth and middle age was still rejecting him.

Brief Autumnal

Green grape, and you refused me.
  Ripe grape, and you sent me packing.
    Must you deny me a bite of your raisin?

             ANONYMOUS (DATE UNCERTAIN)
        (*Translated by* DUDLEY FITTS [1952], 1903–1968)

THE SPECIFIC IMAGE

Our senses note only particulars. We never see color, we see particular *colors;* we never just touch, we touch *something*. For a long time philosophers have been saying that being exists only in individual things. "The individual," says Carl Jung, "is the only reality." The poet E. E. Cummings puts it more catchily: "There's nothing as something as one." *Humanity* does not exist as a thing we can see; but *this* person does, *that* person does. This human preference for the particular is shown in many primitive languages, which may have no word for *tree* but which may have many such words as "oak," "pine," "maple," and "elm." Pound, who urged writers to go in fear of abstractions, and who believed "It is better to present one image in a lifetime than to produce voluminous works," has given us some memorable images.

In a Station of the Metro

The apparition of these faces in the crowd;
  Petals on a wet, black bough.

Alba

As cool as the pale wet leaves of lily-of-the-valley
  She lay beside me in the dawn.
                  [1915]
           EZRA POUND (1885–1972)

Frequently a poem (like life itself) offers only sense details; it professes neither a meaning nor a moral, though it may embody both. The interpretation (as in life itself) will be up to us.

The End of the Weekend

A dying firelight slides along the quirt
Of the cast-iron cowboy where he leans
Against my father's books. The lariat
Whirls into darkness. My girl, in skin-tight jeans,

5   Fingers a page of Captain Marryat,
Inviting insolent shadows in her shirt.

We rise together to the second floor.
Outside, across the lake, an endless wind
Whips at the headstones of the dead and wails
10   In the trees for all who have and have not sinned.
She rubs against me and I feel her nails.
Although we are alone, I lock the door.

The eventual shapes of all our formless prayers,
This dark, this cabin of loose imaginings,
15   Wind, lake, lip, everything awaits
The slow unloosening of her underthings.
And then the noise. Something is dropped. It grates
Against the attic beams.
                  I climb the stairs,

20   Armed with a belt.
                  A long magnesium strip
Of moonlight from the dormer cuts a path
Among the shattered skeletons of mice.
A great black presence beats its wings in wrath.
25   Above the boneyard burn its golden eyes.
Some small grey fur is pulsing in its grip.   [1968]
                      ANTHONY HECHT (1923–2004)

The author presents his evidence—shows what happens—without comment. We decide on the meaning, each of us, as if each had been present, unobserved but observing, in that lakeside cottage.

Filmmakers often use imagery in a similar way:

> There is a famous sequence at the end of Lewis Milestone's *All Quiet on the Western Front* in which the hero, Paul, a German soldier, is shot by a French sniper. The sniper is shown carefully aiming his rifle but all we see of Paul is his hand stretching out to try and touch a butterfly that has come to rest. We recognize it as Paul's hand because we already know he is a butterfly collector, and, because of the sniper, watch it stretching farther in anxious suspense. Then there is a shot, the hand jerks, slowly drops, and lies still. Paul's death is as vivid as if we had seen a full picture of him dying.*

The rifle, the hand, the butterfly—these are the kinds of images the poet also uses. A good way to check on the *visual* imagery in a poem is to ask: What kind of camera work would it take to present this image? Could it be filmed at all?

For examples of a technique like that of cinema, we can go to some of the oldest poems in English, the folk ballads, which move, through graphic

---

*R. Stephenson and Jean R. Debrix, *The Cinema as Art* (Baltimore: Penguin, 1965), p. 207.

scenes generally without transition, from emotional high point to emotional high point.

Sir Patrick Spens

The king sits in Dumferling toune,
　　Drinking the blude-reid wine:
"O whar will I get guid sailor,
　　To sail this schip of mine?"

5　Up and spak an eldern knicht,
　　Sat at the kings richt kne:
"Sir Patrick Spens is the best sailor,
　　That sails upon the se."

The king has written a braid letter,
10　　And signd it wi' his hand;
And sent it to Sir Patrick Spens,
　　Was walking on the sand.

The first line that Sir Patrick red,
　　A loud lauch lauched he:
15　The next line that Sir Patrick red,
　　The teir blinded his ee.

"O wha is this has don this deid,
　　This ill deid don to me;
To send me out this time o' the yeir,
20　　To sail upon the se?

"Mak haste, mak haste, my mirry men all,
　　Our guid schip sails the morne."
"O say na sae, my master deir,
　　For I feir a deadlie storme.

25　"Late, late yestreen I saw the new moone
　　Wi' the auld moone in hir arme;
And I feir, I feir, my deir master,
　　That we will cum to harme."

O our Scots nobles wer richt laith
30　　To weet their cork-heild shoone;
Bot lang owre a' the play wer playd,
　　Thair hats they swam aboone.

O lang, lang, may thair ladies sit
　　Wi' thair fans into their hand,

9/*braid:* *blunt, explicit*
14/*lauch:* *laugh*
16/*ee:* *eye*
17/*wha:* *who*
23/*na sae:* *not so*
25/*yestreen:* *yesterday evening*

26/*auld:* *old*
29/*richt laith:* *right loath*
30/*weet . . . shoone:* *wet . . . shoes*
31/*Bot lang owre a':* *but long before all*
32/*swam aboone:* *floated above*

35 Or eir they se Sir Patrick Spens
    Cum sailing to the land.

O lang, lang, may the ladies stand,
    Wi' thair gold kems in their hair,
Waiting for thair ain deir lords,
40   For they'll se thame na mair.

Haf owre, haf owre to Aberdour,
    It's fiftie fadom deip,
And thair lies guid Sir Patrick Spens,
    Wi' the Scots lords at his feit.

ANONYMOUS (DATE UNCERTAIN)

35/*Or eir: before ever*
38/*kems: combs*

40/*na mair: no more*
41/*Haf owre: half way over*

One can imagine the action here filmed as a short art movie, following the order of the stanzas. The scenario for the first three might run as follows:

1. Shot of king, surrounded by councillors. King's fingers move nervously on stem of wine goblet. He glances at window; storm outside. Tossing branches, fast-moving clouds. King asks his question.
2. Camera goes from face to face of councillors. They look toward window. Gradually all look toward old knight. He answers. Reluctantly?
3. Shot of king's hand, signing letter with great flourish. Shot of Sir Patrick Spens, walking by surf. Stormy background. Small medieval ships drawn up on shore. His men nearby. He is handed the letter.

EXERCISES & DIVERSIONS

A. Since snakes do not have the same sensory equipment as we have, special problems come up for the poet who tries to get into the consciousness of a snake. How successfully is it done here?

Rattler, Alert

Slowly he sways that head that cannot hear,
Two-jeweled cone of horn the yellow of rust,
Pooled on the current of his listening fear.
His length is on the tympanum of earth,
And by his tendril tongue's tasting the air
He sips, perhaps, a secret of his race
Or feels for the known vibrations, heat, or trace
Of smoother satin than the hillwind's thrust
Through grass: the aspirate of my half-held breath,
The crushing of my weight upon the dust,
My foamless heart, the bloodleap at my wrist.

[1946]

BREWSTER GHISELIN (*b.* 1903)

Rattlesnakes, which are deaf, can sense vibrations of the earth through their "tympanum" or eardrum. Their flickering tongues are "chemoreceptive," providing them with a chemical analysis of the environment. They also have infrared temperature-differential receptors to help locate warm-blooded prey. These are the scientific facts. How does the poet present them?

After several lines of "he . . . his" (referring to the snake), we suddenly get the "my" of the observer in the last three lines. What clues are there to the observer's emotional state?

Most of the lines end with a *th* sound or an *s* sound or an *st* sound. Could this use of sound be meaningful? Could the *t*'s of line 5? The *h*'s of line 9?

In the last line, why is "foamless" used of the heart? Why is "bloodleap" a better word here than "pulse"?

B. In Ted Kooser's "Abandoned Farmhouse" (Anthology, p. 524, the concrete details (the shoes, the bed, the worn Bible, the leaky barn, etc.) have a story to tell. Since it could be told more briefly without them ("He was a big, tall, religious man, not a great farmer, married," etc.), why do the details seem to matter so much?

C. 1. Instead of the abstraction *nutriment,* one might use such an image as "juicy cheeseburger on dark rye with dill pickle." What concrete images can you think of that might be used to stand for the following abstractions: *exercise, amusement, wretchedness, locality, velocity, attraction, dryness, spiciness, agitation, deception, insufficiency, authority, success?*

  2. A traffic signal might be used as an image to stand for such abstractions as *safety* or *control.* While walking, riding, or idling, make a list of ten objects that come to your attention. What abstractions (qualities, conditions, processes) could each stand for if mentioned in a poem?

D. In this fragment, Sappho invites the goddess Aphrodite to come visit her in a temple garden. In her description, how many of our senses does the poet involve?

> Leaving Crete, come visit again our temple,
> please, for me. So holy a place, a pleasant
> stand of apple trees, and the altar wreathed in
>   cedary incense.
> Once within, you've water that chuckles cool through
> mazy apple paths, with a dusk of roses
> overgrown. There's sleep in the air: the wind and
>   leaves are like magic.
> Once within, you've pasture for horses grazing;
> Maytime flowers are rich in the grass, the friendly
> heavens breathe . . .

E. All rules have their exceptions. In these lines by Amy Clampitt, could you defend the abstraction *quicknesses* as better here than concrete specification (such as "wrens and sparrows")?

> . . . the branches overhead
> so full of small, unfrightened quicknesses . . .

F. Complete the scenario of "Sir Patrick Spens," using, where effective, concrete details not mentioned in the text but suggested by it. What other poems in this chapter would lend themselves to cinematic treatment?

ESSAY

Read and reread "The End of the Weekend" until you feel you understand the situation. Write a **paraphrase** of the poem, putting it completely in your own words, and "reducing" it to its literal meaning. Now write a brief essay in which you explain the differences between the words Anthony Hecht uses and your own. Consider the following questions as you write:

1. Does it matter that the firelight is "dying"?
2. Why is the girl "inviting" shadows? Why are they "insolent"?
3. Why are the imaginings "loose"?
4. If line 3 of the poem had ended with "lasso" instead of "lariat," would the girl still have been fingering a book by Captain Marryat? If not, how might the line have ended?
5. If they are alone, why does the boy (or is he a man?) lock the upstairs door?
6. What does the image of the "great black presence" have to do with the affair? What effect, if any, did it probably have on the lovers?

POEM

Here is another brief piece of writing by Jim Moore:

Haiku/Touch

Do not feel lonely.
The disappearing world longs
for you to touch it.   [1995]

Take a few minutes and try to imagine that "disappearing world" in concrete images using all five of your senses. Now write a poem about that world in any form you choose. Your only job is to make it vivid even as it disappears.

2

WHAT'S IT LIKE?

Simile, Metaphor, and Other Figures

SIMILE AND METAPHOR

The poet's preference for thinking in images, as we have seen, is not merely a literary mannerism; it is based on the way our body and mind put us in touch with the universe.

In the next two chapters we are going to consider how all of us—including the poets—compare and relate the images that come into our minds. To begin with, we organize them according to resemblances. A thought pattern we use many times a day takes such forms as, "What is she really like?" "What's it like, being in college?" "What's it *like?*" Our effort to understand anything starts by relating it to something better known that it resembles. The earliest mention of coal in Chinese literature refers to it as "ice-charcoal"; all that the poet could do with the unfamiliar substance was to relate it to others that he knew. Over twenty centuries later, two of our astronauts, working in moon dust they had never seen before, could use nothing but *likes* to describe it: "When you put your scoop in, it smooths it out—just like plaster." "I was going to say—like cement." "When you find stuff you don't understand," one scientist said, "you ask yourself, does it look like anything you've ever seen before?"

The mind itself operates by finding likenesses. When a new piece of information is fed into the brain, it is whirled around the circuits until it finds its place with similar things. Otherwise, we would not only learn nothing; we would not even long survive in a world full of hazards we have to identify.

Poets are only acting the way we all do in wondering what things are like. "To what shall I compare thee, dear bridegroom?" asks Sappho. "Shall

I compare thee," Shakespeare wonders, "to a summer's day?" The Song of Songs from the Bible delights in telling what things are like: "As the lily among thorns, so is my love among the daughters. As the apple tree among the trees of the wood, so is my beloved among the sons." The best-known of the Psalms begins, "The Lord is my shepherd."

This need to compare is psychological and emotional. To describe the nature of moon dust, the astronauts had to relate it to something familiar. But poets are not merely trying to convey information; they feel pleasure and give us pleasure in discovering resemblances that no one had noticed before. *It's true,* we feel, when coming on a good comparison. *It's true, but I never realized it!* Such comparisons, the poet James Dickey reminds us, are adventurous.

A California poet, Robinson Jeffers, feeling how "beautiful . . . and a little terrible" it was to watch schools of sardines being netted at night, was reminded that civilizations too are doomed and that a fate like that of the sardines may await our world as well. Although we may not agree with his gloomy prognosis, there is something exciting and even beautiful in the way he relates his two sets of images. The discovery of any surprising likeness is one more clue to the suspicion that there seems to be an order, however deep and mysterious, in the universe.

The Purse-Seine

Our sardine fishermen work at night in the dark of the moon; daylight
   or moonlight
They could not tell where to spread the net, unable to see the
   phosphorescence of the shoals of fish.
They work northward from Monterey, coasting Santa Cruz; off New
   Year's Point or off Pigeon Point
The look-out man will see some lakes of milk-color light on the sea's
   night-purple; he points, and the helmsman
5 Turns the dark prow, the motor-boat circles the gleaming shoal and
   drifts out her seine-net. They close the circle
And purse the bottom of the net, then with great labor haul it in.

                               I cannot tell you
How beautiful the scene is, and a little terrible, then, when the crowded
   fish
Know they are caught, and wildly beat from one wall to the other of
   their closing destiny the phosphorescent
Water to a pool of flame, each beautiful slender body sheeted with
   flame, like a live rocket
10 A comet's tail wake of clear yellow flame; while outside the narrowing
Floats and cordage of the net great sea-lions come up to watch, sighing
   in the dark; the vast walls of night
Stand erect to the stars.

Lately I was looking from a night mountain-top
On a wide city, the colored splendor, galaxies of light: how could I help
but recall the seine-net
Gathering the luminous fish? I cannot tell you how beautiful the city
appeared, and a little terrible.
15 I thought, We have geared the machines and locked all together into
interdependence; we have built the great cities; now
There is no escape. We have gathered vast populations incapable of
free survival, insulated
From the strong earth, each person in himself helpless, on all
dependent. The circle is closed, and the net
Is being hauled in. They hardly feel the cords drawing, yet they shine
already. The inevitable mass-disasters
Will not come in our time nor in our children's, but we and our
children
20 Must watch the net draw narrower, government take all powers—or
revolution, and the new government
Take more than all, add to kept bodies kept souls—or anarchy, the
mass-disasters.

These things are Progress;
Do you marvel our verse is troubled or frowning, while it keeps its
reason? Or it lets go, lets the mood flow
In the manner of the recent young men into mere hysteria, splintered
gleams, cracked laughter. But they are quite wrong.
There is no reason for amazement: surely one always knew that
cultures decay, and life's end is death.   [1938]
ROBINSON JEFFERS (1887–1962)

The discovery of likeness is often expressed by the figures of speech
called **simile** and **metaphor.**

The Latin word "simile" means *alike;* we use simile when we say one
thing is *like* another. "Metaphor" is from the Greek word for *transfer.* In
modern Greece, one can see delivery trucks with the word "ΜΕΤΑΦΟΡΑ"
painted on their sides; they are metaphors on wheels, as it were, transferring
goods from one place to another. When we use metaphor, we transfer to one
thing the identity of something else that we associate with it, as when we say
that the heart of a cruel man is a stone or that a grumpy man is a bear. The
obvious difference between simile and metaphor is that the first, by means of
words such as "like," "as," "as if," "than," compares two terms or images ("I
feel like a wreck"); the second omits the linking word and seems to identify
the two more wholeheartedly ("I'm a wreck!"). Metaphor, since unqualified,
is stronger than simile; since more concentrated, it hits with greater impact.
The two terms cover different intensities of the same process, as the surrealist leader André Breton recognized when he said, "The most exalting word is
the word LIKE, whether it is pronounced or implied." The contemporary poet
Mark Doty would agree:

Metaphor on Wheels

—but what's lovelier
than the shapeshifting

transparence of *like* and *as:*
Clear undulant words?
We look at alien grace

unfettered
by any determined form . . .

We can see how language itself developed out of metaphor by noting the fossil metaphors it still contains: the *leg* of a table, the *mouth* of a river, the *teeth* of the wind.

There may be readers who think that figures of speech are artificial or fancy ways of saying what a plain-speaker could say simply. But the important figures of speech are not mere tricks of rhetoric; they are modes in which our minds really operate. As the biologist Lewis Thomas has written, "The mark of being human is speech and the ready use of metaphor."

Our minds work naturally in metaphor; without it they would fail to function productively. When we say our minds "work" and "function productively," we are relying on a metaphor: The mind is [like] a machine. Our everyday conversation is built ("built" is metaphorical) on a foundation of many such metaphors. The nature of time, for example, is hard to grasp in any physical way. Money is more material: We can jingle it in our pockets or fold it into our wallets. So it is convenient to think *time is money;* that way we physicalize it, put it in terms we can handle. We say we *save* time, *waste* time, *spend* time, have *extra* time to *give* someone, *invest* time in projects, *run out of* time, *budget* our time, live on *borrowed* time. All of these, and many such expressions, are based on the metaphor *time is money.* Wallace Stevens, who was both a poet and vice president of an insurance company, once wrote that "Money is a kind of poetry." His figure surprises us because we usually associate poetry with noncommercial powers, yet money, like poetry, involves the transfer of one thing (wealth) via another (paper). Of course Stevens was a bit rueful in his claim; reverse it to "Poetry is a kind of money" and some people would laugh you out of the room. Nevertheless, in some parts of the world poetry has been equated with bread. Many things in our experience make sense to us only with the help of a metaphor. This has always been true in religion, in which God can be thought of as a father, as a shepherd, as a lord of hosts, and so on. It is equally true in science, and never more so than today, when we are trying to understand the invisible particles in the atom. Niels Bohr, the Nobel Prize-winning physicist, said: "When it comes to atoms, language can only be used as in poetry. The poet, too, is not nearly so concerned with describing facts as with creating images." J. Bronowski has explained further: "All our ways of picturing the invisible are metaphors, likenesses that we snatch from the larger world of eye and ear and touch." We should not forget that language itself is nothing but "figure of speech": We use a word when we mean a thing or an action.

When we say "A is [like] B," we are trying to show, in a fresh and vivid way, something about the nature of A. Good figures jolt us out of accustomed ruts of thinking and surprise us into a pleasant shock of recognition. But since it is the A that is being clarified for us ("Moon dust is like plaster"), the B should be better known, more familiar, in some respect more vivid than the A. The greatest writers prefer very common, "unpoetic" objects for their B's, as Dante does when he compares a winged monster, resting his forepaws on the brink of a cliff, to *a scow* on a riverbank, or when he says that people passing in the moonlight squint, in order to recognize each other, like *an old tailor threading his needle,* or that the mind rests in the truth it has been seeking like *an animal in its den;* or as Villon does when he says that the teeth of a starving man stand out from his shrunken gums like those of *a rake,* or that the body of a hanged man on which the birds feed is more pecked at than *a thimble.*

The B is also likely to be the more concrete of the two terms, as in John Donne's

> Let falsehood like a *discord* anger you. . . .

or in his

> If they are good it would be seen;
> Good is as visible as *green.* . . .

Sometimes a simile or metaphor will determine the structure of an entire poem, as we saw in "The Purse-Seine" and as we see in the following poem, in which "as" introduces the simile.

The Silken Tent

She is as in a field a silken tent
At midday when a sunny summer breeze
Has dried the dew and all its ropes relent,
So that in guys it gently sways at ease,
5   And its supporting central cedar pole,
That is its pinnacle to heavenward
And signifies the sureness of the soul,
Seems to owe naught to any single cord,
But strictly held by none, is loosely bound
10 By countless silken ties of love and thought
To everything on earth the compass round,
And only by one's going slightly taut
In the capriciousness of summer air
Is of the slightest bondage made aware.

[1942]

ROBERT FROST (1874–1963)

As that poem was based on a simile, the next one is based on a metaphor.

My Life Had Stood—A Loaded Gun

My Life had stood—a Loaded Gun—
In Corners—till a Day
The Owner passed—identified—
And carried Me away—

5   And now We roam the Sovereign Woods—
And now We hunt the Doe—
And every time I speak for Him
The Mountains straight reply—

And do I smile, such cordial light
10 Upon the Valley glow—
It is as a Vesuvian face
Had let its pleasure through—

And when at Night—Our good Day done—
I guard My Master's Head—
15 'Tis better than the Eider-Duck's
Deep Pillow—to have shared—

To foe of His—I'm deadly foe—
None stir the second time—
On whom I lay a Yellow Eye—
20 Or an emphatic Thumb—

Though I than He—may longer live
He longer must—than I—
For I have but the power to kill,
Without—the power to die—

[1863?] [1955]

EMILY DICKINSON (1830–1886)

The speaker says her life is a loaded gun—a surprising metaphor for this poem of faithful love. Once that statement has been made, in line 1, the poet is committed to that image: Everything else in the poem should make sense in terms of both life and gun. Here, the life of the speaker belongs to its "owner," the one who "carried Me away." She is also his lifelong protector. In the last stanza, though the words are very simple, their connections may be more difficult: The lines seem to mean that the "Owner" *must* (has just *got* to!) live longer than the speaker, because without him she would have no function in life, nothing to live for.

There is a similar use of metaphor in a poem in which a return to ordinary life after a blissful experience is described in terms of a parachute descending.

Returning

She re-enters her life
the way a parachutist re-enters
the coarser atmosphere of earth,
exchanging the sensual shapes of clouds
5   for cloud-shaped trees rushing
to meet her, their branches sharp,
their soft leaves transitory.

She notices smells,
the scent of pines piercing
10   the surface of memory—
that dark lake submerged in pines
in which her husband
starts to swim
back into sight.

15   And as she lands
in their own garden,
after her brief but brilliant flight,
she pushes the silky parachute from her
as she pushed the white sheet
20   from her breasts
just yesterday.

[1981]
LINDA PASTAN (*b.* 1932)

SIMILE

CAUTION! HAZARDOUS READING!
PROCEED WITH CARE!

In boxes like this, in this chapter and some later ones, various figures of speech are sampled, out of context, in stronger concentration than we are ever likely to find them in actual poems. ("Western Wind" has none at all.)

We should not expect to find brilliant detail in every line of a poem; its presence might be as distracting, and ultimately as numbing, as string after string of exploding firecrackers.

> Deep in the sun-searched growths the dragon-fly
> Hangs like a blue thread loosened from the sky. . . .
>
> DANTE GABRIEL ROSSETTI

> I farm a pasture where the boulders lie
> As touching as a basket full of eggs . . .   ROBERT FROST

> The attic wasps went missing by like bullets . . .   ROBERT FROST

> She rides her hips as
> it were a horse   WILLIAM CARLOS WILLIAMS

> Love without hope, as when the young bird-catcher
> Swept off his tall hat to the Squire's own daughter,
> So let the imprisoned larks escape and fly
> Singing about her head, as she rode by.
>
> ROBERT GRAVES

> Wi' minds like the look on a hen's face . . .   HUGH MacDIARMID

> Each dockpost comes with a pelican . . .
> one languidly unrumples itself and flies
> off like a purposeful overcoat.   WILLIAM MATTHEWS

>   . . . I watch a toad
>   —dusty, huge—cross a blacktop road
>   by hops and halts; landing each
>   time like a splattered
> egg . . .   BRAD LEITHAUSER

>   . . . After we kissed
> I wore my mouth like a neon bowtie for days . . .   ALICE FULTON

> The waitress looks at my face
> as if it were a small tip.   STEPHEN DUNN

> . . . lightning jabbed the building,
> hit apartment 14–E, scattering bricks from the roof
> like beads from a broken necklace.   MARTÍN ESPADA

In the following poem, the writer begins by denying one metaphor ("Marriage is not . . .") only to reestablish another.

Habitation

Marriage is not
a house or even a tent

it is before that, and colder:

the edge of the forest, the edge
5 of the desert
        the unpainted stairs
at the back where we squat
outside, eating popcorn

the edge of the receding glacier
10 where painfully and with wonder
at having survived even
this far

we are learning to make fire   [1976]
                                        MARGARET ATWOOD (*b.* 1939)

In both of these poems (Pastan and Atwood), the figures of speech are explicit. Merely to imply a metaphor can also be effective: to say A is like B without ever naming B, but giving clues to B's identity:

> . . . I looked, and Stella spied,
> Who, hard by, made a window send forth light. . . .
>   SIR PHILIP SIDNEY

Stella's beauty is like a candle, a lamp, or some other source of illumination.

Since "motley" is the many-colored costume of a fool, a poet implies he lives among fools when he writes

> Being certain that they and I
> But lived where motley is worn . . .
>   WILLIAM BUTLER YEATS

Metaphors are implied but not identified in the following lines:

> When we first met and loved, I did not build
> Upon the event with marble . . .
>   ELIZABETH BARRETT BROWNING

> Out in the porch's sagging floor,
> Leaves got up in a coil and hissed,
> Blindly struck at my knee and missed. . . .
>   ROBERT FROST

In "Went Up a Year This Evening" (see Anthology, p. 422), Emily Dickinson writes an entire poem that describes a death in imagery of a balloon ascension—without ever mentioning the balloon.

In "No Second Troy," Yeats has written about a woman whose beauty, intensity, and revolutionary ardor are likely to bring trouble to the world; he implies she is like Helen of Troy, whose glamour led to the destruction of a kingdom.

No Second Troy

Why should I blame her that she filled my days
With misery, or that she would of late
Have taught to ignorant men most violent ways,
Or hurled the little streets upon the great,
5   Had they but courage equal to desire?
What could have made her peaceful with a mind
That nobleness made simple as a fire,
With beauty like a tightened bow, a kind
That is not natural in an age like this,
10   Being high and solitary and most stern?
Why, what could she have done, being what she is?
Was there another Troy for her to burn?   [1910]
WILLIAM BUTLER YEATS (1865–1939)

In addition to the implied image, the poem has two others of an especially powerful sort. The woman has a mind "that nobleness made simple as a fire." Fire is simple, yes; but, like all basic images, it is ambivalent. It is beautiful, vivid, life-giving; it is also ominous and destructive, as the woman is. Her nobility may be simple, but—watch out! Her beauty is "like a tightened bow," its lines gracefully and dynamically curved. But a tightened bow is also threatening, like a pointed revolver. The apparently simple images carry what we could call a *supercharge*.

Or the opposite may happen. The A-is-B equivalence may be sound in one respect, but the B may carry other suggestions that weaken the metaphor. Honey and vinegar, for example, are about the same color. We might say that rich blond hair or suntanned skin was honey-colored, but we could not safely say it was vinegar-colored. The suggestion of sourness in the vinegar image disqualifies it as a metaphor for anything lovely, no matter how right its color might be. We find the same fault in the following lines:

Once more at dawn I drive
The weary cattle of my soul to the mud hole of your eyes.

Another common weakness is what is called a *mixed metaphor*—that is, a metaphor made up of components that do not go together. "Skating on thin ice" and "being in hot water" are sensible enough metaphors (though trite) for hazardous actions and embarrassing predicaments. But if one says, "People who skate on thin ice are likely to find themselves in hot water," one is mixing a metaphor and, unless humor is intended, is writing awkwardly. Mixed metaphors are like double exposures in photography. Some may be deliberate; some may accidentally result in a good picture. Most are plain failures, with results comic, ugly, or merely blurred. We get something like the comedy of mixed metaphor in the "Irish bulls" Carl Sandburg quotes in *The People, Yes:*

> I can never get these boots on till I have worn them for a while . . .
> If all the world were blind what a melancholy sight it would be . . .
> They would cut us into mince-meat and throw our bleeding heads on
>   the table to stare us in the face . . .
> On the dim and faroff shore of the future we can see the footprint of
>   an unseen hand . . .

John Ciardi, in describing the fields just after a spring thaw, begins, "The paper fields . . ." "Paper," then, is his metaphor. He continues the line, "lay crumpled by the road." If the fields are paper, they have to do something paperlike; they have to be "crumpled." A less skillful writer might have said, "The paper fields lie shattered by the road," forgetting that paper cannot shatter. Pablo Neruda, as translated by W. S. Merwin, writes

> The clouds travel like white handkerchiefs of goodbye. . . .

and then continues the image with

> The wind, travelling, waving them in its hands. . . .

Suppose he had written

> The clouds travel like white handkerchiefs of goodbye
> Shipwrecked on the harsh shores of forgetfulness . . .

The image would then have been absurd: Handkerchiefs are not seagoing vessels.

Sometimes, as we saw in "The Silken Tent" and "My Life Had Stood— A Loaded Gun," an image is sustained throughout a poem. A small poem by Robert Frost is a good example.

A Patch of Old Snow

> There's a patch of old snow in a corner
>   That I should have guessed
> Was a blow-away paper the rain
>   Had brought to rest.

5   It is speckled with grime as if
        Small print overspread it,
    The news of a day I've forgotten—
        If I ever read it.   [1916]
                                        ROBERT FROST (1874–1963)

The metaphor ("patch of old snow" equals "a blow-away paper") is
sustained by three words in the second stanza: "print," "news," and "read."
A careless writer might easily have forgotten his newspaper imagery and
written something like

        It is speckled with grime as if
            It were polka-dot cotton,
        Like some mystical code in a dream,
            Or a tune I've forgotten.

But newspapers are not made out of cotton, nor are polka dots much like
a "code," nor is a "tune" related to newspapers or polka dots or a code.

    The poet Al Young (*b.* 1939) often writes about musicians. In his four
lines about a bass player, Vernon Alley, he extends a fiery metaphor:

Up Vernon's Alley

His smile can light up wood as good as pluck.
All sparkle, no match, his finger's on some fuse
hooked up to soul; an ammunition truck.
Whole worlds go up when Vernon plays the blues.   [2001]

    For other poems that develop a single metaphor, see George Herbert's
"Redemption" (Anthology, p. 381) and William Carlos Williams's "To Waken
an Old Lady" (p. 447). In the following poem, a simile is sustained; the basic
image ("Old people are like birds") makes sense on both levels (that of
people and that of birds) throughout the poem.

City Pigeons

Old people are like birds:
the same words flock to the mind's eye
in speaking of them.
They perch in public places,
5   scratch for the world's crumbs, seek
its shiny trifles—
easily ruffled
are quick to realight, alert
and nodding,
10 cheeky occupants of plazas,
monuments' companions, suppliants
in lime-specked groves
to dirty mysteries.   [1968]
                                        HELEN CHASIN (*b.* 1938)

On the other hand, images may be sustained at too great a cost, as they are in this anonymous little verse:

> God took our flower—our little Nell.
> He thought He too would like a smell.

Simile and metaphor, like the other figures of speech, can be overused: Excessive repetition of "like" or "as" can be a tedious mannerism. Unless of course a comic effect is intended, as it is in Michael Ondaatje's "Sweet Like a Crow," which makes playful fun of an eight-year-old girl in Sri Lanka, where Mr. Ondaatje, now living in Canada, was born. His poem begins

> Your voice sounds like a scorpion being pushed
> through a glass tube
> like someone has just trod on a peacock . . .
> like a rusty bible, like someone pulling barbed wire
> across a stone courtyard, like a pig drowning . . .
> a frog singing at Carnegie Hall . . .
> a nose being hit by a mango . . .

and continues through about two dozen other similes of dissonance.

ANALOGY

Any resemblance, in form or function, between otherwise unlike objects can be called **analogy,** which is a kind of reasoning based on metaphor. Since A is like B in some respects, it is possible to suppose that other resemblances follow. A science writer and physicist at the Smithsonian Astrophysical Observatory takes us from metaphor to analogy when he writes that

> Metaphor is critical to science. Metaphor in science serves not just as a pedagogical device . . . but also as an aid to scientific discovery. In doing science, it is almost impossible not to reason by physical analogy, not to form mental pictures, not to imagine balls bouncing and pendulums swinging. Metaphor is part of the process of science.[*]

His opinion of the value of analogy has been confirmed by recent studies of the personal papers of Thomas Edison, which show that

> The new portrait of Edison is marked by his powerful ability—never fully recognized until now—to reason through analogy. It was perhaps this trait more than any flashes of brilliance or cries of "Eureka!" that accounted for his great inventiveness. It is now thought that this hidden ability is what transformed one successful invention into another, eventually producing the phonograph, the incandescent light bulb, systems of electric power generation and motion pictures.[†]

[*]Alan P. Lightman, "Magic on the Mind: Physicists' Use of Metaphor," *The American Scholar,* Winter 1989.
[†]William J. Broad, "Subtle Analogies Found at the Core of Edison's Genius," *New York Times,* March 22, 1985.

METAPHOR

Now is the winter of our discontent
Made glorious summer by this sun of York:
And all the clouds that loured upon our house
In the deep bosom of the ocean buried . . .   WILLIAM SHAKESPEARE

The haughty thistle o'er all danger towers,
In every place the very wasp of flowers.   JOHN CLARE

Out of the chimney of the court-house
A greyhound of smoke leapt and chased
The northwest wind. . . .   EDGAR LEE MASTERS

                              . . . an eagle
Was perched on the jag of a burnt pine,
Insolent and gorged, cloaked in the folded storms
        of his shoulders . . .   ROBINSON JEFFERS

. . . snakes' hypodermic teeth . . .   MARIANNE MOORE

. . . the lion's ferocious chrysanthemum head. . . .
                                                  MARIANNE MOORE

You gave me dandelions . . .

round suns rising
in April, soft moons
blowing away in June . . .   LINDA PASTAN

                          . . . Now
a squirrel quivers a tail

of smoke, serving himself one
acorn in its own brown bowl . . .   MARY JO SALTER

. . . the new moon's just a luminous
zilch . . .   ALICE FULTON

Summer was slack,
a dog chain with its dog gone.   MICHAEL CHITWOOD

Poets too have made powerful use of analogy.

The poet's mind—like the subconscious mind of the dreamer and the prelogical mind of the child—is more moved by similarities and parallels than by stricter forms of logic; analogy seems to be the poet's favorite form of reasoning. When Sidney writes

ANALOGY

And why take ye thought for raiment? Consider the lilies of the field, how they grow; they toil not, neither do they spin: and yet I say unto you, That even Solomon in all his glory was not arrayed like one of these.

MATTHEW 6:28

Old wood inflamed, doth yield the bravest fire,
When younger doth in smoke his virtue spend. . . .

SIR PHILIP SIDNEY

No more be grieved at that which thou hast done:
Roses have thorns, and silver fountains mud;
Clouds and eclipses stain both moon and sun,
And loathsome canker lives in sweetest bud.

WILLIAM SHAKESPEARE

Thin airy things extend themselves in space,
    Things solid take up little place. . . .   ABRAHAM COWLEY

But 'tis too much on so despised a theme:
No man would dabble in a dirty stream. . . .

THE EARL OF ROCHESTER

Nothing in progression can rest on its original plan. We may as well think of rocking a grown man in the cradle of an infant.

EDMUND BURKE

True ease in writing comes from art, not chance,
As those move easiest who have learned to dance.

ALEXANDER POPE

No mud can soil us but the mud we throw . . .

JAMES RUSSELL LOWELL

                    But enough,
For when we have blamed the wind we can blame love . . .

WILLIAM BUTLER YEATS

Thus noble gold down to the bottom goes,
When worthless cork aloft doth floating lie. . . .

he means that since certain values in life are good as gold and others cheap and lightweight as cork, perhaps these values behave like gold and cork in the current of life: The best may sink from sight; the worst stay conspicuously on top.

Sometimes we find an entire poem structured on analogy.

All But Blind

All but blind
    In his chambered hole
Gropes for worms
    The four-clawed Mole.

5   All but blind
    In the evening sky
The hooded Bat
    Twirls softly by.

All but blind
10   In the burning day
The Barn-Owl blunders
    On her way.

And blind as are
    These three to me,
15 So, blind to Some-One
    I must be.

[1901]
WALTER DE LA MARE (1873–1956)

Analogies, like the other figures of speech we are considering, also thrive outside the literary world. A football coach near the end of a winning season was asked if he would change his strategy for the last game. "No," he analogized, "I'm going to dance with the girl that brought me."

SYNESTHESIA

One kind of analogy that works with intersense relationships is called **synesthesia,** from Greek words that mean *blended feeling.* It is the perception or interpretation of the data of one sense in terms of another. The process itself has been seen as regressive. Early in human history, it seems we did not distinguish between the senses as sharply as we do now. Sense data tended to overlap, as they still do in babies, whose world, according to a recent study, is a world of synesthesia, of confusion of the senses.

His world smells to him much as our world smells to us, but he does not perceive odors as coming through his nose alone. He hears odors, and sees odors, and feels them too. His world is a mêlée of pungent aromas—and pungent sounds, and bitter-smelling sounds, and sweet-smelling sights, and sour-smelling pressures against the skin. If we could visit the newborn's world, we would think ourselves inside a hallucinogenic perfumery.*

*Daphne and Charles Maurer, *The World of the Newborn.* (New York: Basic Books, 1988).

SYNESTHESIA

To the bugle, every color is red. EMILY DICKINSON

Dark hills at evening in the west,
Where sunset hovers like a sound
Of golden horns that sang to rest
Old bones of warriors underground . . . EDWIN ARLINGTON ROBINSON

[Of autumn groves] . . . their lion-color in the wood
Roars to miraculous heat and turbulence. ELINOR WYLIE

And Cortez rode up, reining tautly in—
Firmly as coffee grips the taste—and away!— HART CRANE

When we were children words were colored
(Harlot and murder were dark purple). . . . LOUIS MACNEICE

Nothing disturbed it: not the owl that came
rowing out at noon, soundless as fur . . . AMY CLAMPITT

The oriole, a charred and singing coal,
still burns aloud among the monuments . . . AMY CLAMPITT

. . . if I could touch you
my hands would begin to sing . . . MARY OLIVER

The [tenor's] high quavers
That hold like splashes of light on the dark water . . . ROBERT PINSKY

I met a blind girl who thought the sky
tasted like cold metal when it rained . . . ANITA ENDREZZE

In some individuals, called "synesthetes," this miswiring of the brain persists into adulthood. The great scientist Sir Isaac Newton associated musical notes with colors—not only associated them, he *saw* colors when he heard notes, *saw* red when he heard C, *saw* orange when he heard D, and so on. There have been cases of people who perceived taste as color, who saw geometric shapes when they felt pain, or, weirdest of all, who would contort their bodies into certain poses that conformed to sounds they heard—"audiomotor synesthesia," the scientists called it. In all these instances, the cause was in the brain structure itself, not in the imagination of the synesthete, who generally enjoyed, rather than suffered from, the enriched sensibility. Sense centers in the brain, when stimulated, can arouse associated centers.

In speaking, we are all synesthetes. Words like "sweet," "sour," and "bitter" are taste words, but we speak of a sweet smile, a sour note, a bitter sight. Although "stink" is a smell word, we apply it to anything that affects us unpleasantly. "Loud" is a sound word, yet we speak of a loud necktie. We feel blue; we listen to cold words; we see dull colors. Wine experts would be lost without synesthesia: a glance at one of the standard guides reveals that the following words are used to describe various vintages: "hard," "soft," "light," "heavy," "smooth," "rough," "dry," "spotty," "fat," "round," "green," "flinty," "strong," "sturdy," "velvety," "satiny," "firm," "sunny," "harsh."

Synesthesia was a mode of imagery favored by the French Symbolist poets of the nineteenth century (see Chapter 3, pp. 46–66). Charles Baudelaire imagined

> There are perfumes cool as the flesh of children,
> Sweet as oboes, green as the meadows . . .

and Arthur Rimbaud wrote a sonnet to the color of French vowels, which begins

> A black, E white, I red, U green, O blue . . .

ALLUSION

Another recognition of similarity is **allusion,** which follows an "it-reminds-me-of" pattern. An allusion is an incomplete reference to something that those who share our knowledge or background will understand. In conversation we often use such allusions as "There he goes acting like Bill!" or "I hope this evening won't be like the last one." To an outsider, the meaning of such an allusion would be obscure. Poets, naturally at home with poetry, sometimes quote from or allude to other writers (as Pablo Picasso liked to "quote" from other painters by including details from their work in his own paintings). When Frost, writing about the accidental death of a farm boy, calls his poem " 'Out, Out—,' " he assumes we will remember Macbeth's famous remarks on life and death,

> Out, out, brief candle!
> Life's but a walking shadow. . . .

and that his poem will pick up an added pathos from the memory. When Alexander Pope writes his "Intended for Sir Isaac Newton," he trusts we will all hear the allusion to the first chapter of Genesis ("And God said, Let there be light: and there was light").

Intended for Sir Isaac Newton

Nature and Nature's laws lay hid in Night:
God said, *Let Newton be!* and all was Light.

ALEXANDER POPE (1688–1744)

Such poets as Ezra Pound and T. S. Eliot have been particularly fond of widening the range and deepening the meaning of their own poems by evoking lines or fragments from the work of other poems they assume we should be familiar with. For a celebrated example, see Eliot's "The Love Song of J. Alfred Prufrock" and the footnotes to it (Anthology, p. 453). Most poets are familiar enough with their great predecessors to be able to quote from them when quotations are relevant.

Michael Donaghy (1954–2004, an Irish-American native of the Bronx who spent his last years in Britain) alluded in the following poem not only to W. B. Yeats's "An Irish Airman Foresees His Death," but also to the Bible and various New York personages:

Local 32B

The rich are different. Where we have doorknobs,
they have doormen—like me, a cigar store Indian
on the Upper East Side, in polyester, in August.
As the tenants tanned in Tenerife and Monaco
5   I stood guard beneath Manhattan's leaden light
watching poodle turds bake grey in half an hour.
Another hot one, Mr. Rockefeller!
An Irish doorman foresees his death,
waves, and runs to help it with its packages.
10   Once I got a cab for Mr. Pavarotti. No kidding.
No tip either. I stared after him down Fifth
and caught him looking after me, then through me,
like Samson, eyeless, at the Philistine chorus—
Yessir, I put the tenor in the vehicle.
15   And a mighty tight squeeze it was.   [2000]

It's characteristic of Donaghy's quick wit and lightly worn intellect that such a range of references can appear in a poem named for a labor union. That "cigar store Indian" is an allusion to a figure no longer commonly seen by American shoppers—a wooden statue advertising tobacco products. But Donaghy's working-class, Irish background caused him to layer in more historical allusions as well as various associations with opera and prosperous New York neighborhoods.

We do not have to catch all such allusions to understand and enjoy Donaghy's poem, but the meaning of many lines is richer if we do. We see a somewhat different use of allusion in David Mura's "The Natives" (Anthology, p. 554). In reading it, we are several times reminded—as Mura wishes us to be—of Edwin Muir's "The Horses" (Anthology, p. 452).

A wide-ranging fondness for allusion allows the poet to unite widely different areas of experience. In August Kleinzahler's "Watching Dogwood Blossoms Fall in a Parking Lot Off Route 46" (Anthology, p. 542), the petals drifting alongside an industrial highway in New Jersey take his imagination far from the world of strip malls, smokestacks, and semis to the China of a thousand years before, when the great poet Tu Fu, as often in his verse, muses on blossoms drifting by a riverbank. In his reverie of bird-song and love-longing, the orioles, vivid symbols in ancient Chinese love poems, are seen as stirring a sensitive nerve in the old poet.

Marilyn Nelson, in her "Epithalamium and Shivaree" (Anthology, p. 535), ranges even more surprisingly. From her rapt account of the Marriage at Cana (John 2:1–11) and its effect, we are catapulted into a circus world of tightrope walkers with pink parasols jitterbugging on unicycles over the "silver thread" of a river far below.

PERSONIFICATION, MYTHOLOGY

Since we have more in common with people than with other objects of our experience, it is not surprising that many of our comparisons relate things to people. We personify, or see as people, not only inanimate things but also abstractions, movements, or events. In the childhood of the individual, in the childhood of the culture, in the mind of the dreamer, we find extensive use of such **personification.** The child may pet or punish a toy wagon for being good or bad. Early human societies show a tendency toward animism or psychism, toward attributing life to lifeless things. Even in our civilized society, adults reduced to primitive rage break their golf clubs or kick their flat tires. We speak of "friendly" colors or "timid" arguments or "yawning" chasms or chemical "reactions." We project our moods onto landscapes or onto the weather. Robert Burns, when unhappy, wondered how nature could go on being its happy self:

> Ye banks and braes o' bonnie Doon,
>   How can ye bloom so fresh and fair?
> How can ye chant, ye little birds,
>   And I so weary, full o' care. . . .

Eliot called April the "cruellest" month. Projecting the qualities of living things onto the nonliving is what John Ruskin called the "pathetic fallacy." When used mechanically or sentimentally, it can be ridiculous. Or maudlin. Or unintentionally funny: "Dearest, must end this letter. Old Sir Weariness is creeping up on me." But used aptly, it can be vigorous: Seeing a tree in a windstorm, one might imagine tree and storm as wrestling antagonists. Or as Alice Fulton writes:

> It was impossible
> not to personify: the ash and willow
> tore their hair in the breeze . . .

Naomi Shihab Nye personifies the letters on an eye chart:

> The D is desperate.
> The B wants to take a vacation,
> live on a billboard, be broad and brave.
> The E is mad at the R for upstaging him.
> The little c wants to be a big C if possible,
> and the P pauses long between thoughts.

Today we have our own personifications: "Football is king"; "Medical science tells us"; "The economy demands"; "Inflation is threatening." We speak of Jack Frost, Old Man River ("He must know something"), Mr. Clean, Lady Luck. More than one modern poet has transferred his soul into a plant.

A Cut Flower

I stand on slenderness all fresh and fair,
I feel root-firmness in the earth far down,
I catch in the wind and loose my scent for bees
That sack my throat for kisses and suck love.
5   What is the wind that brings thy body over?
Wind, I am beautiful and sick. I long
For rain that strikes and bites like cold and hurts.
Be angry, rain, for dew is kind to me
When I am cool from sleep and take my bath.

10   Who softens the sweet earth about my feet,
Touches my face so often and brings water?
Where does she go, taller than any sunflower
Over the grass like birds? Has she a root?
These are great animals that kneel to us,
15   Sent by the sun perhaps to help us grow.
I have seen death. The colors went away,
The petals grasped at nothing and curled tight.
Then the whole head fell off and left the sky.

She tended me and held me by my stalk.
20   Yesterday I was well, and then the gleam,
The thing sharper than frost cut me in half.
I fainted and was lifted high. I feel
Waist-deep in rain. My face is dry and drawn.
My beauty leaks into the glass like rain.
25   When first I opened to the sun I thought
My colors would be parched. Where are my bees?
Must I die now? Is this a part of life?

[1942]
KARL SHAPIRO (b. 1913)

PERSONIFICATION

When well-appareled April on the heel
Of limping Winter treads . . .

WILLIAM SHAKESPEARE

. . . Danger knows full well
That Caesar is more dangerous than he.

WILLIAM SHAKESPEARE

When "Music, Heavenly Maid," was *very* young,
She did not sing as poets say she sung.
Unlike the mermaids of the fairy tales,
She paid but slight attention to her scales.

CHRISTOPHER PEARSE CRANCH

When I am dead and over me bright April
    Shakes out her rain-drenched hair . . .

SARA TEASDALE

Come, my songs, let us express our baser passions,
Let us express our envy of the man with a steady job
    and no worry about the future.
You are very idle, my songs.
I fear you will come to a bad end.
You stand about on the streets,
You loiter at the corners and bus-stops,
You do next to nothing at all . . .
Insolent little beasts, shameless, devoid of clothing! . . .

EZRA POUND

All through the night the knot in the shoelace
waits for its liberation
and the match on the table packs its head
with anticipation of light.
The faucet sweats out a bead of water
which gathers strength for the free-fall,
while the lettuce in the refrigerator
succumbs to its brown killer . . .

LISEL MUELLER

Meanwhile telephones crouch, getting ready to ring
In locked-up offices

PHILIP LARKIN

The Tiber muddles by,
    stroking its beard of filthy weed . . .

KARL KIRCHWEY

In "To Autumn" (see Anthology, p. 407), John Keats personifies the spirit of that season.

We still like to make up stories, just as our earliest ancestors did, which use personification to explain the great forces of our existence. Such stories, which might explain how the world began or where the sun goes when it sets, we call myths. **Mythology** is a natural product of the symbolizing mind; poets, when not making up myths of their own, are still commenting on the ancient ones. Yeats tells us how, at a time when he thought the world was in need of guidance from above, his imagination "began to play with Leda and the Swan for metaphor." According to his version of the myth, Zeus, in the form of a swan, had forced himself upon Leda, the beautiful queen of Sparta. An offspring of their union was Helen of Troy—hence the reference of the Trojan War near the end of the poem. Yeats tells us that, as he was writing, "bird and lady took such possession of the scene that all politics went out of it." He concentrated on the imagined experience itself, which, for poetry, may be more important than any "ideas" expressed. What would it really be like, he wondered, for a girl to be loved by Zeus in the form of a swan?

Leda and the Swan

A sudden blow: the great wings beating still
Above the staggering girl, her thighs caressed
By the dark webs, her nape caught in his bill,
He holds her helpless breast upon his breast.

5 How can those terrified vague fingers push
The feathered glory from her loosening thighs?
And how can body, laid in that white rush,
But feel the strange heart beating where it lies?

A shudder in the loins engenders there
10 The broken wall, the burning roof and tower
And Agamemnon dead.
               Being so caught up,
So mastered by the brute blood of the air,
Did she put on his knowledge with his power
15 Before the indifferent beak could let her drop?   [1928]
WILLIAM BUTLER YEATS (1865–1939)

A poet may merely refer to an ancient myth, as Walter Savage Landor does when he puts to new use the story about Charon, the aged ferryman who in classical mythology took the souls of the dead across the River Styx in the underworld.

Dirce

Stand close around, ye Stygian set,
  With Dirce in one boat conveyed!

Or Charon, seeing, may forget
  That he is old and she a shade.   [1831]
          WALTER SAVAGE LANDOR (1775–1864)

Landor's quietly written poem is about a girl so beautiful that even when dead and a mere "shade" she might have brought out the potential rapist in Charon, old as he is. Both of these poems, like Auden's "The Shield of Achilles" in a later chapter (p. 96), are based on the mythology of Greece and Rome, which has given us such familiar figures as Aphrodite, Mars, Neptune, Apollo, Bacchus, Pan, and the Sirens. Most of them are rather literary images today; they are not as close to us as such legendary figures as Raven, Coyote, and the Thunderbird are to our Native American poets, whose rich mythology rose out of the belief that all nature was alive—that not only the animals but even the plants, the forests, the mountains, the stars had a consciousness like our own and participated actively in our lives. Leslie Marmon Silko's "Prayer to the Pacific" (Anthology, p. 541) deals with a "myth of origin" like that held by many Indian tribes, for whom North America, thought of as existing on the back of a giant turtle, was their "Turtle Island." Louise Erdrich's "Jacklight" (Anthology, p. 561) is another poem that becomes more meaningful when seen against a background of Native American mythology: of such tales, for example, as those of men mating with or turning into deer, tales which show the close and desirable association of humanity with nature.

EXERCISES & DIVERSIONS

A. Ponder the similes and metaphors in the following lines. Which do you think succeed? Which fail?

  1. Slow time, with woollen feet make thy soft pace,
    And leave no tracks in the snow of her pure face. . . .
                RICHARD LOVELACE

  2. Fain would I kiss my Julia's dainty leg,
    Which is as white and hairless as an egg.
                ROBERT HERRICK

  3. Sweet marmalade of kisses newly gathered. . . .
            MARGARET CAVENDISH

  4. Sweet maidens with tanned faces,
    And bosoms fit to broil. . . .
                JOHN CLARE

  5. And then Llewellyn leapt and fled
    Like one with hornets in his hair. . . .
         EDWIN ARLINGTON ROBINSON

6.   . . . a sow
    Displaying a valentine rump. . . .

                                    ADRIEN STOUTENBURG

7. Think of the storm roaming the sky uneasily
    like a dog looking for a place to sleep in,
    listen to it growling.

                                    ELIZABETH BISHOP

8. . . . a glinting beetle on its back
    struggled like an orchestra

    with Beethoven . . .

                                    CRAIG RAINE

9. The divorce judge has asked for a witness,
    and you wait at the back of the courtroom
    as still as a flag on its stand . . .

                                    TED KOOSER

10. . . . Ted Williams walked to the diamond . . .
    squinting at the pitcher, bat swaying like a memory of trees.

                                    MARTÍN ESPADA

B. How well do you think the imagery (lake, skates, saint, thin ice) works
    in the following love poem, published early in this century?

        Her bosom's like a frozen lake
            On whose cold brink I stand;
        Oh, buckle on my spirit's skates,
            And take me by the hand!

        And lead thou, loving saint, the way
            To where the ice is thin
        That it may break beneath my feet
            And let a lover in.

C. Identify and evaluate the examples of analogy, synesthesia, allusion, and
    personification in the following lines:

    1. Gnats are unnoted wheresoe'er they fly,
        But eagles gazed upon with every eye . . .

                                    WILLIAM SHAKESPEARE

    2. And the hapless soldier's sigh
        Runs in blood down palace walls . . .

                                    WILLIAM BLAKE

3. Let no Sunrise' yellow noise
   Interrupt this Ground . . .

EMILY DICKINSON

4. The sun had laid his chin on the grey wood,
   Weary, with all his poppies gathered round him. . . .

WILLIAM BUTLER YEATS

5. And Tian said, with his hand on the strings of his lute,
   The low sounds continuing
           after his hand left the strings,
   And the sound went up like smoke, under the leaves . . .

EZRA POUND

6. How trumpet and drum paraded before
   The marching young men, how they led
   Us, green and dumb, where the war
           Opened his mouth to be fed . . .

HOWARD NEMEROV

7. it was almost dark when the wind
   breathless from playing
   with water
           came over and stopped
   resting in the bare trees and dry grass . . .

A. R. AMMONS

8. . . . the vacuum cleaner grazes
   over the carpet, lowing,
   its udder a swollen wobble . . .

CRAIG RAINE

9. On either side, those dear old ladies,
   the loosening barns, their little windows
   dulled by cataracts of hay and cobwebs
   hide broken tractors under their skirts . . .

TED KOOSER

10. Country girls full of yum-yum and apple pie . . .

MARGARET BENBOW

D. In attacking the notion, held by some linguists, that there is no such thing as "good English," and that the only standard is what people say, Theodore M. Bernstein, in *The Careful Writer*, uses three analogies: There are more bad fiddlers than good, yet no one hesitates to say there is such a thing as good violin playing; there are more golfers who shoot in the nineties than in the seventies, yet we know there is a right way to play golf; there are more awkward do-it-yourself carpenters than competent professionals, yet we know there are right and wrong ways of doing carpentry work. "In language alone," he concludes, "are the bunglers blessed." Do his analogies constitute good metaphoric reasoning?

E. In the cartoon below, the use of metaphor has led to a failure of communication. Has the poet chosen his metaphors badly? Or has the bird misinterpreted them? Through malice? Through stupidity? (The lazy mind hates metaphor, says Diana in George Meredith's *Diana of the Crossways*.)

F. Would you agree with Alan Shapiro (*b*. 1926) that poets' fondness for metaphor can sometimes obscure reality instead of illuminating it?

Against Poets

Golden leaves,
Russet leaves
Detach, float, spin
By the thousands,
Singly.

Charged with meaning
By poets,
Used as metaphor
For decline, loss,
Separation,

The poets
Come between us
And the leaves
In their meaningless
Beauty.

[1996]

G. 1. This Sally now does like a garment wear
        The beauty of the evening; silent, bare,
        Hips, shoulders, arms, tresses, and temples lie . . .

(Reprinted by permission of John L. Hart FLP, and Creators Syndicate, Inc.)

Coming across this description of a sleeping girl in a poem by
L. E. Sissman, most readers of poetry will remember three lines from
Wordsworth's "Composed upon Westminster Bridge" (Anthology,
p. 399). Notice how corresponding words in the third of these lines are
alike in sound. Is the purpose of the allusion purely humorous?

2.   Amy Clampitt's poem "Real Estate" begins

> Something there is that doesn't
> love a Third Avenue tenement . . .

Page through the poems of Robert Frost in the Anthology
(pp. 438–443), to locate the source of the allusion. Why do you
think the poet wants to remind us of Frost?

ESSAYS

A.   In the introduction to *Harper's Anthology of 20th Century Native
American Poetry* (in which myth is said to be vital to "the orchestration
and recognition of life energies"), Louise Erdrich's "feminist" poem
"Jacklight" (Anthology, p. 561) is said to be "a story of the need for
the violent male principle to be inducted in the deep female woods."
Write an essay in which you agree or disagree with this interpretation.
Write your essay for a reader who may not be familiar with the poem:
Introduce your reader to the poem under discussion; then point out
the interpretation given above and state your own position toward it.
In the rest of your essay, use examples from the poem to make your
case.

B.   Write an essay on the uses of figurative language in April Lindner's
"Girl" (Anthology, p. 565) or Mary Jo Salter's "Boulevard du
Montparnasse" (Anthology, p. 559). How would these poems
be diminished if such figures were not used?

POEMS

A.   Take a simile from any poem or lines in the preceding pages and
rewrite it as an extended metaphor in a poem of your own.

B.   Write a poem alluding to a song or literary work that only someone
of your generation would know. Can you make your poem
comprehensible to readers of other generations?

3

SYMBOLISM

The Broken Coin

Chapter 2 focused on simile and metaphor: on how we can illustrate the nature or quality of something by comparing it to something else with which we are more familiar, or which possesses that quality more vividly. This chapter will focus on another of the ways we handle imagery: on our habit of mentioning an object so that it refers not only to itself but to other realities associated with it.

Our central concern here is with symbolism, but two figures of speech afford a handy introduction to it. Their names are exotic (like so many in medicine, law, and other fields) because they were given by the scholars in Greece who noticed long ago that they are shortcuts we employ regularly in our thinking and in our speech.

SYNECDOCHE, METONYMY

Synecdoche (the Greek means something like *taking as a whole*) is commonly defined as "a part for the whole." A way of perceiving and thinking as well as of speaking, in its commonest form it singles out some part of a thing as important enough to stand for the whole thing, as when we say, "A *sail!*" meaning a whole ship, or "All *hands* on deck," or "Let's count *noses*," or "We need new *blood* in this department." A rancher might be asked, "How many *head* of cattle do you have?"

From the great welter of sensations fed into our brains every second (100 million, according to scientists), our attention focuses on some as standing for larger configurations—that is, we see "a part for the whole." A cave man coming suddenly upon his enemy, perhaps a more primitive type with snarling teeth bared, might later report to his cave wife, "Guess what I saw today! The Fang!" Like so many "rhetorical devices," synecdoche was nearer and dearer to primitive people than to us—for them, the part *was* the whole. This is a common assumption of magic all over the world. Get any part of a person—a lock of hair, a fingernail—or even learn the right name (Rumpelstiltskin!) and that person is subject to your magic power.

We often talk in synecdoche: "She was all eyes" or "Look at Nosey!" or "Here comes Big Mouth" or "She's such a brain" or "How's Twinkle-toes?" When we ask in prayer for "our daily bread," we have more in mind than an all-starch diet. "That's life" is a synecdoche; we see one incident or situation as standing for the nature of existence.

Metonymy is so close it overlaps. If our cave man had run into a more advanced type of enemy, he might have been especially impressed by something the stranger was carrying: a sharp rock fastened with deer hide thongs to a stout stick. If he had had a second escape, he might have reported later, "I saw The Axe today!" A metonymy—the cave man is referring to one thing by using the name of something associated with it. Children use metonymy when they call a dog a "bow-wow," from the associated sound. We use it when we say things like "Are there going to be any big names at the party?" or "His backhand [that is, the ball hit by his backhand] just nicked the line," or "I've been reading Shakespeare," or "I ate the whole plate" (even though the plate is still on the table), or "I drank two bottles." The last is that old favorite—container for thing contained. (James Thurber once thought up its opposite: "Get away from me or I'll hit you with the milk!") Metonymy is used by Shakespeare when he means to tell us that kings, scholars, and physicians must all die in time:

> The scepter, learning, physic must
> All follow this, and come to dust.

Mary Jo Salter (*b.* 1954) has played with such figures in "A Poetics of Sex":

> In bed we find no clean
> division of body and soul:
> anatomy
> is metonymy.
> Kissing your parts, I mean,
> I mean the whole. [1994]

THE SYMBOL

Most of the figures of speech we have been reading about conform so closely to the way we actually think that they are more than mere literary devices. This may be especially true of the one we come to now. According to the

SYNECDOCHE, METONYMY

Scepter and crown
Must tumble down,
And in the dust be equal made
With the poor crooked scythe and spade.   JAMES SHIRLEY

He stood among a crowd at Dromahair;
His heart hung all upon a silken dress . . .   WILLIAM BUTLER YEATS

The boy's first outcry was a rueful laugh,
As he swung toward them holding up the [mangled] hand
Half in appeal, but half as if to keep
The life from spilling . . .   ROBERT FROST

I should have been a pair of ragged claws
Scuttling across the floors of silent seas.   T. S. ELIOT

[Of students on a school bus]
When a cough came from the compound interest problem,
And a sneeze from the third chapter of the Civics book. . . .
                                    JOHN CIARDI

They took my lover's tallness off to war . . .
                                GWENDOLYN BROOKS

And riding the trolley homeward this afternoon
With the errands in my lap. . . .
                                ELEANOR ROSS TAYLOR

We listen while a dustpan eats
the scattered pieces of a quarrel. . . .
                                    VERN RUTSALA

The wind carries wolf . . .
                                    RED HAWK

[Of someone contemplating suicide]
The brown Aspirin bottle
held . . . five hundred bitter wishes . . .
                                    CRAIG RAINE

[Of cows] I would open the blue front door,
and again the field would be full of their munching.
                                    BILLY COLLINS

anthropologist Eli Sagan, the very health of our minds depends on our ability to use symbols:

> A human need as powerful as sex or aggression, a need that can be denied the psyche only at the cost of severe psychic disorder, is the need to create symbols and live in a symbolic world. In Cassirer's terms, it defines the species: *animal symbolicum.* We are a symbol-making animal.

In Chapter 2 we saw that a typical metaphor has an A-is-B pattern, as in "life is a dream." (Even though we express this as "the dream of life" or "this dream-life we live," we are still relying on our basic equation.) In such a pattern, the focus is on the A; we are being told more about the nature of life than about the nature of dreams.

We also saw that in metaphor the B is likely to be better known, more concrete, more of a sense image than the A: The nature of a dream seems more readily grasped than the nature of life.

The **symbol,** an image that stands for more than it denotes literally, is like metaphor in that it transfers meaning from one thing to another. But with symbol the current of interest is reversed: Our concern is directed from the first term to the second. The A is better known, more concrete, more of a sense image than what should be the B—which is often an abstraction the user does not even identify. If the poet mentions a rose, but is really thinking of the nature of beauty, then *rose* is a symbol of beauty. If the poet mentions being halfway along a road, but has in mind a thirty-fifth birthday, then *road* is a symbol of the life span. If *rose* and *road* are seen as symbols, there is no need to refer to beauty or age at all; we will sense that something more is intended than a real rose or a real road. If we think of the metaphoric process as "A is B," we might think of the symbolic one as "A is X," with the X usually unidentified, though clues are given to its identity.

Symbolic images often are physical objects: a hill, a well, a river. They symbolize such abstractions as *spiritual ascent, vitality, time.* A lion is a symbol for fierceness or courage; a fox, for cunning; a rock, for firmness; a torch, for learning. Light is a symbol for knowledge; darkness for ignorance. "Who looks upon a river in a meditative hour," wondered Emerson, "and is not reminded of the flux of all things?" A river, that is, is a symbol for time or change. "Every natural fact," Emerson believed, "is a symbol of some spiritual fact." We often find symbolic meaning in the details of life, as Portia does in *The Merchant of Venice* when she exclaims:

> How far that little candle throws his beams!
> So shines a good deed in a naughty world.

A candle, then, becomes a symbol for the power of virtue. Shelley, perpetually on the lookout for objects he could use as symbols, once admitted to a friend, "You know I always seek in what I see the manifestation of something beyond the present and tangible object." This is why in "To a Skylark" he is able to address the skylark with "Bird thou never wert." For him it is something more than bird.

In Federico García Lorca's "Sleepwalker's Ballad" (p. 340), a young man, dying of gunshot wounds, comes to see for the last time the woman he loves. To her father he says:

> "Friend, what I want is to trade
> this horse of mine for your house,
> this saddle of mine for your mirror,
> this knife of mine for your blanket."

None of this is meant literally; the young man would not have inserted in a Córdoba newspaper a want ad reading: "Will trade horse, saddle, knife for house, mirror, blanket." The objects mentioned are symbols of two ways of life; the dying man means, "I wish I could settle down and marry your daughter."

The use of such symbols, like that of other poetic "devices," is based on the way the mind really works. Our senses are affected by something. They send their electrical message to the brain, which interprets it as an image, a symbol of the original object that moved them. We express the image by using a word that is a symbol of that symbol. When we say anything, we have already built symbol on symbol.

A baby begins to think symbolically early in its development, associating the opening of a door with *food-mother-warmth*. Later, the adult dreams in symbols. For people in an aboriginal world, almost everything is symbolic, stands for something else. The most meaningful symbols are such natural ones as fire, water, air, and earth. Although these symbols are few in number, they have been significant to us for the hundreds of thousands of years of human existence. "No genius," says Carl Jung, "has ever sat down with a pen or a brush in his hand and said, 'Now I am going to invent a symbol.'"

Not a natural symbol, that is. There seem to be symbols we do make up. Most words are invented symbols; so are flags, coats of arms, traffic signs, valentine hearts, mathematical symbols, and the like. Scholars of language would rather refer to these inventions as *signs,* reserving the word "symbol" for what has a natural basis in reality and itself embodies the quality it stands for. A rose, for example, may be a symbol for beauty; it really exists and really is beautiful. When a snowy owl, generally an arctic bird, appeared in Chicago during a recent winter, newspaper accounts described it as "a symbol of desolation"; amid the skyscrapers or along the frozen lakefront, it seemed to embody that very quality.

Howard Nemerov gives us an introductory lecture, with illustrations, on the symbolism of a coin.

Money

An Introductory Lecture

This morning we shall spend a few minutes
Upon the study of symbolism, which is basic
To the nature of money. I show you this nickel.
Icons and cryptograms are written all over
5 The nickel: one side shows a hunchbacked bison
Bending his head and curling his tail to accommodate
The circular nature of money. Over him arches
UNITED STATES OF AMERICA, and, squinched in
Between that and his rump, E PLURIBUS UNUM,
10 A Roman reminiscence that appears to mean
An indeterminately large number of things
All of which are the same. Under the bison
A straight line giving him a ground to stand on
Reads FIVE CENTS. And on the other side of our nickel
15 There is the profile of a man with long hair
And a couple of feathers in the hair; we know
Somehow that he is an American Indian, and
He wears the number nineteen-thirty-six.
Right in front of his eyes the word LIBERTY, bent
20 To conform with the curve of the rim, appears
To be falling out of the sky Y first; the Indian
Keeps his eyes downcast and does not notice this;
To notice it, indeed, would be shortsighted of him.
So much for the iconography of one of our nickels,
25 Which is now becoming a rarity and something of
A collectors' item: for as a matter of fact
There is almost nothing you can buy with a nickel,
The representative American Indian was destroyed
A hundred years or so ago, and his descendants'
30 Relations with liberty are maintained with reservations,
Or primitive concentration camps; while the bison,
Except for a few examples kept in cages,
Is now extinct. Something like that, I think,
Is what Keats must have meant in his celebrated
35 Ode on a Grecian Urn.
                                    Notice, in conclusion,
A number of circumstances sometimes overlooked
Even by experts: (*a*) Indian and bison,
Confined to obverse and reverse of the coin,
40 Can never see each other; (*b*) they are looking
In opposite directions, the bison past
The Indian's feathers, the Indian past
The bison's tail; (*c*) they are upside down
To one another; (*d*) the bison has a human face
45 Somewhat resembling that of Jupiter Ammon.
I hope that our studies today will have shown you

Something of the import of symbolism
With respect to the understanding of what is symbolized.   [1967]

HOWARD NEMEROV (1920–1991)

It helps to remember that the Greek word "symbolon" means something *put together*—originally a coin (or potsherd) broken into two pieces, one of which was given to each of the parties in a legal agreement as identification. This half coin became a *symbol:* It hinted that something more was needed to complete its meaning.

One of the most common symbols in poetry is the heart, which is of course a literal organ of the body, a pump of sorts, but is also associated with countless emotions. Sometimes "heart" means "mind" or "soul," sometimes something more like "desire" or "obsession" or one's whole "being." In "Sailing to Byzantium" (Anthology, p. 432), William Butler Yeats urges the sages depicted in a gold mosaic to "Consume my heart away; sick with desire/ And fastened to a dying animal. . . ." Surely here the heart means something more than a fist-sized piece of flesh in the poet's torso. Perhaps attempting to escape such symbolic associations, the contemporary California poet Thomas Centolella begins one poem as follows:

> "The heart" this, "the heart" that—
> I need something more capacious and durable,
> I need desert, I need ocean, I need a range
> of mountains. . . .

Similarly, the poet Jenn Habel (*b.* 1970) seems to resist the common symbolic associations of "heart," yet at the same time the new figures she gives us pertain to the very things that "heart" once more easily stood for:

Another Poem About the Heart

> When the floor drops out, as it has now,
> you cannot hear the squirrel on the wire
> outside your window, the wheels spinning
> on the road below. You want only pity
> 5   and are presented with the unbelievable
> effrontery of a world that moves on.
> But wait: this is not the person you are.
> You're the kind of person who
> sits in dark theaters crying at the collarbones
> 10   that curve across the dancers' chests,
> at the proof of a perfection they represent;
> a person who goes out walking in a four-day drizzle,
> sees a pot of geraniums and is seized, overcome
> by how they can bring so much (what else
> 15   can you call it?) joy. You love the world,
> are sure, at least, that you have. But be truthful:

you only love freely things that have nothing
to do with you. You're like a matchstick house:
intricately constructed but flimsy and hollow inside.
20 You're a house in love with the trees beside you—
able to look at them all day, aware of how faithful they are—
but unable to forgive that they'd lie down
leaving you exposed and alone in a large enough storm.   [2002]

Surely that matchstick house deprived of its screening trees can bear all sorts of symbolic implications.

One of our problems is knowing a symbol when we see one. Sigmund Freud, twitted because his cigars suggested Freudian symbols, replied tartly that sometimes a cigar was just a cigar. Sometimes the images in a poem are just themselves. An apple is an apple; a rose is a rose. They are impoverished, not enriched, by being seen as symbols. When the poet says "bed" in "Western Wind," we can be pretty sure he means an actual bed. One could read the poem symbolically and decide the lines mean: "When will the breath of the Spirit descend on me with life-giving grace, so that I may rest in the security of true belief with what I love the most—my virtue?" Common sense tells us such a reading is improbable. Finding symbols where there are no symbols can lead to serious distortions of the poems we read, and to distortions of the reality they would show us.

In our daily conversations common sense tells us when symbols are really symbols. When we hear remarks like "I never promised you a rose garden," we know that the promise of a real rose garden is unlikely in the world we live in, so we take it as standing for something else. And so in poems: When physical objects, though they seem to make sense in the context of the poem, make incomplete sense in the world as we know it, we may find we are dealing with symbols. This seems to be happening with the rather odd exchange of property in the poem that follows.

Hope

I gave to Hope a watch of mine: but he
               An anchor gave to me.
Then an old prayer-book I did present:
               And he an optic sent.
5 With that I gave a vial full of tears:
               But he a few green ears.
Ah loiterer! I'll no more, no more I'll bring:
               I did expect a ring.   [1633]

GEORGE HERBERT (1593–1633)

Even if we assumed that "Hope" was not a personification of the virtue of that name, but an actual person named, say, Wilbur P. Hope, junk-shop owner, it is difficult to imagine such an exchange taking place. The third transaction is particularly bizarre—but so is this whole way of doing business. None of this, we soon suspect, is meant literally. The watch suggests, "It's time!" The anchor, a traditional symbol of faith, suggests, "Hold on a while." The old prayer book, "But I've been devout for a long time!" The "optic," or telescope, "Look beyond." The vial, "I've suffered and longed!" The green ears, "Some day the time will be ripe." The ring, "But I want fulfillment, complete joy—like that of a marriage."

Symbolic poems are not less satisfactory when we cannot provide the symbols with an exact meaning. In fact, it often seems the most compelling symbols direct us to an area of speculation rather than to any single reality.

The Sick Rose

O Rose, thou art sick!
The invisible worm
That flies in the night,
In the howling storm,

5   Has found out thy bed
Of crimson joy:
And his dark secret love
Does thy life destroy.

[1794]
WILLIAM BLAKE (1757–1827)

The rose, traditionally a symbol of love and beauty, is here something that has life and is in a bed of vivid joy. The worm is a source of corruption, is secret, works in the dark, is associated with a violent disorder in nature. Many kinds of beauty and love are threatened by many kinds of destructive secret forces. The poem is more powerful in not compelling us to fix on any one of the possibilities; we are free to range among them, feeling the force of now one, now another. A symbol that has to explain itself, that feels apologetic about its presence, is not a healthy symbol.

Robert Frost can be a tricky writer, faking out a hasty reader in poem after poem. Frost himself said he never wrote a nature poem. Instead, he got a great deal of fun—to use a favorite word of his—out of saying one thing and meaning another.

Acquainted with the Night

I have been one acquainted with the night.
I have walked out in rain—and back in rain.
I have outwalked the furthest city light.

I have looked down the saddest city lane.
5   I have passed by the watchman on his beat
And dropped my eyes, unwilling to explain.

I have stood still and stopped the sound of feet
When far away an interrupted cry
Came over houses from another street,

10 But not to call me back or say good-by;
And further still at an unearthly height,
One luminary clock against the sky

Proclaimed the time was neither wrong nor right.
I have been one acquainted with the night. [1928]

ROBERT FROST (1874–1963)

Frost knew about walks in the city at night. Everything about his poem is authentic—and yet suggestions, like widening ripples, fade off into remoteness and mystery. The poem would be poorer if it simply said: "I have known the dark side of life, the loneliness and misery and violence and oppression, the inability of any of our standards to give any ultimately satisfying answer."

Poets who work in symbols are likely to give more care to the vividness of their images than to the abstractions the images stand for. Images can sometimes be so real that we are not at first aware they are symbols, though something a little strange about them may lead us to feel, perhaps only half consciously, that more is going on than we are aware of. If we came to the poem below with no knowledge about the author, we might take it for a literal love poem: A young woman steals away from her house secretly at night, makes her way through the darkness of a sleeping town, meets her lover in a cedar grove by a castle wall, and is made so ecstatically happy that she almost loses consciousness.

The Dark Night

Once in the dark of night
when love burned bright with yearning, I arose
(O windfall of delight!)
and how I left none knows—
5 dead to the world my house, in deep repose;

in the dark, where all goes right,
thanks to a secret ladder, other clothes
(O windfall of delight!)
in the dark, enwrapped in those—
10 dead to the world my house, in deep repose.

There in the lucky dark,
none to observe me; darkness far and wide;
no sign for me to mark,
no other light, no guide
15 except for my heart—the fire, the fire inside!

That led me on
true as the very noon is—truer too!—
to where there waited one
I knew—how well I knew!—
20 in a place where no one was in view.

O dark of night, my guide!
night dearer than anything all your dawns discover!
O night drawing side to side
the loved and lover—
25   she that the lover loves, lost in the lover!

Upon my flowering breast,
kept for his pleasure garden, his alone,
the lover was sunk in rest;
I cherished him—my own!—
30   there in air from plumes of the cedar blown.

In air from the castle wall,
as my hand in his hair moved lovingly at play,
he let cool fingers fall
and the fire there where they lay!
35   all senses in oblivion drift away.

I stayed, not minding me;
my forehead on the lover I reclined.
Earth ending, I went free,
left all my care behind
40   among the lilies falling and out of mind.   [*Sixteenth century*—date uncertain]
SAINT JOHN OF THE CROSS (1549–1591)

But the poet, one of the greatest of Spanish mystics, is writing about the
love between God and the human soul. Günter Grass, the contemporary
German novelist, has said: "I don't know about God. I couldn't write about
God in detail. The only things I know are what I see, hear, feel and smell." If
a person can know anything about God, Saint John probably knew it—but he
also knew that one writes a poem in images of what one sees, hears, feels,
smells—images that, as symbols, carry far more than their physical referents.

THING-POEMS

Sometimes a poem that seems to be a description of an object will offer a
basis for a symbolic reading. Such poems—as written by Rainer Maria Rilke,
for example—have been called *Dinggedichte,* or "thing-poems."

The Merry-Go Round

Jardin du Luxembourg

Under the roof and the roof's shadow turns
this train of painted horses for a while
in this bright land that lingers
before it perishes. In what brave style
5   they prance—though some pull wagons.

And there burns
a wicked lion red with anger . . .

and now and then a big white elephant.

Even a stag runs here, as in the wood,
10 save that he bears a saddle where, upright,
a little girl in blue sits, buckled tight.

And on the lion whitely rides a young
boy who clings with little sweaty hands,
the while the lion shows his teeth and tongue.

15 And now and then a big white elephant.

And on the horses swiftly going by
are shining girls who have outgrown this play;
in the middle of the flight they let their eyes
glance here and there and near and far away—

20 and now and then a big white elephant.

And all this hurries toward the end, so fast,
whirling futilely, evermore the same.
A flash of red, of green, of gray, goes past,
and then a little scarce-begun profile.
25 And oftentimes a blissful dazzling smile
vanishes in this blind and breathless game.   [1908]
                                     RAINER MARIA RILKE (1875–1926)
                                 (*Translated by* C. F. MacIntyre, 1900–1967)

While vividly realistic, the details hint at something beyond themselves—at life itself or some aspect of it.

"No ideas," William Carlos Williams liked to say, "but in things." His "Nantucket" is a thing-poem, though at first it may seem as objective as a well-made Kodachrome.

Nantucket

Flowers through the window
lavender and yellow

changed by white curtains—
Smell of cleanliness—

5 Sunshine of late afternoon—
On the glass tray

a glass pitcher, the tumbler
turned down, by which

a key is lying—And the
10 immaculate white bed   [1935]
                              WILLIAM CARLOS WILLIAMS (1883–1963)

It was Williams who gave us one of the most oddly challenging "thing-poems" in "The Red Wheelbarrow" (Anthology, p. 448). Perhaps Frank O'Hara (1926–1966) had something even more playful in mind when he wrote the following:

Why I Am Not a Painter

I am not a painter. I am a poet.
Why? I think I would rather be
a painter, but I am not. Well,

for instance, Mike Goldberg
5 is starting a painting. I drop in.
"Sit down and have a drink," he
says. I drink; we drink. I look up.
"You have SARDINES in it."
"Yes, it needed something there."
10 "Oh." I go and the days go by
and I drop in again. The painting is
going on, and I go, and the days
go by. I drop in. The painting is
finished. "Where's SARDINES?"
15 All that's left is just
letters, "It was too much," Mike says.

But me? One day I am thinking of
a color: orange. I write a line
about orange. Pretty soon it is a
20 whole page of words, not lines.
Then another page. There should be
so much more, not of orange, of
words, of how terrible orange is
and life. Days go by. It is even in
25 prose, I am a real poet. My poem
is finished and I haven't mentioned
orange yet. It's twelve poems, I call
it ORANGES. And one day in a gallery
I see Mike's painting, called SARDINES.   [1971]

[4]/*Mike Goldberg: a New York artist whose painting,* Sardines, *was finished in 1955.*

If such poems resist symbolic readings, they also toy with the very process of interpretation we engage in when we think symbolically.

Marianne Moore has written a number of poems that go deeper than the descriptions they seem to be. In "A Carriage from Sweden" (see Anthology, p. 450), she admires a country cart because, in a world of increasingly shoddy productions, it is lovingly and honestly made: symbolic of a culture and a way of life she values.

Any poet who uses symbols may be called a symbolist. The label "Symbolist" is given specifically to a school of French poets of the nineteenth century and those poets of other languages, including English, influenced by them. Such poets as Baudelaire, Rimbaud, and Mallarmé shunned direct statement in favor of the magic and musicality of language and the suggestibility of symbols, in their case symbols sometimes highly personal and obscure to others. Baudelaire saw the whole world as a "forest of symbols."

ALLEGORY

The line between metaphor and symbol is not as distinct as that separating mathematical concepts; one cannot always say with assurance where one ends and the other begins. Nor is it clear exactly where symbol gives way to **allegory,** which can be defined as a narrative in which characters and events stand for ideas and actions on another level. Such fables as those of Aesop are a simple form of allegory; they seem to be telling us about animals but are really telling us about human behavior. Such parables as those in the Bible are often allegories; they seem to be telling us about the shepherd and his sheep or the bridegroom and his bride when they are really telling us about God and human beings. Most allegory has a narrative framework, either a short incident or a long story.

A mountain may be a symbol of salvation, a traveler may be a symbol of a human being in this life. But if the traveler takes as much as one step toward the mountain, it seems that traveler and mountain become allegorical figures, because a story has now begun. Even a landscape can be called allegorical if a continuity is found in the symbolism used to describe it—if everything mentioned, that is, stands for something else.

In other ages, when people thought that everything happening in our world corresponded to something in a spiritual world, it was easy to see things allegorically. Today we rarely have this kind of double vision. The modern objection to allegory is to its artificiality. It is easy enough to see that natural objects like rivers and mountains can serve as symbols for a cluster of associations, but when we force such objects, and human characters as well, into a continuous narrative in which they "really mean" something else, it seems we are regimenting them into an unnatural order in which things can no longer be themselves. What is felt to be the main difference between symbolism and allegory is that the symbolic detail is a real thing that suggests other things— as we know a real thing can do. But the allegorical detail exists primarily to stand for something else; the emphasis is more on the abstraction it stands for than on the image itself.

Allegories tend to be long; in a book like this we can consider only such miniature allegories as the sonnet below, which Sir Thomas Wyatt translated from Petrarch. The ship itself is not very real; it exists only to stand for love and its troubles. The cargo is forgetfulness (for which there is not much market in the real world); the oars are desperate thoughts; the wind is the lover's gust of sighs; the rain, the lover's tears. Any one of these similes or metaphors might work in itself; the attempt to coordinate so many may seem, to modern readers, oppressively contrived.

My Galley Chargèd with Forgetfulness

My galley chargèd with forgetfulness
Through sharp seas in winter nights doth pass
'Tween rock and rock, and eke mine enemy, Alas!
That is my lord, steereth with cruelness;
5   And every oar a thought in readiness
As though that death were light in such a case;
An endless wind doth tear the sail apace
Of forcèd sighs and trusty fearfulness.
A rain of tears, a cloud of dark disdain
10 Hath done the wearèd cords great hinderance,
Wreathed with error and eke with ignorance.
The stars be hid that led me to this pain;
Drownèd is reason that should me comfort,
And I remain despairing of the port.   [1557]

SIR THOMAS WYATT (1503–1542)

¹/*chargèd: loaded, cargoed*   ³/*eke: also, moreover*

Kingsley Amis is alluding to Wyatt's poem, not without seriousness, when he describes a modern woman.

A Note on Wyatt

See her come bearing down, a tidy craft!
Gaily her topsails bulge, her sidelights burn!
There's jigging in her rigging fore and aft,
And beauty's self, not name, limned on her stern.

5   See at her head the Jolly Roger flutters!
"God, is she fully manned? If she's one short . . ."
Cadet, bargee, longshoreman, shellback mutters;
Drowned is reason that should me comfort.

But habit, like a cork, rides the dark flood,
10 And, like a cork, keeps her in walls of glass;
Faint legacies of brine tingle my blood,
The tide-wind's fading echoes, as I pass.

Now, jolly ship, sign on a jolly crew:
God bless you, dear, and all who sail in you.   [1956]

KINGSLEY AMIS (*b.* 1922)

Details are handled allegorically. What saves the poem is the feeling that Amis is having affectionate fun with a rather burdensome convention.

Wyatt leaves no doubt that his ship poem is allegorical. We would be mistaken, however, if we read his "They Flee from Me" (see Anthology, p. 371) as if it were (although in puritanical times it has been so read, in the belief that it was improper for a real woman to show up barefoot and in a loose gown in the poet's bedroom). In that poem, Wyatt is complaining, as men will, about what they see as the fickleness of women—real women, not allegorical statues. A few decades after Wyatt, Sir Philip Sidney warned his readers that when he named a woman he meant a *woman:*

> You that with allegory's curious frame
>> Of other's children changelings use to make,
>> With me those pains, for God's sake, do not take . . .
> When I say "Stella," I do mean the same. . . .

His word "curious" (*elaborate* or *worked over*) sums up the objection to allegory, which William Blake characterized as an "inferior kind of poetry."

For the use of allegory in art, see Albrecht Dürer's engraving "The Knight, Death, and the Devil" (p. 141), which shows the Christian knight—or simply the good man—ignoring such spooks and phantoms as death and the devil as he journeys through life toward the Castle of Salvation.

A modern poet, Billy Collins (*b.* 1941), muses on the use of allegory.

The Death of Allegory

I am wondering what became of all those tall abstractions
that used to pose, robed and statuesque, in paintings
and parade about on the pages of the Renaissance
displaying their capital letters like license plates.

5   Truth cantering on a powerful horse,
Chastity, eyes downcast, fluttering with veils.
Each one was marble come to life, a thought in a coat,
Courtesy bowing with one hand always extended,

Villainy sharpening an instrument behind a wall,
10   Reason with her crown and Constancy alert behind a helm.
They are all retired now, consigned to a Florida for tropes.
Justice is there standing by an open refrigerator.

Valor lies in bed listening to the rain.
Even Death has nothing to do but mend his cloak and hood,
15   and all their props are locked away in a warehouse,
hourglasses, globes, blindfolds and shackles.

Even if you called them back, there are no places left
for them to go, no Garden of Mirth or Bower of Bliss.
The Valley of Forgiveness is lined with condominiums
20   and chain saws are howling in the Forest of Despair.

Here on the table near the window is a vase of peonies
and next to it black binoculars and a money clip,

exactly the kind of thing we now prefer,
objects that sit quietly on a line in lower case,

25   themselves and nothing more, a wheelbarrow,
an empty mailbox, a razor blade resting in a glass ashtray.
As for the others, the great ideas on horseback
and the long-haired virtues in embroidered gowns,

it looks as though they have travelled down
30   that road you see on the final page of storybooks,
the one that winds up a green hillside and disappears
into an unseen valley where everyone must be fast asleep.   [1991]

EXERCISES & DIVERSIONS

A.   In the lines that follow, identify and evaluate the synecdoches and
metonymies:

    1.   O you hard hearts, you cruel men of Rome!

                                        WILLIAM SHAKESPEARE

    2.   Thy beauty shall no more be found,
Nor, in thy marble vault, shall sound
My echoing song; then worms shall try
That long preserved virginity,
And your quaint honor turn to dust,
And into ashes all my lust . . .

                                        ANDREW MARVELL

    3.   To see a world in a grain of sand
And a heaven in a wild flower,
Hold infinity in the palm of your hand
And eternity in an hour.

                                        WILLIAM BLAKE

    4.   Today I heard a sweet voice carolling
In the woodlot paths, with laugh and careless cry
Leading her happy mates: apart I stept,
And while the laugh and song went lightly by,
    In the wild bushes I sat down and wept.

                          FREDERICK GODDARD TUCKERMAN

    5.   A fool there was and he made his prayer
(Even as you and I)
To a rag and a bone and a hank of hair
(We called her the woman who did not care)
But the fool he called her his lady fair—
(Even as you and I!)

                                      RUDYARD KIPLING

6. Your enemy, an old foul mouth, had set
    The pack upon him. . . .

WILLIAM BUTLER YEATS

7.   . . . She was starting down,
    Looking back over her shoulder at some fear. . . .

ROBERT FROST

8. [Of the prodigal son near a pigsty]
    The brown enormous odor he lived by
    was too close, with its breathing and thick hair. . . .

ELIZABETH BISHOP

9. And I rode the Greyhound down to Brooklyn
    where I sit now eating woody strawberries
    grown on the backs of Mexican farmers . . .

MAURICE KENNY

10. . . . the last day of school . . .
     Empty chairs where laughter used to sit.

NAOMI SHIHAB NYE

B. In the cartoon that follows, the literary person is happy to detect
    metaphors in natural objects. A road or way can stand for the possible
    ("No way!" we say, for the impossible), a rock for stability, a running
    brook for change, rising ground for aspiration. His metaphors could
    equally well serve as symbols. If you were to label these other objects in
    the cartoon, what qualities, processes, or the like, might each stand for:
    the leaves, the trunk and branches, the horizon, the sky, the book, the
    wristwatch, the glasses, the clothing, the beard, the nose, the signs
    themselves?

C. 1. In "Good Ships" two attractive young people meet at a party,
        but nothing comes of the encounter. The poet seems to feel that it
        is sad that convention smothers the possibilities of romance. How
        does this sonnet differ from "A Note on Wyatt" in form? In
        attitude?

Good Ships

Fleet ships encountering on the high seas
Who speak, and then unto the vast diverge,
Two hailed each other, poised on the loud surge
Of one of Mrs. Grundy's Tuesday teas,
Nor trimmed one sail to baffle the driving breeze.
A macaroon absorbed all her emotion;
His hue was ruddy but an effect of ocean;
They exchanged the nautical technicalities.

It was only a nothing or so until they parted.
Away they went, most certainly bound for port,
So seaworthy one felt they could not sink;
Still there was a tremor shook them, I should think,
Beautiful timbers fit for storm and sport
And unto miserly merchant hulks converted.   [1924]

JOHN CROWE RANSOM (1888–1974)

⁴/**Mrs. Grundy:** *a person embodying conventional propriety and prudery (a character in*
T. Morton's play Speed the Plough *(1798).*

a. Is the ship imagery allegorical? Metaphoric? Symbolic?
b. Can all three overlap?
c. Does the "macaroon" stand for anything?
d. Instead of "ruddy" in line 7, the poet originally wrote "ashy." Which word fits in better with the sea imagery and the situation?

2. **A Fence**

Now the stone house on the lake front is finished and the workmen are beginning the fence.
The palings are made of iron bars with steel points that can stab the life out of any man who falls on them.
As a fence, it is a masterpiece, and will shut off the rabble and all vagabonds and hungry men and all wandering children looking for a place to play.
Passing through the bars and over the steel points will go nothing except Death and the Rain and Tomorrow.   [1916]
                                CARL SANDBURG (1878–1967)

Is it true that this fence, which begins as a real one, becomes more symbolic in every line? Do you think the personifications of the last line (indicated by the capital letters) make the symbolism too insistent?

D. 1. As a cigar is sometimes just a cigar, so the *things* in a poem may be only themselves. The "cellar stairs" of the poem by Thomas Lux (Anthology, p. 534) seem to be solid stairs that we could trust our weight to. Would his poem be enriched or impoverished if we read it as being about a symbolic descent to the underworld?

   2. Would you agree with the following explication of William Carlos Williams's "Nantucket"? Or do you think the critic, Guy T. Wise, is "reading things into" the poem?

> Dr. Williams has written a sharp attack on the New England ethos and its prevailing Puritanism in this deceptively simple little poem. There is nothing vital, nothing natural in the world he shows us—except the flowers, and notice that they are *outside* the room, their actual color "changed" by the veil of curtains they are seen through. There is a "smell of cleanliness"— but we all know what cleanliness is next to, and Dr. Williams knows we know. The sunshine is "late afternoon" sunshine— tired and weak, as sunshine goes. The tray and the pitcher are both glass—a colorless and monotonous little still-life: glass has no character of its own, but simply reflects or shows that of other things. The tumbler, now. Is it fanciful to propose that although Dr. Williams means a drinking-glass, he would like us to think also, by contrast, of the colorful tumblers, or acrobats,

of the circus world, so unlike the staid New Englanders? The tumbler, anyway, is turned down. The expression implies a refusal; the very image in itself is negative. One cannot fill a downturned tumbler—folly to try. Next to the tumbler is a key, obvious symbol of exclusion. There is unmistakable irony in the heavy "And" of the last sentence. The bed is not only dead white, it is "immaculate," which suggests a hypocritical spirituality hardly appropriate to a hotel-room bed.

ESSAYS

A. Write an essay about an event in your own life, or in the life of another person, that seems to have taken on symbolic meaning. As you tell the story, remember to use concrete language, vivid images involving the reader's senses. Try to find a poem in this book that reminds you of the event in some way, and use passages from the poem, as well as examples from life, to illustrate the story you have to tell. How is the meaning of the event like or unlike the meaning of the poem?

B. Write an essay about a "thing-poem" in this chapter (or one you find elsewhere in the book), paying close attention to literal and descriptive details, then investigating possible symbolic implications of those details. Can the poem resist being read symbolically?

POEMS

A. In Dürer's engraving "The Knight, Death, and the Devil" (p. 141), what qualities, processes, or the like, might the following objects serve as symbols for: the hourglass, the dog, the horse, the castle, the towers, the skull, the reins, the thorn trees, the armor, the sword, the lizard? Write a poem in which you use at least some of these objects as parts of an allegory. You might choose to do this in a humorous way.

B. Write a poem, in any form, that describes a simple object or situation so that it picks up symbolic overtones as the poem progresses.

4

DOUBLE VISION

Antipoetry, Paradox, and Irony

Up to now we have been concerned with sense perception, the source of human awareness; with how the mind deals with the images the senses provide, with how it relates and compares them, condensing some into symbols, narrowing its focus onto parts of others. In this chapter we will consider how our mind—and the poet's—handles the conflicting evidence that its images sometimes present, and also how the poet sometimes prefers to withhold an image rather than present it at all.

ANTIPOETRY

Dante mentions that Providence has written the word for *man* ("*omo,*" in old Italian) in the bone structure of the human face. This fancy may no longer strike us with wonder, but perhaps Nature is trying to tell us something by the way our eyes are positioned: Everything we see, we see from two points of view.

Even if this were not a physiological fact, circumstances sometimes force us into a kind of double vision. Native American poets often feel, as the part-Iroquois Gail Tremblay has said, that "we dance in two worlds," or, with Roberta Hill Whiteman of the Oneida tribe, that "our clock / doesn't tock the same as theirs." Linda Hogan feels similarly torn:

> In my left pocket a Chickasaw hand
> rests on the bone of the pelvis.
> In my right pocket
> a white hand.

Similar tension may be felt by others in our society. For all of us, the world we perceive is made up of data both good and bad, with a wide range of the pleasant and unpleasant between the two extremes. If we look back over poems we have read, we find a number of sense details that are not conventionally appealing.

T. S. Eliot mentions "faint stale smells of beer" and

> . . . the yellow soles of feet
> In the palms of both soiled hands.

One false view of poets is that their mission is to give us "beauty" by seeing only the good, the noble, the inspiring in reality. What they show us is likely to be a more meaningful world than the unselective senses give, but not a "nicer" world, not a censored distortion of reality. They avoid images that are conventionally pretty and, for that reason, overused in middling poems of the past. Often their best work is made up of materials previously overlooked and therefore as fresh and unspoiled as experience itself is.

Robert Morgan tells us that in his early twenties he deliberately "started writing about things that I had never seen poems about, like hog pens and manure piles. And people would come up to me and say, 'You're so lucky that you have all this wonderful material to write about.'"

The more consciously "poetic" (in the conventional sense) the materials out of which a poem is made, the poorer the poem is likely to be. Shakespeare goes out of his way to be unpretty in what may be the best winter poem in English.

Winter

When icicles hang by the wall,
And Dick the shepherd blows his nail,
And Tom bears logs into the hall,
And milk comes frozen home in pail;
5   When blood is nipped and ways be foul,
Then nightly sings the staring owl,
To-whit to-who, a merry note,
While greasy Joan doth keel the pot.

When all aloud the wind doth blow,
10   And coughing drowns the parson's saw,
And birds sit brooding in the snow,
And Marion's nose looks red and raw;
When roasted crabs hiss in the bowl,
Then nightly sings the staring owl,
15   *To-whit to-who,* a merry note,
While greasy Joan doth keel the pot.

[1598]
WILLIAM SHAKESPEARE (1564–1616)

[8]/**keel:** *cool by stirring*   [10]/**saw:** *platitude*   [13]/**crabs:** *crabapples*

Not a Christmas-card touch: no decorations, candles, carols. Yet out of this unpromising material Shakespeare has made a poem that gives a feeling of the energy and exhilaration of winter, of the challenge and vitality and sheer fun of it, such as no pretty poem could ever do.

Winter Fairyland in Vermont

(after Shakespeare)

When icicles by silver eaves
Proclaim old Winter's jolly reign,
When woodfires gleam like golden sheaves,
And Frost is blazoning the pane,
5   When lanes are fairylands in white,
And downy owls bejewel the night,
Joan baking, in a flowery blouse,
Sends rich aroma through the house.

When breezes carol merrily,
10 And herald angels tread the snows,
Wee chickadees are fluffs o'glee
And Marion's cheek a blushing rose.
When bowls of popcorn twinkle bright
And downy owls bejewel the night,
15 Joan baking, in a flowery blouse,
Sends rich aroma through the house.

[1974]

FRANCIS P. OSGOOD (*b.* 1910)

No gloomy birds or chapped noses here; everything is directed toward greeting-card charm. But if the roughness has gone out of the poem, so has the life, the convincing vitality.

The poet who sees only those details that flatter our fondest hopes has one eye closed to reality. But no more so than the poet who sees only what is ugly or shocking:

When icicles like frozen spit
Are drooling from the roof's mustache,
When roads are white as chicken shit,
And pimpled skin's a scabby rash. . . .

Seeing everything as foul and joyless has become a more fashionable extreme —more warranted, some believe, by the world we live in. Yet don't dark glasses falsify as surely as rose-colored ones?

Elizabeth Bishop goes beyond the plain to the gorgeously dirty.

Filling Station

Oh, but it is dirty!
—this little filling station,

oil-soaked, oil-permeated
to a disturbing, over-all
5   black translucency.
Be careful with that match!

Father wears a dirty,
oil-soaked monkey suit
that cuts him under the arms,
10   and several quick and saucy
and greasy sons assist him
(it's a family filling station),
all quite thoroughly dirty.

Do they live in the station?
15   It has a cement porch
behind the pumps, and on it
a set of crushed and grease-
impregnated wickerwork;
on the wicker sofa
20   a dirty dog, quite comfy.

Some comic books provide
the only note of color—
of certain color. They lie
upon a big dim doily
25   draping a taboret
(part of the set), beside
a big hirsute begonia.

Why the extraneous plant?
Why the taboret?
30   Why, oh why, the doily?
(Embroidered in daisy stitch
with marguerites, I think,
and heavy with gray crochet.)

Somebody embroidered the doily.
35   Somebody waters the plant,
or oils it, maybe. Somebody
arranges the rows of cans
so that they softly say:
ESSO—SO—SO—SO
40   to high-strung automobiles.
Somebody loves us all.

[1965]
ELIZABETH BISHOP (1911–1979)

25/*taboret:* stool or small table
39/***ESSO:*** *S.O. (Standard Oil), a brand name now replaced by Exxon in the United States.*

Emerson in "The American Scholar" pointed out that with the rise of democracy there came a change in literature: Instead of the sublime and beautiful, "the near, the low, the common, was explored and poeticized." He rejoiced in the fact, finding in these new themes the presence of the spiritual. Emerson would have been pleased by Whitman's registering his preference for the worn, the ragged, the ordinary, instead of the conventionally beautiful, by jotting down a "series of comparisons" he may have intended to use in a poem.

Beauty

series of comparisons

not the beautiful youth with features of bloom & brightness
but the bronzed old farmer & father
not the soldiers trim in handsome uniforms marching off to sprightly
    music with measured step
but the remnant returning thinned out,
5   not the beautiful flag with stainless white, spangled with silver & gold
But the old rag just adhering to the staff, in tatters—the remnant of
    many battle-fields
not the beautiful girl or the elegant lady with   ?   complexion,
But the mechanic's wife at work or the mother of many children,
    middle-aged or old
Not the vaunted scenery of the tourist, picturesque,
10 But the plain landscape, the bleak sea shore, or the barren plain, with
    the common sky & sun,—or at night the moon & stars.   [1928]
                          WALT WHITMAN (1819–1892)

But Whitman, like the other poets we have been reading, did not swing to the easy extreme of the repulsive. In our own century Wallace Stevens commended William Carlos Williams on his "passion for the anti-poetic," by which he meant "the real" as opposed to the sentimental.

The modern Chilean poet Nicanor Parra uses the term "antipoems" for poetry in which "there is humor, irony, sarcasm . . . the author is making fun of himself and so of humanity." His antipoetry is not opposed to poetry as antimatter is to matter; instead of swinging to an extreme of ugliness, it swings away from a rapt and humorless fixation on accepted beauty back toward the human center from which we see the world.

Such "antipoems" are not new or modern. Poets have always been aware that some of our most exciting experiences, if seen honestly, present us with contradictory data and arouse mixed feelings. A good example is Kenneth Fearing's poem "Love, 20¢ the First Quarter Mile" (see Anthology, p. 461). See also Louise Glück's "Mock Orange" (Anthology, p. 530).

For one of the most famous antipoems, we can again go to Shakespeare.

Sonnet 130

My mistress' eyes are nothing like the sun;
Coral is far more red than her lips' red;

If snow be white, why then her breasts are dun;
If hairs be wires, black wires grow on her head.
5   I have seen roses damasked, red and white,
But no such roses see I in her cheeks;
And in some perfumes is there more delight
Than in the breath that from my mistress reeks.
I love to hear her speak, yet well I know
10   That music hath a far more pleasing sound.
I grant I never saw a goddess go;
My mistress when she walks treads on the ground:
   And yet, by heaven! I think my love as rare
   As any she belied with false compare.   [1609]
WILLIAM SHAKESPEARE (1564–1616)

⁵/*damasked: of mingled colors*
⁸/*reeks: is exhaled* (not the modern meaning)

Refusing to be taken in by the clichés of second-rate poetry, Shakespeare looks objectively at the woman he is in love with and tells us only the exciting truth about her.

Robert Graves (whose picture we see on page 74) can look objectively at his own face in the mirror, but his realistic scrutiny does not interfere with romantic enthusiasm.

Antipoems are not automatically better than other poems. They may come to us with a guarantee of authenticity, but the authentic need not be, in itself, interesting or moving. Boring people are no less boring because they really exist. Wordsworth in "Composed upon Westminster Bridge" and Jonathan Swift in "A Description of the Morning" (see Anthology, pp. 399 and 392) have both written morning poems. Wordsworth is solemn, even reverent. Swift, more in the manner of the antipoet, mentions, not without humor, things that are scandalous or ugly. He gives us a different poem but not necessarily a better one.

PARADOX

Heraclitus, the ancient Greek philosopher, wrote, "In the tension of opposites, all things have their being." Centuries later, William Blake entitled one visionary work "The Marriage of Heaven and Hell," writing in it, "Without Contraries is no progression." Our minds operate on balanced opposites (we even say a malfunctioning mind is "unbalanced"). If our instincts of love and death, of love and aggression, are in conflict, that inner tension corresponds with what we find outside. "The sad truth is that man's real life consists of a complex of inexorable opposites—," said Carl Jung, "day and night, birth and death, happiness and misery, good and evil . . . if it were not so, existence would come to an end." We could easily add to Jung's list: woman and man, ebb and flow, heat and cold, inhaling and exhaling—and so on for as long as we wish. Physics would give us examples: Sir Isaac Newton saw the universe itself as made up of equal and opposite pairs, every action having a reaction. So would physiology: We can stand erect only because for every muscle (called an "agonist") pulling us in one direction, there is a paired muscle (called an "antagonist") pulling us the opposite way. Creation and destruction seem to work curiously together.

The way in which the fundamental dualities of life coexist is represented by the Oriental symbol for the Yin and Yang. Originally meaning only the shady side and sunny side of a hill—darkness and light—the words came to stand for the cosmic polarities that make up our existence. The symbol is not merely a neatly halved circle of two colors. The dualities interact and interpenetrate, so that the semicircle of one curves into the semicircle of the other. In the midst of each curving half is a small circle of its opposite: In everything beautiful, there is something ugly; in everything true, something false; in everything male, something female. Poetry has said this in many ways. Shelley wrote:

> Our sincerest laughter
> With some pain is fraught;
> Our sweetest songs are those that tell of saddest thought.

The Face in the Mirror

Grey haunted eyes, absent-mindedly glaring
From wide, uneven orbits; one brow drooping
Somewhat over the eye
Because of a missile fragment still inhering,
5 Skin deep, as a foolish record of old-world fighting.

Crookedly broken nose—low tackling caused it;
Cheeks, furrowed; coarse grey hair, flying frenetic;
Forehead, wrinkled and high;
Jowls, prominent; ears, large; jaw, pugilistic;
10 Teeth, few; lips, full and ruddy; mouth, ascetic.

I pause with razor poised, scowling derision
At the mirrored man whose beard needs my attention,
And once more ask him why
He still stands ready, with a boy's presumption,
15 To court the queen in her high silk pavilion.   [1959]
ROBERT GRAVES (1895–1985)

Robert Graves

Paradox—a statement that seems to imply a contradiction—was a fact of life long before it was a literary figure. In its Greek form, the word meant *contrary to expectation.* We say a person is a paradox when we cannot reconcile his or her apparently contradictory tendencies. We say, "It wasn't like him to do that" or "I wasn't myself last night." No one can miss the fact that human nature is deeply contradictory. Alexander Pope, who had in mind Blaise Pascal's remarks on the "greatness and misery" of man, developed the theme in this excerpt.

From An Essay on Man

Placed on this isthmus of a middle state,
A being darkly wise, and rudely great:
With too much knowledge for the Sceptic side,
With too much weakness for the Stoic's pride,
5 He hangs between; in doubt to act, or rest,
In doubt to deem himself a God, or Beast;
In doubt his Mind or Body to prefer,
Born but to die, and reasoning but to err;
Alike in ignorance, his reason such,
10 Whether he thinks too little, or too much:
Chaos of Thought and Passion, all confused;
Still by himself abused, or disabused;
Created half to rise, and half to fall;
Great lord of all things, yet a prey to all;
15 Sole judge of Truth, in endless Error hurled:
The glory, jest, and riddle of the world! [1732–1734]

ALEXANDER POPE (1688–1744)

It is easy to see how Pope's very style is affected by the play of contraries, with line sometimes balanced against line (line 3 against 4), half line against half line (lines 8 and 13).

Paradox has been found even in Wordsworth's apparently naïve "Composed upon Westminster Bridge" (see Anthology, p. 399)—paradoxical in that the poet attributes to the man-made city such beauty as a romantic poet expects to find only in a pastoral landscape.

Awareness of paradox is often expressed by means of **oxymoron,** which might be translated from the Greek as *cleverly stupid* or paraphrased as *absurd on purpose.* It links, in one syntactical unit, words that seem to cancel each other out: "honest thief," "saintly devil," "beautifully ugly," "terrible beauty," "boring excitement," "dull fun," "militant pacifist," "lucky disaster," "frigid kiss," "living death," "hurry slowly." "Superette" (for a little supermarket) is a kind of one-word oxymoron; so is the much older "bittersweet."

Oxymoron has become a pet figure of speech in our oxymoronic times, freely used by sportswriters and cartoonists. In the 1998 U.S. Open golf tournament, broadcasters were heard to say that Nick Price would be guided by "his favorite oxymoron": Play with cautious aggression. Stephen

OXYMORON

Yes, brother, you may live.
There is a devilish mercy in the judge,
If you'll implore it, that will free your life
But fetter you till death . . .   WILLIAM SHAKESPEARE

A dungeon horrible, on all sides round
As one great furnace flamed; yet from those flames
No light, but rather darkness visible. . . .   JOHN MILTON

. . . seas less hideously serene . . .   EDGAR ALLAN POE

. . . the sweet hell within . . .   WALT WHITMAN

Dancing to a frenzied drum,
Out of the murderous innocence of the sea.
                                            WILLIAM BUTLER YEATS

. . . a soft tumult
of thy hair. . . .   JAMES JOYCE

. . . the ladies in their imperious humility . . .   MARIANNE MOORE

My father moved through dooms of love
through sames of am through haves of give,
singing each morning out of each night
my father moved through depths of height   E. E. CUMMINGS

I eye the statue with an awed contempt. . . .   ROBERT LOWELL

. . . flowerbeds, relentlessly picturesque . . .   AMY CLAMPITT

Dunn seems to feel that recourse to oxymoron may be a help toward healthy thinking:

I love the logic
of oxymorons, and how paradox helps us
not to feel insane.

IRONY

Irony directs our attention, in any of several ways, to a play of opposites. The most familiar form of irony is the statement that means its contrary, as when, in the middle of an icy downpour, we comment, "Lovely weather!" Or "More good news!" on looking at the evening headlines. Sometimes the person to whom irony is directed does not know that the words have a double meaning; even the speaker may not be aware that they have. When Othello is confronted by an armed posse, he greets them with quiet **verbal irony.**

> Keep up your bright swords, for the dew will rust them.

He is ironic in professing concern for the prettiness of their weapons; ironic too in implying that their swords are more likely to be stained by dew than by blood.

There is another kind of irony in Romeo's saying

> If I may trust the flattering truth of sleep,
> My dreams presage some joyful news at hand. . . .

because we know that at any moment he is going to receive a report that Juliet is dead.

Macbeth, after committing murder, looks at his bloody hand and thinks:

> Will all great Neptune's ocean wash this blood
> Clean from my hand? No, this my hand will rather
> The multitudinous seas incarnadine,
> Making the green one red.

He knows the truth of his situation. Lady Macbeth does not: It is ironic when she enters almost immediately with the remark

> A little water clears us of this deed. . . .

We say that situations in life are ironic when there is some striking illustration of the way in which qualities, events, and the like contain something of their opposite—when a result, for example, is the contrary of what was intended. This is sometimes called **dramatic irony.** If one has just been given a driver's license, has just been congratulated by the instructor, and, when driving off, goes into reverse by mistake and backs up over someone, it is especially satisfactory—as irony!—if the person run over is the instructor. Such irony seems to imply pattern or design of some mischievous sort, as if a supreme jokester were planning the scenario of our lives. A writer who has made a study of the worst disasters of the twentieth century warns us to avoid any ship, plane, or building that is publicized as being especially safe.

Thomas Hardy was a poet fascinated by irony. In poem after poem he seems on the lookout for the little circle of the Yin in the twisted half circle of the Yang. One of the best-known of his ironic poems, "The Ruined Maid" (see Anthology, p. 425), is about the hypocritical discrepancy, in Victorian

England, between the way virtue was extolled and its opposite rewarded. Amelia, a girl from the country, has been "ruined" (seduced), with the result that she now is kept in luxury.

In "The Latest Decalogue" (see Anthology, p. 414), Arthur Hugh Clough gives an ironic reading of the ten commandments as they might be observed by a cynical materialist. Issues that arise in idealistic terms—childhood, parenthood, religion, war—often lend themselves to irony. The literature of World War I is rife with it. In the following poem, Wilfred Owen (1893–1918) makes ironic use of the story of Abraham and Isaac from the book of Genesis.

The Parable of the Old Man and the Young

So, Abram rose, and clave the wood, and went,
And took the fire with him, and a knife.
And as they sojourned both of them together,
Isaac the first-born spake and said, My father,
5   Behold the preparations, fire and iron,
But where the lamb for this burnt-offering?
Then Abram bound the youth with belts and straps,
And builded parapets and trenches there,
And stretched forth the knife to slay his son.
10   When lo! An angel called him out of heaven,
Saying, Lay not thy hand upon the lad,
Neither do anything to him. Behold,
A ram, caught in the thicket by its horns;
Offer the Ram of Pride instead of him.
15   But the old man would not do so, but slew his son,
And half the seed of Europe, one by one.   [1920]

The ironies here are multiple, from the use of archaic diction imitating the Bible to the images of modern trench warfare and the vicious twist in the story at the end. Owen was himself killed in action during the last days of the war—yet another dramatic irony compounding the many verbal ironies of his poem.

The ironic view of life has been a favorite with many twentieth-century poets, perhaps because the events of our time have brought home to us the conviction that there is no simple way of looking at things.

In speech, we can make any statement ironic by the tone in which we utter it, the facial expression we assume, the gestures we dramatize it with. The poets' problem is to make irony clear without any of the aids we have in speech. They have only words on the page to work with. They need our intelligent collaboration; we have to be more wide awake than usual when reading poets given to irony. In the following lines, Ramon Guthrie is writing about a political figure posing for press photographers. Most of us will feel that the apparent innocence of the last two lines is really tongue-in-cheek, really ironic, and that the statement is all the more cutting for seeming naïve.

He poses for press photographers
with bowed head, thumb holding his right eyelid shut,
auricular performing the same service for the left,
his three other fingers poised against his forehead.
It takes a very pious man to pray that fervently
with flash-light bulbs exploding all around him. . . .

UNDERSTATEMENT—THE WITHHELD IMAGE

Up to now we have seen what kinds of images poets give us as they select details from the whole range of our experience and not only from what is considered beautiful or pleasant. We turn now to the images they do not give us.

If each of the millions of images pouring in from the senses had an equal claim on our attention, the mind, unable to handle that dazzling overload, would go into shock. Fortunately, we have mechanisms to keep from consciousness all but the most significant details.

Poets too, though they may think in images, work selectively; they give us only so much of what could be a confusing abundance—often give us synecdoches, for example, instead of totalities. They know too how silence sometimes speaks louder than words, and how an image can be most vividly present to us when it is not mentioned at all.

It was Voltaire who said that the way to bore people is to tell them everything. What *not* to say or *not* to do is the secret of many arts. Dizzy Gillespie, the jazz trumpeter, said, "It took me all my life to learn the biggest music lesson of them all—what NOT to play." Robert Frost would agree that the same holds for poetry: "The unsaid part is the best part."

In 480 B.C., a few hundred Greek soldiers found themselves in the narrow pass at Thermopylae, between the mountains and the sea, facing an overwhelmingly larger Persian army. As the foreign troops came on, advance units were surprised to see the Spartans stretched out casually along the shore combing their long hair. A. E. Housman, in "The Oracles," describes the scene:

> The King with half the East at heel is marched from lands of morning;
>   Their fighters drink the rivers up, their shafts benight the air.
> And he that stands will die for nought, and home there's no returning.
>   The Spartans on the sea-wet rock sat down and combed their hair.

The first three lines, in italics, are somewhat pompous and overwritten. They suggest the awe one is supposed to feel before the army of a king so great that he is referred to simply as "*the* King." The last line is different in tone; Housman uses only a detail or two to stir our feelings.

The poet Simonides, writing soon after the battle, was even more terse.

On the Spartan Dead at Thermopylae

Go tell at Sparta, traveler passing by,
That here obedient to her laws we lie.

SIMONIDES (556?–468 B.C.)

This poet was enough of a "professor of the five senses" to recognize one of the times he need not invoke them. Only too many of those he was talking to would have their own memories of a son or a father dead, their own knowledge of what a spear or sword can do to the human flesh one loves. Such images may be more effective when not mentioned at all. Every good writer, poet or not, knows this: Never tell a reader what will leap to the mind without your telling.

What we might call the **withheld image** can be as powerful as the presented one. It is difficult to imagine that "Western Wind" would have been better if it had been explicit, as current fiction often is, about the bedtime activities of the lovers.

The most famous example of the withheld image is in the love scene in which Paolo and Francesca, the adulterous lovers, pause to tell Dante about the day that spelled their ruin:

> One day we read the story of Lancelot, just
>   for pleasure, about how love had gripped him so.
>   Alone we two, no shadow of mistrust.
> Often above the book our eyes met though,
>   met . . . lingered . . . our faces drained of color then.
>   Yet a mere moment worked our overthrow:
> to read how the longed-for loving lips had been
>   kissed and by such a lover, this one, twined
>   still in my arms, to leave them never again,
> pressed, all a-tremble, his two lips to mine.
>   A bawd that book! A bawd its author too!
>   No further reading that day—not a line.

And then the withheld image. Instead of giving us the love scene, Dante leaves it to our imagination by telling us what they didn't do. The movie camera might show their fingers relaxing on the book, then the book itself slipping to the floor.

The question of what to withhold may come up most urgently with themes of sex and violence, always among the great concerns of literature. Such ballads as "Lord Randal" (see Anthology, p. 369) provide us with examples. In it the main images are all withheld. Lord Randal has been meeting his "true-love," and yet there is no love scene. He has just been poisoned, and yet there is no poisoning scene. He is now dying, and yet there is no death scene.

No one would hold that crucial images should always be withheld, love scenes and deathbed scenes never presented. "Lord Randal" shows that powerful effects can be achieved by holding something back—not only certain images but certain facts, the meaning of which we piece together only gradually. Lord Randal might have entered, crying, "Mother, I'm poisoned!" but then his later revelations would have been less gripping than they now are. The poet might have shown the young man swelling and dying; it is probably better he did not. Both sex and violence are such highly charged subjects that any lack of sureness in describing them may set off the safety valve of laughter.

Other poets, in dealing with such horrors, have preferred a different strategy. In Edwin Arlington Robinson's "The Mill" (see Anthology, p. 436), we are given only such clues as will enable us, detective-fashion, to discover the central event. When we realize, without being told directly, that the lines are about a double suicide, the shock will be greater—as if we had stumbled on the bodies in real life.

X. J. Kennedy has presented an unsolved killing so that such details as the motive and the killer's identity are withheld from us, just as they often are in crimes that make the headlines and puzzle the authorities.

Loose Woman

Someone who well knew how she'd toss her chin
    Passing the firehouse oglers, at their taunt,
    Let it be flung up higher than she'd want,
Just held fast by a little hinge of skin.
5 Two boys come from the river kicked a thatch
    Of underbrush and stopped. One wrecked a pair
    Of sneakers blundering into her hair
And that day made a different sort of catch.

Her next-best talent, setting tongues to buzz,
10   Lasts longer than her best. It still occurs
    To wonder had she been our fault or hers
And had she loved him. Who the bastard was,
    Though long they asked and notebooked round about
    And turned up not a few who would have known
15   That white inch where her neck met shoulderbone,
Was one thing more we never did find out.

[1969]
X. J. KENNEDY (*b.* 1929)

The withheld image is part of a good writer's overall strategy. Unskillful writers inflate their style so as to give their material more substance than it has, just as the puffer, or swellfish, gulps water in when panicked so as to appear larger and more formidable than it is. An old anecdote has a preacher writing in the margin of a sermon these directions to himself: "Argument weak here. Shout and pound pulpit." Weak writers rely on language that shouts and pounds. They like "unleashed titanic angers, throbbing and surging; awesome, specter-haunted anguish stalking the blood-soaked realm!"

More mature writers prefer to understate, to say less than they might rather than more, so that the meaning can explode *within the reader,* not just within the words on the page.

In "Michael," Wordsworth ends an account of the heartbreak of an old man by telling how he used to go out to the stone sheepfold he had been working on:

> . . . many and many a day he thither went
> And never lifted up a single stone.

Wallace Stevens called this last line, in its context, "a line of great poetry." Wordsworth does not have to tell why the man did not lift a stone; the meaning is more powerful if it bursts on us. A lesser poet might have said something like

> . . . many and many a day he thither went
> To pour forth tears of anguish and despair.

Frost concludes his story of the accidental death of a farm boy in "Out, Out—" (Anthology, p. 439) by having the doctor listening to his heartbeat:

> Little—less—nothing! and that ended it.
> No more to build on there. And they, since they
> Were not the one dead, turned to their affairs.

When we realize what hopes the parents must have had for the boy's future, the "No more to build on there" is deeply moving. We might have remained unaffected if we had been told how the parents' horror-stricken eyes were fathomless pools of grief and anguish as they saw their brightest hopes trodden underfoot by callous Fate. The last line and a half is so understated it sounds cold, and yet Frost himself found the poem too moving to read in public. If the parents "turned to their affairs"—which would include not only milking the cows but getting in touch with the undertaker—we know with how heavy a heart they did so.

There is a similar powerful reticence in Mark Doty's "Atlantis," which is about friends dying of AIDS. That name itself is never used; it is called

> not even a real word
> but an acronym, a vacant
> four-letter cypher
>
> that draws meanings into itself,
> reconstitutes the world.

In his "Brilliance" (Anthology, p. 560), the disease is never mentioned, though there are clues to its identity.

A form of understatement we all use is called **litotes.** It asserts a truth by denying its opposite. We say, "Not bad!" of a good cup of coffee, or "He's no Adonis" of an unattractive man. E. E. Cummings concludes a lyric with a litotes based on grammar:

> we are for each other:then
> laugh, leaning back in my arms
> for life's not a paragraph
>
> And death i think is no parenthesis

He gives what may be the supreme litotes of all time in his poem on the death of a politician he did not like. If he had not died, says Cummings,

> somebody might hardly never not have been unsorry, perhaps

OVERSTATEMENT

There is a place too for the kind of overstatement called **hyperbole** (in Greek, *throwing beyond the mark*). We frequently say things like "the best evening I ever had" or "the nicest dress I ever saw" or "I never heard such a lie!" Without hyperbole, some teenagers—to use a hyperbole—could hardly get through a sentence. Slang relies on it: "He's awesome!" "That music is too much!" A magazine writer calls it the chronic P.R. malady—we all know that in advertising everything is the best of its kind—or at least it tries harder.

The characters in Shakespeare frequently make remarks that we recognize as hyperbole. When Miranda, in *The Tempest,* wants to tell her father that what he has just said is very interesting, she remarks:

> Your tale, sir, would cure deafness.

The lovesick Duke in *Twelfth Night* ascribes similar curative powers to what he admires:

> Oh, when mine eyes did see Olivia first,
> Methought she purged the air of pestilence!

Hyperbole is not so much a way of writing as a way of seeing—the wildest hyperbole may be expressed in simple words. Perhaps it is an especially American way of seeing; the tall tales of frontier days are based on it. In *The People, Yes,* Sandburg gives a series of American hyperboles:

> They have yarns
> Of a skyscraper so tall they had to put hinges
> On the two top stories so to let the moon go by,

Of one corn crop in Missouri when the roots
Went so deep and drew off so much water
The Mississippi riverbed that year was dry,
Of pancakes so thin they had only one side,
Of "a fog so thick we shingled the barn and six feet out on the fog,"
Of Pecos Pete straddling a cyclone in Texas and riding it to the west
  coast where "it rained out under him,"
Of the man who drove a swarm of bees across the Rocky Mountains
  and the Desert "and didn't lose a bee. . . ."

Hyperboles are not lies; only the very naïve would take literally a statement like Lisel Mueller's

All the fireflies in the world
are gathered in our yard tonight . . .

Graves, in making the concluding statement of "Spoils," is not necessarily ignorant of the properties of matter or of the techniques of safecracking.

Spoils

When all is over and you march for home,
The spoils of war are easily disposed of:
Standards, weapons of combat, helmets, drums
May decorate a staircase or a study,
5   While lesser gleanings of the battlefield—
Coins, watches, wedding-rings, gold teeth and such—
Are sold anonymously for solid cash.

The spoils of love present a different case,
When all is over and you march for home:
10   That lock of hair, these letters and the portrait
May not be publicly displayed; nor sold;
Nor burned; nor returned (the heart being obstinate)—
Yet never dare entrust them to a safe
For fear they burn a hole through two-foot steel.   [1955]

ROBERT GRAVES (1895–1985)

His conclusion, mistaken as it might seem to a metallurgist, makes perfect sense in terms of the nature of emotion, whose effect cannot be insulated by any physical substance: Love letters can continue to sear us, and the writer, wherever we keep them.

EXERCISES & DIVERSIONS

A. The great example of irony in literature is the story of Oedipus as told
   by Sophocles in his play *Oedipus Rex*. The very steps Oedipus takes to

avoid killing his father bring about the crime. Sophocles has Oedipus say many things that we know have a meaning different from what the hero intends. He pronounces, for example, a solemn curse on the killer and says he will investigate the case as thoroughly as if the murdered man had been his father.

Does the following poem have the same kind of "dramatic irony"? The Hunkpapa were a tribe of the Dakota (or Sioux)—some would say the most impressive and prosperous of the Native Americans. The year 1822 would have been a happy one for them; much of the rest of the century was not.

Dakota: October, 1822: Hunkpapa Warrior

New air has come around us.
It is cold enough to make us know we are different
from the things we touch. Before dark, we ride
along the high places or go deep in the long
grass at the edge of our people
and watch for enemies.
We are the strongest tribe of the Sioux. Buffalo
are plentiful, our women beautiful. Life
is good.
What bad thing can be done against us?

[1972]
ROD TAYLOR (*b.* 1947)

1. Is the time of year symbolic or otherwise significant in the poem?
2. Is the time of day?
B. What elements of antipoetry are there in T. S. Eliot's "Preludes" (pp. 10–11)?
C. How effective is understatement or "the withheld image" in B. H. Fairchild's "Brazil" (Anthology, p. 533)?
D. How effective as paradox do you consider each of these examples?

1. Hope is a good breakfast, but it is a bad supper.

SIR FRANCIS BACON

2. Greatly his foes he dreads, but more his friends;
He hurts me most who lavishly commends.

CHARLES CHURCHILL

3. Beware the fury of a patient man.

JOHN DRYDEN

4. He who praises everybody praises nobody.

SAMUEL JOHNSON

5. You purchase pain with all that joy can give,
   And die of nothing but a rage to live.

   ALEXANDER POPE

6. Man learns from history that man learns nothing from history.

   HEGEL

7. You ought certainly to forgive them as a christian, but never to admit them in your sight, or allow their names to be mentioned in your hearing.

   JANE AUSTEN

8. No people do so much harm as those who go about doing good.

   BISHOP MANDELL CREIGHTON

9. It has long been an axiom of mine that little things are infinitely the most important.

   SIR ARTHUR CONAN DOYLE

10. Packed in my skin from head to toe
    Is one I know and do not know.

    EDWIN MUIR

11. The cure for loneliness is solitude.

    MARIANNE MOORE

12. If time matters, and of course it does, take a plane;
    If time is even more important, go by ship.

    HOLLIS SUMMERS

E. How much poets should withhold is their own decision. They may want to tantalize us into "exploratory behavior." Difficulty is part of the fun in guessing games and detective stories; we are willing to spend time examining anything that gets our interest. (Some obscure poems never do—they are merely boring.) The poem that follows has been called "a famous puzzle-piece."

The Emperor of Ice-Cream

Call the roller of big cigars,
The muscular one, and bid him whip
In kitchen cups concupiscent curds.
Let the wenches dawdle in such dress
As they are used to wear, and let the boys
Bring flowers in last month's newspapers.
Let be be finale of seem.
The only emperor is the emperor of ice-cream.

Take from the dresser of deal,
10 Lacking the three glass knobs, that sheet
On which she embroidered fantails once
And spread it so as to cover her face.
If her horny feet protrude, they come
To show how cold she is, and dumb.
15 Let the lamp affix its beam.
The only emperor is the emperor of ice-cream.   [1923]

WALLACE STEVENS (1879–1955)

The setting is a house in which preparations are being made for the
final ceremonies for the dead.

1. (lines 1–2) Is there an element of irony, of play of opposites, in that
    the man making ice cream is the type he is?
2. (line 3) Why the highfalutin diction (not used elsewhere in the
    poem) and the gooey lushness of sound?
3. (lines 4–6) Why are the "wenches" described as "dawdling" in
    their everyday dresses? Why is it mentioned that the florists use last
    month's newspapers?
4. (line 7) Recall what a "finale" is. Some might paraphrase the line
    as meaning: Whatever seems to be true of life and death, whatever
    one likes to think about them, what we see in this house is the
    reality; ice cream and the horny feet of the dead are facts of our
    existence. Would you prefer to paraphrase it differently? How?
5. (line 8) Is the ice cream, which is real enough, also a symbol? If so,
    of what? Of the sweetness of life? Of the coldness of death? Of
    both combined?
6. (line 8) Is the emperor the "muscular one"? Or is the emperor the
    ruling principle that the ice cream represents? Or both?
7. (lines 9–16) Why does the diction change in the second stanza?
8. (line 10) Why does the poet bother to mention that the dresser has
    three missing knobs? Are they symbolic? (Trust your common
    sense.)
9. (lines 10–12) Is it ironic that the sheet she embroidered now covers
    the woman's face? "Fantails" can refer to either goldfish or pigeons.
    Stevens tells us he meant pigeons. Would the goldfish image have
    been as good? Are the pigeons (or goldfish) symbolic?
10. (line 13) Is it impolite or "not nice" of Stevens to mention that the
    dead woman has callused feet? With what tone does he seem to say
    this? Of fastidiousness? Of contempt? Or—?
11. (line 15) Is the lamp—what lamp?—to be affixed so that it focuses
    on the feet? Or on what?
12. After asking ourselves such questions, should we still feel that
    the poem is a puzzle, with too much withheld to make an
    interpretation possible?

ESSAYS

A.   At one time Stevens picked "The Emperor of Ice-Cream" as his favorite poem, giving what might seem paradoxical reasons. He said that it wore "a deliberately commonplace costume" and yet had "something of the essential gaudiness of poetry." Write an essay in which you point out how—and why—the commonplace and the gaudy coexist in the poem.

B.   Find another poem in this book, preferably one that has not been discussed in class, in which the chief effect the poet apparently intends (beauty, sordidness, strength, weakness, for example) is combined with elements of its opposite. Write an essay on this poem in which you discuss the "tension of opposites" in its nature.

POEMS

A.   Write a poem about someone you love, using a list of his or her faults as a basis for praise. See John Frederick Nims's "Love Poem" (Anthology, p. 475) for an example.

B.   Write a poem of either love or hate for a person, place, or thing, but do not use the word "love" or the word "hate" anywhere in your poem.

TWO

The Emotions

5

THE COLOR OF THOUGHT

Emotions in Poetry

THE ROLE OF EMOTION

Up to now (to repeat an outline given earlier) we have been concerned with the source of human awareness, sense perception: with how the mind deals with the images the senses provide; with how it relates and compares them, condensing some into symbols, narrowing its focus onto parts of others; with how it handles conflicting evidence; and with how it presents, or chooses not to present, all this in poetry.

This chapter will be about emotion, the reaction of the mind-body combination to the objects or situations that sense images make it aware of. Emotion, like imagery, is conditioned by our physiological history; we can no more feel a disembodied emotion than perceive a disembodied image.

Why do cats dislike getting their feet wet? Charles Darwin, fascinated by the behavior of animals, thought he knew. About 3000 B.C. the Egyptians domesticated the native wildcat to serve as a guard animal. As cats slowly spread over the world, they retained the racial preferences of the almost waterless land of their ancestors.

Darwin also tried to account for human facial expressions as inherited from our ancestors. When we express scorn or rage by sneering, we curl back our lip to bare the once large canine teeth, although it has been a long time since we, in our endless armaments race, have considered our dental weaponry of much account.

Psychologists believe that the mind also inherits predispositions. Certain images affect us more powerfully than any experience of our own would seem to account for. Psychologists like Carl Jung, poets like William Butler Yeats believe that such images have an inherited potential: We are moved by them because of their significance for us throughout our history. These reactions have been encoded in the nervous system itself, in the biochemistries of memory. **Archetypal image** is the term Jung has used for those patternings whose unconscious charge can stir and disturb us. Birth, love, guilt, death, rebirth are examples of such archetypal themes. So are sibling rivalry, the need for or envy of a father figure or earth mother, the quest for some kind of Grail, ideas of heaven or hell. We can think of images that affect us as if from long ago: the sun, darkness, the sea, mountains, trees, caves, shelter, storms, war—all the basic realities that helped determine our happiness or misery, our survival or extinction, throughout our history.

Certain passages of poetry touch us as if there were indeed such memories:

> The Son of Morn in weary Night's decline,
> The lost Traveller's Dream under the Hill.

It is not necessary to know what Blake meant to find his lines strangely haunting. Almost every word is rich with emotions that go back as far as human memory.

Emotional experience: This, more than anything else, is what poetry gives us. And this is what we value as much as anything in life and what we are willing to go to almost any extreme for. Our lives—if fully human—are afloat on seas of emotion; we live more richly there than we live in any geographical world.

We do not have to believe in the ideas of a poem to share its experience: A pacifist can enjoy Homer; an atheist, Dante. But we do have to believe in its emotions. If the poem seems to fake anything there, it is not likely to involve us.

The poet, unlike the philosopher, is not primarily a thinker. "The poet who 'thinks,'" T. S. Eliot reminds us, "is merely the poet who can express the emotional equivalent of thought." Robert Frost said that a poem "is never a thought to begin with. . . . A poem begins with a lump in the throat . . . a home-sickness or a love-sickness. . . . A complete poem is one where an emotion has found its thought and the thought has found the words."

Though emotion may be hard to define, we know very well what it feels like. We know that strong emotion has a marked and instant physical effect on us. It influences our heartbeat, our breathing, the distribution of our blood flow (we flush or grow pale), our visceral activities, glandular secretions, the temperature and electrical conductivity of the skin. Emotion affects all of our internal rhythms—and the rhythms of our poetry. Its physiological aspects could hardly be better illustrated than in the poem of Sappho we have read (p. 8); in it she describes herself as being almost paralyzed with fear and love.

If this seems to be a poetic flight of fancy, we might recall that emotion releases adrenalin into the bloodstream, and that an excess of adrenalin, instead of assisting muscular activity, interferes with the reconversion of lactic acid to the needed glycogen, so that, under great emotional stress, we can become muscularly handicapped. Sappho is right in feeling she may faint. A greatly increased heartbeat *(tachycardia)* will result in reduced circulation, since the heart then operates less efficiently as a pump; and as the brain gets less blood, one becomes dizzy and may lose consciousness. Sappho did not know all this, but she did know what she was feeling, what her body image had become, and she did know that poets report in images.

It is no wonder that poetry, which is physical and emotional, affects sensitive readers in a physical way. William James, the psychologist, was susceptible: "In listening to poetry . . . we are often surprised at the cutaneous shiver which like a sudden wave flows over us, and at the heart-swelling and the lachrymal effusion that unexpectedly catch us at intervals." Emily Dickinson judged poetry by its physical effect:

> If I read a book [and] it makes my whole body so cold no fire ever can warm me I know *that* is poetry. If I feel physically as if the top of my head were taken off, I know *that* is poetry. These are the only way[s] I know it.

So did A. E. Housman: "Experience has taught me, when I am shaving of a morning, to keep watch over my thoughts, because, if a line of poetry strays into my memory, my skin bristles so that the razor ceases to act."

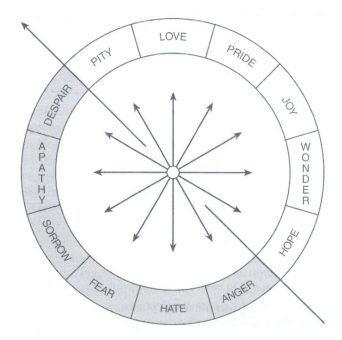

We can visualize the emotions as a color wheel (p. 93) like the ones we see in art-supply shops, a wheel in which selected colors are arranged, like spokes, according to their prismatic, or "spectral," order. We make more colors by adding white to get tints, black to get shades. If we start blending the colors themselves, there is no end to the number we can make, just as there is no end to the number or complexity of our emotions.

Colors opposite each other on *their* wheel are complementary: When mixed, they cancel each other out, giving us black or a neutral shade of gray. But when emotions are mixed, as they usually are, each can remain distinct. When we feel a passionate love and hate for the same person, the blend is anything but gray.

It would be possible to classify poems as belonging to this or that segment of the wheel. One could make collections of love poems, poems of joy, poems of wonder, and the rest. The more poems we read, the more we find they are not confined to the happier emotions, the brighter half of the wheel. Life never promised us a rose garden. Poets deal with all the possibilities of existence, with all that has happened to men and women before and after the fall in Eden. Dante, one of the greatest of poets, wrote an "Inferno" as well as a "Paradiso."

For a poem that deals with deep depression in a manner contemporary poets would be likely to use, see William Matthews's "Mood Indigo" (Anthology, p. 527). In "The Woodspurge" (see Anthology, p. 421), Dante Gabriel Rossetti has written a poem of "perfect grief." Yeats in his old age admits to unbecoming passions:

The Spur

You think it horrible that lust and rage
Should dance attention upon my old age;
They were not such a plague when I was young;
What else have I to spur me into song?   [1938]

Dick Davis (*b.* 1945), disillusioned with love, bids it a vehement farewell in his poem "Desire":

A myth that you believed in once, it's gone
And you can't credit that you've been so stupid:
Damn the whole crew, you say, damn Venus, damn
Her sparrows, damn her little bastard Cupid.   [1980]

Another contemporary poet, Heather McHugh (*b.* 1948) has this to say about a relationship:

Earthmoving Malediction

Bulldoze the bed where we made love,
bulldoze the goddamn room.

Let rubble be our evidence
and wreck our home.

5   I can't give touching up by inches,
can't give beating up
by heart. So set
the comforter on fire and turn the dirt

to some advantage—palaces of
10   pigweed, treasuries of turd. This fist
will vindicate the hand; the tooth
and nail refuse to burn, and I

must not look back, as
Mrs. Lot was named for such
15   a little—something
in a cemetery,

or a man. Bulldoze the coupled
ploys away, the cute exclusives
in the social mall. We dwell

20   on earth, where beds are brown,
where swoops are fell. Bulldoze
it all, up to the pearly gates:

if paradise comes down
there is no other hell.   [1988]

Hate poetry, or **invective,** goes back at least to the ancient Greeks.

Epitaph of Nearchos

Rest lightly O Earth upon this wretched Nearchos
That the dogs may have no trouble in dragging him out.

AMMIANUS (*second century* A.D.)
(*Translated by* DUDLEY FITTS, 1903–1968)

One of the most outspoken poems of disgust, revulsion, and probably self-recrimination is Shakespeare's "Sonnet 129" (see Anthology, p. 375).

Altogether different emotions are expressed by Michael McFee (*b*. 1954):

Time Enough

"We have to stop," she said when kissed.
"We really have to stop," she said when kissed,
lifting her always-ticking wrist.

"We must be quick," she said at one.
5   "Listen, we must be quick," she said at one,
her bare skin savored by the sun.

At two she said nothing at all.
At two she said nothing, nothing at all,
asleep in a delicious sprawl.

10   "I've got to leave," she said at three.
"I've got to leave *right now*," she said at three,
then slowly lifted up one knee.

"I must be home," she said, "by four.
I must be home *or else*," she said, "by four."
15   Her clothes kept waiting on the floor.

"I don't have time for an affair.
I simply don't have time for this affair,"
she said, refastening her hair,

she said, unfastening her hair,
20   she said, again refastening her hair
in the dim mirror's lazy glare.   [2002]

Though we could classify poems according to their predominant emotion, there is no particular gain in doing so. In most poems we get not one emotion in a solo, but rather duets or quartets or even symphonies of many emotions. W. H. Auden's poem "The Shield of Achilles" is about a contemporary world in which human beings have "lost their pride," or can be made to lose it. This depersonalized totalitarian world, hideous with the crime that accompanies poverty and urban demoralization, is contrasted with the world of dance, music, and "ritual pieties" that Homer has shown us. In the *Iliad*, Book xviii, the sea goddess Thetis, because of love for her son Achilles, asks the crippled blacksmith Hephaestos to make a new set of armor for him. As we read the poem, we are whirled completely around the wheel of emotion: Not a one is left untouched. Thetis looks in hope at the human possibilities and is brought to dismay—close to despair—by the contemporary reality.

The Shield of Achilles

She looked over his shoulder
        For vines and olive trees,
Marble well-governed cities
        And ships upon untamed seas,
5   But there on the shining metal
        His hands had put instead
An artificial wilderness
        And a sky like lead.

A plain without a feature, bare and brown,
10   No blade of grass, no sign of neighbourhood,
Nothing to eat and nowhere to sit down,
        Yet, congregated on its blankness, stood
        An unintelligible multitude,

A million eyes, a million boots in line,
15 Without expression, waiting for a sign.

Out of the air a voice without a face
    Proved by statistics that some cause was just
In tones as dry and level as the place:
    No one was cheered and nothing was discussed;
    Column by column in a cloud of dust
20 They marched away enduring a belief
Whose logic brought them, somewhere else, to grief.

        She looked over his shoulder
           For ritual pieties,
        White flower-garlanded heifers,
25   Libation and sacrifice,
        But there on the shining metal
           Where the altar should have been,
        She saw by his flickering forge-light
30   Quite another scene.

Barbed wire enclosed an arbitrary spot
    Where bored officials lounged (one cracked a joke)
And sentries sweated for the day was hot:
    A crowd of ordinary decent folk
35   Watched from without and neither moved nor spoke
As three pale figures were led forth and bound
To three posts driven upright in the ground.

The mass and majesty of this world, all
    That carries weight and always weighs the same
40 Lay in the hands of others; they were small
    And could not hope for help and no help came:
    What their foes liked to do was done, their shame
Was all the worst could wish; they lost their pride
And died as men before their bodies died.

45   She looked over his shoulder
           For athletes at their games,
        Men and women in a dance
           Moving their sweet limbs
        Quick, quick, to music,
50   But there on the shining shield
        His hands had set no dancing-floor
        But a weed-choked field.

A ragged urchin, aimless and alone,
    Loitered about that vacancy; a bird
55 Flew up to safety from his well-aimed stone:
    That girls are raped, that two boys knife a third,
    Were axioms to him, who'd never heard
Of any world where promises were kept,
Or one could weep because another wept.

60   The thin-lipped armourer,
        Hephaestos, hobbled away,
Thetis of the shining breasts
        Cried out in dismay
At what the god had wrought
65   To please her son, the strong
Iron-hearted man-slaying Achilles
        Who would not live long.

               [1955]

W. H. AUDEN (1907–1973)

SENSE AND SENTIMENTALITY

Our remarks on emotion bring us back to where we began our discussion of poetry: back to the role of the senses and to the fact that the poet is, as Federico García Lorca said, a "professor of the five bodily senses." It is through the image that poetry can best convey emotion—either through the image of the object that arouses it, or through the image of its physical effect. Frost describes his walk at night (p. 54) and Marianne Moore her Swedish carriage (Anthology, p. 450) so that, without being told what to feel, we share the writer's emotions.

Poems may not be subject to the same emotional disorders that bring certain of their readers to the psychoanalyst's couch, but they suffer from their own kinds of unbalance. These fall into the general classes of *too little* and *too much*. Some poems fail to involve us because they seem to feel no passion and arouse none in us: frigid poems. Perhaps they substitute intellect or wit for passion; they may be nothing more than exercises in ingenuity. James Russell Lowell felt this in the work of Edgar Allan Poe,

> Who has written some things quite the best of their kind,
> But the heart somehow seems all squeezed out by the mind.

To an unresponsive and unsympathetic reader all poems are frigid. Because poets strong enough to be self-controlled may only imply their feelings instead of letting them gush forth, they may appear to be unfeeling to the insensitive reader. Often, instead of directly revealing emotion, poets will show us something that is a clue to it. Exactly as in real life: We can often tell from people's appearance and behavior what their emotional state is, though they say nothing about it. The less they say, the more moved we may be. Such reticence is characteristic of much of the world's great poetry. As the eleventh-century Chinese poet Wei T'ai puts it:

> Poetry presents the thing in order to convey the feeling. It should be precise about the thing and reticent about the feeling, for as soon as the mind [of the reader] responds and connects with the thing, the feeling shows in the words: this is how poetry enters deeply into us. If the poet presents directly feelings which overwhelm him, and keeps nothing back

to linger as an aftertaste, he stirs us superficially; he cannot start the hands and feet involuntarily waving and tapping in time . . . set heaven and earth in motion and call up the spirits!★

A more common emotional malady is that of "too muchness," or **sentimentality**—emotion in excess of its object, emotion gone out of control and taking over, as cancer cells take over in the body. Sentiment itself—opinion colored by feeling—may be a very good thing: Lincoln's Gettysburg Address expresses noble sentiments. Sentimentality is the disease to which sentiment is subject.

That our grief for even the most worthy of objects can be excessive is the warning given in a folk ballad that probably goes back many centuries.

The Unquiet Grave

"The wind doth blow today, my love,
　　And a few small drops of rain;
I never had but one truelove,
　　In cold grave she was lain.

5　　"I'll do as much for my truelove
　　As any young man may;
I'll sit and mourn all at her grave
　　For a twelvemonth, and a day."

The twelvemonth and a day being up,
10　　The dead began to speak,
"Oh who sits weeping on my grave,
　　And will not let me sleep?"

"'Tis I, my love, sits on your grave
　　And will not let you sleep,
15　For I crave one kiss of your clay-cold lips
　　And that is all I seek."

"You crave one kiss of my clay-cold lips,
　　But my breath smells earthy strong;
If you have one kiss of my clay-cold lips
20　　Your time will not be long:

"'Tis down in yonder garden green,
　　Love, where we used to walk,
The finest flower that ere was seen
　　Is withered to a stalk.

25　"The stalk is withered dry, my love,
　　So will our hearts decay;
So make yourself content, my love,
　　Till God calls you away."

ANONYMOUS (DATE UNCERTAIN)

★Translated by A. C. Graham in *Poems of the Late T'ang* (London: Penguin, 1965).

Excessive grief, which can turn into sentimental brooding, is a vexation to the dead—and so also to the living.

Apathy and despair can be sentimental. If we enjoy wallowing in our own miseries, they become forms of self-pity. Love can be sentimental when lovers are "in love with love"—when they care more about tending their own emotional hothouses than about the well-being of those they love. Or it can be sentimental when the object of their feelings—an animal, perhaps—deserves less than the fullness of human love.

Emotion is healthy when it is of the kind and in the amount that its object deserves: when what we love is really lovable, when what we fear is really fearful. It might seem better to love anything, to feel joy in anything, than to love nothing and feel no joy. But is it? In a play by Christopher Marlowe, a character sends a pot of poisoned rice pudding to a community of nuns. When they all fall sick and die, he exclaims happily, "How sweet the bells ring, now the nuns are dead!" And he goes cheerfully on to his next project, that of poisoning all the monks in a neighboring monastery. The joy and love he feels in his activity will probably seem ill-conceived to most of us.

Excessive pity, even for a worthy cause, can quite incapacitate one for a normal life: The morning papers could keep someone who is pity-prone in futile tears the whole day long. Aristotle thought an overabundance of emotion so harmful to the psyche that he defended Greek tragedy as a necessary release from pity and fear. Healthy emotion is directed to something outside ourselves; sentimentality indulges the emotion for its own sake. Sentimentalists, concerned more with cherishing their own feelings than with the object of those feelings, are saying, in effect, "Look how tender I am! How sensitive to beauty! How capable of deep emotions! How rich in sympathy!" Since they may feel that their unusual sensitivity is unappreciated, they may easily fall into self-pity.

To experience any emotion is engrossing—we never feel so alive as when we are emotionally aroused. So we are tempted to fake our emotions, to build them up deliberately into more than they are. To sustain such fake passion, we have to create or falsify its objects. Sentimentalists hallucinate, turn the world into a warm nest in which they can coddle their own snug feelings. They see only so much of reality as confirms them in their enjoyment of the more tender and tearful emotions. They like things that are cute and quaint and tiny; they can, indeed, miniaturize even the strongest and noblest objects until they become of a size to merit pity and tears.

Writers of sentimental poetry like to play on our stock responses—those built-in automatic reactions we have to many things we think dear and familiar: childhood; barefoot boys; home, sweet home; the old porch swing; the old oaken bucket; old rocking chairs; dust-covered toys; the fidelity of dogs. It was no doubt the sentimentalists' doting views on dogs and toddlers that led W. C. Fields, a lifelong crusader against sentimentality in art and life, to behave so as to win the admiring tribute from Leo Rosten: "Any man who hates dogs and babies can't be all bad."

The innocent happiness of childhood is particularly dear to sentimental-ists. They choose not to know (at least in their rosy moods) about unhappy childhoods—like that of Yeats, who said, "Indeed I remember little of child-hood but its pain." Judging by psychiatric reports and newspaper stories, the lives of many children are unhappy: Only a mindlessly sentimental view of childhood would deny that. Nor are the parents invariably blissful: Any parent knows that children, lovable as they are, can be exasperating, simply because they are little individuals who want what they want. A parent of young children, coming home tired after a hard day at the office, is not likely to find the little ones in the pose described by William Cullen Bryant:

> And some to happy homes repair,
> Where children, pressing cheek to cheek,
> With mute caresses shall declare
> The tenderness they cannot speak.

Even Wordsworth, great poet that he was, slipped into sentimental child wor-ship when he hailed his "six years' darling of a pigmy size" as "best philo-sopher . . . Mighty prophet! Seer blest!"—titles that his philosophic friend Coleridge dryly dismissed with the remark that "Children at this age give us no such information of themselves." Or, as the comedian Joe E. Lewis used to say, "Out of the mouths of babes comes mostly oatmeal."

Few of us could imagine a greater catastrophe than the death of a child, yet how often such subjects lie behind bad poems. The emotions involved may be quite real, but the expression of those emotions is either too full of stock phrasings or attitudes, or deaf to its lack of proportionality. Julia Moore (1847–1920), once called "the Sweet Singer of Michigan," described the death of "Little Libbie" as follows:

> While eating dinner, this dear little child
>   Was choked on a piece of beef.
> Doctors came, tried their skill a while,
>   But none could give relief. . . .
> Her friends and schoolmates will not forget
>   Little Libbie that is no more;
> She is waiting on the shining step,
>   To welcome home friends once more.   [1876]

There are kind and sensitive people who would read this poem with guffaws of derision—not out of sadism, but simply because they find it unbelievable.

For an extreme contrast, suppose we look at one of the best poems about the death of a child.

Bells for John Whiteside's Daughter

There was such speed in her little body,
And such lightness in her footfall,

It is no wonder her brown study
Astonishes us all.

5   Her wars were bruited in our high window.
We looked among orchard trees and beyond
Where she took arms against her shadow,
Or harried unto the pond

The lazy geese, like a snow cloud
10 Dripping their snow on the green grass,
Tricking and stopping, sleepy and proud,
Who cried in goose, Alas,

For the tireless heart within the little
Lady with rod that made them rise
15 From their noon apple-dreams and scuttle
Goose-fashion under the skies!

But now go the bells, and we are ready,
In one house we are sternly stopped
To say we are vexed at her brown study,
20 Lying so primly propped.   [1924]

JOHN CROWE RANSOM (1888–1974)

³/**brown study:** *deep absorption, day-dreaming*   ⁵/**bruited:** *sounded*

This is a real little girl. No doubt lovable—but still, in her vitality, a vexation to those around. No escape from the little voice! She dies, but there is nothing melodramatic about her death—no touching deathbed scenes. Nor is her "angelic beauty" described as she lies there "primly propped." There are no professions of anguish or despair or of heavenly hope from the relatives. We know, without being told, that here is a sorrow too deep for words, and that what we are confronted with is one of the mysteries of our existence. Another poem about the death of a child that manages great feeling while remaining unsentimental is Dana Gioia's "Planting a Sequoia" (Anthology, p. 545). And of course Frost's "Out, Out—" (Anthology, p. 439) is almost brutal in its honesty about such a subject.

Here, for comparison, are two more baby poems, one sentimental and one not.

Étude Réaliste (I)

A baby's feet, like sea-shells pink,
    Might tempt, should heaven see meet,
An angel's lips to kiss, we think,
    A baby's feet.

5 Like rose-hued sea-flowers toward the heat
    They stretch and spread and wink
Their ten soft buds that part and meet.

No flower-bells that expand and shrink
　　Gleam half so heavenly sweet
10　As shine on life's untrodden brink
　　A baby's feet.   [1892]
　　　　　ALGERNON CHARLES SWINBURNE (1837–1909)

(The poet-priest Gerard Manley Hopkins, though devoted to a holy life, said of Swinburne's "*rot* about babies" that it made him side with King Herod, notorious for his Massacre of the Innocents.)

A Song for the Middle of the Night

By way of explaining to my son the following curse by Eustace Deschamps: "Happy is he who has no children; for babies bring nothing but crying and stench."

Now first of all he means the night
　　You beat the crib and cried
And brought me spinning out of bed
　　To powder your backside.
5　I rolled your buttocks over
　　And I could not complain:
Legs up, la la, legs down, la, la,
　　Back to sleep again.

Now second of all he means the day
10　You dabbled out of doors
And dragged a dead cat Billy-be-damned
　　Across the kitchen floors.
I rolled your buttocks over
　　And made you sing for pain:
15　Legs up, la la, legs down, la, la,
　　Back to sleep again.

But third of all my father once
　　Laid me across his knee
And solved the trouble when he beat
20　The yowling out of me.
He rocked me on his shoulder
　　When razor straps were vain:
Legs up, la la, legs down, la la,
　　Back to sleep again.

25　So roll upon your belly, boy,
　　And bother being cursed.
You turn the household upside down,
　　But you are not the first.
Deschamps the poet blubbered too,
30　For all his fool disdain:
Legs up, la la, legs down, la la,
　　Back to sleep again.   [1957]
　　　　　　　　　JAMES WRIGHT (1927–1980)

Sentimentalists tend to overvalue the companionship of an animal, since its response to them is less critical than that of a human being and, therefore, more flattering. All the better if the animal has a sad fate, which, by encouraging their own pity and self-pity, permits them to drop a gentle tear. We think of the "trembling maid, of her own gentle voice afraid" in Thomas Moore's "Lalla Rookh":

> Oh! ever thus from childhood's hour,
> I've seen my fondest hopes decay;
> I never loved a tree or flower,
> But 'twas the first to fade away.
> I never nursed a dear gazelle,
> To glad me with its soft black eye,
> But when it came to know me well,
> And love me, it was sure to die!

Such sentimentality arouses not only disbelief but derision in sensible readers. Few lines in English have been more honored with parody, which taunts our self-pitying little gazelle-nurser with such lines as those of James Payn:

> I've never had a piece of toast
> Particularly long and wide,
> But fell upon the sanded floor,
> And always on the buttered side.

Even cat lovers may feel that Rod McKuen goes overboard in his love for his cat Sloopy. For years, the poet tells us, it had been Rod and Sloopy "against the world." Then one day Rod did not come home. A day later he came running through the snow, "screaming *Sloopy Sloopy*," only to find her gone!

> I was a madman
> to have stayed away
>   one minute more
> than the appointed hour.

Sloopy, he reflects, is now a bitter cat, and

> I'm bitter too
> and not a free man any more. . . .
>
>   Looking back
> perhaps she's been
> the only human thing
> that ever gave back love to me.

McKuen, sentimentally, treats Sloopy as if she were human. May Swenson, on the other hand, tries to imagine how a cat might really experience the world.

Cat & the Weather

Cat takes a look at the weather:
snow;
puts a paw on the sill;
his perch is piled, is a pillow.

5 Shape of his pad appears:
will it dig? No,
not like sand,
like his fur almost.

But licked, not liked:
10 too cold.
Insects are flying, fainting down.
He'll try

to bat one against the pane.
They have no body and no buzz,
15 and now his feet are wet;
it's a puzzle.

Shakes each leg,
then shakes his skin
to get the white flies off;
20 looks for his tail,

tells it to come on in
by the radiator.
World's turned queer
somehow: all white,

25 no smell. Well, here
inside it's still familiar.
He'll go to sleep until
it puts itself right.

[1963]
MAY SWENSON (1919–1990)

Emotions are to be evaluated with reference to their object. It is precisely such an evaluation that William Stafford is concerned to make in his poem about an unborn fawn: Should one risk human lives in a probably vain effort to save the fawn?

Traveling Through the Dark

Traveling through the dark I found a deer
dead on the edge of the Wilson River road.
It is usually best to roll them into the canyon:
that road is narrow; to swerve might make more dead.

5   By glow of the tail-light I stumbled back of the car
and stood by the heap, a doe, a recent killing;
she had stiffened already, almost cold.
I dragged her off; she was large in the belly.

My fingers touching her side brought me the reason—
10   her side was warm; her fawn lay there waiting,
alive, still, never to be born.
Beside that mountain road I hesitated.

The car aimed ahead its lowered parking lights;
under the hood purred the steady engine.
15   I stood in the glare of the warm exhaust turning red;
around our group I could hear the wilderness listen.

I thought hard for us all—my own swerving—,
then pushed her over the edge into the river.   [1962]

        WILLIAM STAFFORD (1914–1993)

Emotions of course are real, and perhaps the only real subjects for poetry; it's just that some emotions (about the death of a loved one or a family pet, say) easily become traps for our sentimental tendencies. The question for the poet, then, is how to write about the genuine without falling into these traps. Poets have been devising strategies to avoid sentimentality since ancient times. Notice how skillfully it is done by Richard Wilbur (*b.* 1920) in the poem below.

The Pardon

    My dog lay dead five days without a grave
In the thick of summer, hid in a clump of pine
And a jungle of grass and honeysuckle-vine.
I who had loved him while he kept alive

5   Went only close enough to where he was
To sniff the heavy honeysuckle-smell
Twined with another odor heavier still
And hear the flies' intolerable buzz.

Well, I was ten and very much afraid.
10   In my kind world the dead were out of range
And I could not forgive the sad or strange
In beast or man. My father took a spade

And buried him. Last night I saw the grass
Slowly divide (it was the same scene
15   But now it glowed a fierce and mortal green)
And saw the dog emerging. I confess

I felt afraid again, but still he came
In the carnal sun, clothed in a hymn of flies,
And death was breeding in his lively eyes.
20   I started in to cry and call his name,

Asking forgiveness of his tongueless head.
. . . I dreamt the past was never past redeeming:
But whether this was false or honest dreaming
I beg death's pardon now. And mourn the dead.   [1950]

In Wilbur's poem one transitional moment would be line 9, a statement given a line of its own, distancing the speaker in time from his subject. Wordsworth said that poetry is "emotion recollected in tranquility," but Wilbur's subject is not always viewed in a state of calm. A nightmare breaks through the artful surface of the poem.

EXERCISES & DIVERSIONS

A. In "The Shield of Achilles" (pp. 96–98), Auden shows the horror of a contemporary world by contrasting it with an ancient world of naturalness, order, "ritual pieties," and the dance. Many of his details allude to the eighteenth book of the *Iliad*, but there the artwork on the shield is not as sweetly innocent as that which Thetis hopes for in Auden's poem. The world of Homer is less idealized: Hephaestos depicts a murder trial and a city at war, in which appear the figures of Discord, Tumult, and Fate, whose cloak is soaked red with human blood. In the peaceful countryside there is a gory scene of a lion gorging on a dead bull.

1. Does Auden oversimplify in his comparison of the ancient world to the modern one?

2. Is it ironic that Achilles, the representative of the ancient world, is himself "iron-hearted," "man-slaying," and doomed to an early death?

3. In scenes of the modern world, what effective use is made of the withheld image? What is *not* shown?

4. What effective synecdoches or metonymies occur? Why is "boots" (line 14) a better word than "shoes"?

5. Auden's idea might be expressed (oversimply) as: The conditions of contemporary life do not permit the full development of human potential as well as older civilizations did. Show the steps by which the poet turns this idea into images.

6. Why would the contemporary civilization Auden shows be hostile to poetry? What details indicate that all emotion has been stifled?

7. Some readers will feel a Biblical allusion in the number of the victims of modern tyranny (line 36). Others may feel that when Auden says that his "multitude" is "waiting for a sign" (line 15), he is alluding to the twelfth chapter of St. Matthew, in which some of the scribes and Pharisees tell Christ they would like to see "a sign" (a miracle). Would the allusion—if it is there—seem ironic?

8. In Homer's depiction of the shield, there is no "sacrifice," no "flower-garlanded heifers," no "altar" (fourth stanza). All are found in John Keats's "Ode on a Grecian Urn":

> Who are these coming to the sacrifice?
>   To what green altar, O mysterious priest,
> Lead'st thou that heifer lowing at the skies,
>   And all her silken flanks with garlands dressed?

Would you guess that Auden is making a deliberate allusion to the Keats poem? Or is this an involuntary echo? A mere coincidence?

9. The urchin (line 53) is described as "aimless," but his stone is "well-aimed." In a freshman writing class would this be called "clumsy repetition," or is it intentional?

10. Other words seem to be used with special effect, so that we almost do a double take with them. With derivation (see dictionary) and connotations in mind, weigh the use of "artificial" (line 7), "feature" (line 9), "neighbourhood" (line 10), "congregated" (line 12), "unintelligible" (line 13), "cheered" (line 19), "enduring" (line 21), "arbitrary" (line 31), "vacancy" (line 54), "axioms" (line 57).

11. What is the effect of the unusually high percentage of monosyllabic words in the sixth stanza?

12. Why is Hephaestos described as "thin-lipped" (line 60)? The usual epithet for Thetis is ἀ ργυρόπεζα ("silver-footed"). Why, in line 62, did not Auden write "Thetis of the silver feet"?

13. When stanzas are used in a poem, they are generally the same throughout. We can see at a glance that two kinds of stanzas are used here. Why is the shift appropriate in this poem?

14. What is the inner logic of the stanzas? Do the second and third stanzas, for example, relate to the first? The fifth and sixth to the fourth?

15. Is it true that all the emotions named on the emotion wheel (p. 93) are felt as present in this poem?

16. The addition of one more stanza would make the structure symmetrical. Where should it be? Can you see any reason for its absence? (Heroic project for literary aspirants: Try writing the "missing" stanza so it fits in with the others in all respects.)

B. The philosopher Jean-Paul Sartre saw emotion as the process by which we escape, when frustrated by reality, into a make-believe world. For example, a man who gets the worst of it in an argument escapes from the world of logic (where he cannot win) to the world of rage (where he can win). His face reddens, his muscles swell, he jumps to his feet with a threatening "Oh yeah? Maybe you'd like a punch in the nose!" Or a rejected woman sulks in a corner, her eyes dull so she cannot see the real world, her muscles lax so she cannot cope with it. She escapes into a despair that says the world is not worthwhile anyway. For Sartre, emotion is symbolic activity, magical behavior—a way of transforming what we cannot deal with.

1. Can you find poems in this chapter in which someone uses emotion as an escape from reality?

2. Can you recall poems in earlier chapters in which emotion was used in this way?

3. As opposed to Sartre, the physician-writer Gustav Eckstein holds, in *The Body Has a Head,* that "without emotion there is nothing that could be called mind. Clarification of thought depends on it." What poems have we read in which emotion seems to stimulate thought rather than distort it?

4. Do you feel that although Sartre's theory may not fit all emotions, it does fit sentimental ones, which are a kind of magical behavior aimed at transforming reality? Cite examples.

C. Sentimentality, which gives free access to unearned emotions, is at home in the popular arts—the movies, TV, best-selling fiction, advertising—which show us not the world as it is but the world as magically transformed into what we would like it to be.

Yes, the Agency Can Handle That

You recommend that the motive, in Chapter 8, should be changed from ambition to a desire, on the heroine's part, for doing good; yes, that can be done.

Installment 9 could be more optimistic, as you point out, and it will not be hard to add a heartbreak to the class reunion in Chapter 10.

Script 11 may have, as you say, too much political intrigue of the sordid type; perhaps a diamond-in-the-rough approach would take care of this. And 12 has a reference to war that, as you suggest, had better be removed; yes.

This brings us to the holidays, that coincide with our prison sequence. With the convicts' Christmas supper, if you approve, we can go to town.

Yes, this should not be difficult. It can be done. Why not?

And script 600 brings us to the millennium, with all the fiends of hell singing Bach chorales.

And in 601 we explore the Valleys of the Moon (why not?), finding in each of them fresh Fountains of Youth.

And there is no mortal ill that cannot be cured by a little money, or lots of love, or by a friendly smile; no.

And few human hopes go unrealized; no.

And the rain does not ever, anywhere, fall upon corroded monuments and the graves of the forgotten dead. [1940]

KENNETH FEARING (1902–1961)

1. The "agency" is preparing a series of programs for mass presentation. Is it true that the revisions they say they are willing to make are all in the direction of sentimental treatment of the material?
2. Do you think the poem has the same speaker—an agency executive—throughout? Or does the poet himself begin to cut in with his own voice? If so, where?
3. What is the basis of the irony we get toward the close? Why does the irony become stronger as it becomes more concrete?
4. Is the poem essentially an attack on sentimental taste? On what grounds does the poet seem to think of sentimentality as a kind of falsehood?
5. "Yes, this should not be difficult" (line 5). Is it true that the sentimental treatment of a theme is easier than the emotionally honest treatment?

D. Poems not written as allegories can sometimes be read allegorically. Could Archibald MacLeish's "Eleven" (pp. 7–8) be read as a poem about the poetic process, in that the child, hating the "Think now, Think . . . ," leaves the world of thought to get back to the world of sensation, imagination, and feeling?

ESSAYS

A. One of the most difficult tasks of the critic is to convey the experience of reading a poem, as well as its meanings or technical workings. In other words, a critic must be able to feel emotions and convey them to readers. Choose a poem from this book—preferably one with complex emotions—and write an essay in which you attempt to describe these effects and, where possible, how they seem to be created in the poem. You'll want to read the poem several times, even aloud, and perhaps take notes from your experience of it. Feel free to write in the first person in this paper. One possible thesis could derive from the poet's apparent intentions. Or you could ask why readers of our time should care about what this poem achieves. Strive to be vivid and clear in your prose, engaging the readers' senses as well as their minds.
B. Write an essay on Auden's "The Shield of Achilles" (pp. 96–99) in which you try to pinpoint the poem's emotional effect.

POEMS

A. All of us have personal images (of things, of people, of places, of seasons) that affect us deeply, perhaps because they condense memories and associations from childhood. Think of examples in your own mind, and write a poem making use of such images so that others can be made to feel their power.

B.   What objects do you think you tend to be sentimental about? Let yourself write a frankly sentimental poem about such an object. Now rewrite it so that, while still heartfelt, it has no traces of sentimentality.

THREE

The Words

6

MACHINE FOR MAGIC

The Fresh Usual Words

LIVING WORDS

Up to now we have been considering how the senses give us images that are a picture of our world, and how these images affect us with desire or aversion or any of the other emotions.

When we have given examples, however, we have had to anticipate still another element of poetry: the *words* through which the image and emotion are expressed.

In the mind of poets and their readers, image, emotion, and word all interact. And they interact with other elements we have not yet come to, such as sound and rhythm and the shape of sentences. Neither the poem nor the poet's mind is compartmentalized as neatly as a table of contents would seem to indicate.

The fact that we are moving on now to the role of words in poetry does not mean that we can put imagery and emotion behind us, as if we had "finished" them. What we have said about the two ought to be kept in mind and retested as we contemplate what is almost the only way we have of sharing them: the spoken word.

The painter Edgar Degas, not content with doing his graceful paintings of dancing girls, also wanted to write poems. Finding the literary work difficult, he complained to his friend, the celebrated poet Mallarmé, that he could not seem to write well, although he was "full of ideas." Mallarmé's famous answer was: "My dear Degas, poems are not made out of ideas; they're made out of *words*." The best ideas, even though they turn into images, are of no avail *as poems* unless the words are right—just as a statue of even the noblest subject is a failure if the wood cracks or the marble shatters. Poems are made out of *words*.

And poets are necessarily in love with words. As the poet W. H. Auden has put it:

> . . . a poet is, before anything else, a person who is passionately in love with language . . . [this] is certainly the sign by which one recognizes whether a young man is potentially a poet or not. "Why do you want to write poetry?" If the young man answers: "I have important things to say," then he is not a poet. If he answers, "I like hanging around words listening to what they say," then maybe he is going to be a poet.*

The Chilean poet Pablo Neruda (1904–1973), winner of the Nobel Prize in literature in 1971, is even more enraptured with the magic of words:

> It's the words that sing, they soar and descend. . . . I bow to them. . . . I love them, I cling to them, I run them down, I bite into them, I melt them down. . . . I love words so much. . . . The unexpected ones . . . The ones I wait for greedily or stalk until, suddenly, they drop. . . . Vowels I love. . . . They glitter like colored stones, they leap like silver fish, they are foam, thread, metal, dew. . . . I run after certain words. . . . They are so beautiful that I want to fit them all into my poem. . . . I catch them in midflight, as they buzz past, I trap them, clean them, peel them, I set myself in front of the dish, they have a crystalline texture to me, vibrant, ivory, vegetable, oily, like fruit, like algae, like agates, like olives. . . . And then I stir them, I shake them, I drink them, I gulp them down, I mash them, I garnish them, I let them go. . . . I leave them in my poem like stalactites, like slivers of polished wood, like coals, pickings from a shipwreck, gifts from the waves. . . . Everything exists in the word.†

So it seems is Eudora Welty, who in a television documentary told how her passion for words made them seem real objects: "Held in the mouth, the moon became a word. It had the roundness of a Concord grape."‡

Many poets have found their dictionary fascinating reading. "For several years," confessed Emily Dickinson, "my Lexicon—was my only companion." In his *Cantos* Ezra Pound quotes his friend Ford Madox Ford with approval:

> . . . get a dictionary
> and learn the meaning of words.

Many poets have told us that their poems started not with an idea but with a phrase or two that pleased them—phrases for which they then had to find the appropriate idea. This procedure, which will seem in reverse to most of us, is

---

*W. H. Auden, "Squares and Oblongs," in *Poets at Work*, ed. C. D. Abbott (New York: Harcourt, Brace & Co., 1948), p. 171.

†Pablo Neruda, *Memoirs*, translated by Hardie St. Martin (New York: Farrar, Straus and Giroux, 1977), p. 53.

‡"Eudora Welty: One Writer's Beginnings," *The American Experience* (BBC, January 1989).

so common that the French poet Paul Valéry admitted that poets have more trouble finding ideas to fit their words than words to fit their ideas.

Poetry consists not so much in saying memorable things as in saying things memorably. The interplay of image and emotion is not yet poetry; without the word it would remain forever silent, unshared, locked in the core of the individual. The poets' job is to make out of words a machine that will transmit what is in their minds to the minds of others—a machine so finely built that those others will admire it at least as much for its own perfection as for the message it transmits.

To some, "machine" may seem too unpoetic a metaphor. And yet it was the poet William Carlos Williams who called a poem "a small (or large) machine made out of words." He was echoing what Valéry had already said more than once: "A poem is really a kind of machine for producing the poetic state of mind by means of words."

When poets are constructing one of their magic-machines, they are not so much *saying* something as *making* something out of words, just as a sculptor is making something out of stone; a painter, something out of shapes and colors; a composer, something out of sounds.

Much of our nonpoetic speech aims at communicating information. We say, "Jacksonville is five miles away," or "The room will cost sixty dollars a night." It does not matter what words we use provided the message is clear; we may forget the exact words once they have served their purpose. But poets care *how* they say what they say. "All the fun's in how you say a thing," said Robert Frost. Poets care about the sound and length of words, their suggestions, their rhythm when put together. They want to say something not only right for the occasion, but something that will keep forever. They are getting back, in short, to language as a kind of magic.

The words on pages 118–119 show us two kinds of diction. On the left-hand page we have words that are very much alive and have been so for centuries; these are the kinds of words the best poets will prefer to use. On the right-hand page we have words and combinations of words that may once have been part of the living language but have long since lost their vitality; these are the kinds of words good poets generally avoid.

"Moon, Sun, Sleep, Birds, Live" of Kenneth Patchen is like a working model of a poem, cut away to give us a vivid glimpse of the moving parts.

It might be hard to state the "meaning" of this page of poetry, in which the words of the title, dramatized by typography, stand out in a field of seven little poems. Around this composition is a frame of about a hundred words, some related by association of ideas. The page, capable of being read in many ways, seems to be notes for a meditation on existence and language, on words as expressing the basic realities of our lives. It is also a lesson in the language of poetry. The vocabulary it uses is taken from the best words available to the poet—nearly all are what Joseph Conrad called the "fresh usual words" and André Breton "*les mots sans rides,*" the unwrinkled words. These have endured, as alive today as in Shakespeare's time. They are still the words we

Moon, Sun, Sleep, Birds, Live

rain wind light cold cold dark late stem gate bar flame knife garden blue
noise morning son loud art alive net tiger storm lily job tear maker shove

mirror

Moon

work

coast SUN star

deer good

frog soul

tunnel   I am the music you make book

grave   the blue wings of the ocean lift

noose   the crying of the black swan world

supper body

beauty   I am the friend

SLEEP

stone

fear   of your childhood town

heights weave

garden

Birds

It is in my heart to wish you center

taste no sorrow break

climb no pain afraid

will   for I am the will of your last being no betrayal skill

look   the shudder of the breaking open thing

wing   of terrible gates O thou art good laugh

valley and wise grow

rule   I am the cave and the light and kindling three

name   the watch God keeps a new fire keep

knock   when His children go mad force

angel   I am the death you seek other

shadow

LIVE

the life you are afraid charm

terror to know soar

quest *behold this eye of blood!* fence

power rise tree knowledge innocence fall hand thorn get father chain spool
law peace turtle grass snow prayer life black deep first tie hit see eye

[1942]
KENNETH PATCHEN (1911–1972)

opalescent   proffered   beauteous   waning   haunting   witchery
ethereal   lightsome   behest   wrought   sought   supernal
sunder   sever   besmirch   benison   ope   sup   smite
darkling   thrice   rhapsodic   wend   illume   boon   waft
tranced   pageantry   array   mart   lave   rive   clime
crystalline   deem   filigree   silhouette   arabesque   furled   steed
enmeshed   cacophony   sere   damsel   samite   etched
mystic   morsel   abode   aureole   endowed   saraband
alchemy   sibylline   trancèd   labyrinthine   fray   plangent
ween   rhythm (of life, etc.)   chaste (moonlight, etc.)
symphony (of life, of the city, etc.)   tracery (of branches, etc.)
happy haunts   endearing grace   eyes' tender light   fierce beauty
sadly yearn   one brief space   teeming life   life's evening
sunset glow   silvery laugh   unison divine   first faint blush of dawn
swaying in the breeze   wee fleeting touch   radiant smile
willing hands   heavy laden   wondrous tales   beauty's elixir
light and gay   friends of yesteryear   long-cherished dreams
piny grove   'neath the starlit canopy   the kiss of the breeze
kindly deeds   broken dreams   peacefully sleeping
mute orchestras of spring   murmured hymn   cannot fathom
thousands cheered   memories of lost days   snow-capped peaks
cadenced words of pure delight   dew-kissed flowers   allotted span
golden deeds   star-jeweled sky   earth's pageantries   rippling stream
bitter tears   mystic mingling   numbered days   softly pervades
seething humanity   rhapsodic balm   would that I could
falls in benediction   the young wind   harborward   sighing winds
timeless flight   the thrill of nature's lyre   ancient days
loved familiar things   the verdant earth in glad array
dream-fraught musings   amorous troubadours   haunting mood
the days of wine and roses   brooding quietude   solemn majesty
muted rage   soul aglow   naked trees   mountains towering high
quick suspicion   feathered songsters choiring in the blue
untethered sails   night's soft fragrance   the tender morn
caressing ripples   nocturnal paeans of glee   the star-sweet night
bleak winter tolls its knell   nameless grace   last aching memory
the musings fancy sired   the petalled flowers   sequestered ways
the rose dewy-eyed   woe-enfolded cypresses   dread surmise
rock-bound coast   heaven's vaulted reach   chill-winged rain

use for many of our deepest experiences. A large number come to us as sense impressions: "rain," "wind," "light," "cold," and others.

Most are "thing words" ("lily," "tiger," "star") rather than terms for abstractions; what we said about *concrete* and *abstract* in Chapter 1 holds too for the poet's vocabulary. Some directly express emotions; many more name objects that have long been charged with emotion: "flame," "knife," "garden," "morning," among them. All are rich in **connotation,** the suggestions that words accumulate in addition to their **denotation,** or dictionary meaning. (See Exercises & Diversions, A. 2., p. 137, for examples of these terms.)

The vitality of Patchen's vocabulary is clear if we contrast his page with a page of words that are dead or close to dying, words we would not be likely to use if we had anything urgent or passionate to say. One cannot insist that poets will never use any of these; sometimes they have their reasons for trying to revive a dead word, or even for laying it forth in state. Some words too have precise technical applications that retain their vigor, such as "opalescent" when used of gemstones, or "witchery" when used of superstitions in colonial New England. They shrivel and die when put to such use as "The heavenly rainbow wafts her opalescent witchery o'er the verdant earth." (Compare the simplicity of Wordsworth's "The rainbow comes and goes, / And lovely is the rose.") A poem with a high percentage of such verbiage has little chance of coming to life. The deadest words are the merely "poetic" ones, words once alive but long since embalmed. Some readers, seeing them only in poetry of the past and thinking of them as uncontaminated by daily handling, may believe them especially worthy of the poet's attention. But devotion to such words or phrases is a kind of necrophilia.

A number of our examples of dead diction ("bitter tears," "thousands cheered") have become **clichés.** "Cliché" was originally a printing term for a single piece of type with words so often used together that it was handy to have them in one piece. Clichés have caught on because when first used they were apt and striking: "sadder but wiser," "tired but happy," "strong as an ox," "cool as a cucumber," "blissful ignorance," "get down to brass tacks," "far be it from me," "this historic occasion," "add insult to injury," "last but not least," "at this point in time." Some recent clichés a columnist has called our attention to are "ballpark figure," "meaningful dialogue," "world-class," "a level playing field," "window of opportunity," and "no problem." Each may have been effective the first few times it was used; all have become stale with overuse. The first man to compare the cheeks of a girl to a rose, said Salvador Dalí, was obviously a poet; the first to repeat it was possibly an idiot.

Most revolutions in poetry aim at getting back to a more natural language. "The *norm* for a poet's language," said T. S. Eliot, "is the way his contemporaries talk." Pound has insisted on this norm again and again. "Good god! isn't there one of them that can write natural speech without copying clichés?" Poetry, he liked to repeat, ought to be at least as well written as prose. It ought to use no expression that one would not use under the stress of emotion in real life.

The greatness of Frost lies partly in that he was one of the few who brought poetry back to natural speech. One early poem, however, has about every fault that "poetic diction" can have, and is sentimental as well. Yet it has a couple of lines—one line in particular—that the young Frost recognized as prophetically good. The first third of the poem, "My Butterfly," reads:

> Thine emulous fond flowers are dead, too,
> And the daft sun-assaulter, he
> That frighted thee so oft, is fled or dead:
> Save only me
> 5   (Nor is it sad to thee!)—
> Save only me
> There is none left to mourn thee in the fields.
>
> The gray grass is scarce dappled with the snow;
> Its two banks have not shut upon the river;
> 10   But it is long ago—
> It seems forever—
> Since first I saw thee glance,
> With all thy dazzling other ones,
> In airy dalliance,
> 15   Precipitate in love,
> Tossed, tangled, whirled and whirled above,
> Like a limp rose-wreath in a fairy dance. . . .

Amid much faded literary diction, the good line stands out in all its plainness:

> Its two banks have not shut upon the river.

The metaphor—ice like closing doors—is only implied. The plainest words are used—"shut," for example, instead of the more genteel "closed." A young person who liked his poetry "poetic" about 1890 might have written:

> King Winter hath not clanged
> His crystal portals o'er the finny chamber.

And typical readers might have thought, "How poetic!"

But Frost, with rare independence, knew better than the other young poets and typical readers of his time. Once, when he went outside after a difficult or boring day, he felt a little tingle of pleasure at the way a crow powdered him with falling snow as it stirred.

Dust of Snow

> The way a crow
> Shook down on me
> The dust of snow
> From a hemlock tree

₅   Has given my heart
A change of mood
And saved some part
Of a day I had rued.   [1923]
                                    ROBERT FROST (1874–1963)

This is no more than a small poem about a small experience, like those so dear to writers of *haiku* (see p. 318). Although every word is fitted into a rhythm and about one out of four has a rhyming sound, all fall easily into their natural place. The feeling, communicated more through the little dance of rhythm and rhyme than through what is said, would have gone flat if Frost had merely annotated the experience:

The way that a crow
shook down right on me
some snow, sort of like dust,
from a high hemlock bough
has given my heart
a different feeling about things,
and partly saved
a day I felt had been wasted.

For some, this constitutes "writing a poem"—just putting it down any old way. Frost made his statement memorable by giving it verve and lilt. A less direct poet might have felt such plain language was inadequate for such an experience; he might have inflated it with preachments and poetic diction:

Pulverous Silver Essence!

How dear the ways of Nature! Lo, yon crow
Precipitated earthward, even on me,
A pulverous silver essence, dust of snow,
White benefactions of a hemlock tree;

₅   Bequeathing (legacy unto my heart!)
Transfigurations of an erstwhile mood,
Redeeming a jeweled modicum, wee part
Of one diurnal unit I had rued.

Many readers would consider our dressed-up version more "poetic" than Frost's unassuming sentence. Other readers, more cerebral, might prefer it this way.

Wittgenstein and the Crow

Event
as instanced in
"the progress of phenomena":
Item: the avian

5   disbursal of elate frigidities
from a species Old Pop Longfellow saluted
as second in his paradigm of murmurers.
Which same
affords me *möglichkeit*
of shifting psyche-gears:
thereby reclaiming data stamped KAPUT.

It seems unlikely that either version would fix itself in the memory quite as successfully as Frost's original.

Some of the best poems are made up of very simple words:

all, along, any, ashore, back, bar, cannot, comes, day, deep, ever, far, glass, ground, gull, hull, keep, land, like, long, look, more, one, pass, people, raising, reflects, sand, sea, ship, standing, takes, truth, turn, vary, water, watch, way, wetter, when, wherever

Not a rare word here, not a "poetic" one. And yet out of these words, plus a couple of *the*'s and *a*'s, Frost made a poem (about "the response of mankind to the empty immensity of the universe") that the critic Lionel Trilling said he often thought "the most perfect poem of our time."

Neither Out Far Nor In Deep

The people along the sand
All turn and look one way.
They turn their back on the land.
They look at the sea all day.

5   As long as it takes to pass
A ship keeps raising its hull;
The wetter ground like glass
Reflects a standing gull.

The land may vary more;
10   But wherever the truth may be—
The water comes ashore,
And the people look at the sea.

They cannot look out far.
They cannot look in deep.
15   But when was that ever a bar
To any watch they keep?

[1936]
ROBERT FROST (1874–1963)

Emily Dickinson is another poet who can get eye-opening effects, make us do the double take that fixes our attention, by using ordinary words in a way that is rich and strange. What could we make of a list of words like this?

acre, alone, attended, barefoot, boggy, bone, boy, breathing, closes, comb, cool, cordiality, corn, divides, feel, feet, fellow, floor, further, gone, grass, know, likes, may, met, more, narrow, nature, never, noon, notice, occasionally, once, opens, passed, people, rides, secure, seen, several, shaft, spotted, stooping, sudden, sun, then, thought, tighter, too, transport, unbraiding, when, whiplash, with, without, wrinkled, zero

Emily Dickinson managed. Out of these plain words she made one of the best poems ever written about one of Nature's creatures.

A Narrow Fellow in the Grass

A narrow Fellow in the Grass
Occasionally rides—
You may have met Him—did you not
His notice sudden is—

5　The Grass divides as with a Comb—
A spotted shaft is seen—
And then it closes at your feet
And opens further on—

He likes a Boggy Acre
10　A Floor too cool for Corn—
Yet when a Boy, and Barefoot—
I more than once at Noon

Have passed, I thought, a Whip lash
Unbraiding in the Sun
15　When stooping to secure it
It wrinkled, and was gone—

Several of Nature's People
I know, and they know me—
I feel for them a transport
20　Of cordiality—

But never met this Fellow
Attended, or alone
Without a tighter breathing
And Zero at the Bone—

[1865]
EMILY DICKINSON (1830–1886)

A more conventional poet might have shuddered, at the close, with

I gasp, and icy chills go
Up and down my spine!

But look at the originality of Emily Dickinson's last two lines!
Many of the words in the two lists above have one syllable. English, unlike Spanish or Italian, uses monosyllables for many of the basic realities:

day, night, birth, death, boy, girl, love, hate, youth, age, and many others. Concentrations of monosyllables can have powerful effects, as in the last lines of Shakespeare's "Sonnet 18":

> So long as men can breathe or eyes can see,
> So long lives this, and this gives life to thee.

They can be forceful too when played off against the longer Latinate words that English is rich in, as in the following lines from *Macbeth:*

> Will all great Neptune's ocean wash this blood
> Clean from my hand? No, this my hand will rather
> The multitudinous seas incarnadine,
> Making the green one red.

There are exceptions—here as elsewhere—to almost everything we are saying. The bigger, rarer word may be the effective one:

> Sometimes these cogitations still amaze
> The troubled midnight and the noon's repose.
>
> T. S. ELIOT (1888–1965)

Eliot uses "cogitations" with a kind of self-mockery: His speaker is not only a thinker, he is that more deliberate thing, a cogitator, and therefore all the more amazed to confront emotional realities. Keith Waldrop startles us with polysyllables:

> Some brat has chalked the word *screw*
> at the edge of my drive, and doodled
> around it unequivocal hieroglyphics.

"Unequivocal hieroglyphics" is ironic because of the very discrepancy between the level of the language and the frank reality it refers to.

LESS IS MORE

One quality of memorable speech is concentration: much in little. Of a mother punishing her child with such ineffectual fury that the child himself feels sorry for her weakness, John Ciardi writes:

> She beat so hard it hurt me not to hurt.

To describe how daughters drift away from their mothers:

> And still they grew away because they grew.

To describe the long period over which a widow received insurance payments:

Two mailmen died before his mail stopped coming.

The beauty of conciseness is like that of the globe or sphere (in many cultures a symbol of spiritual perfection)—both cover the greatest volume with the minimum surface area.

Break, Break, Break

Break, break, break,
   On thy cold gray stones, O Sea!
And I would that my tongue could utter
   The thoughts that arise in me.

5 O well for the fisherman's boy,
   That he shouts with his sister at play!
O well for the sailor lad,
   That he sings in his boat on the bay!

And the stately ships go on
10   To their haven under the hill;
But O for the touch of a vanish'd hand,
   And the sound of a voice that is still!

Break, break, break,
   At the foot of thy crags, O Sea!
15 But the tender grace of a day that is dead
   Will never come back to me.   [1842]
            ALFRED, LORD TENNYSON (1809–1892)

We appreciate the leanness of this lament for bygone days if we contrast it with another that has a high fat content. "Retrospection," an anonymous poem of the late nineteenth century, begins:

When we see our dreamships slipping
   From the verge of youth's green slope—
Loosening from the transient moorings
   At the golden shore of hope—
5 Vanishing, like airy bubbles,
   On the rough, tried sea of care,
Then the soul grows sick with longing
   That is almost wild despair.

Far behind lies sunny childhood—
10   Fields of flowers our feet have trod
When our vision-bounded Eden
   Held no mystery but God;
When in dreams we spoke with angels,
   When awake, with brooks and birds,
15 Reading in the breeze and sunshine
   Love's unspoken, tender words. . . .

And so on, through five more stanzas of the same.

Poetry, as we quoted before, ought to be at least as well written as prose. Some of the material in the rest of this chapter may seem to refer not just to poetry but to prose as well—indeed to good writing in general. And it does: Though good writing will not guarantee a good poem, bad writing will guarantee a bad one.

Some parts of speech are more necessary than others. Nouns and verbs are the most important, the most existential—nouns referring to the forms that being can take, verbs to their activity. Adjectives and adverbs are hangers-on, with little independent existence of their own. Used weakly, they are decorative rather than structural, hence attractive to the apprentice writer, who needs surface decoration to cover up the architectural flaws. Humpty Dumpty, in telling Alice about words, says, "They've a temper some of them; particularly verbs, they're the proudest—adjectives you can do anything with, but not verbs." In his writings on style, Pound constantly warns against adjectives. Perhaps nothing so weakens a poem as to have the nouns "chaperoned" (as Pound said) by adjectives, or the verbs by adverbs. Adjective fanciers are surprised at how many poems are almost without their favorite part of speech. In the poems that follow, notice how few adjectives there are, what kind they are, and for what occasions they seem to be saved.

Along the Field as We Came By

Along the field as we came by
A year ago, my love and I,
The aspen over stile and stone
Was talking to itself alone.
5 Oh, who are these that kiss and pass?
A country lover and his lass;
Two lovers looking to be wed;
And time shall put them both to bed,
But she shall lie with earth above,
10 And he beside another love.

And sure enough beneath the tree
There walks another love with me,
And overhead the aspen heaves
Its rainy-sounding silver leaves;
15 And I spell nothing in their stir,
But now perhaps they speak to her,
And plain for her to understand
They talk about a time at hand
When I shall sleep with clover clad,
20 And she beside another lad.

[1896]
A. E. HOUSMAN (1859–1936)

3/*stile: steps over a wall or fence*

One can imagine these lines bedizened—but hardly improved!—with modifiers:

> Along the sunny summer field as gayly we came by,
> Just one enchanted year ago, my blushing love and I,
> The trembling aspen over stile and over rocky stone
> Was talking to its solitary single self alone:
> "O who are these enamored ones who coyly kiss and pass?
> A lusty country lover and his winsome-dimpled lass;
> Two young and tender lovers looking fondly to be wed;
> And cruel and jealous time will put them separately to bed;
> The sad and hapless girl will lie with damp old earth above;
> And he—O heedless he!—beside another buxom love. . . ."

The airman in a poem of Yeats uses hardly an adjective in explaining why he took part in World War I. (As an Irishman, he could not hate the Germans or love the English; his impulse to enlist came from an existential love of adventure.)

An Irish Airman Foresees His Death

I know that I shall meet my fate
Somewhere among the clouds above;
Those that I fight I do not hate,
Those that I guard I do not love;
5 My country is Kiltartan Cross,
My countrymen Kiltartan's poor,
No likely end could bring them loss
Or leave them happier than before.
Nor law, nor duty bade me fight,
10 Nor public men, nor cheering crowds,
A lonely impulse of delight
Drove to this tumult in the clouds;
I balanced all, brought all to mind,
The years to come seemed waste of breath,
15 A waste of breath the years behind
In balance with this life, this death.

[1919]
WILLIAM BUTLER YEATS (1865–1939)

Gerard Manley Hopkins uses hardly any adjectives in "Spring and Fall" (see Anthology, p. 429), which is about the sorrow of a child as she watches the leaves drop. (She is really grieving, the poet tells her, over the fact of mortality—as Homer did when he said that the generations of men were like the generations of leaves.)

What we have been saying about modifiers is a caution, not a rule. Adjectives and adverbs tend to run to fat, to be sagging appendages on the bone and muscle of poetry. But just as we need some fat for the health and contour of the body, so we need some adjectives in poetry: for precision, for luxuriance, sometimes even for a needed sense of muchness.

The most useless adjectives duplicate the meaning of their noun, or express a quality implied by it. We have no need of them in such expressions as

> celestial stars, fragrant flowers, vernal spring, deep abyss, empty chasm, cold winter sun, flaming pyre, fair beauty, soft whispers, sweet perfume, loud strife, bleak waste, stimulating wine, dark forebodings, nobly enshrined.

If the nouns did not have their usual qualities—if the stars were *infernal,* or the spring *wintry,* or the strife *quiet*—the fact might be interesting enough to deserve an adjective.

Adjectives do little except dilute the poetry in such phrases from Bryant as

> busy artisan, weary traveller, beaten drums, mighty ocean, golden grain, balmy evening, pathless desert, stubborn flint, yielding wax, sultry July, chill north wind.

Doubled adjectives can add fat to a poem, especially when the meanings overlap, as in "flushed and angry cheek," "gay and gaudy hue," "bleak and barren mountains," "this region, desolate and drear," "icy Alpine height." Sometimes there are reasons for accumulating adjectives, as when Shakespeare wants to give a sense of the muchness of something in

> How weary, stale, flat and unprofitable
> Seem to me all the uses of the world!

or in

>   . . . I grant him bloody,
> Luxurious, avaricious, false, deceitful,
> Sudden, malicious, smacking of every sin
> That has a name . . .

As many as three adjectives together tend to drag, but John Milton uses that very drag expressively in describing how his coy Eve yields to Adam with "sweet, reluctant, amorous delay."

Adjective-prone writers tend to favor such hyphenated expressions as "the day-tired town" or "her life-glad form" or "age-forgotten songs." Some hyphenated expressions are natural: "the spring-fed lake," "the air-conditioned theater," "salt-caked tugs." But new ones made up only for poetic effect may call attention to themselves as unnatural intruders. They can also be imprecise. Does "She entered the wood, deer-cautious" mean she was cautious as a deer, or cautious because there were deer around? With such expressions as the following, we suspect the writer has made a self-conscious effort to lift natural English to a more "poetic" level: "brook-gladdened mead-ows," "hate-lashed storms," "terror-tinged yearning," "chimneys sulphur-flamed," "fruit-ripe with child," "thirst-inviting brook," "pine-bemurmured ridge." Pound, however, makes good use of elaborate hyphenization for mockery in the following little poem.

The Bath Tub

As a bathtub lined with white porcelain,
When the hot water gives out or goes tepid,
So is the slow cooling of our chivalrous passion,
O my much praised but-not-altogether-satisfactory lady.   [1915]

EZRA POUND (1885–1972)

And Hopkins can be richly expressive in such phrases as his "dapple-dawn-drawn Falcon" ("The Windhover," Anthology, p. 428).

A writer careful about adjectives and adverbs, keeping them in reserve for special effects, can make them vigorous and vivid.

A raven low in the air, with stagnant eyes. . . .

WALTER DE LA MARE

You lay still, brilliant with illness, behind glass. . . .

THOMAS KINSELLA

The old farmer, his scarlet face
Apologetic with whiskey. . . .

JAMES WRIGHT

Morning comes, frail with mist . . .

CRAIG RAINE

Sometimes surprising effects can result from transferring a modifier from the noun it really belongs with to an associated noun. We often use such transfers in ordinary speech—as when we say we had a "noisy evening," even though it was the *we*, not the evening, that was noisy. We speak of "giddy heights," of a "shivery horror movie," of "dishonest money." Sir Philip Sidney said he did not "aspire to Caesar's bleeding fame." Other examples:

. . . clarions
That in the battle blowen bloody sounds. . . .

GEOFFREY CHAUCER

O, most wicked speed, to post
With such dexterity to incestuous sheets!

WILLIAM SHAKESPEARE

His brow is wet with honest sweat. . . .

HENRY WADSWORTH LONGFELLOW

Contemporary poets are still transferring adjectives:

And all throughout a Breughel matinee
Those buxom waltzes ran. . . .

JAMES MERRILL

Humpty Dumpty may have found verbs the hardest words of all, but writers have coped with them. (John Berryman says of Ernest Hemingway, who prided himself on coping, "He verbed for forty years.") Here are some interesting verbs performing:

. . . over a field
Snapping with grasshoppers. . . .

FREDERICK GODDARD TUCKERMAN

Song-sparrows were wound up for the summer.

ELIZABETH BISHOP

At night the factories
struggle awake.

ELIZABETH BISHOP

Scolding your pipe against a tree. . . .

MARCIA MASTERS

Rudolph Reed was oaken.
His wife was oaken too.
And his two good girls and his good little man
Oakened as they grew. . . .

GWENDOLYN BROOKS

The Hammond organ lubricates the air. . . .

MILLER WILLIAMS

. . . his grey eyes
brittled into ice . . .

MARY OLIVER

And the dancers are dressing. They tease
Their toes into shoes.

BRIGIT PEGEEN KELLY

. . . your window upstairs where
white curtains, loose with air, would blouse
like sails . . .

ELISE PASCHEN

Such vivid verbs are often compressed metaphors: The Reeds are strong as oak; they *are* oak; as they grow stronger, they oaken.

Poets, like other writers, achieve concentration by packing double meanings into single words. This kind of double-talk—these puns—is by no means confined to poetry. We often see slogans like these:

DRIVE AS IF YOUR LIFE DEPENDED ON IT.

ARE YOU DYING FOR A CIGARETTE?

Today we think of puns as the kind of humor more likely to evoke groans than laughter. But puns were taken more seriously in earlier times. When John Donne put his future in jeopardy by marrying Sir George More's underage daughter without the father's consent, someone—probably not Donne himself—composed a one-liner:

John Donne,   Anne Donne,   Un-done.

Donne himself was not joking when he wrote, during an illness that might have been fatal, his poem "A Hymn to God the Father," with its punning:

When Thou hast done, Thou hast not Donne,
    For I have more.

(Some critics even think that "more" is a pun on his wife's name.)

Some puns play on different meanings of the same word, as in George Starbuck's lines:

The world has a glass center.
I saw the sign for it.
TOLEDO, GLASS CENTER OF THE WORLD.

Others play on different words that sound alike.

On His Books

When I am dead, I hope it may be said,
"His sins were scarlet, but his books were read."   [1924]
HILAIRE BELLOC (1870–1953)

Some might feel there is something like a playful pun in the way William Stafford relates the name of a legendary lady to the landscape of a county named for her.

Godiva County, Montana

She's a big country. Her undulations
roll and flow in the sun. Those flanks

quiver when the wind caresses the grass.
Who turns away when so generous a body
5   offers to play hide-and-seek all summer?
One shoulder leans bare all the way up
the mountain; limbs range and plunge
wildly into the river. We risk our eyes
every day; they celebrate; they dance
10   and flirt over this offered treasure.
"Be alive," the land says. "Listen—
this is your time, your world, your pleasure."   [1998]

Richard Wilbur has written a series of quatrains based on puns. Here are two of them:

If a sheepdog ate a cantaloupe,
Would it make him frisk like an antelope?
Would he feel all pleased and jolly?
Or would he be a Melon Collie?

When Jack came tumbling down the hill,
The record shows that sister Jill
"Came tumbling after." Was he her
Roll Model, then, as I infer?

Surly readers might feel he has done well to call the series *Some Atrocities.*

Besides storing their words with multiple meanings, writers can give them more charge by making full use of their connotations (see page 120). Words, like people, can be interesting because of their background, because of where they have been and the company they have kept in the past.

When the Normans came to England from France in 1066, the language of the natives was Old English (or Anglo-Saxon), which gave us many of the words for down-to-earth realities. French became the language of the court; words of French ancestry are redolent of courtliness, chivalry, romance. For centuries Latin was the language of the church and of scholarship; words patently from the Latin can still suggest erudition or pedantry. In ordinary speech we do not separate these three components, but a high concentration of any one can make itself felt as unusual. In "The Wanderer," W. H. Auden makes use of Old English derivatives, some few of them odd enough to call for the dictionary. Such words, as opposed to the more cultivated French and Latin ones, evoke a rugged and heroic life in a primitive northern setting. Auden's poem is about the archetypal figure of the seeker, the adventurer, the pioneer who leaves his home, his establishment, to fare forth into new territory.

The Wanderer

Doom is dark and deeper than any sea-dingle.
Upon what man it fall

In spring, day-wishing flowers appearing,
Avalanche sliding, white snow from rock-face,
5   That he should leave his house,
No cloud-soft hand can hold him, restraint by women;
But ever that man goes
Through place-keepers, through forest trees,
A stranger to strangers over undried sea,
10   Houses for fishes, suffocating water,
Or lonely on fell as chat,
By pot-holed becks
A bird stone-haunting, an unquiet bird.

There head falls forward, fatigued at evening,
15   And dreams of home,
Waving from window, spread of welcome,
Kissing of wife under single sheet;
But waking sees
Bird-flocks nameless to him, through doorway voices
20   Of new men making another love.

Save him from hostile capture,
From sudden tiger's leap at corner;
Protect his house,
His anxious house where days are counted
25   From thunderbolt protect,
From gradual ruin spreading like a stain;
Converting number from vague to certain,
Bring joy, bring day of his returning,
Lucky with day approaching, with leaning dawn.   [1933]
                                      W. H. AUDEN (1907–1973)

¹/*dingle:* deep cleft or hollow   ¹²/*becks: brooks*
¹¹/*fell:* high waste land or pasture
chat: a European thrush

The first eighteen words are from Old English; not until we come to
"flowers" do we have a word that derives, through Old French, from the
Latin. We can see how different the poem would sound if we Latinized it:

Fate is more obscure and profound than any ocean-valley . . .

The vocabulary keeps us in an Old English world until we reach

Save him from hostile capture,

which is pure Latin-French. So is

Converting number from vague to certain,

and words like "sudden," "protect," "anxious," "gradual." As the wanderer returns home, he returns to a more genteel vocabulary.

Hopkins, though a professor of Greek and Latin, favored native English words. In "The Windhover" (see Anthology, p. 428) there are almost no words whose Latin ancestry would be obvious. The vocabulary is basically Old English, but what is unusual is the large number of words, all crucial to the meaning, that suggest a French world of chivalry, adventure, and even romance: "minion," "dauphin," "falcon," "achieve," "mastery," "beauty," "valour," "buckle," "billion," "dangerous," "chevalier," "sillion," "vermilion." That the language has so French, so chivalric, a cast is appropriate: The poet, seeing a kind of knightly adventurousness in the daring falcon, thinks of Christ, his chevalier or supreme knight-figure.

The eighteenth century was particularly fond of a sonorous Latinate vocabulary, as in the italicized words in these lines from Samuel Johnson's "The Vanity of Human Wishes":

> Let *Observation* with *extensive* view,
> Survey mankind from China to Peru. . . .
>
> *Delusive Fortune* hears the *incessant* call,
> They mount, they shine, *evaporate,* and fall. . . .
>
> The form *distorted justifies* the fall,
> And *detestation* rids the *indignant* wall. . . .

Even when such words are the natural ones for their meaning, an accumulation of them can sound learned or pompous.

But sometimes words come to us with a halo of ghostly images: apparitions from the underworld of etymology. "Deliberate" comes from the Latin *librare* (*to weigh*), which is itself from *libra* (*a pound*—whence our abbreviation *lb.*—and the *scales* on which *pounds* were weighed). When we remember that the word has to do with weights and balances, then it becomes a pictogram: We see the weighted mechanisms shifting as the bridge begins to rise in Richard Wilbur's line:

> Deliberately the drawbridge starts to rise. . . .

We become more sensitive to ordinary words by realizing how haunted they are. Merely turning the pages of a dictionary will stir up quite a few ghosts. "Alarm" is more exciting when we realize it is a cry, "To arms!" (*All' arme!* in Italian). An ordinary "derrick" becomes a grislier part of the industrial landscape if we remember that it was named after a certain Derrick, a famous London hangman. "Nonchalant" means *not heating up*. To be nonchalant is to "cool it." "Curfew" has a setting when we know it comes from two Old French words we would now spell *couvre-feu: cover the fire*—put it out for the night. A curfew for teenagers picks up interesting symbolic overtones if we think of it as meaning "time to put the fires out." "Dexterity" refers to the right hand, most people's best hand; "sinister" refers to the left, or unlucky, side: To speak of a magician, or a ball handler, as having "sinister dexterity" gives us a curious punning oxymoron. Sensitive to the personality and history of words, writers make full use of them as resources. Frost has noticed that when people say they are in favor of a *revolution* in any respect they mean they want to keep things exactly as they are: a *revolution* means that something wheel-like goes all the way around and ends up where it was. Revolutionaries should be in favor of half revolutions:

> Yes, revolutions are the only salves.
> But they're one thing that should be done by halves.

Let's finish with two contemporary American poems that take pleasure in various kinds of words.

The Word for Everything

There is the word for you
and beside it the word *me*,
though neither of us knows which they are.
There is the word for the two of us, together
5 or apart. Together
and apart.
There is the word for chair,
the word *clear*.

There is the word for this moment, too,
10 though no one can pronounce it.
It is not now,
though there is the word *now*,
and the word *slow*.
Between them is the word
15 one does not hear,
the word these words look for,

here by the clear chair
deep in the slow now.

[1996]
ROGER MITCHELL (*b.* 1935)

Remembering the Ardèche

April plunges the classroom into light,
aisles of elm trees glitter beyond the window,
and I must pause midsentence, wondering
where you are. En route, no doubt,
5 chasing the easy skirts of camomile
along the Dordogne, south to Gascony;

while I remain suspended in my lecture,
fistfuls of wit cast before flocks of students
who long for the spring migrations,
10 chafing at their confinement from the weather.
I wear my patience like a light green dress
and wear it thin.

     It must have been in April
you and I walked together all the way
from Langogne to Aubenas,
15 never once meeting a window set in a wall
to sever inner from outer; only the high
clearstory of sunny clouds raised upon hills.   [1984]

             EMILY GROSHOLZ (b. 1950)

EXERCISES & DIVERSIONS

A. 1. For a view of words unlike that of Pablo Neruda or Eudora Welty, see the poem by Vern Rutsala (Anthology, p. 513). Why is his attitude so unlike theirs?

2. When Federico García Lorca's speaker (p. 340) says he would like to trade his horse, saddle, and knife for a house, mirror, and blanket, he is not thinking of the **denotation,** or dictionary meaning, of the words ("**horse:** a large, solid-hoofed, herbivorous quadruped, *Equus caballus* . . .") but of the **connotation,** or cluster of associations, each has. The horse connotes an outdoor life of wandering, adventure, and peril; the saddle connotes homelessness, discomfort, and hardship; the knife, passion and violence. The objects for which he would like to trade connote safety, comfort, and settled domesticity. The words in Patchen's poem (p. 118) are rich in connotation. "Rain," in the upper left-hand corner, suggests coolness, fertility, flowers, freshness, renewal, purity, snugness by the fire; but it also connotes chilliness, discomfort, loneliness, gloom, deprivation (as in "to save for a rainy day"). What association clusters go along with each of these words: gate, fence, flame, snow, garden, coast, lily, thorn, mirror, shadow, star, stone?

3. Do any other words in Patchen's poem strike you as being especially strong in connotation?

4. Does it seem to you that such words—or what they stand for—could be symbols of what they connote? Is "rain," for example, a fertility symbol?

B. Evaluate the worth of each adjective in the following examples:

1. This done, he took the bride about the neck
And kissed her lips with such a clamorous smack
That at the parting all the church did echo. . . .

            WILLIAM SHAKESPEARE

2. Poor world, said I, what wilt thou do
    To entertain this starry Stranger?
  Is this the best thou couldst bestow,
    A cold and not too cleanly manger?
  Contend, ye powers of heaven and earth,
    To fit a bed for this huge birth.

RICHARD CRASHAW

3. For everything that's lovely is
  But a brief, dreamy, kind delight. . . .

WILLIAM BUTLER YEATS

4. The sky was like a waterdrop
    In shadow of a thorn,
  Clear, tranquil, beautiful,
    Dark, forlorn. . . .

WALTER DE LA MARE

5. The autumn night receives us, hoarse with rain. . . .

LOUISE BOGAN

6. The responsible sound of the lawnmower. . . .

WILLIAM STAFFORD

7. . . . barefoot gulls
  designing the sands. . . .

WILLIAM STAFFORD

8. [Of a beggar]
    How much money would erase him in a dream,
    his lids inflamed, his bare feet biblical
    with sores? . . . The bay across the street
    is affluent with sun. . . .

RICHARD HUGO

9. . . . in Aspen,
  no poverty or crime, each day
  a cruise in the blond, expensive streets . . .

STEPHEN DUNN

10. . . . I was the clerk periscopic
  behind the desk of a welfare hotel . . .

MARTÍN ESPADA

C. In the light of matters discussed in this chapter, comment on the
  following quotations:

1. O shut the door! and when thou hast done so,
  Come weep with me—past hope, past cure, past help!

WILLIAM SHAKESPEARE

2. And worse I may be yet. The worst is not
   As long as we can say, "This is the worst."

WILLIAM SHAKESPEARE

3. And the ox, with sleek hide, and with low-swimming head;
   And the sheep, little-kneed, with a quick-dipping nod;
   And a girl, with her head carried on in a proud
   Gait of walking, as smooth as an air-swimming cloud.

WILLIAM BARNES

4. The loud vociferations of the street
   Become an indistinguishable roar. . . .

HENRY WADSWORTH LONGFELLOW

5. [Of a deer]
   We do not discern those eyes
       Watching in the snow . . .
   We do not discern those eyes
       Wondering, aglow,
         Fourfooted, tiptoe. . . .

THOMAS HARDY

6. *"Chelidon urbica urbica"*
   I cried on the little bird,
   Meticulously enunciating each syllable of each word. . . .

WALTER DE LA MARE

7. Mellifluous as bees, these brittle men
   droning of Honeyed Homer give me hives. . . .

GEORGE STARBUCK

D. In Jarrell's "The Knight, Death, and the Devil," which is based on Albrecht Dürer's engraving (p. 141), there are many hyphenated modifiers. Do they seem to work here? Is there anything, for example, in the texture of the engraving itself to which they correspond?

The Knight, Death, and the Devil

Cowhorn-crowned, shockheaded, cornshuck-bearded,
Death is a scarecrow—his death's-head a teetotum
That tilts up toward man confidentially
But trimmed with adders; ringlet-maned, rope-bridled,
The mare he rides crops herbs beside a skull.
He holds up, warning, the crossed cones of time:
Here, narrowing into now, the Past and Future
Are quicksand.
          A hoofed pikeman trots behind.
His pike's claw-hammer mocks—in duplicate, inverted—
The pocked, ribbed, soaring crescent of his horn.

A scapegoat aged into a steer; boar-snouted;
His great limp ears stuck sidelong out in air;
A dewlap bunched at his breast; a ram's-horn wound
Beneath each ear; a spur licked up and out
From the hide of his forehead; bat-winged, but in bone;
His eye a ring inside a ring inside a ring
That leers up, joyless, vile, in meek obscenity—
This is the devil. Flesh to flesh, he bleats
The herd back to the pit of being.
In fluted mail; upon his lance the bush
Of that old fox; a sheep-dog bounding at his stirrup,
In its eyes the cast of faithfulness (our help,
Our foolish help); his dun war-horse pacing
Beneath in strength, in ceremonious magnificence;
His castle—some man's castle—set on every crag:
So, companioned so, the knight moves through this world.
The fiend moos in amity, Death mouths, reminding:
He listens in assurance, has no glance
To spare for them, but looks past steadily
At—at—
        a man's look completes itself.

The death of his own flesh, set up outside him;
The flesh of his own soul, set up outside him—
Death and the devil, what are these to him?
His being accuses him—and yet his face is firm
In resolution, in absolute persistence;
The folds of smiling do for steadiness;
The face is its own fate—*a man does what he must*—
And the body underneath it says: *I am.*

        [1955]

        Randall Jarrell (1914–1965)

E. What kinds of pictures haunt these words from their etymological past?
(Consult a good dictionary.)

    fool, generous, companion, lunacy, planet, maudlin, tawdry, sabo-
    tage, pandemonium, tangerine, bungalow, chivalrous, cavalier,
    bedlam, gargoyle, focus, exaggerate, disaster, dilapidated, carnival,
    carnation, carnage, carnal, horde

F. Examine the use of adjectives preceding their nouns in "The
Woodspurge" (Anthology, p. 421), "Love, 20¢ the First Quarter Mile"
(Anthology, p. 461), and "Spoils" (p. 84). Why is the use of adjectives
so very different in "Leda and the Swan" (p. 40)? Could any of the
adjectives there be omitted without loss?

G. How successful is the diction in these excerpts from the poems of
Kevin Pilkington (the first two about animals drinking)?

Albrecht Dürer, *The Knight, Death, and the Devil*

1. A stream runs down
    a deer's throat . . .
2. . . . A calf walks
    over to the clear water
    then drinks its face.
3. You sit in a bar on 2nd Ave.
    with a woman you want
    but notice the distance
    in her eyes has the extra
    mile that even another drink
    could never help you reach.

ESSAYS

A. Find a poem in this book that you like for its **diction,** or word choice. Look up every noun, verb, and modifier in a dictionary, and write down what you learn about word origins. Also note any denotative or connotative meanings you can think of. Now reread the poem. How has it changed for you? Write an essay introducing your reader to this poem and leading up to a specific thesis about the author's use of diction. Remember to quote from the poem for evidence and to discuss those quotations in detail. Try to make your reader see how important word choice has been to the success of the poem.

B. Think for a moment about the difference between words and pictures. In this chapter you have the Jarrell poem and the Dürer etching, but elsewhere in the book you will find color inserts of poems based upon paintings. Write an essay on one of these poem-painting pairs, dwelling particularly on the nature of the poet's words. What sort of diction is used, and how does the poet's technique compare to that of the visual artist?

POEMS

A. Write a descriptive poem (of, say, a dozen lines, in any rhythm) about a familiar object, or anything of interest to you. Do not use any adjectives until the last line; then try to use, effectively, a series of three.

B. Make a list of your five favorite nouns, five favorite verbs, and three favorite modifiers. Try writing a poem using all of these words in any combination.

C. Spend some time reading the etymologies of words in a good dictionary, paying particular attention to words from Germanic or Anglo-Saxon roots and those of Latinate roots. Now, try to write a poem made entirely of words from the Germanic or Anglo-Saxon, allowing yourself a minimum of Latinate diction.

FOUR

The Sounds

7

GOLD IN THE ORE

Sound as Meaning

This chapter may look as if it were about some such abstraction as acoustical theory. It is actually about the way we use our bodies—instruments of flesh and bone—to produce the sounds we call voice: the sounds of poetry and all human speech. We can realize how sensitive the mouth is and what care the brain takes of it if we contemplate a "homunculus" (see p. 146)—a representation of the way a human being would look if the proportions of the body corresponded to the brain area devoted to each part. More brain space is needed for the mouth than for all the rest of the body except the hands.

We can think of words as having not only a mind (their meanings) but also a body—the structure of sound in which their meanings live. Most poets, who are not Platonic in their love for language, care as much for the body of their words as for the mind. They like to feel words in the mouth, as Kay Ryan does in the following poem:

Crustacean Island

There could be an island paradise
where crustaceans prevail.
Click, click, go the lobsters
with their china mitts and
5   articulated tails.
It would not be sad like whales
with their immense and patient sieving
and the sobering modesty
of their general way of living.
10   It would be an island blessed
with only cold-blooded residents

and no human angle.
It would echo with a thousand castanets
and no flamencos.

[1996]
KAY RYAN (*b.* 1945)

Wallace Stevens is speaking for many good poets when he says "words above everything else, are, in poetry, sounds." The sound of poetry, what Robert Frost called "the gold in the ore," is what we turn to now.

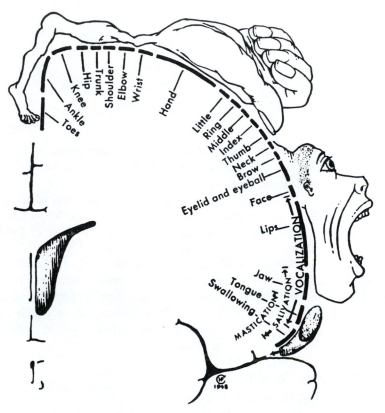

(From *The Cerebral Cortex of Man* by Penfield and Bamussen. Copyright © 1950 Macmillan. Reprinted by permission of The Gale Group.)

A poem comes to us first as speech, on sound waves that register as barometric changes against the drums and gauges of the ear, an apparatus so sensitive it takes notice if the pressure against it varies by 1 part in 10 billion. "A breath of the mouth becomes a picture of the world," said Johann Gottfried von Herder, ". . . everything that man has ever thought and willed . . . depends on a moving breath of air."

We hear poems even when we seem to be taking them silently from the page. Tiny wires attached to the speech areas of the throat have picked up electrical currents—evidence that the muscles were being stimulated during silent reading. The body participates sympathetically with what it experiences. Colors affect us physically: Experiments have shown that fixing the eyes on pure red can raise blood pressure and accelerate heartbeat, whereas fixing the eyes on pure blue can have a tranquilizing effect. Images of sound must affect us no less profoundly, since as very young children we were more at home in the world of sound (which we had known even before birth) than in the world of sight. The rest of this chapter will be about the physical nature of speech. This is not theoretical material to be merely read; these are physical facts to be acted out physically—to be felt and tried in the mouth as we read.

Not Sense

The tongue shapes and molds sound. Speech
becomes sensation in the mouth vibrating
on the palate and the teeth—touch
done with more than fingertips transmutes
5   itself to rhythm in the ear. Words outleap
meaning and turn into a way to move.
We speak the names that objects will become.
Voice wakes the light, and we begin to see
the shadows leaves can make against the wood.
10   We say Earth spins, and suddenly the clouds
move like ghosts of old ones bringing rain
that loves the growing things upon the ground.
I listen to your breath against my skin
and wait for you to name the way you feel,
15   to tell me where you've been and where you go,
to find the shape of things we share and have
to give. I lean and whisper words to let you see
the beauty that I watch when I'm with you.
My tongue slips nimbly past my teeth
20   and finds lips ready to caress
the line of small round scars that mark
your cheek. Nothing mars the surface
of your skin; what is is graceful and words
could never see it any other way. I watch with senses
25   more perceptive than my eyes, and let you touch me
more than once or twice. Your voice says little;
sound echoes in my senses like the wind.
You fill the dark passages of form with murmurs
that inhabit me until I learn it's sound not sense
30   that fills the world, that keeps me warm.   [1990]

GAIL TREMBLAY (b. 1945)

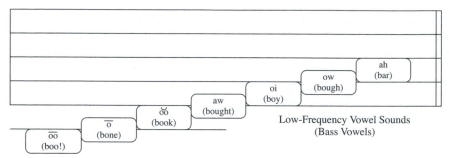

Frequency Scale of English Vowel Sounds

VOWELS AND ASSONANCE

Our speech sounds are conventionally divided into vowels and consonants. With vowels the airflow from the lungs is not impeded. If we pronounce *a e i o u*, we can feel that we are nowhere obstructing the breath but only, by raising our tongue, rounding our lips, and the like, reshaping the instrument it flows through. How we manage so complicated a process would astound us if we thought about it.

Our feats of hearing are equally incredible. We follow as many as twenty distinct sounds a second; we notice sounds that fade into nothingness in a few thousandths of a second; and we do so while turning this complicated acoustic input into electrochemical nerve impulses that the brain can process. The most complicated sound patterns a poet ever uses are as nothing compared to the patterns we handle habitually.

Vowels are in a way like musical notes; we can set up a vowel scale (rather like a musical scale) based on the frequencies that the sounds have in themselves. Sound, as we know, travels in waves. Since it travels at constant speed, the shorter the waves, the more per second—the higher, that is, the frequency of the sound. Shortwave sounds are high-frequency sounds, shrill sounds, like the *ee* of "whee!" The longer the waves, the fewer per second, and the slower and deeper the sound seems to be. The *oo* of "moon" is a low-frequency sound.

A difficulty we run into in making up a vowel scale is that vowels are not notes, but chords made up of tones and overtones from the resonating system of throat, mouth, and head. Some of our fifteen sounds, the diphthongs, are two chords sounded in sequence. The *i* sound of "good-by" is a run-together *áh-ee*. Several other sounds are also vowels in motion—"glides" from one sound into another. Our scale, though it would not provide a basis for laboratory experiment, is on the whole accurate for American speech, and it serves well enough for the reading of poetry.

The "upness" and "downness" of vowel sounds affect us physically in different ways. The *ee* sound, at the top of the scale, comes in a pattern of waves that could be diagramed like this:

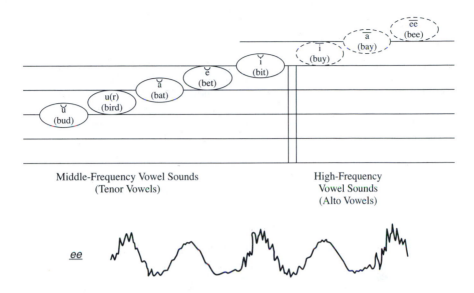

Middle-Frequency Vowel Sounds
(Tenor Vowels)

High-Frequency
Vowel Sounds
(Alto Vowels)

ee

in contrast to the wave pattern of the *oo* sound, at the bottom of the scale:

oo

The high-frequency *ee* is busier, gives the ear more to process. Its greater activity suggests greater vitality, speed, excitement than the slower-moving, more sluggish waves of the *oo*.

Few categories in our experience are richer in emotional suggestion than upness and downness. We associate being "up" or "high" with an increase in vitality, being "down" or "low" with a lessening of it. Our heart "sinks" when we feel grief, the physical effect of which Charles Darwin describes as follows: "The muscles [become] flaccid; the eyelids droop; the head hangs on the contracted chest; the lips, cheeks, and lower jaw all sink downward from their own weight."★ The last phrase explains why downness is bad: When we give up or lose strength, gravitation takes over. All growth, aspiration, striving is an upward thing, almost against the nature of matter itself.

High-frequency vowels go well with expressions of excitement, exhilaration, vivacity. James Joyce, one of the most sound-conscious of writers,

★Charles Darwin, *The Expression of the Emotions in Man and Animals* (Chicago: University of Chicago Press, 1965), p. 167.

provides a good example of their use in an exultant passage from *A Portrait of the Artist as a Young Man:*

> He was alone. He was unheeded, happy and near to the wild heart of life.
> He was alone and young and wilful and wildhearted, alone amid a waste
> of wild air and brackish waters and the seaharvest of shells and tangle
> and veiled grey sunlight and gayclad lightclad figures, of children and
> girls and voices childish and girlish in the air.

Probably no poet has ever so deliberately written in the high-frequency range as Dylan Thomas did when he urged his dying father to keep up his courage to the end.

Do Not Go Gentle into That Good Night

> Do not go gentle into that good night,
> Old age should burn and rave at close of day;
> Rage, rage against the dying of the light.
>
> Though wise men at their end know dark is right,
> Because their words had forked no lightning they
> Do not go gentle into that good night.
>
> Good men, the last wave by, crying how bright
> Their frail deeds might have danced in a green bay,
> Rage, rage against the dying of the light.
>
> Wild men who caught and sang the sun in flight,
> And learn, too late, they grieved it on its way,
> Do not go gentle into that good night.
>
> Grave men, near death, who see with blinding sight
> Blind eyes could blaze like meteors and be gay,
> Rage, rage against the dying of the light.
>
> And you, my father, there on the sad height,
> Curse, bless, me now with your fierce tears, I pray.
> Do not go gentle into that good night.
> Rage, rage against the dying of the light.

[1952]
DYLAN THOMAS (1914–1953)

The rhyming sounds, throughout, are $\bar{\imath}$ ("night") and $\bar{a}$ ("day"). With these are many high, bright $\bar{e}$'s ("deed"). The effect is not only in the high-frequency vowels themselves, but in the fact that they occur about twice as often here as they do in the normal run of English speech. The unlooked-for percentage must come as a shock of excitement, an aural pick-me-up, to the sensitive, if largely subconscious, mechanisms of the brain.

A more somber poem gives a very different concentration of sound.

Once by the Pacific

The shattered water made a misty din.
Great waves looked over others coming in,
And thought of doing something to the shore
That water never did to land before.
5 The clouds were low and hairy in the skies,
Like locks blown forward in the gleam of eyes.
You could not tell, and yet it looked as if
The shore was lucky in being backed by cliff,
The cliff in being backed by continent;
10 It looked as if a night of dark intent
Was coming, and not only a night, an age.
Someone had better be prepared for rage.
There would be more than ocean-water broken
Before God's last *Put out the Light* was spoken.   [1928]

ROBERT FROST (1874–1963)

A scary poem. Something in the universe, it implies, is threatening our existence; things are going to get worse before they get better. The vowel sounds
gravitate toward the lower, darker notes: There are more than twice as many
aw's, *oo*'s, and *o*'s as we are used to hearing in spoken English.

The larger an object is and the more volume it has, the more slowly it is
likely to vibrate. The long strings in a piano give us the deep tones; a double
bass can go lower than a violin. Avalanches and stormy seas have deeper
reverberations than hailstones on the roof—not merely louder. The larger
object produces a low-frequency sound.

Since low notes are related to largeness, they also evoke what is powerful
or awesome or ominous or gloomy. We think of them as *dark* notes, perhaps
because our experience of caverns and other reverberating hollows is associated with the dark. (The voice of the great singer Caruso was said to "darken"
as over the years it shifted from tenor toward baritone.)

Vowels have their characteristic resonance from the shape and size of the
cavities in which they resound—that is, from the way in which we make use
of the resonating chambers of mouth and head. The larger the hollow in
which a vowel sound vibrates, the deeper the sound and the more clearly our
nerves and muscles tell us that *we ourselves* are embodying largeness, hollow-
ness, darkness. If we could see—which heaven forbid!—a cross section of the
head of a person pronouncing "*ee*," it would look rather like the left-hand
figure below. The front part of the tongue has been raised to permit only a
narrow stream of air to pass through. Such a high front vowel, tensely produced, can suggest not only speed, brightness, and vitality but also littleness,
as in "needle" or "teeny-weeny." It *is* a littleness, and we are doing a kind of
charade of littleness by squeezing the mouth to the narrowest opening that
permits any sound at all.

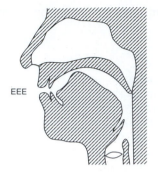 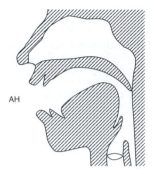

People producing an *ah* sound (right-hand figure, above) have to make the mouth a noticeably larger resonating chamber: have to make a sensitive part of the body, very close to the brain, a more sonorous cavern for the deeper, more solemn, more awesome sound. Not only do the sounds we produce have certain qualities, but our bodies, in producing them, are trying to be *like* those very qualities.

Sounds also affect us through the memories they arouse of what we have heard in life. The 10 billion neurons of the brain have almost infinite inter-connections. Hearing certain sounds cannot fail to remind us of surf or thunder or the hiss of a snake or the whine of the winter wind through telephone wires on the prairie. Or of feet echoing in an empty street at night, the scream of brakes, the siren of a fire truck. Sounds like these can be deeply emotional, bringing, as we have learned, their messages of life and death.

For many reasons, then, the sounds of human speech are charged with emotional potential. Poets have always felt this. When Shelley begins his "Ode to a Skylark" with a line that features the four highest-frequency vowels, he sets the poem in the key of these vowels:

> Hail to thee, blithe spirit!

When Frost uses almost all of the bass vowels in the first two lines of "An Old Man's Winter Night," his introductory chords prepare us to expect the worst:

> All out-of-doors looked darkly in at him
> Through the thin frost, almost in separate stars. . . .

Once we have uttered a sound, we take pleasure in repeating it. We find repetition in magic spells, in solemn oaths, in orations, in ads, as well as in the speech noises a baby makes for its own pleasure. When a sound is clearly struck in a poem, it tends to attract similar sounds. At the beginning of Gary Snyder's "Oil," many of the sounds that we hear can be heard again within the next few syllables:

soft rainsqualls on the swells
south of the Bonins, late at night. Light
from the empty mess-hall
throws back bulky shadows
of winch and fairlead
over the slanting fantail where I stand. . . .

Repetition of a vowel sound ("soft"/"squalls"; "rain"/"late") is known as **assonance.**

Each of the fifteen vowel sounds of our scale has its own character or tone color. Skillful writers and sensitive readers are aware of the differences, just as one is aware of the differences between the tones of a flute, a violin, and a bassoon. But since poets for the most part work with the language as it is, and since words that combine a desired sound and an appropriate meaning are not always available, the use of expressive sound in poetry is not to be expected as a regular thing. The most we can say is that poets are sensitive to the sounds they are making and use them expressively when they see the opportunity. The benefit that most of us, as readers, derive from meditating at least briefly on the quality of individual sounds is that we come to participate more completely, more physically, in the experience of the poem. The remarks that follow—we repeat—should be tested in the mouth.

Writers or readers who wanted to master the keyboard of sound could concentrate on each of the fifteen vowel sounds in turn, noticing what happens in their mouth when they pronounce it, listening to its quality and deciding on its emotional possibilities, thinking of words in which it seems especially expressive, and watching for it to turn up in the poetry they are reading. They would not be surprised to discover that, just as such symbols as "earth" and "sea" have room at the same time for opposite connotations, so one sound can be appropriate for opposite emotions—the shrill *i* of "strike" can serve for either exultation or despair. Sounding this diphthong, they would feel how it originates as an *ah* in the lax back region of the throat but climbs instantly into the vibrant *ee* region. They could feel it move in their mouth. They might guess that since more energy goes into its production than into that of a pure vowel, it has more energy to convey. They might well decide that it is the most dynamic of the high-frequency vowels, that it strikes the ear more forcibly than the others, has more audibility. They might come upon Sylvia Plath using it almost brutally for its cutting power in

Christ! they are panes of ice,
A vice of knives . . .

or upon James Tate dramatizing its shrillness in

. . . sirens malign
the sky . . .

or upon Coleridge using its brightness and sparkle in

> . . . in silent icicles,
> Quietly shining to the quiet moon.

We could work through all the vowel sounds in this way—though we do not have the time or space to do so here. Suppose we pick out only a few for examination.

Even the dullest vowel sound has its individuality. The little *i* (of "bit") has been a favorite with writers trying to depict things that are brisk, quick, little, slim, glittery. Plato thought it especially apt for showing movement. Many would feel that "skinny-dipping" sounds more like what it means than "nude bathing" does. The effect is in the thin, glittery vowels. "Shivery hickory" sounds right for a baseball bat. Robert Fitzgerald uses it in his well-known baseball poem ("Cobb Would Have Caught It," Anthology, p. 471), which has other quick-moving *i* sequences as well:

> . . . the baseman
> Gathers a grounder in fat green grass,
> Picks it stinging and clipped as wit
> Into the leather: a swinging step
> Wings it deadeye down to first. . . .

It is easy to find other examples of expressive *i*'s:

> Slim pickerel glint
> in the water. . . .
>
> DONALD HALL

> [a bird] flits nimble-winged in thickets. . . .
>
> SYLVIA PLATH

The short *ŭ* sound has a definite but disreputable personality. It has been called the "shudder vowel"—the *uh* or *ugh* we make when feeling horror or disgust. Pronouncing it is like clearing the throat or ejecting something from the mouth. The slang word "upchuck" (for *vomit*) has the appropriate sound. (Slang is frequently more sound-conscious than standard English.) An investigation of hundreds of monosyllables has shown that the *ŭ* of "mud" has generally undesirable connotations. One scholar has listed many *uh* words that express dislike, disgust, or scorn: "blunder," "bungle," "clumsy," "humdrum," "slum," "slush," "muck," "muddle," "slut." We could all think of others: "dump," "crummy," "sludge," "chump," "bunk," "punk," "runt," "pus," "muss," "fuzz," "puffy," "repugnant."

When we sort of push a grunt up, with tongue, cheek, and lips left slack, what comes out is an "*uh*." We use it as the hesitation sound, when we don't quite know, uh, what to say. The archaic word "ugsome" meant *repulsive*.

Any observation we make about sound and sense will have *many* exceptions. These in no way disprove the expressiveness of sound; they merely show that in some words that particular element is inert or subordinate to other considerations. We can think of pleasant *uh* words: "young love," "summer," "cuddle," "comfort," "slumber," "lullaby," "yummy."

Man saying "Ugh!"

E. E. Cummings has combined the pleasant-unpleasant associations of *ŭ* and its slushy sound in his poem about the "mud-luscious," "puddle-wonderful" world of children.

Chansons Innocentes, I

in Just-
spring   when the world is mud-
luscious the little
lame balloonman

5   whistles   far   and wee
and eddieandbill come
running from marbles and
piracies and it's
spring

10   when the world is puddle-wonderful
the queer
old balloonman whistles
far   and   wee
and bettyandisbel come dancing

15 from hop-scotch and jump-rope and
its
spring
and
    the
20   goat-footed

balloonMan   whistles
far
and
wee
                                       [1923]

E. E. CUMMINGS (1894–1962)

The seven low-frequency vowel sounds, resonated from the back of the mouth, owe their deeper tone to the larger volume of air set in motion. To many, *aw* will seem the most powerful of the vowel sounds, a hollow reverberation from far back in the throat, rougher, grander, larger than the even lower-frequency *oh* and *oo* sounds. The Canadian poet Christian Bök often plays with such sounds in both prose and verse. Here is one example:

Vowels

loveless vessels

we vow
solo love

we see
5 love solve loss

else we see
love sow woe

selves we woo
we lose

10 losses we levee
we owe

we sell
loose vows

so we love
15 less well

so low
so level

wolves evolve
                                       [2001]

CHRISTIAN BÖK (*b.* 1966)

CONSONANTS AND ALLITERATION

Vowels are produced by an unimpeded flow of breath. How expressive they can be in themselves we can see in Margaret Benbow's use of them in "Crazy Arms: Earlene Remembers" (Anthology, p. 531), in which the familiar vowels, *a e i o u,* by themselves turn into the impassioned cries of overlusty lovers. Consonants are produced by interference that sets up an audible turbulence or cuts off the airflow completely. It might seem that the fewer consonants we use, the more musical our speech would be. But consonant power is one of the glories of English. Hawaiian, by contrast, has a high percentage of vowels and cannot pronounce two consonants together—"Merry Christmas" comes out "Mele Kalikimaka." It is the consonants that give shape and energy to our speech. Richard Wilbur has this in mind in his poem on Saint Teresa of Avila, who had to

> lock the O of ecstasy within
> The tempered consonants of discipline.

Robert Pinsky too has found them rugged. Of children learning a new language he writes:

> We took their language into our mouths and chewed
> (Some of the consonants drove us nearly crazy . . .)

Like vowels, consonants have their distinctive characters, which are felt more emphatically in repetition. Such repetition at the beginning of words or syllables is called **alliteration.**

The most vowel-like of the consonants are *w* and *y. W* is double *U*—an *oo* sound. When we read "Western Wind," we begin "*oo-estern oo-ind, hoo-en oo-ill . . .,*" with the *oo*'s gliding so rapidly into the following vowel that we are hardly aware of their "*oo*ness" at all. Vowel-like *w*'s alliterate smoothly:

> O sylvan Wye! thou wanderer through the woods. . . .
> WILLIAM WORDSWORTH

> It is a red bird that seeks out his choir
> Among the choirs of wind and wet and wing. . . .
> WALLACE STEVENS

It may be that the two *w*'s help account for the popularity of the western wind among poets.

In the opinion of many, the common American *r* is more vowel than consonant. Except for custom, "bird" could just as well be spelled "brd." But since *r* has a dark throaty quality—especially when combined with a guttural like *g*—we use it to represent the growl or *grrrr* of an animal or angry man.

Ben Jonson was not the first to call it the dog's letter. François Villon put his French *r* (then rolled) to amusing use when he wrote a ballade (p. 315) to a lady he was angry at; for twenty-eight lines his rhymes, all ending in *r*, snarl and snap at her.

The *r* and *l* are both called *liquids*. They seem to flow on or around the tongue instead of being clicked or popped or hissed forth. Probably *l* would win a popularity contest for the prettiest vowel sound. Lord Byron makes fun of the overuse of soft *l*'s:

> When amatory poets sing their loves
> In liquid lines mellifluously bland. . . .

He would probably not have objected to the less conspicuous *l*'s with which Yeats' old woman wonders:

> What lively lad most pleasured me
> Of all that with me lay?

Down-to-earth theorists have noticed that the sound seems to be formed low in the mouth, near the surface of the tongue and the inner surface of the lower teeth, which are more bathed in saliva than other parts of the mouth. Saliva-bathed or not, *l* does go well with liquidity:

> And on a sudden, lo! the level lake
> And the long glories of the winter moon.
>
> ALFRED, LORD TENNYSON

> I hear lake water lapping with low sounds by the shore. . . .
>
> WILLIAM BUTLER YEATS

The *m*, *n*, and *ng* sounds are known as *nasals;* the airflow is diverted into the nasal passages to vibrate there. We can feel the change in our mouth by sounding the three in sequence: "bam," "ban," "bang."

We use an *m* sound—sometimes conventionalized as "yum!"—for warm appreciation. Probably no other consonant is so expressive by itself. In reply to "Do you like my dress?" a perfectly intelligible answer would be "Mmm-mmmmm!" The sound is prolonged, not broken off; is internal (behind closed lips) and hence warm and cherished; is associated with the affectionate and sensitive lips, which bring the human child the first pleasure it knows—food and the warm presence of its mother. It has been noticed that *m* occurs in the word for *mother* in many languages, presumably because this is the sound happy babies make. Because it is about the only sound we can make with closed lips, we hum it when engaged in such pleasurable activities as eating something or kissing someone.

The sound of *n* is somewhat higher in tone, more a whine than a hum; *n* seems to pick up a bony hardness from being sounded near the roof of the mouth. We might think of mosquitoes as going "*Nnnnnn,*" but not "*Mmmmmm.*"

The *ng* sound has a metallic resonance that qualifies it for many sound words: "bang," "boing," "bong," "clang," "ding-dong," "gong," "jangle," "ping," "ring."

The seven sounds we have so far discussed have been called semi-vowels; they would probably be thought of as the most musical of the consonants.

The sounds known as *fricatives* are produced by audible friction over something that interferes with the airflow from the lungs. They include *h; f, c; th* ("thing"), *dh* ("that"); *s, z; sh, zh* ("pleasure"). The *h* is only a roughness in the breath, the rasp of air through the vocal cords as they get in place for the vowel that follows.

In *f* and *v*, turbulence is heard as the air passes between the lower lip and the upper teeth. Both sounds can be pleasantly soft, though they are not necessarily so.

> Duncan is in his grave;
> After life's fitful fever he sleeps well. . . .
>
> WILLIAM SHAKESPEARE

> Snow falling and night falling fast, oh, fast
> In a field I looked into going past. . . .
>
> ROBERT FROST

When the breath hisses between tongue and teeth, the result is an *s* sound. Jonson spoke of it with mixed feelings: "a most easy and gentle letter, and softly hisseth against the teeth . . . it is called the serpent's letter." Ancient critics looked down on it as "more suited to a brute beast than to a rational being." Tennyson tried to get rid of *s*'s; he called it "kicking the geese out of the boat." Robert Graves says his deathbed advice will be: "The art of poetry consists in knowing exactly how to manipulate the letter S." Graves finds Shelley particularly crude in his handling of *s* sounds, as in these lines from "Ode to the West Wind":

> Thou on whose stream, mid the steep sky's commotion,
> Loose clouds like earth's decaying leaves are shed. . . .

> . . . when to outstrip thy skiey speed
> Scarce seemed a vision. . . .

In processing sound tracks for recordings, technicians make use of a device called a *de-esser* to get rid of the hiss. Writers, however, sometimes make their lines hiss on purpose. One famous example is the conspiratorial whisper of Macbeth:

> . . . if the assassination
> Could trammel up the consequence and catch,
> With his surcease, success. . . .

Many of the sounds we have been considering can change their character in the company of other sounds. The *sn* and *st* might be taken as typical.

Of the words that start with *sn,* only a few are pleasant: "snow," "snuggle," "snug," and some others. Most are unpleasant: "snag," "snare," "snake," "sneak," "snide," "snitch," "snob," "snoop," "snub." One large group of *sn* words has to do with the nose: "sneeze," "sniff," "snuffle," "snivel," "snoot," "snore," "snort," "snout," "snuff," "sneer." Darwin thought that "sneer" and "snarl" were related, and that both were produced by muscular contractions like those of a snarling dog, with lip drawn back to expose the threatening canine teeth.

Many words beginning with *st* mean things that "stand steady" or are "stable" or "stabilized"; or that support something, like "staff," "stake," "stem," "stilt," "stirrup," "strut," "stud"; or that are somehow strong, like "stern," "stiff," "strict," "stubborn," "sturdy," "stag," "steed"; or that show energetic action, like "stalk," "stamp," "storm," "stun."

> How bowed the woods beneath their sturdy stroke!
>
> THOMAS GRAY

> And she who seemed eaten by cankering care
> In statuesque sturdiness stalks. . . .
>
> THOMAS HARDY

Robert Graves, often a skeptic in these matters, commends the muscular *str* words as being like what they mean: "strain," "strength," "strangle," "struggle," "strike," "strive," and many others.

Sh, sounded farther back in the mouth, is less sharp but has more body than *s.* We use it, as a kind of "white noise," to overpower other sounds when we say, "Shhhh!" or "Hush!"—whereas "Sssss!" is to get attention or express disapproval.

The final group of consonants—*p, b; t, d; k, g*—called *stops* (or *plosives* or *explosives*), are more drastic. They cut off the air for a moment, let pressure build up behind the barrier of lips or tongue, then release it with a tiny explosion. With *p* and *b,* the most forceful of the consonant sounds, it is the lips that block and explode the air. Repetitions of *p* call instant attention to themselves by sounding like the "Peter Piper picked . . ." tongue twister. The *b* can be almost as obstreperous. When Shakespeare wants to make fun of excessive alliteration (consonant repetition), *b* is the letter he chooses for his ridicule:

> Whereat, with blade, with bloody blameful blade,
> He bravely broached his boiling bloody breast. . . .

Woman saying "Sn—!"

Plath uses *p* and *b* for the texture of rocky soil:

What flinty pebbles the ploughblade upturns. . . .

Other contemporaries have used these stops for abrupt physical motion:

The lobbed ball plops, then dribbles in the cup. . . .

ROBERT LOWELL

Plop, plop. The lobster toppled in the pot. . . .

JOHN BERRYMAN

Robert Browning put the exuberance of *b* to good use in describing the buxom abundance of a woman's body:

Was a lady such a lady, cheeks so round and lips so red,—
On her neck the small face buoyant, like a bell-flower on its bed,
O'er the breast's superb abundance where a man might base his head?

A *p* (and a *b* almost as well) can express rejection by holding back the air and then violently expelling it, as in "Pooh!" or "Bunk!" Comic strips use the spit sound "*Ptui!*" for disgust. (The classical Greek word for "spit" was almost the same— *ptuo.*) Such words originate, it seems, in the natural mouth movements of the act of spitting. When we pronounce *p* or *sp*, the muscles of the mouth mimic disgust—which means that, if disgust happens to be what we feel, we can throw ourselves more completely, with more body English, into what we are saying.

When we pronounce *t* or *d*, the air is stopped by the tongue tip, which is clicked against the ridge behind the teeth. The effect is neater, trimmer than with the more explosive *p* and *b;* clocks and watches show a sense of fitness in saying "ticktock" instead of "bing bang."

When we pronounce *k* or *g* (a hard *g*, as in "guttural," not as in "gesture"), the airflow is stopped farther back toward the throat by the bunched-up back of the tongue. Particularly when reinforced with *r* or the deeper vowels, these give us the most throaty sound available—as in "choke," "crow," "gag," "gargle."

Crows crowd croaking overhead. . . .

JOHN CLARE

Not only sands and gravels
Were once more on their travels,
But gulping muddy gallons
Great boulders off their balance
Bumped heads together dully
And started down the gully. . . .

ROBERT FROST

Alliteration is as old as language. Babies alliterate before they can speak a sentence: "da-da," "bye-bye." We all know what alliteration can do for a slogan or catch phrase. Political sloganeers revel in it. Alliterative phrases have entwined themselves into the language we use every day. One could find hundreds of examples like "house and home," "rack and ruin," "spick and span," "rough and ready," "a dime a dozen," "in the fourth and final quarter." Driving into Tennessee from the north, one passes a restaurant–gas station called "Tank 'n' Tummy," among fireworks dealers known as "Goofy Goober," "Lonely Luke," "Crazy Chris," and—with assonance—"Loco Joe." Somebody believes in sound values!

Alliteration can, like any useful thing, be vulgarized by overuse. Politicians and advertisers are probably the most flagrant offenders. But poets have also been at fault. Edmund Spenser, coming on the line

For lofty love doth loathe a lowly eye . . .

objected to this "playing with the letter." Good alliteration, however, is much more than a literary gewgaw. It can create a bond of identity between words, hinting that if they have a sound in common, perhaps they have something more:

Love me little, love me long,
Is the burden of my song.

ANONYMOUS

Lay hands upon these traitors and their trash. . . .

WILLIAM SHAKESPEARE

It can also represent, by its muchness of sound, any kind of muchness:

Great England's glory and the world's wide wonder. . . .

EDMUND SPENSER

Before polygamy was made a sin;
When man, on many, multiplied his kind,
Ere one to one was cursedly confined. . . .

JOHN DRYDEN

> Fish, flesh and fowl, commend all summer long
> Whatever is begotten, born, and dies. . . .
>
> WILLIAM BUTLER YEATS

> *Flammantia moenia mundi,* Lucretius wrote,
> Alliterating like a Saxon—all those M's mean majesty. . . .
>
> ROBINSON JEFFERS

Or weary repetition:

> The plowman homeward plods his weary way. . . .
>
> THOMAS GRAY

It may link words together by sound only to contrast their meaning:

> The graceful with the gross combined,
> The stately with the stinking. . . .
>
> ARTHUR HUGH CLOUGH

It may be a mark of abundant energy:

> To leap large lengths of miles when thou art gone. . . .
>
> WILLIAM SHAKESPEARE

Clinging alliteration can stand for clinging things:

> Nor cast one longing lingering look behind . . .
>
> THOMAS GRAY

> . . . the stale
> steak grease stuck to her fuzzy leaves. . . .
>
> THEODORE ROETHKE

In writing about the bewildering death of a little girl (pp. 101–102), John Crowe Ransom uses stiff alliteration for two kinds of immobility:

> In one house we are sternly stopped
> To say we are vexed at her brown study,
> Lying so primly propped.

Assonance (p. 153) can serve the same purposes as alliteration, though often more subtly.

EXERCISES & DIVERSIONS

A. About such matters as we have been discussing in this chapter, the Roman critic Quintilian once wrote: "Studies of this kind harm only those who stick in them, not those who pass through them." Explore the implications of this remark, particularly in regard to our treatment of sound.

B. 1. *Whisper* the words "June," "Joan," "John," "Jan," "Jen," "Gin," "Jane," "Jean," in that order. Can you feel how the vowel sounds move progressively up the scale? Now *whisper* them in reverse order. Can you feel them move down the scale?

2. What do you notice about the use of sound in Pound's "Alba" (p. 12)?

3. Shakespeare's "Sonnet 129" (Anthology, p. 375) was referred to earlier as a poem of disgust or revulsion. The poem is full of expressively ugly sounds. Point them out.

C. In each of the following lines of poetry, some sound effect is conspicuous. Decide, with each, if it is too conspicuous. Or are the sounds appropriate and expressive?

1. Thou wretched, rash, intruding fool, farewell!

WILLIAM SHAKESPEARE

2. I'll lug the guts into the neighbor room. . . .

WILLIAM SHAKESPEARE

3. Oh for that night! When I in Him
Might live invisible and dim.

HENRY VAUGHAN

4. I saw, alas! some dread event impend. . . .

ALEXANDER POPE

5. The fair breeze blew, the white foam flew,
The furrow followed free;
We were the first that ever burst
Into that silent sea.

SAMUEL TAYLOR COLERIDGE

6. Over the water the old ghost strode. . . .

THOMAS LOVELL BEDDOES

7. Like some black mountain glooming huge aloof. . . .

JAMES RUSSELL LOWELL

8. A vacant sameness grays the sky. . . .

THOMAS HARDY

9. The mother looked him up and down,
And laughed—a scant laugh with a rattle.

EDWIN ARLINGTON ROBINSON

10. Some morning from the boulder-broken beach. . . .

ROBERT FROST

11. Tossed
    by the muscular sea,
    we are lost,
    and glad to be lost
    in troughs of rough
    love.

MAY SWENSON

12.   . . . Then back to housework,
    we hunched over our ironing or bunched
    in froggy squats beside our soapy buckets,
    backs buckling, all elbows and buttocks.

JULIA ALVAREZ

D. 1. Think of ten common alliterating phrases like "might and main," "friend or foe," "sink or swim."

   2. We discussed words beginning with *sn* and *st*. Do you find any pattern in words beginning with *bl* and *br*? (Recall words you know, like "blare" and "brisk," or skim a dictionary.)

ESSAYS

A. In 1655 Milton wrote one of his greatest sonnets to protest an atrocity of the time, the slaughter in the mountains of more than a thousand members of the Vaudois by the Duke of Savoy. How is sound used expressively? (Notice that sounds at the end of lines are especially prominent—even more so when they happen to rhyme.)

On the Late Massacre in Piedmont

Avenge, O Lord, thy slaughtered saints, whose bones
    Lie scattered on the Alpine mountains cold,
    Even them who kept thy truth so pure of old
    When all our fathers worshiped stocks and stones
Forget not: in thy book record their groans
    Who were thy sheep and in their ancient fold
    Slain by the bloody Piedmontese that rolled
    Mother with infant down the rocks. Their moans
The vales redoubled to the hills, and they
    To Heaven. Their martyred blood and ashes sow
    O'er all th' Italian fields where still doth sway
The triple tyrant: that from these may grow
    A hundredfold, who having learnt thy way
    Early may fly the Babylonian woe.

[1673]
JOHN MILTON (1608–1674)

Write an essay in which you paraphrase the poem; then offer a thesis about Milton's expressive use of sound. In the body of the paper, discuss this usage in detail, using plenty of quoted examples. For a conclusion, don't merely reiterate your opening; instead, ask yourself why contemporary readers might care about such expressive sound, and try to write a defense of this aspect of poetry. As an alternative, try this essay assignment with a poem by Richard Wilbur or another contemporary poet.

B.   Now look at a poem deliberately written in the English alliterative tradition based upon the Anglo-Saxon roots of the language—Richard Wilbur's "Junk" (p. 236). Read the whole section in which the poem appears, on "Strong-Stress Rhythms," so you get the idea. Write an essay on Wilbur's uses of sound patterns in the poem, paying particular attention to alliteration and assonance and how they contribute to meaning.

POEMS

A.   Write a short poem on an "up" theme using many high-frequency vowels. Do the same on a "down" theme, using many low-frequency vowels. (You might also enjoy reversing the process to see what happens: Write on an "up" theme using "down" vowels, and vice versa.)

B.   Write a curse poem or invective against someone or something you despise. Use as much alliteration as you can to produce the sound of bitterness.

8

WORKING WITH GOLD

Rhyme and Music

LANGUAGE AS MIMICRY

Poetry used to be magic. Far away and long ago, poetic formulas, perhaps in rhyme or some other form of sound-play, were thought to bring rain or put a curse on an enemy or charm someone into loving. In all such spells, as we recall from fairy tales, the sound was as important as the sense. Origen, the third-century theologian from Egypt who wrote in Greek, mentions certain charms found useful in ridding one's house of devils; he cautions, however, that they will not work in translation. Not because devils are poor linguists, but because the power of the formula lay in the sound itself. The aspects of language we will be concerned with in this chapter may seem more a matter of magic than of science.

Some 15,000 years ago, when the glaciers of the last Ice Age drove our ancestors into cave openings near the Mediterranean, reindeer, natives of the Arctic tundra, roamed freely over what are now the resort areas of the Riviera. Earth dwellers had been human for hundreds of thousands of years before the Ice Age, but they come before us with particular vividness when we see the cave drawings made in those centuries. These exist for us in a soundless world. "Many of the painted caves are really very terrifying places; the silence is intense, broken only occasionally by a distant boom when a drop of water falls from the roof into some silent pool below."* But the artist did not live in a world of silence. Ice and gravel crackled underfoot; thunder roared and re-echoed; animals made the same cries and growls that animals make today.

*M. Burkitt, *The Old Stone Age* (New York: New York University Press, 1956), p. 216.

Bison and wild boar from the caves of Altamira, Spain

The people who did these sensitive drawings must have used their built-in sound systems to imitate animals or the sounds of nature. Crouched by the fire near the cave mouth and listening to thunder reverberating among the rocks, they must have amused or frightened themselves by making thunder sounds deep in the throat—probably bursting into wild, delighted laughter at their success or lack of it. Likely enough, the earliest words for thunder would be thunder sounds—as "thunder" itself seems to be.

When our cave dwellers let rumbling sounds roll around in their throats, they were beginning to use what we call **onomatopoeia.** The Greek word means *name making,* as if something in nature made its own name by sounds associated with it—as a dog does for a child when it seems to say "bow-wow." Brigit Pegeen Kelly has observed that

> the baby
>
> . . . thought they were cows. "Moo,"
> He said. "Mooooo." He names things by their sounds.

These verbal mimicries are as deeply rooted in human nature as the desire to draw is; some people even think they account for the origin of language. We know that children find them expressive: Not only the "choo-choo" and "tick-tock" they learn from others, but also the words they originate themselves, like the "ffttt" one little boy made up as a name for soda water or the "pooh" one little girl called a match, from the sound made in blowing it out. Onomatopoetic words occur in languages all over the world. Comic strips rely heavily on them. One had this sound track for a fight sequence: "KAK . . . BTAK . . . FTAK . . . BUTOOP . . . YAG-GHHHH . . . KAPOWK . . . FOOM . . . SZAK . . . BOK. . . ." "Thump," "thud," and other such words may have originated as *btak* or *foom* sounds long ago. Dictionaries show many words described as "of imitative origin"—"giggle," "gargle," "whiz," "bang," "pop," "sizzle," among them. A dictionary of American slang gives a long list of more recent inventions, such as "beep," "bebop," "boing," "burp," "clunk," "ding-a-ling," "plunk," "putt-putt," "smooch," "yackety-yak."

If our cave dwellers of 15,000 years ago did rumble their thunder sounds, they were doing no more than others had done long before them and would be doing long afterward. John Keats made thunder sounds in his way:

> A shout from the whole multitude arose,
> That lingered in the air like dying rolls
> Of abrupt thunder, when Ionian shoals
> Of dolphins bob their noses through the brine. . . .

Six deep *oh* sounds, the dull *u*'s of "abrupt thunder," and perhaps the *ah*'s of "dolphins bob."

Another cave painting shows women or long-haired men climbing a high tree to rob a swarm of wild bees of its honey. The bee-robbers would surely have talked of their experience, and talking of it would surely have made sounds like *mmmmmmmmmmmm* or *uuuuzzzz* or *buzzzz* to describe the angry bees. If so, they would have been doing what Tennyson did thousands of years later in his lines

> The moan of doves in immemorial elms,
> And murmuring of innumerable bees. . . .

As Thomas Lux would have it in his "Onomatopoeia," this figure of speech, far from being the exclusive property of academics, is really best understood by people who live physically, *in their bodies:*

> The word sounds like the thing.
> The sound of the word next to
> the sound of another word
> sounds like the thing feels
> or you desire it to feel. You want
> this alive
>   . . . what you want
> to be known must be known
> cellularly, belly-wise,

or on the tongue: *cerulean blue,*
for example, or *punch drunk.*
Those who live elsewhere
than their bodies don't buy it, don't like it,
this in-the-body . . .

Some are skeptical of onomatopoeia because, although dogs, cats, falling objects, thunder, and the like make the same sounds all over the world, speakers of different languages have different words to represent the sounds. We may think we hear "bow-wow" when a dog barks. But a Spaniard hears "¡guau! ¡guau!"; a Frenchman, "ouâ-ouâ"; a German, "wauwau"; a Swede, "vov-vov." Hawaiian dogs bark in vowels: "aoaoao." Russian dogs go "ГАВ, ГАВ." Ancient Greek dogs said, "βαύ, βαύ." If human beings cannot even agree on how a dog barks, some may feel, what good is onomatopoeia?

But these dog sounds do have something in common. One can hardly imagine a language in which barking would be represented by "twee-twee" or "siss-zizz." The barks are unlike because different languages have different ways of putting letters together. A French dog would not say "bow-wow" because French uses a *w* only in foreign words. Why should French dogs bark like foreigners in their own country?

Such sound words are produced by the limited resources of our vocal equipment, which pretends, not very successfully, to be something else. And which has to produce a word that can be written down. But how can we spell the way a dog barks? Or spell the sound of the rain or the rush of wind in the trees or any of the nonhuman sounds? Our onomatopoetic words are like imitations done in another medium—as when Sergei Prokofiev, in *Peter and the Wolf,* uses different musical instruments to represent human and animal noises. The sound of a clarinet is not really like that of a cat, or an oboe like that of a duck, or three French horns like that of a wolf. "Sizzle" is a good onomatopoetic word, yet we could stand in the kitchen and say "sizzle" until we were blue in the face and no one would really think bacon was cooking.

Since onomatopoeia, like other sound effects we have considered, communicates little by itself, it can only reinforce or dramatize a meaning we already know is there. Its utility, therefore, is very limited. We seldom find a poem constructed wholly for sound effects, like the one below.

Player Piano

My stick fingers click with a snicker
And, chuckling, they knuckle the keys;
Light-footed, my steel feelers flicker
And pluck from these keys melodies.

5 My paper can caper; abandon
Is broadcast by dint of my din,
And no man or band has a hand in
The tones I turn on from within.

At times I'm a jumble of rumbles,
10   At others I'm light like the moon,
But never my numb plunker fumbles,
Misstrums me, or tries a new tune.   [1954]

JOHN UPDIKE (*b.* 1932)

In onomatopoeia, the sound of a word is supposed to imitate a sound associated with its meaning. Suppose though we are dealing not with sound at all, but with some other category of experience. Are words then in any way like what they mean? Children think they are. A five-year-old, in Colorado for the first time, was heard to exclaim, "Those are mountains, daddy? There ought to be a bigger word for *those!*" So do poets. Alexander Pope was thinking like the child when he wrote:

I'd call them mountains, but can't call them so,
For fear to wrong them with a name too low. . . .

In an ideal language, some believe, sound and sense would be in perfect accord. Humpty Dumpty was thinking along these lines when he asked Alice what her name meant:

"*Must* a name mean something?" Alice asked doubtfully.
"Of course it must," Humpty Dumpty said with a short laugh,
"my name means the shape I am—and a good handsome shape it is,
too. With a name like yours, you might be any shape, almost."

Humpty Dumpty's idea of the meaningfulness of names is at least as old as the second chapter of Genesis: "the Lord God formed every beast of the field, and every fowl of the air; and brought them unto Adam to see what he would call them: and whatsoever Adam called every living creature, that was the name thereof." Biblical scholars point out that for the Hebrews names were thought of as symbols, magic keys to the nature, character, or role of the bearer. John Hollander's poem "Adam's Task" is about Adam giving appropriate names to the strange beasts:

Thou, paw-paw-paw; thou, glurd; thou, spotted
    Glurd; thou, whitestap, lurching through
The high-grown brush; thou, pliant-footed,
    Implex; thou, awagabu. . . .

We would have to see these fabulous animals to judge the appropriateness of the names. A "glurd" might glow, like Blake's tiger (though in a sort of a blur), as it glides. An "awagabu" sounds waggy and sinuous—perhaps a bit like the "ongologo," a word some primitive tribes use for the centipede. An "ongologo" would have to have a lot of something.

Plato, in his *Cratylus,* may be the first philosopher to have discussed an ideal language based on sound. In the dialogue, Socrates (who is sometimes tongue-in-cheek) entertains the notion that words should not be merely arbitrary or conventional, but natural as well—something in their being should correspond to the nature of what they denote. The letter *r* belongs in words of motion because (in the trilled *r*) there is more activity in the mouth than for any other sound. *L* is for looseness or fluidity, since the tongue seems to slip in pronouncing it. But the heavier *g* in front of *l* will slow it down and make it sticky—as in our word "glue." If we could use such likenesses, says Socrates, "this would be the most perfect state of language."

Such a language might be ideal, and it would certainly be fun to use. But Plato knew that a language like that had never existed and never would, since only certain categories of objects, qualities, or experiences can be matched up with certain sounds. Some sounds may be *harder, faster, larger, stickier* than other sounds, but how can they be more *possible,* more *true,* or more *virtuous?*

In everyday life, the sound of a word is not of much immediate importance. No one would refuse to cry "Fire!" or "Help!" out of a feeling that the word had an inappropriate combination of vowels and consonants.

But a good writer, the critic Herbert Read believes, will pick and choose among the existing words for those that "by some subtle combination of vowel and consonant suggest by a seeming appropriateness the quality or kind of object named." Beyond simple onomatopoeia, he finds two subtly appropriate classes of words: those in which movement of lips, tongue, and cheek, together with suggestive sound, simulate the action described—as in "blare," "flare," "brittle," "whistle," "creep," "scrabble," "puddle," "shiver," "fiddle," "sling," "globe"—and those in which sounds are not imitative, but suggestive musical equivalents—as in "swoon," "mood," "sheen," "horror," "smudge," "jelly."

We can figure out the "magic" of most of these. "Blare" and "flare" have a big, loose lip movement. "Brittle" breaks in two in the middle. "Sling" hisses—*sssss*—and then lets go suddenly—*llll-ING!* "Mood" is a deep-inside sound. "Horror" catches in the throat. Even some very ordinary words strike us as having a physical rightness about them. The word "match" moved a classical scholar to exclaim, "How admirably it catches the scrape of sulphurated stick on emery!" The Danish philologist Otto Jespersen likes the word "roll," as in *rolling along.* It is a word we can keep rolling around in our mouth; *r, o,* and *l* can all be sounded as long as we want or we have breath for. Whereas the Russian word for "roll" (*katat'* or *katit'*) sounds like something bumping along on square wheels. "Level" is a word like its meaning, sounding almost the same forward or backward and ending as levelly as it began. "Uneven," however, has that little bump of an accent sticking up in the middle. One well-known maker of jams and jellies has shown that it knows people are sensitive to sound suggestion by turning its own unattractive name to account. "With a name like Smucker's," say the ads, "it has to be good."

What we are dealing with is a form of synesthesia (pp. 33–35) that tries to provide an equivalent in sound for appearance, smell, taste, touch, and movement. Most of us know that there are analogies between the senses, and that the imagination likes to play with them. Very hot curry, for example, has a taste that suggests a bright color—yellow or red—rather than a pastel gray or lavender. Anyone sensuously alive feels these correspondences. Saint Augustine, among other things a professor of rhetoric, was well aware of synesthesia as a source of vocal appropriateness. After speaking of sound-words used to denote actual sounds, he says, "But since there are things which have no sound, for these the analogy of touch comes into play: if they touch the sense smoothly or roughly, smoothness or roughness of touch is heard in the letters."

The reason poets like to unite sound and sense should be clear from all we have been saying about poetry, which speaks not merely for the brain but for the whole human being, body and mind. When sound goes along with sense, the meaning of a poem becomes *physicalized*. It resists the authoritarianism of the intellect, which claims the right to force a meaning on any combination of sounds, regardless of their nature. Appropriate sound invites the body to participate in the being of a poem, just as the poet's body participated in its creation.

The following poem opens up in its uses of sound the very acts of writing and reading, and even the problems of a poetic career:

Making Poetry

"You have to inhabit poetry
if you want to make it."

And what's "to inhabit"?

To be in the habit of, to wear
5   words, sitting in the plainest light,
in the silk of morning, in the shoe of night;
a feeling bare and frondish in surprising air;
familiar . . . rare.

And what's "to make"?

10   To be and to become words' passing
weather; to serve a girl on terrible
terms, embark on voyages over voices,
evade the ego-hill, the misery-well,
the siren hiss of *publish, success, publish,*
15   *success, success, success.*

And why inhabit, make, inherit poetry?

Oh, it's the shared comedy of the worst
blessed; the sound leading the hand;
a wordlife running from mind to mind

20　through the washed rooms of the simple senses;
one of those haunted, undefendable, unpoetic
crosses we have to find.　　　　　　　　　　　　　　　[1985]
ANNE STEVENSON (*b.* 1933)

A REASON FOR RHYME?

When we say "neither rhyme nor reason," we imply that rhyme lies outside the domain of reason. In a way it does, though we can see some of the reasons for its appeal. If in the pages that follow we seem to be devoting inordinate attention to it, we are doing so because it can stand for those other "magical" devices of sound that poets use to keep their language from being too purely rational.

Poetry, of course, does not *have* to rhyme. Many of the poems we have read are without rhyme and live quite happily that way. All we are doing in this section is investigating what rhyme has to contribute when it is present. With it we are back once more in the world of magic and unreason.

When Byron writes

> There's not a sea the passenger e'er pukes in
> Turns up more dangerous breakers than the Euxine

his lines are vitalized by the rhyme. The effect is gone if we read:

> There's not a sea the passenger e'er pukes in
> Turns up more dangerous breakers than the Black Sea.

The ingenuity and impudence of linking by sound the folksy "pukes in" with the classical name for the Black Sea are what give these lines their electric tingle. Good rhyme likes to spark a current of thought or emotion between two poles.

Expressions like "fair and square," "rough and tough," "moaning and groaning," and such reduplicating ones as "shilly-shally," "hocus-pocus," "walkie-talkie," and "fender bender," show how rhyme has worked itself into the fabric of the language. As fast as slang changes, it still retains its fondness for rhyme. One decade says, "See you later, alligator"; another says "super-duper" or "slick chick." Furry Lewis, the blues composer, says:

> The time when you get a blues . . . you have to go all over it again until you rhyme it. It got to be rhymed up if you call yourself being with the blues. If it ain't rhymed up it don't sound good to me or nobody else.

This poem is modeled on a blues song. Notice its rhymes as well as its uses of repetition:

A Poem for Myself

(Or Blues for a Mississippi Black Boy)

I was born in Mississippi;
I walked barefooted thru the mud.
Born black in Mississippi,
Walked barefooted thru the mud.
5   But, when I reached the age of twelve
I left that place for good.
Said my daddy chopped cotton
And he drank his liquor straight.
When I left that Sunday morning
10   He was leaning on the barnyard gate.
Left her standing in the yard
With the sun shining in her eyes.
And I headed North
As straight as the Wild Goose Flies,
15   I been to Detroit & Chicago
Been to New York city too.
I been to Detroit and Chicago
Been to New York city too.
Said I done strolled all those funky avenues
20   I'm still the same old black boy with the same old blues.
Going back to Mississippi
This time to stay for good
Going back to Mississippi
This time to stay for good—
25   Gonna be free in Mississippi
Or dead in the Mississippi mud.

[1973]

ETHERIDGE KNIGHT (1931–1991)

Michael McFee's "Time Enough" (p. 95) is also a sort of blues number.

Probably the commonest objection to rhyme is that it prevents poets from saying what they want to say—which (defenders of rhyme would retort) is like hurdlers complaining that the hurdles get in their way. In any field, power shows itself in the ease with which obstacles are overcome.

Another objection is that rhyme is associated with so much bad poetry that it is no longer fit to associate with good poetry. Bad rhyming can be boring, can give us "the sure returns of still expected rhyme"—like the "June"/"moon" and the "breeze"/"trees" that Pope objected to:

Where'er you find the cooling western breeze,
In the next line it whispers through the trees. . . .

There are other expected rhymes: "breath" can bring up only "death"; "mountains" are fond of "fountains"; "anguish" means that someone is bound to "languish"; and "kiss" leads to "bliss" so inevitably that Byron could make fun of the pair:

> "Kiss" rhymes to "bliss" in fact as well as verse—
> I wish it never led to something worse. . . .

Rhyme is made up of a sameness plus a difference, as in *poet / know it / show it*. The sameness, the fixed element, is an accented vowel sound (1). Sounds coming *after* the accented vowel sound must be the same (2). The difference, the variable, is what comes *before* the accented vowel sound (3).

(1)	(2)	(3)
p | o | et	po | et |	p | o et
kn | ow | it	know | it |	kn | ow it
sh | ow | it	show | it |	sh | ow it

Rhyme, by no means peculiar to English, seems to be an almost universal phenomenon. Chances are it goes back, long before written records, to the very beginnings of verse. We do not have to be experts in African languages to recognize it in a song of the Gabon Pygmies:

> Msore i nia n'fare,
> Msore i nia n'sare.

Nor do we have to know Swahili to recognize the rhyme in four consecutive lines ending with *jehazi, ngazi, wazi, mjakazi*. Rhyme occurs in Chinese verse from the earliest times; one authority deplores that most translations give us no inkling of this. Long before the time of the medieval monks in England, rhyme flourished in Ireland and Wales. Irish missionaries may have brought it to the continent. Or perhaps it came from Arabia, whose culture may have given the Provençal poets of the twelfth century their interest in elaborate rhyming, of which Ezra Pound gives some idea in his adaptation of a little Provençal poem.

Alba

When the nightingale to his mate
Sings day-long and night late
My love and I keep state
In bower,
5   In flower,
'Till the watchman on the tower

Cry:
>   "Up! Thou rascal, Rise,
>   I see the white
> 10   Light
>   And the night
>   Flies."

[1917–1920]
EZRA POUND (1885–1972)

Rhyme was so important in old Persian poetry that the quatrains of Omar Khayyám (Anthology, p. 408) were arranged according to rhyming sounds. It is so built into the syntax of Greek and Latin (in which the endings of nouns, adjectives, and verbs make up a constant chiming) that there was no need to seek additional rhyme for the end of lines. This is true also of Japanese, in which all words end with a vowel or an *n,* so that it is almost impossible to find a haiku without rhyming words.

Many reasons have been given for the appeal of rhyme. One of the oldest is that we like to see any stunt skillfully performed: We like to watch acrobats and tightrope walkers and jugglers. Good rhyming is a feat of skill with words.

Another reason is based on a psychological tendency that we feel even more clearly in music. It has been called "the law of return," which holds that it is better to return to any starting point—to get back to home base—than not to return—a law that operates both in primitive melodies of two or three notes and in complex orchestral music. Prominent sounds arouse in us the expectation of hearing them again. Ogden Nash plays on this sense of expectation in a special way; we know that when one of his rhymes is about to come up it may be an outrageous one, and we wait for it with the kind of pleasure-pain with which we see an upheld tray of glassware tipping and about to crash to the floor. (See "Very Like a Whale," Anthology, p. 463.)

History, we say, repeats itself, and it does so with effects like those of rhyme. Characters today may remind us of Napoleon or Julius Caesar, as if individuals were rhyming with each other. Periods in history are like other periods. Pound uses such correspondences in his *Cantos,* and even uses the word "rhyme" to refer to them.

What is called "rhyming of ideas" is found also in such ceremonial songs as those of the Apache Indians, whose "Corn Ceremony" begins:

> At the east where the black water lies stands the large corn, with staying roots, its large stalk, its red silk, its long leaves, its tassel dark and spreading, on which there is the dew.
> At the sunset where the yellow water lies stands the large pumpkin with its tendrils, its long stem, its wide leaves, its yellow top on which there is pollen.

Then, too, our experience of physical reality accustoms us to corresponding pairs—left and right, up and down, far and near, and many others.

The supreme experience of bilateral symmetry is the human body, with its almost perfect correspondence of right and left. When we walk, our two sides swing forward not only in rhythm but in something very like rhyme—ankle rhymes with ankle, knee with knee, hip with hip, wrist with wrist, shoulder with shoulder. The best defense of the naturalness of rhyme is the sight of any healthy man or woman walking down the street—*left, right, left, right*—rhyme in motion.

Another theory of the nature of rhyme is even more physical. According to Goethe, words rhyming are words making love, words snuggling, in as close a union as possible, almost fusing but—*vive la différence*—still a little different, just as the two sexes are different:

> One sound, it seems, fits snugly with another.
> And when a word is nestled in our ear,
> Another comes beside it with caresses. . . .

English poets, long before Goethe's time, have spoken of "the kiss of rhyme," and Derek Walcott, in his contemporary Homeric narrative poem *Omeros*, has a ghostly voice insist that

> . . . Rhyme . . . is the language's
> desire to enclose the loved world in its arms. . . .

The Mexican poet Octavio Paz has eroticized rhyme still further by calling it "a copulation of sounds."

Some people imagine that rhyme interferes with the rational processes of thought by obliging us to distort what we originally had in mind. But are rational processes so important? In many of us, even in poets, they can be dull and predictable. An interruption, a few detours and unexpected turns, might make a trip with them less routine. The necessity of finding a rhyme may jolt the mind out of its ruts, force it to turn wildly across the fields in some more exhilarating direction. Force it out of the world of reason into the world of mystery, magic, and imagination, in which relationships between sounds may be as exciting as a Great Idea. In his celebrated novel, Marcel Proust refers to "good poets whom the tyranny of rhyme forces into the discovery of their finest lines." It is surprising that the intellectual Hegel defended rhyme by saying that without such devices words become "mentalized"—we forget they have a body and use them only as tools to communicate.

When two words rhyme, their meanings also interact: Each can take on something of the meaning of the other. This is what the poet Jim Hall had in mind when he wrote:

> Any kid knows that rhyming flowers
> with towers
> makes a rose all of a sudden a mile high. . . . .

A Defense of Rhyme

Rhyme can also intensify a word by amplifying its sound. When John Clare, in "The Parish," wanted to show us a pretentious ignoramus, he might have written:

> Young Farmer Bigg, of this same flimsy sort,
> Wise among fools, and with the wise an ass. . . .

"Ass," the key word, is not especially resonant here. But Clare wrote:

> Young Farmer Bigg, of this same flimsy class,
> Wise among fools, and with the wise an ass. . . . .

And then we really hear the word.

Yet another reason for rhyme is in its structural possibilities. It can even serve as a scaffolding for poetry not yet built. Some of Shelley's manuscripts show that he left certain lines blank except for the rhyme, which furnished not only necessary sounds but key ideas. We can see how rhyme works as a kind of structural blueprint, below, in a complicated stanza like that of John Donne's "The Canonization," in which the speaker is telling others to do whatever they want as long as they do not interfere with his love:

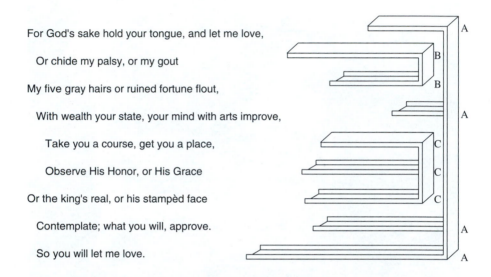

For God's sake hold your tongue, and let me love,

 Or chide my palsy, or my gout

My five gray hairs or ruined fortune flout,

 With wealth your state, your mind with arts improve,

  Take you a course, get you a place,

  Observe His Honor, or His Grace

Or the king's real, or his stampèd face

 Contemplate; what you will, approve.

So you will let me love.

We can also set up a rhyme scheme to see how successfully we can resist it—by treating it as an opponent rather than as a teammate. This wrestling match with rhyme, which is now on top, now underneath, is seen in Browning's poem "My Last Duchess" (see Anthology, p. 412). The poem is in rhyming couplets, yet many of the rhymes are hurried over as if not there because the movement of the sentence will not allow us to pause for them.

In "Musée des Beaux Arts" (see color insert section), W. H. Auden makes rhyme almost inconspicuous by having, in lines of uneven length, rhyming words the sense will not let us linger on. Some of these rhymes are far apart. The story itself is from the eighth book of Ovid's *Metamorphoses:* To escape from Crete, the artificer Daedalus has made wings of feathers held together by wax for himself and his son Icarus. The son, though warned, in his exuberance flies too high; when the heat of the sun melts the wax, Icarus plunges headlong into the sea, only his legs visible in the painting, but unnoticed by those on land.

But perhaps the last reason for the use of rhyme is the best of all: People find it fun. Poetry has been seen as the supreme example of the play spirit in human beings. "The hitting of the mark by rhyme" is part of the game—as in the many target games we like to play. Children love all such word play; the use of rhyme has been seen as a subconscious recollection of the fun of childhood. "I rhyme for fun," declared Robert Burns. Gary Snyder says, "If you start teaching poetry on the grade school level, use rhyme, they love it. . . . Children love word play, music of language." There have always been reformers, of course, who disapprove of fun, especially when they think they have something portentous to say.

The rhyme we have been talking about and giving examples of is called **end rhyme** (see note on **rhyme scheme,** p. 194). Rhymes within the line, **internal rhymes,** are also common:

> Once upon a midnight dreary, while I pondered, weak and weary. . . .

Marianne Moore uses internal rhyme as a structural principle in her "A Carriage from Sweden" (Anthology, p. 450). We notice easily enough the end rhymes in lines 2 and 3 of each stanza. But one could probably read the poem for years and not notice that in the first line of every stanza the third syllable rhymes with the last one—"there"/"air," "may"/"away," "resined"/"wind," and so on—or that in the last line of every stanza the first syllable rhymes with the eighth (in one stanza, the ninth)—"*some*-thing"/"*home*," "*in*tegrity"/"*vein*," "*A*dolphus"/"de*cay*," for example.

OFF-RHYME OR SLANT RHYME

What we call rhyme in Marianne Moore's poem does not always fit the definition given some pages back. "*Some*thing" and "*home*," "*in*tegrity" and "*vein*" do not have the same vowel sound; "some" calls for "hum," not "home"; "in" calls for "vin," not "vein." This kind of "imperfect rhyme"— also called "**off-rhyme,**" "**slant rhyme,**" "oblique rhyme," "near rhyme," "half rhyme"—has been deliberately employed by some earlier poets and many modern ones.

Emily Dickinson uses it so often that it becomes characteristic. Her earliest work shows she could rhyme perfectly when she wanted to, but for some reason she became fond of the little dissonance of off-rhyme. Instead of rhymes like "June"/"moon" she prefers "June"/"men," "June"/"mean," or "June"/"moan." She often has rhymes like "port"/"chart," "affair"/"more," or "wheel"/"mill." She seems to feel that a vowel can rhyme with any other vowel: "know"/"withdrew," "dough"/"sky," "sky"/"tree."

No poet has called attention to the expressive value of off-rhyme more movingly than Wilfred Owen in his poems of World War I. Owen wrote in both full rhyme, as in the first poem below, and off-rhyme, as in the second. The use of off-rhyme in itself does not guarantee a better or more original or even more "modern" poem, but it does offer a different kind of music.

Anthem for Doomed Youth

What passing-bells for these who die as cattle?
    Only the monstrous anger of the guns.
    Only the stuttering rifles' rapid rattle
Can patter out their hasty orisons.
No mockeries now for them; no prayers nor bells,
    Nor any voice of mourning save the choirs,—
The shrill, demented choirs of wailing shells;
    And bugles calling for them from sad shires.

What candles may be held to speed them all?
    Not in the hands of boys, but in their eyes
Shall shine the holy glimmers of good-byes.
    The pallor of girls' brows shall be their pall;
Their flowers the tenderness of patient minds,
And each slow dusk a drawing-down of blinds.

Arms and the Boy

Let the boy try along this bayonet-blade
How cold steel is, and keen with hunger of blood;
Blue with all malice, like a madman's flash;
And thinly drawn with famishing for flesh.

Lend him to stroke these blind, blunt bullet-leads
Which long to nuzzle in the hearts of lads,
Or give him cartridges of fine zinc teeth,
Sharp with the sharpness of grief and death.

For his teeth seem for laughing round an apple.
There lurk no claws behind his fingers supple;
And God will grow no talons at his heels,
Nor antlers through the thickness of his curls.

                              [1920]
                      WILFRED OWEN (1893–1918)

The rhymes in "Arms and the Boy" are all off-rhyme. But there is something special about the first three pairs: The vowel sounds change while the consonants before and after remain the same, so that we have a framing of "bl-d," "fl-sh," and "l-ds" with different vowel sounds in the middle. This pattern is known as **consonance.** Most of the rhyming pairs drop to a deeper vowel sound in the second word—an effect like that of a flatted "blue note" in music. Off-rhymes are like discords; they suggest that something is irregular and disturbed, has somehow failed or fallen short. They have been popular with many poets of our time, who feel that a discordant medium is appropriate for a discordant age. Such a poet was Thomas McGrath (1916–1990) who uses off-rhymes for much of the following poem:

Remembering the Children of Auschwitz

We know the story. The children
Are lost in the deep forest—
Though it is the same forest
In which we all are born.

5 But somehow it has changed:
A new kind of darkness,
Or something they never noticed,
Has colored the pines and the larches.

And now appears the Bird,
10 (Bird of a strange dreaming)
To lead them, as tales foretold,
Over the little streams

Into the garden of order
Where trees no longer menaced,
15 And a little house was protected
Inside its candy fences.

And all seemed perfectly proper:
The little house was covered
with barbwire and marzipan;
20 And the Witch was there; and the Oven.

Perhaps they never noticed—
After all that disorder
Of being lost—that they'd come
To the Place named in the stories.

25 Perhaps there was even peace—
A little—after disorder,
Before they awoke into
A dream of deeper horror.

And now the Bird will never
30 Take them across the river
(Though they knew how to walk on water).
They become part of the weather.

They have become the Ascensions.
When we lift up our eyes,
35 In any light, we see them:
Darkening all our skies.

[1983]

[33]/**Ascensions:** *alludes to the Ascension of Christ*

How ironic, we might wonder, is that final full rhyme of "eyes" and skies"?

THE MUSIC OF POETRY

What we call the "music" of poetry is only by analogy like the music we hear from the singing voice or from musical instruments. A number of poets have been unwilling to have their poems turned into songs; as one French poet said when a composer requested such permission, "I thought I had already set it to music." Vachel Lindsay went so far as to say, "Sheet music, piano music, orchestras and the like should not be in the same room with verses, as a general rule." What the poets mean, of course, is that poetry makes its own kind of music, which is not that of singers or instrumentalists.

When we say that language is euphonious, we mean that it is pleasant to the ear. But we probably also mean that we pronounce it so easily that there is a pleasure in the physical movements, as there is in any muscular activity we perform with ease. (A French poet-critic has written a book of more than 500 pages on the "muscular pleasure" of poetry.) Eurhythmics is the art of moving our body in harmony with music or the spoken word; euphony might be thought of as oral eurhythmics. Its opposite is cacophony, the harsh or inharmonious use of language—harsh to listen to because harsh to pronounce. We cannot, as we say, "get our tongue around it."

But as Gilbert White says in *The Natural History and Antiquities of Selborne:*

> Sounds do not always give us pleasure according to their sweetness and melody; nor do harsh sounds always displease. We are more apt to be captivated or disgusted with the associations which they promote than with the notes themselves. Thus the shrilling of the field-cricket, though sharp and stridulous, yet marvellously delights some hearers, filling their minds with a train of summer ideas of everything that is rural, verdurous, and joyous.

Harsh lines in poetry may also please us because their very harshness may help dramatize the meaning.

Poets deliberately write rough lines to give a sense of physical effort, as Pope did:

> When Ajax strives some rock's vast weight to throw,
> The line too labors, and the words move slow. . . .

Our tongue muscles have as much trouble with the *xstr, s/s, ksv,* and *t/t* of the first line as Ajax had with his rock.

In his poem "The Haystack in the Floods," William Morris has lines that invite the participation of our facial muscles:

> . . . A wicked smile
> Wrinkled her face, her lips grew thin,

> A long way out she thrust her chin:
> "You know that I should strangle you
> While you were sleeping, or bite through
> Your throat, by God's help. . . ."

Such effects are more muscular than musical.

Even though we have found that it is possible to arrange vowels in a kind of scale, the relationships between them are not like those between musical notes. We can sing *do mi so do* and feel a pleasurable harmony in the intervals. There is no such pleasure in saying $\overline{oo}$ *ah ă ee*. The tones do get higher but the intervals are not related, although we sometimes get a general sense of vowels ascending, as in Shakespeare's lines

> Like to the lark at break of day arising
> From sullen earth, sings hymns at heaven's gate. . . .

Or we may feel the vowels dropping, as in Walt Whitman's evocation

> When lilacs last in the dooryard bloom'd. . . .

or Emily Dickinson's description

> The thunder gossiped low. . . .

The simplest way to make a sound ring out is to repeat it immediately, as Shakespeare does in phrases like "brave day" or "time's scythe." Or to repeat it after an unstressed syllable, as he does in "ragged hand" or "mortal war." Dickinson liked this simple figure—"stumbling buzz," "satin cash." So did Sylvia Plath—"gristly-bristled," "cuddly mother." Such linked repetitions of sound turn up everywhere in poetry.

Often we find two sounds interlocked:

> Under the glassy, cool, translucent wave. . . .

> JOHN MILTON

Or we find one pair of sounds bracketing another:

> And chaste Diana haunts the forest shade. . . .

> ALEXANDER POPE

> In which sad light a carvèd dolphin swam. . . .

> T. S. ELIOT

These three simple arrangements—linked, interlocked, bracketed—can be used to build up more involved combinations. Consonants can be patterned in the same way. Such figures are generally not systematic. What poets do is repeat sounds when they feel that the repetition would be pleasant or meaningful.

Most poets, we find, care very much about such sound effects and work hard at them. A friend of Keats tells us that one of the poet's "favorite topics . . . was the principle of melody in verse . . . particularly in the management of open and close vowels ["height"/"hit," "load"/"lid," and the like]." Keats's theory, "worked out by himself . . . was, that the vowels should be so managed as not to clash one with another so as to mar the melody,—and yet that they should be interchanged, like differing notes of music to prevent monotony."

Keats also believed that certain sounds are more or less appropriate for certain feelings, and can be all the more expressive if skillfully repeated. The first stanza of the "Ode to a Nightingale" (see Anthology, p. 405) is a good example.

In the first line, dark, dull vowel sounds ("heart," "drowsy," "numbness") are contrasted with the shriller ones ("aches," "pains"). All the sounds of line 1 are repeated in the stanza, but none so much as the dull *u* of "numbness," which recurs in "drunk," "some," "dull," "one," "sunk." The next sequence to notice is the short *e* followed by a nasal—"sense," "hemlock," "emptied," "envy." The repetition of this unexciting little vowel is monotonous, like the numbness that Keats, for all his "aches" and "pains," says he is feeling. These *en*'s and *em*'s are vitalized by the brighter vowel in the "beechen green" of line 9. Rather gloomy vowels set the tone for the first few lines of the stanza, but the song of the nightingale (which Keats thinks of as a Dryad, or tree goddess) brings in a run of excited vowels such as we have not heard before: "light-wingèd Dryad of the trees." The four prominent syllables even make up a little tune or figure at the top of the vowel scale. The keen *ee* sound becomes even clearer in "beechen green." The last line is tonally interesting: The prominent syllables slide down the scale to the throaty *oh*, only to rise to the very top in a final *ee* that echoes the other happy *ee* sounds.

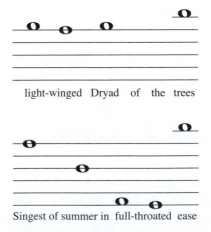

light-winged Dryad of the trees

Singest of summer in full-throated ease

An early poem of Yeats—which owed something to his reading of Thoreau's *Walden*—"set the professors agog," said Yeats, "by the arrangements of the vowel sounds."

The Lake Isle of Innisfree

I will arise and go now, and go to Innisfree,
And a small cabin build there, of clay and wattles made:
Nine bean-rows will I have there, a hive for the honeybee,
And live alone in the bee-loud glade.

5   And I shall have some peace there, for peace comes dropping slow,
Dropping from the veils of the morning to where the cricket sings;
There midnight's all a glimmer, and noon a purple glow,
And evening full of the linnet's wings.

I will arise and go now, for always night and day
10   I hear lake water lapping with low sounds by the shore;
While I stand on the roadway, or on the pavements grey,
I hear it in the deep heart's core.   [1893]
WILLIAM BUTLER YEATS (1865–1939)

²/**wattles:** *interwoven sticks or branches*

All we find is what has been standard practice among sound-conscious poets—a pleasant variety of vowels that lets us range freely over the scale (as in the *ī, i, oh, ow,* and *ee* of the first line); certain clearly felt repetitions amid the variety (as in "clay"/"made," "nine"/"hive"); uses of vowel and consonant sounds that are right for their meaning (as the three little *i*'s of "cricket sings" and "linnet's wings"); and perhaps an occasional progression up or down the scale, as in the descending *ee ŭ ah oh* of "peace comes dropping slow" and the similar *ee ah aw* of "deep heart's core."

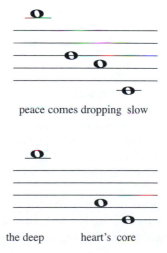

peace comes dropping slow

the deep   heart's core

In recordings made later, Yeats himself dwelt on the vowel sounds almost the way a singer would; he explained the strangeness of his reading by saying that he cared very much about the sound of his lines.

There are many pretty effects in this short poem. One we might overlook is in

I hear lake water lapping with low sounds by the shore . . .

Thirteen vowel sounds, eleven of them different. The sound of the water is always changing and yet is always the same too, as the continued *l*'s are hinting.

Robert Penn Warren has spoken about the enjoyment we feel in participating physically in the experience of a poem: "a pleasure, just the way the muscles get into play. In your whole vocal apparatus. . . . It's just a wonderful workout, a sense of kinetic involvement in the lines. This release, this muscular play . . . just the physical pleasure of a well-turned line is something."

The poem that aroused Warren's gymnastic sensibilities is Milton's "Lycidas" (see Anthology, p. 383). Edward King, a Cambridge acquaintance of Milton, was drowned while on his way to visit his family in Ireland. King had written some poetry and was planning to become a clergyman. Milton thought about himself: He too was a young student with plans and ambitions. Were they indeed worth the effort and sacrifice if life could be ended by a sudden mindless accident? He thought about the church of his time, which seemed in need of such young men as the one it had just lost. Milton dreamed of heaping his friend's body with all the flowers of the countryside, which themselves would grieve for the dead young man—but he was too tough and level-headed to go along with such poetic fancies, which he knew were a "false surmise" (line 153). The body itself had not been recovered. It was tossing somewhere in the hundreds of miles of wild ocean between the Hebrides and the far-off coast of Spain.

Milton has put some readers off by writing his poem in the form of a pastoral elegy: He imagines that he and his friends are song-loving shepherds in an idyllic culture. The use of such imagery was an old form of make-believe— it had its conventional rules just as games have theirs. What, after all, is more artificial in the world of nature than a tennis court or a golf course? And yet they offer us better scope for certain activities than natural terrain would. And so, for some, do such conventions as those of the pastoral. Milton chose to play the game that way, with an ancient form of "let's pretend" that no doubt represents the desire for a simple life in significant rapport with the environment. He knew poets had been playing that game for at least 2,000 years. He takes the name "Lycidas" from earlier works of that type; he refers to places in Sicily and Italy because they are associated with Theocritus and Vergil, who wrote the best pastoral poetry of antiquity. But he also deliberately breaks with their kind of poetry by making his indignant attack on the corruption of the church, by referring to his own literary status and ambitions, and by admitting not only Apollo and Jove into his poetic world but also—and far more significantly—the founder of Christianity, who triumphantly walked the waves that had engulfed a young Christian. (An **elegy** is a lament for the dead, or a meditation on the thoughts that death arouses.)

The power of Milton's music makes itself felt in the first line with the three resonant *or* sounds, echoing within a few lines in "forced" and "before," and recurring in key passages later, most impressively in the six lines beginning with line 58: "Orpheus," "bore," "roar," "gory," "shore." Together, *aw* and *r* make up what must be the strongest combination of vowel and consonant in English. The virile *r*, which we are told Milton pronounced "very hard," seems to be a favorite sound of his—there are eighteen in the first five lines of "Lycidas." This is typical of the music of the poem, which is strong and resonant more often than conventionally melodious. Robert Lowell calls the brusque third line "a very great line in its context . . . largely through sound." The sound itself is "harsh and crude," a roughness in the mouth that is pleasantly chunky to munch on. Many of the most memorable lines are equally rough-textured—really a "workout."

Though the "music" of poetry is very different from the music of instruments or the singing voice, we all know works in which poetry and song come companionably together—each incomplete without the company of the other. It should be remembered that though this book is mostly about poetry as speech, the title poem, "Western Wind," is itself a song lyric. One of the best-known early songs in English, dating perhaps to the thirteenth century, is this:

Sumer Is Icumen In

Sumer is icumen in.
Lhude sing cuccu.
Groweth sed and bloweth med
and springeth the wde nu.
5   Sing cuccu.

Awe bleteth after lomb.
Lhouth after calve cu.
Bulluc sterteth, bucke verteth.
Murie sing cuccu.
10   Cuccu, cuccu,
wel singes thu, cuccu.
Ne swik thu naver nu.

Sing cuccu nu. Sing cuccu.
Sing cuccu. Sing cuccu nu.

[1]/*Sumer: warm spring weather* is **icumen:** *has come*
[3]/*bloweth: blossoms med: mead, meadow*
[4]/*wde nu: wood now*

[6]/*Awe: ewe*
   cu: cow
   verteth: farts
[7]/*Lhouth: Loweth*
[8]/*sterteth: leaps, starts*
[12]/*Don't ever stop now*

Ezra Pound had some fun with this song in his "Ancient Music":

Ancient Music

Winter is icummen in,
Lhude sing Goddamm,
Raineth drop and staineth slop,
And how the wind doth ramm!
5   Sing! Goddamm.
Skiddeth bus and sloppeth us,
An ague hath my ham.
Freezeth river, turneth liver,
                    Damn you, sing: Goddamm.
10   Goddamm, Goddamm, 'tis why I am, Goddamm,
                    So 'gainst the winter's balm.
Sing Goddamm, damm, sing, Goddamm,
Sing goddamm, sing goddamm, DAMM.   [1915]

One has only to follow the career of a popular songwriter like Bob Dylan to know how folk and ballad traditions have infused the parallel worlds of poetry and song.

The Streets of Laredo

As I walked out in the streets of Laredo,
As I walked out in Laredo one day,
I spied a young cowboy all wrapped in white linen,
All wrapped in white linen as cold as the clay.

5   'I see by your outfit that you are a cowboy'—
These words he did say as I boldly stepped by,
'Come sit down beside me and hear my sad story;
I'm shot in the breast and I know I must die.

'It was once in the saddle I used to go dashing,
10   Once in the saddle I used to go gay;
First to the ale-house and then to the jail-house,
Got shot in the breast and I'm dying today.

'Get six jolly cowboys to carry my coffin;
Get six pretty maidens to carry my pall;
15   Put bunches of roses all over my coffin,
Roses to deaden the clods as they fall.

'Oh, beat the drum slowly and play the fife lowly,
Play the dead march as you carry me along;
Take me to the green valley and lay the sod o'er me,
20   For I'm a young cowboy and I know I've done wrong.

'Go gather around you a crowd of young cowboys
And tell them the story of this, my sad fate;

Tell one and the other before they go further
To stop their wild roving before it's too late.

25 'Go fetch me a cup, a cup of cold water
To cool my parched lips,' the cowboy then said.
Before I returned, the spirit had left him
And gone to its Maker—the cowboy was dead.

We beat the drum slowly and played the fife lowly,
30 And bitterly wept as we carried him along;
For we all loved our comrade, so brave, young and handsome,
We all loved our comrade although he'd done wrong.

ANONYMOUS (DATE UNCERTAIN)

We may even come across poems which, though not written for or set to music, seem haunted by echoes of traditional ballad tunes.

Lord Lovelace

Lord Lovelace rode home from the wars,
   His wounds were black as ice,
While overhead the winter sun
   Hung out its pale device.

5 The lance was tattered in his hand,
   Sundered his axe and blade,
And in a bloody coat of war
   Lord Lovelace was arrayed.

And he was sick and he was sore
10   But never sad was he,
And whistled bright as any bird
   Upon an April tree.

'Soon, soon,' he cried, 'at Lovelace Hall
   Fair Ellen I shall greet,
15 And she with loving heart and hand
   Will make my sharp wounds sweet.

'And Young Jehan the serving-man
   Will bring the wine and bread,
And with a yellow link will light
20   Us to the bridal bed.'

But when he got to Lovelace Hall
   Burned were both wall and stack,
And in the stinking moat the tower
   Had tumbled on its back.

25 And none welcomed Lord Lovelace home
   Within the castle shell,
And ravaged was the land about
   That Lord Lovelace knew well.

Long in his stirrups Lovelace stood
30   Before his broken door,
And slowly rode he down the hill
    Back to the bitter war.

Nor mercy showed he from that day,
    Nor tear fell from his eye,
35   And rich and poor both fearful were
    When Black Lovelace rode by.

This tale is true that now I tell
    To woman and to man,
As Fair Ellen is my wife's name
40   And mine is Young Jehan.

[1970]
CHARLES CAUSLEY (1917–2003)

EXERCISES & DIVERSIONS

A. 1. Say the following words over slowly to yourself, feeling them in the mouth. In which ones does the sound seem to go well with the sense? Can you always say why?
Slump, murmur, spoon, fork, encumber, cucumber, curt, fife, bassoon, abrupt, cluster, sullen, moody, lackadaisical, brisk, brusque, languid, robust, keen, dull, smooth, rough, woofer, tweeter, hiccup, glee, glum, glimmer, glow, flip, flop, fluff, drip, droop, creak, croak, glut, gulp, gobble, cantankerous, gleam, gloom, flabbergast, lollipop, gorge, oily, shudder, pomp, tinsel.

2. Could the meaning of any be reversed (where possible) without loss of expressiveness? Could "slump," for example, just as well mean *to straighten up,* "murmur" mean *to howl?*

3. List a dozen or so other words that seem to you to be like their meanings.

4. List a dozen or so words (such as "instantaneously") that seem to be conspicuously unlike their meanings.

B. Think about the relationship between sound and sense in the following lines of poetry. What do you conclude about each?

1. Life is as tedious as a twice-told tale
Vexing the dull ear of a drowsy man. . . .

WILLIAM SHAKESPEARE

2. They err that would bring style so basely under:
The lofty language of the law was thunder.

THOMAS RANDOLPH

3. The luscious clusters of the vine
    Upon my mouth do crush their wine. . . .

ANDREW MARVELL

4. Dear, damned, distracting town, farewell!

ALEXANDER POPE

5. But when loud surges lash the sounding shore,
    The hoarse, rough verse should like the torrent roar. . . .

ALEXANDER POPE

6. Oh what a tangled web we weave,
    When first we practice to deceive!

SIR WALTER SCOTT

7.   . . . Lee Cauldwell
    Rode by the stable wondering why his lips
    Twitched with such bitter anger. . . .

ROBINSON JEFFERS

8. And the gray air haunted with hawks. . . .

ROBINSON JEFFERS

9. More beautiful and soft than any moth
    With burring furred antennae feeling its huge path
    Through dusk, the air liner with shut-off engines
    Glides over suburbs. . . .

STEPHEN SPENDER

10.   . . . And now today
    When bombastic bards belligerently bray
    For asses' ears in poems called profound . . .

CHARLES MARTIN

C. How is rhyme used in these two short poems by Timothy Murphy
    (b. 1951)?

Twice Cursed

Bristling with fallen trees
and choked with broken ice
the river threatens the house.
I'll wind up planting rice
if the spring rains don't cease.
What ancestral curse
prompts me to farm and worse,
convert my woes to verse?

Poet's Prayer

When I die and go to hell,
as I most certainly shall
(being such an unbeliever)
good Lord, please deliver
my soul to that shady dell
where the pagan poets dwell.
And there, Lord, let me seek
masters of trope and rhyme—
the infernal and the sublime—
and toil until the end of time
to learn Latin and Greek.

[1998]

D. The way the rhymes are arranged in a poem or in a stanza is called the **rhyme scheme.** We diagram it by using small letters in alphabetical order. Four lines ending, for example, in *hill, home, till, roam* have the rhyme scheme *a b a b.* Lines ending in *sea, dune, June, free* have the rhyme scheme *a b b a. Bird, grass, fly, heard, pass, sky* would give *a b c a b c.*

Examine the use of rhyme in the following poems, noticing especially the rhyme scheme, the use of perfect rhyme and off-rhyme, the expressiveness of the rhyme:

1. "The End of the Weekend," p. 12.
2. "In My Craft or Sullen Art," p. 348.
3. "The Woodspurge," p. 421.
4. "Bells for John Whiteside's Daughter," p. 101.
5. "A Narrow Fellow in the Grass," p. 124.

E. 1. How does Milton arrange his rhymes in "Lycidas"? What little figures, such as *a b a b* or *a b b a,* do you find? Are any lines left unrhymed? If so, does there seem to be a reason? Does Milton use off-rhyme?

2. Pick out some lines that seem especially smooth and some that seem especially rough.

F. 1. In the rest of the "Ode to a Nightingale" (see Anthology, p. 405), does Keats use sound as richly as in the first stanza? Pick out another stanza for close analysis.

2. How does Robinson use sound expressively in "The Dark Hills"?

The Dark Hills

Dark hills at evening in the west,
Where sunset hovers like a sound
Of golden horns that sang to rest
Old bones of warriors under ground,

Far now from all the bannered ways
Where flash the legions of the sun,
You fade—as if the last of days
Were fading, and all wars were done.   [1920]

EDWIN ARLINGTON ROBINSON (1869–1935)

ESSAYS

A. Read over the text of "The Streets of Laredo" (p. 190) and note anything in the song that seems to work without the benefit of the melody. What elements would you call poetic? How important is narrative in terms of making the piece cohere? Are there other poems in this book that seem to work in similar ways? Does anything in this song lyric detract from it as a poem on the page? Write an essay in which you address the question of whether songs and poems have anything at all in common, and try to defend your position with examples. You might consider some currently popular songs; ask yourself whether the lyrics could really stand by themselves without the benefit of melody and studio recording techniques.

B. Peruse the lyrics of several popular songs you have always enjoyed in any genre: rap, rock, rhythm and blues, folk, and so on. Choose a lyric that you think is particularly well written for its precise use of diction as well as its sound effects and write an essay defending that lyric as a poem. If you can't think of any songs, some titles from Bob Dylan that might prove useful are "Subterranean Homesick Blues," "Boots of Spanish Leather," and "Stuck Inside of Mobile with the Memphis Blues Again."

POEMS

A. Compose a poem in which the lines end with the words below in the order given. Find possible connections between the words, so that your poem gives a logical account of something. Since we have not yet discussed rhythm, use any rhythm you want to, free or not. But if you do happen to use a line that has five beats (strong accents) as in

What's in a name? That which we call a rose
By any other name would smell as sweet. . . .

you will have written a Shakespearean sonnet.

————————————————————————————————————— quiet
————————————————————————————————————— kiss
————————————————————————————————————— riot
————————————————————————————————————— abyss
————————————————————————————————————— trees
————————————————————————————————————— June
————————————————————————————————————— peas
————————————————————————————————————— prune
————————————————————————————————————— crystal
————————————————————————————————————— bar
————————————————————————————————————— pistol
————————————————————————————————————— guitar
————————————————————————————————————— brooded
————————————————————————————————————— concluded

Such an exercise, called *bouts-rimés* (rhymed endings), has been a favorite game of poets.

B.   Think of a melody you love and compose new words to fit the tune. Put your lyric aside for twenty-four hours. When you look at it with fresh eyes, try to push the melody out of your mind and treat this lyric as a poem without music. Question every word as rigorously as you can, and try to intensify the "music" of the words without the benefit of any other music to accompany the poem.

FIVE

The Rhythms

9

THE DANCER AND THE DANCE

The Play of Rhythms

RHYTHM

Our very existence, like that of the universe we live in, is a system of rhythms. Biologists know of more than a dozen human rhythmical cycles, from that of the heart pulsing 100,000 times a day to that of the alpha waves of the brain pulsing almost ten times as fast. Even before we were born, consciousness may have come to us as an awareness of rhythm—the hammock-like swinging as our mother walked, the intimate beating of her heart and our own matching hers in double time. Long ago people guessed that the heartbeat might be the source of our speech rhythms as well. The Greek physician Galen quotes an earlier medical writer as saying that the heart's weak-strong diastole and systole, whose sound is described as *lub-DUBB* or *ka-BOOM,* is like the weak-strong iambic foot (as in the word "alive"). By "foot" we mean one of the units whose repetition will give us a rhythm; the word goes back to primitive times when the swing of a rhythm might be accentuated by a stamping foot. This particular unit, a weaker syllable followed by a stronger one (*ka-BOOM*), has been called "iambic" since the Greeks identified and named it more than 2,000 years ago.

Jason Sommer, in "For Whoever Reads My Book in Solitude," associates the reading of poetry with the reader's awareness of her iambic pulse beat:

> . . . Brows arched, one page she reads
> over and over, then goes on . . .
> . . . nothing moves, only the iamb
> of pulse at her temple, tapping also
> in her crossed-over leg, trembling the book.

A basic rhythm in many languages, it may indeed be echoing the most basic of physical rhythms. The emotional importance we attach to the heart is shown by our taking it as the symbol of love, although it is not the heart but the hypothalamus at the base of the brain that is the physical home of our emotions. A shepherdess in Elizabethan poetry can rejoice that

> My true love hath my heart, and I have his,
> By just exchange, one for the other given. . . .

There is less demand among lovers for the hypothalamus. Researchers have shown that the heartbeat rhythm, even produced mechanically, has a soothing effect on babies; not only Madonnas in art but live mothers in the supermart prefer to hold their babies so that the child's head is to the left, close to the beating heart of the mother.

> Hunched in the dark beneath his mother's heart,
> The fetus sleeps and listens; dropped into light,
> He seeks to lean his ear against the breast
> Where the known rhythm holds its secret place. . . .
>
> JOHN UPDIKE

A Swedish pediatric journal has even reported that holding the baby on the right may be an early sign of a disturbed infant-mother relationship.

Some have held that, since the beat of the accents in most poetry is a little faster than the heartbeat, the rhythm acts as a tonic. We know that excitement, anticipation, emotion can speed up the heart or cause it to spark contractions so close together that we get the sensation of a skipped beat. Grief and depression can slow it down. One of Shakespeare's young women says of a false lover, "he grieves my very heartstrings . . . it makes me have a slow heart." We will see that all these effects have their correlation with the rhythms of poetry.

Walking, too, with our legs and arms swinging in pendulum time, has developed our feeling for rhythms. Goethe composed many of his poems while walking. So did the young Robert Frost, swinging as his pendulum the schoolbooks he carried at the end of a strap. The kind of work that men and women did for countless centuries—sowing, mowing, woodchopping, spinning, rocking the cradle—encouraged rhythmical expressions. Robert Graves believes that our most vigorous rhythms originated in the ringing of hammers on the anvil and the pulling of oars through the sea.

We feel rhythms also in the world outside, with its alternations of day and night, its revolving seasons, its pulsing of waves on the shore, and its swaying of trees in the wind. There are times when rhythm has a stronger hold on us than our most sacred concerns. Through rhythm, an authority on the dance has said, we reunite ourselves with the ecstasy and terror of a moving universe. No wonder people have been fascinated by the nature of rhythm. Thomas Jefferson, while serving as minister to France, even took time out from his diplomatic duties to write about it in his "Thoughts on English Prosody." The term **prosody,** arising from the Greek word for "tune," now refers to our various theories about verse, including those segments of organized rhythm we call **meter** (more about this later in the chapter).

Though rhythm is not easy to define, we can agree that it is a pattern of recurrence: Something happens with such regularity that we can resonate with it, anticipate its return, and move our body in time with it.

The Elizabethan George Puttenham said that the effect of rhythm was "to inveigle and appassionate the mind"—to involve and excite us. A rhythm that we hear can set up sympathetic reactions—we tap a foot, drum with our fingers, nod in time to it. Rhythm can also affect the way we feel: Psychiatric research has discovered that rhythmical body movements can lead to altered states of consciousness. Rhythm is contagious. It is also hypnotic. We find it difficult, by the ocean, to count to a hundred waves without feeling our mind drift away into a kind of trance. In taking possession of us, it leaves less of our attention for other concerns. Its trancelike effect explains its connection with magic; the language used in primitive ceremonies all over the world is rhythmical. Its affinity with ecstacy (*being outside or beyond oneself*) is well known.

Rhythmical speech has also been thought of as distancing or framing (as in a picture or on a stage) the material it deals with. Its sustained cadence—not exactly what we are used to in actual speech—tells us we are in another world, a make-believe world like that of the theater, in which experience is presented to us without the obligations it involves in real life.

REPETITION AS RHYTHM

One of the simplest forms of rhythm, and one of the most emphatic and passionate, is repetition. Among the most emotional paragraphs in William Faulkner's *Absalom, Absalom!* is the last one, in which Quentin is asked why he hates the South:

> "I dont hate it," Quentin said quickly, at once, immediately; "I dont hate it," he said. *I dont hate it,* he thought, panting in the cold air, the iron New England dark; *I dont I dont; I dont hate it! I dont hate it!*

Whenever poetry begins, it seems to begin with repetition—which is a form of *dwelling on* something. Certain African tribes have a song in celebration of the new moon, which is thought to bring rain:

> New moon, come out, give water for us,
> New moon, thunder down water for us.
> New moon, shake down water for us.

Here is a more modern use of evocative repetition:

Counting the Beats

You, love, and I,
(He whispers) you and I,
And if no more than only you and I
What care you or I?

5 Counting the beats,
Counting the slow heart beats,
The bleeding to death of time in slow heart beats,
Wakeful they lie.

Cloudless day,
10 Night, and a cloudless day,
Yet the huge storm will burst upon their heads one day
From a bitter sky.

Where shall we be,
(She whispers) where shall we be,
15 When death strikes home, O where then shall we be
Who were you and I?

Not there but here,
(He whispers) only here,
As we are, here, together, now and here,
20 Always you and I.

Counting the beats,
Counting the slow heart beats,
The bleeding to death of time in slow heart beats,
Wakeful they lie.   [1951]
                              ROBERT GRAVES (1895–1985)

Probably no poet has made more systematic use of repetition as a rhythmical principle than Walt Whitman.

From Leaves of Grass

I am the poet of the body,
And I am the poet of the soul.

The pleasures of heaven are with me, and the pains of hell are with
    me,
The first I graft and increase upon myself. . . . the latter I translate into
    a new tongue.

5 I am the poet of the woman the same as the man,
And I say it is as great to be a woman as to be a man,
And I say there is nothing greater than the mother of men.

I chant a new chant of dilation or pride,
We have had ducking and deprecating about enough,
10   I show that size is only development.

Have you outstript the rest? Are you the President?
It is a trifle. . . . they will more than arrive there every one, and still
    pass on.

I am he that walks with the tender and growing night;
I call to the earth and sea half-held by the night.

15   Press close barebosomed night! Press close magnetic nourishing night!
Night of south winds! Night of the large few stars!
Still nodding night! Mad naked summer night!

Smile O voluptuous coolbreathed earth!
Earth of the slumbering and liquid trees!
20   Earth of departed sunset! Earth of the mountains misty-topt!
Earth of the vitreous pour of the full moon just tinged with blue!
Earth of shine and dark mottling the tide of the river!
Earth of the limpid gray of clouds brighter and clearer for my sake!
Far-swooping elbowed earth! Rich apple-blossomed earth!
25   Smile, for your lover comes!

Prodigal! you have given me love! . . . therefore I to you give love!
O unspeakable passionate love!

Thruster holding me tight and that I hold tight!
We hurt each other as the bridegroom and the bride hurt each other.

[1855]

WALT WHITMAN (1819–1892)

Such repetitions consist of patterns of word arrangement. Other elements of design can be repeated, so that we have a rhythm like that of a painting. If we "read" Kandinsky's *Lines of Marks* below, we find the artist repeating and varying a few simple motifs: the bar, the circle, the triangle, the crescent.

Dylan Thomas's "Fern Hill" (see Anthology, p. 479) has not only an elaborate rhythmical structure for the ear but also a painterly use of thematic materials. The colors green and gold (for grass and sunlight) are used throughout. Five of the six stanzas make mention of singing or music. There are many echoes in syntax or diction: "green and carefree," "green and golden," "green and dying"; "happy as the grass was green," "happy as the heart was long."

THE RHYTHM OF ACCENT

The repetition of words, images, or motifs gives us a kind of rhythm. But what we mean when speaking of the rhythm of poetry is more often a pattern of sound in the syllables themselves.

Wassily Kandinsky, *Lines of Marks*

If we were writing in a language like ancient Greek, in which the length of syllables was prominent, we could make a pattern by alternating long and short ones, as if they were quarter notes and eighth notes. If we were writing in a tonal language like Chinese, we could make a pattern by alternating pitch. But in English, in which accent is more prominent than length or pitch, we generally make a pattern out of accented and unaccented syllables. There are several ways in which we can do this. The one we will consider first is the commonest in our poetry. Called **syllable-stress** or **accentual-syllabic,** it takes into account both the number of syllables in the pattern and the arrangement of their accents.

Most of us have a practical grasp of what a syllable is, perhaps based on the way dictionaries divide up words: mo-lec-u-lar; syn-co-pat-ed; un-pre-ten-tious. We recognize syllables as the little lumps of sound words can be crumbled into—a vowel nucleus with whatever consonants may attach themselves to either side. There are occasional options. Words like "fire" or "hour" are pronounced sometimes as one syllable, sometimes as two (fi-er, hou-er). Other words have a certain play or give: cu-ri-ous or cur-yus; sen-su-al or sench-wul; fa-vor-ite or fav-rite; mur-der-ous or murd-rous.

Certain syllables are made more prominent than others by being *accented*—we also say *stressed* or *emphasized*. We put noticeably more energy into pronouncing them than we do into syllables that have no accent. Nearly all of us (unless tone-deaf) recognize accents when we hear them: What we *imPORT,* we call "IMports"; what we *reJECT,* we call "REjects." A TV show some years ago got a laugh by having a character talk about "po-LOP-onies" when he meant "polo ponies." Few of us would immediately recognize the name of an American city if we heard it pronounced "Phil-AD-el-FEE-a, Pen-SYL-va-NIGH-a." We are more sensitive than we may be aware of to accents and their displacement.

Speech has a tendency to alternate accented and unaccented syllables, much as we tend to impose a rhythm on any series of sounds. The language likes to rhythmicize itself. We shift the accent in "reSTORE" to get a better rhythm in "RESTorAtion." Longer words, as Jefferson noticed, move in rhythm: tubérculósis, enthúsiástically, indústriálizátion.

There are, of course, many degrees of the kind of emphasis we call accent. We need subtle differences to distinguish, in speaking, between "What's in the road ahead?" and "What's in the road—a head?" Or, to take a hackneyed example, between "the greenhouse," "the green house," and "the Greene house." Linguists admit four degrees of stress, though no doubt, for anyone sensitive enough to catch them, there are many in between. But whether there are four or forty, all we need for the rhythms of poetry are *two*. Does a syllable have *more* or *less* stress, mass, energy than the syllables around it? How much more does not matter. More or less alone can make waves of sound. Like alternations of tension and relief, like the *lub-DUBB* of the heart-beat, like inhaling and exhaling, like yin and yang and the antithetical play of existence, our rhythm is an interaction between *two* principles, *two* kinds of accent, not among three or more.

The writer who is using accents for rhythm makes sure that they come in waves, as so much energy does in the physical world. What we feel in accentual rhythm is a regular surge of *more* and *less* in the natural flow of the language.

When we go surfing on a rhythm, we take the crests and hollows without particularly analyzing their dynamics. We ride the lines like this:

The ^{CUR} few ^{TOLLS} the ^{KNELL} of ^{PART} ing ^{DAY,}

very much as we would have pronounced the words anyway, even if we had not been riding the rhythm (which ought to be in the *natural* pronunciation of the words, and not in any artificial singsong we impose on them). We may be content to take these waves of rhythm as they come, as one can be happy merely watching the surf along the shore. But if we really care about waves, we have to immobilize the flux (as with a camera) to see the wave as a surge of rotating particles that themselves move forward hardly at all.

If we could similarly immobilize the waves of the commonest English rhythm (called "iambic"), we would find every unit of trough and crest to be made up of a dip and swell in the accents—of an unstressed syllable and a stressed one, as in "reJOICE," "to LOVE," "at HOME." The unit whose repetition makes up any rhythm is called a **foot,** a term that, as we said, takes us back to the supposed association of poetry with the dance, when each rhythmic unit was marked by a beat of the dancer's foot.

A NOTE ON SCANSION

If we are to isolate any unit of rhythm-particles for our inspection, we need a set of symbols—some would say *signs*—to stop the action and show what is happening. The process of applying these symbols is what we call **scansion**—its *scan* analogous to the medical CAT scan. Many find it a dreary affair. It seems pedantic and destructive to represent a living line of verse by anything so lifeless as

$$\smile - | \smile - | \smile - | \smile - | \smile - |.$$

This is certainly not the same thing as a line of poetry. Agreed. But we take for granted the utility of such simplified schemes in many activities. Compared with the color and drama of a football game, the diagram of a play is also dry and pedantic. Yet it is difficult to imagine a professional quarterback looking at the diagram and snarling, "Who needs that kind of stuff? I just plan to get out there and heave the old pigskin." Our line of scansion is misleadingly stiff: It suggests that all accented syllables are exactly the same and all unaccented ones exactly the same, rigid as the stone ups and downs along a battlement. In fact the syllables are quite uneven, like a series of waves on a lake or the undulations of a hilly horizon.

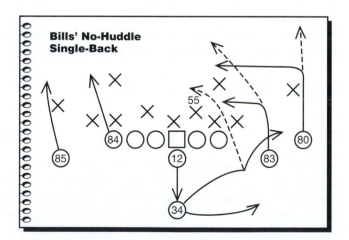

Musical notes are sometimes used with poetry to show how the particles of rhythm are related. The first two lines of George Meredith's "Love in the Valley" might be analyzed as:

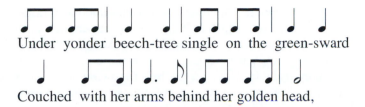

Under yonder beech-tree single on the green-sward

Couched with her arms behind her golden head,

But speech has nothing like so metronomic a regularity. Music is in the world of chronometric time; the metronome, even though the performer may tease and worry it now and then, sets the standard. But the rhythm of poetry exists also in the free-flowing world of psychological time, the kind of time in which, as Romeo says, "Sad hours seem long," or in which happiness, to paraphrase Goethe, can make the day race by on flashing feathers. Time, in the rhythms of poetry, is subjective—as elastic as Dali's famous watch, drooped like a pancake over its tree branch. One could pause for a couple of seconds after a word in poetry ("beech-tree," for example, in the first line of Meredith's poem) and not affect the basic rhythm. Musical scansion is not of much use to us.

A more modern type of scansion, that of structural linguistics, attempts to show four degrees of stress, four degrees of pitch, and four kinds of connective pauses between words. But a system that turns a simple line of Yeats into

Speéch + aftèr + lóng sílènce; ît + ís + ríght . . .

is more complex than we need. Readers do not listen that way; poets do not write that way. When Theodore Roethke quotes from a nursery rhyme:

Hinx, minx, the old witch winks,

he says he feels it as "five stresses [accents] out of a possible six." He does not say he feels it as "three primaries, a secondary, and a tertiary."

All that matters is *more* or *less;* an easy way to indicate the two is the traditional one—a firm straight line for the accented syllable (—) and a sagging little curve for the slack one (◡).★ (Some scanners prefer to tilt the straight line skyward (´) to indicate accent.)

Sometimes the pattern of accents is unmistakable,

The cŭr|fĕw tōlls|thĕ knēll|ŏf pārt|ĭng dāy. . . .

Nothing to hesitate over here. Where we find ourselves hesitating, the thing to do is to mark the accents we are sure of. There is no doubt about words

★Cf. E. E. Cummings's use of these marks in his ms. of "rose tree," p. 354.

like "de̽līght," "rĕmēmbĕr," "āppĕtīte," or (usually) about phrases like "thĕ cāt," "tŏ thĕ stōre," "yŏu wānt tŏ." We generally get enough pieces of the pattern from the known words to complete the rest of it for ourselves by filling it in with matching parts—testing them by means of natural pronunciation to see if they really fit. Once we get into the swing of a rhythm, we are pretty sure how it is going to continue. But scansion is not an exact science like mathematics. Stressed and unstressed syllables are not always as instantly identifiable as even and odd numbers are. Occasionally we come across a line that no two of us will scan in exactly the same way; we might even scan the same line a little differently on different days or in different moods. But even when we differ about details, we are generally in agreement about the basic rhythm.

IAMBIC PENTAMETER

The rhythmical line we will be using for the examples that follow in this section is the commonest line in the poetry of our language, the **iambic pentameter.** *Iambic* because for over twenty centuries that has been the name of the trough-and-crest unit (⌣ —), as in "to da̦nce" or "enjoy." If the word sounds classroomy to us now, we might recall that it originally meant something violent and abusive. In ancient Greece a girl named Iambé personified the obscene songs (in iambics) sung to relieve emotional tension at religious mystery rites. *Pentameter* because there are five of these iambs to a line. Among all people, five is the natural unit of counting off (a glance at the hand will show why). The fiveness of the line may have another physiological basis. Since the ratio between a somewhat excited pulse rate and the normal rate of breathing (seventeen breaths a minute) is about five to one, we would not be too far off in thinking of iambic pentameter as a breathful of heartbeats. Hugh Kenner imagines Homer in the throes of composition: "the muse singing as his chest contracted, his breath governing the line, his heart beating against the stresses." Recalling this rhythm might even help us save a life. In cardiopulmonary resuscitation—the technique for keeping alive victims of "sudden death" by mouth-to-mouth breathing and rhythmical pressure on the chest—the ratio between the substitute propulsion of chest pressure and the substitute breathing is never far from five to one. It seems evident that our breathing can influence and be influenced by rhythm, and that a real connection exists between the two. Some Eskimos, we are told, have the same word for "poetry" as they have for "breath."

Pick up any anthology that covers poetry in English, and you will find that at least two-thirds of it is in iambic pentameter. It has been called the most important meter in the North European world. Chaucer, who got it from the ten- or eleven-syllable line of French and Italian poetry, is given credit for establishing it in English, though there was a basis for it in our earlier native verse.

Iambics, to be so thoroughly accepted, must have seemed natural—like the way people really talk. Aristotle heard them in the language of everyday Greek. Hopkins commented, "and the same holds for English." Richard Blackmur once said, after listening to recorded poetry in thirty-odd languages, that he could hear the iambic base in all but one.

More iambic pentameters are uttered every day here in America than Shakespeare and all his fellows wrote in a lifetime. When George Starbuck wonders:

> Whaddaya do for action in this place?

he is writing in a cadence we often fall into without knowing it.

> I'd like to introduce a friend of mine.
>
> Please fill 'er up—and better check the oil.
>
> Suppose you take your damn feet off the chair.
>
> Deposit fifty cents for overtime.
>
> Cheeseburger special and a glass of beer.
>
> For rent: one-room apartment near the lake.
>
> Eleven times eleven comes to what?
>
> I'd like to know exactly what she said.

It's easy to find lines as natural as this in the poets; in Conrad Aiken, for example, lines like

> I'll meet you Thursday night at half past ten.
>
> How do you like the way I've done my hair?
>
> Boy, if I told you half of what I know. . . .
>
> I told him straight, if he touched me, just once more,—
> That way, you know,—I'd kill him. And I did.

In Frost, lines like:

> I didn't make you know how glad I was
> To have you come and camp here on our land. . . .
>
> He burned his house down for the fire insurance. . . .
>
> I might have, but it doesn't seem as if.
>
> It's knowing what to do with things that counts.

Leonard Bernstein thought that iambic pentameter was in on the birth of the blues, out of which jazz and so much modern music was to evolve. The writers of blues lyrics did not use it because it was "classic"; they used it for the same reason that Shakespeare and the Elizabethan dramatists did—it embodies a basic speech pattern:

> I hate to see that evenin' sun go down. . . .

> Goin' lay my head right on the railroad track,
> [Be]cause my baby, she won't take me back. . . .

> The man I love's got low-down ways for true. . . .

> Woke up this mornin', blues all round my bed. . . .

VARIATIONS ON IAMBIC

The model in our head against which we are measuring our examples in this section is schematized as

$$\smile-\mid\smile-\mid\smile-\mid\smile-\mid\smile-\mid$$

What we say about it will hold for other metrical patterns as well. But we will not expect lines of living poetry to match this or any other model exactly. There is no merit, as we will soon show, in mere regularity; even the heart departs from its 72 beats a minute to meet the needs of life situations. We can sometimes find perfectly regular iambics, as in Shakespeare's

> When I do count the clock that tells the time . . .

or in his

> Of hand, of foot, of lip, of eye, of brow. . . .

In "Sonnet 66" we have almost eleven consecutive lines (from the "behold" of line 2 through line 12) with only one variation from strict meter—the little stumble that comes in, appropriately enough, with the "tongue-tied" of line 9.

Sonnet 66

> Tired with all these, for restful death I cry:
> As, to behold desert a beggar born,
> And needy nothing trimmed in jollity,
> And purest faith unhappily forsworn,
> 5 And gilded honor shamefully misplaced,
> And maiden virtue rudely strumpeted,
> And right perfection wrongfully disgraced,

And strength by limping sway disablèd,
And art made tongue-tied by authority,
10 And folly (doctor-like) controlling skill,
And simple truth miscalled simplicity,
And captive good attending captain ill.
  Tired with all these, from these would I be gone,
  Save that, to die, I leave my love alone.   [1609]
                WILLIAM SHAKESPEARE (1564–1616)

²/**desert:** *true merit*   ⁶/**strumpeted:** *treated like a harlot*
³/**needy nothing:** *a penniless nonentity* ⁸/**limping sway:** *defective authority*
trimmed in jollity: *showily dressed* ¹¹/**simplicity:** *idiocy*

But nothing so regular is to be found elsewhere in the sonnets, or rarely anywhere in good poetry. Shakespeare has a reason here for his unvarying rhythm: He is writing about the monotony of the world's injustice, which has its own dreary pattern of recurrence.

If we were tapping our fingers to music and the music suddenly stopped, we could go on tapping without breaking the rhythm, just as we could continue a wavy line, if it ended, with a dotted line of similar waves.

Our expectation of continuing rhythm is so strong that we can even feel an accent where perhaps there is none, as we imagine we hear a ticktock pattern in the undifferentiated ticks of a clock. If we are led to expect an accent on syllables 2, 4, 6, 8, and 10, we are inclined to stress these syllables. When Shakespeare, in "Sonnet 68," complains about such "bastard signs" of beauty as the wearing of wigs from the hair of persons now dead, he writes:

Before the golden tresses of the dead,
The right of sepulchers, were shorn away
To live a second life on second head. . . .

Our anticipation of the rhythm we are now moving in leads us to expect an accent on "of" (the eighth syllable) in the first line, and on the last syllable of "sepulchers" (the sixth syllable) in the second line. There is no real accent on either; but since we expect to hear one, and since nothing insists we cannot hear one, we *think* accent without sounding it.

But sometimes an apparently misplaced accent is too strong to ignore, and then we have a genuine variation in the rhythm. When Shakespeare begins a line with "To the wide world," we cannot imagine that it should be pronounced, "To THE wide WORLD" or any other way except "To the WIDE WORLD." Such variations are the life of rhythm.

The iambic foot is made up of two particles, or syllables, the first having less mass or energy than the second ($\smile$—). But, in place of the normal foot, we find that four options are possible.

1. Pyrrhic ($\smile$ $\smile$)

The first option is a foot of two syllables, neither of which has an accent, as in the lines from "Sonnet 68" discussed above. This foot is called a **pyrrhic** ($\smile$ $\smile$).

> When I have seen the hungry ocean gain
> Advan | tăge ŏn | the king | dŏm ŏf | the shore. . . .
>
> WILLIAM SHAKESPEARE

> A horse! A horse! My king | dŏm fŏr | a horse! . . .
>
> WILLIAM SHAKESPEARE

> I feel the ladder sway | ăs thĕ | boughs bend. . . .
>
> ROBERT FROST

Very often such options as this have no expressive function. But a pyrrhic foot, in giving us *less* than we expect, just may dramatize some kind of *less*ness—the erosion of the shore, perhaps, or the sense of the boughs giving as the ladder leans against them. Its weakness helps the very line stagger as we read:

> While through the window masked with flowers
> A lone wasp stag | gĕrs frŏm | the dead. . . .
>
> J. V. CUNNINGHAM

2. Spondee (— —)

The second option is a foot of two syllables, both of which have an accent. This is called a **spondee** (— —). We hear it in expressions like "dead beat" (very tired), as opposed to "deadbeat" (one who avoids paying debts); or in expressions like "dead weight," "dead end," "Dead Sea," as opposed to "deadeye," "deadwood," "deadline," each of which accents the first syllable.

Since the spondee packs as much mass as possible into a two-syllable foot, it can reinforce notions of muchness, weightiness, or slowness. Since its very density makes it take longer to pronounce, it can dramatize extent or duration.

> Was it the proud | fūll sāil | of his | grēat vērse, |
> Bound for the prize of all | tōō prē | cious you . . . ? |
>
> WILLIAM SHAKESPEARE

Yet once more ere thou hate me, one |fŭll kīss. . . . |

A. C. SWINBURNE

The long |dāy wānes, |the slow |mōŏn clīmbs, |the deep
Mōăns rōŭnd |with many voices. . . .

ALFRED, LORD TENNYSON

I laid down my |lōng nĕt |in the |bĭg tīde |. . . . |

BREWSTER GHISELIN

Clotted spondees have been used for frozen blood:

And though I think this heart's |blōŏd frōze |nōt fāst |
It ran |tōō smāll |to spare |ōne drŏp |for dream |ing. . . .

JOHN CROWE RANSOM

Spondees can also slow down the line so that details can be contemplated:

Reign in my thoughts! |faīr hānd! |sweēt ēye! |rāre vōīce! |

SAMUEL DANIEL

Since the pyrrhic foot gives us less than we expect, and the spondee more, they are sometimes combined as a kind of double foot (˘ ˘ — —) in which the second half compensates for the first:

                 . . . They may seize
Ŏn thĕ whīte wōn |dĕr ŏf deār Jūl |iet's hand. . . .

WILLIAM SHAKESPEARE

Let Rome in Tiber melt |ănd thĕ wīde ārch |
Ŏf thĕ rānged ēm |pire fall! . . .

WILLIAM SHAKESPEARE

Ănd thĕ mīnd whīrls |ănd thĕ heārt sīngs |
And ă shōut greēts |the daring one.

ROBERT FROST

3. Trochee (—˘)

The third option reverses the iambic foot from ˘— to —˘. "Happy," "token," "over" are examples of this foot (the **trochee**). Trochees are so common at the beginning of iambic lines that we hardly feel them as variations.

To be or not to be, that is the question.
|Whēthĕr |'tis nobler in the mind to suffer. . . .

They also fit in easily after a strong pause within the line:

> Did heaven look on,
> And would not take their part? | Sīnfŭl | Macduff,
> They were all struck for thee! | Naūght thăt | I am. . . .

But elsewhere, when a trochee substitutes for an iamb, the effect can be like that of strain or abrupt dislocation. A trochee among iambs is out of place, its movement going counter to the tilt of the line. In these examples from Shakespeare a trochee is found roughing the meter, calling attention to some violence in the thought:

> With time's injurious hand | crūshed ănd | o'erworn . . .

> | Lēt mĕ | nōt tŏ | the marriage of true minds
> Admit impediments . . .

> How weary, stale, | flāt, ănd | unprofitable
> Seem to me all the uses of this world!

> By the clock 'tis day,
> And yet dark night | strānglĕs | the traveling lamp . . .

> This tyrant, whose sole name | blīstĕrs | our tongue. . . .

Yeats provides us with an expressive example of a reversed foot:

> O she had not these ways
> When all the wild | sūmmĕr | was in her gaze.

Going along with the meter, we want to read "the WILD sumMER," but cannot. So, with some feeling of strain, we do violence to the meter, which itself is made to rebel as the words recall the woman's rebellious youth.

Perhaps it has taken our ear a few centuries to get used to this midline trochee. Even Jefferson, in so many ways willing to declare his independence, did not easily go along with it. Of the reversed foot in Milton's

> To do aught good | nēvĕr | will be our task,

he says, "it has not a good effect." What Jefferson disliked about the irregularity is probably what we like—the shock value of the energetic dislocation. Milton's "never" stands out defiantly against accepted laws of meter, as it would never do if placed tamely after "will."

We can also think of the trochee among iambs as a kind of backspin or underspin or reverse English, as in Allen Tate's

> The going years, | caūght ĭn | an after-glow,
> Reverse like balls | ēnglĭshed | upon green baize. . . .

Here the word "englished" is itself englished, its —⌣ spinning against the ⌣—'s of the line.

The last foot of the line, especially sensitive to reversal, is almost never trochaic. But where most writers might have given us the regular

> All good hydraulic systems leak a bit

William Harmon dares to write:

> All good hydraulic systems leak slightly.

4. Anapest (⌣ ⌣—)

The fourth option is a foot of three syllables with the accent on the last (⌣ ⌣ —), as in "disagree," "reproduce," "to the woods." This foot (the **anapest**) adds an extra syllable, as one would do in a series of *de DUM de DUM*'s if one occasionally slipped in a *de de DUM*. Pleasant in itself as a change of pace, it can be expressive in suggesting a burst of speed, something impulsive and capricious, like a skip or little caper interrupting our normal stride. Substitute anapests are common, as in Browning's "Fra Lippo Lippi":

> The world and life's too big to pass|for a dream . . .
>
> Scarce had they turned the corner when a titter,
>
> Like the skip|ping of rab|bits by moon|light—three slim shapes. . . .

All four of these options are of common occurrence in poetry. In Shakespeare we even find occasional lines in which four of the five feet are non-iambic:

> |Pluck the|keen teeth|from the|fierce ti|ger's jaws . . .
>
> |Let me|not to|the mar|riage of|true minds. . . .

But he does not let the number of syllables fall short of ten—fall short of five feet of at least two syllables. Iambic pentameter cares about not only accent but also number of syllables—it may add two or three to the ten, but it practically never drops any. On rare occasions though, in what is called a "headless" line, the first syllable may be dropped, as in T. S. Eliot's

> Wipe your hand across your mouth, and laugh.

An extra syllable at the end of the line is so common it is hardly felt as an irregularity:

> To be or not to be, that is|the ques|tion. . . .

Sometimes we even find two unaccented syllables hanging over at the end of a line, as in Shakespeare's

> I, that am rudely stamped, and want love's maj | ĕstў. . . .

Much of this chapter has been an account of the structure of iambic pentameter. If we wish to stop the flow of that rhythm to examine the mechanics of the individual wave, we should now be able to do so.

A pleasant poem for this kind of study is Edward FitzGerald's translation of *The Rubáiyát* (or *Quatrains*) of Omar Khayyám, the twelfth-century Persian poet, mathematician, and astronomer (see Anthology, p. 408). Rhythmically, the stanzas are easy to follow, since they have a more regular swing than most of the poems we have been reading. And yet in them we can find all the variations described on the preceding pages.

METER AND RHYTHM

In speaking of music, Igor Stravinsky stresses the distinction between meter and rhythm, a distinction that holds also in poetry. In music, meter is what the metronome is doing; rhythm, what the composer or performer actually gives us. In poetry, **meter** (from the Greek word for *measure*) is the basic scheme, the ⌣—|⌣—|⌣—|⌣—|⌣—, apart from any realization in words— what our mind could continue with if all sound stopped. **Rhythm** (from the Greek word for *flow*) is the way the words of the poem move, often coinciding with the meter but sometimes not. Meter is like the abstract idea of a dance as a choreographer might plan it with no particular performers in mind; rhythm is like a dancer interpreting the dance in a personal way.

A difference between the rhythm of music and the rhythm of poetry is that speech, unlike music, is not metronomic. The poet Walter de la Mare reminds us that if we tried to talk emotionally in time with a metronome, the results could only be comic. Human speech has more rhythmic freedom than a metronome permits. In music, rhythmic freedom is what the great guitarist Andrés Segovia used to stress in the master classes he gave: He wanted constant variation from, and yet with regard to, the basic metrics; he tried to discourage his students from letting themselves become too metronomic. Such warnings are probably even more important in poetry, in which servitude to meter can be as destructive as total contempt for it.

What we feel in the iambic line—or in the other strong-stress lines we shall consider in the next chapter—is an interplay of two movements at once: that of the meter, which our mind holds and anticipates, and that of the actual words of the poem as we hear them. The two are seldom identical. As Robert Frost, with the help of a pun, puts it:

> The tune is not the meter, not the rhythm,
> But a resultant that arises from them.
> Tell them Iamb, Jehovah said, and meant it.

In expecting, in iambic verse, another iambic foot, the mind is right most of the time. When it is not right, it does a double take, and the questionable foot, subconsciously, gets more attention than if it were regular.

As we brought out in our discussion of variations, iambic pentameter is monotonous if we think of it merely as meter. Of course: Monotony is the only virtue of a metronome. But good poets do not write iambic pentameter as a meter; they use it as a rough gauge for their rhythms. There are as many rhythms based on iambic pentameter as there are individual—really individual—writers. No one would confuse the iambics of Shakespeare with those of Pope or Milton or Tennyson or Yeats or Cummings. Some poets prefer **end-stopped** lines, which conclude with a pause generally marked by the punctuation. In the excerpt from Pope's "An Essay On Man" (p. 75), every line is end-stopped. The excerpt from Milton's *Paradise Lost* (just below) shows a strong preference for **run-on** lines: In over two-thirds of the lines the sense carries us over to the next line without a pause. The rhythmical effect, called **enjambment,** is very different. Poets differ also in the way they handle the **caesura** (the word means *a cut*)—the pause that tends to fall near the middle of most lines. In scansion it is marked by a double bar (||). In the passage from Book I of *Paradise Lost* in which Milton, in two long sentences, describes Satan and the fallen angels, we see how the poet varies his rhythm by varying the internal pauses. The numbers to the right of the lines indicate the syllable after which the caesura falls (the extra syllables of anapests are omitted from the count). Some readers might feel the pause is elsewhere.

He scarce had ceased || when the superior fiend 4
Was moving toward the shore; || his ponderous shield 6
Etherial temper, || massy, || large and round, 5,7
Behind him cast; || the broad circumference 4
Hung on his shoulders like the moon, || whose orb 8
Through optic glass || the Tuscan artist views 4
At evening || from the top of Fiesole, 3
Or in Valdarno, || to descry new lands, 5
Rivers or mountains || in her spotty globe. 5
His spear, || to equal which the tallest pine 2
Hewn on Norwegian hill, || to be the mast 6
Of some great admiral, || were but a wand, 6
He walked with || to support uneasy steps 3
Over the burning marl, || not like those steps 6
On heaven's azure, || and the torrid clime 5
Smote on him sore besides, || vaulted with fire; 6
Nathless he so endured, || till on the beach 6
Of that inflamèd sea, || he stood and called 6
His legions, || angel forms, || who lay entranced 3,6
Thick as autumnal leaves || that strow the brooks 6
In Vallombrosa, || where the Etrurian shades 5
High overarched embower; || or scattered sedge 6
Afloat, || when the fierce winds Orion armed 2
Hath vexed the Red Sea coast, || whose waves o'erthrew 6

25   Busiris ‖ and his Memphian chivalry,   3
     While with perfidious hatred ‖ they pursued   7
     The sojourners of Goshen, ‖ who beheld   7
     From the safe shore ‖ their floating carcasses   4
     And broken chariot wheels, ‖ so thick bestrown   6
30   Abject and lost lay these, ‖ covering the flood,   6
     Under amazement ‖ of their hideous change   5

Individual style is largely a matter of the interplay between meter and rhythm (an interplay that is also called "variation," "tension," "substitution," or "counterpoint"). For deviations to be felt at all, there has to be something to deviate from. The offbeats of African music are effective because the sense of a regular beat has been established in the mind of the listener. Musicians cannot have offbeats unless they have a metrical beat to be "off." And so in poetry—if the meter is a loose one, the variations will be weak.

The tensions of Beethoven's *Grosse Fugue* are said to have pushed music to extreme limits, almost shattering the tonal system. Working against a rigid meter makes it possible for Yeats to get a similar effect in a poem in which his vision of imminent world chaos throws the last line into confusion, beneath the metrical ruins of which there lies, almost buried, the iambic meter.

The Second Coming

     Turning and turning in the widening gyre
     The falcon cannot hear the falconer;
     Things fall apart; the centre cannot hold;
     Mere anarchy is loosed upon the world,
5   The blood-dimmed tide is loosed, and everywhere
     The ceremony of innocence is drowned;
     The best lack all conviction, while the worst
     Are full of passionate intensity.

     Surely some revelation is at hand;
10   Surely the Second Coming is at hand.
     The Second Coming! Hardly are those words out
     When a vast image out of *Spiritus Mundi*
     Troubles my sight: somewhere in sands of the desert
     A shape with lion body and the head of a man,
15   A gaze blank and pitiless as the sun,
     Is moving its slow thighs, while all about it
     Reel shadows of the indignant desert birds.
     The darkness drops again; but now I know
     That twenty centuries of stony sleep
20   Were vexed to nightmare by a rocking cradle,
     And what rough beast, its hour come round at last,
     Slouches towards Bethlehem to be born?   [1921]
                       WILLIAM BUTLER YEATS (1865–1939)

[12]/*Spiritus Mundi: the "Soul of the World," a kind of storehouse of archetypal memories*

The poem also illustrates all of the variations previously described. Here, the variations are expressive. Not all variations are. Some bring nothing more than a pleasant variety to the verse. As with sound itself, correspondence between expressiveness and idea is only occasional. When variations are meaningful, they strike with double effect.

An earlier poem by Yeats, "He Remembers Forgotten Beauty," shows how a passionate rhythm can override mathematical meter (which here has four beats instead of the five of pentameter):

> When my arms wrap you round I press
> My heart upon the loveliness
> That has long faded from the world. . . .

While there are wrong ways of scanning these lines ("Whēn mў|ārms wrăp|yōu rŏund|Ī prĕss . . .") there is no one right way. Here is one possible way of feeling the stresses:

> Whĕn mȳ|ārms wrāp|yōu rōund|Ĭ prĕss
> Mў hēart|ŭpŏn|thĕ lōve|lĭnĕss
> Thăt hăs|lōng făd|ĕd frŏm|thĕ wōrld. . . .

One might even stress every syllable in the first line. Instead of the four expected accents, it has anywhere from five to eight. There is much more mass and energy than we expect in this line, fewer of the slacks or sags of unaccented syllables. Metrically, this may be the tightest embrace in poetry. The second line is different, with only two strong accents, one on "heart" and one on the "love-" in "loveliness." ("Upon" itself has an accent, but it is relatively weak as we read this line.) The gap in the middle, between "heart" and "loveliness," is as if the rhythm, in its excitement, had skipped a beat. The definite accents in the third line are on "long," "fad-" (of "faded"), and "world." The spondee "long fad-" helps dramatize muchness and length of time. The slack of "-ed from the" has about as many unaccented syllables as the meter would tolerate between "fad-" and "world," so that what has *faded* is distanced by the rhythm itself.

In "Effort at Speech between Two People" (see Anthology, p. 475), written in the early 1930s by Muriel Rukeyser, then a college sophomore, there is even more freedom within the feet. It is not always easy to isolate the units within these free-flowing lines, but there tend to be five accentual crests in each. The rhythm returns to a regular line (12, 15, 20, and others) often enough so that we know what the metrical basis is.

LINE LENGTH

Up to now we have used the pentameter, or five-beat line, for our examples. But a line may have any number of feet from one to about eight—at which point we run out of breath. In Matthew Arnold's "Dover Beach," somewhat more than half of the lines are pentameter; the rest have from two to four feet. We might feel that a more determined pattern would be inappropriate for this melancholy reverie.

Dover Beach

The sea is calm to-night.
The tide is full, the moon lies fair
Upon the straits; on the French coast the light
Gleams and is gone; the cliffs of England stand,
5   Glimmering and vast, out in the tranquil bay.
Come to the window, sweet is the night-air!
Only, from the long line of spray
Where the sea meets the moon-blanched land,
Listen! you hear the grating roar
10   Of pebbles which the waves draw back, and fling,
At their return, up the high strand,
Begin, and cease, and then again begin,
With tremulous cadence slow, and bring
The eternal note of sadness in.

15   Sophocles long ago
Heard it on the Ægæan, and it brought
Into his mind the turbid ebb and flow
Of human misery; we
Find also in the sound a thought,
20   Hearing it by this distant northern sea.

The Sea of Faith
Was once, too, at the full, and round earth's shore
Lay like the folds of a bright girdle furled.
But now I only hear
25   Its melancholy, long, withdrawing roar,
Retreating, to the breath
Of the night-wind, down the vast edges drear
And naked shingles of the world.

Ah, love, let us be true
30   To one another! for the world, which seems
To lie before us like a land of dreams,
So various, so beautiful, so new,
Hath really neither joy, nor love, nor light,
Nor certitude, nor peace, nor help for pain;
35   And we are here as on a darkling plain
Swept with confused alarms of struggle and flight,
Where ignorant armies clash by night.

[1867]

MATTHEW ARNOLD (1822–1888)

²⁸/**shingles:** *rocky beaches*

Poems with one foot to the line (**monometer**) are rare. Lines of two feet (**dímeter**) are about as short as we are likely to find.

Question

Body my house
my horse my hound
what will I do
when you are fallen

5   Where will I sleep
How will I ride
What will I hunt

Where can I go
without my mount
10   all eager and quick
How will I know
in thicket ahead
is danger or treasure
when Body my good
15   bright dog is dead

How will it be
to lie in the sky
without roof or door
and wind for an eye

20   With cloud for shift
how will I hide?

[1954]
MAY SWENSON (1910–1989)

Theodore Roethke has written a waltz poem in lines of three feet (**trímeter**).

My Papa's Waltz

The whiskey on your breath
Could make a small boy dizzy;
But I hung on like death:
Such waltzing was not easy.

5   We romped until the pans
Slid from the kitchen shelf;
My mother's countenance
Could not unfrown itself.

The hand that held my wrist
10   Was battered on one knuckle;
At every step you missed
My right ear scraped a buckle.

You beat time on my head
With a palm caked hard by dirt,
15   Then waltzed me off to bed
Still clinging to your shirt.   [1948]
                                        THEODORE ROETHKE (1908–1963)

Lines of four feet (**tetrámeter**) are the commonest after pentameter.
Four-stress lines are faster, crisper than five-stress ones—appropriate to the
theme of Andrew Marvell's best-known poem, "To His Coy Mistress" (see
Anthology, p. 390), which seems to tell us that time is of the essence.

The six-foot line (**hexámeter**) is also known, when iambic, as the
Alexandrine (from an Old French poem on Alexander the Great). With its
tendency to break in two in the middle, this line can drag in English, as in the
second of these lines by Pope:

A needless Alexandrine ends the song,
That like a wounded snake, drags its slow length along.

In "The Cold Heaven" (see Anthology, p. 432), the long line helps us visualize the stretching winter landscape and the vistas of past and future it evokes.

Lines of seven feet (**heptámeter**) were popular, as "fourteeners," in the
sixteenth century. They have also been much used since:

There's not a joy the world can give like that it takes away. . . .
                                        GEORGE GORDON, LORD BYRON

Oh, East is East, and West is West, and never the twain shall meet. . . .
                                        RUDYARD KIPLING

. . . there is no joy in Mudville—mighty Casey has struck out.
                                        ERNEST L. THAYER

They also turn up in modern song lyrics:

I want you to tell me, little girl, just where did you
        stay last night . . .

The seven feet often break up into four and three, the well-known **ballad
stanza,** as in "Sir Patrick Spens" (p. 14) or such hymns as John Newton's
"Amazing Grace":

Amazing grace, how sweet the sound,
        That saved a wretch like me;
I once was lost but now am found,
        Was blind but now I see.

Lines of eight feet (**octámeter**), though rarer, are found in some well-known poems, among them Tennyson's trochaic "Locksley Hall," which begins:

> Comrades, leave me here a little, while as yet 'tis early morn:
> Leave me here, and when you want me, sound upon the bugle horn . . .

and in Poe's "The Raven":

> Once upon a midnight dreary, while I pondered, weak and weary. . . .

EXERCISES & DIVERSIONS

A. If Yeats's "The Second Coming" (p. 218), written in 1919, is indeed a political poem, as the woman in the cartoon believes, what political forces does it seem to refer to? Is it better, for the poem, that they are left vague and unspecified? Why has the phrase "slouching toward Bethlehem" lent itself to journalistic use in our time?

B. What purpose, if any, does repetition serve in the following quotations?

1. There was a crooked man, and he walked a crooked mile,
    He found a crooked sixpence against a crooked stile;
    He bought a crooked cat, which caught a crooked mouse,
    And they all lived together in a little crooked house.

    ANONYMOUS

2. This is my play's last scene; here heavens appoint
    My pilgrimage's last mile; and my race,
    Idly yet quickly run, hath this last pace;
    My span's last inch, my minute's latest point. . . .

    JOHN DONNE

3. But O the heavy change, now thou art gone,
    Now thou art gone, and never must return!

    JOHN MILTON

(© by Nicole Hollander. Reprinted by permission.)

4. They all are gone, and thou art gone as well!
   Yes, thou art gone!

MATTHEW ARNOLD

[Is this as effective as No. 3?]

5. There passed a weary time. Each throat
   Was parched, and glazed each eye.
   A weary time! a weary time!
   How glazed each weary eye. . . .

SAMUEL TAYLOR COLERIDGE

C. Each of the following examples of iambic lines makes use of one or
   more of the optional feet. Find and identify them. Besides adding
   variety to the line, which variations are expressive?

1. Sidney is dead, dead is my friend, dead is the world's delight. . . .

FULKE GREVILLE

2. What is your substance, whereof are you made,
   That millions of strange shadows on you tend?

WILLIAM SHAKESPEARE

3. Bear thine eyes straight, though thy proud heart go wide. . . .

WILLIAM SHAKESPEARE

4.   O, I could prophesy,
   But that the earthy and cold hand of death
   Lies on my tongue. . . .

WILLIAM SHAKESPEARE

5. Cover her face; mine eyes dazzle; she died young.

JOHN WEBSTER

6. The grim eight-foot-high iron-bound serving-man. . . .

JOHN DONNE

7. Come, keen iambics, with your badger's feet,
   And badger-like, bite till your teeth do meet.

JOHN CLEVELAND

8. And the white breast of the dim sea. . . .

WILLIAM BUTLER YEATS

9. O body swayed to music, O brightening glance,
   How can we know the dancer from the dance?

WILLIAM BUTLER YEATS

10. And if by noon I have too much of these,
      I have but to turn on my arm, and lo,
      The sun-burned hillside sets my face aglow. . . .

ROBERT FROST

11. Divinity must live within herself . . .
      Elations when the forest blooms; gusty
      Emotions on wet roads on autumn nights. . . .

WALLACE STEVENS

12. Tudor indeed is gone and every rose,
      Blood-red, blanch-white that in the sunset glows
      Cries: "Blood, Blood, Blood!" against the gothic stone
      Of England, as the Howard or Boleyn knows.

EZRA POUND

13. And if the child goes out at evening, stands
      Cold in the cobbled street, and claps cold hands. . . .

CONRAD AIKEN

14. On a cold night I came through the cold rain
      And false snow to the wind shrill on your pane
      With no hope and no anger and no fear:
      Who are you? and with whom do you sleep here?

J. V. CUNNINGHAM

15. Against that torn mouth no kiss comes to bless,
      I answer to the shame I can't confess,
      The old wound coiled up bitterly in me,
      The one your love relieves but cannot free.

SUZANNE J. DOYLE

D. 1.   Out of some subway scuttle, cell or loft
          A bedlamite speeds to thy parapets,
          Tilting there momently, shrill shirt ballooning,
          A jest falls from the speechless caravan.

      This stanza, from Hart Crane's "Proem: To Brooklyn Bridge," describes how, from some obscure and humble lodging, a deranged man will sometimes rush to the bridge, balance a moment dizzily on the railing, then leap to his death. Show how the interplay between meter and rhythm is expressive in every line (especially lines 2 and 3).

   2.   One of the last sonnets of Marilyn Hacker's sequence of love poems, *Love, Death, and the Changing of the Seasons,* is about the end of the relationship. The agitation and distress the speaker feels are reflected in the meter of the first ten lines, which is frequently irregular. Point out how and where.

Who would divorce her lover with a phone
call? You did. Like that, it's finished, done—
or is for you. I'm left with closets of
grief (you moved out your things next day). I love
you. I want to make the phone call this
time, say, pack your axe, cab uptown, kiss
me, lots. I'll run a bubble bath; we'll sing
in the tub. We worked for love, loved it. Don't sling
that out with Friday's beer cans, or file-card it
in a drawer of anecdotes . . .

E. Paul Thompson (*The Work of William Morris*) uses the following
passage from "The Defense of Guenevere" to show that

> odd deviations from the normal iambic beat . . . become masterly
> devices for creating tension. . . . a secondary rhythm drags against
> the weakened primary meter, so that a purely physical description
> of Guenevere takes on a sense of sexual shame. . . . The fourth line,
> clumsy according to conventional metrical standards, is here bril-
> liantly effective. Morris had in fact created a new verse form, like
> stammering direct speech.

Do you feel that the "odd deviations" do, indeed, have this effect?

But knowing now that they would have her speak,
She threw her wet hair backward from her brow,
Her hand close to her mouth touching her cheek,
As though she had had there a shameful blow,
And feeling it shameful to feel ought but shame
All through her heart, yet felt her cheek burned so,

She must a little touch it. . . .

WILLIAM MORRIS

F. On the Countess Dowager of Pembroke

Underneath this sable hearse
Lies the subject of all verse:
Sidney's sister, Pembroke's mother:
Death, ere thou hast slain another,
Fair, and learn'd, and good as she,
Time shall throw a dart at thee.

[1621]
WILLIAM BROWNE (1591–1643)

The meter of this famous little poem, which appears in many
anthologies, might seem undecidable, since four of the lines are
—◡— ◡—◡—, either iambs with the first syllable omitted, or
trochees with the last omitted. Winifred Nowottny (*The Language Poets*

Use) thinks the poem's brief magnificence comes in part from a change in rhythm. The first three lines are trochaic, except for one reversed foot (can you find it?). But with the word "Death," a reversal of attitude, from mourning to triumph, is accompanied by a reversal of rhythm, to rising iambs. Do you believe this is a sensible analysis of the rhythm?

G. The four-stress lines in Marvell's "To His Coy Mistress" were described as "faster, crisper" than pentameter would have been. Pentameter would sound like this:

> Had we but world enough and time, this coy-
> ness, lady, were no crime. We would sit down
> And think which way to walk and pass our long
> Love's day. Thou by the Indian Ganges' side
> Shouldst rubies find; I by the tide of Humber. . . .

Is that really slower? What if we doubled the lines? Twice as slow?

> Had we but world enough and time, this coyness, lady, were no crime.
> We would sit down and think which way to walk and pass our long
>   love's day. . . .

If tetrameters are fast, would dimeters be twice as fast?

> Had we but world
> Enough and time,
> This coyness, lady,
> Were no crime.
> We would sit down
> And think which way
> To walk and pass
> Our long love's day. . . .

What happens if we read in monometers?

> Had we
> But world
> Enough
> And time,
> This coyness,
> Lady,
> Were
> No crime. . . .

Does it seem that a change in the line length really affects the tempo?

H. Anthony Hecht's "The Dover Bitch" (Anthology, p. 492) looks at
    Arnold's "Dover Beach" from a fresh perspective. So, more tersely,
    does Katherine McAlpine's "That Ghastly Night in Dover":

> The sea was calm, and sweet was the night air,
> but what a bore! One whiff of ocean breeze
> started his blathering all night long, I swear—
> stuff about naked shingles and Sophocles.   [1997]

Does either express serious reservations about Arnold's poem, or are
they merely playful takeoffs on it?

ESSAYS

A. If you count the syllables in Frost's "Acquainted with the Night"
    (p. 54), you will find that every line has ten syllables, and you can be
    reasonably sure that you are reading pentameter verse. A count of
    eight syllables is often present for tetrameter, six for trimeter, and so
    on. But not all verse is so easily measured. Some poems contain so
    many variations, so many kinds of feet, that the pattern may not be
    immediately clear. Reread Tennyson's "Break, Break, Break" (p. 126)
    and you will see that syllable count alone is hardly a helpful guide to
    the poem's meters. You will have to "hear" that most lines contain three
    feet, or three clearly accented syllables among the relatively unaccented
    ones.

    Now try scanning the poem, noting the variety of feet you discover
    and any moments of ambiguity. If you call lines 1 and 13 trimeter, then
    they are made of three monosyllabic feet. What else can you say about
    the effect of these lines on the rhythms of the poem? Now, are there
    any lines in the poem that are clearly not trimeter? What meter is used
    instead, and why do you suppose this happened? When you read the
    poem aloud, what happens when the meter changes?

    Write an essay in which you discuss the uses of meter in the poem,
    all the while keeping your reader aware of the connections between
    rhythm and meaning, tone and apparent intent. What is this poem
    meant to accomplish, and how does Tennyson marshal his poetic
    techniques to make it happen? Feel free to make use of any knowledge
    you find useful, not just the study of meter.

B. Study the use of long and short lines in Arnold's "Dover Beach."
    Now study it in Hart Crane's "My Grandmother's Love Letters"
    (Anthology, p. 492). See if you can determine the meter in each line of
    each poem, just for practice. Now decide which of the two you will
    write a short essay about in which you make use of your observations
    about meter and metrical variation to make a case for deliberate formal

strategies in the poem. You may of course allude to all the other technical lessons you have learned about poetry so far in this book.

POEMS

A. 1. Make up a dozen or so iambic pentameters of the kind you might use in conversation, like "This English class has really been a bore" or "You got your tickets for the game tonight?"

2. Compose a dozen or so lines of realistic dialogue in iambic pentameter.

3. Write a few lines of perfectly regular iambic pentameter; then a few that use pyrrhic feet (⌣ ⌣) for *less*ness; a few that use spondees (— —) for *more*ness or fullness; a few that use trochees (— ⌣) for abruptness or violence; and a few that use anapests (⌣ ⌣ —) for speed or impulse.

B. Begin to write in the voice of a character unlike yourself, but do so in blank verse (unrhymed pentameter). This character is telling a story to someone else about a problem he or she has. As you tell the tale, try to use your measured lines and line breaks to dramatic effect, so your enjambments underline or emphasize the psychology of your character. See if you can't work the poemw toward a "killer ending," a final line that has real power and memorability.

10

DIFFERENT DRUMMERS

Alternative Forms of Meter

OTHER SYLLABLE-STRESS RHYTHMS

The iambic—or heartbeat—rhythm has been the one most often used in our poetry over the centuries. But other metrical units are also vigorous. Three such units are frequently used.

Trochee

We have already noticed the trochee (— ⏑) as an option in the iambic line. It can also constitute a rhythm by itself. The word means *running* or *speedy*. Certain common phrases fall into trochaic patterns: "brēad ănd | būttĕr," "sālt ănd | pēppĕr," "cūp ănd | saucĕr," "hēad ănd | shōuldĕrs," "rōugh ănd | rēadӯ," "hīgh ānd | mīghtӯ," "frēē ănd | ēasӯ." Trochaic lines can become monotonous, as they sometimes do in Longfellow's "The Song of Hiawatha":

> By the shores of Gitche Gumee,
> By the shining Big-Sea-Water,
> Stood the wigwam of Nokomis,
> Daughter of the Moon, Nokomis.
> Dark behind it rose the forest,
> Rose the black and gloomy pine-trees,
> Rose the firs with cones upon them;
> Bright before it beat the water,
> Beat the clear and sunny water . . .

In Philip Larkin's poem about a mine disaster, the old rhythm (which Longfellow imitated from an ancient Finnish meter) is successfully revived ("The Explosion," see Anthology, p. 488). You can also find this meter in William Blake's "The Tyger" (Anthology, p. 397), W. H. Auden's "Lullaby" (p. 465), and in the third part of Auden's elegy for Yeats (p. 466). A trochaic rhythm in longer lines is used in Poe's "The Raven." The first stanza should be enough to recall the swing of this famous poem:

> Once upon a midnight dreary, while I pondered, weak and weary,
> Over many a quaint and curious volume of forgotten lore—
> While I nodded, nearly napping, suddenly there came a tapping,
> As of some one gently rapping, rapping at my chamber door—
> " 'Tis some visitor," I muttered, "tapping at my chamber door—
>   Only this and nothing more."

The meter is trochaic octameter, with lines 2 and 4 **catalectic** (*cut short, docked of their final syllable*). Line 6 is tetrameter, also catalectic. If we read the poem naturally, we notice how the individual feet often bond together in pairs:

> While I nodded, | nearly napping, | suddenly there | came a
>   tapping. . . .

Such rhythms, in which two feet tend to fuse into a unit, are called **dipodic**.

The iambic foot, discussed in Chapter 9, is known as a **rising rhythm,** since the energy concentrates at the end of the foot. The trochee is a **falling rhythm.**

Dactyl and Anapest

The two basic three-syllable feet are the **dactyl** (— ‿ ‿) and the **anapest** (‿ ‿ —). The first name is from the Greek word for *finger.* In Greek it had a long syllable followed by two short ones, as the finger has a long bone and two shorter ones. In English the dactyl has an accented syllable followed by two unaccented ones, as (twice) in "innocent bystander." Its opposite, with two unaccented syllables followed by an accented one, is called "anapest," from a word that means *reversed.* We have already mentioned the anapest as an option in iambic verse. Both feet occur in their natural state in English —the dactyl, for example, in a sentence like, "Look at him finish the pint in a gulp or two!"; the anapest in, "For an option on cattle you'd mortgage your house?"

Triple rhythms are busier and faster than double ones; on the other hand, they are lighter, less solid. Triple rhythms are often found in light verse: "Thĕre wăs | ă yoŭng lād | y̆ frŏm Dāl | lăs. . . ." The distinction between

Michelangelo, Detail from *The Creation*

"rising" and "falling" rhythms holds true also for triple feet—anapests lift, dactyls dip.

Byron's "The Destruction of Sennacherib" (based on 2 Kings 19) is written in anapestic tetrameters, though with an iamb sometimes substituted for the first foot and with some variant feet we might feel are more like —⏑— or ⏑—— than the basic ⏑⏑—. (See the Table of Feet, p. 234, for their names.)

The Destruction of Sennacherib

The Assyrian came down like the wolf on the fold,
And his cohorts were gleaming in purple and gold;
And the sheen of their spears was like stars on the sea,
When the blue wave rolls nightly on deep Galilee.

5   Like the leaves of the forest when summer is green,
That host with their banners at sunset were seen:
Like the leaves of the forest when autumn hath blown,
That host on the morrow lay withered and strown.

For the Angel of Death spread his wings on the blast,
10 And breathed in the face of the foe as he passed;
And the eyes of the sleepers waxed deadly and chill,
And their hearts but once heaved—and for ever grew still!

And there lay the steed with his nostril all wide,
But through it there rolled not the breath of his pride;
15 And the foam of his gasping lay white on the turf,
And cold as the spray of the rock-beating surf.

And there lay the rider distorted and pale,
With the dew on his brow, and the rust on his mail;
And the tents were all silent, the banners alone,
20   The lances unlifted, the trumpet unblown.

And the widows of Ashur are loud in their wail,
And the idols are broke in the temple of Baal;
And the might of the Gentile, unsmote by the sword,
Hath melted like snow in the glance of the Lord!   [1815]
                    GEORGE GORDON, LORD BYRON (1788–1824)

Robert Frost puts the swingy meter to very different use in his "Blueberries," which begins:

You ought to have seen what I saw on my way
To the village, through Patterson's pasture today:
Blueberries as big as the end of your thumb. . . .

Dactylic rhythms, though less common in English, can be found. They predominate in Thomas Hardy's "The Voice," which begins:

Woman much missed, how you call to me, call to me,
Saying that now you are not as you were
When you had changed from the one who was all to me,
But as at first, when our day was fair.

William Carlos Williams, not often attracted to traditional rhythms, felt the rightness of the lively dactyl to describe the dancers in a famous painting ("The Dance," see Anthology, p. 448):

Ĭn | Breūghĕl's greāt | pīcturĕ, Thĕ | Kērmĕss
thē | dāncĕrs gŏ | roūnd, thĕy gŏ | roūnd ănd
ă | roūnd. . . .

Bouncy irregularities that seem to swing the rhythm into anapests for a phrase or two help enliven the rollicking dance.

To feel and enjoy the waves of rhythm in a poem, we don't have to be familiar with the terminology, any more than we have to know what "fuel injection" or "universal joint" means if we drive a car. Such terms, though, are a convenience in discussion.

If you study the Table of Feet (p. 234) you will begin to realize how, in English verse, the two-syllable units predominate, with three-syllable feet most often used as substitutions. However, occasionally one encounters such exotic fauna as Timothy Murphy's "Harvest of Sorrows," a near-monorhyme in which the dominant foot is the amphibrach:

TABLE OF FEET

The four basic feet in English versification are:

IAMB	‿—	*as in*	recalled
TROCHEE	—‿		only
ANAPEST	‿‿—		in a dream
DACTYL	—‿‿		memories

These next four, none of which could constitute a meter in itself, are found as occasional substitutes for a basic foot:

Pyrrhic	‿‿	of the
Spondee	——	old loves
Tribrach	‿‿‿	of a re-
Molóssos	———	mote lost land

Some of the following, borrowed from Greek or Latin prosody, are also found as occasional substitutes for a basic foot.

Amphímacer (or cretic)	—‿—	overgrown
Amphibrach	‿—‿	remembers
Bácchius	‿——	the closed door
Antibácchius	——‿	too rudely

Harvest of Sorrows

When swift brown swallows
return to their burrows
and diamond willows
leaf in the hollows,
5   when barrows wallow
and brood sows farrow,
we sow the black furrows
behind our green harrows.

When willows yellow
10   in the windy hollows,
we butcher the barrows
and fallow the prairies.
The silo swallows
a harvest of sorrows;
15   the ploughshare buries
a farmer's worries.

Now harried sparrows
forage in furrows.
Lashing the willows,
20 the north wind bellows
while farmers borrow
on unborn barrows.
Tomorrow, tomorrow
the sows will farrow.

[1998]
TIMOTHY MURPHY (*b.* 1951)

⁵/**barrows:** *castrated pigs*
⁶/**farrow:** *give birth to young pigs*

STRONG-STRESS RHYTHMS

Up to now we have been illustrating only one of the several ways of metering sounds in English. Since it takes into account both the number of syllables and the placing of the accents, it has been called the **syllable-stress** (or **accentual-syllabic**) **system.** But it might just as well, more simply, be thought of as standard rhythm. Because of the interplay between meter and rhythm—that is, between expectation and actuality—standard rhythm produces what we could call, by analogy, something like a stereo effect. In listening to it, we are hearing two voices at once. Other systems have more the nature of monaural sound.

One of them counts only accents, disregarding number of syllables. The other counts only number of syllables, disregarding where the accents fall. The first of these, the **strong-stress system** (often called **accentual meter**), is the older, going back to the verse line of Anglo-Saxon times. The Old English (or Anglo-Saxon) line is made up of two halves. In each half are two strongly stressed syllables, as in W. H. Auden's

Wāving from wīndow,   sprēad of wēlcome . . .

Since the number of unaccented syllables does not matter, there can be a great variety of lengths and patterns—from four syllables, all stressed, in a line like

rōugh rōads,   rōck-strēwn

to over twenty syllables in the unlikely but possible

due to the rūthlessness of the rūmorings,   due to
the Perūvians' incommunicabĩlity. . . .

In theory these two lines are equivalent, since each has four strong beats; in practice, however, lines as gangling as the second one seldom or never occur.

Originally, the four accented syllables were emphasized by alliteration, an ancient feature of Germanic languages. The commonest pattern was to have the first three stresses alliterating (or all beginning with a vowel). Later on, derivatives of strong-stress rhythms have only the four stresses without alliteration, as in the stark little Resurrection poem of the fifteenth century.

I Have Labored Sore

I have labored sore   and suffered death,
and now I rest   and draw my breath;
but I shall come   and call right soon
heaven and earth   and hell to doom;
5   and then shall know   both devil and man,
what I was   and what I am.

ANONYMOUS (FIFTEENTH CENTURY)

4/**doom:** *judgment*

Ezra Pound, in his version of the Anglo-Saxon "The Seafarer," often uses the old pattern:

Nārrow nīghtwatch   nīgh the shīp's head . . .

Chīll its chaīns are;   chāfing sīghs. . . .

Richard Wilbur has used Old English rhythm in a poem which, by its form alone, points up a contrast between our modern world of plastics and unseasoned wood and an older world of well-made tools and furnishings.

Junk

Huru Welandes
                                        worc ne geswiceð
monna ænigum
                                        ðara ðe Mimming can
heardne gehealdan.
                                                Waldere★

An axe angles
                    from my neighbor's ashcan;
It is hell's handiwork,
                                the wood not hickory,
The flow of the grain
                    not faithfully followed.

★The epigraph, taken from a fragmentary Anglo-Saxon poem, concerns the legendary smith Wayland, and may roughly be translated: "Truly, Wayland's handiwork—the sword Mimming which he made—will never fail any man who knows how to use it bravely." [Wilbur's note]

The shivered shaft
                    rises from a shellheap
Of plastic playthings,
                        paper plates,
And the sheer shards
                    of shattered tumblers
That were not annealed
                    for the time needful.
At the same curbside,
                    a cast-off cabinet
Of wavily-warped
                    unseasoned wood
Waits to be trundled
                    in the trash-man's truck.
Haul them off! Hide them!
                            The heart winces
For junk and gimcrack,
                        for jerrybuilt things
And the men who make them
                            for a little money,
Bartering pride
                    like the bought boxer
Who pulls his punches,
                    or the paid-off jockey
Who in the home stretch
                    holds in his horse.
Yet the things themselves
                    in thoughtless honor
Have kept composure,
                    like captives who would not
Talk under torture.
                    Tossed from a tailgate
Where the dump displays
                        its random dolmens,
Its black barrows
                    and blazing valleys,
They shall waste in the weather
                            toward what they were.
The sun shall glory
                    in the glitter of glass-chips,
Foreseeing the salvage
                    of the prisoned sand,
And the blistering paint
                        peel off in patches,
That the good grain
                    be discovered again.
Then burnt, bulldozed,
                        they shall all be buried

To the depth of diamonds,

in the making dark

Where halt Hephaestus

keeps his hammer

30   And Wayland's work

is worn away.   [1961]

RICHARD WILBUR (b. 1921)

In the first twelve lines, there are eleven different arrangements of accented and unaccented syllables.

Auden's "The Wanderer" (p. 133) has the feeling of Old English rhythms and often the very pattern:

Doom is dark and deeper than any sea-dingle. . . .

Waving from window, spread of welcome. . . .

In his book-length *The Age of Anxiety,* Auden went back to even stricter strong stress:

Ingenious George reached his journey's end
Killed by a cop in a comfort station,
Dan dropped dead at his dinner table,
Mrs. O'Malley with Miss de Young
Wandered away into wild places. . . .

Such four-beat patterns are common in nursery rhyme, such as this old one (anonymous, and of uncertain date) that varies the pattern with two three-beat lines:

How many miles to Babylon?
Three score miles and ten.
Can I get there by candle-light?
Yes, and back again.
If your heels are nimble and light,
You can get there by candle-light.

One phenomenon noticed by students of accentual meter in recent decades is the rise of rap music, songs that often make use of four-beat patterns in syncopated lines. These four lines are from "Rapper's Delight" by the Sugarhill Gang:

i said by the way baby what's your name
said I go by the name of lois lane
and you could be my boyfriend you surely can
just let me quit my boyfriend called superman

Many of E. E. Cummings's poems—including some of those that seem most modern—come from the older tradition.

if everything happens that can't be done

if everything happens that can't be done
(and anything's righter
than books
could plan)
⁵ the stupidest teacher will almost guess
(with a run
skip
around we go yes)
there's nothing as something as one

¹⁰ one hasn't a why or because or although
(and buds know better
than books
don't grow)
one's anything old being everything new
¹⁵ (with a what
which
around we come who)
one's everyanything so

so world is a leaf so tree is a bough
²⁰ (and birds sing sweeter
than books
tell how)
so here is away and so your is a my
(with a down
²⁵ up
around again fly)
forever was never till now

now i love you and you love me
(and books are shuter
³⁰ than books
can be)
and deep in the high that does nothing but fall
(with a shout
each
³⁵ around we go all)
there's somebody calling who's we

we're anything brighter than even the sun
(we're everything greater
than books
⁴⁰ might mean)
we're everyanything more than believe

> (with a spin
> leap
> alive we're alive)
> 45   we're wonderful one times one   [1944]
>   E. E. CUMMINGS (1894–1962)

In a poem that seems "everything new," Cummings's "anything old" is a rhythm going back at least seven centuries. If we reassemble one of the stanzas Cummings has disguised by his typographical layout, we find four regular strong-stress lines of four beats followed by one of three beats:

> if ēverything hăppens   that căn't be dōne
> (and ānything's rīghter   than bōoks could plān)
> the stūpidest tēacher   will ālmost gūess
> with a rūn skīp   arōund we go yēs
> there's nōthing as sōmething as ōne

His lines on the page are symmetrically divided and subdivided. Though the poem seems all spontaneity, it is worked out with a precision almost mathematical.

Most poets who use the four-beat, strong-stress pattern today use a simplified form of it:

> Summer will rise till the houses fear;
> streets will hear underground streams. . . .
>
>   WILLIAM STAFFORD

> I slept under   rhododendron
> All night   blossoms fell
> Shivering on   a sheet of cardboard
> Feet stuck   in my pack
> Hands deep   in my pockets. . . .
>
>   GARY SNYDER

James Merrill, in the last poem of his last book, published in the year of his death (1996), has lines of similarly spaced strong stress, with echoes of its ancient alliteration:

> O heart green acre   sown with salt
> by the departing   occupier . . .
>
> evening star   salt of the sky
> First the grave   dissolving into dawn
>
> then the crucial   recrystallizing
> from inmost depths   of clear dark blue

Strong-stress rhythm, based on accent, the most energetic element of speech, serves to communicate physical energy, as in one of the best-known of American baseball poems, Robert Fitzgerald's "Cobb Would Have Caught It" (see Anthology, p. 471).

Finally, we should add that strong-stress or accentual meters are commonly found in songs—not just the obvious rap music with its four-beat pattern, but also other song lyric traditions. W. H. Auden, for example, borrowed an opening line from the folk song tradition and went on to write one of his most engaging poems in a three-beat measure:

As I Walked Out One Evening

As I walked out one evening
   Walking down Bristol Street,
The crowds upon the pavement
   Were fields of harvest wheat.

5 And down by the brimming river
   I heard a lover sing
Under an arch of the railway:
   "Love has no ending.

"I'll love you, dear, I'll love you
10   Till China and Africa meet,
And the river jumps over the mountain
   And the salmon sing in the street,

"I'll love you till the ocean
   Is folded and hung up to dry
15 And the seven stars go squawking
   Like geese about the sky.

"The years shall run like rabbits,
   For in my arms I hold
The Flower of the Ages,
20   And the first love of the world."

But all the clocks in the city
   Began to whirr and chime:
"Oh let not Time deceive you,
   You cannot conquer Time.

25 "In the burrows of the Nightmare
   Where justice naked is,
Time watches from the shadow
   And coughs when you would kiss.

"In headaches and in worry
30   Vaguely life leaks away,
And Time will have his fancy
   Tomorrow or today.

"Into many a green valley
   Drifts the appalling snow;

35 Time breaks the threaded dances
   And the diver's brilliant bow.

"O plunge your hands in water,
   Plunge them in up to the wrist;
Stare, stare in the basin
40 And wonder what you've missed.

"The glacier knocks in the cupboard,
   The desert sighs in the bed,
And the crack in the teacup opens
   A lane to the land of the dead.

45 "Where the beggars raffle the banknotes
   And the Giant is enchanting to Jack,
And the Lily-white Boy is a Roarer,
   And Jill goes down on her back.

"O look, look in the mirror,
50 O look in your distress;
Life remains a blessing
   Although you cannot bless.

"O stand, stand at the window
   As the tears scald and start;
55 You shall love your crooked neighbor
   With your crooked heart."

It was late, late in the evening,
   The lovers they were gone;
The clocks had ceased their chiming,
60 And the deep river ran on.

[1940]
W. H. AUDEN (1907–1973)

SPRUNG RHYTHM

Strong-stress rhythm is so old that poets keep calling it "new" when they re-discover it. In 1800 Coleridge said that the meter of his "Christabel" seemed irregular because "it was founded on a new principle: namely, that of count-ing in each line the accents, not the syllables." More influential was the "new prosody" that Gerard Manley Hopkins calls "sprung rhythm." By "sprung" he means *abrupt,* as when one accent directly follows another. We also say a thing is *sprung* when it is forced out of its proper position by its own tension or by that of things pressing against it. Unaccented syllables can be *sprung* out of a line by the pressure of accents around them—as when we say "I'll go" for "I will go."

Hopkins explained that in sprung rhythm "one stress makes a foot," no matter how many unstressed syllables are with it. Some of the stresses he marked in his poems are the kind we do use in speech, but could not easily guess from a printed text. Characteristic of sprung rhythm is the way stresses jostle against one another, unbuffered by unaccented syllables in between. In "Spring and Fall" (see Anthology, p. 429), we see this happening. In the thirteenth line, for example, two *had*'s have been sprung out, leaving the accents to clash together, as marked:

> What héart [had] héard of, ghóst [had] guéssed. . . .

We have now seen examples of the two basic rhythmical systems of English versification: the syllable-stress system and the strong-stress system. Both have given us great poetry. If the syllable-stress system has given us more, it may only be because it has seemed more all-purpose than the bouncy and emphatic strong-stress system.

A WORD ABOUT QUANTITY

A third metrical system tried to impose itself on English around 1580 and for a decade or so thereafter. Classicists wanted to meter English as if it were Greek or Latin—by *length* of syllable rather than by accent. Although we recognize that some syllables take longer to say than others—that "home" is longer than "him" and "strength" is longer than "sit"—our ear does not divide syllables into long and short consciously enough for us to feel a pattern in the arrangement. Metering by *quantity*—length of syllable—was a failure in English.

But the study of classical meters did bring in some new rhythms, once the long and short syllables were replaced by accented and unaccented ones.

The poems of Sappho, on pages 8 and 16, transpose her quantitative rhythm into accentual ones. It is not surprising to find Sapphic stanzas* in translations of Sappho, but the use to which Timothy Steele puts something like them may come as a surprise.

Sapphics Against Anger

Angered, may I be near a glass of water;
May my first impulse be to think of Silence,
Its deities (who are they? do, in fact, they
        Exist? etc.).

5   May I recall what Aristotle says of
The subject: to give vent to rage is not to
Release it but to be increasingly prone
        To its incursions.

---

*The Sapphic stanza, transposed to our accentual feet, consists of three lines of — ⌣ | — ⌣ | — ⌣ ⌣ | — ⌣ | — ⌣ and one of — ⌣ ⌣ | — ⌣.

May I imagine being in the *Inferno,*
10   Hearing it asked: "Virgilio mio, who's
That sulking with Achilles there?" and hearing
       Virgil say: "Dante,

That fellow, at the slightest provocation,
Slammed phone receivers down, and waved his arms like
15   A madman. What Attila did to Europe,
       what Genghis Khan did

To Asia, that poor dope did to his marriage."
May I, that is, put learning to good purpose,
Mindful that melancholy is a sin, though
20   Stylish at present.

Better than rage is the post-dinner quiet,
The sink's warm turbulence, the streaming platters,
The suds rehearsing down the drain in spirals
       In the last rinsing.

25   For what is, after all, the good life save that
Conducted thoughtfully, and what is passion
If not the holiest of powers, sustaining
       Only if mastered.

             [1986]
      TIMOTHY STEELE (*b.* 1948)

These are based on the Sapphic stanzas of ancient classical poetry. The more complicated Alcaic stanza★ has also been brought over into English; its meter is illustrated by this version of the first stanza of Ode I, ix of Horace:

You see how, white with snows to the north of us,
Soracte looms; how snow's over everything:
    the burdened pines no longer buoyant,
       streams at a stand in the winter weather.

A difficulty with such meters in English is their rigidity. We enjoy variations. But a Sapphic line is a Sapphic line (see Frost's "For Once, Then, Something" for a great example of this classical hendecasyllabic), and the writer has almost no freedom to carry accents. Steele has not always tried to apply the template exactly. He gives us the look and feel of a classical stanza while allowing the flexibility of contemporary speech.

SYLLABIC METER

A fourth and totally different system—by number of syllables alone, with no regard for accent—is winningly presented by James Tate in his poem about a student in a poetry workshop.

★Two lines of $\asymp$ |$-\smile$|$-$ $-$|$-\smile\smile$|$-\smile$ $\asymp$ followed by one line of $\asymp$| $-\smile$|$-$ $-$|$-\smile$ $-$ $\asymp$ and one of $-\smile$ $\smile$|$-\smile\smile$|$-\smile$|$-$ $\asymp$.

Miss Cho Composes in the Cafeteria

You are so small, I
am not even sure
that you are at all.

To you, I know I
5   am not here: you are
rapt in writing a

syllabic poem
about gigantic,
gaudy Christmas trees.

10   You will send it home
to China, and they
will worry about

you alone amid
such strange customs. You
15   count on your tiny

bamboo fingers; one,
two, three—up to five,
and, oh, you have one

syllable too much.
20   You shake your head in
dismay, look back up

to the tree to see
if, perhaps, there might
exist another

25   word that would describe
the horror of this
towering, tinselled

symbol. And . . . now
you've got it! You jot
30   it down, jump up, look

at me and giggle.   [1967]

JAMES TATE (*b.* 1943)

Tate has written his poem exactly as little Miss Cho is writing hers. His, too, is a **syllabic** poem—here, with five syllables to the line, with one significant exception. In such poems all that matters, metrically, is the number of syllables, not their accent.

The American poet Ron Rash often uses syllabic forms derived from the Welsh. In the following brief poem he writes heptasyllabic (or seven-syllable) lines, giving further definition to his stanzas with subtle rhyming:

Scarecrow

He said this land would kill him,
and when it did his widow
left the hoe where he dropped it
on his death-row, staked his clothes

5   to raise his stark shade over
tall corn stalks like the black pall
she laid across his casket.
All that summer, into fall

she allowed no harrowing plow
10   where his heart failed, not until
five Aprils passed and the last
rag on the rotting cross fell.

[2000]

RON RASH (*b.* 1953)

Syllabic poems can have lines of any manageable number of syllables. The odd numbers seem more attractive—five and seven are particular favorites.

Sometimes syllabic verse is arranged in more complex stanzas. In Dylan Thomas's "Fern Hill" (see Anthology, p. 479) the fourth line of every stanza has six syllables:

Time let me hail and climb. . . .

The third and fifth lines have nine:

The night above the dingle starry. . . .

Lines 1, 2, 6, and 7 of each stanza have fourteen syllables. Two of the twenty-four lines are excessive by one syllable, but only a finger-counter would notice. It seems unlikely that our ear will catch any exact number of syllables above about five, since nothing in our speech has accustomed us to attach any importance to such reckoning.

Marianne Moore's "A Carriage from Sweden" (see Anthology, p. 450) has eight syllables in lines 1, 2, 3, and 5 of each stanza (with two exceptions); line 4 of each stanza (with one exception) has nine.

They say there is a sweeter air
    where it was made, than we have here;
    a Hamlet's castle atmosphere.
At all events there is in Brooklyn
something that makes me feel at home.

Romance languages such as French and Italian had long evolved traditions of syllabic verse, but English language poets developed such interests mainly in the twentieth century. It was encouraged by the example of Japanese poetry, based on syllable count since Japanese has no accent noticeable enough to base a rhythm on. (See the remarks on *tanka* and *haiku* in Chapter 12, pp. 317–318.) The most eminent practitioners of syllabics in English have been Marianne Moore and W. H. Auden, who was influenced by her. The trim, crisp lines of both no doubt owe something to the careful attention that syllabics demand, but the greatness of their work does not consist in their ability to count syllables. A series of counted syllables in itself is hardly a source of excitement or emotion in poetry. Someone in a passion may resort to stress rhythms ("You SON of a BITCH!") but is not likely to count syllables. Good syllabic poems are good because of their use of words, or because of their imagery, or because they have an overrhythm that we feel more strongly than the enumeration of syllables, as in Thomas's "Fern Hill" or in many poems of Moore and Auden.

EXERCISES & DIVERSIONS

A. Students of the poetry of Calvin are aware that the six-year-old shows considerable promise in this field, as in so many others (see pp. 248–249). We may be surprised, knowing his character, that his technique is at present solidly traditional. But probably the precocious child realizes that one can experiment creatively only with a solid grounding in the fundamentals. His avant-garde period may still lie ahead of him, when he achieves more maturity of outlook and expertise, say, at the age of eight or nine. If we check his line endings in the poem on p. 248 and the one across the page from it, we find that he employs only perfect rhymes, like those in the very earliest poems of Emily Dickinson, before she had yet ventured into the off-rhymes for which she is known.

   The first two lines of the poem on the next page are in the same meter as the beginning of William Browne's poem on page 226:

   BROWNE: Underneath this sable hearse . . .
   CALVIN: Still and quiet feline form . . .

1. But what kind of change does he make in the next two lines? Is it the same kind of change that Nowottny says Browne makes?
2. Would you say that some of Calvin's lines are catalectic?
3. Find examples of the foot named Bacchius (⌣ — —) in Byron and Calvin.
4. Find examples of the foot named Amphimacer (— ⌣ —) in Calvin.
5. Would you judge from the reaction of Hobbes that he is less sensitive to good poetry than Calvin is? More sensitive?

B.   How would you describe the rhythm of each of these examples?

1. Thou preparest a table before me in the presence of mine enemies:
     thou anointest my head with oil; my cup runneth over.
     Surely goodness and mercy shall follow me all the days of my life:
     and I will dwell in the house of the Lord for ever.

Psalm 23: 5–6

2. 'Tis the middle of night by the castle clock,
     And the owls have awakened the crowing cock;
     Tu—whit!——Tu—whoo!
     And hark, again! the crowing cock,
     How drowsily it crew.

SAMUEL TAYLOR COLERIDGE

3. This is the forest primeval. The murmuring pines and the hemlocks. . . .

HENRY WADSWORTH LONGFELLOW

4. O my agèd Uncle Arly!
     Sitting on a heap of barley
          Thro' the silent hours of night,–
     Close beside a leafy thicket:–
     On his nose there was a cricket,–
     In his hat a railway-ticket;–
          (But his shoes were far too tight.)

EDWARD LEAR

5. A was an archer, who shot at a frog,
     B was a butcher, and had a great dog.
     C was a captain, all covered with lace,
     D was a drunkard, and had a red face.
     E was an esquire, with pride on his brow,
     F was a farmer, and followed the plough.

MY TIGER, IT SEEMS, IS RUNNING 'ROUND NUDE.
THIS FUR COAT MUST HAVE MADE HIM PERSPIRE.
IT LIES ON THE FLOOR—SHOULD THIS BE CONSTRUED
AS A PERMANENT CHANGE OF ATTIRE?
PERHAPS HE CONSIDERS ITS COLORS PASSÉ,
OR MAYBE IT FIT HIM TOO SNUG
WILL HE WANT IT BACK? SHOULD I PUT IT AWAY?
OR USE IT RIGHT HERE AS A RUG?

I WONDER WHEN SCHOOL STARTS.

> G was a gamester, who had but ill-luck,
> H was a hunter, and hunted a buck. . . .

ANONYMOUS

6. When the hounds of spring are on winter's traces,
    The mother of months in meadow or plain
Fills the shadows and windy places
    With lisp of leaves and ripple of rain;
And the brown bright nightingale amorous
Is half assuaged for Itylus,
For the Thracian ships and the foreign faces,
    The tongueless vigil, and all the pain.

ALGERNON CHARLES SWINBURNE

7. There are strange things done in the midnight sun
    By the men who moil for gold;
The Arctic trails have their secret tales
    That would make your blood run cold;
The Northern Lights have seen queer sights
    But the queerest they ever did see
Was that night on the marge o' Lake Lebarge
    I cremated Sam McGee.

ROBERT W. SERVICE

8. Winter and Summer I sing of her grace,
    As the rose is fair, so fair is her face,
    Both Summer and Winter I sing of her,
    And snow makyth me to remember her. . . .

EZRA POUND

9. No mice in the heath run, no song-birds fly
    For fear of the buzzard that floats in the sky.

He soars and he hovers, rocking on his wings,
He scans his wide parish with a sharp eye,
He catches the trembling of small hidden things,
He tears them in pieces, dropping them from the sky. . . .

ROBERT GRAVES

10. High-piled haycocks edge to the cliffs, like beehive
Huts with long views seaward, a dozen fledgling
Monks all perched there, settled in under storm cowls,
     Watching the ocean . . .

J. D. MCCLATCHY

11. I'm a riddle in nine syllables,
An elephant, a ponderous house,
A melon strolling on two tendrils. . . .

SYLVIA PLATH

C. Is there anything like "sprung rhythm" in Tennyson's "Break, Break, Break" (p. 126) or in Campion's "It Fell on a Summer's Day" (see Anthology, p. 376)?
D. Gary Snyder's "Bubbs Creek Haircut" begins:

High ceilingd and the double mirrors, the
     calendar a splendid alpine scene—scab barber—
in stained white barber gown, alone, sat down, old man
A summer fog gray San Francisco day
I walked right in.   on Howard Street
               haircut a dollar twenty-five.
Just clip it close as it will go.
     "now why you want your hair cut back like that."
     —well I'm going to the Sierras for a while
Bubbs Creek and on across to upper Kern . . .

Can you find any iambic pentameters in these free-looking lines?

ESSAYS

A. Choose a poem written either in strong-stress meter or syllabics and write an essay defending or attacking the ways in which form is used in the poem. You will have to read the poem very attentively, noting any effects of rhythm, line breaks, diction, or rhetoric that contribute to your argument. Try to convince your readers that they should care about how techniques are used in this poem.
B. Study the uses of meter in Auden's "In Memory of W. B. Yeats" (Anthology, p. 466) and write a brief essay on how his formal choices affect the tone and impact of his poem.

POEMS

A. Write a short poem in strong-stress rhythms on a subject that seems
    appropriate to their energetic character.
B. Write a short poem in trochaic tetrameter (most likely catalectic). Use
    one of the examples cited on page 231 for your template.
C. Write a poem in syllabics, of any line length (or combination of line
    lengths) you prefer.

11

REMOVING THE NET

"Free Verse," Concrete Poetry, Prose Poems

SOME BACKGROUND ON FREE VERSE

What we commonly call **free verse** has existed for a long time. Such ancient poetries as the Sumerian and the Hebrew relied not on meter for their formal definition but on repetition and parallelism (see the discussion of sentence structure in Chapter 12). However, in most Asian and European poetry of the last three millennia, some form of meter has been a defining principle. There have been exceptions to this, as we can see in poems by Christopher Smart and Walt Whitman. But from Sappho to the twentieth century, meter remained one of the poet's most essential tools. Some would argue that it still is so, but other forms of poetry have played an extraordinary role in modern times, even dominating the field.

For the purposes of a textbook like *Western Wind* we needn't rehearse the entire history of arguments about free verse. We know that some poets have objected to it. Robert Frost famously said, "Writing free verse is like playing tennis with the net down," and more than one modern poet has responded something like "Yes, it's so much harder, because you have to imagine the net." In the twentieth century there were arguments in all the arts about *form,* and if we seem to have arrived at a place where multiple approaches can be sanctioned and enjoyed, we must still try to understand how these forms work.

To be brief, the modern free verse era arises in the nineteenth century with the aesthetic populism of Whitman and the literary movement we call Modernism, which is characterized in part by a breakdown of traditional forms in virtually all of the arts. French writers of the late nineteenth century experimented with prose poetry and, in the case of such figures as Arthur Rimbaud (1854–1891) and Stephane Mallarmé (1842–1898), unpatterned lines that came to be called *vers libre.* Just as Whitman's long, rolling lines had puzzled and offended some readers yet found passionate defenders in surprising places, Modernist *vers libre* both confused and energized the literary world. In many people's minds, such techniques as rhyme and meter were associated with moribund artificiality. And indeed, if one studies late nineteenth-century poetry in English, one can easily see why meter came to feel merely a decorative instead of an essential element.

Novelist, poet, and editor Ford Madox Ford (1873–1939) claimed to have invented a new method of writing by 1898. In this technique, "no exigency of meter must interfere with the personal cadence of the writer's mind or the pressure of recorded emotion." But just what is this "personal cadence of the writer's mind," and is it sufficient to say that all ways of organizing and valuing verse are merely subjective? Over the last century or so, theories of free verse have led to the production of marvelous poems, but the theories themselves can be maddeningly vague. While we will allude to several of those theories, it does seem as if the proof is in the pudding; it is more useful to discuss specific poems than it is to generalize about free verse technique.

So, if free verse is *verse* without a pattern of the sort we have seen in most of the last two chapters, just how is it organized? Does the word "free" mean "chaotic" or can we see certain tendencies that are indeed formal?

A good place to start is with the short-lived literary movement known as **Imagism,** which arose in London around 1912, following theories of such poets as T. E. Hulme (1883–1917) and Ezra Pound (1885–1972). In a sequence of short essays for the Chicago journal *Poetry,* later collected as "A Retrospect" (1918), Pound set down three highly influential rules:

1. Direct treatment of the "thing" whether subjective or objective.
2. To use absolutely no word that does not contribute to the presentation.
3. As regarding rhythm: to compose in the sequence of the musical phrase, not in the sequence of a metronome.

Thus, Imagist poems tend to be short, spare depictions of images, written in lines with no pattern of stresses or syllables. The single most famous example of such a poem would be Pound's "In a Station of the Metro" (p. 12). Another example would be this little poem by Pound's friend H. D.:

Oread

Whirl up, sea—
whirl your pointed pines,
splash your great pines
on our rocks,
5   hurl your green over us,
cover us with your pools of fir.   [1915]

HILDA DOOLITTLE (1886–1961)

The title here refers to a mountain nymph in classical mythology.

If some form of Imagism remains one of the most important trends in all of modern poetry, valuing concrete diction, brevity, and lines without meter, it is also true that most of the original Imagists tried other forms of organization. In the following poem by William Carlos Williams, for example, definition of line and image may be less important than sentence grammar. Notice how deliberately Williams uses parts of speech like verbs and prepositions, how the pattern of short sentences following the first long sentence contributes to the poet's evocation of his paternal grandmother.

Dedication for a Plot of Ground

This plot of ground
facing the waters of this inlet
is dedicated to the living presence of
Emily Dickinson Wellcome
5   who was born in England, married,
lost her husband and with
her five year old son
sailed for New York in a two-master,
was driven to the Azores;
10   ran adrift on Fire Island shoal,
met her second husband
in a Brooklyn boarding house,
went with him to Puerto Rico
bore three more children, lost
15   her second husband, lived hard
for eight years in St. Thomas,
Puerto Rico, San Domingo, followed
the oldest son to New York,
lost her daughter, lost her "baby,"
20   seized the two boys of
the oldest son by the second marriage
mothered them—they being
motherless—fought for them
against the other grandmother
25   and the aunts, brought them here
summer after summer, defended
herself here against thieves,
storms, sun, fire,
against flies, against girls
30   that came smelling about, against
drought, against weeds, storm-tides,
neighbors, weasels that stole her chickens,
against the weakness of her own hands,
against the growing strength of
35   the boys, against wind, against
the stones, against trespassers,
against rents, against her own mind.

> She grubbed this earth with her own hands,
> domineered over this grass plot,
> blackguarded her oldest son
> into buying it, lived here fifteen years,
> attained a final loneliness and—

40

> If you can bring nothing to this place
> but your carcass, keep out.   [1917]
>
>   WILLIAM CARLOS WILLIAMS (1883–1963)

Poems like this help us understand what the critic Charles O. Hartman means when he writes, " 'Free' is properly a synonym for 'nonmetrical,' and it follows that *the prosody of free verse is rhythmic organization by other than numerical modes.*"★

There is plenty of precedent here. When the English Bible appeared, the English ear became habituated to its cadences—two or three simple groupings, generally parallel, and, as translated, in free rhythms:

> The heavens declare the glory of God; and the firmament showeth his handiwork.
> Day unto day uttereth speech, and night unto night showeth knowledge.

The most familiar and musical of free rhythms are Walt Whitman's, vigorous as his own zest and confidence, spacious as the American vistas he loved to sing. In "Out of the Cradle Endlessly Rocking," his great poem of love and death, we are easily caught up in the surge of his biblical cadence. The best way to read this poem the first few times is to ride the rhythm without trying to analyze its nature (see Anthology, p. 416).

When we do try to analyze it, we notice that often the rhythm comes on waves of parallel syntax—as in the twenty-two-line first sentence, or the fourteen-line sentence beginning with line 130. Whitman professed to dislike regularity, yet his numerous revisions show that he worked for it, changing many lines to bring them into an iambic dance. Though his lines vary greatly in length and are made up of many kinds of feet, almost always the cells of rhythm join in strands according to their natural affinity.

He has both rising lines,

> When the li̽|lac-scent| was in the air|and Fifth-|month
> grass|was grow|ing . . .

and falling ones,

> Out of the|cradle|endlessly|rocking. . . .

★*Free Verse: An Essay on Prosody,* Princeton University Press, 1980, pp. 24–25.

He has the same foot—or almost the same foot—running through a line:

Oūt from thĕ|pātchĕs ŏf|brīĕrs ănd|blāckbĕrriĕs. . . .

Often we come on a familiar shape in the surf of rhythm—perhaps an iambic pentameter or two:

Blow up sea-winds along Paumanok's shore;
I wait and I wait till you blow my mate to me . . .

perhaps hexameters:

I, chanter of pains and joys, uniter of here and hereafter,
Taking all hints to use them, but swiftly leaping beyond them. . . .

Rhythmical figures are likely to be repeated. The first line has the same figure twice (— ◡ ◡ — ◡), the Sapphic combination of dactyl and trochee. Sometimes he uses this motif without the final unaccented syllable, so that it becomes the choriambus (— ◡ ◡ —). Whitman may not have thought in these terms, but he did feel in these rhythms. These two figures, in the first dozen lines, make up nearly the whole texture:

— ◡ ◡ — ◡   — ◡ ◡ —

Out of the cradle
endlessly rocking
Out of the mocking-
musical shuttle
Out of the Ninth-month
Over the sterile
sands and the fields be-   -yond where the child
                                  leaving his bed
                                  wander'd alone

bareheaded, barefoot
Down from the shower'd
Up from the mystic
twining and twisting   they were alive
Out from the patches
briers and blackber-

                                  chanted to me
                                  memories sad

risings and fallings
under that yellow   -risen and swol-
                                  yearning and love
                                  there in the mist
                                  never to cease

Sound attracts sound, we said, in speaking of alliteration and assonance. And units of rhythm attract similar units. If we find one amphimacer (—⏑—), chances are we will find another, and then another:

> Sāt thĕ lōne | sīngĕr wōn | dĕrfŭl | cāusĭng tēars . . .
>
> Whāt ĭs thāt | līttlĕ blāck | thīng Ĭ sēe . . . ?

Little wonder the lines are so musical.

About a half century after Whitman, a rhythm like his turns up in the work of Carl Sandburg:

> I am the prairie, mother of men, waiting,
> They are mine, the threshing crews eating beefsteak,
>   the farm boys driving steers to the railroad cattle pens . . .

LINE BREAKS

We have already seen that anyone who writes in verse, with or without meter, cares deeply about enjambment, the movement from one line to another. If writing in lines is one of the poet's chief distinctions, then using that movement to full effect will be an important goal. Notice what happens when, in Williams's "Dedication for a Plot of Ground," he begins to put verbs at the beginnings of lines—they're like little engines pushing the lines into alertness. Sometimes it's not only the line break but also a change of another sort that gives free verse enjambments their power, as in these two lines from Theodore Roethke's "Elegy for Jane":

> Oh, when she was sad, she cast herself down into such a pure depth,
> Even a father could not find her.

Here the movement from that long, drawn-out line to a shorter one is part of the power. But so, surely, is beginning the second of the two lines with a firmly stressed syllable.

Often line breaks are subtler. In the following short poem, notice the effect of the one clear enjambment from line 4 to line 5:

A Man Said to the Universe

A man said to the universe:
"Sir, I exist!"
"However," replied the universe,
"The fact has not created in me
5   A sense of obligation."

[1895]

STEPHEN CRANE (1871–1900)

While it is true that we have difficulty making generalizations about how a poet breaks his or her lines—it's often by intuition and practice as much as design—line breaks remain hugely important to the free verse poem. Try reading aloud the following short poem, pausing just slightly at the end of each line:

The Ache of Marriage

The ache of marriage:

thigh and tongue, beloved,
are heavy with it,
it throbs in the teeth

5   We look for communion
and are turned away, beloved,
each and each

It is leviathan and we
in its belly
10 looking for joy, some joy
not to be known outside it

two by two in the ark of
the ache of it.

                          [1964]
             DENISE LEVERTOV (1923–1997)

[8]/*leviathan:* the great fish that swallowed Jonah in the Old Testament

Sometimes free verse is organized in little stanzas or paragraphs:

Psalm

Veritas sequitur . . .

In the small beauty of the forest
The wild deer bedding down—
That they are there!

               Their eyes
5 Effortless, the soft lips
Nuzzle and the alien small teeth
Tear at the grass

             The roots of it
Dangle from their mouths
10 Scattering earth in the strange woods.
They who are there.

             Their paths
Nibbled thru the fields, the leaves that shade them
Hang in the distances
15 Of sun

The small nouns
Crying faith
In this in which the wild deer
Startle, and stare out.   [1965]
                                    GEORGE OPPEN (1908–1984)

Epigraph: **veritas sequitur:** *Latin, "Truth follows . . ." The allusion is to Thomas Aquinas, who said "Truth follows upon the being of things."*

For a change of pace, examine the jazzy syncopation of Suzanne Lummis's lines in the following poem:

Morning After the 6.1

At work we tell
and tell of disasters, wrack
of flood tides, windchill, uncontained
fires, eye of storm, core of volcano.
5   Remember the Sylmar when the ground
pitched like the deck of a ship?
the power lines jerked and snapped;
electricity bolted into the dark like
unspeakable language.
10   We are too happy to work. Survival
has gone to our heads like pirate rum.
Dead, stand back and make way—
we are the living.   [2005]
                                    SUZANNE LUMMIS (*b.* 1951)

[5]/ *Sylmar: part of Los Angeles thought to have been the epicenter for the 1971 earthquake, which became known as "the Sylmar."*

Again, as you encounter free verse, look at the pacing of the lines and think about how they are organized. We will conclude this section with one more contemporary example:

The Killer Instinct

No one can quite

get over it. It is summer and revenge
lies sweetly in the fields
with her legs open,
                    her Bo Peep
5   petticoats in ribbons.
                    Et tu,
cutie? Not

far away, alternate worlds
queue up

                to be auditioned,
                                chatting
10   despairingly among themselves,

        but nobody's called back. Revenge,

        our wretched darling, shakes the straw
        out of her hair
                        and shines herself
        into the reddest apple
15   on the highest bough.
                                Hanging tough
        through hundreds of such afternoons,
        worried into life
                        by lightning's play
        on elemental soup, her stalwart heart
        will rise again, slough off
20   loose brilliance
                        like a firecracker,
        and pack more melodies than Mozart.

        Love, revenge, remaindering . . .
        is this the end?
                        —The world pumps on,
        with all its gently pitiless muzak.

[1999]

RACHEL LODEN (*b.* 1948)

THE VARIABLE FOOT

William Carlos Williams, though he wrote poems in free verse, came to feel it was "not the answer." He rejected its looseness, going so far as to say that "free verse wasn't verse at all," since "all art is orderly." He did believe, however, that the traditional rhythms were no longer appropriate for the American idiom.

Williams thought he found his cue in the theories of Albert Einstein. If everything in our world is relative (this of course was never Einstein's thought), why not have a relative or "variable" foot in poetry? The three-line "triadic" units that he began to work with represented his "new measure." He advised us to count each line as a single beat—each line, that is, is considered a foot. Though his theory was far from clear to many of his readers, it enabled him to write some very good poems.

The Descent

        The descent beckons
                as the ascent beckoned.
                        Memory is a kind
        of accomplishment,

5   a sort of renewal
                         even
     an initiation, since the spaces it opens are new places
                inhabited by hordes
                     heretofore unrealized,
10 of new kinds—
                since their movements
                     are toward new objectives
     (even though formerly they were abandoned).

     No defeat is made up entirely of defeat—since
15 the world it opens is always a place
                formerly
                     unsuspected. A
     world lost,
                a world unsuspected,
20   beckons to new places
     and no whiteness (lost) is so white as the memory
     of whiteness   .

     With evening, love wakens
                though its shadows
25   which are alive by reason
     of the sun shining—
                grow sleepy now and drop away
                    from desire   .

     Love without shadows stirs now
30   beginning to awaken
                     as night
     advances.

     The descent
                made up of despairs
35   and without accomplishment
     realizes a new awakening:
                which is a reversal
     of despair.

                For what we cannot accomplish, what
40 is denied to love,
                what we have lost in the anticipation—
                    a descent follows,
     endless and indestructible   .   [1948]

                    WILLIAM CARLOS WILLIAMS (1883–1963)

    In his best poems the lines do move expressively, often doubling back on themselves as if in halting or agonized meditation:

     The descent beckons
            as the ascent beckoned.
                 Memory is a kind. . . .

The isolation of some words forces us to ponder their meaning—the implications of "even," for example, in line 6 or "formerly" in line 16. Other lines (17, 21) hurry us urgently ahead.

Though Williams denied that the iamb fits American speech, the very words he used to make his denial are themselves iambic, especially if we change his "is not" to the more American "'s not":

The ĭ | ămb's nōt | thĕ nōr | măl mēas | ŭre ŏf | Āmēr | ĭcăn spēech . . .

Whatever he may have said about iambs, he retains many of them in his "new rhythm." A late poem, "Asphodel, That Greeny Flower," begins:

Ŏf ās | phŏdēl, | thăt grēen | y̆ flōw | ĕr,
　　　lĭke ă būt | tĕrcūp
　　　　　ŭpōn | ĭts brānch | ĭng stēm—
săve thăt | ĭt's grēen | ănd wōod | ĕn—
5　　　　Ī cōme, | my̆ swēet, |
　　　　　tŏ sīng | tŏ yōu . . .

We can tell one "variable foot" from another by the way each is placed on the page. Such positioning on the page—sometimes called **spatial prosody** or **visual prosody**—has been encouraged in our time by the use of the typewriter, since its precise spacing can indicate, as Charles Olson (one modern theorist) has said, "the breath, the pauses, the suspensions even of syllables." He explains, in his essay "Projective Verse":

> If a contemporary poet leaves a space as long as the phrase before it, he means that space to be held, by the breath, an equal length of time. If he suspends a word or syllable at the end of a line . . . he means that time to pass that it takes the eye . . . to pick up the next line.

Olson makes use of the multiple margin of the typewriter by moving it to the right or left to indicate progress, regress, or return. Spacing becomes one more analogy poets can use. (Cummings, of course, had done this decades before Olson reduced it to a system.)

CONCRETE POETRY AND SHAPED POETRY

Typography can even be made to act out what it is saying, as in this poem, which shows us the two *likes* being attracted.

Like Attracts Like

like   attracts   like

like   attracts   like

like   attracts   like

like   attracts   like

like   attracts   like

like attracts like

like attracts like

likeattractslike

likeattractlike

likattraclike

likttralike

liktralike

likliks

[1967]
EMMETT WILLIAMS (*b.* 1925)

Constructions like this one, which use typography to make a little picture of their subject on the page, are known as **concrete** or **spatialist poetry;** it has enjoyed a vogue not only in recent decades but as long ago as the days of ancient Greece, where it was known as *technopaignia,* or *playing around with technique.* We see an example from the seventeenth century in George Herbert's "Easter-Wings" (see Anthology, p. 382). Poems have been designed in the shape of swans, neckties, watches, automobiles—almost anything.

Hansjörg Mayer (*b.* 1943) shows us the bubbliness and drippiness of oil by splashing on the page the letters that make up the word:

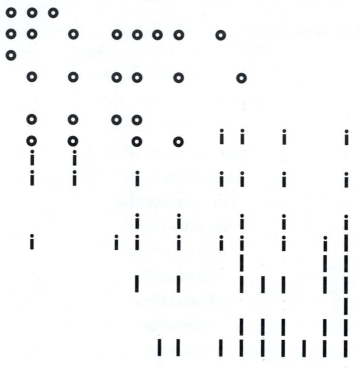

[1969]
HANSJÖRG MAYER (*b.* 1943)

In a contemporary example of *carmina figuata,* as "shaped poetry" came to be called in Latin, Jan D. Hodge gives us the image of a carousel figure. However, Hodge is also using an aural technique in his dactylic and anapestic rhythms, matching the motion of the object he describes.

Carousel

for Evelyn Conley

```
              why is
      a      carousel sad
     and exact why is it
  turning forever around      in
my head? why is its music     its
movement as real as glass?    when
 if  at all will the melody   end?
  dreamlike my memories die   into
    animals   prancing around in a
    formal    procession to nowhere
    calico   horses pace    up and              down
    and a    tiger a    lion a zebra         move round
      to       the    music alongside a    bracket of swans as
             a    host of golden haired cherubs lean down from   the
                 clouds and throw kisses  at cherubs that reaching from
                 mirrors throw kisses at  them and the kisses are   lost
      on the    wind and the music and  movement and kisses all   waft
    over water to                  me                    in  this
     dream of a carousel wishes hitch  rides on the horses the lion
      the zebra parading past mirrors  where cherubs reach up from
      the sky      to throw kisses at cherubs who ride on the   soft
       light          of clouds and    kisses and horses       and
      wishes              ride             sadly around        and
       around             till            they waste           on
         the              wind            and music
       comes              over            the water
         to               call            in a  sigh
                          for             a circle
                          of              animals
                                      lost   in a
                                    song       on
                                    the
                                    wind
```

[1997]

JAN D. HODGE (*b.* 1942)

THE PROSE POEM

"The prose poem is like a dog that talks," wrote Charles Simic, and indeed there is something unlikely about the form. Charles Baudelaire, who began his "Little Poems in Prose" in the 1850s, was the best known but not the first of the writers of prose poems in France, where the form arose. While it remains difficult to define, examples of good prose poetry abound from writers as diverse as T. S. Eliot, W. H. Auden, James Wright, and Russell Edson. In writing such works, the poet gives up all the advantages of the line and the line break, yet strives to create a poem-like object—something that strikes us as being essentially memorable, intense, and intentional. Sometimes the prose poem crosses genres with the short-short stories of fiction writers, or "sudden fiction." The following prose poem by Robert Hass may be a case in point:

A Story About the Body

The young composer, working that summer at an artist's colony, had watched her for a week. She was Japanese, a painter, almost sixty, and he thought he was in love with her. He loved her work, and her work was like the way she moved her body, used her hands, looked at him directly when she made amused and considered answers to his questions. One night, walking back from a concert, they came to her door and she turned to him and said, "I think you would like to have me. I would like that too, but I must tell you that I have had a double mastectomy," and when he didn't understand, "I've lost both my breasts." The radiance that he had carried around in his belly and chest cavity—like music—withered very quickly, and he made himself look at her when he said, "I'm sorry. I don't think I could." He walked back to his own cabin through the pines, and in the morning he found a small blue bowl on the porch outside his door. It looked to be full of rose petals, but he found when he picked it up that the rose petals were on top; the rest of the bowl—she must have swept them from the corners of her studio—was full of dead bees.

[1989]
Robert Hass (*b.* 1941)

Other prose poems are more intensely lyrical:

Part of Eve's Discussion

It was like the moment when a bird decides not to eat from your hand, and flies, just before it flies, the moment the rivers seem to still and stop because a storm is coming, but there is no storm, as when a hundred starlings lift and bank together before they wheel and drop, very much like the moment, driving on bad ice, when it occurs to you your car could spin, just before it slowly begins to spin, like the moment just before you forgot what it was you were about to say, it was like that, and after that, it was still like that, only all the time.

[1988]

MARIE HOWE (b. 1950)

Like the free verse poet, the prose poet has to work by instinct. But good poets in meter often feel the same way. They proceed by studying models of the form. The prose poet will be particularly attuned to questions of narrative detail—what to leave out—and sentence rhythms. To finish, look at an example of the prose poem as elegant meditation:

Trains in Winter

Over first coffee, I ride the diner and look out at snow fallen deep in gorges. At winter stations, a locomotive can freeze to the rails, and a mountain night turn so cold it makes the rails snap. Some trains in heavy snow overtake a moose herd along a roadbed, then sweep a few cows into the ravine, or maybe a bull crossing a trestle will go on through, catching his legs between the ties. I've seen icebergs melting in a Newfoundland cove, their fresh water icing to a clear glaze. I've heard of sister ships passing at sea, on their last crossing, while on deck a few passengers wave. Tapestries in smoking rooms, shipboard mysteries. There is so much tonnage to our lives, as if civility required an enormous effort, if only for a little sweetness, a little wine.

Hope's the pure country I was born to, where trains run on schedule in their periodic and beneficent sadness. I want to forget the casual insults that often pass for humor, and imagine the letters lovers might write, or the letters friends send every winter as their sentences cross the distance of a page. Their words are like a train arriving in Los Angeles while another train approaches the desert, and still another leaves the Chicago yards. Tonight I want to lie in my bed and listen to trains moving across America toward a place still humanly possible, desirable if difficult, a day's journey away.

[2004]

JAY MEEK (b. 1937)

EXERCISES & DIVERSIONS

A.   Iris

a burst of iris so that
come down for
breakfast
we searched through the
rooms for
that

        sweetest odor and at
        first could not
        find its

        source then a blue as
        of the sea
        struck

        startling us from among
        those trumpeting
        petals

                                        [1962]
                    WILLIAM CARLOS WILLIAMS (1883–1963)

Line breaks indicate a pause, however slight (if only while the eye
returns to the left-hand margin); stanza breaks indicate a stronger
pause. When a reviewer objected that in "Iris" the breaks were
arbitrary, eccentric, against the habits of ordinary speech, an admirer
of Williams countered that they were expressive and "functional." The
break between "its" and "source," for example, dramatizes the poet's
halting bewilderment as he looks for the source of the fragrance. Would
you agree that Williams's "visual prosody" (the way of indicating
rhythm by the spacing on the page) is meaningful? Are his line breaks
natural pauses?

B. Here is a poem originally written in lines but typed now in prose, "Not
Waving but Drowning," by Stevie Smith.

    Nobody heard him, the dead man, but still he lay moaning: I was much
    further out than you thought and not waving but drowning. Poor chap,
    he always loved larking and now he's dead it must have been too cold
    for him his heart gave way, they said. Oh, no no no, it was too cold
    always (still the dead one lay moaning) I was much too far out all my
    life and not waving but drowning.

    Try breaking it into lines and stanzas yourself. When you are done,
    look at how Smith did it (Anthology, p. 464). What do you learn about
    line breaks from this comparison?

C. Find a poem you like written in lines. Now write it out as prose. Is it as
effective?

D. In each of the following examples, what is effective or ineffective about
the verse technique?

    1. *Starglow* dwarf china rose shrubthorn
        lantern fashion-fare airing car-tire crushed
        young's churning old rambler's flown
        to sky can cut back. . . .

                                        LOUIS ZUKOVSKY

    2. My head and shoulders, and my book
        In the cool shade, and my body

Stretched bathing in the sun, I lie
Reading beside the waterfall—
Boehme's "Signature of All Things."

KENNETH REXROTH

3. The pact that we made was the ordinary pact
    of men & women in those days

    I don't know who we thought we were
    that our personalities
    could resist the failures of the race

ADRIENNE RICH

4. Do not wake me, for I am not ready
    to speak, to break the spell
    fixed in these sleeping stones.

JOHN HAINES

5. And who can stand to be
    made up for good? And who can face
    being adored? I swear

    there is no frame
    that I would keep you in.

HEATHER McHUGH

E. Examine long-lined poems by Walt Whitman, Robinson Jeffers,
    Kenneth Fearing, and C. K. Williams. Read examples aloud. How are
    these long lines organized, and how does each poet differ tonally from
    the others?
F. Examine short-lined poems by Kay Ryan, Yusef Komunyakaa, and
    Gary Soto. How effective are these lines and line breaks?

ESSAYS

A. Once you have tried out exercises E. and F. above, write an essay about
    one poet's use of line length. What appears to determine the length of
    his or her free-verse lines? How does the poet use sentence syntax,
    repetition, line breaks, imagery, and other organizing tools? How do
    these technical choices contribute to the meaning of the poem?
B. Write a defense of or an attack on prose poetry as a genre.
C. Write an essay on visual or concrete poetry. You may look up more
    examples on your own. What technical observations are you called
    upon to make about composition, color, or lack thereof? If this book
    most often views poetry as speech, how can you describe a particular
    poet's non-aural poems?

POEMS

A. Take a poem of yours that does not seem to have come to life yet. If it is in short lines, rewrite it in longer lines. If it is in long lines, rewrite it in shorter ones. How will stanza breaks, lines breaks, and enjambments be useful as you revise? What needs to be added? What subtracted?

B. Try writing a poem in your own version of Williams's "variable foot."

C. Collect lines and images from periodicals and see if you can compose a collage poem.

D. Write a prose poem of one-half page or less, making use of either one long sentence, a series of short sentences, or a deliberate change of sentence rhythms.

SIX

The Mind

12

THE SHAPE OF THOUGHT

Sentences and Structure

THE SENTENCE

Up to now we have been dealing with the more physical aspects of poetry: sensation, emotion, voice with its sounds and rhythms. All of these, of course, we experience in our consciousness. What the brain does not register might as well not exist for us. Even our sensuality has nothing but mind to reside in.

But there are elements of poetry that seem to have a more intellectual character than those we have looked at. One of these is the way poets organize the sentences of their poems. The sentence represents, in greatly simplified form, an act of the mind. In *greatly* simplified form: Since the brain has more cells to work with than there are people on this planet, any mental process is almost infinitely complex. When the mind can simplify its complexities so that they can be expressed in words, they naturally come forth as sentences. As Ernest Fenollosa, the student of Oriental languages, put it: "The sentence form was forced upon primitive man by nature itself."

"To write a poem," said Robert Frost, "is to go a-sentencing." A writer's state of mind, or that of the characters he or she creates, can determine the shape of the sentences that reveal that state of mind. Such shapes can be not only expressive but also symbolic of their content. In psychological experiments, people have been asked to draw lines they felt would express certain emotional states. Lines felt as beautiful were smoothly curved, unbroken, symmetrical. Lines felt as ugly were jagged, with mixed angles and irregular twists. Sentences can express us and affect us in much the same way. At a celebration once held at Rutgers for the centennial of the birth of James Joyce,

one of the subjects under consideration was the effect the nonlinear sentence
might have on the nervous system.

When at the beginning of Shakespeare's *Richard III* the future king is
confident, exulting in thoughts of his coming triumphs, his language flows
forth in harmonious sentences:

> Now is the winter of our discontent
> Made glorious summer by this sun of York;
> And all the clouds that loured upon our house
> In the deep bosom of the ocean buried.
> Now are our brows bound with victorious wreaths,
> Our bruisèd arms hung up for monuments,
> Our stern alarums changed to merry meetings,
> Our dreadful marches to delightful measures.
> Grim-visaged War hath smoothed his wrinkled front,
> And now, instead of mounting barbèd steeds
> To fright the souls of fearful adversaries,
> He capers nimbly in a lady's chamber
> To the lascivious pleasing of a lute. . . .

But when toward the close of the play he is guilt-ridden, terrified by ghosts
that tell him to despair and die, his sentences are abrupt, staccato:

> The lights burn blue. It is now dead midnight.
> Cold fearful drops stand on my trembling flesh.
> What do I fear? Myself? There's none else by.
> Richard loves Richard: that is, I am I.
> Is there a murderer here? No. Yes, I am.
> Then fly. What, from myself? Great reason why!
> Lest I revenge. What, myself upon myself? . . .

When poets, or other writers, can give their sentences a shape that will
dramatize their meaning, they try to do so. When Eugenio Montale, later
awarded the Nobel Prize, took as a symbol the life cycle of the eel, he wrote
his poem (the original of course in Italian) in one long sentence—an incomplete
one at that. The effect is to dramatize, in the very thrust of the words,
the tireless energy that shows itself in nature. Is not this vitality, the poet asks,
like the life force that sparkles so beautifully in the eyes of a woman?

The Eel

> The eel, the
> siren of sleety seas, abandoning
> the Baltic for our waters,
> our estuaries, our
> 5 freshets, to lash upcurrent under the brunt
> of the flood, sunk deep, from brook to brook and then

trickle to trickle dwindling,
more inner always, always more in the heart
of the rock, thrusting
10   through ruts of the mud, until, one day,
explosion of splendor from the chestnut groves
kindles a flicker in deadwater sumps,
in ditches pitched
from ramparts of the Appennine to Romagna;
15   eel: torch and whip,
arrow of love on earth,
which nothing but our gorges or bone-dry
gutters of the Pyrenees ushers back
to edens of fertility;
20   green soul that probes
for life where only
fevering heat or devastation preys,
spark that says
the whole commences when the whole would seem
25   charred black, an old stick buried;
brief rainbow, twin
to that within your lashes' dazzle, that
you keep alive, inviolate, among
the sons of men, steeped in your mire—in this
30   not recognize a sister?   [1957]

EUGENIO MONTALE (1896–1981)

Short sentences, or sentences made up of short elements, may express a nervous discharge of energy, as in the poems of Emily Dickinson. Gwendolyn Brooks uses three-word sentences to express energy recklessly expended.

We Real Cool

The Pool Players.
Seven at the Golden Shovel.

We real cool. We
Left school. We

Lurk late. We
Strike straight. We

5   Sing sin. We
Thin gin. We

Jazz June. We
Die soon.   [1960]

GWENDOLYN BROOKS (1917–2000)

Very long sentences or very short ones are the extremes. In between are many possibilities.

USE OF CONNECTIVES

The very way the parts of a sentence are held together may be significant. A series of connectives like "and . . . and . . . and" can be childish—or it can be solemnly impressive, as in the first chapter of Genesis:

> In the beginning God created the heaven and the earth. And the earth was without form, and void; and darkness was upon the face of the deep. And the Spirit of God moved upon the face of the waters. And God said, "Let there be light": and there was light.

Frost uses many *and*'s for drowsy monotony at the beginning of "Out, Out—," in which a fatal accident happens because people are tired after a long day's work (see Anthology, p. 439).

When conjunctions are omitted, the tone can be one of abruptness and energy, as in Caesar's famous *"Veni, vidi, vici"*—"I came, I saw, I conquered." The omission of connectives that express logical relationships ("therefore," "because," "if," "although," and the like) is common in primitive languages. We might represent a typical pattern as: "Man hungry. He shoot arrow. Kill deer. Man happy." Poetry, caring more for the sensory details than for the logical relationship between them, is especially inclined to use this kind of construction. It is called **parataxis,** or *setting side by side.* The author of the poem "Western Wind" never specifies the connection between the wind and the rain and his love. Dreams, too, work purely by means of parataxis; since they have no easy way of indicating logical relationships, they set objects, persons, or situations meaningfully next to one another. So do some poems.

The Message

The door that someone opened wide
The door that someone shut again
The chair where someone came to sit
The cat that someone cuddled there
5   The fruit that someone bit into
The letter someone read and read
The chair that someone overturned
The door that someone opened wide
The road where someone's running yet
10 The woods that someone's passing through
The river someone's jumping in
The hospital where someone's dead.

[1972]
JACQUES PRÉVERT (1900–1977)

It has been suggested that such parataxis makes us feel the poem is coming into being as we read it. Life, we might even say, is all parataxis: It presents us with situations and events; we have to determine their logical relationships.

PARALLELISM

One of the most ancient and powerful ways of organizing a sentence is to give corresponding parts corresponding expression. **Parallelism,** which is a kind of rhythm, is to be found in the poetry of all languages. We recognize it in such biblical cadences as those of Psalm 19, already quoted in the previous chapter, or in William Carlos Williams's "Dedication for a Plot of Ground." We recognize it too in the characteristic rhythms of Walt Whitman.

I Hear America Singing

I hear America singing, the varied carols I hear,
Those of mechanics, each one singing his as it should be blithe and
    strong,
The carpenter singing his as he measures his plank or beam,
The mason singing his as he makes ready for work, or leaves off work,
5   The boatman singing what belongs to him in his boat, the deckhand
    singing on the steamboat deck,
The shoemaker singing as he sits on his bench, the hatter singing as he
    stands,
The wood-cutter's song, the ploughboy's on his way in the morning, or
    at noon intermission or at sundown.
The delicious singing of the mother, or of the young wife at work, or of
    the girl sewing or washing,
Each singing what belongs to him or her and to none else,
10 The day what belongs to the day—at night the party of young fellows,
    robust, friendly,
Singing with open mouths their strong melodious songs.   [1867]
                            WALT WHITMAN (1819–1892)

Parallel structures, by reinforcing each other, strengthen the sentence, paragraph, or poem they make up. Suppose we want to tell how once in battle a horseshoe nail fell out of a horseshoe, so that the horse was crippled and couldn't be managed—was in fact useless—with the result that horse and rider became ineffective as a combat unit. Since that rider played a key role in the battle plan, his loss led to the defeat of his army, so that the government also fell. All because a nail was lost!

    Concentrating these gangling elements into parallel clauses, we get the famous verses quoted by Benjamin Franklin and hung as a reminder in the offices of the Anglo-American Supply Quarters in London in World War II:

For want of a nail, the shoe was lost,
For want of a shoe, the horse was lost,
For want of a horse, the rider was lost,
For want of a rider, the battle was lost,
For want of a battle, the kingdom was lost,
And all for the want of a horseshoe nail.

In the following poem, reasons to love America are made more urgent and conflicted by the parallel usage of the conjunction "because."

Learning to Love America

because it has no pure products

because the Pacific Ocean sweeps along the coastline
because the water of the ocean is cold
and because land is better than ocean

5   because I say we rather than they

because I live in California
I have eaten fresh artichokes
and jacarandas bloom in April and May

because my senses have caught up with my body
10   my breath with the air it swallows
my hunger with my mouth

because I walk barefoot in my house

because I have nursed my son at my breast
because he is a strong American boy
15   because I have seen his eyes redden when he is asked who he is
because he answers I don't know

because to have a son is to have a country
because my son will bury me here
because countries are in our blood and we bleed them

20   because it is late and too late to change my mind
because it is time.   [1998]

SHIRLEY GEOK-LIN LIM (*b*. 1944)

When two or more lines begin with the same word, it is called **anaphora.**

Sometimes the parallel elements are crisscrossed, as in lines 4 and 6 of this passage from Yeats's "Easter 1916":

The horse that comes from the road,
The rider, the birds that range
From cloud to tumbling cloud,
Minute by minute they change;
A shadow of cloud on the stream
Changes minute by minute. . . .

This figure is called **chiasmus,** from the X-shaped Greek letter *chi*. A simple example would be: "I like football; baseball I hate."

Parallelism that contrasts words or ideas (often by means of "but" or a word like it) is called **antithesis;** it emphasizes conflicting materials by setting them sharply together. Alexander Pope, like other poets of the rational eighteenth century, likes to strike sparks by clashing the flint of one idea against the steel of another:

> Authors are partial to their wit, 'tis true,
> But are not critics to their judgment too?

> True wit is nature to advantage dressed,
> What oft was thought, but ne'er so well expressed.

SENTENCE STRUCTURE

Breaking up the shape of the sentence, some have felt, might enable us to get closer to the complex reality it oversimplifies. Some of the experiments of James Joyce and others have been directed to this end. So have some of the ancient figures of speech, which, as we have seen, are really ways of thinking.

Inversion of the normal word order is one of the most obvious of these figures of speech. Sometimes even good writers have been known to wrench words out of the natural order because they "need them there" for the rhyme or the rhythm; this is always an ugliness:

> Fast to the roof cleave may my tongue
> If mindless I of thee be found. . . .
>
> THOMAS CAMPION

> . . . Old acquaintances
>   Seem do we. . . .
>
> THOMAS HARDY

Not all inversions are bad. Some we hear in colloquial speech. "But nice she is!" "A genius he is *not!*" Only our sense of spoken English tells us which inversions come naturally.

Milton uses inversion well when he says of Satan:

>   Him the Almighty Power
> Hurled headlong flaming from the ethereal sky
> With hideous ruin and combustion down
> To bottomless perdition . . .

This is upside-down—but so was Satan. When Andrew Marvell says of fate:

> And therefore her decrees of steel
> Us as the distant poles have placed. . . .

we can see that he is dramatizing the worldwide separation of the lovers by isolating "us" in the sentence.

E. E. Cummings uses inversion expressively in his little poem about the glance exchanged between a poisoned mouse and its poisoner.

Me up at does

Me up at does

out of the floor
quietly Stare

a poisoned mouse

5   still who alive

is asking What
have i done that

You wouldn't have   [1963]

                                   E. E. CUMMINGS (1894–1962)

Normally we look down on the helpless mouse. In this poem it is the reproachful upward glance of the mouse that is more telling; the words reverse as the electrical charge of the glance does.

Parenthesis also interrupts the conventional order of syntax in the interests of fidelity to thought. In a love poem of the Elizabethan Nicholas Breton, Coridon is so enraptured with his Phillida that he can speak hardly a line without exclamations of parenthetic enthusiasm:

Fair in a morn (O fairest morn,
   Was never morn so fair!)
There shone a sun, though not the sun
   That shineth in the air.
5   For the earth and from the earth
   (Was never such a creature!)
Did come this face (was never face
   That carried such a feature!).
Upon a hill (O blessèd hill,
10   Was never hill so blessèd!)
There stood a man (was never man
   For woman so distressèd!). . . .

In Shakespeare's *Cymbeline* the guilty Iachimo is less happily distraught; his stricken parentheses play havoc with the sentence:

Upon a time (unhappy was the clock
That struck the hour!)—it was in Rome (accursed
The mansion where!)—'twas at a feast (Oh, would
Our viands had been poisoned, or at least
Those which I heaved to head!)—the good Posthumus
(What should I say? . . .)

We see a particularly emotional parenthesis (using dashes) in Frost's "Out, Out—" (Anthology, p. 439):

> . . . Then the boy saw all—
> Since he was old enough to know, big boy
> Doing a man's work, though a child at heart—
> He saw all spoiled.

There are other ways to break up the normal sentence structure to follow the working of the mind. We can start a sentence according to one pattern and abruptly abandon it midcourse for another. "What I'd really like to—how about a long walk?" We all use the device, called **anacolúthon** *(not following)*, when impulse or a better thought cancels what we were about to say. Peter Viereck's unhappy and ungrammatical lover is entangled in it the moment he says "is" in the first line.

To Helen of Troy (N.Y.)

> I sit here with the wind is in my hair;
> I huddle like the sun is in my eyes;
> I am (I wished you'd contact me) alone.
>
> A fat lot you'd wear crape if I was dead.
> It figures, who I heard there when I phoned you;
> It figures, when I came there, who has went.
>
> Dogs laugh at me, folks bark at me since then;
> "She is," they say, "no better than she ought to";
> I love you irregardless how they talk.
>
> You should of done it (which it is no crime)
> With me you should of done it, what they say.
> I sit here with the wind is in my hair.   [1967]

Peter Viereck (b. 1916)

The incoherence of passion can also shatter the structure of a sentence, as when King Lear struggles to express himself to his unnatural daughters:

> I will have such revenges on you both
> That all the world shall—I will do such things—
> What they are, yet I know not. . . .

We can also start a sentence and abruptly cut it off, perhaps with the "or else—!" that we know can speak louder than words. This is called **aposiopé-sis** *(falling silent)*. "Either you clean up your room, or else—!" Yeats likes to let passion interfere with sentence structure:

> Hanrahan rose in frenzy there
> And followed up those baying creatures towards—
>
> O towards I have forgotten what—enough!

In the poem that follows, the speaker is too choked with rage to continue.

Beyond Words

That row of icicles along the gutter
Feels like my armory of hate;
And you, you . . . you, you utter . . .
You wait!

[1947]
ROBERT FROST (1874–1963)

One of the poems of Alice Fulton, which is a favorite of her readers, dramatizes an aposiopesis.

What I Like

Friend—the face I wallow toward
through a scrimmage of shut faces.
Arms like towropes to haul me home, aide-
memoire, my lost childhood docks, a bottled ark
in harbor. *Friend*—I can't forget
how even the word contains an *end*.
We circle each other in a scared bolero,
imagining stratagems: postures and imposters.
Cold convictions keep us solo. I ahem
and hedge my affections. Who'll blow the first kiss,
land it like the lifeforces we feel
tickling at each wrist? It should be easy
easy to take your hand, whisper down this distance
labeled hers or his: what I like about you is

[1983]
ALICE FULTON (b. 1952)

John Clare, the nineteenth-century poet who spent the last decades of his
life in a benevolent insane asylum, was indifferent to sentence structure and
punctuation in the wild tumble of words in his love song to Mary.

Remember Dear Mary

Remember dear Mary love cannot deceive
Loves truth cannot vary dear Mary believe
You may hear and believe it believe it and hear
Love could not deceive those features so dear
Believe me dear Mary to press thy soft hand
Is sweeter than riches in houses and Land

Where I pressed thy soft hand at the dewfall o' eve
I felt the sweet tremble that cannot deceive
If love you believe in Belief is my love
As it lived once in Eden ere we fell from above
To this heartless this friendless this desolate earth
And kept in first love Immortality's birth

'Tis there we last meet I adore thee and love thee
Theres nothing beneath thee around thee above thee
15　I feel it and know it I know so and feel
If your love cannot show it mine cannot conceal
But knowing I love I feel and adore
And the more I behold—only loves thee the more　　　[date uncertain]

JOHN CLARE (1793–1864)

Besides traveling at different paces and in different manners, sentences can also take us through different sectors of the language, or even break into regions not previously explored. The rest of this chapter will present a few samplings of the many kinds of terrain in which poets can go a-sentencing.

THINKING ABOUT DICTION

Language has many levels, from the crudest to the most sublime. Poets avail themselves of an appropriate level—or sometimes get ironic effects by seeking out a deliberately inappropriate one.

We are familiar with the language governments use in their press releases. We know that if our side has suffered a humiliating rout, official headlines can make things seem all right with "BRILLIANT STRATEGIC RETREAT CONFUSES FOE!" Robert Graves writes in this mode about the Battle of Marathon (490 B.C.), in which the outnumbered Athenians won a surprising victory over the "barbarians," as they called the Persians. Generally we read the Athenian version, as given by Herodotus: "There fell in the battle of Marathon, on the side of the barbarians, about six thousand and four hundred men; on that of the Athenians, one hundred and ninety-two." Graves imagines how the Persian press releases might have explained the incident at home.

The Persian Version

Truth-loving Persians do not dwell upon
The trivial skirmish fought near Marathon.
As for the Greek theatrical tradition
Which represents that summer's expedition
5　Not as a mere reconnaissance in force
By three brigades of foot and one of horse
(Their left flank covered by some obsolete
Light craft detached from the main Persian fleet)
But as a grandiose, ill-starred attempt
10　To conquer Greece—they treat it with contempt;
And only incidentally refute
Major Greek claims, by stressing what repute
The Persian monarch and the Persian nation
Won by this salutary demonstration:

15 Despite a strong defence and adverse weather
All arms combined magnificently together.   [1951]
ROBERT GRAVES (1895–1985)

Drawing on the horror movies of the late-late shows in his poem about
cat people, Edward Field uses a diction that accepts in a matter-of-fact way
the melodramatic improbabilities of such films.

Curse of the Cat Woman

It sometimes happens
that the woman you meet and fall in love with
is of that strange Transylvanian people
with an affinity for cats.

5 You take her to a restaurant, say, or a show,
on an ordinary date, being attracted
by the glitter in her slitty eyes and her catlike walk,
and afterwards of course you take her in your arms
and she turns into a black panther
10 and bites you to death.

Or perhaps you are saved in the nick of time
and she is tormented by the knowledge of her tendency:
That she daren't hug a man
unless she wants to risk clawing him up.

15 This puts you both in a difficult position—
panting lovers who are prevented from touching
not by bars but by circumstance:
You have terrible fights and say cruel things
for having the hots does not give you a sweet temper.

20 One night you are walking down a dark street
and hear the pad-pad of a panther following you,
but when you turn around there are only shadows,
or perhaps one shadow too many.

You approach, calling, "Who's there?"
25 and it leaps on you.
Luckily you have brought along your sword
and you stab it to death.

And before your eyes it turns into the woman you love,
her breast impaled on your sword,
30 her mouth dribbling blood saying she loved you
but couldn't help her tendency.

So death released her from the curse at last,
and you knew from the angelic smile on her dead face
that in spite of a life the devil owned,
35 love had won, and heaven pardoned her.   [1967]
EDWARD FIELD (b. 1924)

CREATING NEW WORDS

Probably the first step toward new ways of sentencing is a reworking of the word itself. New insights, new awarenesses sometimes demand new words; or new words can prove to be new insights. In each quotation that follows is a word we would not find in an ordinary dictionary, and yet the meaning is clear:

> . . . Over him arches
> UNITED STATES OF AMERICA, and, squinched in
> Between that and his rump, E PLURIBUS UNUM. . . .
>
> HOWARD NEMEROV

> . . . fields and hedges, the scarlotry of
> maple leaves. . . .
>
> A. R. AMMONS

"Squinched" and "scarlotry" are made up of words we know: the first, of such words as "squeeze," "scrunch," "pinch"; the second, of "scarlet" and "harlotry." They are like the "portmanteau" words that Lewis Carroll made up so successfully: "chortle" (from "chuckle" and "snort"), "galumph" (from "gallop" and "triumph").

Of an "antique spaniel" who can hardly walk, Mark Doty writes:

> . . . when he falls
> and looks up from those droozed,
> ancient eyes . . .

We are not likely to find "droozed" in any dictionary. Yet we can guess what it means by relating it to words it resembles.

In a poem about Robert Frost, May Swenson, without inventing new words, uses typography to reveal the words that are hidden in other words. Part of it reads:

> Lots of trees in the fo
> rest but this one's an O
> a K that's plan
> ted hims elf . . .

> His sig nature's on the he art
> of his time. . . .

Spelling "forest" as fo / rest emphasizes the "rest" (or peace) in that forest— even for an enemy or "fo." The "oak" is an O / a K because it is a fine oak, an OK oak. Frost, as oak, has not merely planted himself but *plan*ned to plant "hims" (hymns) and is *elf*ish, mischievous. "His sig nature" emphasizes its *natural*ness; his heart is a kind of "he art," or masculine art. In these few lines are many more such ghostly conjurings. In a Halloween poem she switches consonants as children like to do: A frosty night becomes the "A Nosty Fright" of her title, and familiar plants are disguised as "the sack-eyed blusan and the wistle theed," in a world of nine peedles and risted twoots.

Not all poets are inclined to break up or invent words. Some, like classic poker players, prefer to stick with the game as it is. On their side would be Frost himself, who stubbornly declares, "We play the words as we find them. We make them do."

John Berryman, in his "Dream Songs" (see Anthology, p. 476), has devised what often sounds like a new language. He has done this by combining various voices that range from hieratic English in the grand style to dialect and baby talk—a selection from the many tones possible to a psyche split many ways.

The nonadventure of "4" is typical of the poet's manner. ("Mr. Bones," or "Sir Bones," is the name for the end man in a minstrel show who clacked out castanetlike rhythms on the "bones.") "22" becomes clear if we recall that Thomas Jefferson and John Adams both died on the Fourth of July, 1826. Adams, knowing that death was near, roused himself to say, "Thomas Jefferson survives." But Jefferson had died a few hours before Adams did. The twelve characters of the first two stanzas might be seen as typical of the TV-watching public that makes up the nation such men as Jefferson and Adams founded. The poem might have a solemn message: We are unworthy of the heroes who founded our country. But it never takes so indignant or preachy a tone. For all of their basic passion, the voices themselves are colloquial and—in their dark way—amusing.

A poet who goes further in conjuring up a language of his own is Cummings.

wherelings whenlings

wherelings whenlings
(daughters of ifbut offspring of hopefear
sons of unless and children of almost)
never shall guess the dimension of

5   him whose
each
foot likes the
here of this earth

whose both
10   eyes
love
this now of the sky

—endlings of isn't
shall never

15 begin
to begin to

imagine how(only are shall be were
dawn dark rain snow rain
-bow &
20 a

moon
's whis-
per
in sunset

25 or thrushes toward dusk among whippoorwills or
tree field rock hollyhock forest brook chickadee
mountain. Mountain)
whycoloured worlds of because do

not stand against yes which is built by
30 forever & sunsmell
(sometimes a wonder
of wild roses

sometimes)
with north
35 over
the barn

[1940]
E. E. CUMMINGS (1894–1962)

Cummings does only one thing that seems new here: He lets any part of speech serve for any other part. Conjunctions can be nouns, adverbs can be adjectives, pronouns can be verbs—anything can be anything. We might think of this as a modern invention, but the practice is so old that the grammarians had many names for it.

The Old English suffix "-ling" has many meanings. It can mean *having the quality of,* as "darlings" are *dear,* and "hirelings" are *hired.* It can mean *concerned with,* as "worldlings" are concerned with the *world.* It can be a diminutive, as in "gosling" and "suckling." Often it has unfavorable overtones, as in "hireling." When Cummings refers to "wherelings" and "whenlings," he means *petty* people, concerned with the local and the temporary instead of the spiritual; wondering "Where am I?" and "When will I . . . ?" instead of living and doing—always conditional, tentative, irresolute. They live in a nonexistent future, vacillating between "hope" and "fear." They will not do things "unless"; they do them only "almost." People who are really alive care about not the *where* of this earth but "the here of this earth"; what their eyes love is not the *when* of the sky but "this now of the sky." Unless we really live, really *are,* it can never be said of us that we *were*—it will be as if we had never existed. "Whycoloured worlds" (those of whining *why? why? why?*) can never stand against "yes," which for Cummings means the wholehearted acceptance of life and living.

His poem "anyone lived in a pretty how town" (see Anthology, p. 458) is easy to follow once we realize that "anyone," like the medieval Everyman, is a typical human being who marries a typical "noone" (a nobody, as outsiders might think), lives a typical life, dies a typical death, and has what we think of as a typical hereafter.

EXERCISES & DIVERSIONS

A. What matters discussed in this chapter are illustrated by the following quotations?

1. Were I (who to my cost already am
    One of those strange, prodigious creatures, man)
    A spirit free to choose. . . .

    THE EARL OF ROCHESTER

2. Ask of the learn'd the way, the learn'd are blind,
    This bids to serve, and that to shun mankind;
    Some place the bliss in action, some in ease,
    Those call it pleasure, and contentment these;
    Some sunk to beasts, find pleasure end in pain;
    Some swelled to gods, confess ev'n virtue vain;
    Or indolent, to each extreme they fall,
    To trust in everything, or doubt of all.

    ALEXANDER POPE

3. But how shall I . . . make me room there:
    Reach me a . . . Fancy, come faster—
    Strike you the sight of it? look at it loom there,
    Thing that she . . . There then! the Master. . . .

    GERARD MANLEY HOPKINS

4. Lived a woman wonderful,
        (May the Lord amend her!)
    Neither simple, kind, nor true,
    But her Pagan beauty drew
    Christian gentlemen a few
        Hotly to attend her.

    RUDYARD KIPLING

5. If you have revisited this town, thin Shade,
    Whether to look upon your monument
    (I wonder if the builder has been paid). . . .

    WILLIAM BUTLER YEATS

6. The mountain held the town as in a shadow.
   I saw so much before I slept there once. . . .
   Near me it seemed. . . .

   ROBERT FROST

7. Troops went by the house and down the road and the dust they raised
   powdered the leaves of the trees. The trunks of the trees too were dusty
   and the leaves fell early that year and we saw the troops marching
   along the road and the dust rising and leaves, stirred by the breeze,
   falling and the soldiers marching and afterwards the road bare and
   white except for the leaves.

   ERNEST HEMINGWAY

8. . . . the last helicopter has thwonked back to the Marine base . . .

   CHARLES WRIGHT

9. The rabbit with his pink, distinctly, eyes. . . .

   JOHN UPDIKE

10. There's a kind of white moth, I don't know
    what kind, that glimmers, it does,
    in the daylight . . .

    MARY OLIVER

B. 1. If a poem is written in stanzas (units of the same shape and length), should each stanza be a sentence? If you look back over poems we have read, does it seem that sentences have a tendency to fit the stanza shape, so that stanzas are likely to end with a period?

2. How could a writer use form expressively by *not* stopping for the stanza break but by overriding it?

3. This stanzaic enjambment happens in "A Carriage from Sweden" (p. 450) and in "Bells for John Whiteside's Daughter" (p. 101)— with what effect in each?

4. Go a-sentencing through some of the poems we have read earlier, noticing—for this once at least—the interplay between sentence structure and the demands of the form. Point out some interesting effects.

C. 1. In "Acquainted with the Night" (p. 54), the length of the sentences, in number of lines, is 1, 1, 1, 1, 2, 7, 1. Is this structure related to meaning?

2. In "The End of the Weekend" (p. 12), what is the longest sentence? The shortest? Is the length significant?

D. 1. Quite a few expressions in "Curse of the Cat Woman" (p. 284) take on a special tone. How would you describe the tone of "It sometimes happens" (line 1), "that strange Transylvanian people" (line 3), "an affinity for cats" (line 4), "her tendency" (line 12), "or perhaps one shadow too many" (line 23), "Luckily you have brought along your sword" (line 26), "the woman you love" (line 28), "her breast impaled on" (line 29)?

2. In a differently handled poem, the last four lines might well be a hopeless tissue of clichés and sentimentality. What saves them here?

ESSAYS

A. Find a poem in this book in which the creative use of sentence structure seems especially important. Ask yourself what intellectual and emotional effects are produced by the poem's grammatical and rhetorical techniques; then write an essay defending or attacking the poem for its use of such techniques.

B. Many poems imply by technical or other means a realm of experience that cannot be expressed. Find such a poem in this book, and write an essay on the unspoken elements in the poem. As you conclude your essay, try to take a further step of clarifying the relationship of word to world. It will be difficult, but try it.

POEMS

A. Write a bad poem—sentimental, cliché-ridden—of about a dozen lines, ending up with the last four lines of Field's poem.

B. Write a list poem using either parataxis or parallelism.

C. Write a poem using deliberate anacolúthon or aposiopesis.

13

GOLDEN NUMBERS

On Nature and Form

If we leaf through a book of verse, we notice immediately that poetry, unlike prose, favors special conformations; it likes to arrange itself in shapes on the page. These shapes in space originally represented shapes in time—shapes to be heard if we were listening to a recitation rather than looking at a book.

In its love for shapeliness and proportion, poetry is like mathematics. Many readers, however, believe that poetry and mathematics are opposed in spirit. Such readers may be repelled by the pages that follow, with their drawings that seem to be straight out of Euclid. But no mathematical background is required—there are no problems to solve. The drawings are only to marvel at. And to be seen as analogies: They are really telling us something about the nature of poetry; and about nature itself.

To decide in advance that a poem will have seventeen syllables or fourteen lines or that it will be constructed in stanzaic units of this or that size or shape may seem arbitrary and artificial. When a poem begins to germinate in the poet's mind, could it not grow simply and naturally, the way a flower grows, instead of being forced to follow a pattern? This seems a good question—but it shows little knowledge of how flowers do grow. Nature has been working on its flowers for some millions of years; a close look at them, as at anything in the natural world, will show why Pythagoras said that all things are number, why Plato said that God always geometrizes.

If we take a close look at the head of a sunflower, we see two sets of spirals whirling in opposite directions. The florets that make them up are not of any random number. Typically, there are twenty-one going clockwise and thirty-four going counterclockwise—numbers that a mathematician would come on with a thrill of recognition. They belong to the series of "golden numbers" called the Fibonacci sequence (after a thirteenth-century

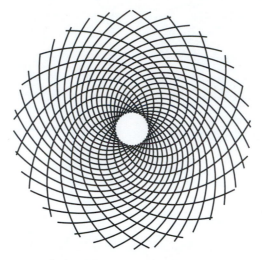

Spiral Pattern in the Sunflower

Italian mathematician), in which each number is the sum of the two preceding ones: 1, 1, 2, 3, 5, 8, 13, 21, 34, 55, and so on. Although the sequence may look like an artificial curiosity, it turns up again and again in nature—in the way rabbits breed, in the generation of bees, in the number and pattern of leaves or petals on certain plants, in the spirals of the sunflower. The sequence has been used by modern artists in placing units in their paintings and by modern musicians in planning the durations within their rhythms.

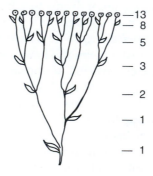

Sneezewort

A further strangeness about the series is that the ratio between consecutive numbers, after the first few, remains about the same, coming closer and closer to a stabilization in which the smaller number is to the larger as .618 is to 1. This .618 ratio—familiar to the ancient Greeks and to most designers, artists, and architects ever since—is that of the Golden Section, a way of proportioning dimensions so that the parts (many believe) have the most aesthetically pleasing relationship to each other and to the whole.

In this division, the lesser part is to the greater as the greater is to the whole: *CB* : *AC* :: *AC* : *AB*. This sectioning or "Section" is what Pound had in mind when in his Canto XC he says of architects he admired: "Builders kept the proportion."

It is also a ratio we have perceived, without being aware of it, in many things in nature. The human body, besides having bilateral symmetry, seems to have proportioned itself in accordance with the Golden Section. The length from the top of the head to the navel and the length from the navel to the toes have the ratio of about .618 to 1. These two divisions are subdivided. The length from navel to knee is to the length from knee to sole as 1 is to .618. In reverse order, navel to throat and throat to top of head are related as 1 is to .618. The architect Le Corbusier, who has planned buildings on the basis of the Golden Section, has even devised a scale for designers based on the proportions of the human body.

If bodily proportions might have given the Greeks a feeling for the Golden Section, geometry would have suggested it with more precision. The mysterious appeal of the ancient pentagram, or "endless knot," one of the most famous of all magic signs, owes much to its play of proportion. This star-shaped figure fairly glitters with its two hundred .618's. *B* cuts both *AC* and *AD* so as to give Golden Sections. *BE* is .618 of *AB*, and so on. The followers of Pythagoras used the pentagram as their secret sign. It stood not only for health and love but for the human body itself, which was thought to be organized in fives: five senses, four limbs and a head, five fingers (their three bones having the golden proportion).

Since the pentagram also stood for the letters in the name "Jesus," it was thought to be an object of fear to hellish spirits. When Mephistopheles finds the pentagram's *Drudenfuss*, or "wizard's foot," drawn on Faust's threshold,

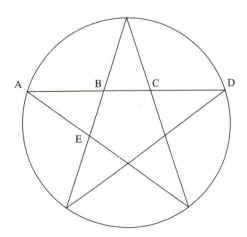

it takes some trickery to get by it. Its shape—as with good poems—is its power. In the pentagram—as in good poems—mathematics and magic come together. We are affected by precise relationships we are not conscious of.

If we take a line divided according to the Golden Section, bend the shorter part upward, and then complete the rectangle, we have the golden rectangle with its "divine proportion," which, with the Section itself, is supposed to have had an important influence on ancient art and architecture, determining, it may be, the structure of the pyramids and of the Parthenon, which fits neatly into it. Certainly it made itself felt in the Renaissance (Da Vinci made use of it) and ever since, right down to the architecture of Le Corbusier and the art of Seurat and Mondrian. In 1912 one group of artists even exhibited in Paris as the "Golden Section" painters. It was with them that Marcel Duchamp first showed his *Nude Descending a Staircase.* We can still find this proportion in modern buildings and in many common objects—envelopes, playing cards, magazines. Numerous psychological tests have shown that we prefer these dimensions in a rectangle, perhaps because the proportions correspond with our oval field of vision.

The golden rectangle has been called "the rectangle of the whirling squares." If we divide it by the Golden Section so that one part is a square, the smaller area will itself be a second golden rectangle within the first (A). If we divide the smaller rectangle in the same way, the same thing will happen—another square, another golden rectangle (B). We can continue in this way, making smaller and smaller squares as we whirl around clockwise. If we then connect, with an evenly curving line, corresponding points of all the squares (C), we will have one of the most beautiful curves in mathematics and one of the most beautiful lines in nature—the logarithmic spiral, whose allure moved one admirer to ask that it be engraved on his tombstone.

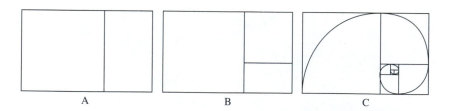

A   B   C

This graceful curve, which seems to have been artificially constructed at a drawing board, probably appears most spectacularly in the nautilus seashell, a favorite of collectors. As the creature in the seashell grows, it moves onward, in a spiral, into larger and larger chambers, all of them having the same proportions. Oliver Wendell Holmes found a moral here, which he expressed, by means of a stanza form that itself expands, in "The Chambered Nautilus":

> Build thee more stately mansions, O my soul,
>   As the swift seasons roll!
> Leave thy low-vaulted past!
>   Let each new temple, nobler than the last,
> Shut thee from heaven with a dome more vast
>   Till thou at last art free,
> Leaving thine outgrown shell by life's unresting sea.

We find this same curve in the sunflower head and the daisy, in the pinecone and the pineapple, all of which have their opposing spirals in Fibonacci numbers. We find it where the time element of living growth has left its shape on matter—in the curling horns of mountain goats, in the tusks of elephants, in the claws of a cat, the beak of a parrot. It appears in transitory fashion in the coil of an elephant's trunk or a monkey's tail, in a lock of hair falling naturally.

Part of the pleasure we feel in contemplating this spiral may come from our awareness of its continuous proportion, which, in a world of change, gives us the reassurance of what remains similar to itself. Certain well-managed patterns in poetry may have an analogous effect.

If there is such elaborate patterning everywhere in nature, it would seem not unnatural for poets to wish to incorporate—far more modestly and on a far tinier scale—some such symmetries in their own work. They cannot of course hope to work with the geometrical precision of nature. Most trust their own sense of proportion, developed from study, contemplation, and exercise. However, Dante does give a mathematical framework to his *Divine Comedy*. Its three parts, written in units of three lines, have thirty-three cantos, with a thirty-fourth canto in the first part that brings all to the perfect one hundred.

Contrived as this patterning may seem to be, we can hardly call it artificial. Nature—in the seashell, in the daisy, in a lock of hair—far outdoes our artists in the use of mathematical symmetry. All that matters, in any art, is that the calculation and effort should not show, that we see the ease and elegance of the achievement but not the labor that went into it. It is important to realize that imposing a form is not in any way unnatural—Parthenon and nautilus owe their beauty to the same kind of mathematical harmony.

William Blake once wrote: "Without Minute Neatness of Execution the Sublime cannot Exist! Grandeur of ideas is founded on Precision of Ideas." Yeats saw no contradiction between calculated precision and human passion. He once praised Lady Gregory's house as a place in which "passion and precision have been one." He insisted to a friend that "the very essence of genius, of whatever kind, is precision." In "The Statues" he is concerned with the relationship between passion, beauty, and mathematical precision.

The Statues

Pythagoras planned it. Why did the people stare?
His numbers, though they moved or seemed to move
In marble or in bronze, lacked character.
But boys and girls, pale from the imagined love
Of solitary beds, knew what they were,
That passion could bring character enough,
And pressed at midnight in some public place
Live lips upon a plummet-measured face.

No! Greater than Pythagoras, for the men
That with a mallet or a chisel modelled these
Calculations that look but casual flesh, put down
All Asiatic vague immensities,

And not the banks of oars that swam upon
The many-headed foam at Salamis.
15 Europe put off that foam when Phidias
Gave women dreams and dreams their looking-glass.

One image crossed the many-headed, sat
Under the tropic shade, grew round and slow,
No Hamlet thin from eating flies, a fat
20 Dreamer of the Middle Ages. Empty eyeballs knew
That knowledge increases unreality, that
Mirror on mirror mirrored is all the show.
When gong and conch declare the hour to bless
Grimalkin crawls to Buddha's emptiness.

25 When Pearse summoned Cuchulain to his side,
What stalked through the Post Office? What intellect,
What calculation, number, measurement, replied?
We Irish, born into that ancient sect
But thrown upon this filthy modern tide
30 And by its formless spawning fury wrecked,
Climb to our proper dark, that we may trace
The lineaments of a plummet-measured face.　　　　[1939]

WILLIAM BUTLER YEATS (1865–1939)

In the first stanza, Pythagoras is given credit for the emphasis on pro-portion in Greek sculpture, which might seem cold to a cold observer. But boys and girls saw their dreams of love embodied in these perfect shapes.

In the second stanza, the spirit of the sculptors, even more than the courage of Greek sailors, is seen as defending the precision of Athenian ideals against the abstractions of Eastern thought. (In 480 B.C. at Salamis, the Greeks defeated the much larger Persian fleet. Phidias was the probable designer of the statuary on the Parthenon.)

In the third stanza, an Eastern Buddha figure, fat and dreamy, out of contact with the physical world and the passionate precision of mathematics, is seen taking over as the Greek spirit declines. ("Gong and conch" suggest an Oriental call to prayer; "Grimalkin" is an old cat or an old woman.)

In the fourth stanza, the Easter Rising of 1916 in Dublin is recalled, when, under the command of Patrick Pearse, Irish nationalist forces seized the Post Office. Cuchulain (Coo-hóo-lin) was a legendary Irish hero whose statue was set up in the Post Office when it was rebuilt after the shelling. Here, Cuchulain (and Pearse) represents "intellect . . . calculation, number, measurement," like that of ancient Athens at its best. These qualities, Yeats believed, were desirable in the formlessness of the modern world.

Yeats would have agreed with one of the conclusions of this section: There is nothing unnatural in our desire to find form and pattern in our experience. We can hardly keep from doing so. When we look at the starry skies, all we really see are swarms of bright specks. But we have never been content to see that way. We see hunters and great bears and rocking chairs

. . . And pressed at midnight in some public place
Live lips upon a plummet-measured face. . . .

Roman copy of the *Diadoumenos* of Polykleitos

and dippers. Or we see figures like lions and scorpions and fish, which we name Leo and Scorpio and Pisces, relating them to long-dead languages. We like to believe there are connections between these imaginary creatures and the temperament and fate of human beings born under them. Everywhere we like to find the reassurance of form.

Part of the shapeliness of poems comes from the way some of their parts correspond. This is true not only of poems. A popular song some decades back declared, "I met a million-dollar baby in the five-and-ten-cent store." The lover had to meet his girl in *that* store so that "million dollar" could be played off against "five-and-ten-cent." Sing, "I met a million-dollar baby in the local dry-goods store," and the contrast is lost. When Dolly Parton sings about women who end up with "a man they can't remember on a night they can't forget," we again have a significant contrast.

Often a speaker in Shakespeare completes a pattern by echoing a word or image the preceding speaker had used, as Cassius echoes Casca in *Julius Caesar:*

> CASCA: Indeed, they say the senators tomorrow
> Mean to establish Caesar as a king,
> And he shall wear his crown by sea and land
> In every place save here in Italy.
> CASSIUS: I know where I will wear this dagger then;
> Cassius from bondage will deliver Cassius. . . .

In *A Comedy of Errors,* Egeon, about to be executed, is comforted to find correspondences even in disaster:

> Yet this my comfort: when your words are done,
> My woes end likewise with the evening sun.

Poets still like to find such correspondences, as Kevin Pilkington does in

> He's leaning on his cane
> the way all of us
> have leaned on him for years.

We can also look for correspondences between the content of a poem and its shape. But the shape of a poem, like its sound, cannot express much apart from the meaning. We might feel a nervous quality in short, fitful, uneven lines, or sustained power in long, even ones, as we might get a sense of crescendo or decrescendo from the shape of stanzas. Blake probably felt that the short lines of his "The Fly" were appropriate—flies do not go in for long-distance flights:

> Little fly,
> Thy summer's play
> My thoughtless hand
> Has brushed away.
>
> Am not I
> A fly like thee. . . .

He probably thought that the long lines of his "Holy Thursday" were appropriate for its processional content. His own drawing shows a long line of children across the page, above and below the verses:

> 'Twas on a Holy Thursday, their innocent faces clean,
> The children walking two & two in red & blue & green. . . .

John Donne seems particularly fond of a stanza form that dramatizes a crescendo, an excitement mounting to a climax. Lines (as heard, but not necessarily as printed) are shorter toward the beginning of a stanza, longer toward the end, though in no regular progression. Rhymes also tend to amass, to intensify, toward the close. This is the pattern in which he thinks and feels.

The Anniversary

All kings and all their favorites,
All glory of honors, beauties, wits,
The sun itself, which makes times as they pass,
Is elder by a year now than it was
5   When thou and I first one another saw:
All other things to their destruction draw,
    Only our love hath no decay;
This, no tomorrow hath nor yesterday;
Running, it never runs from us away,
10 But truly keeps his first, last, everlasting day.

Two graves must hide thine and my corse;
If one might, death were no divorce.
Alas, as well as other princes, we
(Who prince enough in one another be)
15 Must leave at last in death these eyes and ears,
Oft fed with true oaths and with sweet salt tears;
    But souls where nothing dwells but love
(All other thoughts being inmates) then shall prove
This, or a love increased there above,
20 When bodies to their graves, souls from their graves remove.

[11]/*corse: corpse*   [18]/*inmates: mere tenants*

And then we shall be thoroughly blest,
But we no more than all the rest;
Here upon earth we're kings, and none but we
Can be such kings, nor of such subjects be.
25   Who is so safe as we? where none can do
Treason to us, except one of us two.
    True and false fears let us refrain;
Let us love nobly, and live, and add again
Years and years unto years, till we attain
30 To write threescore: this is the second of our reign.   [1633]

                              JOHN DONNE (1572–1631)

There is the same kind of gathering intensity, dramatized by the form, in "A Valediction: Of Weeping" (see Anthology, p. 378), which begins with the image of a woman's face, at parting, reflected in the falling tears of her lover. In these poems Donne's stanza form moves from less to more, with a sense of mounting excitement. The line arrangement Christina Rossetti chooses for her "An Easter Carol" is appropriate for the exuberance she feels. It begins:

Spring bursts today,
For Christ has risen and all the world's at play.

Flash forth, thou Sun.
The rain is over and gone, its work is done. . . .

We get just an opposite effect—from more to less—in the sense of deprivation with which a poem ascribed to Francis Bacon opens:

The world's a bubble, and the life of man
    Less than a span;
In his conception wretched, from the womb
    So to the tomb. . . .

In Robert Herrick's happier poem, "The Thanksgiving," the lineation again follows a psychological motive—that of curtailment, littleness, humility. It begins:

Lord, Thou hast given me a cell
    Wherein to dwell;
And little house, whose humble roof
    Is weather-proof;
Under the spars of which I lie
    Both soft and dry;
Where Thou my chamber for to ward
    Hast set a guard
Of harmless thoughts, to watch and keep
    Me, while I sleep. . . .

The adjectives—"little," "humble"—go with the curtailed form, in which Herrick takes a four-beat line and then cuts it in half. Something like the sadness of deprivation is to be felt in the short last line of the stanza that Keats uses in "La Belle Dame sans Merci" (see Anthology, p. 403). In David Wagoner's poem "The Other Side of the Mountain," a short line has a different effect, that of heels digging in to resist the momentum of the long line:

> To walk downhill you must lean partially backwards,
> Heels digging in,
> While your body gets more help than it can use
> In following directions. . . .

Sometimes a poet will deliberately echo a familiar form to exploit its ironic possibilities. In 1650 Andrew Marvell wrote his stately "An Horation Ode Upon Cromwell's Return from Ireland" in a stanza of two tetrameters followed by two trimeters, its dignity apparent in such stanzas as those on the ceremonial execution of King Charles:

> He nothing common did or mean
> Upon that memorable scene:
>   But with his keener eye
>   The axe's edge did try:
> Nor called the gods with vulgar spite
> To vindicate his helpless right,
>   But bowed his comely head
>   Down as upon a bed . . .

Readers who recall Marvell's well-known poem will feel the ghost of its form haunting Robert B. Shaw's "Shut In" (Anthology, p. 538).

The shape of verse forms may be expressive, as the spiral of the nautilus expresses the life force that shaped it, or as the snowflake expresses the molecular geometry within. At other times the shape seems arbitrary or accidental—though if a verse form continues to live, it must somehow fit the way we feel and think. If the logic of a form eludes us, we might think of it as we think of games. Why *three* strikes in baseball? Why *four* balls? Why the rigidly fixed forms of Olympic events, the 440s and 880s? Without rules, games are impossible. We know what rage a hard-core poker player feels when a slap-happy beginner, given dealer's choice, makes up a fancy variant of his or her own: free-form poker. Too many wild cards, and the game is meaningless.

The next section will consider some of the forms available to writers. Few poets have written in all of them; some have confined themselves to one or two; most have tried their hand at several. Certain poets, like Thomas Hardy, prefer to make up their own shapes. As Kipling said:

> There are nine and sixty ways of constructing tribal lays,
>   *And—every—single—one—of—them—is—right!*

Nature often prefers to work in fixed forms. The snowflake, after millions of years, is still a hexagonal structure. Yet no two seem to be alike.

FIXED STANZA FORMS

Some forms have no fixed number of lines—they run on until they end. **Blank verse**—unrhymed iambic pentameter—is the most familiar. Shakespeare's plays are prevailingly in blank verse. We have seen it in MacLeish's

"Eleven" (p. 457) and Frost's "Out, Out—" (Anthology, p. 439). Other forms are arranged in **stanzas,** identical units of groups of lines. The Italian word *stanza* means a *room,* a *stopping place.* (Nonstanzaic divisions, as in blank verse, can be called *verse paragraphs.*)

We can find poems of just one line:

> "Good-bye," said the river, "I'm going downstream."
> HOWARD NEMEROV (1920–1991)

Two-liners are often used for *epigrams,* from a Greek word that meant *write on*—on a tombstone, say, or on a temple wall. Since such writings tend to be brief (especially when carved in stone), we use the word for any pithy poem, often a rhyming two-liner, whose point deflates some kind of affectation or pretension, as in X. J. Kennedy's "On a Given Book":

> I slumbered with your sonnets on my bosom:
> The net result of trying to peruse 'em.   [1985]
> X. J. KENNEDY (b. 1929)

or Bruce Bennett's "On Being Immortalized in Bronze":

> No matter how distinguished, when you're dead
> you'll end up with a pigeon on your head.   [1998]
> BRUCE BENNETT (b. 1940)

Or they may serve for more affectionate purposes, as in Dick Davis's translation of an early Persian poet, Amareh (11th century):

> I'll hide within my poems as I write them
> Hoping to kiss your lips as you recite them.

Many poems are composed in **couplets** (units of two lines): Blake's poem about the tiger (Anthology, p. 397); Swift's about the morning (Anthology, p. 392); Marvell's about his mistress (Anthology, p. 390). The "heroic couplets" of Dryden and Pope (called "heroic" because they were used in early translations of the heroic poems of Homer and Vergil) were, for a century, the favorite verse form.

THREE-LINE STANZAS

Rhyme schemes, as we mentioned before, are diagramed by using the same letter for each rhyming sound. Lines ending with *roam, sea, home, free* would be indicated by *a b a b;* lines ending with *sky, earth, mirth, fly* by *a b b a.* Unrhymed lines are indicated by an *x.*

Three-line units are constructed most simply by having them rhyme *a a a, b b b,* and so on.

Taken Up

Tired of earth, they dwindled on their hill,
Watching and waiting in the moonlight until
The aspens' leaves quite suddenly grew still,

No longer quaking as the disc descended,
5   That glowing wheel of lights whose coming ended
All waiting and watching. When it landed

The ones within it one by one came forth,
Stalking out awkwardly upon the earth,
And those who watched them were confirmed in faith:

10   Mysterious voyagers from outer space,
Attenuated, golden—shreds of lace
Spun into seeds of the sunflower's spinning face—

Light was their speech, spanning mind to mind:
We come here not believing what we find—
15   *Can it be your desire to leave behind*

The earth, which those called angels bless,
Exchanging amplitude for emptiness?
And in a single voice they answered *Yes,*

Discord of human melodies all blent
20   To the unearthly strain of their assent.
Come then, the Strangers said, and those that were taken, went.   [1978]
CHARLES MARTIN (b. 1942)

For another example, see Frost's "Provide, Provide" (Anthology, p. 441).

In "Acquainted with the Night" (p. 54), Frost uses the most celebrated of three-line units, **terza rima,** the "triple rhyme" that Dante and others had used (p. 80). The rhyme scheme is *a b a, b c b, c d c,* and so on, with the middle rhyme of each **tercet** (group of three) becoming the first and third rhyme of the following group. The interconnection of tercets, the way one leads to and sustains the next, gives this form a continuity and momentum such as few others have. Shelley's "Ode to the West Wind" (see Anthology, p. 401) is written in sections of terza rima, each closed with a couplet. Here is a contemporary example of terza rima by the Hungarian-English poet George Szirtes:

Like a Black Bird

Like a black bird against snow, he flapped
Over the path, his overcoat billowing
In the cold wind, as if he had trapped

The whole sky in it. We watched trees swing
5   Behind him, lurching drunkenly, blurred
Bare twigs and branches, scrawny bits of string,

And as we gazed ahead the snowflakes purred
In our ears, whispering the afternoon
Which grew steadily darker and more furred.

10   His face was in shadow, but we'd see it soon.
As he approached, it slowly gathered shape:
His nose, in profile, was a broken moon,

His hat a soft black hill bound round with tape,
His raised lapels held his enormous eyes
15   Between them. The winter seemed to drape

Itself about him as if to apologize
For its own fierceness, hoping to grow warm
Through physical contact, and we, likewise,

Ran towards him, against a grainy storm
20   Of light and damp. It was so long ago
And life was then in quite another form,

When there were blacker days and thicker snow.   [2004]
GEORGE SZIRTES (*b.* 1948)

Four-Line Stanzas

The commonest stanza form in European literature is the **quatrain,** or
four-line stanza. Psychologists may account for its popularity by recalling
that Carl Jung, with much support from mythology and religious symbols,
thought the nucleus of the psyche normally expressed itself in a fourfold
structure. For Blake, the number 4 stood for perfection; for Pound (in "Canto
91"), "the whole creation [was] concerned with FOUR." Dante Gabriel
Rossetti's "The Woodspurge" (see Anthology, p. 421) is an expressive
example of a quatrain in monorhyme (*a a a a*), but that rhyme scheme is unusual. The quatrain most often used is the **ballad stanza,** of which we have
seen many examples ("Western Wind," p. 6; "Sir Patrick Spens," p. 14;
"The Unquiet Grave," p. 99). Lines 1 and 3 are iambic tetrameter (or
sometimes $\smile— |\smile— |\smile— |\smile$); lines 2 and 4 are iambic trimeter. The
rhyme scheme is *a b a b*, or, more often, *x a x a*, as in "Western Wind" and
in most of the poems of Emily Dickinson, who did most of her work in this
simplest of forms. Wordsworth favored the *a b a b* stanza in his Lucy poems.

A Slumber Did My Spirit Seal

A slumber did my spirit seal;
    I had no human fears:

She seemed a thing that could not feel
    The touch of earthly years.

5 No motion has she now, no force;
    She neither hears nor sees;
Rolled round in earth's diurnal course,
    With rocks, and stones, and trees.   [1800]

WILLIAM WORDSWORTH (1770–1850)

Another well-known quatrain is Tennyson's "In Memoriam" stanza: four tetrameters rhyming *a b b a* in "envelope" fashion—the *a*-rhymes enclose the stanza:

Ring out, wild bells, to the wild sky,
    The flying cloud, the frosty light.
    The year is dying in the night;
Ring out, wild bells, and let him die.

Ring out the old, ring in the new,
    Ring, happy bells, across the snow:
    The year is going, let him go;
Ring out the false, ring in the true.

The following quatrain poem by Dick Davis (who lived for eight years in Iran) rhymes every other line, as if to suggest both awkwardness and resolution. The poem is also a fine example of extended metaphor.

On the Iranian Diaspora

You've seen a child intent on carrying
A cup brimful of water from the sink
—Step by careful step—to the kitchen table,
And then triumphantly sit down to drink.

5 This is the task the exile undertakes;
The heavy cup he balances is full
Of reminiscence and desire—the depth
In which he sees a world before the Fall.

He walks a narrow corridor where strangers
10 Jostle the vessel he cannot refill,
He sees the liquid that his life depends on
Lurch in his trembling hands, and spill, and spill.

There is no table where he could set down
His awkward, emptying charge; his stiff arms ache;
15 As there is less to drink his thirst increases;
It is a thirst which he will never slake.   [1989]

Five-Line Stanzas

There are many possible ways of combining rhymes and line lengths in five-line stanzas. No one form has become standard. A common practice is to take a familiar quatrain and add an additional rhyming line. Poe uses three different arrangements (as the indentations indicate) in one of his best poems.

To Helen

Helen, thy beauty is to me
　　Like those Nicéan barks of yore,
That gently, o'er a perfumed sea,
　　The weary, way-worn wanderer bore
5　　To his own native shore.

On desperate seas long wont to roam,
　　Thy hyacinth hair, thy classic face,
Thy Naiad airs have brought me home
　　To the glory that was Greece,
10　And the grandeur that was Rome.

Lo! in yon brilliant window-niche
　　How statue-like I see thee stand,
　　The agate lamp within thy hand!
Ah, Psyche, from the regions which
15　　Are Holy-Land!

[1845]
EDGAR ALLAN POE (1809–1849)

2/**Nicéan:** *several ancient cities were*
named Nicea
8/**Naiad:** *a water nymph*

14/**Psyche:** *the soul personified as a*
goddess

Six-Line Stanzas

Stanzas of six lines or more are likely to be made up of simpler elements. The "Venus-and-Adonis stanza" (named for Shakespeare's poem) is a quatrain with a couplet added: *a b a b c c*. One of the most individual six-line units is the "Burns stanza" or "Scottish stanza," an *a a a b a b*, in which the *a*'s are tetrameter, the *b*'s dimeter. Robert Burns's "To a Mouse" begins:

Wee, sleeket, cowran, tim'rous beastie,
O, what a panic's in thy breastie!
Thou need na start awa sae hasty,
　　Wi' bickering brattle!
5　I wad be laith to rin an' chase thee,
　　Wi' murd'ring pattle!

I'm truly sorry Man's dominion
Has broken Nature's social union,
An' justifies that ill opinion,
      Which makes thee startle,
At me, thy poor, earth-born companion,
      An' fellow-mortal! . . .

[1]/**sleeket, cowran:** *glossy, cowering*   [5]/**wad be laith to rin:** *would be loath to run*
[3]/**na start awa sae:** *not start away so*   [6]/**pattle:** *shovel*
[4]/**wi' bickering brattle:** *with hasty scuttle, hurry-scurry*

Catherine Tufariello's beautiful poem below uses a sestet made of an envelope quatrain (rhymed *abba*) followed by a couplet:

This Child

This child, in whose improbable red hair
My mother soon will see a fair colleen—
The dormant Shea genes slipped from quarantine—
While yours will find a beauty to compare
With her own mother Rose, a *gingy* too,
Belongs, for this first night, to me and you.

Strait-jacketed, the sometime acrobat
Lies still now, punch-drunk from the din and glare
That hauled her howling, flailing, from her lair
Like a furious pink rabbit from a hat.
She has fine lungs (Italian, we suppose),
Whether an Irish or a Jewish Rose.

So furtively you'd think a watchful warden
Might interrupt, we pull the cap away—
Conspirators again, as on the day
We took our vows in the judge's tiny garden,
Hopeful and ignorant of what they'd mean,
Framed with magnolia's cream and tangled green.

She's really here, resistant as the world,
Marvelous as an unexpected joke,
A gift to be unwrapped. Shyly we stroke
Damp head, clown feet, tease starfish hands uncurled,
The copper down, startlingly bright and fine,
Closing the circuit between your hand and mine.

Meanwhile, neither of her world nor of this,
She gazes past us, toward the sunless void
She'd crossed to meet us like an asteroid—
The proof of an absurd hypothesis
We'd stubbornly defended all the same,
While all the time we hoarded this pure flame.

[2003]

CATHERINE TUFARIELLO (*b.* 1963)

Seven-Line Stanzas

Among the seven-line possibilities, *a b a b b c c,* called **rhyme royal** (apparently because it was used by a poet-king of Scotland), stands out as especially attractive. We see it in Wyatt's "They Flee from Me" (see Anthology, p. 371) and, among modern poems, in the wider stanzas of W. H. Auden's "The Shield of Achilles" (p. 96).

Eight-Line Stanzas

The best-known eight-line stanza, an iambic pentameter *a b a b a b c c,* is called **ottava rima,** or "eighth rhyme." Its most brilliant success in English is in *Don Juan.* Byron's passion and wit find themselves at home with the elaborate buildup of the triple rhyme, followed by the opportunity for a sudden wisecrack or anticlimax in the concluding couplet:

> And Julia's voice was lost, except in sighs,
> > Until too late for useful conversation;
> The tears were gushing from her gentle eyes,
> > I wish, indeed, they had not had occasion;
> But who, alas, can love, and then be wise?
> > Not that remorse did not oppose temptation:
> A little still she strove, and much repented,
> And whispering "I will ne'er consent"—consented.

But ottava rima can be used seriously too, as in Yeats's "The Statues" (p. 296), "Among School Children" (see Anthology, p. 433), and many of his more thoughtful later poems. There are, of course, a great many other ways of building up an eight-line stanza out of simpler elements.

Nine-Line Stanzas

The classic nine-line form is the Spenserian stanza, devised for *The Faerie Queene.* The iambic lines, the first eight of which are pentameter and the last of which is an alexandrine, are richly rhymed: *a b a b b c b c c.* This stanza form was a favorite of the Romantic poets. A stanza from Byron and one from Shelley will show how the form moves through its elaborate pattern, pivoting on the fifth line to begin almost a new movement and closing with the longer, slower line—an effect like the concluding chords of a piece of music:

> There is a pleasure in the pathless woods,
> There is a rapture on the lonely shore,
> There is a society, where none intrudes,
> By the deep sea, and music in its roar:
> 5   I love not man the less, but nature more,

From these our interviews, in which I steal
From all I may be, or have been before,
To mingle with the universe, and feel
What I can ne'er express, yet cannot all conceal.

GEORGE GORDON, LORD BYRON

He has outsoared the shadow of our night;
Envy and calumny and hate and pain,
And that unrest which men miscall delight,
Can touch him not and torture not again;
5 From the contagion of the world's slow stain
He is secure, and now can never mourn
A heart grown cold, a head grown gray in vain;
Nor, when the spirit's self has ceased to burn,
With sparkless ashes load an unlamented urn.

PERCY BYSSHE SHELLEY

Although today it seems somewhat literary, this stanza form continues to come to life with the right handling.

John Updike has chosen Spenserians for "The Dance of the Solids," which is about the atomic structure of solid-state matter. His scientific terminology is almost a burlesque of Spenser's courtly abstractions. One of the eleven stanzas reads:

The *Polymers*, those giant Molecules,
Like Starch and Polyoxymethylene,
Flesh out, as protein serfs and plastic fools,
This Kingdom with Life's Stuff. Our time has seen
The synthesis of Polyisoprene
And many cross-linked Helixes unknown
To *Robert Hooke;* but each primordial Bean
Knew Cellulose by heart. *Nature* alone
Of Collagen and Apatite compounded Bone.

FIXED FORMS FOR POEMS

Besides the fixed stanza forms, there are designs for the complete poem. The most famous—and most notorious—is the **sonnet,** which has no rival in popularity. It has been a favorite of some of the best poets—and some of the worst. The name is from the Italian *sonetto,* which means *little sound* or *little song.* Part of its appeal is in its brevity—a sonnet can easily be read in less than sixty seconds. But, though brief, the sonnet is ingeniously organized, its fourteen iambic pentameter lines rhyming in various ways. The Italian (or Petrarchan) sonnet is divided into an octave (eight lines) and a sestet (six lines). Readers seem to feel, for some reason, something satisfying in the proportion: Their 6:8:14 relationship comes very close to the 5:8:13 of the Fibonacci sequence and the Golden Section. The octave of the Italian sonnet, with its many interrelated symmetries, has a rhyme scheme of *a b b a a b b a*. The sestet combines two or three rhymes in almost any possible way, although final couplets are generally avoided. Common patterns are *c d c d c d* or *c d e c d e*.

Since a sonnet of this kind needs four rhymes for both *a*'s and *b*'s, it is not an easy form to use in English. Yet poets continue to write Petrarchan sonnets. George Meredith chose it to express cosmic fear and awe, with space imagery like that of the telephotography of the astronauts.

Lucifer in Starlight

On a starred night Prince Lucifer uprose.
Tired of his dark dominion swung the fiend
Above the rolling ball in cloud part screened,
Where sinners hugged their spectre of repose.
5 Poor prey to his hot fit of pride were those.
And now upon his western wing he leaned,
Now his huge bulk o'er Afric's sands careened,
Now the black planet shadowed Arctic snows.
Soaring through wider zones that pricked his scars
10 With memory of the old revolt from Awe,
He reached a middle height, and at the stars,
Which are the brain of heaven, he looked, and sank.
Around the ancient track marched, rank on rank,
The army of unalterable law.   [1883]

GEORGE MEREDITH (1828–1909)

The rhyme scheme of the English (or Shakespearean) sonnet is less demanding: *a b a b, c d c d, e f e f, g g*—three quatrains and a final couplet.

Sonnet 29

When, in disgrace with fortune and men's eyes,
I all alone beweep my outcast state,
And trouble deaf heaven with my bootless cries,
And look upon myself and curse my fate,
5 Wishing me like to one more rich in hope,
Featured like him, like him with friends possessed,
Desiring this man's art, and that man's scope,
With what I most enjoy contented least;
Yet in these thoughts myself almost despising,
10 Haply I think on thee, and then my state,
Like to the lark at break of day arising
From sullen earth, sings hymns at heaven's gate;
    For thy sweet love remembered such wealth brings,
    That then I scorn to change my state with kings.   [1609]

WILLIAM SHAKESPEARE (1564–1616)

3/**bootless:** *useless, unavailing*   10/**haply:** *perhaps, by chance*

Contemporary poets are still finding new ways of handling it.

Why Did The

Because the cackling of the cocks and hens
Had raised his hackles for too many years.
Because the pecking order made no sense,
But simply fattened the inferiors.
5   Because the smells—not only of the yard,
But of the mental air—had made him sick,
With every hatchling hurrying to discard
The truths he had been raised on as a chick.
Because his spirit was oppressed by Freud,
10   The prince of darkness, and by Darwin's laws
That left the whole farm falling into void
No fowl could find a reason for. Because
The barnyard now seemed ready to explode,
With hope in flight, the chicken crossed the road.   [2003]

THOMAS CARPER (*b.* 1936)

E. E. Cummings wrote many sonnets in both the Italian and English mode. Though thought of as experimental, Cummings turned to the sonnet more often than to any other form: More than one-fourth of his published poems are sonnets.

Edmund Spenser, inventor of the Spenserian stanza, devised a matching sonnet form that bears his name. It rhymes *a b a b, b c b c, c d c d, e e.*

Many poets have taken liberties with the traditional arrangements of the rhymes. Gwendolyn Brooks, like some poets before her, eases the Italian pattern into an *a b b a c d d c* octave in one of her sonnets.

The Rites for Cousin Vit

Carried her unprotesting out the door.
Kicked back the casket-stand. But it can't hold her,
That stuff and satin aiming to enfold her,
The lid's contrition nor the bolts before.
5   Oh oh. Too much. Too much. Even now, surmise,
She rises in the sunshine. There she goes,
Back to the bars she knew and the repose
In love-rooms and the things in people's eyes.
Too vital and too squeaking. Must emerge.
10   Even now she does the snake-hips with a hiss,
Slops the bad wine across her shantung, talks
Of pregnancy, guitars and bridgework, walks
In parks or alleys, comes haply on the verge
Of happiness, haply hysterics. Is.   [1949]

GWENDOLYN BROOKS (*b.* 1917)

In the following sonnet, in which the octave has the same pattern that Gwendolyn Brooks used, although the sestet differs, A. E. Stallings shows how her sonnets can handle, with ease, grace, and wit, even strong personal grief.

Sine Qua Non

Your absence, father, is nothing. It is nought—
The factor by which nothing will multiply,
The gap of a dropped stitch, the needle's eye
Weeping its black thread. It is the spot
5 Blindly spreading behind the looking glass.
It is the startled silences that come
When the refrigerator stops its hum,
And crickets pause to let the winter pass.

Your absence, father, is nothing—for it is
10 Omega's long last O, memory's elision,
The fraction of impossible division,
The element I move through, emptiness,
The void stars hang in, the interstice of lace,
The zero that still holds the sum in place.   [2002]

A. E. STALLINGS (*b.* 1968)

Title: ***Sine Qua Non:*** *Latin, without which not. In this case a precondition for existence.*

Quite a few sonnets, like the two above, refuse to fit into any class. Some are hybrid—half Italian, half English. Some, like Shelley's "Ozymandias" (see Anthology, p. 401), have original rhyme schemes. Some, still called "sonnets," have more or less than fourteen lines, or more or less than five feet to the line. Hopkins, thinking mathematically, kept the proportions but changed the size in his "curtal" (*curtailed*) sonnet. Instead of the 8:6 ratio he used $6:4\frac{1}{2}$ (or 4 and a fraction).

Pied Beauty

Glory be to God for dappled things—
    For skies of couple-color as a brinded cow;
        For rose-moles all in stipple upon trout that swim;
Fresh-firecoal chestnut-falls; finches' wings;
5 Landscape plotted and pieced—fold, fallow, and plough;
    And áll trádes, their gear and tackle and trim.

All things counter, original, spare, strange;
    Whatever is fickle, freckled (who knows how?)
        With swift, slow; sweet, sour; adazzle, dim;
10 He fathers-forth whose beauty is past change:
            Praise him.   [1877] [1918]

GERARD MANLEY HOPKINS (1844–1889)

Often sonnets are composed in sequences. For a short one of these, see R. S. Gwynn's "Body Bags" (Anthology, p. 540).

Of the other fixed forms used in English, the oldest and most elaborate is the **sestina.** Invented by a Provençal poet in the twelfth century, the sestina comes as close as any poetic form to the elaborate mathematical patterns in nature. It has six-line stanzas and a three-line **envoy** (*short concluding stanza*). The same six words that end the lines in the first stanza return in the other stanzas as line-end words (three of them have to occur midline in the envoy). Their arrangement is different in each stanza, according to a set pattern, which readers sufficiently interested will easily discover in Anthony Hecht's "The Book of Yolek" (Anthology, p. 493).

Of the forms that have come to us from French poetry, one of the best known is the **ballade** (not to be confused with the English and Scottish ballad). François Villon (fifteenth century) is the most celebrated writer of **ballades;** his poem that follows illustrates (in translation) the pattern most often followed: three stanzas of eight lines each rhyming *a b a b b c b c C*, and a four-line envoy rhyming *b c a C.*[*] (Capital letters in such formulas mean that the whole line recurs as a **refrain,** which is the name for a line or lines repeated at regular intervals, like the chorus of a song.)

Ballade to His Mistress

F   alse beauty who, although in semblance fair,
R   ude art in action, and hast cost me dear,
A   s iron harsh, and harder to outwear,
N   ame that did spell the end of my career,
5   C   harm that dost mischief, builder of my bier,
O   gress who dost thy lover's death require,
Y   outh without pity! Womankind, dost hear?
S   hould help a man, not drag him in the mire!

M   uch better had it been to seek elsewhere
10   A   id and repose, and keep my honour clear,
R   ather than thus be driven by despair
T   o flee in anguish and dishonour drear.
'H   elp, help!' I cry. 'Ye neighbours all, draw near;
E   ach man fetch water for my raging fire!'
15   Compassion bids that every true compeer
        Should help a man, not drag him in the mire.

V   anished soon will be thy beauty rare,
I   ts blossom will be withered and sere.
I   could find cause for laughter, were I there,
20   L   iving and eating still. But nay, 'twere sheer
L   unacy, for by then I'ld be thy peer,
O   ld, ugly as thyself, and sans desire.
N   ow drink amain! For drinking and good cheer
        Should help a man, not drag him in the mire.

[*] The translation does the envoy as *a c a C.*

25   Prince of all lovers, I do scarcely dare
To ask thine aid, lest I provoke thine ire;
But ev'ry honest heart, by God I swear,
Should help a man, not drag him in the mire.

FRANÇOIS VILLON (1431–1463?)
(*English version by Norman Cameron, 1905–1953*)

The lines all end with an angry *r* sound, as we mentioned on page 158; most begin with the letters of his name or that of his mistress. A poem in which the first letters of each line spell out the alphabet, a name, or a secret message (possibly censorable) is called an **acrostic.**

Some other forms deriving from Old French poetry look alike and have similar names: **rondel, roundel, rondeau.** They tend to be bookish—the kind of thing literary folk like to try their hand at instead of doing crossword puzzles, or that young writers attempt once or twice as a stunt. A simpler form of the rondel, the **triolet,** with repetitions at middle and end (*A B a A a b A B*) is familiar in English. Here is one by Wendy Cope:

Valentine

My heart has made its mind up
And I'm afraid it's you.
Whatever you've got lined up,
My heart has made its mind up
5   And if you can't be signed up
This year, next year will do.
My heart has made its mind up
And I'm afraid it's you.

[1992]
WENDY COPE (*b.* 1945)

The same form is poignantly adapted, with some variation, in this poem.

1904

The things they did together, no one knew.
It was late June. Behind the old wood-shed
wild iris was in blossom, white and blue,
but what those proud ones did there no one knew,
5   though some suspected there were one or two
who led the others where they would be led.
Years passed—but what they did there no one knew,
those summer children long since safely dead.

[1987]
FREDERICK MORGAN (1922–2004)

A^1
b
A^2

a
b
A^1

a
b
A^2

a
b
A^1

a
b
A^2

a
b
A^1
A^2

The **villanelle** (a *villanella* was originally an Italian country song or dance) became a French verse form in the sixteenth century and was taken up by English dilettante poets in the nineteenth. At first it seemed only a literary plaything:

> A dainty thing's the villanelle;
> It serves its purpose passing well. . . .

But for some reason it has attracted the interest of some of the best poets of our time. A nineteen-line poem, consisting of five tercets followed by a quatrain and having only two rhymes, it repeats the first line (A^1) and the third line (A^2) according to the scheme at the left. It looks as if, with the villanelle, we are back with the complexities of the sunflower. When Dylan Thomas wrote "Do Not Go Gentle into That Good Night" (p. 150), his passionate exhortation to his dying father, he chose this "dainty thing" and made it resonant with love, grief, and indignation—one of the best examples we have of how a poet with enough vitality can breathe life into a form apparently long dead. Robinson, Auden, Roethke and Bishop are others who have used the villanelle for serious purposes.

The shape of poetry in English has also been influenced by Japanese poetry. In Japanese, a syllabic language with little accentual stress, the classical form for more than a thousand years has been the **tanka,** a thirty-one-syllable poem whose five lines have 5, 7, 5, 7, 7 syllables. This one is from the tenth century:

> Lying here alone,
> So lost in longings for you
> I forget to comb
> My tangled tresses—oh for
> Your hand caressing them smooth!

LADY IZUMI SHIKIBU (tenth century)

The tanka may have influenced one American invention, the **cinquain,** with its 2, 4, 6, 8, 2 syllables.

Cinquain: A Warning

> Just now
> Out of the strange
> Still dusk . . . as strange, as still . . .
> A white moth flew. Why am I grown
> 5   So cold?

[1915]
ADELAIDE CRAPSEY (1878–1914)

As tanka developed, poets began to write them jointly in a series called **renga** (revived by the Mexican poet Octavio Paz and his friends). One would contribute the first three lines of 5, 7, 5 syllables, another the two lines of 7, 7, and so on.

From the first link of renga came the seventeen-syllable **hokku,** or **haiku,** popular in Japan from the seventeenth century on. In this concentrated, one-breath verse form, there is generally a suggestion of season or a "season word" in a tersely described incident or observation that suggests more than it says, stirring a mood by presenting a picture. Often a comparison is implied, as in these two of Bashō's:

> Evening darkens. Hunched
> On a withered bough, a crow.
> Autumn in the air.
>
> Lightning in the clouds!
> In the deeper dark is heard
> A night-heron's cry.

BASHŌ (seventeenth century)

Brilliantly adapted as haiku is to Japanese culture and the Japanese language, it has seldom attracted the major American poets, though the apparent simplicity has endeared it to numerous poetry lovers. Richard Wilbur, one of the few well-known poets to use it, has combined the form of the haiku with imagery of the bullfight.

Sleepless at Crown Point

> All night, this headland
> Lunges into the rumpling
> Capework of the wind.

[1976]
RICHARD WILBUR (b. 1921)

An exotic form that one sees increasingly these days is the **pantoum,** originally a Malayan form brought into French in the nineteenth century and noticed by Victor Hugo. Of any length, the rhyming pantoum is made up of quatrains in which the second and fourth lines of each stanza become the first and third of the next one; the concluding stanza repeats lines from the first stanza.

Black Helicopters

> Gather your families. Lift your eyes.
> They'll take your daughters and your sons.
> Black helicopters rule the skies.
> The New World Order wants your guns.

5   They'll take your daughters and your sons
For schooling that is "outcome based."
The New World Order wants your guns
And getting them is just a taste,

For schooling that is "outcome based"—
10   Condoms for kids instead of prayer—
And taking them is just a taste:
Look at the uniforms they wear!

Condoms for kids instead of prayer.
Soon there'll be nowhere left to go.
15   Look at the uniforms they wear!
What's further out than Idaho?

Soon there'll be nowhere left to go.
Dust clouds are rising on the road.
(What's further out than Idaho?)
20   Look to the heavens. Lock and load.

Dust clouds are rising on the road.
Gather your families, lift your eyes.
Look to the heavens. Lock and load.
Black helicopters rule the skies.

[2000]

R. S. GWYNN (*b.* 1948)

Three fixed forms generally handled as light verse are the **limerick,** the **clerihew,** and the **double dactyl.** The first is so well known that we hardly need an example—which is just as well, since no limerick worth its salt would want to be found in respectable company.

The clerihew, named for E. C(lerihew) Bentley, has two generally mismated couplets with comic rhymes that present the "potted biography" of a famous person.

Sir Isaac Newton

Sir Isaac Newton
Wasn't much for your rootin' an' tootin'.
Probably what made him a grouch
Was those apples kept plonkin' him—*ouch!*

ANONYMOUS

The double dactyl was conceived by the poet Anthony Hecht and a classicist friend. Here are two of them, the first untitled:

Higgledy-piggledy
Ludwig van Beethoven
Bored by requests for some
Music to hum,

5 Finally answered with
Oversimplicity,
"Here's my Fifth Symphony:
Duh, duh, duh, DUM!"

[1966]
E. William Seaman (*b.* 1927)

Tact

Patty-cake, patty-cake,
Marcus Antonius,
What do you think of the
African Queen?

5 Gubernatorial
Duties require my
Presence in Egypt. Ya
Know what I mean?

[1966]
Paul Pascal (*b.* 1925)

The form consists of two quatrains, the last lines of each rhyming. All lines except these two have two full dactyls; the rhyming lines have only $—\smile\smile\,|—$. The first line is a sort of nonsense invocation, like "Ibbety-bibbety" or the above. The second line has to be a double dactyl name: Laurence Olivier, Anna Karenina, or the like. Somewhere in the poem, ideally in the sixth line, there has to be a double dactyl word like "partheno-genesis," "gynecological," "Mediterranean." These are heavy obligations for so light a form, and yet a number of disporting poets have met them triumphantly.

Such unserious poems as these can help us make a serious point about form in poetry. A free-verse limerick is improbable. What happens to the rhyme is part of the fun:

There was a young lady of Tottenham,
Who'd no manners, or else she'd forgotten 'em;
   At tea at the vicar's
   She tore off her knickers,
Because, she explained, she felt 'ot in 'em.

Anonymous

Liberate this into free verse, and we get:

A young lady, a native of Tottenham,
Had no manners, or else they slipped her mind;
   At the vicar's tea
   She tore her knickers off,
Explaining that she found them uncomfortably warm.

The first was at least a limerick and, for some, a passing smile. But the second is a nothing. If we saw it by itself, we might even be puzzled as to its intention. So with the double dactyl about Antony and Cleopatra. If we denude it of its form and leave it as naked meaning, we get something like:

"Mark Antony, what do you think of Cleopatra?"
"Well, I have to stay in Egypt anyway, since I'm the governor.
    Get it?"

Not very funny. Form is power.

EXERCISES & DIVERSIONS

A. One of the best-known poems of A. E. Housman begins as follows:

With rue my heart is laden
    For golden friends I had,
For many a rose-lipt maiden,
    For many a lightfoot lad.

His second stanza is one of these two. Can you be fairly sure which is his? And why?

By brooks that murmur softly	By brooks too broad for leaping
The lightfoot boys are laid;	The lightfoot boys are laid;
The rose-lipt girls are sleeping	The rose-lipt girls are sleeping
In many a misty glade.	In fields where roses fade.

B. 1. In "The Statues," check on the rhymes. Why are the final couplets of each stanza likelier to have perfect rhymes than other lines do? Why are there no off-rhymes in the last stanza, though there had been in earlier stanzas?

2. What sounds are repeated in lines 7 and 8? Are they expressive?

3. Do you notice any expressive irregularities (or regularities) in the rhythm?

4. In "The White Statue," Olive Custance (Lady Alfred Douglas) wrote:

. . . I yearn
To press warm lips against your cold white mouth.

Are her lines as effective poetically as the last two lines of Yeats in the first stanza of "The Statues"?

C. 1. Leafing through sections of this book you have already read, do you notice any stanza shapes that look unusual or interesting? Upon examination, do they prove to be expressive in any way? Merely decorative? Or—?

2. In poems you have read, do you recall any "correspondences" like those between "million-dollar baby" and "five-and-ten-cent store"? Would the following lines of Albert Goldbarth qualify?

> Now: sun through the blinds.
> The staves it makes.
> And then the first notes of birdsong.

D. This section has been making a case for the naturalness of form. But suppose one lives a chaotic life, or lives in a chaotic age that has little sense of form. Is it then more natural to write formless poetry? Or do you think that the more disorder artists feel around them, the more obligation they have to create what order they can? Which of the following statements would you agree with?

1. Art had to be confused to express confusion; but perhaps it was truest, so.

HENRY ADAMS

2. [The poetry of primitive people] gives order and harmony to their sudden overmastering emotions and their tumbling thoughts . . . a solid center in what would otherwise be chaos. . . .

C. M. BOWRA

3. [Deeply troubled poets, like Thomas Hardy,] tend to use strict forms as a kind of foothold, a fixed point in an uncertain cosmos.

KENNETH MARSDEN

4. The more [a poet] is conscious of an inner disorder and dread, the more value he will place on tidiness in the work as a *defense*, as if he hoped that through his control of the means of expressing his emotions, the emotions themselves, which he cannot master directly, might be brought to order.

W. H. AUDEN

E. How would you describe the stanza forms or rhyme schemes used in "Rattler, Alert" (p. 15), "Counting the Beats" (p. 202), "My Life Had Stood—A Loaded Gun" (p. 23), "All But Blind" (p. 33), "A Note on Wyatt" (p. 60), "The Ruined Maid" (Anthology, p. 425), "Dust of Snow" (p. 121), "anyone lived in a pretty how town" (Anthology, p. 458), "Out, Out—" (Anthology, p. 439), "Me up at does" (p. 280)?

F. 1. Of the six-line stanzas in the poems listed below, are any two alike? Do some stanza designs seem more successful than others? "The End of the Weekend" (p. 12), "It Fell on a Summer's Day" (Anthology, p. 376), "A Last Confession" (Anthology, p. 435), "Dream Songs, 22" (Anthology, p. 476), "Remember Dear Mary" (p. 282).

2. Ask yourself the same questions about these eight-line stanzas: "Winter" (p. 68), "The Mill" (Anthology, p. 436), "Loose Woman" (p. 81).

3. How many different five-line stanzas do you notice among the poems read?

G. 1. The sonnets listed below are all irregular in some way. How? "With How Sad Steps, O Moon" (Anthology, p. 373), "Leda and the Swan" (p. 40), "Good Ships" (p. 63), "Anthem for Doomed Youth" (p. 182).

2. Milton's "On the Late Massacre in Piedmont" (p. 165) breaks with the Italian sonnet scheme in one small respect, yet the difference makes itself felt so strongly that this is called a "Miltonic sonnet." What is different about it?

H. The ballad stanza is also called "common meter" (C.M.), especially when used in hymns. Why is the following stanza form called "short meter" (S.M.)?

I Look into My Glass

I look into my glass,
And view my wasting skin,
And say, "Would God it came to pass
My heart had shrunk as thin!"

5 For then, I, undistrest
By hearts grown cold to me,
Could lonely wait my endless rest
With equanimity.

But Time, to make me grieve,
10 Part steals, lets part abide;
And shakes this fragile frame at eve
With throbbings of noontide.

[1898]
THOMAS HARDY (1840–1928)

Why is the following (from "Greensleeves") called "long meter" (L.M.)?

Alas, my love! you do me wrong
To cast me off discourteously;
And I have lovèd you so long,
Delighting in your company. . . .

ESSAYS

A. Yeats once imagined his ideal audience as a solitary fisherman, in particular a fly-fisherman, who would know something about skill and grace as well as the ways of nature. He wanted his poem for that fisherman to be "cold and passionate," a phrase that describes many of Yeats's best poems. It seems that "cold," logical organization, often on display in stanza forms or the movement from one stanza to another, can be a help to the poet who wants to convey feeling and complexity. Choose a poem that attracts you for its use of stanza form. Notice whether the stanzas are end-stopped or enjambed, and ask yourself whether these formal choices are necessary and compelling. Now write an essay in which you explain the poem's meaningful effects, including those of stanzaic organization.

B.   Study the stanzaic work of one poet (say Dickinson, Yeats, Frost, or Auden) and write an essay on how that poet uses the constraints of stanza form to create a passionate human voice.

POEMS

A.   Write a poem using the letters of your own name (or somebody else's) as first letters of each line.

B.   Write a dozen or so lines of terza rima on a theme that exploits its forward movement.

C.   Write a stanza of rhyme royal or ottava rima (perhaps in the manner of Byron), or a Spenserian stanza, or three or four haiku.

D.   Would it be harder to write a passable example of a sonnet or a double dactyl? (Write one of each and see.)

E.   Write a villanelle or a sestina.

F.   Write two stanzas in stanza forms that, as far as you know, have never been used before.

14

A HEAD ON ITS SHOULDERS

From Realism to Surrealism

COMMON SENSE

Although complicated ratios and formulas play a part in our sense of proportion, the mathematics that appears openly in poetry will be very simple, like the addition in A. E. Housman's lines

> —To think that two and two are four
>   And neither five nor three
> The heart of man has long been sore,
>   And long 'tis like to be.

Or like the *a:b::c:d* in Frost's "The Oven Bird":

> He says the leaves are old and that for flowers
> Mid-summer is to spring as one to ten. . . .

Simple computations glow into family love and solicitude in a poem by Miller Williams.

A Poem for Emily

Small fact and fingers and farthest one from me,
a hand's width and two generations away,
in this still present I am fifty-three.
You are not yet a full day.

5 When I am sixty-three, when you are ten,
and you are neither closer nor as far,
your arms will fill with what you know by then,
the arithmetic and love we do and are.

When I by blood and luck am eighty-six
10 and you are someplace else and thirty-three
believing in sex and god and politics
with children who look not at all like me,

sometime I know you will have read them this
so they will know I love them and say so
15 and love their mother. Child, whatever is
is always or never was. Long ago,

a day I watched awhile beside your bed,
I wrote this down, a thing that might be kept
awhile, to tell you what I would have said
20 when you were who knows what and I was dead
which is I stood and loved you while you slept.

[1986]
MILLER WILLIAMS (*b.* 1930)

Only occasionally do the poets go into higher mathematics, as Aleda Shirley does when she writes in her poem "Cant"

> . . . I linger by this window and close
> in on the future in much the way the sequence
>
> .9, .99, .999, . . . grows ever nearer but will never
> reach the number one, its asymptotic limit.

Nor do we normally expect to find much in the way of formal reasoning in poetry. But poets are not mindless; frequently we find a structure of logic in even their most imaginative poems. A good example is Andrew Marvell's "To His Coy Mistress" (Anthology, p. 390), in which we find a logical process developing as follows:

Lines		
1–2:	If . . .
3–20:	Then . . .
21–32:	But . . .
33–44:	Therefore . . .
45–46:	Thus . . .

In "The Subverted Flower" (see Anthology, p. 442), a poem by Frost about a sexual misunderstanding between two young people, we are shown not only the geometry of human behavior, but that geometry as embodied, as seen through the distorting glass of a young man's embarrassed passion. The young people are more than psyches. They have physical bodies with shining hair and lips and hands; they stand waist-deep in goldenrod and fern; they ache and struggle and are panicked.

Wallace Stevens frequently lets a poem originate in a philosophic problem, but he sees to it that the problem is given a poetic solution. We can observe how he deals with philosophic thought by looking at his "Sunday Morning" (see Anthology, p. 444), a poem that wonders whether one should live for this world or for that afterlife which most religions offer.

A real voice in a real body in a real world, it is a vivid example of how poets philosophize. The thoughts of the poem are involved with physical sensations. Philosophical and religious questions come up because the woman is physically happy: She is enjoying her leisure, in comfortable undress, with the taste and fragrance of coffee and oranges, the warmth and gaiety of the sun, the brightly colored bird at liberty on the rug. All her senses are alive in the first few lines of the poem, which never leaves the sensory world.

In much of this book we have been concerned with what we could call the physiology of poetry. We have stressed, too, that poetry has much in common with primitive or childlike ways of apprehending reality, that it seems more at home with dreams and visions than with syllogisms or statistics. George Santayana, philosopher as well as poet, knew what he was talking about when he said that he was "an ignorant man, almost a poet."

But poetry, related as it is to dream and impulse and mysterious influences from our distant past, certainly has a head on its shoulders. It may even be said to be a matter of common sense. If this statement seems shocking, in pages to come we will also find justice done to poetry's invaluable elements of irrationality.

All we mean by common sense is a sense of the way the world is. When you lift a forkful of mashed potatoes toward your face, common sense tells you it goes in your mouth, not in your ear. You can, of course, protest the weary sameness of things by putting it in your ear, though common sense tells you the consequences will be unpleasant. Common sense tells you to move if you are standing in the street and see a four-wheeled, two-ton object hurtling toward you. It tells you not to step outside the window for a breath of air if you are on the fortieth floor. In our philosophic moods we may wonder what is "really real," but in the details of our everyday living we have a pretty sound idea.

Ezra Pound, when presented with the notion that intelligence involved "some repressing and silencing of poetry," reacted indignantly: He offered a reward "for any authenticated case of intellect having stopped a chap's writing poesy! You might as well claim that railway tracks stop the engine. No one ever claimed that they would make it go." Gary Snyder, in "What You Should Know to Be a Poet," specifies, "Your own six senses, with a watchful and elegant mind."

The function of mind in poetry is worth stressing because there are readers who think poets work better when they turn their mind off and let imagination and emotion take over. Imagination and emotion are necessary sources of poetry, but few good poets would agree that they ought to be in charge. "Every true poet is necessarily a first-rate critic," said Paul Valéry.

Dylan Thomas insisted that images, regardless of where they come from, "must go through the rational processes of the intellect." Sylvia Plath thought the mind should be in control—even when dealing with the extremist situations that led to her suicide:

> I think my poems come immediately out of the sensuous and emotional experiences I have, but I must say I *cannot* sympathize with these cries from the heart that are informed by nothing except, you know, a needle or a knife, or whatever it is. I believe one should be able to control and manipulate experiences, even the most terrifying, like madness, like being tortured . . . and should be able to manipulate these experiences with an informed and intelligent mind.*

An example of intellect controlling poetry when everything else has gone awry is one of the last poems of John Berryman, a poem (as events were to show) that is almost a suicide note.

He Resigns

Age, and the deaths, and the ghosts.
Her having gone away
in spirit from me. Hosts
of regrets come & find me empty.

5 I don't feel this will change.
I don't want any thing
or person, familiar or strange.
I don't think I will sing

any more just now;
10 or ever. I must start
to sit with a blind brow
above an empty heart.

[1989]
JOHN BERRYMAN (1914–1972)

Unable to keep his life together, the poet keeps his poem more tightly together (*a b a b* in iambic trimeter) than anything he had written in years, instead of simply letting it "flow" from the depths of his agony.

There are readers who consider "poetry" and "common sense" in opposition. Poetry, they think, is some kind of lovely supersense: cloud castles in the airy blue. Most poets, more down to earth than their readers, would agree with Robert Graves that a poem should make prose sense as well as poetic sense. Even ecstatic poetry, thinks Graves, is no exception: A poem cannot make "more than sense" unless it first makes sense.

*Transcribed from *The Poet Speaks,* Argo recording No. RG 455, Record Five (London: Argo Record Company Ltd., 1965).

The painter Miró, for all of his visionary surrealism, believed in keeping in mind his goal of communicating with others. "We Catalans," he said, "believe you must always plant your feet firmly on the ground if you want to be able to jump in the air." Certainly the greatest of the Spanish mystical poets, Saint John of the Cross, believed in making sense even when he was talking about experiences beyond any images our minds could hold or any words we could find to express them. Of such poems of his as "The Dark Night" (p. 55), the Spanish poet Jorge Guillén has written: "We are immediately fascinated by these forms that do not break with the laws of our world." At first this may seem to be low praise. What it means is that the poet shows a reverence and love for the beauty and integrity of the universe.

Few readers are as eagle-eyed as Graves, who can be hard on poetry he thinks deficient in sense. He even finds much to object to in one of Wordsworth's most famous poems.

The Solitary Reaper

Behold her, single in the field,
Yon solitary Highland Lass!
Reaping and singing by herself;
Stop here, or gently pass!
5   Alone she cuts and binds the grain,
And sings a melancholy strain;
O listen! for the Vale profound
Is overflowing with the sound.

No Nightingale did ever chaunt
10 More welcome notes to weary bands
Of travellers in some shady haunt,
Among Arabian sands:
A voice so thrilling ne'er was heard
In spring-time from the Cuckoo-bird,
15 Breaking the silence of the seas
Among the farthest Hebrides.

Will no one tell me what she sings?—
Perhaps the plaintive numbers flow
For old, unhappy, far-off things,
20 And battles long ago:
Or is it some more humble lay,
Familiar matter of to-day?
Some natural sorrow, loss, or pain,
That has been, and may be again?

25 Whate'er the theme, the Maiden sang
As if her song could have no ending;
I saw her singing at her work,
And o'er the sickle bending:—
I listened, motionless and still;

30 And, as I mounted up the hill,
    The music in my heart I bore,
    Long after it was heard no more.   [1807]
                                WILLIAM WORDSWORTH (1770–1850)

Graves protests that "There are only two figures in sight: Wordsworth and the Highland Lass—yet he cries, 'Behold her!' Do any of you find that reasonable?" If he is talking to himself, why say, "Behold her," when he has already done so, or "O listen!" when he cannot help listening, since the vale is "overflowing with the sound"? Graves also finds the poem wordy. If we were cabling the sense of the first stanza, we could say it in twelve words instead of forty three:

SOLITARY HIGHLAND LASS REAPING BINDING GRAIN STOP MELANCHOLY SONG OVERFLOWS PROFOUND VALE

Wordsworth uses four expressions for loneliness: "single," "solitary," "alone," "by herself." Graves also objects to the natural science of the poem: "occasional nightingales . . . penetrate to the more verdurous parts of Arabia Felix, but only as winter migrants, when heavy rains provide them with grubs and caterpillars, and never nest there; consequently they do not '*chaunt*.'" The Hebrides, he says, are far from silent: "The islands enjoy a remarkably temperate climate, because of the Gulf Stream; and the cuckoo's arrival coincides with the equinoctial gales." "Cuckoo-bird" he considers baby talk. He goes on to wonder why Wordsworth asks: "Will no one tell me what she sings?" Who could? he wonders, since no one is present except the poet and the single, solitary Highland Lass, all alone and by herself. He concludes by defining a good poem as "one that makes complete sense; and says all it has to say memorably and economically; and has been written for no other than poetic reasons."★

Some poems show a more flagrant violation of common sense, which even naïve readers will be startled at. We need no background in highway engineering or the theory of bridge construction to feel that something is wrong in the world of a poem like the one below.

Building the Bridge

An old man, going a lone highway,
Came, at the evening, cold and gray,
To a chasm, vast, and deep, and wide,
Through which was flowing a sullen tide.

5 The old man crossed in the twilight dim;
   The sullen stream had no fears for him;

★From Robert Graves, "Legitimate Criticism of Poetry," *Five Pens in Hand* (New York: Doubleday and Company, 1958), pp. 45–48.

But he turned, when safe on the other side,
And built a bridge to span the tide.

"Old man," said a fellow pilgrim, near,
10 "You are wasting strength with building here;
Your journey will end with the ending day;
You never again must pass this way;
You have crossed the chasm, deep and wide,—
Why build you the bridge at eventide?"

15 The builder lifted his old gray head:
"Good friend, in the path I have come," he said,
"There followeth after me today
A youth, whose feet must pass this way.
This chasm, that has been naught to me,
20 To that fair-haired youth may a pitfall be.
He, too, must cross in the twilight dim;
Good friend, I am building the bridge for *him*."   [date uncertain]

WILL ALLEN DROMGOOLE (1860–1934)

Assuming there can be a "lone" highway, traveled only by an old man, a fellow pilgrim, and a fair-haired youth, this one is an example of bad planning: A chasm, vast and deep and wide, has somehow been overlooked by the highway department. We are not told how the old man crossed it, though that is an interesting question. Did he swim, keeping his old gray head above the water? We might wonder, too, why he bothered to cross at all if he was thinking about building a bridge. Why not start building it from the near bank instead of swimming over and then building the bridge back from the far side? Generally the construction of such a bridge requires a little planning and a good supply of heavy materials. It normally takes time, too, especially with just one old man, working in dim light, to drive the pilings and swing the beams into place.

Such a poem breaks violently with the laws of our world. We can see how remote from reality it is by putting it not into one of Mr. Graves' cables, but into journalese.

Man, 70, Builds Bridge over Vast Chasm

Commuters long accustomed to swimming the deep, cold waters that roll in Vast Chasm, four miles north of town, were agreeably surprised this morning to find a gleaming steel structure spanning the tide.

"Twarn't there last night is all I know," said long-time resident Wilson Finozzle. "Sure is nice not to get soaked in them deep, cold waters, a-coming home with the vittles of an evening. Ain't read a dry newspaper since I was knee-high to a grasshopper."

"It was nothing," said the gray-haired builder, from his cell in the county jail, where he is being held on charges of bridge building without a permit. "I did it for a fair-haired youth. Wouldn't anybody?"

Will Allen Dromgoole's poem is well intentioned, meant to present us with an edifying example of noble conduct. Nobody would quarrel with her message. But she settles on images so improbable in terms of the world we live in that we are more likely to laugh than to listen seriously. When poetry is working on two levels, that of intended meaning and that of imagery, it has to make sense on *both* levels. One cannot hold back his laughter because "the poet doesn't really mean it that way" or because "it's only a figure of speech." For poets to claim our indulgence for what they *meant* to say is as futile as for golfers to demand that their ball be placed where they *meant* to hit it: Unfulfilled intentions count as little in the world of literature as in the world of sports.

When Christ in the New Testament (Luke 10) wants to show that we should be kind to others, there is no nonsense about how we ought to build bridges across chasms in the dark. Instead we are given the simple parable of the good Samaritan. We might expect Gerard Manley Hopkins, one of the finest of religious poets and presumably partial to the otherworldly, to be sympathetic to departures from prosaic common sense. But he was not. When, in 1886, he was shown a poem by the young William Butler Yeats, he thought it "a strained and unworkable allegory about a young man and a sphinx on a rock in the sea," and wanted to ask questions like "How did it get there?" and "What did it eat?" Hopkins explained: "People think such criticisms very prosaic, but common sense is never out of place anywhere, neither on Parnassus nor on Tabor nor on the Mount where our Lord preached . . . parables all taken from real life."

An affront to our common sense is a reason for **parody,** which Pound once said he supposed "the best criticism." The parodist feels that some feature of a poem is so lacking in balance that he deliberately exaggerates its faults, to the point of comedy, to show how absurd they are. The poems of Housman mention a fair number of love-stricken lads who kill themselves or rush off to death in battle or are hanged for murder. Occasionally the maudlin self-punishment leads to a ridiculous situation, like that in "The True Lover," in which a lad who has cut his throat pays a last call on his love, pleading, "Take me in your arms a space." She does:

> She heard and went and knew not why;
> Her heart to his she laid. . . .

By and by she notices that her lad seems not to be breathing (though he can talk in rather long sentences) and has no heartbeat. There is also an odd salty wetness about him. He explains why:

> "Oh like enough 'tis blood, my dear,
> For when the knife has slit
> The throat across from ear to ear
> 'Twill bleed because of it."

This may bring tears to the susceptible eyes of those whose medical knowl-edge is limited. Level-headed readers, who refuse to believe what Housman is telling them, are more likely to laugh. Hugh Kingsmill is parodying this aspect of Housman when he writes:

> What, still alive at twenty-two,
> A clean, upstanding chap like you?
> Sure, if your throat 'tis hard to slit,
> Slit your girl's, and swing for it.
>
> Like enough, you won't be glad,
> When they come to hang you, lad:
> But bacon's not the only thing
> That's cured by hanging from a string. . . .

Parody, although it has to be funny to make its point, is a serious literary exercise that amounts to a criticism of some excess or defect in the original. Fundamentally, it is a protest against some violation of common sense.

UNCOMMON SENSE

We generally look at the world with the eyes of common sense and, in survival situations, we are obliged to do so; yet there are times when we can disregard its warnings. In our dreams or daydreams all rules are suspended. We hardly need the Dadaists and Surrealists of the twentieth century to tell us what the sensible Horace admitted long ago—on occasion it is fun to act in a crazy way (*dulce est desipere in loco*). And before him the intellectual Greeks, who produced the Parthenon and the sculpture of the classical period, had also allowed for the irrational in human life. Sappho would prob-ably have been the first to admit that she was not behaving sensibly in letting love take over as it did.

We can point to nature as acting like a zany in producing flying fish and the duckbill platypus. If we look through a telescope at spiral nebulae or through a microscope at the cellular structure of our own bodies, what we see is so like surrealist art we can hardly tell one from another. Nature is contin-ually doing things at which our reason boggles—so much so that philoso-phies of absurdity and meaninglessness have been based on its caprice. As have religions: In "A Masque of Reason," Frost has Jehovah explain to Job:

> But it was of the essence of the trial
> You shouldn't understand it at the time.
> It had to seem unmeaning to have meaning.

Unreason, then, common enough in the universe, has a right to its place in poetry. According to Yeats, who spoke out strongly for the identity of passion and precision and for the mathematical basis of beauty, all great poetry contains an irrational element.

Arguably, one of Yeats's favorite words in later years was "rage," and it was something about the passion engendered by such extreme emotion that engaged him. Perhaps this contemporary poem by a woman, Terese Svoboda, is in part a response to the masculine rage of Yeats:

Old God

Ah, to be old and rage uncontrollably,
to command the sun and moon to stop
and yet be treated like a dog,
house training at ten and two
5   or we'll weight your walker. Flatline

the sun does daily, and the dog
howls anyway. I read where men's bodies
can be made twenty years younger,
only men's—we're so simple. I totter
10 toward a diamond of yellow light,

where the same geese snatch bread
ad nauseam. No one wants to see
them past their prime—they fly elsewhere
for their duplicate unsexed deaths.
15 Why feed them? I parade,

leg by leg, back to my barracks,
my rage rising over a horizon
of sleeping nieces. Weep wombs,
for what you hold is
20 not yourself, over and over.

[2002]
TERESE SVOBODA (b. 1951)

But welcome as occasional unreason may be, our minds are in for a surprise when we first come on a poem like "What the Violins Sing in Their Baconfat Bed," by Jean Arp, an Alsatian Dadaist and Surrealist best known for his sculpture and painting. The poem has lines that could be put into English as

the elephant is in love with the millimeter

the snail dreams of lunar defeat
its slippers are pallid and drained
like a gun made of Jell-O that's held by a neodraftee . . .

5   the lion sports a mustache that is pure gothic of the flamboyant type
his skin is calm
he laughs like a blot from a bottle of oink

the lobster goes *grrr* like a gooseberry
he is wise with the savvy of apples

10 has the bleeding-heart ways of a plum
he is fiendish in sex like a pumpkin

the cow takes a path that's pathetic
it peters out in a pond of flesh . . .

the butterfly stuffed is a popover made of papaya
15 papaya popovers grow into papapaya papapovers
papapaya papapovers grow into grandpapapaya grandpapapovers . . .

To ask what this poem means is a wrong approach. The question is: What does it do? Such poems certainly jolt us out of habitual ways of perceiving and thinking. Probably they also amuse us. The writing is very specific—anything but abstract. The "thought" is hard to follow. But it is not meant to be "thought." Instead, it is experience, as dreams are or as the inspection of natural oddities is. If it seems an insult to our ordinary ways of thinking, then the writer would consider it a success.

The Dadaist movement came into existence about the middle of the First World War. If our common sense could lead to the folly of war, the Dadaists felt, perhaps it was time to try another approach—that of "not-sense." They did absurd things in the hope of shocking society into an awareness of the bankruptcy of traditional procedures. They preferred chance to logic as determining a literary work.

Surrealism, which took over from Dadaism in 1922, was not just a literary movement. Surrealists hoped to promote their revolution by releasing the untapped forces of the unconscious, the marvels of dream, fantasy, hallucination, and chance; they professed to think spontaneity better than effort.

One form their spontaneity took was that of automatic writing. In this process, one writes down quickly, without thinking, whatever comes into his or her head. If the words begin to make sense, the writer is on the wrong track and should start over. It was soon found that automatic writing produced almost nothing of interest. For one thing, it was easy to fake. André Breton later admitted it had been "a continuous disaster."

Actually, the Surrealists' devotion to spontaneity and absence of control was never complete. Most surrealist art was not at all spontaneous. Tzara spent five years writing and rewriting one of his books. Breton worked for six months on a thirty-word poem, probably setting an all-time record for deliberation. The painter André Masson was seen to throw away from sixty to a hundred attempts at an automatic drawing before he got one with the "spontaneous" feeling he wanted.

We can see what the Surrealists were up to more vividly in their painting than in their literature. René Magritte, too rational to be a regular member of the group, was like them in setting out to defy common sense. In his art he puts things where we least expect them, or shows them made out of materials we least expect them to be made out of.

We see a boot, but the boot is sprouting real toes. We see a house as at midnight—windows lighted, façade glowing in the pallor of a streetlamp —and yet the sky behind the midnight roof and trees is a noon sky. Out of a plain fireplace in a plain room, a little locomotive may come chugging. Every object is painted with perfect fidelity to nature, and yet nature itself is transformed.

Similar transformations of reality are present in the typical surrealist image—in Breton's "soluble fish" or "white-haired revolver." No objects are too remote to be coupled. As in collage, one can paste anything next to anything. The Surrealists thought there was something "sublime" in the way the mind could reconcile contraries and find unity in the unlike. But what the French mathematician Henri Poincaré observed about combining, in mathematics, elements from different domains is also true in poetry: "Most combinations so formed would be entirely sterile."

The Surrealists invented many kinds of word games, and even returned with enthusiasm to the games of their childhood, since this was one more way of flouting the prudential time-is-money world of adults. In their favorite game, the first player would write down a word, fold over the paper so the word could not be seen, pass the folded paper to the next player, who would add a word, fold the paper again, and pass it on. When all had contributed, the composition would be read. The game was called "Cadavre exquis" (*exquisite corpse*) from the first sentence that resulted: "The exquisite corpse shall drink the young wine." The results sound like lines from surrealist poetry. They are not, of course, pure chance. Unless the words have the logic of syntax, they are mere gibberish ("The drank young the shall exquisite wine corpse").

The Surrealists not only made up objects in their imagination but also took a fresh look at ordinary things, particularly the "found objects" that chance presented them with. Marcel Duchamp once picked up an ordinary iron bottle-rack, signed his name to it, and declared it art. The group also composed "surrealist objects," of which the most famous were a fur-lined cup, saucer, and spoon. Not all inversions of actual experience surprise or amuse us: Surrealism lends itself to schlock confections as easily as any other set of mannerisms does and may remind us of the words of Dr. Johnson that the poet Derek Walcott quotes as an epigraph to his poem "Nearing Forty":

> The irregular combination of fanciful invention may delight awhile by that novelty of which the common satiety of life sends us all in quest. But the pleasures of sudden wonder are soon exhausted and the mind can only repose on the stability of truth.

As the discoveries of science become more and more fantastic, poems based on them approach the condition of the surreal.

Palindrome

There is less difficulty—indeed, no logical difficulty at all—in imagining two portions of the universe, say two galaxies, in which time goes one way in one galaxy and the opposite way in the other. . . . Intelligent beings in each galaxy would regard their own time as "forward" and time in the other galaxy as "backward."

—MARTIN GARDNER in *Scientific American*

Somewhere now she takes off the dress I am
putting on. It is evening in the antiworld
where she lives. She is forty-five years away
from her death, the hole which spit her out
5   into pain, impossible at first, later easing,
going, gone. She has unlearned much by now.
Her skin is firming, her memory sharpens,
her hair has grown glossy. She sees without glasses,
she falls in love easily. Her husband has lost his
10   shuffle, they laugh together. Their money shrinks,
but their ardor increases. Soon her second child
will be young enough to fight its way into her
body and change its life to monkey to frog to
tadpole to cluster of cells to tiny island to
15   nothing. She is making a list:
        Things I will need in the past
          lipstick
          shampoo
          transistor radio
20   Alice Cooper
          acne cream
          5-year diary with a lock
She is eager, having heard about adolescent love
and the freedom of children. She wants to read
25   *Crime and Punishment* and ride on a roller coaster
without getting sick. I think of her as she will
be at fifteen, awkward, too serious. In the
mirror I see she uses her left hand to write,
her other to open a jar. By now our lives should
30   have crossed. Somewhere sometime we must have
passed one another like going and coming trains,
with both of us looking the other way.   [1986]

                        LISEL MUELLER (*b.* 1924)

What seem at first to be nonsense poems may sometimes explode into disturbing fragments of sense.

Our Bog Is Dood

Our Bog is dood, our Bog is dood,
They lisped in accents mild,

But when I asked them to explain
They grew a little wild.
5 How do you know your Bog is dood
My darling little child?

We know because we wish it so
That is enough, they cried,
And straight within each infant eye
10 Stood up the flame of pride,
And if you do not think it so
You shall be crucified.

Then tell me, darling little ones,
What's dood, suppose Bog is?
15 Just what we think, the answer came,
Just what we think it is.
They bowed their heads. Our Bog is ours
And we are wholly his.

But when they raised them up again
20 They had forgotten me
Each one upon each other glared
In pride and misery
For what was dood, and what their Bog
They never could agree.

25 Oh sweet it was to leave them then,
And sweeter not to see,
And sweetest of all to walk alone
Beside the encroaching sea,
The sea that soon should drown them all,
30 That never yet drowned me.

[1966]
Stevie Smith (1902–1971)

Is this a nonsense poem? Or is it a serious poem about the psychology of controversy, religious or political? The word "Bog" does mean *God* in Slavic languages, though why we should invoke that meaning here is not evident to common sense. "Dood" might be baby talk for *good,* or it might mean *dead,* or it might mean nothing. The little ones in the poem, at least, do not agree on its meaning.

A continual source of nonsense or of surrealist revelation is the world of our dreams, daydreams, and fantasies.

The curious fact that some dreams are in black and white, not in color, is thought to mean that the dreamer is regressing to a primitive stage of human development when we did see in black and white, as some animals still do. In going back so unimaginably far, the dreaming mind falls again into primitive ways of thinking in which reason counts for little. Dream, like myth and fairy tale, prefers emotion, imagery, and symbol to logic and ideas. Every dreamer is a surrealist.

Our waking thoughts have to deal with objects that are hard, sharp, heavy, explosive. A wrong decision can be the end of us. Dreams have no such obligations. We can be run over by dream trains or fall out of dream skyscrapers and be none the worse for it. In dreams we are indestructible. We are free to reassign the properties of matter. Like the surrealist image, anything can become anything else. Time and space lose their power. Elizabeth Bishop mentions

> The armored cars of dreams, contrived to let us do
> so many a dangerous thing . . .

Dreams can be poems in themselves. A student in a writing workshop once described a dream that was better than any of her poems. She might well have taken lessons from her unconscious:

> I dreamed I was standing somewhere in the middle of a great desert. Off on the horizon I could see some beautiful purple mountains, their peaks bathed in golden light. Suddenly I heard a drumming of hooves, which grew louder and louder. Then I could see the horse coming. As he got near me, I was surprised to see that he had two heads. One head was well shaped and even noble, like a horse in Greek sculpture; its eyes were fixed on the distant mountains. The other head was ugly, misshapen; it had twisted fangs and bloodshot eyes. As the horse ran past me, the noble head did not look in my direction; but the ugly head kept its eyes leeringly on me, twisting around to do so. I fell to my knees and worshipped the two-headed horse.

This is probably a better image than the dreamer could have found consciously for a young girl's view of sex as both idealistic and threatening. Among modern poets, both Frost and Edwin Muir (see Anthology) have admitted using their own dreams as subjects for poems.

If Coleridge is telling the truth, one classic of English poetry (see Anthology, p. 399) was written in a dream. The poet, who said he was publishing his "Kubla Khan" as a "psychological curiosity" rather than for any "supposed *poetic* merits," tells how he fell asleep in his chair as a result of a pain-relieving drug, just as he was reading how Kublai Khan, the great thirteenth-century Mongolian ruler of China, built his summer palace at Xamdu.

He awakened later with the memory of a two- to three-hundred-line poem in his head, which he immediately began to write down. He had reached line 54 when he was interrupted by "a person on business from Porlock." When he returned to his room he found "to his no small surprise and mortification" that he had forgotten all the rest except for some scattered fragments. The poem as we have it seems to be a spontaneous production of the sleeping mind, which did not, however, create it from nothing. Scholars have traced most of the material of the poem to Coleridge's own reading.

Not even the subconscious can dredge up much of interest from a shabbily furnished mind.

Unfortunately, the subconscious—like a baseball player who hits one home run in a lifetime career—does not have an impressive record as a writer of finished poems. We have to take Coleridge's word for it that the subconscious finished even this one.

A poem that was not composed in a dream but that looks at the world through a dreamlike haziness, with occasional surrealist images, is one of the gypsy ballads of the Spanish poet Federico García Lorca.

Sleepwalker's Ballad

  Green I love you green.
Green of the wind. Green branches.
The ship far out at sea.
The horse above on the mountain.
5 Shadows dark at her waist,
she's dreaming there on her terrace,
green of her cheek, green hair,
with eyes like chilly silver.
Green I love you green.
10 Under that moon of the gypsies
things are looking at her
but she can't return their glances.

  Green I love you green.
The stars are frost, enormous;
15 a tuna cloud floats over
nosing off to the dawn.
The fig tree catches a wind
to grate in its emery branches;
the mountain's a wildcat, sly,
20 bristling its acrid cactus.
But—who's on the road? Which way?
She's dreaming there on her terrace,
green of her cheek, green hair,
she dreams of the bitter sea.

25 "Friend, what I want is to trade
this horse of mine for your house,
this saddle of mine for your mirror,
this knife of mine for your blanket.
Friend, I come bleeding, see,
30 from the mountain pass of Cabra."
"I would if I could, young man;
I'd have taken you up already.
But I'm not myself any longer,
nor my house my home any more."
35 "Friend, what I want is to die

in a bed of my own—die nicely.
An iron bed, if there is one,
between good linen sheets.
I'm wounded, throat and breast,
40   from here to here—you see it?"
"You've a white shirt on; three hundred
roses across—dark roses.
There's a smell of blood about you;
your sash, all round you, soaked.
45   But I'm not myself any longer,
nor my house my home any more."
"Then let me go up, though; let me!
at least to the terrace yonder.
Let me go up then, let me!
50   up to the high green roof.
Terrace-rails of the moonlight,
splash of the lapping tank."

    So they go up, companions,
up to the high roof-terrace;
55   a straggle of blood behind them,
behind, a straggle of tears.
Over the roofs, a shimmer
like little tin lamps, and glassy
tambourines by the thousand
60   slitting the glitter of dawn.

    Green I love you green,
green of the wind, green branches.
They're up there, two companions.
A wind from the distance leaving
65   its tang on the tongue, strange flavors
of bile, of basil and mint.
"Where is she, friend—that girl
with the bitter heart, your daughter?"
"How often she'd wait and wait,
70   how often she'd be here waiting,
fresh of face, hair black,
here in green of the terrace."

    There in her terrace pool
was the gypsy girl, in ripples.
75   Green of her cheek, green hair,
with eyes like chilly silver.
Icicles from the moon
held her afloat on the water.
Night became intimate then—
80   enclosed, like a little plaza.
Drunken, the Civil Guard
had been banging the door below them.

Green I love you green.
Green of the wind. Green branches.
85   The ship far out at sea.
The horse above on the mountain.   [1928]
FEDERICO GARCÍA LORCA (1899–1936)

Since insanity is the supreme form (next to suicide) of the mind's crying out against itself, the Surrealists were interested in the visions of madness—though not as much as we might have expected, possibly because the more insane people are, the more incoherent they are likely to become. Their rantings can be as boring as the sane person's platitudes.

In Mark Irwin's "X" we might think for a moment that the speaker is behaving with a kind of insanity, or claiming to, but the poem opens up profound levels of sensitivity. Even Irwin's typographical choice of leaving extra space between each line is difficult to rationalize, though it seems to open up the poem as we experience it, letting a little air into the subject. Irwin's nine lines work by a kind of lyrical probing, offering unexpected juxtapositions even as they begin with a logical assertion.

X

Because every thought is either memory or desire, the world

pulls away on both sides. Anyone's wish is a bird, and a wish

unfulfilled the unwinged skull, but a seed—fuzzy—pushes

its past toward tomorrow, all flutter and ecstasy. That's why

whenever I see people touch, I place a small white X where they

stood. Chalk, wind. Rock of sugar. Rock of salt. We spend our lives

licking at both. We sleep, eat, cry, sing. I like most when

it snows, when I must reinvent the shivering marvel of each

X, as knowledge is recollection, and love all discovery without delay.

                                                                    [2000]
MARK IRWIN (b. 1953)

A COMPARISON

Thinking about levels of reason and unreason in poetry, it might be well to consider two different translations of the same poem in a language with which some of us are not familiar, Chinese. The great Li Po (also spelled Li Bai), who lived in the eighth century, has been hugely influential on modern poetry in English. Here is one of Li Po's better-known poems, as translated by Arthur Waley (1889–1966):

Drinking Alone by Moonlight

A cup of wine, under the flowering trees;
I drink alone, for no friend is near.
Raising my cup I beckon the bright moon,
For he, with my shadow, will make three men,
5 The moon, alas, is no drinker of wine;
Listless, my shadow creeps about at my side.
Yet with the moon as friend and the shadow as slave
I must make merry before the Spring is spent.
To the songs I sing the moon flickers her beams;
10 In the dance I weave my shadow tangles and breaks.
While we were sober, three shared the fun;
Now we are drunk, each goes his own way.
May we long share our odd, inanimate feast,
And meet at last on the Cloudy River of the sky.   [1919]

14/*Cloudy River of the sky: the Milky Way*

Here is a more recent version by Vikram Seth (*b.* 1952):

Drinking Alone with the Moon

A pot of wine among the flowers.
I drink alone, no friend with me.
I raise my cup to invite the moon.
He and my shadow and I make three.

5 The moon does not know how to drink;
My shadow mimes my capering;
But I'll make merry with them both—
And soon enough it will be Spring.

I sing—the moon moves too and fro.
10 I dance—my shadow leaps and sways.
Still sober, we exchange our joys.
Drink—and we'll go our separate ways.

Let's pledge—beyond human ties—to be friends,
And meet where the Silver River ends.   [1992]

Most of us can't say which is the more accurate of the two translations, though if we read Seth's *Three Chinese Poets* (1992) we can see a good argument for using rhyme in a translation from the Chinese. Both poets make English sonnets, Waley's left unrhymed. But compare the specific terms used, as well as the grammar of sentences, and we might agree that in Waley's translation there is just a bit more of an anxious irrationality, in Seth's more of a reasonable resolve. This is not to say that either translation is the one we absolutely must choose, only that a translator strongly influenced by Modernism

(Waley) and one steeped in English as well as Chinese formalism (Seth) might bring different emotional material to the same poem.

EXERCISES & DIVERSIONS

A. 1. In "The Subverted Flower" (Anthology, p. 442), what is meant by the flower symbolism of the first four lines? How is the flower "subverted"?

   2. From whose point of view (through whose consciousness) is the situation presented? The boy's? The girl's? The poet's?

B. 1. Is it fair to say that "Sunday Morning" (Anthology, p. 443) is a dialogue with one speaker represented by the "She said" and words in quotation marks? Who is the other speaker? Is there ever a third?

   2. If you summarized in a sentence the meaning of each stanza of "Sunday Morning," would the sentences add up to a logical argument? A logical proof of anything? Does their logical validity affect their poetic validity?

C. In the first of the passages that follow, the Duchess of Newcastle is very sensible in writing about "What Is Liquid." In the second, Marvell is not very sensible in suggesting how one might get a supply of tears for an especially mournful bereavement.

   1. All that doth flow we cannot liquid name,
      Or else would fire and water be the same;
      But that is liquid which is moist and wet;
      Fire that property can never get:
      Then 'tis not cold that doth the fire put out,
      But 'tis the wet that makes it die, no doubt.

   2. Hastings is dead, and we must find a store
      Of tears untouched, and never wept before.
      Go stand betwixt the morning and the flowers;
      And, ere they fall, arrest the early showers.

   Yet most would agree that Marvell's lines are better poetry. Does this show that our discussion has overestimated the importance of common sense in poetry?

D. A poem that uses imagery to make a point ought to make sense on *both* levels—that of the intended meaning and that of the imagery. Are both levels well managed in these poems: "The Tyger" (Anthology, p. 397), "Traveling Through the Dark" (p. 105), "Neither Out Far Nor In Deep" (p. 123), "The Eel" (p. 274), "Dover Beach" (p. 220)?

E. **Travesty** and **burlesque** are akin to parody. The first (related to "transvestite") means that garments are changed—a lofty style, for example, shifted to a vulgar or comic one. Travesty drags something down—we speak of a "travesty of justice." Burlesque (from the Italian *burla,* joke) is less literary or critical than parody. It tries to be funny just for the fun of it.

I Never Plucked—A Bumblebee

I never plucked—a Bumblebee—
Without I marvelled—"Ouch!"—
Wise Nature—hath such ways to show—
Her children—"Mustn't touch!"

I never chewed—a Beetle up—
Sans pouting—"Icky-poo!"
Did Beetle taste— like "Choc-o-late"—
He were extinctive now.

I never did me—this or that—
Without—I something said.
I put a Pumpkin—on my neck—
And used to call it—"Head"—

Till Robin—cocked his dapper eye—
Impeachment—sir—of me?
As one who—off his rocker flip—
Or fruitcake—nutty be?

ANONYMOUS

1. The verses above are a takeoff on what famous poet?
2. Would you classify them as parody, travesty, or burlesque—or a combination of any two or all three?
3. What elements of style of the famous poet have been selected for attention?

F. "Kubla Khan" (Anthology, p. 399) illustrates almost all the technical points about poetry that we have been discussing.

1. Are there any lines that do not engage one of our senses?
2. Have all the senses been involved by the time the poem ends?
3. Is the vocabulary simple? Does it have a high percentage of "thing-words"?
4. Can you find examples of the functional use of assonance and alliteration?
5. Why did the writer change the historic "Kublai" and "Xamdu" to "Kubla" and "Xanadu" in the poem?
6. How many rhymes can you find on a single sound? How many lines apart can the rhymes be?
7. What two line-lengths are used? Is the shift from one to the other significant? Is there ever a third?
8. Can you find all the "options" mentioned in our treatment of iambic verse? Are those that you find used expressively?

9. Does the poem, in its own way and as far as it goes, "make sense"? Are there any surrealist details?
10. Do you think it odd that the most celebrated of all dream poems is so craft-conscious?

ESSAYS

A. Do you recall any poems that you read with such disbelief that you found yourself noticing faults with as sharp an eye as Robert Graves' in this chapter? Write a Gravesian analysis of a poem you find particularly vulnerable. Feel free to look outside this textbook for such a poem.
B. Find a poem that works by a kind of unreason or a logic that seems like what we call "uncommon sense." Write an essay noting the poem's challenges to sense, then making a case for its emotional or experiential validity.

POEMS

A. The painter Sophie Taeuber (wife of Jean Arp) describes a dream she once had:

> Last night I dreamt that I was on a beach. . . . I heard the voices of my friends grow fainter and fainter. I was alone, and, while the night fell, my index finger wrote the word "happy" on the sand, as though it had been impelled by an outside force. While tracing the letters, I saw the word sink into the stone. A muffled, whispering noise made me look up. It was a great slab of rock which had broken loose and was poised ominously above me. And the thought flashed into my mind that if it crushed me that very moment, all that would be left of me would be the single word "happy."

Describe a dream of your own in a way that brings out its kinship with poetry.
B. Now rewrite this dream in verse.
C. Make up a half-dozen or so surrealist images consisting of noun and adjective, like Breton's "soluble fish" or "white-haired revolver."
D. Invent a half-dozen or so interesting surrealist objects, like the fur-lined breakfast set.
E. Write a parody (or travesty or burlesque) of any poem or poet that strikes your fancy. (Suggested titles: "Walt Whitman Among the Yellow Pages," "The Coy Mistress Replies," "anyone lived in a pretty (huh?) town," "The Ruby Yacht of Omar K. Yamm." Or, better, make up your own.)

15

ADAM'S CURSE

Inspiration and Effort

How do poems come into being at all?

Some people believe they are produced by a mysterious something called "inspiration." Poets, in this view, are a sort of medium; they have nothing to do but sit there and let themselves be played on by celestial fingers.

Inspiration

How often have I started out
With no thought in my noddle,
And wandered here and there about,
Where fancy bade me toddle;
5   Till feeling faunlike in my glee
I've voiced some gay distiches,
Returning joyfully to tea,
A poem in my britches.

A-squatting on a thymy slope
10   With vast of sky about me,
I've scribbled on an envelope
The rhymes the hills would shout me;
The couplets that the trees would call,
The lays the breezes proffered . . .
15   Oh, no, I didn't *think* at all—
I took what Nature offered.

For that's the way you ought to write—
Without a trace of trouble;
Be super-charged with high delight

[6]/**distiches:** *distiches (sic) are units of two lines. The plural is pronounced disticks; Service mispronounces it to rhyme with britches.*

347

20 And let the words out-bubble;
Be voice of vale and wood and stream
Without design or proem:
Then rouse from out a golden dream
To find you've made a poem.

25 So I'll go forth with mind a blank,
And sea and sky will spell me;
And lolling on a thymy bank
I'll take down what they tell me;
As Mother Nature speaks to me
30 Her words I'll gaily docket,
So I'll come singing home to tea
A poem in my pocket.   [1907]

ROBERT W. SERVICE (1874–1958)

"Read from some humbler poet," wrote Longfellow, "Whose songs gushed from his heart." Robert Service is one of those humbler poets, and his songs do indeed "gush." Poets of higher intensity work against greater resistance. The account Dylan Thomas gives of how he composed is very different. Instead of toddling around out-bubbling, he works—he *labors* at the *exercise* of his *craft* or *art*, which is *sullen* because words, like marble, are resistant material.

In My Craft or Sullen Art

In my craft or sullen art
Exercised in the still night
When only the moon rages
And the lovers lie abed
5 With all their griefs in their arms,
I labour by singing light
Not for ambition or bread
Or the strut and trade of charms
On the ivory stages
10 But for the common wages
Of their most secret heart.

Not for the proud man apart
From the raging moon I write
On these spindrift pages
15 Nor for the towering dead
With their nightingales and psalms
But for the lovers, their arms
Round the griefs of the ages,
Who pay no praise or wages
20 Nor heed my craft or art.   [1946]

DYLAN THOMAS (1914–1953)

A good poem is likely to seem so spontaneous, so easy, so natural, that we can hardly imagine the poet sweating over it—crossing out lines, scrawling in between them, making out lists of rhymes or synonyms. But enough of the poets' scribbled-over manuscripts are extant—under lock and key in rare-book rooms or under glass in museums—for us to know that most poets did indeed find their muse a difficult mistress.

A poem that seems spontaneous may have come into being after a long and painful birth. All that matters is that the finished poem seem spontaneous. In his "Adam's Curse" (Anthology, p. 431) Yeats tells us with what difficulty his own poems were written:

>   ... A line will take us hours maybe;
> Yet if it does not seem a moment's thought,
> Our stitching and unstitching has been naught.
>   ... It's certain there is no fine thing
> 5 Since Adam's fall but needs much laboring. ...

Toujours travailler—always keep on working—was a motto of the sculptor Rodin. The greater the artist (there are few exceptions to this), the harder that artist works. It was Picasso, and not some industrious office manager, who said, "Man invented the alarm clock."

Most writers work hard over their lines to make it seem they have not worked at all. When Keats said that unless poetry came "as naturally as the leaves to a tree, it had better not come at all," by "naturally" he cannot have meant *effortlessly,* as his own much worked-over manuscripts demonstrate. No poets have been so divinely gifted that they did not have to struggle to find themselves: "A good poet's made," said Ben Jonson, "as well as born." Nearly all poets would agree with Edwin Muir that "to write naturally, especially in verse, is one of the most difficult things in the world; naturalness does not come easily to the awkward human race, and is an achievement of art." As for easy writing, the dramatist Richard Brinsley Sheridan has summed that up for us: "Easy writing's cursed hard reading."

Ideas suddenly and unaccountably flashing into the light of consciousness are called inspirations. We get them in any field in which our minds move with knowledge and experience. They are more often foolish than wise, but even when they are promising, we usually have to work out the details. Poets find that words or lines will suddenly be "given" to them, as if flashed on a mental screen. But they then have to work out the continuity that will complete the poem. Without these given lines, these inspirations, probably no poems come into being. It would be possible for us to know all there was to know about the theory and technique of poetry, and yet never be able to write a poem. It seems that we cannot *will* to do anything creative, although we can will to bring about conditions favorable to inspiration and can will to work on the inspiration once it comes. Technique *in itself* can do little; it is valuable only in the service of passion and inspiration.

The ratio between inspiration and deliberate effort differs in different artists. Music came easily to Mozart, but not to Beethoven, who had to jot down his ideas, rework them again and again, sometimes completing a theme twenty-five years after the idea for it struck him. His way of composing, compared with Mozart's, was stodgy and plodding, but the music that resulted

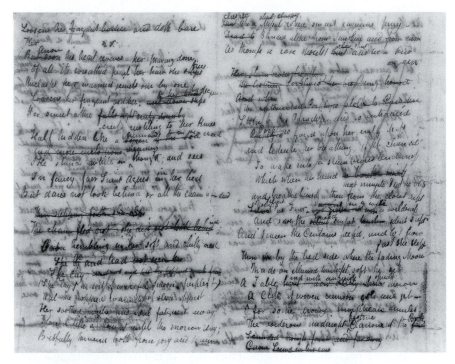

John Keats's manuscript, "The Eve of St. Agnes," stanzas 26–29.

was no less "inspired." So too with poets. Some work rapidly, some slowly. The number of flashes of inspiration that go into the process may have little to do with the quality of the poem that results. Frost considered unfinished one poem he had begun to work on fourteen years before; he left another "lying around nameless" for forty years because he could not find a fourth line that suited him.

It should be stressed again that our inspirations are as specialized as our minds are. If our whole bent is toward Romance philology or football strategy, we will not come up with inspirations in the field of economic theory. Inspirations follow commonsense rules: We get only the inspirations we are qualified to receive. And unless we have laid the groundwork by conscious planning and hard work, there is no inspiration to be hoped for.

"Chance," said Pasteur, "favors the prepared mind." Poets have to condition their minds to produce and handle inspirations. If they have a vocabulary of only a few hundred words, the unconscious has very little to work with. If they have taken little notice of the world around, their minds will suffer from a poverty of images. If they have not read other poets, they will not know when they are original and when they are not—as if a young physicist, scorning the achievements of the past, were to spend his time reinventing the wheel.

The influence of a well-conditioned conscious mind extends to the unconscious, which continues to work, often more originally and brilliantly, with

A manuscript of Walt Whitman's "Come, Said My Soul," the title-page
epigraph in several editions of *Leaves of Grass*.

the patterns we have consciously set up. All the artist's work, before the fact of inspiration, is a way of programming the unconscious along desirable lines.

Malcolm Cowley's description of Hart Crane's writing habits shows that apparently wild bursts of spontaneity were based on months or even years of careful thought:

> There would be a Sunday afternoon party. . . . Hart would be laughing twice as hard as the rest of us . . . he would be drinking twice as much hard cider and contributing more than his share of the crazy metaphors and overblown epithets. Gradually he would fall silent and a little later we would find that he had disappeared. . . .
>
> An hour later . . . he would appear in the kitchen or on the croquet court. . . . In his hands would be two or three sheets of typewritten manuscript, with words crossed out and new lines scrawled in. "Read that," he would say. "Isn't that the *grrrrea*test poem ever written!" . . .
>
> I later discovered that Hart would have been meditating over that particular poem for months or even years, scribbling verses on pieces of paper that he carried in his pockets and meanwhile waiting for the moment of pure inspiration when he could put them all together. . . .
>
> Painfully, perseveringly—and dead sober—Hart would revise his poem, clarifying its images, correcting its meter and searching through dictionaries and thesauruses for exactly the right word. . . . Even after the poem had been completed, the manuscript mailed to *Poetry* or the *Dial* and perhaps accepted, he would still have changes to make.*

The knowledge of how to make something of our insights is what we call **technique.** Those who care about communicating their insights care very much about technique, which Ezra Pound said he believed in "as a test of a man's sincerity." Those who do not care about it are like the writer who, as James Russell Lowell said,

> . . . might have been poet, but that, in its stead, he
> Preferred to believe that he was so already.

"Trifles," Michelangelo is reported to have said, "make perfection, and perfection is no trifle." When Frost once digressed into a discussion of some technical point at a reading of his poems, a member of the audience objected:

> "But Mr. Frost, when you're writing your *beautiful* poems, you can't really be thinking of technical things like that? You can't really like *those!*"
> "Like 'em?" Frost growled, "I revel in 'em!"

Dylan Thomas is even more emphatic:

> What I like to do is to treat words as a craftsman does his wood or stone or what-have-you, to hew, carve, mould, coil, polish and plane them into patterns, sequences, sculptures, fugues of sound. . . .
>
> I am a painstaking, conscientious, involved and devious craftsman in words. . . . I use everything and anything to make my poems work and move in the direction I want them to: old tricks, new tricks,

---

*Malcolm Cowley, *Exile's Return* (New York: Viking, 1941), pp. 145–147.

puns, portmanteau-words, paradox, allusion, paronomasia, paragram, catachresis, slang, assonantal rhymes, vowel rhymes, sprung rhythm. . . . The inventions and contrivances are all part of the joy that is part of the painful, voluntary work.*

A worker in a more popular field, the film director Federico Fellini, told Ray Bradbury that the rumors that he makes up a script as he shoots are "stupid gossip. It's absolutely impossible to improvise. Making a movie is a mathematical operation. It is like sending a missile to the moon. Art is a scientific operation." Fellini himself, according to Woody Allen, was ruled by "technical passion." "All artistic problems," Allen went on to say, "are really technical." Artists in every medium (except for some Surrealists) downplay the role of chance in what they create, and in denying it, they return not to some sophisticated world but to the world of the child and of primitive people. For early cultures, there was no such thing as chance; everything had its cause. And so for children: As Piaget has observed, "The idea of chance is absent from the mentality of a child."

Preoccupation with technique can protect writers from the tyranny of the spontaneous, the zombielike acceptance of absolutely everything—trash and treasure alike—that floats up from the depths of the psyche. It can also encourage the objectivity they need to judge their own work, a quality not easy to maintain if they let themselves be swept away by the self-indulgence of their own emotions.

Their own emotions!—there are literary aspirants who think that the strength of their own emotions is enough to invigorate the poems they write. "But I felt it so strongly! So sincerely! It came from my heart!" they are likely to protest when the worth of their work is questioned. Unfortunately their own feelings are beside the point. Readers are not mind readers or heart readers; they will feel only what the words and rhythms tell them to feel. Genuine feeling guarantees nothing. "All bad art," said Oscar Wilde, "springs from genuine feeling"—genuine feeling, that is, which the artist does not have the skill, the technique, to put on canvas, to show in stone, or to embody in a passionate work of words. Significant emotion, as T. S. Eliot said, is that "which has its life in the poem and not in the history of the poet." Our expression of an emotion may be so clichéd, so incoherent, so fulsome as to be wholly inadequate to what we really feel, or think we feel. The Russian poet Bella Akhmadulina has warned us about this: When struck by what seems a brilliant inspiration, she admitted in an interview, she immediately grew distrustful of it, was careful "not to confuse the intensity of the feeling with the worth of what I've written." The two are not the same, much as some apprentice writers wish they were. Often when we are carried away by what seems the inspired quality of any work of art, we forget that only technique enabled the artist to share those raptures with us. The dancer Rudolf Nureyev seemed "wild and spontaneous" when dancing "Swan Lake" with

*James Scully, *Modern Poets on Modern Poetry* (New York: McGraw-Hill, 1965), pp. 196–197.

```
rosetree, rosetree
—you're a song to see;whose
every(any)where
opening poems are;
until no small most
miracle is almost
glimpse by wonder
(people of a person)
blossoms the myriad
soul of beatitude
(and from all nothing
gluttons come seething)
each in roguish
(bigger than a wish no)
whom of fragrance
dances a honeydunce;
whirling's a frantic
ego gigantic
out,if stumble
should the brigand,welcome
she'll some another me
(dreamtree;truthtree;
when cannot measure
a now of your treasure)
lovetree!not a
glory you're today but
must(to quite disappear)
three,four,five times declare
dying unfatal—
a heart her each petal
```

A worksheet of E. E. Cummings—one of the 175 sheets for his nine-stanza "rose tree." Numbers to the left of the lines indicate the number of syllables; yet the scansion, in the conventional marks for long and short syllables, shows that the poet was also working with accent. The worksheets also have lists of rhymes, indications of vowel and consonant patterns, and various other charts and graphs. Cummings obviously took tremendous care as he composed his apparently artless poems.

Margot Fonteyn, yet, as Miss Fonteyn tells us in her *Autobiography,* "It was paradoxical that the young boy everyone thought so wild and spontaneous in his dancing cared desperately about technique." Technique is how we communicate passion in the arts—but we need hardly say that the passion has to be there to begin with.

After inspiration has struck and has been recorded more or less satisfactorily in a first draft, poets begin their laborious process of revision. The process is only natural—it assumes that our first thoughts are not always our best ones. In life we often modify the phraseology that first occurred to us—if we have a chance to. We can see how studiously we revise after we have been put down by someone else's clever remark. Perhaps all we can do at the time is mutter something like, "Oh, yeah? Look who's talking!"—not exactly a brilliant comeback. All the way home we may be mulling, "What I *should* have said to that guy was . . ." As the days go by and we continue to revise, what we should have said gets better and better. The French have the expression *"l'esprit de l'escalier"* (staircase wit) for the kind of remark that occurs to us, just too late, as we are leaving the place where we should have made it. Revision is precisely this what-I-should-have-said process. And even though it relies a great deal on reason and calculation, it can be very passionate. Nor is it shutting the door on inspiration. It is merely giving inspiration, which takes its own sweet time, a second chance to strike—and a third, and a fourth, until we feel it is right on target.

Poets, with very few exceptions, take pleasure in the work of revision. The Surrealists revised extensively. D. H. Lawrence said, "It has taken me twenty years to say what I started to say, incoherently, when I was nineteen, in this poem." E. E. Cummings could begin a poem with "O sweet spontaneous earth," but he did not let spontaneity interfere with his own painstaking craftsmanship. Sometimes he wrote 100 or 200 versions of a poem before he felt it was right.

Often, lines that look as if they had occurred to poets in a moment of inspiration turn out to have been revised into their perfection. Whitman's line

> Out of the cradle endlessly rocking

benefited immeasurably from revision. His original inspiration was the toneless

> Out of the rocked cradle . . .

which he varied many ways before he got the simple music he wanted. Whitman, though elsewhere he may have loafed and invited his soul, was a hard worker at his poetry, doing prodigious amounts of revision over the decades.

William Blake is another poet often thought of as inspired, which indeed he claimed to be. "The Authors," he said of his work, "are in Eternity." But an editor familiar with his manuscripts corrects that impression:

It was Blake's belief . . . that long passages, or even whole poems, were merely transcribed by him from the dictation of spirits. The evidence of extant MSS., however, shows that he himself saw nothing final or absolute in this verbal inspiration, but submitted these writings like any others to such successive changes as at length satisfied his artistic conscience. . . . Blake's meticulous care in composition is everywhere apparent in the poems preserved in rough draft. . . . There we find the first crude version, or single stanza around which his idea was to take shape, followed by alteration on alteration, re-arrangement after re-arrangement, deletions, additions and inversions, until at last the poem as in the case of "The Tiger" attains its perfect form.* [cf. pp. 358–359]

Sometimes poets, in addition to making lesser changes, feel that the whole poem should be reconceived and restructured, as Lawrence does when he reduces the five stanzas of his early "The Piano" to the three stanzas of "Piano."

The Piano

Somewhere beneath that piano's superb sleek black
Must hide my mother's piano, little and brown, with the back
That stood close to the wall, and the front's faded silk both torn,
And the keys with little hollows, that my mother's fingers had worn.

5 Softly, in the shadows, a woman is singing to me
Quietly, through the years I have crept back to see
A child sitting under the piano, in the boom of the shaking strings
Pressing the little poised feet of the mother who smiles as she sings.

The full throated woman has chosen a winning, living song
10 And surely the heart that is in me must belong
To the old Sunday evenings, when darkness wandered outside
And hymns gleamed on our warm lips, as we watched mother's fingers glide.

Or this is my sister at home in the old front room
Singing love's first surprised gladness, alone in the gloom.
15 She will start when she sees me, and blushing, spread out her hands
To cover my mouth's raillery, till I'm bound in her shame's heart-spun bands.

A woman is singing me a wild Hungarian air
And her arms, and her bosom, and the whole of her soul is bare,
And the great black piano is clamouring as my mother's never could clamour
20 And my mother's tunes are devoured of this music's ravaging glamour.
                                          [1911]

Piano

Softly, in the dusk, a woman is singing to me;
Taking me back down the vista of years, till I see

*John Sampson, Ed., *The Poetical Works of William Blake* (Oxford University Press, 1913).

A child sitting under the piano, in the boom of the tingling strings
And pressing the small, poised feet of a mother who smiles as she
   sings.

5   In spite of myself, the insidious mastery of song
Betrays me back, till the heart of me weeps to belong
To the old Sunday evenings at home, with winter outside
And hymns in the cosy parlour, the tinkling piano our guide.

So now it is vain for the singer to burst into clamour
10 With the great black piano appassionato. The glamour
Of childish days is upon me, my manhood is cast
Down in the flood of remembrance, I weep like a child for the past.

                                   [1918]
                    D. H. LAWRENCE (1885–1930)

In the earlier poem the poet, or the character he imagines, is listening to "a wild Hungarian air." The music puts him in mind of a very different kind of music, that of hymns sung at home when he was small enough to sit under the old-fashioned square piano. But the soft music he remembers is swallowed up in the "ravaging glamour" of the wild new music.

In the second version, the childhood memory of music at home is more powerful than the effect of the sexy singer. The poem becomes a lament for the lost innocence of childhood.

A critical poll might well select Yeats as the greatest poet of the twentieth century. No poet ever derived less from inspiration or worked harder at hammering his poems into shape. Yeats found writing an "intense unnatural labor that reduces composition to four or five lines a day." He even said he did much of his work by the critical, rather than the imaginative, faculty. We can get some idea of the labor that went into his poetry by looking at the fifth stanza of "Among School Children" (see Anthology, p. 433), which could be summarized as saying: If a mother could see her baby as he will be sixty years later, would all the trouble of his birth seem worthwhile? (Lines 3 and 4 refer to the Platonic notion that the child exists before birth and would like to return to that earlier world unless the memory of it were destroyed by "the drug.")

Yeats's manuscripts show that he started out with a list of possible rhymes for the stanza:

lap	fears	lap
shape	~~tears~~	made
	~~years~~	escape
	~~forth~~ birth	betrayed
	forth	shape
		head

These are obviously not words that just happened to rhyme, as if Yeats were going through the alphabet. The ideas these words stand for are a framework for the way he thought his stanza might develop.

The first two drafts of William Blake's "The Tyger" (see Anthony, p. 397)

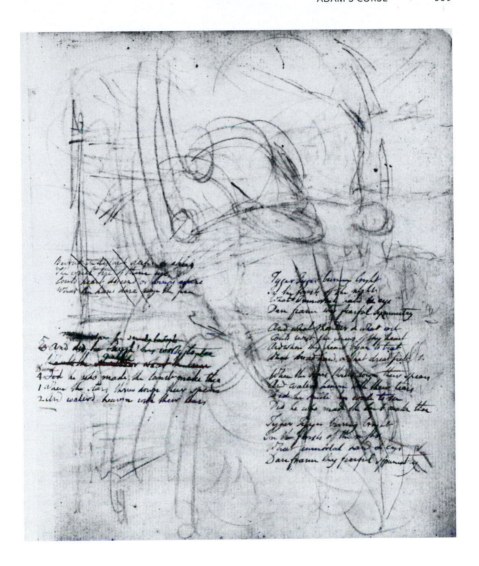

What mother of a child shrieking the first scream
Of a soul
Of a soul struggling to leave
Degradation of the——
What mother with a child upon her breast
Shedding there its tears, all the despair
Of the soul betrayed into the flesh
What youthful mother, rocking on her lap

A fretful thing that knows itself betrayed
Still knowing that it is betrayed[?]
Still half remembering that it [is] betrayed
A thing, the ~~oblivious honey has~~ generative honey had betrayed

And struggles with vain clamor to escape
And that shrieks out and struggles to escape
And that must sleep, ~~or~~ shriek struggle to escape

Before its memory and apprehension fade
Before its   the memories of its freedom fade
As its drugged memories gleam or fade
As it
As still but half drugged memories decide
As its drugged memories may decide
Where some brief memories or the drug decide
~~As flitting~~   As sudden memories or the drug decide

Would think—[if] it came before her in a vision
Would think—had she ~~foreknown~~ foreknowledge of that shape
Would think her son could she foreknow that shape
Would think her son, ~~could she foreknow~~ did she but see that shape

~~The image~~ What the child would be at sixty years
Her son with sixty winters on his head
With maybe sixty winters on   upon his head
With sixty or more winters upon his head
With sixty or more winters on ~~his~~ its head

———— What youthful mother, a shape upon her lap

———— Honey of generation had betrayed,

———— And that must sleep, shriek, struggle to escape

———— As recollection or the drug decide,

———— Would think her son, did she but see that shape

———— With sixty or more winters on its head,

A compensation for the pang of his birth,
Or the uncertainty of his setting forth?

On facing pages 360 and 361 we have, on the right-hand page, the clear, simple, and logical lines that finally made up the stanza. The last two lines seem to have come to Yeats easily—or he may have worked hard at them on a manuscript sheet now lost. But the other lines came only after a difficult struggle with alternative versions, printed on the left-hand page (which is mostly a rubble of undistinguished language). Work sheets preliminary to these may well have been lost or destroyed. Yeats may have made many choices in his own head before writing a word down.

He would make further changes as he dictated. He could then go to work on the neatly typed copy, making so many revisions that it would have to be retyped. And so on. If the poem had appeared in a magazine, he might further rework it before book publication. Even after the book appeared, the revisions continued. Many years after he wrote some of his early poems, he revised them in his later manner—turning "early Yeats" into "late Yeats."

When we see how easily the poem reads, it is hard to remember what must have been the pangs of its birth and the uncertainties of its setting forth.

EXERCISES & DIVERSIONS

A.   A. E. Housman has this to say about the composition of his "I Hoed and Trenched and Weeded": "Two of the stanzas, I do not say which, came into my head, just as they are printed. . . . A third stanza came

Not all writers believe in revision.

with a little coaxing after tea. One more was needed, but it did not come: I had to turn to and compose it myself, and that was a laborious business. I wrote it thirteen times, and it was more than a twelve-month before I got it right."

Can you guess which two stanzas came easily, which came with a little coaxing, and which came with difficulty? If one stanza does seem to you least inspired and most worked over, would you agree with Housman that he finally "got it right"? Or should he have given it a few more tries?

I Hoed and Trenched and Weeded

I hoed and trenched and weeded,
    And took the flowers to fair:
I brought them home unheeded;
    The hue was not the wear.

So up and down I sow them
    For lads like me to find,
When I shall lie below them,
    A dead man out of mind.

Some seed the birds devour,
    And some the season mars,
But here and there will flower
    The solitary stars,

And fields will yearly bear them
    As light-leaved spring comes on,
And luckless lads will wear them
    When I am dead and gone.

                                     [1896]
                           A. E. HOUSMAN (1859–1936)

B.   1.   In the twenty-five or more years that FitzGerald spent on his five editions of *The Rubáiyát* (Anthology, p. 408), he tried many of the stanzas several ways. Here are three versions of his original stanza XII. Can you see a progressive improvement?

"How sweet is mortal Sovranty!"—think some:
Others—"How blest the Paradise to come!"
    Ah, take the Cash in hand and waive the Rest;
Oh, the brave Music of a *distant* Drum!

Some for the Glories of This World; and some
Sigh for the Prophet's Paradise to come;
    Ah, take the Cash, and let the promise go,
Nor heed the music of a distant Drum!

Some for the Glories of This World; and some
Sigh for the Prophet's Paradise to come;

> Ah, take the Cash, and let the Credit go,
> Nor heed the rumble of a distant Drum!

2. Is there a progressive improvement in the changes made in what was originally stanza LXXIV? (No one holds that *all* revisions are improvements.)

> Ah, Moon of my Delight, who know'st no wane,
> The Moon of Heav'n is rising once again:
>   How oft hereafter rising shall she look
> Through this same Garden after me—in vain!

> But see! The rising Moon of Heav'n again—
> Looks for us, Sweet-heart, through the quivering Plane:
>   How oft hereafter rising will she look
> Among those leaves—for one of us in vain!

> Yon rising Moon that looks for us again—
> How oft hereafter will she wax and wane;
>   How oft hereafter rising look for us
> Through this same Garden—and for *one* in vain!

C. Here is an example of "early Yeats" turned into "late Yeats." In what do the differences chiefly consist? Imagery? Emotion? Diction? Rhythm? Form? Does the meaning change?

The Lamentation of the Old Pensioner

(1890 version)

> I had a chair at every hearth,
>   When no one turned to see,
> With 'Look at that old fellow there,
>   And who may he be?'
> And therefore do I wander now,
>   And the fret lies on me.

> The road-side trees keep murmuring.
>   Ah, wherefore murmur ye,
> As in the old days long gone by,
>   Green oak and poplar tree?
> The well-known faces are all gone:
>   And the fret lies on me.

(1925 version)

> Although I shelter from the rain
> Under a broken tree,
> My chair was nearest to the fire
> In every company
> That talked of love or politics,
> Ere Time transfigured me.

Though lads are making pikes again
For some conspiracy,
And crazy rascals rage their fill
At human tyranny,
My contemplations are of Time
That has transfigured me.

There's not a woman turns her face
Upon a broken tree,
And yet the beauties that I loved
Are in my memory;
I spit into the face of Time
That has transfigured me.

WILLIAM BUTLER YEATS (1865–1939)

D.   In 1941 Walter de la Mare published this quatrain in an American magazine.

The Stone

Folded hands and darkened eyes—
        Here one loved too well now lies;
What her name was, Stone, declare;
        Thou could'st not say how fair!

When he included it in a book of poems nine years later, it was very different.

Slim Cunning Hands

Slim cunning hands at rest, and cozening eyes—
Under this stone one loved too wildly lies;
How false she was, no granite could declare;
        Nor all earth's flowers, how fair.   [1950]

WALTER DE LA MARE (1873–1956)

An American poet laureate, Howard Nemerov, whose work is represented in this book, said in a radio interview that he found the new version so moving that he could not read it without tears. What exactly has de la Mare done, line by line, almost word by word, that made such a difference in a poem originally rather dull?

ESSAYS

A.   Look closely at the two versions of D. H. Lawrence's poem about the piano, asking yourself such questions as these:

1.   Why is the description of the mother's old worn piano omitted in the later version?

2. The nightclub singer is a brilliant figure. Does the later version suffer by making no mention of her?
3. Why is the original fourth stanza, pleasant in itself, omitted in the later version?
4. Why are "shaking strings" changed to "tingling strings"?
5. Why is "darkness" changed to "winter"?

Now write an essay in which you compare these two versions, defending one over the other. Use quotations to make your case, analyzing them closely. Feel free to make use of any technical language you have learned from this book.

B. Write an essay comparing Thomas's "In My Craft or Sullen Art" to Yeats's "Adam's Curse." How do the two poems differ? What visions of poetry do they contain? What visions of romantic love? Are these visions related?

POEMS

A. Find a first-person poem you've written that does not satisfy you. Revise it in second or third person.
B. Examine Yeats's way of intensifying verses—boiling them down. Take a long poem of yours and boil it down, cutting at least 50 percent of the lines.
C. Take a short poem of yours and dig deeper into the emotional material. Really try to question your statements with greater skepticism. Write your way further into the material, making a longer poem. Then challenge every line, every word, for its accuracy, cutting anything that does not hold up.

Anthology

ANONYMOUS (date uncertain)

Lord Randal

"O where hae ye been, Lord Randal, my son?
O where hae ye been, my handsome young man?"
"I hae been to the wild wood; mother, make my bed soon,
For I'm weary wi' hunting, and fain wald lie down."

5   "Where gat ye your dinner, Lord Randal, my son?
Where gat ye your dinner, my handsome young man?"
"I din'd wi' my true-love; mother, make my bed soon,
For I'm weary wi' hunting, and fain wald lie down."

"What gat ye to your dinner, Lord Randal, my son?
10 What gat ye to your dinner, my handsome young man?"
"I gat eels boil'd in broo; mother, make my bed soon,
For I'm weary wi' hunting, and fain wald lie down."

"What became of your bloodhounds, Lord Randal, my son?
What became of your bloodhounds, my handsome young man?"
15 "O they swell'd and they died; mother, make my bed soon,
For I'm weary wi' hunting, and fain wald lie down."

"O I fear ye are poison'd, Lord Randal, my son!
I fear ye are poison'd, my handsome young man!"
"O yes! I am poison'd; mother, make my bed soon,
20 For I'm sick at the heart, and I fain wald lie down."

[1]/*hae: have*
[4]/*fain wald: would like to*
[5]/*gat: got*
[11]/*broo: broth, juice*

The Wife of Usher's Well

There lived a wife at Usher's Well,
   And a wealthy wife was she;
She had three stout and stalwart sons,
   And sent them oer the sea.

5 They hadna been a week from her,
   A week but barely ane,
Whan word came to the carline wife
   That her three sons were gane.

They hadna been a week from her,
10   A week but barely three,
Whan word came to the carlin wife
   That her sons she'd never see.

[7]/*carline: an old woman, a witch, or a hag*

"I wish the wind may never cease,
  Nor fashes in the flood,
15 Till my three sons come hame to me,
  In earthly flesh and blood."

It fell about the Martinmass,
  When nights are lang and mirk,
The carlin wife's three sons came hame,
20 And their hats were o the birk.

It neither grew in syke nor ditch,
  Nor yet in ony sheugh;
But at the gates o Paradise,
  That birk grew fair eneugh.

• • •

25 "Blow up the fire, my maidens,
  Bring water from the well;
For a' my house shall feast this night,
  Since my three sons are well."

And she has made to them a bed,
30 She's made it large and wide,
And she's taen her mantle her about,
  Sat down at the bed-side.

Up then crew the red, red cock,
  And up and crew the gray;
35 The eldest to the youngest said,
  " 'T is time we were away."

The cock he hadna crawd but once,
  And clappd his wings at al,
When the youngest to the eldest said,
40 "Brother, we must awa.

"The cock doth craw, the day doth daw,
  The channerin worm doth chide;
Gin we be mist out o our place,
  A sair pain we maun bide.

45 "Fare ye weel, my mother dear!
  Fareweel to barn and byre!
And fare ye weel, the bonny lass
  That kindles my mother's fire!"

---

[14]/**fashes:** _troubles_   [22]/**sheugh:** _furrow, or a trough for slops_
[20]/**birk:** _birch_   [42]/**channerin:** _devouring_
[21]/**syke:** _trench_   [46]/**byre:** _stable, or cattle shed_

SIR THOMAS WYATT (1503–1542)

They Flee from Me

They flee from me that sometime did me seek
With naked foot stalking in my chamber.
I have seen them gentle, tame and meek
That now are wild and do not remember
5   That sometime they put themself in danger
To take bread at my hand, and now they range
Busily seeking with a continual change.

Thankèd be fortune, it hath been otherwise
Twenty times better, but once in special,
10   In thin array, after a pleasant guise,
When her loose gown from her shoulders did fall
And she me caught in her arms long and small,
Therewith all sweetly did me kiss,
And softly said, "Dear heart, how like you this?"

15   It was no dream; I lay broad waking.
But all is turnèd through my gentleness
Into a strange fashion of forsaking;
And I have leave to go of her goodness,
And she also to use newfangleness.
20   But since that I so kindly am servèd,
I would fain know what she hath deservèd.   [1557]

19/**newfangleness:** *desire for change*   20/**kindly:** *according to [her and my]*
nature (also the modern meaning)

CHRISTOPHER MARLOWE (1564–1593)

The Passionate Shepherd to His Love

Come live with me and be my love,
And we will all the pleasures prove
That valleys, groves, hills, and fields,
Woods, or steepy mountain yields.

5   And we will sit upon the rocks,
Seeing the shepherds feed their flocks,
By shallow rivers, to whose falls
Melodious birds sing madrigals.

And I will make thee beds of roses
10   And a thousand fragrant posies,
A cap of flowers, and a kirtle
Embroidered all with leaves of myrtle;

11/**kirtle:** *long dress*

A gown made of the finest wool,
Which from our pretty lambs we pull;
15 Fair linèd slippers for the cold,
With buckles of the purest gold;

A belt of straw and ivy buds
With coral clasps and amber studs:
And if these pleasures may thee move,
20 Come live with me and be my love.

The shepherd swains shall dance and sing
For thy delight each May morning:
If these delights thy mind may move,
Then live with me and be my love.

[1600]

SIR WALTER RALEIGH (1552?–1618)

The Nymph's Reply to the Shepherd

If all the world and love were young,
And truth in every shepherd's tongue,
These pretty pleasures might me move
To live with thee and be thy love.

5 Time drives the flocks from field to fold,
When rivers rage and rocks grow cold;
And Philomel becometh dumb;
The rest complains of cares to come.

The flowers do fade, and wanton fields
10 To wayward winter reckoning yields:
A honey tongue, a heart of gall,
Is fancy's spring, but sorrow's fall.

Thy gowns, thy shoes, thy beds of roses,
Thy cap, thy kirtle, and thy posies
15 Soon break, soon wither, soon forgotten,
In folly ripe, in reason rotten.

Thy belt of straw and ivy buds,
Thy coral clasps and amber studs,
All these in me no means can move
20 To come to thee and be thy love.

But could youth last, and love still breed,
Had joys no date, nor age no need,
Then these delights my mind might move
To love with thee and be thy love.

[1600]

7/*Philomel: the nightingale*

SIR EDMUND SPENSER (1552?–1599)

One Day I Wrote Her Name Upon the Strand

One day I wrote her name upon the strand,
   But came the waves and washèd it away.
   Again I wrote it with a second hand,
   But came the tide and made my pains his prey.
5 "Vain man," said she, "that dost in vain essay
   A mortal thing so to immortalize;
   For I myself shall like to this decay,
   And eke my name be wipèd out likewise."
"Not so," quod I, "let baser things devise
10 To die in dust, but you shall live by fame;
   My verse your virtues rare shall eternize,
   And in the heavens write your glorious name:
Where, whereas death shall all the world subdue,
   Our love shall live, and later life renew."   [1595]

⁸/*eke: also*   ⁹/*quod: said*

SIR PHILIP SIDNEY (1554–1586)

With How Sad Steps, O Moon

With how sad steps, O moon, thou climb'st the skies,
   How silently, and with how wan a face.
   What, may it be that even in heavenly place
That busy archer his sharp arrows tries?
5 Sure, if that long-with-love-acquainted eyes
   Can judge of love, thou feel'st a lover's case;
   I read it in thy looks; thy languisht grace,
To me that feel the like, thy state descries.

Then, even of fellowship, O moon, tell me
10 Is constant love deemed there but want of wit?
Are beauties there as proud as here they be?
   Do they above love to be loved, and yet
Those lovers scorn whom that love doth possess?
Do they call virtue there ungratefulness?   [1598]

⁹/*of fellowship: as a friend in the same situation*   ¹⁴/*call virtue . . . ungratefulness: call ungratefulness a virtue*

WILLIAM SHAKESPEARE (1564–1616)

From *Sonnets*

18

Shall I compare thee to a summer's day?
Thou art more lovely and more temperate.
Rough winds do shake the darling buds of May,
And summer's lease hath all too short a date.
5   Sometime too hot the eye of heaven shines,
And often is his gold complexion dimmed;
And every fair from fair sometime declines,
By chance, or nature's changing course, untrimmed;
But thy eternal summer shall not fade,
10   Nor lose possession of that fair thou owest,
Nor shall death brag thou wanderest in his shade,
When in eternal lines to time thou growest.
    So long as men can breathe or eyes can see,
    So long lives this, and this gives life to thee.   [1609]

[8]/*untrimmed: stripped of its trimming*   [10]/*owest: own*

73

That time of year thou mayst in me behold
When yellow leaves, or none, or few, do hang
Upon those boughs which shake against the cold,
Bare ruined choirs where late the sweet birds sang.
5   In me thou seest the twilight of such day
As after sunset fadeth in the west,
Which by and by black night doth take away,
Death's second self, that seals up all in rest.
In me thou seest the glowing of such fire
10   That on the ashes of his youth doth lie,
As the deathbed whereon it must expire,
Consumed with that which it was nourished by.
    This thou perceivest, which makes thy love more strong,
    To love that well which thou must leave ere long.   [1609]

116

Let me not to the marriage of true minds
Admit impediments; love is not love
Which alters when it alteration finds,
Or bends with the remover to remove.
5   Oh no, it is an ever-fixèd mark
That looks on tempests and is never shaken;
It is the star to every wandering bark,
Whose worth's unknown, although his height be taken.
Love's not time's fool, though rosy lips and cheeks

10 Within his bending sickle's compass come;
Love alters not with his brief hours and weeks,
But bears it out even to the edge of doom.
    If this be error and upon me proved,
    I never writ, nor no man ever loved.   [1609]

129

The expense of spirit in a waste of shame
Is lust in action; and, till action, lust
Is perjured, murderous, bloody, full of blame,
Savage, extreme, rude, cruel, not to trust;
5 Enjoyed no sooner but despisèd straight;
Past reason hunted, and no sooner had,
Past reason hated as a swallowed bait
On purpose laid to make the taker mad;
Mad in pursuit, and in possession so;
10 Had, having, and in quest to have, extreme;
A bliss in proof, and proved, a very woe,
Before, a joy proposed; behind, a dream.
    All this the world well knows, yet none knows well
    To shun the heaven that leads men to this hell.   [1609]

[1]/**expense of spirit:** *expenditure of*   [11]/**in proof:** *while experienced*
vital energy

THOMAS CAMPION (1567–1620)

My Sweetest Lesbia, Let Us Live and Love

My sweetest Lesbia, let us live and love,
And though the sager sort our deeds reprove,
Let us not weigh them. Heaven's great lamps do dive
Into their west, and straight again revive;
5 But, soon as once set is our little light,
Then must we sleep one ever-during night.

If all would lead their lives in love like me,
Then bloody swords and armour should not be;
No drum nor trumpet peaceful sleeps should move,
10 Unless alarm came from the camp of love.
But fools do live and waste their little light,
And seek with pain their ever-during night.

When timely death my life and fortune ends,
Let not my hearse be vexed with mourning friends;
15 But let all lovers, rich in triumph, come
And with sweet pastimes grace my happy tomb:
And, Lesbia, close up thou my little light,
And crown with love my ever-during night.   [1601]

It Fell on a Summer's Day

It fell on a summer's day
While sweet Bessie sleeping lay
In her bower, on her bed,
Light with curtains shadowèd,
5   Jamey came; she him spies,
Opening half her heavy eyes.

Jamey stole in through the door;
She lay slumbering as before;
Softly to her he drew near;
10   She heard him, yet would not hear.
Bessie vowed not to speak;
He resolved that dump to break.

First a soft kiss he doth take;
She lay still, and would not wake.
15   Then his hands learned to woo;
She dreampt not what he would do,
But still slept, while he smiled
To see love by sleep beguiled.

Jamey then began to play;
20   Bessie as one buried lay,
Gladly still through this sleight
Deceived in her own deceit.
And since this trance began,
She sleeps every afternoon.   [1601]

¹²/***dump:*** *reverie*   ²¹/***sleight:*** *trick*

THOMAS NASHE (1567–1601)

Adieu, Farewell Earth's Bliss

Adieu, farewell earth's bliss!
This world uncertain is:
Fond are life's lustful joys;
Death proves them all but toys.
5   None from his darts can fly;
I am sick, I must die.
      Lord, have mercy on us.

Untitled in the play in which it occurs, this poem is sometimes given (by editors) some such title as "In Time of Pestilence."

³/***fond:*** *foolish*   ⁴/***toys:*** *trifles*

Rich men, trust not in wealth:
Gold cannot buy you health;
10   Physic himself must fade.
All things to end are made;
The plague full swift goes by.
I am sick, I must die.
     Lord, have mercy on us.

15   Beauty is but a flower
Which wrinkles will devour;
Brightness falls from the air;
Queens have died young and fair;
Dust hath closed Helen's eye.
20   I am sick, I must die.
     Lord, have mercy on us.

Strength stoops unto the grave;
Worms feed on Hector brave.
Swords may not fight with fate;
25   Earth still holds ope her gate.
Come, come, the bells do cry.
I am sick, I must die.
     Lord, have mercy on us.

Wit with his wantonness
30   Tasteth death's bitterness;
Hell's executioner
Hath no ears for to hear
What vain art can reply.
I am sick, I must die.
35   *Lord, have mercy on us.*

Haste therefore, each degree,
To welcome destiny:
Heaven is our heritage;
Earth but a player's stage.
40   Mount we unto the sky!
I am sick, I must die.
     Lord, have mercy on us.   [1600]

29/*wantonness: playfulness*   36/*degree: social level*

JOHN DONNE (1572–1631)

The Sun Rising

          Busy old fool, unruly sun,
            Why dost thou thus
Through windows, and through curtains call on us?
Must to thy motions lovers' seasons run?

5   Saucy pedantic wretch, go chide
            Late school boys, and sour prentices,
         Go tell court-huntsmen that the King will ride,
         Call country ants to harvest offices;
      Love, all alike, no season knows, nor clime,
10   Nor hours, days, months, which are the rags of time.

            Thy beams, so reverend and strong
            Why shouldst thou think?
      I could eclipse and cloud them with a wink,
      But that I would not lose her sight so long:
15   If her eyes have not blinded thine,
            Look, and tomorrow late, tell me
         Whether both the Indias of spice and mine
         Be where thou left'st them, or lie here with me.
      Ask for those Kings whom thou saw'st yesterday,
20   And thou shalt hear: all here in one bed lay.

            She's all states, and all princes, I,
            Nothing else is.
      Princes do but play us; compared to this,
      All honor's mimic; all wealth alchemy.
25   Thou, sun, art half as happy as we,
            In that the world's contracted thus;
         Thine age asks ease, and since thy duties be
         To warm the world, that's done in warming us.
      Shine here to us, and thou art everywhere;
30   This bed thy center is, these walls, thy sphere.   [1633]

[24]/**alchemy:** *false gold, fraudulence (alchemy professed to be able to transmute base metals into gold)*

A Valediction: Of Weeping

            Let me pour forth
         My tears before thy face, whilst I stay here,
         For thy face coins them, and thy stamp they bear,
         And by this mintage they are something worth,
5   For thus they be
            Pregnant of thee;
         Fruits of much grief they are, emblems of more,
         When a tear falls, that thou falls which it bore,
     So thou and I are nothing then, when on a diverse shore.

10   On a round ball
         A workman that hath copies by, can lay
         An Europe, Afric, and an Asia,
         And quickly make that, which was nothing, all;
           So doth each tear,
15   Which thee doth wear,

[2]/**whilst I stay:** *before I leave (the speaker is about to go on a sea voyage)*   [3]/**coins:** *is reflected in them, like the face on a coin*

A globe, yea world, by that impression grow,
   Till thy tears mixed with mine do overflow
This world, by waters sent from thee, my heaven dissolvèd so.

      O more than moon,
20   Draw not up seas to drown me in thy sphere,
   Weep me not dead, in thine arms, but forbear
   To teach the sea, what it may do too soon;
         Let not the wind
         Example find,
25   To do me more harm, than it purposeth;
   Since thou and I sigh one another's breath,
Whoe'er sighs most, is cruellest, and hastes the other's death.   [1633]

A Valediction: Forbidding Mourning

As virtuous men pass mildly away,
   And whisper to their souls, to go,
Whilst some of their sad friends do say,
   The breath goes now, and some say, no:

5   So let us melt, and make no noise,
   No tear-floods, nor sigh-tempests move;
'Twere profanation of our joys
   To tell the laity our love.

Moving of the earth brings harms and fears,
10   Men reckon what it did and meant,
But trepidation of the spheres,
   Though greater far, is innocent.

Dull sublunary lovers' love
   (Whose soul is sense) cannot admit
15 Absence, because it doth remove
   Those things which elemented it.

But we by a love, so much refined,
   That ourselves know not what it is,
Inter-assurèd of the mind,
20   Care less, eyes, lips, and hands to miss.

Our two souls therefore, which are one,
   Though I must go, endure not yet
A breach, but an expansion,
   Like gold to airy thinness beat.

8/**laity:** *ordinary people, not ordained in the religion of love*
9/**moving of the earth:** *earthquakes*
11/**trepidation of the spheres:** *movements in the distant heavens (specifically, what astronomers call "the precession of the equinoxes": apparent shifts in the heavens because of the wobbling of the earth on its axis)*
13/**sublunary:** *beneath the moon, earthly*
16/**elemented:** *made up its elements*
24/**gold:** *gold can be hammered so thin it would take 2,000 sheets to make up the thickness of this page*

25 If they be two, they are two so
        As stiff twin compasses are two:
    Thy soul, the fixed foot, makes no show
        To move, but doth, if the other do.

    And though it in the center sit,
30   Yet when the other far doth roam,
    It leans, and hearkens after it,
        And grows erect, as that comes home.

    Such wilt thou be to me, who must
        Like the other foot, obliquely run;
35 Thy firmness makes my circle just,
        And makes me end, where I begun.   [1633]

26/*compasses: a draughtsman's compass for drawing circles; not a mariner's compass*

Death Be Not Proud

    Death be not proud, though some have callèd thee
    Mighty and dreadful, for thou art not so;
    For those whom thou think'st thou dost overthrow
    Die not, poor death, nor yet canst thou kill me.
5   From rest and sleep, which but thy pictures be,
    Much pleasure, then from thee much more must flow,
    And soonest our best men with thee do go,
    Rest of their bones, and soul's delivery.
    Thou art slave to fate, chance, kings, and desperate men,
10 And dost with poison, war, and sickness dwell,
    And poppy, or charms can make us sleep as well,
    And better than thy stroke; why swell'st thou then?
    One short sleep past, we wake eternally,
    And death shall be no more; death, thou shalt die.   [1633]

11/*poppy: one kind of poppy is the source of opium*

BEN JONSON (1573?–1637)

On My First Son

    Farewell, thou child of my right hand, and joy.
        My sin was too much hope of thee, loved boy;
    Seven years thou wert lent to me, and I thee pay,
        Exacted by thy fate, on the just day.
5   Oh, could I lose all father now. For why
        Will man lament the state he should envý?—
    To have so soon 'scaped world's and flesh's rage,
        And, if no other misery, yet age.

1/*child of my right hand: the meaning of Benjamin (the boy's name) in Hebrew*

Rest in soft peace, and, asked, say here doth lie
10   Ben Jonson his best piece of poetry.
For whose sake, henceforth, all his vows be such
    As what he loves may never like too much.   [1616]

ROBERT HERRICK (1591–1674)

Delight in Disorder

A sweet disorder in the dress
Kindles in clothes a wantonness:
A lawn about the shoulders thrown
Into a fine distraction;
5 An erring lace, which here and there
Enthralls the crimson stomacher;
A cuff neglectful, and thereby
Ribbons to flow confusedly;
A winning wave, deserving note,
10 In the tempestuous petticoat;
A careless shoe-string, in whose tie
I see a wild civility,
Do more bewitch me, than when art
Is too precise in every part.   [1648]

[3]/*lawn: sheer linen*   [6]/*stomacher: a sort of dickey worn
beneath the laces of the bodice*

GEORGE HERBERT (1593–1633)

Redemption

Having been tenant long to a rich Lord,
    Not thriving, I resolvèd to be bold,
    And make a suit unto him, to afford
A new small-rented lease, and cancel the old.
5 In heaven at his manor I him sought:
    They told me there, that he was lately gone
    About some land, which he had dearly bought
Long since on earth, to take possession.
I straight returned, and knowing his great birth,
10   Sought him accordingly in great resorts;
    In cities, theatres, gardens, parks, and courts:
At length I heard a ragged noise and mirth
    Of thieves and murderers: there I him espied,
    Who straight, *Your suit is granted,* said, and died.   [1633]

Easter-Wings

Lord, who createdst man in wealth and store,
Though foolishly he lost the same,
Decaying more and more
Till he became
5   Most poor:
With thee
Oh let me rise
As larks, harmoniously,
And sing this day thy victories:
10   Then shall the fall further the flight in me.

My tender age in sorrow did begin:
And still with sicknesses and shame
Thou didst so punish sin,
That I became
15   Most thin.
With thee
Let me combine.
And feel thy victory:
For, if I imp my wing on thine,
20   Affliction shall advance the flight in me.   [1633]

¹⁹/*imp:* *in falconry, to graft feathers onto an injured wing*

The Pulley

When God at first made man,
Having a glass of blessings standing by—
Let us (said he) pour on his all we can;
Let the world's riches, which dispersèd lie,
5   Contract into a span.

So strength first made a way,
The beauty flowed, then wisdom, honor, pleasure:
When almost all was out, God made a stay,
Perceiving that, alone of all His treasure,
10   Rest in the bottom lay.

For if I should (said he)
Bestow this jewel also on My creature,
He would adore My gifts instead of Me,
And rest in Nature, not the God of Nature:
15   So both should losers be.

Yet let him keep the rest,
But keep him with repining restlessness;
Let him be rich and weary, that at least,
If goodness lead him not, yet weariness
20   May toss him to My breast.   [1633]

EDMUND WALLER (1606–1687)

Go, Lovely Rose

Go, lovely rose,
Tell her that wastes her time and me
That now she know,
When I resemble her to thee,
5   How sweet and fair she seems to be.

Tell her that's young
And shuns to have her graces spied,
That hadst thou sprung
In deserts where no men abide,
10   Thou must have uncommended died.

Small is the worth
Of beauty from the light retired:
Bid her come forth,
Suffer herself to be desired,
15   And not blush so to be admired.

Then die, that she
The common fate of all things rare
May read in thee,
How small a part of time they share
20   That are so wondrous sweet and fair.   [1645]

JOHN MILTON (1608–1674)

Lycidas

*In this monody the author bewails a learned friend, unfortunately drowned
in his passage from Chester on the Irish Seas, 1637. And by occasion
foretells the ruin of our corrupted clergy, then in their height.*

Yet once more, O ye laurels, and once more,
Ye myrtles brown, with ivy never sere,
I come to pluck your berries harsh and crude,
And with forced fingers rude
5   Shatter your leaves before the mellowing year.
Bitter constraint and sad occasion dear
Compels me to disturb your season due;

See comments, p. 189.
monody: *originally, an ode sung by one person; a lament*

1–2/**laurels . . . myrtles . . . ivy:**
*three kinds of evergreen foliage
symbolizing poetry*

2/**sere:** *dry, withered*
3/**crude:** *not yet ripe*
6/**dear:** *heartfelt, grievous*

For Lycidas is dead, dead ere his prime,
Young Lycidas, and hath not left his peer.
10   Who would not sing for Lycidas? he knew
Himself to sing, and build the lofty rhyme.
He must not float upon his watery bier
Unwept, and welter to the parching wind,
Without the meed of some melodious tear.
15   Begin then, sisters of the sacred well
That from beneath the seat of Jove doth spring;
Begin, and somewhat loudly sweep the string.
Hence with denial vain and coy excuse;
So may some gentle muse
20   With lucky words favour my destined urn,
And as he passes turn,
And bid fair peace be to my sable shroud.
        For we were nursed upon the self-same hill,
Fed the same flock, by fountain, shade, and rill;
25   Together both, ere the high lawns appeared
Under the opening eyelids of the morn,
We drove a-field, and both together heard
What time the gray-fly winds her sultry horn,
Battening our flocks with the fresh dews of night,
30   Oft till the star that rose at evening, bright,
Toward heaven's descent had sloped his westering wheel.
Meanwhile the rural ditties were not mute,
Tempered to the oaten flute;
Rough satyrs danced, and fauns with cloven heel
35   From the glad sound would not be absent long;
And old Damœtas loved to hear our song.
        But O the heavy change, now thou art gone,
Now thou art gone, and never must return!
Thee, shepherd, thee the woods and desert caves,
40   With wild thyme and the gadding vine o'ergrown,
And all their echoes, mourn.
The willows and the hazel copses green
Shall now no more be seen,
Fanning their joyous leaves to thy soft lays.
45   As killing as the canker to the rose,
Or taint-worm to the weanling herds that graze,
Or frost to flowers, that their gay wardrobe wear,
When first the white-thorn blows;
Such, Lycidas, thy loss to shepherd's ear.

[14]/**meed**: *gift*
[15]/**sisters**: *the Muses*
[28]/**gray-fly**: *name of several insects, some beetlelike*
[29]/**battening**: *feeding, fattening*
[33]/**oaten**: *made of an oat straw*

[36]/**Damœtas**: *unidentified (an elderly professor?)*
[45]/**canker**: *destructive bug or caterpillar*
[46]/**taint-worm**: *intestinal worm that infests young cattle*
   weanling: *newly weaned*

50 Where were ye, nymphs, when the remorseless deep
    Closed o'er the head of your loved Lycidas?
    For neither were ye playing on the steep
    Where your old bards, the famous druids, lie,
    Nor on the shaggy top of Mona high,
55 Nor yet where Deva spreads her wizard stream.
    Ay me, I fondly dream!
    Had ye been there—for what could that have done?
    What could the muse herself that Orpheus bore,
    The muse herself, for her enchanting son,
60 Whom universal nature did lament,
    When by the rout that made the hideous roar
    His gory visage down the stream was sent,
    Down the swift Hebrus to the Lesbian shore?
        Alas! what boots it with uncessant care
65 To tend the homely, slighted, shepherd's trade,
    And strictly meditate the thankless muse?
    Were it not better done, as others use,
    To sport with Amaryllis in the shade,
    Or with the tangles of Neæra's hair?
70 Fame is the spur that the clear spirit doth raise
    (That last infirmity of noble mind)
    To scorn delights and live laborious days;
    But the fair guerdon when we hope to find,
    And think to burst out into sudden blaze,
75 Comes the blind fury with the abhorrèd shears,
    And slits the thin-spun life. "But not the praise,"
    Phœbus replied, and touched my trembling ears:
    "Fame is no plant that grows on mortal soil
    Nor in the glistering foil
80 Set off to the world, nor in broad rumour lies;
    But lives and spreads aloft by those pure eyes
    And perfect witness of all-judging Jove;

53/**druids:** *an order of ancient Celtic priest-poet-magicians*
54/**Mona:** *the island of Anglesey, off the northern coast of Wales*
55/**Deva:** *the river Dee, thought to have prophetic powers, which flows through Chester and empties into the Irish Sea*
56/**fondly:** *foolishly*
58/**Orpheus:** *legendary Greek poet and musician, son of the muse Calliope, torn to pieces by angered Thracian women. His head—still singing—was swept down the river Hebrus (in Thrace) and across the Aegean to the island of Lesbos.*

64/**what boots it:** *what good does it do*
65/**shepherd's trade:** *poetry, in this pastoral world*
67/**use:** *habitually do*
68–69/**Amaryllis . . . Neæra:** *women's names, borrowed from classical poetry*
73/**guerdon:** *reward*
75/**fury:** *death—of the three fates, the one that cuts the thread of our life*
77/**Phœbus:** *Apollo, god of beauty, poetry, etc. His touching or pulling the ear is a gesture of reproof.*
79/**foil:** *gold or silver leaf placed to increase the brightness of precious stones*

As he pronounces lastly on each deed,
Of so much fame in heaven expect thy meed."
85   O fountain Arethuse, and thou honoured flood,
Smooth-sliding Mincius, crowned with vocal reeds,
That strain I heard was of a higher mood:
But now my oat proceeds,
And listens to the herald of the sea,
90 That came in Neptune's plea.
He asked the waves, and asked the felon winds,
What hard mishap hath doomed this gentle swain?
And questioned every gust of rugged wings
That blows from off each beakèd promontory:
95 They knew not of his story;
And sage Hippotades their answer brings,
That not a blast was from his dungeon strayed;
The air was calm, and on the level brine
Sleek Panope with all her sisters played.
100 It was that fatal and perfidious bark,
Built in the eclipse, and rigged with curses dark,
That sunk so low that sacred head of thine.
     Next Camus, reverend sire, went footing slow,
His mantle hairy, and his bonnet sedge,
105 Inwrought with figures dim, and on the edge
Like to that sanguine flower inscribed with woe.
"Ah! who hath reft," quoth he, "my dearest pledge?"
Last came, and last did go,
The pilot of the Galilean lake;
110 Two massy keys he bore of metals twain
(The golden opes, the iron shuts amain).
He shook his mitred locks, and stern bespake:
"How well could I have spared for thee, young swain,
Enow of such as, for their bellies' sake,
115 Creep and intrude and climb into the fold!
Of other care they little reckoning make
Than how to scramble at the shearers' feast,
And shove away the worthy bidden guest.

85/**Arethuse:** *a spring in Sicily, symbolic here of Sicilian pastoral poetry*
86/**Mincius:** *Italian river near Vergil's birthplace, symbolic here of Italian pastoral poetry*
88/**oat:** *see line 33*
89/**herald of the sea:** *The sea god Triton*
96/**Hippotades:** *Aeolus, god of the winds*
99/**Panope:** *a sea nymph*

103/**Camus:** *the river Cam, representing Cambridge University*
104/**hairy:** *with the fur trimming of an academic gown (?)*
sedge: *a water plant with a flaglike flower*
106/**flower:** *the hyacinth, the design on whose petals was thought to be the Greek for* Alas!
109/**pilot:** *probably Saint Peter with the keys of heaven and a bishop's cap (miter)*
111/**amain:** *with force*
114/**enow:** *enough*

Blind mouths! that scarce themselves know how to hold
120 A sheep-hook, or have learnt aught else the least
That to the faithful herdman's art belongs!
What recks it them? What need they? They are sped;
And when they list, their lean and flashy songs
Grate on their scrannel pipes of wretched straw;
125 The hungry sheep look up, and are not fed,
But swoln with wind and the rank mist they draw,
Rot inwardly, and foul contagion spread;
Besides what the grim wolf with privy paw
Daily devours apace, and nothing said.
130 But that two-handed engine at the door
Stands ready to smite once, and smite no more."
      Return, Alpheus; the dread voice is past
That shrunk thy streams; return, Sicilian muse,
And call the vales, and bid them hither cast
135 Their bells and flowrets of a thousand hues.
Ye valleys low, where the mild whispers use
Of shades and wanton winds and gushing brooks,
On whose fresh lap the swart star sparely looks,
Throw hither all your quaint enamelled eyes,
140 That on the green turf suck the honeyed showers,
And purple all the ground with vernal flowers.
Bring the rathe primrose that forsaken dies,
The tufted crow-toe, and pale jessamine,
The white pink, and the pansy freaked with jet,
145 The glowing violet,
The musk-rose, and the well-attired woodbine,
With cowslips wan that hang the pensive head,
And every flower that sad embroidery wears;

119/**blind mouths:** *a concentrated way of saying that bad clergymen are all greedy mouths and fail to see what they should see*
120/**a sheep-hook:** *a symbol of the pastor's life, perhaps a bishop's staff*
121/**herdman:** *pastor, clergyman*
122/**What recks it them?:** *What do they care?*
   they are sped: *they have prospered*
123/**list:** *want to*
124/**scrannel:** *thin, scratchy*
   straw: *cf. l, 33*
128/**wolf:** *apparently the Catholics, in their attempt to make converts*
130/**two-handed engine:** *Many guesses have been made about this ominous and mysterious object, among them a two-handed sword*

belonging to God or Saint Michael; the two houses of Parliament; Puritan zeal; the approaching civil war; the combined forces of England and Scotland; etc. The fact that it cannot be identified with certainty makes it the more ominous.
132/**Alpheus:** *a Greek river whose waters were thought to flow unmixed through the sea to rise in the "fountain Arethuse" of line 85*
136/**use:** *are frequent*
138/**swart star:** *Sirius, the Dog Star, associated with the hot weather that burns or tans, makes swart*
142/**rathe:** *early*
143/**crow-toe:** *wild hyacinth*
144/**freaked:** *streaked whimsically (freakishly). Milton made up the word.*
146/**woodbine:** *honeysuckle*

Bid amaranthus all his beauty shed,
150 And daffodillies fill their cups with tears,
To strew the laureate hearse where Lycid lies.
For so to interpose a little ease,
Let our frail thoughts dally with false surmise,
Ay me! whilst thee the shores and sounding seas
155 Wash far away, where'er thy bones are hurled,
Whether beyond the stormy Hebrides,
Where thou perhaps under the whelming tide
Visit'st the bottom of the monstrous world;
Or whether thou, to our moist vows denied,
160 Sleep'st by the fable of Bellerus old,
Where the great vision of the guarded mount
Looks toward Namancos and Bayona's hold;
Look homeward, angel, now, and melt with ruth;
And O ye dolphins, waft the hapless youth.
165   Weep no more, woeful shepherds, weep no more,
For Lycidas, your sorrow, is not dead,
Sunk though he be beneath the watery floor;
So sinks the day-star in the ocean bed,
And yet anon repairs his drooping head,
170 And tricks his beams, and with new-spangled ore
Flames in the forehead of the morning sky:
So Lycidas sunk low, but mounted high,
Through the dear might of him that walked the waves,
Where, other groves and other streams along,
175 With nectar pure his oozy locks he laves,
And hears the unexpressive nuptial song,
In the blest kingdoms meek of joy and love.
There entertain him all the saints above,
In solemn troops and sweet societies,
180 That sing, and singing in their glory move,
And wipe the tears for ever from his eyes.
Now, Lycidas, the shepherds weep no more;

149/**amaranthus:** *an imaginary flower thought never to fade*
151/**laureate:** *crowned with laurel*
153/**false surmise:** *the notion that the body of Lycidas is available, and that flowers have any real concern for him*
156/**Hebrides:** *islands off the western coast of Scotland*
160/**Bellerus:** *a fabulous figure apparently invented by Milton, named for Bellerium, or Land's End in Cornwall*
161/**great vision:** *Saint Michael, who was said to appear on the* pyramidal island off Cornwall named for him
162/**Namancos and Bayona:** *place names of an old region and a city in northwest Spain, about 500 miles south of the guarded mount, across the Atlantic*
163/**angel:** *Saint Michael*
ruth: *pity*
164/**dolphins:** *probably an allusion to the early Greek poet Arion, saved from drowning by a dolphin. There are other legends of dolphin rescues.*
168/**day-star:** *sun*
170/**tricks:** *trims*
173/**him:** *Christ*
176/**unexpressive:** *inexpressible*

Henceforth thou art the genius of the shore,
In thy large recompense, and shalt be good
185 To all that wander in that perilous flood.
     Thus sang the uncouth swain to the oaks and rills,
While the still morn went out with sandals gray;
He touched the tender stops of various quills,
With eager thought warbling his Doric lay:
190 And now the sun had stretched out all the hills,
And now was dropt into the western bay.
At last he rose, and twitched his mantle blue:
To-morrow to fresh woods and pastures new.   [1645]

183/**genius:** *protective local deity*   188/**stops . . . quills:** *finger-holes . . . pipes*
186/**uncouth:** *unknown, obscure*   189/**Doric:** *Much Greek pastoral poetry*
                                                  was in the Doric dialect.

On His Blindness

When I consider how my light is spent,
     Ere half my days, in this dark world and wide,
     And that one talent which is death to hide
     Lodged with me useless, though my soul more bent
5 To serve therewith my Maker, and present
     My true account, lest he returning chide,
     "Doth God exact day-labor, light denied?"
     I fondly ask; but patience to prevent
That murmur, soon replies, "God doth not need
10   Either man's work or his own gifts; who best
     Bear his mild yoke, they serve him best, his state
Is kingly. Thousands at his bidding speed
     And post o'er land and ocean without rest:
     They also serve who only stand and wait."   [1673]

8/**fondly:** *foolishly*   13/**post:** *travel rapidly*

ANNE BRADSTREET (1612–1672)

To My Dear and Loving Husband

If ever two were one, then surely we.
If ever man were loved by wife, then thee;
If ever wife was happy in a man,
Compare with me, ye women, if you can.
5 I prize thy love more than whole mines of gold,
Or all the riches that the East doth hold.
My love is such that rivers cannot quench,
Nor aught but love from thee give recompense.
Thy love is such I can no way repay,
10 The heavens reward thee manifold, I pray.
Then while we live, in love let's so perséver
That when we live no more, we may live ever.   [1678]

ANDREW MARVELL (1621–1678)

To His Coy Mistress

Had we but world enough, and time,
This coyness, Lady, were no crime.
We would sit down and think which way
To walk and pass our long love's day.
5   Thou by the Indian Ganges' side
Shouldst rubies find; I by the tide
Of Humber would complain. I would
Love you ten years before the Flood,
And you should, if you please, refuse
10 Till the conversion of the Jews.
My vegetable love should grow
Vaster than empires, and more slow;
An hundred years should go to praise
Thine eyes and on thy forehead gaze;
15 Two hundred to adore each breast,
But thirty thousand to the rest;
An age at least to every part,
And the last age should show your heart.
For, Lady, you deserve this state,
20 Nor would I love at lower rate.
      But at my back I always hear
Time's wingèd chariot hurrying near;
And yonder all before us lie
Deserts of vast eternity.
25 Thy beauty shall no more be found,
Nor, in thy marble vault, shall sound
My echoing song; then worms shall try
That long preserved virginity,
And your quaint honor turn to dust,
30 And into ashes all my lust:
The grave's a fine and private place,
But none, I think, do there embrace.
      Now therefore, while the youthful hue
Sits on thy skin like morning dew,
35 And while thy willing soul transpires
At every pore with instant fires,
Now let us sport us while we may,
And now, like amorous birds of prey,
Rather at once our time devour
40 Than languish in his slow-chapped power.

2/**coyness:** *shyness, reserve, disdain*
10/**conversion of the Jews:** *which, it was thought, would not come about until the end of time*

40/**slow-chapped:** *slow-jawed, devouring slowly*

Let us roll all our strength and all
Our sweetness up into one ball,
And tear our pleasures with rough strife
Through the iron gates of life:
45 Thus, though we cannot make our sun
Stand still, yet we will make him run.   [1681]

KATHERINE PHILIPS (1631–1664)

An Answer to Another Persuading a Lady to Marriage

Forbear, bold youth; all's heaven here,
    And what you do aver
To others, courtship may appear;
    'Tis sacrilege to her.

5 She is a public deity;
    And were't not very odd
She should depose herself to be
    A petty household god?

First make the sun in private shine
10   And bid the world adieu,
That so he may his beams confine
    In compliment to you:

But if of that you do despair,
    Think how you did amiss
15 To strive to fix her beams, which are
    More bright and large than this.   [1667]

[15]/*fix: confine to one place*

APHRA BEHN (1640–1689)

Song: Love Armed

Love in fantastic triumph sate,
    Whilst bleeding hearts around him flowed,
For whom fresh pains he did create,
    And strange tyrannic power he showed:
5 From thy bright eyes he took his fire,
    Which round about in sport he hurled;
But 'twas from mine he took desire,
    Enough to undo the amorous world.

From me he took his sighs and tears;
10   From thee, his pride and cruelty;
From me, his languishments and fears;
    And every killing dart from thee.

Thus thou and I the god have armed
    And set him up a deity;
15 But my poor heart alone is harmed,
    Whilst thine the victor is, and free. [1684]

JONATHAN SWIFT (1667–1745)

A Description of the Morning

Now hardly here and there an hackney-coach,
Appearing, showed the ruddy morn's approach.
Now Betty from her master's bed had flown,
And softly stole to discompose her own.
5 The slipshod prentice from his master's door
Had pared the dirt, and sprinkled round the floor.
Now Moll had whirled her mop with dextrous airs,
Prepared to scrub the entry and the stairs.
The youth with broomy stumps began to trace
10 The kennel-edge, where wheels had worn the place.
The small-coal man was heard with cadence deep,
Till drowned in shriller notes of chimney-sweep,
Duns at his lordship's gate began to meet,
And Brickdust Moll had screamed through half the street.
15 The turnkey now his flock returning sees,
Duly let out a-nights to steal for fees;
The watchful bailiffs take their silent stands;
And schoolboys lag with satchels in their hands. [1711]

9/*broomy stumps: worn-down brooms*
10/*kennel: gutter, open sewer*
13/*duns: creditors*
14/*brickdust: an abrasive used for cleaning*
15/*turnkey: jailer*

THOMAS GRAY (1716–1771)

Elegy Written in a Country Churchyard

The curfew tolls the knell of parting day,
The lowing herd wind slowly o'er the lea,
The ploughman homeward plods his weary way,
And leaves the world to darkness and to me.

5 Now fades the glimmering landscape on the sight,
And all the air a solemn stillness holds,
Save where the beetle wheels his droning flight,
And drowsy tinklings lull the distant folds;

Save that from yonder ivy-mantled tower
10 The moping owl does to the moon complain
Of such, as wandering near her secret bower,
Molest her ancient solitary reign.

Beneath those rugged elms, that yew-tree's shade,
Where heaves the turf in many a moldering heap,
15 Each in his narrow cell forever laid,
The rude forefathers of the hamlet sleep.

The breezy call of incense-breathing morn,
The swallow twittering from the straw-built shed,
The cock's shrill clarion, or the echoing horn,
20 No more shall rouse them from their lowly bed.

For them no more the blazing hearth shall burn,
Or busy housewife ply her evening care;
No children run to lisp their sire's return,
Or climb his knees the envied kiss to share.

25 Oft did the harvest to their sickle yield;
Their furrow oft the stubborn glebe has broke;
How jocund did they drive their team afield!
How bowed the woods beneath their sturdy stroke!

Let not Ambition mock their useful toil,
30 Their homely joys, and destiny obscure;
Nor Grandeur hear with a disdainful smile
The short and simple annals of the poor.

The boast of heraldry, the pomp of power,
And all that beauty, all that wealth e'er gave,
35 Awaits alike the inevitable hour:
The paths of glory lead but to the grave.

Nor you, ye proud, impute to these the fault,
If Memory o'er their tomb no trophies raise,
Where through the long-drawn aisle and fretted vault
40 The pealing anthem swells the note of praise.

Can storied urn or animated bust
Back to its mansion call the fleeting breath?
Can Honour's voice provoke the silent dust,
Or Flattery soothe the dull cold ear of Death?

45 Perhaps in this neglected spot is laid
Some heart once pregnant with celestial fire;
Hands that the rod of empire might have swayed,
Or waked to ecstasy the living lyre.

But Knowledge to their eyes her ample page,
50 Rich with the spoils of time, did ne'er unroll;
Chill Penury repressed their noble rage,
And froze the genial current of the soul.

---

[16]/**rude:** *lacking the advantages of education and culture*
[26]/**glebe:** *soil*

[39]/**fretted:** *ornately carved*
[43]/**provoke:** *call forth*

Full many a gem of purest ray serene,
The dark unfathomed caves of ocean bear;
55 Full many a flower is born to blush unseen,
And waste its sweetness on the desert air.

Some village Hampden, that with dauntless breast
The little tyrant of his fields withstood;
Some mute inglorious Milton here may rest,
60 Some Cromwell, guiltless of his country's blood.

The applause of listening senates to command,
The threats of pain and ruin to despise,
To scatter plenty o'er a smiling land,
And read their history in a nation's eyes

65 Their lot forbade; nor circumscribed alone
Their growing virtues, but their crimes confined;
Forbade to wade through slaughter to a throne,
And shut the gates of mercy on mankind;

The struggling pangs of conscious truth to hide,
70 To quench the blushes of ingenuous shame,
Or heap the shrine of Luxury and Pride
With incense kindled at the Muse's flame.

Far from the madding crowd's ignoble strife,
Their sober wishes never learned to stray;
75 Along the cool sequestered vale of life
They kept the noiseless tenor of their way.

Yet even these bones from insult to protect,
Some frail memorial still erected nigh,
With uncouth rhymes and shapeless sculpture decked,
80 Implores the passing tribute of a sigh.

Their name, their years, spelt by the unlettered Muse,
The place of fame and elegy supply;
And many a holy text around she strews,
That teach the rustic moralist to die.

85 For who, to dumb Forgetfulness a prey,
This pleasing anxious being e'er resigned,
Left the warm precincts of the cheerful day,
Nor cast one longing lingering look behind?

On some fond breast the parting soul relies,
90 Some pious drops the closing eye requires;
Even from the tomb the voice of Nature cries,
Even in our ashes live their wonted fires.

---

[57]/**Hampden:** *John Hampden, who
in 1637 refused to pay an illegal tax
levied by the king*

[73]/**madding:** *acting like madmen*
[92]/**wonted:** *accustomed, usual*

For thee, who mindful of the unhonoured dead
Dost in these lines their artless tale relate,
95   If chance, by lonely contemplation led,
Some kindred spirit shall inquire thy fate,

Haply some hoary-headed swain may say,
"Oft have we seen him at the peep of dawn
Brushing with hasty steps the dews away
100   To meet the sun upon the upland lawn.

"There at the foot of yonder nodding beech
That wreathes its old fantastic roots so high,
His listless length at noontide would he stretch,
And pore upon the brook that babbles by.

105   "Hard by yon wood, now smiling as in scorn,
Muttering his wayward fancies he would rove;
Now drooping, woeful-wan, like one forlorn,
Or crazed with care, or crossed in hopeless love.

"One morn I missed him on the customed hill,
110   Along the heath, and near his favorite tree;
Another came; nor yet beside the rill,
Nor up the lawn, nor at the wood was he;

"The next, with dirges due, in sad array,
Slow through the church-way path we saw him borne.
115   Approach and read (for thou canst read) the lay,
Graved on the stone beneath you agèd thorn."

The Epitaph

Here rests his head upon the lap of earth
A youth to Fortune and to Fame unknown;
Fair Science frowned not on his humble birth,
120   *And Melancholy marked him for her own.*

Large was his bounty, and his soul sincere;
Heaven did a recompense as largely send:
He gave to Misery all he had, a tear;
He gained from Heaven ('twas all he wished) a friend.

125   *No farther seek his merits to disclose,*
Or draw his frailties from their dread abode,
(There they alike in trembling hope repose)
The bosom of his Father and his God.

[1753]

---

⁹⁵/**if chance:** *if it happens that*
⁹⁷/**haply:** *perhaps*
  swain: *countryman*
¹¹¹/**rill:** *brook*

¹¹⁵/**lay:** *poem*
¹¹⁹/**Science:** *learning, knowledge*
¹²⁰/**Melancholy:** *sensibility, as well as the*
modern meaning

CHRISTOPHER SMART (1722–1771)

From Jubilate Agno

For I will consider my Cat Jeoffry.
For he is the servant of the Living God duly and daily serving him.
For at the first glance of the glory of God in the East he worships in his way.
For is this done by wreathing his body seven times round with elegant quickness.
5   For then he leaps up to catch the musk, which is the blessing of God upon his prayer.
For he rolls upon prank to work it in.
For having done duty and received blessing he begins to consider himself.
For this he performs in ten degrees.
For first he looks upon his fore-paws to see if they are clean.
10   For secondly he kicks up behind to clear away there.
For thirdly he works it upon stretch with the fore-paws extended.
For fourthly he sharpens his paws by wood.
For fifthly he washes himself.
For Sixthly he rolls upon wash.
15   For Seventhly he fleas himself, that he may not be interrupted upon the beat.
For Eighthly he rubs himself against a post.
For Ninthly he looks up for his instructions.
For Tenthly he goes in quest of food.
For having considered God and himself he will consider his neighbour.
20   For if he meets another cat he will kiss her in kindness.
For when he takes his prey he plays with it to give it a chance.
For one mouse in seven escapes by his dallying.
For when his day's work is done his business more properly begins.
For he keeps the Lord's watch in the night against the adversary.
25   For he counteracts the powers of darkness by his electrical skin and glaring eyes.
For he counteracts the Devil, who is death, by brisking about the life.
For in his morning orisons he loves the sun and the sun loves him.
For he is of the tribe of Tiger.
For the Cherub Cat is a term of the Angel Tiger.
30   For he has the subtlety and hissing of a serpent, which in goodness he suppresses.
For he will not do destruction if he is well-fed, neither will he spit without provocation.

"Jubilate Agno" means "Rejoice in the Lamb."

[6]/**upon prank:** *prankishly, playfully*
[11]/**works it upon stretch:** *stretches ergetically*
[14]/**upon wash:** *upon having washed*
[15]/**upon the beat:** *on his daily round*
[26]/**brisking . . . :** *living briskly, positively*

For he purrs in thankfulness, when God tells him he's a good Cat.
For he is an instrument for the children to learn benevolence upon.
For every house is incomplete without him and a blessing is lacking in
    the spirit. . . .   ([1759–1760] 1939)

WILLIAM BLAKE (1757–1828)

The Tyger

Tyger, Tyger, burning bright,
In the forests of the night,
What immortal hand or eye
Could frame thy fearful symmetry?

5 In what distant deeps or skies
Burnt the fire of thine eyes?
On what wings dare he aspire?
What the hand dare seize the fire?

And what shoulder, & what art,
10 Could twist the sinews of thy heart?
And when thy heart began to beat,
What dread hand? & what dread feet?

What the hammer? what the chain?
In what furnace was thy brain?
15 What the anvil? What dread grasp
Dare its deadly terrors clasp?

When the stars threw down their spears
And watered heaven with their tears,
Did he smile his work to see?
20 Did he who made the Lamb make thee?

Tyger, Tyger, burning bright,
In the forests of the night,
What immortal hand or eye
Dare frame thy fearful symmetry?   [1794]

London

I wander through each chartered street,
Near where the chartered Thames does flow,
And mark in every face I meet
Marks of weakness, marks of woe.

5 In every cry of every Man,
In every Infant's cry of fear,
In every voice, in every ban,
The mind-forged manacles I hear.

How the Chimney-sweeper's cry
10   Every blackening Church appals;
And the hapless Soldier's sigh
Runs in blood down Palace walls.

But most through midnight streets I hear
How the youthful Harlot's curse
15   Blasts the new born Infant's tear,
And blights with plagues the Marriage hearse.   [1794]

A Poison Tree

I was angry with my friend:
I told my wrath, my wrath did end.
I was angry with my foe:
I told it not, my wrath did grow.

5   And I watered it in fears,
Night and morning with my tears;
And I sunnèd it with smiles,
And with soft deceitful wiles.

And it grew both day and night,
10   Till it bore an apple bright;
And my foe beheld it shine,
And he knew that it was mine,

And into my garden stole,
When the night had veiled the pole:
15   In the morning glad I see
My foe outstretched beneath the tree.   [1794]

WILLIAM WORDSWORTH (1770–1850)

She Dwelt among the Untrodden Ways

She dwelt among the untrodden ways
       Beside the springs of Dove,
A maid whom there were none to praise
       And very few to love:

5   A violet by a mossy stone
       Half hidden from the eye!
Fair as a star, when only one
       Is shining in the sky.

She lived unknown, and few could know
10   When Lucy ceased to be;
But she is in her grave, and oh,
       The difference to me!   [1800]

The World Is Too Much With Us

The world is too much with us; late and soon,
Getting and spending, we lay waste our powers:
Little we see in Nature that is ours;
We have given our hearts away, a sordid boon!
5   This sea that bares her bosom to the moon;
The winds that will be howling at all hours,
And are up-gathered now like sleeping flowers;
For this, for everything, we are out of tune;
It moves us not.—Great God! I'd rather be
10 A pagan suckled in a creed outworn;
So might I, standing on this pleasant lea,
Have glimpses that would make me less forlorn;
Have sight of Proteus rising from the sea;
Or hear old Triton blow his wreathèd horn.   [1807]

13–14/*Proteus . . . Triton: sea-gods of Greek mythology*

Composed upon Westminster Bridge

September 3, 1802

Earth has not anything to show more fair:
Dull would he be of soul who could pass by
A sight so touching in its majesty:
This City now doth, like a garment, wear
5   The beauty of the morning; silent, bare,
Ships, towers, domes, theatres, and temples lie
Open unto the fields, and to the sky;
All bright and glittering in the smokeless air.
Never did sun more beautifully steep
10 In his first splendour, valley, rock, or hill;
Ne'er saw I, never felt, a calm so deep!
The river glideth at his own sweet will:
Dear God! the very houses seem asleep;
And all that mighty heart is lying still!   [1807]

SAMUEL TAYLOR COLERIDGE (1772–1834)

Kubla Khan

In Xanadu did Kubla Khan
A stately pleasure-dome decree:
Where Alph, the sacred river, ran
Through caverns measureless to man
5   Down to a sunless sea.
So twice five miles of fertile ground

With walls and towers were girdled round:
And there were gardens bright with sinuous rills,
Where blossomed many an incense-bearing tree;
10 And here were forests ancient as the hills,
Enfolding sunny spots of greenery.

But oh! that deep romantic chasm which slanted
Down the green hill athwart a cedarn cover!
A savage place! as holy and enchanted
15 As e'er beneath a waning moon was haunted
By woman wailing for her demon-lover!
And from this chasm, with ceaseless turmoil seething,
As if this earth in fast thick pants were breathing,
A mighty fountain momently was forced:
20 Amid whose swift half-intermitted burst
Huge fragments vaulted like rebounding hail,
Or chaffy grain beneath the thresher's flail:
And 'mid these dancing rocks at once and ever
It flung up momently the sacred river.
25 Five miles meandering with a mazy motion
Through wood and dale the sacred river ran,
Then reached the caverns measureless to man,
And sank in tumult to a lifeless ocean:
And 'mid this tumult Kubla heard from far
30 Ancestral voices prophesying war!
        The shadow of the dome of pleasure
        Floated midway on the waves;
        Where was heard the mingled measure
        From the fountain and the caves.
35 It was a miracle of rare device.
A sunny pleasure-dome with caves of ice!

        A damsel with a dulcimer
        In a vision once I saw:
        It was an Abyssinian maid,
40   And on her dulcimer she played,
        Singing of Mount Abora.
        Could I revive within me
        Her symphony and song,
        To such a deep delight 'twould win me,
45 That with music loud and long,
I would build that dome in air,
That sunny dome! those caves of ice!
And all who heard should see them there,
And all should cry, Beware! Beware!
50 His flashing eyes, his floating hair!
Weave a circle round him thrice,
And close your eyes with holy dread,
For he on honey-dew hath fed,
And drunk the milk of Paradise.   [1816]

PERCY BYSSHE SHELLEY (1792–1822)

Ozymandias

I met a traveller from an antique land
Who said: Two vast and trunkless legs of stone
Stand in the desert. Near them, on the sand,
Half sunk, a shattered visage lies, whose frown,
5   And wrinkled lip, and sneer of cold command,
Tell that its sculptor well those passions read
Which yet survive, stamped on these lifeless things,
The hand that mocked them and the heart that fed;
And on the pedestal these words appear:
10 "My name is Ozymandias, king of kings:
Look on my works, ye Mighty, and despair!"
Nothing beside remains. Round the decay
Of that colossal wreck, boundless and bare,
The lone and level sands stretch far away.   [1819]

Ozymandias: the Greek form of Usermare-setepenre (Ramses the Great), who reigned in Egypt from 1304 until 1237 B.C.E. He left many colossal statues of himself.

Ode to the West Wind

I

O wild west wind, thou breath of autumn's being,
Thou from whose unseen presence the leaves dead
Are driven like ghosts from an enchanter fleeing,

Yellow, and black, and pale, and hectic red,
5   Pestilence-stricken multitudes! O thou
Who chariotest to their dark wintry bed

The wingèd seeds, where they lie cold and low,
Each like a corpse within its grave, until
Thine azure sister of the spring shall blow

10 Her clarion o'er the dreaming earth, and fill
(Driving sweet buds like flocks to feed in air)
With living hues and odours plain and hill:

Wild spirit, which art moving everywhere;
Destroyer and preserver; hear, O hear!

II

15 Thou on whose stream, 'mid the steep sky's commotion,
Loose clouds like earth's decaying leaves are shed,
Shook from the tangled boughs of heaven and ocean,

Angels of rain and lightning: there are spread
On the blue surface of thine airy surge,
20 Like the bright hair uplifted from the head

Of some fierce Maenad, even from the dim verge
Of the horizon to the zenith's height,
The locks of the approaching storm. Thou dirge

Of the dying year, to which this closing night
25   Will be the dome of a vast sepulchre,
Vaulted with all thy congregated might

Of vapours, from whose solid atmosphere
Black rain, and fire, and hail will burst: O hear!

III

Thou who didst waken from his summer dreams
30   The blue Mediterranean, where he lay,
Lulled by the coil of his crystalline streams,

Beside a pumice isle in Baiae's bay,
And saw in sleep old palaces and towers
Quivering within the wave's intenser day,

35   All overgrown with azure moss and flowers
So sweet, the sense faints picturing them! Thou
For whose path the Atlantic's level powers

Cleave themselves into chasms, while far below
The sea-blooms and the oozy woods which wear
40   The sapless foliage of the ocean, know

Thy voice, and suddenly grow gray with fear,
And tremble and despoil themselves: O hear!

IV

If I were a dead leaf thou mightest bear;
If I were a swift cloud to fly with thee;
45   A wave to pant beneath thy power, and share

The impulse of thy strength, only less free
Than thou, O uncontrollable! if even
I were as in my boyhood, and could be

The comrade of thy wanderings over heaven,
50   As then, when to outstrip thy skiey speed
Scarce seemed a vision; I would ne'er have striven

As thus with thee in prayer in my sore need.
O! lift me as a wave, a leaf, a cloud!
I fall upon the thorns of life! I bleed!

55   A heavy weight of hours has chained and bowed
One too like thee: tameless, and swift, and proud.

---

[21]/*Maenad: a woman inspired to
frenzy by Dionysus*

[32]/*Baiae: an ancient Roman resort near
Naples, now submerged*

V

Make me thy lyre, even as the forest is:
What if my leaves are falling like its own?
The tumult of thy mighty harmonies

60 Will take from both a deep autumnal tone,
Sweet though in sadness. Be thou, spirit fierce,
My spirit! Be thou me, impetuous one!

Drive my dead thoughts over the universe,
Like withered leaves, to quicken a new birth;
65 And, by the incantation of this verse,

Scatter, as from an unextinguished hearth
Ashes and sparks, my words among mankind!
Be through my lips to unawakened earth

The trumpet of a prophecy! O wind,
70 If winter comes, can spring be far behind?   [1820]

JOHN CLARE (1793–1864)

Autumn

The thistledown's flying, though the winds are all still,
On the green grass now lying, now mounting the hill,
The spring from the fountain now boils like a pot;
Through stones past the counting it bubbles red-hot.

5 The ground parched and cracked is like overbaked bread,
The greensward all wracked is, bents dried up and dead.
The fallow fields glitter like water indeed,
And gossamers twitter, flung from weed unto weed.

Hill-tops like hot iron glitter bright in the sun,
10 And the rivers we're eying burn to gold as they run;
Burning hot is the ground, liquid gold is the air;
Whoever looks round sees Eternity there.   ([1842–1864] 1920)

6/**bents:** *stalky grass*   8/**gossamers:** *fine floating cobwebs*
                                               twitter: *tremble, quiver*

JOHN KEATS (1795–1821)

La Belle Dame sans Merci

A Ballad

I

O what can ail thee, knight-at-arms,
    Alone and palely loitering?

The title means "The Beautiful Lady without Mercy."

The sedge has withered from the lake,
 And no birds sing.

II

5 O what can ail thee, knight-at-arms!
  So haggard and so woe-begone?
The squirrel's granary is full,
 And the harvest's done.

III

I see a lily on thy brow,
10 With anguish moist and fever dew,
And on thy cheeks a fading rose
 Fast withereth too.

IV

I met a lady in the meads,
 Full beautiful—a faery's child,
15 Her hair was long, her foot was light,
 And her eyes were wild.

V

I made a garland for her head,
 And bracelets too, and fragrant zone;
She looked at me as she did love,
20 And made sweet moan.

VI

I set her on my pacing steed,
 And nothing else saw all day long,
For sidelong would she bend, and sing
 A faery's song.

VII

25 She found me roots of relish sweet,
  And honey wild, and manna dew,
And sure in language strange she said—
 "I love thee true."

VIII

She took me to her elfin grot,
30 And there she wept, and sighed full sore,
And there I shut her wild wild eyes
 With kisses four.

IX

And there she lullèd me asleep,
 And there I dreamed—Ah! woe betide!
35 The latest dream I ever dreamed
  On the cold hill side.

X

I saw pale kings and princes too,
    Pale warriors, death-pale were they all;
They cried—"La Belle Dame sans Merci
40   Hath thee in thrall!"

XI

I saw their starved lips in the gloam,
    With horrid warning gapèd wide,
And I awoke and found me here,
    On the cold hill's side.

XII

45 And this is why I sojourn here,
    Alone and palely loitering,
Though the sedge is withered from the lake,
    And no birds sing.

[1820]

18/*zone: belt*

Ode to a Nightingale

1

My heart aches, and a drowsy numbness pains
    My sense, as though of hemlock I had drunk,
Or emptied some dull opiate to the drains
    One minute past, and Lethe-wards had sunk:
5 'Tis not through envy of thy happy lot,
    But being too happy in thine happiness,—
        That thou, light-wingèd Dryad of the trees,
        In some melodious plot
Of beechen green, and shadows numberless,
10   Singest of summer in full-throated ease.

2

O, for a draught of vintage! that hath been
    Cooled a long age in the deep-delvèd earth,
Tasting of Flora and the country green,
    Dance, and Provençal song, and sunburnt mirth!
15 O for a beaker full of the warm South,
    Full of the true, the blushful Hippocrene,
        With beaded bubbles winking at the brim,
        And purple-stainéd mouth;

2/*hemlock: a poisonous plant, and its juice, medically used as a powerful sedative*
4/*Lethe: A river in the underworld whose waters caused the drinker to forget his past*

7/*Dryad: a wood-nymph*
13/*Flora: goddess of flowers*
14/*Provençal: of Provence, in the south of France, home of the medieval troubadours*
16/*Hippocrene: a spring in Greece sacred to the Muses*

That I might drink, and leave the world unseen,
20   And with thee fade away into the forest dim:

3

Fade far away, dissolve, and quite forget
    What thou among the leaves hast never known,
The weariness, the fever, and the fret
    Here, where men sit and hear each other groan;
25 Where palsy shakes a few, sad, last gray hairs,
        Where youth grows pale, and spectre-thin, and dies;
        Where but to think is to be full of sorrow
            And leaden-eyed despairs,
        Where Beauty cannot keep her lustrous eyes,
30   Or new Love pine at them beyond to-morrow.

4

Away! away! for I will fly to thee,
    Not charioted by Bacchus and his pards,
But on the viewless wings of Poesy,
    Though the dull brain perplexes and retards:
35 Already with thee! tender is the night,
        And haply the Queen-Moon is on her throne,
            Clustered around by all her starry Fays;
                But here there is no light,
        Save what from heaven is with the breezes blown
40   Through verdurous glooms and winding mossy ways.

5

I cannot see what flowers are at my feet,
    Nor what soft incense hangs upon the boughs,
But, in embalmèd darkness, guess each sweet
    Wherewith the seasonable month endows
45 The grass, the thicket, and the fruit-tree wild;
        White hawthorn, and the pastoral eglantine;
            Fast fading violets covered up in leaves;
            And mid-May's eldest child,
        The coming musk-rose, full of dewy wine,
50   The murmurous haunt of flies on summer eves.

6

Darkling I listen; and, for many a time
    I have been half in love with easeful Death,
Called him soft names in many a musèd rhyme,
    To take into the air my quiet breath;

---

[32]/**Bacchus:** *god of wine*
    pards: *leopards*
[33]/**viewless:** *invisible*

[37]/**Fays:** *fairies*
[43]/**embalmèd:** *perfumed*
[51]/**darkling:** *in the dark*

55 Now more than ever seems it rich to die,
    To cease upon the midnight with no pain,
      While thou art pouring forth thy soul abroad
        In such an ecstasy!
    Still wouldst thou sing, and I have ears in vain—
60   To thy high requiem become a sod.

       7

Thou wast not born for death, immortal Bird!
    No hungry generations tread thee down;
The voice I hear this passing night was heard
    In ancient days by emperor and clown:
65 Perhaps the self-same song that found a path
    Through the sad heart of Ruth, when, sick for home,
      She stood in tears amid the alien corn;
        The same that oft-times hath
Charmed magic casements, opening on the foam
70   Of perilous seas, in faery lands forlorn.

       8

Forlorn! the very word is like a bell
    To toll me back from thee to my sole self!
Adieu! the fancy cannot cheat so well
    As she is famed to do, deceiving elf.
75 Adieu! adieu! thy plaintive anthem fades
    Past the near meadows, over the still stream,
      Up the hill-side; and now 'tis buried deep
        In the next valley-glades:
    Was it a vision, or a waking dream?
80   Fled is that music:—Do I wake or sleep?   [1820]

66/**Ruth:** see the Book of Ruth,   73/**fancy:** imagination
in the Old Testament

To Autumn

Season of mists and mellow fruitfulness,
    Close bosom-friend of the maturing sun;
Conspiring with him how to load and bless
    With fruit the vines that round the thatch-eaves run;
5 To bend with apples the mossed cottage-trees,
    And fill all fruit with ripeness to the core;
      To swell the gourd, and plump the hazel shells
    With a sweet kernel; to set budding more,
And still more, later flowers for the bees,
10 Until they think warm days will never cease,
      For summer has o'er-brimmed their clammy cells.

Who hath not seen thee oft amid thy store?
    Sometimes whoever seeks abroad may find

Thee sitting careless on a granary floor,
15　　　Thy hair soft-lifted by the winnowing wind;
Or on a half-reaped furrow sound asleep,
　　　Drowsed with the fumes of poppies, while thy hook
　　　　　Spares the next swath and all its twinèd flowers:
And sometime like a gleaner thou dost keep
20　　　Steady thy laden head across a brook;
　　　Or by a cider-press, with patient look,
　　　　　Thou watchest the last oozings hours by hours.

Where are the songs of spring? Ay, where are they?
　　　Think not of them, thou hast thy music too,—
25　While barrèd clouds bloom the soft-dying day,
　　　And touch the stubble-plains with rosy hue;
Then in a wailful choir the small gnats mourn
　　　Among the river sallows, borne aloft
　　　　　Or sinking as the light wind lives or dies;
30　And full-grown lambs loud bleat from hilly bourn;
　　　Hedge-crickets sing; and now with treble soft
　　　The red-breast whistles from a garden-croft;
　　　　　And gathering swallows twitter in the skies.　　　[1820]

17/**hook:** *hooked knife, sickle*　　　30/**bourn:** *enclosure*
28/**sallows:** *willows*　　　32/**garden-croft:** *small garden next to house*

EDWARD FITZGERALD (1809–1883)

From The Rubáiyát of Omar Khayyám

I

Awake! for Morning in the Bowl of Night
Has flung the Stone that puts the Stars to Flight:
　　　And Lo! the Hunter of the East has caught
The Sultán's Turret in a Noose of Light.

III

5　And, as the Cock crew, those who stood before
The Tavern shouted—"Open then the Door!
　　　You know how little while we have to stay,
And, once departed, may return no more."

Stanzas with Roman numbers only are from the first edition of 1859; those with b *numbers are from the second edition of 1868; those with* c *from the fifth edition of 1889.*

VII

Come, fill the Cup, and in the Fire of Spring
10 The Winter Garment of Repentance fling:
  The Bird of Time has but a little way
To fly—and Lo! the Bird is on the Wing.

XII c

A Book of Verses underneath the Bough,
A Jug of Wine, a Loaf of Bread—and Thou
15   Beside me singing in the Wilderness—
Oh, Wilderness were Paradise enow!

XIII c

Some for the Glories of This World; and some
Sigh for the Prophet's Paradise to come;
  Ah, take the Cash, and let the Credit go,
20 Nor heed the rumble of a distant Drum!

XVIII b

Think, in this battered Caravanserai
Whose Portals are alternate Night and Day,
  How Sultán after Sultán with his Pomp
Abode his destined Hour, and went his way.

XXIV b

25 I sometimes think that never blows so red
The Rose as where some buried Cæsar bled;
  That every Hyacinth the Garden wears
Dropt in her Lap from some once lovely Head.

XIX

And this delightful Herb whose tender Green
30 Fledges the River's Lip on which we lean—
  Ah, lean upon it lightly! for who knows
From what once lovely Lip it springs unseen!

XXIII b

And we, that now make merry in the Room
They left, and Summer dresses in new bloom,
35   Ourselves must we beneath the Couch of Earth
Descend—ourselves to make a Couch—for whom?

XXVII c

Myself when young did eagerly frequent
Doctor and Saint, and heard great argument
  About it and about: but evermore
40 Came out by the same door where in I went.

16/enow: enough   21/**Caravanserai**: *inn primarily for caravans*

XXXII

There was a Door to which I found no Key:
There was a Veil past which I could not see:
    Some little Talk awhile of ME and THEE
There seemed—and then no more of THEE and ME.

LXXVI b

45 The Moving Finger writes; and, having writ,
Moves on: nor all your Piety nor Wit
    Shall lure it back to cancel half a Line,
Nor all your Tears wash out a Word of it.

LXXI

And much as Wine has played the Infidel,
50 And robbed me of my Robe of Honour—well,
    I often wonder what the Vintners buy
One half so precious as the Goods they sell.

LXXII

Alas, that Spring should vanish with the Rose!
That Youth's sweet-scented Manuscript should close!
55   The Nightingale that in the Branches sang,
Ah, whence, and whither flown again, who knows!

CVIII b

Ah, Love! could you and I with Fate conspire
To grasp this sorry Scheme of Things entire,
    Would not we shatter it to bits—and then
60 Re-mould it nearer to the Heart's Desire!

LXXIV

Ah, Moon of my Delight, who know'st no wane,
The Moon of Heaven is rising once again:
    How oft hereafter rising shall she look
Through this same Garden after me—in vain!

LXXV

65 And when Thyself with shining Foot shall pass
Among the Guests Star-scattered on the Grass,
    And in thy joyous Errand reach the Spot
Where I made one—turn down an empty Glass!
                             [1859]

ALFRED, LORD TENNYSON (1809–1892)

Ulysses

It little profits that an idle king,
By this still hearth, among these barren crags,
Matched with an aged wife, I mete and dole

Unequal laws unto a savage race,
5 That hoard, and sleep, and feed, and know not me.
I cannot rest from travel; I will drink
Life to the lees. All times I have enjoyed
Greatly, have suffered greatly, both with those
That loved me, and alone; on shore, and when
10 Thro' scudding drifts the rainy Hyades
Vext the dim sea. I am become a name;
For always roaming with a hungry heart
Much have I seen and known,—cities of men
And manners, climates, councils, governments,
15 Myself not least, but honored of them all,—
And drunk delight of battle with my peers,
Far on the ringing plains of windy Troy.
I am a part of all that I have met;
Yet all experience is an arch wherethro'
20 Gleams that untravelled world whose margin fades
For ever and for ever when I move.
How dull it is to pause, to make an end,
To rust unburnished, not to shine in use!
As tho' to breathe were life! Life piled on life
25 Were all too little, and of one to me
Little remains; but every hour is saved
From that eternal silence, something more,
A bringer of new things; and vile it were
For some three suns to store and hoard myself,
30 And this gray spirit yearning in desire
To follow knowledge like a sinking star,
Beyond the utmost bound of human thought.
      This is my son, mine own Telemachus,
To whom I leave the sceptre and the isle,—
35 Well-loved of me, discerning to fulfil
This labor, by slow prudence to make mild
A rugged people, and thro' soft degrees
Subdue them to the useful and the good.
Most blameless is he, centred in the sphere
40 Of common duties, decent not to fail
In offices of tenderness, and pay
Meet adoration to my household gods,
When I am gone. He works his work, I mine.
      There lies the port; the vessel puffs her sail;
45 There gloom the dark broad seas. My mariners,
Souls that have toiled, and wrought, and thought with me,—
That ever with a frolic welcome took
The thunder and the sunshine, and opposed
Free hearts, free foreheads,—you and I are old;

---

[10]/**Hyades:** *a group of stars whose rising was thought to indicate rain*

[42]/**meet:** *appropriate*

[48]/**opposed:** *resisted with*

50   Old age hath yet his honor and his toil.
Death closes all; but something ere the end,
Some work of noble note, may yet be done,
Not unbecoming men that strove with Gods.
The lights begin to twinkle from the rocks;
55   The long day wanes; the slow moon climbs; the deep
Moans round with many voices. Come, my friends,
'Tis not too late to seek a newer world.
Push off, and sitting well in order smite
The sounding furrows; for my purpose holds
60   To sail beyond the sunset, and the baths
Of all the western stars, until I die.
It may be that the gulfs will wash us down;
It may be we shall touch the Happy Isles,
And see the great Achilles, whom we knew.
65   Tho' much is taken, much abides; and tho'
We are not now that strength which in old days
Moved earth and heaven, that which we are, we are,—
One equal temper of heroic hearts,
Made weak by time and fate, but strong in will
70   To strive, to seek, to find, and not to yield.   [1842]

---

[63]/**the Happy Isles:** *in classical mythology, the home of the virtuous dead*

ROBERT BROWNING (1812–1889)

My Last Duchess

Ferrara

That's my last Duchess painted on the wall,
Looking as if she were alive. I call
That piece a wonder, now: Frà Pandolf's hands
Worked busily a day, and there she stands.
5   Will't please you sit and look at her? I said
"Frà Pandolf" by design, for never read
Strangers like you that pictured countenance,
The depth and passion of its earnest glance,
But to myself they turned (since none puts by
10   The curtain I have drawn for you, but I)
And seemed as they would ask me, if they durst,
How such a glance came there; so, not the first
Are you to turn and ask thus. Sir, 'twas not
Her husband's presence only, called that spot

Ferrara: *a center of art and culture in northern Italy during the Renaissance*

[3]/**Frà Pandolf:** *an imaginary artist. Frà is short for Frate (Brother)*

15 Of joy into the Duchess' cheek: perhaps
    Frà Pandolf chanced to say "Her mantle laps
    Over my lady's wrist too much," or "Paint
    Must never hope to reproduce the faint
    Half-flush that dies along her throat:" such stuff
20 Was courtesy, she thought, and cause enough
    For calling up that spot of joy. She had
    A heart—how shall I say?—too soon made glad,
    Too easily impressed; she liked whate'er
    She looked on, and her looks went everywhere,
25 Sir, 'twas all one! My favor at her breast,
    The dropping of the daylight in the West,
    The bough of cherries some officious fool
    Broke in the orchard for her, the white mule
    She rode with round the terrace—all and each
30 Would draw from her alike the approving speech,
    Or blush, at least. She thanked men,—good! but thanked
    Somehow—I know not how—as if she ranked
    My gift of a nine-hundred-years-old name
    With anybody's gift. Who'd stoop to blame
35 This sort of trifling? Even had you skill
    In speech—(which I have not)—to make your will
    Quite clear to such an one, and say, "Just this
    Or that in you disgusts me; here you miss,
    Or there exceed the mark"—and if she let
40 Herself be lessoned so, nor plainly set
    Her wits to yours, forsooth, and made excuse,
    —E'en then would be some stooping; and I choose
    Never to stoop. Oh sir, she smiled, no doubt,
    Whene'er I passed her; but who passed without
45 Much the same smile? This grew; I gave commands;
    Then all smiles stopped together. There she stands
    As if alive. Will't please you rise? We'll meet
    The company below, then. I repeat,
    The Count your master's known munificence
50 Is ample warrant that no just pretence
    Of mine for dowry will be disallowed;
    Though his fair daughter's self, as I avowed
    At starting, is my object. Nay, we'll go
    Together down, sir. Notice Neptune, though,
55 Taming a sea-horse, thought a rarity,
    Which Claus of Innsbruck cast in bronze for me!   [1842]

56/**Claus of Innsbruck:** *an imaginary artist*

EMILY BRONTË (1818–1848)

Remembrance

Cold in the earth—and the deep snow piled above thee,
Far, far removed, cold in the dreary grave!
Have I forgot, my only love, to love thee,
Severed at last by time's all-severing wave?

5   Now, when alone, do my thoughts no longer hover
Over the mountains, on that northern shore;
Resting their wings where heath and fern-leaves cover
Thy noble heart for ever, ever more?

Cold in the earth—and fifteen wild Decembers,
10 From those brown hills, have melted into spring:
Faithful, indeed, is the spirit that remembers
After such years of change and suffering!

Sweet love of youth, forgive, if I forget thee
While the world's tide is bearing me along;
15 Other desires and other hopes beset me,
Hopes which obscure, but cannot do thee wrong.

No later light has lightened up my heaven,
No second morn has ever shone for me;
All my life's bliss from thy dear life was given,
20 All my life's bliss is in the grave with thee.

But when the days of golden dreams had perished,
And even despair was powerless to destroy,
Then did I learn how existence could be cherished,
Strengthened, and fed without the aid of joy.

25 Then did I check the tears of useless passion—
Weaned my young soul from yearning after thine;
Sternly denied its burning wish to hasten
Down to that tomb already more than mine.

And, even yet, I dare not let it languish,
30 Dare not indulge in memory's rapturous pain;
Once drinking deep of that divinest anguish,
How could I seek the empty world again?

                                                          [1846]

ARTHUR HUGH CLOUGH (1819–1861)

The Latest Decalogue

Thou shalt have one God only; who
Would be at the expense of two?
No graven images may be
Worshipped, except the currency;

5   Swear not at all; for, for thy curse,
Thine enemy is none the worse;
At church on Sunday to attend
Will serve to keep the world thy friend;
Honour thy parents; that is, all
10   From whom advancement may befall;
Thou shalt not kill; but needst not strive
Officiously to keep alive;
Do not adultery commit;
Advantage rarely comes of it;
15   Thou shalt not steal; an empty feat,
When it's so lucrative to cheat;
Bear not false witness; let the lie
Have time on its own wings to fly;
Thou shalt not covet; but tradition
20   Approves all forms of competition.

The sum of all is, thou shalt love,
If anybody, God above;
At any rate shall never labour
More than thyself to love thy neighbour.   [1849]

WALT WHITMAN (1819–1892)

From Leaves of Grass

I think I could turn and live awhile with the animals. . . . they are so
    placid and self-contained,
I stand and look at them sometimes half the day long.
They do not sweat and whine about their condition,
They do not lie awake in the dark and weep for their sins,
5   They do not make me sick discussing their duty to God,
Not one is dissatisfied. . . . not one is demented with the mania of
    owning things,
Not one kneels to another nor to his kind that lived thousands of years
    ago,
Not one is respectable or industrious over the whole earth.

So they show their relations to me and I accept them;
10   They bring me tokens of myself. . . . they evince them plainly in their
    possession.

I do not know where they got those tokens,
I must have passed that way untold times ago and negligently dropt
    them,
Myself moving forward then and now and forever,
Gathering and showing more always and with velocity,
15   Infinite and omnigenous and the like of these among them;

---

¹⁵/*omnigenous: of all kinds*

Not too exclusive toward the reachers of my remembrancers,
Picking out here one that shall be my amie,
Choosing to go with him on brotherly terms.

A gigantic beauty of a stallion, fresh and responsive to my caresses,
20 Head high in the forehead and wide between the ears,
Limbs glossy and supple, tail dusting the ground,
Eyes well apart and full of sparkling wickedness. . . . ears finely cut and
    flexibly moving.

His nostrils dilate. . . . my heels embrace him. . . . his well built limbs
    tremble with pleasure. . . . we speed around and return.
I but use you a moment and then I resign you stallion. . . . and do not
    need your paces, and outgallop them,
25 And myself as I stand or sit pass faster than you.   [1855]

16/*remembrancer: one who reminds*   17/*amie: the French word means friend
(feminine); later changed to "one that I love"*

Out of the Cradle Endlessly Rocking

Out of the cradle endlessly rocking,
Out of the mocking-bird's throat, the musical shuttle,
Out of the Ninth-month midnight,
Over the sterile sands and the fields beyond, where the child
    leaving his bed wander'd alone, bareheaded, barefoot,
5 Down from the shower'd halo,
Up from the mystic play of shadows twining and twisting as if they
    were alive,
Out from the patches of briers and blackberries,
From the memories of the bird that chanted to me,
From your memories sad brother, from the fitful risings and fallings
    I heard
10 From under that yellow half-moon late-risen and swollen as if with
    tears,
From those beginning notes of yearning and love there in the mist,
From the thousand responses of my heart never to cease,
From the myriad thence-arous'd words,
From the word stronger and more delicious than any,
15 From such as now they start the scene revisiting,
As a flock, twittering, rising, or overhead passing,
Borne hither, ere all eludes me, hurriedly,
A man, yet by these tears a little boy again,
Throwing myself on the sand, confronting the waves,
20 I, chanter of pains and joys, uniter of here and hereafter,
Taking all hints to use them, but swiftly leaping beyond them,
A reminiscence sing.

3/**Ninth-month:** *the Quaker name for September*

Once Paumanok,
When the lilac-scent was in the air and Fifth-month grass was
    growing,
25 Up this seashore in some briers,
Two feather'd guests from Alabama, two together,
And their nest, and four light-green eggs spotted with brown,
And every day the he-bird to and fro near at hand,
And every day the she-bird crouch'd on her nest, silent, with bright
    eyes,
30 And every day I, a curious boy, never too close, never disturbing them,
Cautiously peering, absorbing, translating.
Shine! shine! shine!
Pour down your warmth, great sun!
While we bask, we two together.

35 *Two together!*
Winds blow south, or winds blow north,
Day come white, or night come black,
Home, or rivers and mountains from home,
Singing all time, minding no time,
40 *While we two keep together.*

Till of a sudden,
May-be kill'd, unknown to her mate,
One forenoon the she-bird crouch'd not on the nest,
Nor return'd that afternoon, nor the next,
45 Nor ever appear'd again.

And thenceforward all summer in the sound of the sea,
And at night under the full of the moon in calmer weather,
Over the hoarse surging of the sea,
Or flitting from brier to brier by day,
50 I saw, I heard at intervals the remaining one, the he-bird,
The solitary guest from Alabama.

Blow! blow! blow!
Blow up sea-winds along Paumanok's shore;
I wait and I wait till you blow my mate to me.

55 Yes, when the stars glisten'd,
All night long on the prong of a moss-scallop'd stake,
Down almost amid the slapping waves,
Sat the lone singer wonderful causing tears.

He call'd on his mate,
60 He pour'd forth the meanings which I of all men know.

Yes my brother I know,
The rest might not, but I have treasur'd every note,

---

[23]/**Paumanok:** *the Indian name for Long Island*

For more than once dimly down to the beach gliding,
Silent, avoiding the moonbeams, blending myself with the shadows,
65 Recalling now the obscure shapes, the echoes, the sounds and sights
    after their sorts,
The white arms out in the breakers tirelessly tossing,
I, with bare feet, a child, the wind wafting my hair,
Listen'd long and long.

Listen'd to keep, to sing, now translating the notes,
70 Following you my brother.

Soothe! soothe! soothe!
Close on its wave soothes the wave behind,
And again another behind embracing and lapping, every one close,
But my love soothes not me, not me.
75 *Low hangs the moon, it rose late,*
It is lagging—O I think it is heavy with love, with love.

O madly the sea pushes upon the land,
With love, with love.

O night! do I not see my love fluttering out among the breakers?
80 *What is that little black thing I see there in the white?*

Loud! loud! loud!
Loud I call to you, my love!
High and clear I shoot my voice over the waves,
Surely you must know who is here, is here,
85 *You must know who I am, my love.*

Low-hanging moon!
What is that dusky spot in your brown yellow?
O it is the shape, the shape of my mate!
O moon do not keep her from me any longer.

90 *Land! land! O land!*
Whichever way I turn, O I think you could give me my mate back again if
    you only would,
For I am almost sure I see her dimly whichever way I look.

O rising stars!
Perhaps the one I want so much will rise, will rise with some of you.

95 *O throat! O trembling throat!*
Sound clearer through the atmosphere!
Pierce the woods, the earth,
Somewhere listening to catch you must be the one I want.

Shake out carols!
100 *Solitary here, the night's carols!*
Carols of lonesome love! death's carols!
Carols under that lagging, yellow, waning moon!

O under that moon where she droops almost down into the sea!
O reckless despairing carols.

105　*But soft! sink low!*
Soft! let me just murmur,
And do you wait a moment you husky-nois'd sea,
For somewhere I believe I heard my mate responding to me,
So faint, I must be still, be still to listen,
110　*But not altogether still, for then she might not come immediately to me.*

Hither my love!
Here I am! here!
With this just-sustain'd note I announce myself to you,
This gentle call is for you my love, for you.

115　*Do not be decoy'd elsewhere,*
That is the whistle of the wind, it is not my voice,
That is the fluttering, the fluttering of the spray,
Those are the shadows of leaves.
O darkness! O in vain!
120　*O I am very sick and sorrowful.*

O brown halo in the sky near the moon, drooping upon the sea!
O troubled reflection in the sea!
O throat! O throbbing heart!
And I singing uselessly, uselessly all the night.

125　*O past! O happy life! O songs of joy!*
In the air, in the woods, over fields,
Loved! loved! loved! loved! loved!
But my mate no more, no more with me!
We two together no more.

130　The aria sinking,
All else continuing, the stars shining,
The winds blowing, the notes of the bird continuous echoing,
With angry moans the fierce old mother incessantly moaning,
On the sands of Paumanok's shore gray and rustling,
135　The yellow half-moon enlarged, sagging down, drooping, the face of
　　the sea almost touching,
The boy ecstatic, with his bare feet the waves, with his hair the
　　atmosphere dallying,
The love in the heart long pent, now loose, now at last tumultuously
　　bursting,
The aria's meaning, the ears, the soul, swiftly depositing,
The strange tears down the cheeks coursing,
140　The colloquy there, the trio, each uttering,
The undertone, the savage old mother incessantly crying,
To the boy's soul's questions sullenly timing, some drown'd secret
　　hissing,
To the outsetting bard.

Demon or bird (said the boy's soul,)
145   Is it indeed toward your mate you sing? or is it really to me?
For I, that was a child, my tongue's use sleeping, now I have heard you,
Now in a moment I know what I am for, I awake,
And already a thousand singers, a thousand songs, clearer, louder and
    more sorrowful than yours,
A thousand warbling echoes have started to life within me, never to die.

150   O you singer solitary, singing by yourself, projecting me,
O solitary me listening, never more shall I cease perpetuating you,
Never more shall I escape, never more the reverberations,
Never more the cries of unsatisfied love be absent from me,
Never again leave me to be the peaceful child I was before what there
    in the night,
155   By the sea under the yellow and sagging moon,
The messenger there arous'd, the fire, the sweet hell within,
The unknown want, the destiny of me.

O give me the clew! (it lurks in the night here somewhere,)
O if I am to have so much, let me have more!
160   A word then, (for I will conquer it,)
The word final, superior to all,
Subtle, sent up—what is it?—I listen;
Are you whispering it, and have been all the time, you sea-waves?
Is that it from your liquid rims and wet sands?

165   Whereto answering, the sea,
Delaying not, hurrying not,
Whisper'd me through the night, and very plainly before daybreak,
Lisp'd to me the low and delicious word death,
And again death, death, death, death,
170   Hissing melodious, neither like the bird nor like my arous'd child's
    heart,
But edging near as privately for me rustling at my feet,
Creeping thence steadily up to my ears and laving me softly all over,
Death, death, death, death, death.

Which I do not forget,
175   But fuse the song of my dusky demon and brother,
That he sang to me in the moonlight on Paumanok's gray beach,
With the thousand responsive songs at random,
My own songs awaked from that hour,
And with them the key, the word up from the waves,
180   The word of the sweetest song and all songs,
That strong and delicious word which, creeping to my feet,
(Or like some old crone rocking the cradle, swathed in sweet garments,
    bending aside,)
The sea whisper'd me.   [1881]

---

[144]/**demon:** *here and in line 175, a demigod or attendant spirit (more often spelled "daemon" or "daimon")*

When I Heard the Learn'd Astronomer

When I heard the learn'd astronomer,
When the proofs, the figures, were ranged in columns before me,
When I was shown the charts and diagrams, to add, divide, and
    measure them,
When I sitting heard the astronomer where he lectured with much
    applause in the lecture-room,
5   How soon unaccountable I became tired and sick,
Till rising and gliding out I wander'd off by myself,
In the mystical moist night-air, and from time to time,
Look'd up in perfect silence at the stars.   [1865]

Reconciliation

Word over all, beautiful as the sky,
Beautiful that war and all its deeds of carnage must in time be utterly
    lost,
That the hands of the sisters Death and Night incessantly softly wash
    again, and ever again, this soil'd world;
For my enemy is dead, a man divine as myself is dead,
5   I look where he lies white-faced and still in the coffin—I draw near,
Bend down and touch lightly with my lips the white face in the
    coffin.   [1866]

DANTE GABRIEL ROSSETTI (1828–1882)

The Woodspurge

The wind flapped loose, the wind was still,
Shaken out dead from tree and hill:
I had walked on at the wind's will,—
I sat now, for the wind was still.

5   Between my knees my forehead was,—
My lips, drawn in, said not Alas!
My hair was over in the grass,
My naked ears heard the day pass,

My eyes, wide open, had the run
10 Of some ten weeds to fix upon;
Among those few, out of the sun,
The woodspurge flowered, three cups in one.

From perfect grief there need not be
Wisdom or even memory:
15 One thing then learnt remains to me,—
The woodspurge has a cup of three.   [1870]

The woodspurge has small greenish-yellow flowers.

EMILY DICKINSON (1830–1886)

Went Up a Year This Evening

Went up a year this evening!
I recollect it well!
Amid no bells nor bravoes
The bystanders will tell!
5   Cheerful—as to the village—
Tranquil—as to repose—
Chastened—as to the Chapel
This humble Tourist rose!
Did not talk of returning!
10 Alluded to no time
When, were the gales propitious—
We might look for him!
Was grateful for the Roses
In life's diverse bouquet—
15 Talked softly of new species
To pick another day;
Beguiling thus the wonder
The *wondrous* nearer drew—
Hands bustled at the moorings—
20 The crowd respectful grew—
Ascended from our vision
To Countenances new!
A Difference—A Daisy—
Is all the rest I knew!   ([c. 1859] 1955)

I Heard a Fly Buzz—When I Died

I heard a Fly buzz—when I died—
The Stillness in the Room
Was like the Stillness in the Air—
Between the Heaves of Storm—

5   The Eyes around—had wrung them dry—
And Breaths were gathering firm
For that last Onset—when the King
Be witnessed—in the Room—

I willed my Keepsakes—Signed away
10 What portion of me be
Assignable—and then it was
There interposed a Fly—

With Blue—uncertain—stumbling Buzz—
Between the light—and me—
15 And then the Windows failed—and then
I could not see to see—   ([c. 1862] 1955)

PAOLO UCCELLO, *Saint George and the Dragon*. Oil on canvas, 56.5 × 74 cm. The National Gallery, London. Photo © National Gallery Picture Library.

Not my Best Side

I

Not my best side, I'm afraid.
The artist didn't give me a chance to
Pose properly, and as you can see,
Poor chap, he had this obsession with
5 Triangles, so he left off two of my
Feet. I didn't comment at the time
(What, after all, are two feet
To a monster?) but afterwards
I was sorry for the bad publicity.
10 Why, I said to myself, should my conqueror
Be so ostentatiously beardless, and ride
A horse with a deformed neck and square hoofs?
Why should my victim be so
Unattractive as to be inedible,
15 And why should she have me literally

Plate 1

On a string? I don't mind dying
Ritually, since I always rise again,
But I should have liked a little more blood
To show they were taking me seriously.

II

20 It's hard for a girl to be sure if
She wants to be rescued. I mean, I quite
Took to the dragon. It's nice to be
Liked, if you know what I mean. He was
So nicely physical, with his claws
25 And lovely green skin, and that sexy tail,
And the way he looked at me,
He made me feel he was all ready to
Eat me. And any girl enjoys that.
So when this boy turned up, wearing machinery,
30 On a really *dangerous* horse, to be honest
I didn't much fancy him. I mean,
What was he like underneath the hardware?
He might have acne, blackheads or even
Bad breath for all I could tell, but the dragon—
35 Well, you could see all his equipment
At a glance. Still, what could I do?
The dragon got himself beaten by the boy,
And a girl's got to think of her future.

III

I have diplomas in Dragon
40 Management and Virgin Reclamation.
My horse is the latest model, with
Automatic transmission and built-in
Obsolescence. My spear is custom-built,
And my prototype armour
45 Still on the secret list. You can't
Do better than me at the moment.
I'm qualified and equipped to the
Eyebrow. So why be difficult?
Don't you want to be killed and/or rescued
50 In the most contemporary way? Don't
You want to carry out the roles
That sociology and myth have designed for you?
Don't you realize that, by being choosy,
You are endangering job prospects
55 In the spear- and horse-building industries?
What, in any case, does it matter what
You want? You're in my way.   [1978]

U. A. FANTHORPE (b. 1929)

Plate 2

Musée des Beaux Arts

About suffering they were never wrong,
The Old Masters: how well they understood
Its human position; how it takes place
While someone else is eating or opening a window or just walking dully along;
5   How, when the aged are reverently, passionately waiting
For the miraculous birth, there always must be
Children who did not specially want it to happen, skating
On a pond at the edge of the wood:
They never forgot
10   That even the dreadful martyrdom must run its course
Anyhow in a corner, some untidy spot
Where the dogs go on with their doggy life and the torturer's horse
Scratches its innocent behind on a tree.

In Brueghel's *Icarus,* for instance: how everything turns away
15   Quite leisurely from the disaster; the ploughman may
Have heard the splash, the forsaken cry,
But for him it was not an important failure; the sun shone
As it had to on the white legs disappearing into the green
Water; and the expensive delicate ship that must have seen
20   Something amazing, a boy falling out of the sky,
Had somewhere to get to and sailed calmly on.

[1940]

W. H. AUDEN (1907–1973)

PIETER BRUEGHEL THE ELDER, *Landscape with the Fall of Icarus.* Musées Royaux des Beaux-Arts, Brussels. Photo Scala/Art Resource.

Plate 3

PIERO DELLA FRANCESCA, *Madonna del Parto*. Cemetery
Chapel, Monterchi, Sansepolcro, Scala/Art Resource.

San Sepolcro

In this blue light
    I can take you there,
snow having made me
    a world of bone
5   seen through to. This
    is my house,

my section of Etruscan
    wall, my neighbor's
lemontrees, and, just below
10   the lower church,
the airplane factory.
    A rooster

crows all day from mist
    outside the walls.
15 There's milk on the air,
    ice on the oily
lemonskins. How clean
    the mind is,

Plate 4

holy grave. It is this girl
20   by Piero
della Francesca, unbuttoning
        her blue dress,
her mantle of weather,
        to go into

25 labor. Come, we can go in.
        It is before
the birth of god. No-one
        has risen yet
to the museums, to the assembly
30   line—bodies

and wings—to the open air
        market. This is
what the living do: go in.
        It's a long way.
35 And the dress keeps opening
        from eternity

to privacy, quickening.
        Inside, at the heart,
is tragedy, the resent moment
40   forever stillborn,
but going in, each breath
        is a button

coming undone, something terribly
        nimble-fingered
45 finding all of the stops.   [1983]

                              JORIE GRAHAM (*b*. 1951)

Plate 5

GUSTAV KLIMT, *The Kiss,* 1907–1908. Oesterreichische Galerie, Vienna. Photo Erich Lessing/
Art Resource.

Short Story on a Painting of Gustav Klimt

They are kneeling upright on a flowered bed
   He
         has just caught her there
              and holds her still
₅   Her gown
         has slipped down
              off her shoulder
He has an urgent hunger
        His dark head
₁₀   bends to hers
              hungrily

Plate 6

And the woman the woman
    turns her tangerine lips from his
      one hand like the head of a dead swan
15   draped down over
              his heavy neck
      the fingers
        strangely crimped
          tightly together
20   her other arm doubled up
        against her tight breast
     her hand a languid claw
        clutching his hand
     which would turn her mouth
25   to his
    her long dress made
      of multicolored blossoms
      quilted on gold
    her Titian hair
30   with blue stars in it
    And his gold
      harlequin robe
        checkered with
          dark squares
35   Gold garlands
      stream down over
        her bare calves &
        tensed feet
Nearby there must be
40   a jeweled tree
      with glass leaves aglitter
      in the gold air
It must be
    morning
45   in a faraway place somewhere
They
    are silent together
      as in a flowered field
    upon the summer couch
50   which must be hers
  And he holds her still
      so passionately
    holds her head to his
      so gently so insistently
55   to make her turn
      her lips to his
Her eyes are closed
    like folded petals
She
60 will not open
     He
      is not the One   [1976]
     LAWRENCE FERLINGHETTI (*b.* 1919)

Plate 7

PAUL DELVAUX, *The Village of the Mermaids*, 1942. Oil on panel, 104.3 × 124.1 cm. Gift of Mr. and Mrs. Maurice E. Culberg, 1951.73. Photograph © 1999, The Art Institute of Chicago.

Paul Delvaux: The Village of the Mermaids

Oil on canvas, 1942

Who is that man in black, walking
away from us into the distance?
The painter, they say, took a long time
finding his vision of the world.

5   The mermaids, if that is what they are
under their full-length skirts,
sit facing each other
all down the street, more of an alley,
in front of their gray row houses.

10 They all look the same, like a fair-haired
order of nuns, or like prostitutes
with chaste, identical faces.
How calm they are, with their vacant eyes,
their hands in laps that betray nothing.

15 Only one has scales on her dusky dress.

It is 1942; it is Europe,
and nothing fits. The one familiar figure
is the man in black approaching the sea,
and he is small and walking away from us.   [1989]

LISEL MUELLER (*b.* 1924)

Plate 8

I Started Early—Took My Dog

I started Early—Took my Dog—
And visited the Sea—
The Mermaids in the Basement
Came out to look at me—

5 And Frigates—in the Upper Floor
Extended Hempen Hands—
Presuming Me to be a Mouse—
Aground—upon the Sands—

But no Man moved Me—till the Tide
10 Went past my simple Shoe—
And past my Apron—and my Belt
And past my Bodice—too—

And made as He would eat me up
As wholly as a Dew
15 Upon a Dandelion's Sleeve—
And then—I started—too—

And He—He followed—close behind—
I felt His Silver Heel
Upon my Ankle—Then my Shoes
20 Would overflow with Pearl—

Until We met the Solid Town—
No One He seemed to know—
And bowing—with a Mighty look—
At me—The Sea withdrew—   ([c. 1862] 1955)

Because I Could Not Stop for Death

Because I could not stop for Death—
He kindly stopped for me—
The Carriage held but just Ourselves—
And Immortality.

5 We slowly drove—He knew no haste
And I had put away
My labor and my leisure too,
For His Civility—

We passed the School, where Children strove
10 At Recess—in the Ring—
We passed the Fields of Gazing Grain—
We passed the Setting Sun—

Or rather—He passed Us—
The Dews drew quivering and chill—
15 For only Gossamer, my Gown—
My Tippet—only Tulle—

16/**Tippet:** *long scarf or shoulder cape*

We paused before a House that seemed
A Swelling of the Ground—
The Roof was scarcely visible—
20   The Cornice—in the Ground—

Since then—'tis Centuries—and yet
Feels shorter than the Day
I first surmised the Horses' Heads
Were toward Eternity—   ([c. 1863] 1955)

Tell All the Truth but Tell It Slant

Tell all the Truth but tell it slant—
Success in Circuit lies
Too bright for our infirm Delight
The Truth's superb surprise
5   As Lightning to the Children eased
With explanation kind
The Truth must dazzle gradually
Or every man be blind—   ([c. 1868] 1955)

The Bustle in a House

The Bustle in a House
The Morning after Death
Is solemnest of industries
Enacted upon Earth—

5   The Sweeping up the Heart
And putting Love away
We shall not want to use again
Until Eternity.   ([c. 1866] 1955)

CHRISTINA ROSSETTI (1830–1894)

Up-Hill

Does the road wind up-hill all the way?
    Yes, to the very end.
Will the day's journey take the whole long day?
    From morn to night, my friend.

5   But is there for the night a resting-place?
    A roof for when the slow dark hours begin.
May not the darkness hide it from my face?
    You cannot miss that inn.

Shall I meet other wayfarers at night?
10   Those who have gone before.
Then must I knock, or call when just in sight?
    They will not keep you standing at that door.

Shall I find comfort, travel-sore and weak?
    Of labour you shall find the sum.
15 Will there be beds for me and all who seek?
    Yes, beds for all who come.   [1862]

THOMAS HARDY (1840–1928)

The Ruined Maid

"O 'Melia, my dear, this does everything crown!
Who could have supposed I should meet you in Town?
And whence such fair garments, such prosperi-ty?"—
"O didn't you know I'd been ruined?" said she.

5 —"You left us in tatters, without shoes or socks,
Tired of digging potatoes, and spudding up docks;
And now you've gay bracelets and bright feathers three!"—
"Yes: that's how we dress when we're ruined," said she.

—"At home in the barton you said 'thee' and 'thou,'
10 And 'thik oon,' and 'theäs oon,' and 't'other'; but now
Your talking quite fits 'ee for high compa-ny!"—
"Some polish is gained with one's ruin," said she.

—"Your hands were like paws then, your face blue and bleak
But now I'm bewitched by your delicate cheek,
15 And your little gloves fit as on any la-dy!"—
"We never do work when we're ruined," said she.

—"You used to call home-life a hag-ridden dream,
And you'd sigh, and you'd sock; but at present you seem
To know not of megrims or melancho-ly!"—
20 "True. One's pretty lively when ruined," said she.

—"I wish I had feathers, a fine sweeping gown,
And a delicate face, and could strut about Town!"—
"My dear—a raw country girl, such as you be,
Cannot quite expect that. You ain't ruined," said she.   [1901]

6/*spudding up docks:* digging up *weeds*
9/***barton:*** *farmyard*

10/***thik oon . . . theäs oon:*** *that one . . . this one*
18/***sock:*** *sigh*
19/***megrims:*** *headache, depression*

The Self-Unseeing

Here is the ancient floor,
Footworn and hollowed and thin,
Here was the former door
Where the dead feet walked in.

5 She sat here in her chair,
Smiling into the fire;
He who played stood there,
Bowing it higher and higher.

Childlike, I danced in a dream;
10 Blessings emblazoned that day;
Everything glowed with a gleam;
Yet we were looking away!   [1901]

The Man He Killed

"Had he and I but met
By some old ancient inn,
We should have sat us down to wet
Right many a nipperkin!

5 "But ranged as infantry,
And staring face to face,
I shot at him as he at me,
And killed him in his place.

"I shot him dead because—
10 Because he was my foe,
Just so: my foe of course he was;
That's clear enough; although

"He thought he'd 'list, perhaps,
Off-hand like—just as I—
15 Was out of work—had sold his traps—
No other reason why.

"Yes; quaint and curious war is!
You shoot a fellow down
You'd treat if met where any bar is,
20 Or help to half-a-crown."   [1909]

4/*nipperkin: a measure of beer or*
wine—about a half pint
13/*'list: enlist*

15/*traps: belongings*
20/*half-a-crown: about half a dollar*

The Oxen

Christmas Eve, and twelve of the clock,
    "Now they are all on their knees,"
An elder said as we sat in a flock
    By the embers in hearthside ease.

5 We pictured the meek mild creatures where
    They dwelt in their strawy pen,
Nor did it occur to one of us there
    To doubt they were kneeling then.

So fair a fancy few would weave
10   In these years! Yet, I feel,
If someone said on Christmas Eve,
      "Come; see the oxen kneel,

"In the lonely barton by yonder coomb
      Our childhood used to know,"
15   I should go with him in the gloom,
      Hoping it might be so.   [1917]

According to an old legend, oxen kneel on Christmas Eve in honor of Christ's birth.

13/**barton:** *farmyard*   **coomb:** *valley*

In Time of "The Breaking of Nations"

I

Only a man harrowing clods
      In a slow silent walk
With an old horse that stumbles and nods
      Half asleep as they stalk.

II

5   Only thin smoke without flame
      From the heaps of couch-grass;
Yet this will go onward the same
      Though Dynasties pass.

III

Yonder a maid and her wight
10   Come whispering by:
War's annals will fade into night
      Ere their story die.   [1917]

Though written during World War I, this poem expresses a feeling that moved Hardy during the Franco-Prussian War in 1870. The title alludes to Jeremiah 51:20, where God's judgment against Babylon is reported: "Thou art my battle axe and weapons of war: for with thee will I break in pieces the nations."

6/**couch-grass:** *rough grass that*   9/**wight:** *man*
spreads like a weed

GERARD MANLEY HOPKINS (1844–1889)

God's Grandeur

The world is charged with the grandeur of God.
    It will flame out, like shining from shook foil;
    It gathers to a greatness, like the ooze of oil
Crushed. Why do men then now not reck his rod?
5 Generations have trod, have trod, have trod;
    And all is seared with trade; bleared, smeared with toil;
    And wears man's smudge and shares man's smell: the soil
Is bare now, nor can foot feel, being shod.

And for all this, nature is never spent;
10 There lives the dearest freshness deep down things;
And though the last lights off the black West went
    Oh, morning, at the brown brink eastward, springs—
Because the Holy Ghost over the bent
    World broods with warm breast and with ah! bright wings.   [1918]

[2]/**shook foil:** gold foil, which when shaken gives off a dazzle of light
[4]/**reck his rod:** pay attention to his power

[3-4]/**ooze of oil/Crushed:** olive oil, or various aromatic oils extracted by crushing

The Windhover

To Christ our Lord

I caught this morning morning's minion, king-
    dom of daylight's dauphin, dapple-dawn-drawn Falcon, in his
      riding
    Of the rolling level underneath him steady air, and striding
High there, how he rung upon the rein of a wimpling wing
5 In his ecstasy! then off, off forth on swing,
    As a skate's heel sweeps smooth on a bow-bend: the hurl and
      gliding
    Rebuffed the big wind. My heart in hiding
Stirred for a bird,—the achieve of, the mastery of the thing!

Brute beauty and valour and act, oh, air, pride, plume, here
10 Buckle! AND the fire that breaks from thee then, a billion
Times told lovelier, more dangerous, O my chevalier!
    No wonder of it: shéer plód makes plough down sillion
Shine, and blue-bleak embers, ah my dear,
    Fall, gall themselves, and gash gold-vermilion.

The windhover is a small hawk that hangs or hovers with its head into the wind.

[1]/**minion:** darling, favorite
[2]/**dauphin:** prince
[4]/**rung upon the rein:** pivoted on a wing tip (probably). A horse being trained is said to "ring on the rein"

when it goes in a circle on the end of a long rein.
  wimpling: rippling, pleated
[10]/**buckle:** lock together
[12]/**sillion:** furrow (French, sillon)

Felix Randal

Felix Randal the farrier, O is he dead then? my duty all ended,
Who have watched his mould of man, big-boned and hardy-
    handsome
Pining, pining, till time when reason rambled in it and some
Fatal four disorders, fleshed there, all contended?

5   Sickness broke him. Impatient, he cursed at first, but mended
Being anointed and all; though a heavenlier heart began some
Months earlier, since I had our sweet reprieve and ransom
Tendered to him. Ah well, God rest him all road ever he offended!

This seeing the sick endears them to us, us too it endears.
10 My tongue had taught thee comfort, touch had quenched thy tears,
Thy tears that touched my heart, child, Felix, poor Felix Randal;

How far from then forethought of, all thy more boisterous years,
When thou at the random grim forge, powerful amidst peers,
Didst fettle for the great grey drayhorse his bright and battering
    sandal!   [1918]

[1]/*farrier: blacksmith*
[7]/***reprieve and ransom:*** *confession and communion*
[8]/***all road ever:*** *in whatever ways*

[13]/***random:*** *roughly built of irregular stones*
[14]/***fettle:*** *prepare*

Spring and Fall

to a young child

Márgarét, áre you gríeving
Over Goldengrove unleaving?
Leáves, líke the things of man, you
With your fresh thoughts care for, can you?
5   Áh! ás the heart grows older
It will come to such sights colder
By and by, nor spare a sigh
Though worlds of wanwood leafmeal lie;
And yet you *will* weep and know why.
10 Now no matter, child, the name:
Sórrow's spríngs áre the same.
Nor mouth had, no nor mind, expressed
What heart heard of, ghost guessed:
It ís the blight man was born for,
15 It is Margaret you mourn for.   [1918]

[8]/***wanwood:*** *a coined expression for woods wan in autumn*

leafmeal: *(1) in leafy pieces (cf. piecemeal); (2) ground to leafy meal*
[13]/***ghost:*** *spirit*

A. E. HOUSMAN (1859–1936)

To an Athlete Dying Young

The time you won your town the race
We chaired you through the market-place;
Man and boy stood cheering by,
And home we brought you shoulder-high.

5   To-day, the road all runners come,
Shoulder-high we bring you home,
And set you at your threshold down,
Townsman of a stiller town.

Smart lad, to slip betimes away
10   From fields where glory does not stay
And early though the laurel grows
It withers quicker than the rose.

Eyes the shady night has shut
Cannot see the record cut,
15   And silence sounds no worse than cheers
After earth has stopped the ears:

Now you will not swell the rout
Of lads that wore their honours out,
Runners whom renown outran
20   And the name died before the man.

So set, before its echoes fade,
The fleet foot on the sill of shade,
And hold to the low lintel up
The still-defended challenge-cup.

25   And round that early-laurelled head
Will flock to gaze the strengthless dead,
And find unwithered on its curls
The garland briefer than a girl's.   [1896]

[9]/*betimes: early, in good time*   [23]/*lintel: the horizontal piece of stone or timber over a door or window*

Loveliest of Trees, the Cherry Now

Loveliest of trees, the cherry now
Is hung with bloom along the bough,
And stands about the woodland ride
Wearing white for Eastertide.

5   Now, of my threescore years and ten,
Twenty will not come again,
And take from seventy springs a score,
It only leaves me fifty more.

And since to look at things in bloom
10 Fifty springs are little room,
About the woodlands I will go
To see the cherry hung with snow.   [1896]

WILLIAM BUTLER YEATS (1865–1939)

Adam's Curse

We sat together at one summer's end,
That beautiful mild woman, your close friend,
And you and I, and talked of poetry.
I said, 'A line will take us hours maybe;
5 Yet if it does not seem a moment's thought,
Our stitching and unstitching has been naught.
Better go down upon your marrow-bones
And scrub a kitchen pavement, or break stones
Like an old pauper, in all kinds of weather;
10 For to articulate sweet sounds together
Is to work harder than all these, and yet
Be thought an idler by the noisy set
Of bankers, schoolmasters, and clergymen
The martyrs call the world.'
                    And thereupon
15 That beautiful mild woman for whose sake
There's many a one shall find out all heartache
On finding that her voice is sweet and low
Replied, 'To be born woman is to know—
Although they do not talk of it at school—
20 That we must labour to be beautiful.'

I said, 'It's certain there is no fine thing
Since Adam's fall but needs much labouring.
There have been lovers who thought love should be
So much compounded of high courtesy
25 That they would sigh and quote with learned looks
Precedents out of beautiful old books;
Yet now it seems an idle trade enough.'

We sat grown quiet at the name of love;
We saw the last embers of daylight die,
30 And in the trembling blue-green of the sky
A moon, worn as if it had been a shell
Washed by time's waters as they rose and fell
About the stars and broke in days and years.

I had a thought for no one's but your ears:
35 That you were beautiful, and that I strove
To love you in the old high way of love;
That it had all seemed happy, and yet we'd grown
As weary-hearted as that hollow moon.   [1904]

The Cold Heaven

Suddenly I saw the cold and rook-delighting heaven
That seemed as though ice burned and was but the more ice,
And thereupon imagination and heart were driven
So wild that every casual thought of that and this
5   Vanished, and left but memories, that should be out of season
With the hot blood of youth, of love crossed long ago;
And I took all the blame out of all sense and reason,
Until I cried and trembled and rocked to and fro,
Riddled with light. Ah! when the ghost begins to quicken,
10   Confusion of the death-bed over, is it sent
Out naked on the roads, as the books say, and stricken
By the injustice of the skies for punishment?   [1912]

[1]/**rook:** *crow*

Sailing to Byzantium

I

That is no country for old men. The young
In one another's arms, birds in the trees
—Those dying generations—at their song,
The salmon-falls, the mackerel-crowded seas,
5   Fish, flesh, or fowl, commend all summer long
Whatever is begotten, born, and dies.
Caught in that sensual music all neglect
Monuments of unageing intellect.

II

An aged man is but a paltry thing,
10   A tattered coat upon a stick, unless
Soul clap its hands and sing, and louder sing
For every tatter in its mortal dress,
Nor is there singing school but studying
Monuments of its own magnificence;
15   And therefore I have sailed the seas and come
To the holy city of Byzantium.

III

O sages standing in God's holy fire
As in the gold mosaic of a wall,
Come from the holy fire, perne in a gyre,
20   And be the singing-masters of my soul.
Consume my heart away; sick with desire
And fastened to a dying animal

[1]/**that:** *Ireland—though it might be any place in the physical world* [18]/**gold mosaic:** *Byzantine mosaics show their saints (or "sages") against a background of gold tiles that glitter like fire.* [19]/**perne:** *whirl, spin*

It knows not what it is; and gather me
Into the artifice of eternity.

IV

25 Once out of nature I shall never take
My bodily form from any natural thing,
But such a form as Grecian goldsmiths make
Of hammered gold and gold enamelling
To keep a drowsy Emperor awake;
30 Or set upon a golden bough to sing
To lords and ladies of Byzantium
Of what is past, or passing, or to come.   [1928]

Byzantium, later named Constantinople and now Istanbul, was the capital of the eastern Roman empire and a famous artistic and religious center. Yeats uses it as symbolic of the life of the spirit.

27–32/*Yeats tells us that he had read somewhere about artificial singing birds in a gold and silver tree in the Emperor's palace in Byzantium.*

Among School Children

I

I walk through the long schoolroom questioning;
A kind old nun in a white hood replies;
The children learn to cipher and to sing,
To study reading-books and histories,
5 To cut and sew, be neat in everything
In the best modern way—the children's eyes
In momentary wonder stare upon
A sixty-year-old smiling public man.

II

I dream of a Ledaean body, bent
10 Above a sinking fire, a tale that she
Told of a harsh reproof, or trivial event
That changed some childish day to tragedy—
Told, and it seemed that our two natures blent
Into a sphere from youthful sympathy,
15 Or else, to alter Plato's parable,
Into the yolk and white of the one shell.

III

And thinking of that fit of grief or rage
I look upon one child or t'other there

1/*schoolroom: Yeats's duties as a senator of the Irish Free State included occasional school inspections.*
9/**Ledaean:** *like that of the daughter (Helen of Troy) whom Leda bore. The father was Zeus in the form of a swan. Cf. "Leda and the Swan," p. 40.*

15/**Plato's parable:** *In a myth that Plato recounts in his* Symposium, *men and women were once united in double bodies, till Zeus, fearing their power, separated them "as you might divide an egg with a hair."*

And wonder if she stood so at that age—
20   For even daughters of the swan can share
Something of every paddler's heritage—
And had that colour upon cheek or hair,
And thereupon my heart is driven wild:
She stands before me as a living child.

IV

25   Her present image floats into the mind—
Did Quattrocento finger fashion it
Hollow of cheek as though it drank the wind
And took a mess of shadows for its meat?
And I though never of Ledaean kind
30   Had pretty plumage once—enough of that,
Better to smile on all that smile, and show
There is a comfortable kind of old scarecrow.

V

What youthful mother, a shape upon her lap
Honey of generation had betrayed,
35   And that must sleep, shriek, struggle to escape
As recollection or the drug decide,
Would think her son, did she but see that shape
With sixty or more winters on its head,
A compensation for the pang of his birth,
40   Or the uncertainty of his setting forth?

VI

Plato thought nature but a spume that plays
Upon a ghostly paradigm of things;
Solider Aristotle played the taws
Upon the bottom of a king of kings;
45   World-famous golden-thighed Pythagoras
Fingered upon a fiddle-stick or strings
What a star sang and careless Muses heard:
Old clothes upon old sticks to scare a bird.

---

[19]/**she:** *the woman of the Ledaean body, whom Yeats was long in love with*
[20]/**daughters of the swan:** *girls of divine birth, like Helen*
[26]/**Quattrocento:** *of the 1400s—the Italian Renaissance*
[34]/**had betrayed:** *by bringing it into this life out of a happier preexistence*
[41-42]/**Plato . . . things:** *Plato thought the world we see was only an imitation of true reality, only a kind of froth (spume) on a spiritual framework (ghostly paradigm) of that reality.*

[43-44]/**solider Aristotle:** *"solider" because he took the physical world more seriously and based his investigations on it*
    taws: *a schoolmaster's leather strap. Aristotle was the tutor of the boy who was to become Alexander the Great.*
[45-47]/**Pythagoras:** *he was interested in music, geometry, arithmetic, astronomy. Legend had it that his thighbone was of gold.*
[48]/**old clothes:** *even the greatest men, like the three just mentioned, are no better than scarecrows in old age*

VII

Both nuns and mothers worship images,
50 But those the candles light are not as those
That animate a mother's reveries,
But keep a marble or a bronze repose.
And yet they too break hearts—O Presences
That passion, piety or affection knows,
55 And that all heavenly glory symbolise—
O self-born mockers of man's enterprise:

VIII

Labour is blossoming or dancing where
The body is not bruised to pleasure soul,
Nor beauty born out of its own despair,
60 Nor blear-eyed wisdom out of midnight oil.
O chestnut-tree, great-rooted blossomer,
Are you the leaf, the blossom or the bole?
O body swayed to music, O brightening glance,
How can we know the dancer from the dance?   [1928]

A Last Confession

What lively lad most pleasured me
Of all that with me lay?
I answer that I gave my soul
And loved in misery,
5 But had great pleasure with a lad
That I loved bodily.

Flinging from his arms I laughed
To think his passion such
He fancied that I gave a soul
10 Did but our bodies touch,
And laughed upon his breast to think
Beast gave beast as much.

I gave what other women gave
That stepped out of their clothes,
15 But when this soul, its body off,
Naked to naked goes,
He it has found shall find therein
What none other knows,
And give his own and take his own
20 And rule in his own right;
And though it loved in misery
Close and cling so tight,
There's not a bird of day that dare
Extinguish that delight.   [1929]

The speaker is an old woman, looking back on a lifetime of emotional experience.

EDWIN ARLINGTON ROBINSON (1869–1935)

The Mill

The miller's wife had waited long,
　　The tea was cold, the fire was dead;
And there might yet be nothing wrong
　　In how he went and what he said:
5　"There are no millers any more,"
　　Was all that she had heard him say;
And he had lingered at the door
　　So long that it seemed yesterday.

Sick with a fear that had no form
10　She knew that she was there at last;
And in the mill there was a warm
　　And mealy fragrance of the past.
What else there was would only seem
　　To say again what he had meant;
15　And what was hanging from a beam
　　Would not have heeded where she went.

And if she thought it followed her,
　　She may have reasoned in the dark
That one way of the few there were
20　Would hide her and would leave no mark:
Black water, smooth above the weir
　　Like starry velvet in the night,
Though ruffled once, would soon appear
　　The same as ever to the sight.　　　　　　　　　[1920]

21/*weir: dam*

Mr. Flood's Party

Old Eben Flood, climbing alone one night
Over the hill between the town below
And the forsaken upland hermitage
That held as much as he should ever know
5　On earth again of home, paused warily.
The road was his with not a native near;
And Eben, having leisure, said aloud,
For no man else in Tilbury Town to hear:

"Well, Mr. Flood, we have the harvest moon
10　Again, and we may not have many more;
The bird is on the wing, the poet says,
And you and I have said it here before.
Drink to the bird." He raised up to the light
The jug that he had gone so far to fill,

11/*See The Rubáiyát of Omar Khayyám, VII (p. 408).*

15 And answered huskily: "Well, Mr. Flood,
    Since you propose it, I believe I will."

    Alone, as if enduring to the end
    A valiant armor of scarred hopes outworn,
    He stood there in the middle of the road
20 Like Roland's ghost winding a silent horn.
    Below him, in the town among the trees,
    Where friends of other days had honored him,
    A phantom salutation of the dead
    Rang thinly till old Eben's eyes were dim.

25 Then, as a mother lays her sleeping child
    Down tenderly, fearing it may awake,
    He set the jug down slowly at his feet
    With trembling care, knowing that most things break;
    And only when assured that on firm earth
30 It stood, as the uncertain lives of men
    Assuredly did not, he paced away,
    And with his hand extended paused again:

    "Well, Mr. Flood, we have not met like this
    In a long time; and many a change has come
35 To both of us, I fear, since last it was
    We had a drop together. Welcome home!"
    Convivially returning with himself,
    Again he raised the jug up to the light;
    And with an acquiescent quaver said:
40 "Well, Mr. Flood, if you insist, I might.

    "Only a very little, Mr. Flood—
    For auld lang syne. No more, sir; that will do."
    So, for the time, apparently it did,
    And Eben evidently thought so too;
45 For soon amid the silver loneliness
    Of night he lifted up his voice and sang,
    Secure, with only two moons listening,
    Until the whole harmonious landscape rang—

    "For auld lang syne." The weary throat gave out;
50 The last word wavered, and the song was done.
    He raised again the jug regretfully
    And shook his head, and was again alone.
    There was not much that was ahead of him,
    And there was nothing in the town below—
55 Where strangers would have shut the many doors
    That many friends had opened long ago.   [1921]

20/*Roland: Roland, in command of the rear guard of Charlemagne's army, was ambushed and outnumbered in the pass of Roncevaux in the Pyrenees. Out of pride, he refused to sound until too late the horn that would have brought the Emperor to his rescue.*

WALTER DE LA MARE (1873–1956)

The Listeners

'Is there anybody there?' said the Traveller,
    Knocking on the moonlit door;
And his horse in the silence champed the grasses
    Of the forest's ferny floor:
5 And a bird flew up out of the turret,
    Above the Traveller's head:
And he smote upon the door again a second time;
    'Is there anybody there?' he said.
But no one descended to the Traveller;
10   No head from the leaf-fringed sill
Leaned over and looked into his grey eyes,
    Where he stood perplexed and still.
But only a host of phantom listeners
    That dwelt in the lone house then
15 Stood listening in the quiet of the moonlight
    To that voice from the world of men:
Stood thronging the faint moonbeams on the dark stair,
    That goes down to the empty hall,
Hearkening in an air stirred and shaken
20   By the lonely Traveller's call.
And he felt in his heart their strangeness,
    Their stillness answering his cry,
While his horse moved, cropping the dark turf,
    'Neath the starred and leafy sky;
25 For he suddenly smote on the door, even
    Louder, and lifted his head:—
'Tell them I came, and no one answered,
    That I kept my word,' he said.
Never the least stir made the listeners,
30   Though every word he spake
Fell echoing through the shadowiness of the still house
    From the one man left awake:
Ay, they heard his foot upon the stirrup,
    And the sound of iron on stone,
35 And how the silence surged softly backward,
    When the plunging hoofs were gone.   [1912]

ROBERT FROST (1874–1963)

Mending Wall

Something there is that doesn't love a wall,
That sends the frozen-ground-swell under it,
And spills the upper boulders in the sun;
And makes gaps even two can pass abreast.

5   The work of hunters is another thing:
I have come after them and made repair
Where they have left not one stone on a stone,
But they would have the rabbit out of hiding,
To please the yelping dogs. The gaps I mean,
10   No one has seen them made or heard them made,
But at spring mending-time we find them there.
I let my neighbor know beyond the hill;
And on a day we meet to walk the line
And set the wall between us once again.
15   We keep the wall between us as we go.
To each the boulders that have fallen to each.
And some are loaves and some so nearly balls
We have to use a spell to make them balance:
"Stay where you are until our backs are turned!"
20   We wear our fingers rough with handling them.
Oh, just another kind of outdoor game,
One on a side. It comes to little more:
There where it is we do not need the wall:
He is all pine and I am apple orchard.
25   My apple trees will never get across
And eat the cones under his pines, I tell him.
He only says, "Good fences make good neighbors."
Spring is the mischief in me, and I wonder
If I could put a notion in his head:
30   "*Why* do they make good neighbors? Isn't it
Where there are cows? But here there are no cows.
Before I built a wall I'd ask to know
What I was walling in or walling out,
And to whom I like to give offense.
35   Something there is that doesn't love a wall,
That wants it down." I could say "Elves" to him,
But it's not elves exactly, and I'd rather
He said it for himself. I see him there
Bringing a stone grasped firmly by the top
40   In each hand, like an old-stone savage armed.
He moves in darkness as it seems to me,
Not of woods only and the shade of trees.
He will not go behind his father's saying,
And he likes having thought of it so well
45   He says again, "Good fences make good neighbors."   [1914]

"Out, Out—"

The buzz saw snarled and rattled in the yard
And made dust and dropped stove-length sticks of wood,
Sweet-scented stuff when the breeze drew across it.
And from there those that lifted eyes could count
5   Five mountain ranges one behind the other

Under the sunset far into Vermont.
And the saw snarled and rattled, snarled and rattled,
As it ran light, or had to bear a load.
And nothing happened: day was all but done.
10 Call it a day, I wish they might have said
To please the boy by giving him the half hour
That a boy counts so much when saved from work.
His sister stood beside them in her apron
To tell them "Supper." At the word, the saw,
15 As if to prove saws knew what supper meant,
Leaped out at the boy's hand, or seemed to leap—
He must have given the hand. However it was,
Neither refused the meeting. But the hand!
The boy's first outcry was a rueful laugh,
20 As he swung toward them holding up the hand
Half in appeal, but half as if to keep
The life from spilling. Then the boy saw all—
Since he was old enough to know, big boy
Doing a man's work, though a child at heart—
25 He saw all spoiled. "Don't let him cut my hand off—
The doctor, when he comes. Don't let him, sister!"
So. But the hand was gone already.
The doctor put him in the dark of ether.
He lay and puffed his lips out with his breath.
30 And then—the watcher at his pulse took fright.
No one believed. They listened at his heart.
Little—less—nothing!—and that ended it.
No more to build on there. And they, since they
Were not the one dead, turned to their affairs.   [1916]

"Out, Out—": The title is from Macbeth, *V, v:*
                    Out, out, brief candle!
                    Life's but a walking shadow.

For Once, Then, Something

Others taunt me with having knelt at well-curbs
Always wrong to the light, so never seeing
Deeper down in the well than where the water
Gives me back in a shining surface picture
5 Me myself in the summer heaven godlike
Looking out of a wreath of fern and cloud puffs.
Once, when trying with chin against a well-curb,
I discerned, as I thought, beyond the picture,
Through the picture, a something white, uncertain,
10 Something more of the depths—and then I lost it.
Water came to rebuke the too clear water.
One drop fell from a fern, and lo, a ripple
Shook whatever it was lay there at bottom,
Blurred it, blotted it out. What was that whiteness?
15 Truth? A pebble of quartz? For once, then, something.   [1923]

To Earthward

Love at the lips was touch
As sweet as I could bear;
And once it seemed too much;
I lived on air

5   That crossed me from sweet things,
The flow of—was it musk
From hidden grapevine springs
Down hill at dusk?

I had the swirl and ache
10   From sprays of honeysuckle
That when they're gathered shake
Dew on the knuckle.

I craved strong sweets, but those
Seemed strong when I was young;
15   The petal of the rose
In was that stung.

Now no joy but lacks salt
That is not dashed with pain
And weariness and fault;
20   I crave the stain

Of tears, the aftermark
Of almost too much love.
The sweet of bitter bark
And burning clove.

25   When stiff and sore and scarred
I take away my hand
From leaning on it hard
In grass and sand,

The hurt is not enough:
30   I long for weight and strength
To feel the earth as rough
To all my length.   [1923]

Provide, Provide

The witch that came (the withered hag)
To wash the steps with pail and rag,
Was once the beauty Abishag,

The picture pride of Hollywood.
5   Too many fall from great and good
For you to doubt the likelihood.

---

³/**Abishag:** *the young woman (I Kings 1:1–4) found to attend King David when he was old and ailing*

Die early and avoid the fate.
Or if predestined to die late,
Make up your mind to die in state.

10 Make the whole stock exchange your own!
If need be occupy a throne,
Where nobody can call *you* crone.

Some have relied on what they knew;
Others on being simply true.
15 What worked for them might work for you.

No memory of having starred
Atones for later disregard,
Or keeps the end from being hard.

Better to go down dignified
20 With boughten friendship at your side
Than none at all. Provide, provide!   [1936]

The Subverted Flower

She drew back; he was calm:
"It is this that had the power."
And he lashed his open palm
With the tender-headed flower.
5 He smiled for her to smile,
But she was either blind
Or willfully unkind.
He eyed her for a while
For a woman and a puzzle.
10 He flicked and flung the flower,
And another sort of smile
Caught up like fingertips
The corners of his lips
And cracked his ragged muzzle.
15 She was standing to the waist
In goldenrod and brake,
Her shining hair displaced.
He stretched her either arm
As if she made it ache
20 To clasp her—not to harm;
As if he could not spare
To touch her neck and hair.
"If this has come to us
And not to me alone—"

16/**brake:** *tall ferns*

18/*he stretched her either arm:* he stretched each of his arms toward her

25 So she thought she heard him say;
Though with every word he spoke
His lips were sucked and blown
And the effort made him choke
Like a tiger at a bone.
30 She had to lean away.
She dared not stir a foot,
Lest movement should provoke
The demon of pursuit
That slumbers in a brute.
35 It was then her mother's call
From inside the garden wall
Made her steal a look of fear
To see if he could hear
And would pounce to end it all
40 Before her mother came.
She looked and saw the shame:
A hand hung like a paw,
An arm worked like a saw
As if to be persuasive,
45 An ingratiating laugh
That cut the snout in half,
An eye become evasive.
A girl could only see
That a flower had marred a man,
50 But what she could not see
Was that the flower might be
Other than base and fetid:
That the flower had done but part,
And what the flower began
55 Her own too meager heart
Had terribly completed.
She looked and saw the worst.
And the dog or what it was,
Obeying bestial laws,
60 A coward save at night,
Turned from the place and ran.
She heard him stumble first
And use his hands in flight.
She heard him bark outright.
65 And oh, for one so young
The bitter words she spit
Like some tenacious bit
That will not leave the tongue.
She plucked her lips for it,
70 And still the horror clung.
Her mother wiped the foam
From her chin, picked up her comb,
And drew her backward home.

[1942]

WALLACE STEVENS (1879–1955)

Sunday Morning

I

Complacencies of the peignoir, and late
Coffee and oranges in a sunny chair,
And the green freedom of a cockatoo
Upon a rug mingle to dissipate
5   The holy hush of ancient sacrifice.
She dreams a little, and she feels the dark
Encroachment of that old catastrophe,
As a calm darkens among water-lights.
The pungent oranges and bright, green wings
10 Seem things in some procession of the dead,
Winding across wide water, without sound.
The day is like wide water, without sound,
Stilled for the passing of her dreaming feet
Over the seas, to silent Palestine,
15 Dominion of the blood and sepulchre.

II

Why should she give her bounty to the dead?
What is divinity if it can come
Only in silent shadows and in dreams?
Shall she not find in comforts of the sun,
20 In pungent fruit and bright, green wings, or else
In any balm or beauty of the earth,
Things to be cherished like the thought of heaven?
Divinity must live within herself:
Passions of rain, or moods in falling snow;
25 Grievings in loneliness, or unsubdued
Elations when the forest blooms; gusty
Emotions on wet roads on autumn nights;
All pleasures and all pains, remembering
The bough of summer and the winter branch.
30 These are the measures destined for her soul.

III

Jove in the clouds had his inhuman birth.
No mother suckled him, no sweet land gave
Large-mannered motions to his mythy mind.
He moved among us, as a muttering king,
35 Magnificent, would move among his hinds,
Until our blood, commingling, virginal,
With heaven, brought such requital to desire

See comments (p. 327).

See comments (p. 327).

[35]/*hinds: farm servants*

The very hinds discerned it, in a star.
Shall our blood fail? Or shall it come to be
40 The blood of paradise? And shall the earth
Seem all of paradise that we shall know?
The sky will be much friendlier then than now,
A part of labor and a part of pain,
And next in glory to enduring love,
45 Not this dividing and indifferent blue.

IV

She says, "I am content when wakened birds,
Before they fly, test the reality
Of misty fields, by their sweet questionings;
But when the birds are gone, and their warm fields
50 Return no more, where, then, is paradise?"
There is not any haunt of prophecy,
Nor any old chimera of the grave,
Neither the golden underground, nor isle
Melodious, where spirits gat them home,
55 Nor visionary south, nor cloudy palm
Remote on heaven's hill, that has endured
As April's green endures; or will endure
Like her remembrance of awakened birds,
Or her desire for June and evening, tipped
60 By the consummation of the swallow's wings.

V

She says, "But in contentment I still feel
The need of some imperishable bliss."
Death is the mother of beauty; hence from her,
Alone, shall come fulfillment to our dreams
65 And our desires. Although she strews the leaves
Of sure obliteration on our paths,
The path sick sorrow took, the many paths
Where triumph rang its brassy phrase, or love
Whispered a little out of tenderness,
70 She makes the willow shiver in the sun
For maidens who were wont to sit and gaze
Upon the grass, relinquished to their feet.
She causes boys to pile new plums and pears
On disregarded plate. The maidens taste
75 And stray impassioned in the littering leaves.

VI

Is there no change of death in paradise?
Does ripe fruit never fall? Or do the boughs
Hang always heavy in that perfect sky,
Unchanging, yet so like our perishing earth,
80 With rivers like our own that seek for seas

[54]/*gat them:* got them, betook themselves

They never find, the same receding shores
That never touch with inarticulate pang?
Why set the pear upon those river-banks
Or spice the shores with odors of the plum?
85 Alas, that they should wear our colors there,
The silken weavings of our afternoons,
And pick the strings of our insipid lutes!
Death is the mother of beauty, mystical,
Within whose burning bosom we devise
90 Our earthly mothers waiting, sleeplessly.

VII

Supple and turbulent, a ring of men
Shall chant in orgy on a summer morn
Their boisterous devotion to the sun,
Not as a god, but as a god might be,
95 Naked among them, like a savage source.
Their chant shall be a chant of paradise,
Out of their blood, returning to the sky;
And in their chant shall enter, voice by voice,
The windy lake wherein their lord delights,
100 The trees, like serafin, and echoing hills,
That choir among themselves long afterward.
They shall know well the heavenly fellowship
Of men that perish and of summer morn.
And whence they came and whither they shall go
105 The dew upon their feet shall manifest.

VIII

She hears, upon that water without sound,
A voice that cries, "The tomb in Palestine
Is not the porch of spirits lingering.
It is the grave of Jesus, where he lay."
110 We live in an old chaos of the sun,
Or old dependency of day and night,
Or island solitude, unsponsored, free,
Of that wide water, inescapable.
Deer walk upon our mountains, and the quail
115 Whistle about us their spontaneous cries;
Sweet berries ripen in the wilderness;
And, in the isolation of the sky,
At evening, casual flocks of pigeons make
Ambiguous undulations as they sink,
120 Downward to darkness, on extended wings.   [1923]

The Snow Man

One must have a mind of winter
To regard the frost and the boughs
Of the pine-trees crusted with snow;

And have been cold a long time
5 To behold the junipers shagged with ice,
The spruces rough in the distant glitter

Of the January sun; and not to think
Of any misery in the sound of the wind,
In the sound of a few leaves,

10 Which is the sound of the land
Full of the same wind
That is blowing in the same bare place

For the listener, who listens in the snow,
And, nothing himself, beholds
15 Nothing that is not there and the nothing that is.   [1923]

The Sense of the Sleight-of-Hand Man

One's grand flights, one's Sunday baths,
One's tootings at the weddings of the soul
Occur as they occur. So bluish clouds
Occurred above the empty house and the leaves
5 Of the rhododendrons rattled their gold,
As if someone lived there. Such floods of white
Came bursting from the clouds. So the wind
Threw its contorted strength around the sky.

Could you have said the bluejay suddenly
10 Would swoop to earth? It is a wheel, the rays
Around the sun. The wheel survives the myths.
The fire eye in the clouds survives the gods.
To think of a dove with an eye of grenadine
And pines that are cornets, so it occurs,
15 And a little island full of geese and stars:
It may be that the ignorant man, alone,
Has any chance to mate his life with life
That is the sensual, pearly spouse, the life
That is fluent in even the wintriest bronze.   [1942]

WILLIAM CARLOS WILLIAMS (1883–1963)

To Waken an Old Lady

Old age is
a flight of small
cheeping birds
skimming
5 bare trees
above a snow glaze.
Gaining and failing

they are buffetted
by a dark wind—
10 But what?
On harsh weedstalks
the flock has rested,
the snow
is covered with broken
15 seedhusks
and the wind tempered
by a shrill
piping of plenty.   [1921]

The Red Wheelbarrow

so much depends
upon

a red wheel
barrow

5 glazed with rain
water

beside the white
chickens   [1923]

The Dance

In Breughel's great picture, The Kermess,
the dancers go round, they go round and
around, the squeal and the glare and the
tweedle of bagpipes, a bugle and fiddles
5 tipping their bellies (round as the thick-
sided glasses whose wash they impound)
their hips and their bellies off balance
to turn them. Kicking and rolling about
the Fair Grounds, swinging their butts, those
10 shanks must be sound to bear up under such
rollicking measures, prance as they dance
in Breughel's great picture, The Kermess.   [1944]

[1]/**Kermess:** *an outdoor festival, here in celebration of a wedding*

EZRA POUND (1885–1972)

The River-Merchant's Wife: A Letter

While my hair was still cut straight across my forehead
I played about the front gate, pulling flowers.
You came by on bamboo stilts, playing horse,

You walked about my seat, playing with blue plums.
5 And we went on living in the village of Chokan:
Two small people, without dislike or suspicion.

At fourteen I married My Lord you.
I never laughed, being bashful.
Lowering my head, I looked at the wall.
10 Called to, a thousand times, I never looked back.

At fifteen I stopped scowling,
I desired my dust to be mingled with yours
Forever and forever and forever.
Why should I climb the look out?

15 At sixteen you departed,
You went into far Ku-to-yen, by the river of swirling eddies,
And you have been gone five months.
The monkeys make sorrowful noise overhead.
You dragged your feet when you went out.
20 By the gate now, the moss is grown, the different mosses,
Too deep to clear them away!
The leaves fall early this autumn, in wind.
The paired butterflies are already yellow with August
Over the grass in the West garden;
25 They hurt me. I grow older.
If you are coming down through the narrows of the river Kiang,
Please let me know beforehand,
And I will come out to meet you
        As far as Cho-fu-Sa.   [1915]

                                                   By Rihaku

Rikahu is the Japanese name for the famous Chinese poet Li Po (eighth century).
Pound's version of the Chinese poem is based on the English notes of the scholar
Ernest Fenollosa.

MARIANNE MOORE (1887–1972)

A Grave

Man looking into the sea,
taking the view from those who have as much right to it as you have to
    it yourself,
it is human nature to stand in the middle of a thing,
but you cannot stand in the middle of this;
5 the sea has nothing to give but a well excavated grave.
The firs stand in a procession, each with an emerald turkey foot at the
    top,
reserved as their contours, saying nothing;
repression, however, is not the most obvious characteristic of the sea;
the sea is a collector, quick to return a rapacious look.

10 There are others besides you who have worn that look—
whose expression is no longer a protest; the fish no longer investigate
    them
for their bones have not lasted:
men lower nets, unconscious of the fact that they are desecrating a
    grave,
and row quickly away—the blades of the oars
15 moving together like the feet of water spiders as if there were no such
    thing as death.
The wrinkles progress among themselves in a phalanx—beautiful
    under networks of foam,
and fade breathlessly while the sea rustles in and out of the seaweed;
the birds swim through the air at top speed, emitting catcalls as
    heretofore—
the tortoise shell scourges about the feet of the cliffs, in motion
    beneath them;
20 and the ocean, under the pulsation of lighthouses and noise of bell buoys,
advances as usual, looking as if it were not that ocean in which
    dropped things are bound to sink—
in which if they turn and twist, it is neither with volition nor
    consciousness.   [1924]

A Carriage from Sweden

They say there is a sweeter air
        where it was made, than we have here;
        a Hamlet's castle atmosphere.
At all events there is in Brooklyn
5   something that makes me feel at home.

No one may see this put-away
        museum-piece, this country cart
        that inner happiness made art;
and yet, in this city of freckled
10 integrity it is a vein

of resined straightness from north-wind
        hardened Sweden's once-opposed-to-
        compromise archipelago
of rocks. Washington and Gustavus
15 Adolphus, forgive our decay.

Seats, dashboard and sides of smooth gourd-
        rind texture, a flowered step, swan-
        dart brake, and swirling crustacean-

14–15/**Gustavus Adolphus:** *the Swedish monarch and military leader whose reign*
(1611–1632) marks one of the greatest epochs of Swedish history

tailed equine amphibious creatures
20   that garnish the axletree! What

a fine thing! What unannoying
      romance! And how beautiful, she
      with the natural stoop of the
snowy egret, gray-eyed and straight-haired,
25   for whom it should come to the door—

of whom it reminds me. The split
      pine fair hair, steady gannet-clear
      eyes and the pine-needled-path deer-
swift step; that is Sweden, land of the
30   free and the soil for a spruce tree—

vertical though a seedling—all
      needles: from a green trunk, green shelf
      on shelf fanning out by itself.
The deft white-stockinged dance in thick-soled
35   shoes! Denmark's sanctuaried Jews!

The puzzle-jugs and hand-spun rugs,
      the root-legged kracken shaped like dogs,
      the hanging buttons and the frogs
that edge the Sunday jackets! Sweden,
40   you have a runner called the Deer, who

when he's won a race, likes to run
      more; you have the sun-right gable-
      ends due east and west, the table
spread as for a banquet; and the put-
45   in twin vest-pleats with a fish-fin

effect when you need none. Sweden,
      what makes the people dress that way
      and those who see you wish to stay?
The runner, not too tired to run more
50   at the end of the race? And that

cart, dolphin-graceful? A Dalen
      lighthouse, self-lit?—responsive and
      responsible. I understand;

24/*snowy egret:* a heron with a
beautiful curved neck
27/*gannet:* a sea bird that dives from
high up to seize its prey under water
35/*Denmark's sanctuaried Jews:*
During World War II, Sweden took in
and protected Jews from Denmark,
who were persecuted when that
country was overrun by the Nazis.

37/*kracken:* sea-monsters
38/*frogs:* ornamental braided loops for
button and buttonhole
51/*Dalén:* In 1912 Nils Gustaf Dalén
(1869–1937) won the Nobel Prize in
physics for contributions he made in
coastal lighting. Among his inventions was
a device that would start up an acetylene
flame at twilight and extinguish it at dawn.

it's not pine-needle-paths that give spring
55 when they're run on, it's a Sweden

of moated white castles—the bed
    of white flowers densely grown in an S
    meaning Sweden and stalwartness,
skill, and a surface that says
60 Made in Sweden: carts are my trade.   [1944]

EDWIN MUIR (1887–1959)

The Horses

Barely a twelvemonth after
The seven days war that put the world to sleep,
Late in the evening the strange horses came.
By then we had made our covenant with silence,
5 But in the first few days it was so still
We listened to our breathing and were afraid.
On the second day
The radios failed; we turned the knobs; no answer.
On the third day a warship passed us, heading north,
10 Dead bodies piled on the deck. On the sixth day
A plane plunged over us into the sea. Thereafter
Nothing. The radios dumb;
And still they stand in corners of our kitchens,
And stand, perhaps, turned on, in a million rooms
15 All over the world. But now if they should speak,
If on a sudden they should speak again,
If on the stroke of noon a voice should speak,
We would not listen, we would not let it bring
That old bad world that swallowed its children quick
20 At one great gulp. We would not have it again.
Sometimes we think of the nations lying asleep,
Curled blindly in impenetrable sorrow,
And then the thought confounds us with its strangeness.
The tractors lie about our fields; at evening
25 They look like dank sea-monsters couched and waiting.
We leave them where they are and let them rust:
'They'll moulder away and be like other loam'.
We make our oxen drag our rusty ploughs,
Long laid aside. We have gone back
Far past our fathers' land.
30   And then, that evening
Late in the summer the strange horses came.
We heard a distant tapping on the road,
A deepening drumming; it stopped, went on again
And at the corner changed to hollow thunder.

35 We saw the heads
Like a wild wave charging and were afraid.
We had sold our horses in our fathers' time
To buy new tractors. Now they were strange to us
As fabulous steeds set on an ancient shield
40 Or illustrations in a book of knights.
We did not dare go near them. Yet they waited,
Stubborn and shy, as if they had been sent
By an old command to find our whereabouts
And that long-lost archaic companionship.
45 In the first moment we had never a thought
That they were creatures to be owned and used.
Among them were some half-a-dozen colts
Dropped in some wilderness of the broken world,
Yet new as if they had come from their own Eden.
50 Since then they have pulled our ploughs and borne our loads,
But that free servitude still can pierce our hearts.
Our life is changed; their coming our beginning.   [1956]

T. S. ELIOT (1888–1965)

The Love Song of J. Alfred Prufrock

*S'io credesse che mia risposta fosse
A persona che mai tornasse al mondo,
Questa fiamma staria senza più scosse.
Ma per ciò che giammai di questo fondo
Non tornò vivo alcun, s'i'odo il vero,
Senza tema d'infamia ti rispondo.*

Let us go then, you and I,
When the evening is spread out against the sky
Like a patient etherised upon a table;
Let us go, through certain half-deserted streets,
5 The muttering retreats
Of restless nights in one-night cheap hotels
And sawdust restaurants with oyster-shells:
Streets that follow like a tedious argument
Of insidious intent
10 To lead you to an overwhelming question . . .
Oh, do not ask, "What is it!"
Let us go and make our visit.

The epigraph is from Dante's Inferno, *XXVII, 61–66. The speaker, Guido da Montefeltro, condemned to hell as an evil counselor, is enclosed in a tongue-shaped flame which speaks for him. He says: "If I thought that my answer were to a person who would ever return to the world [and tell others], this flame would move no more [in speech]; but since from this depth no one ever returned alive, if what I hear is true, I'll answer without fear of disgrace."*

In the room the women come and go
Talking of Michelangelo.

15   The yellow fog that rubs its back upon the window-panes,
The yellow smoke that rubs its muzzle on the window-panes
Licked its tongue into the corners of the evening,
Lingered upon the pools that stand in drains,
Let fall upon its back the soot that falls from chimneys,
20 Slipped by the terrace, made a sudden leap,
And seeing that it was a soft October night,
Curled once about the house, and fell asleep.

    And indeed there will be time
For the yellow smoke that slides along the street,
25 Rubbing its back upon the window-panes;
There will be time, there will be time
To prepare a face to meet the faces that you meet;
There will be time to murder and create,
And time for all the works and days of hands
30 That lift and drop a question on your plate;
Time for you and time for me,
And time yet for a hundred indecisions,
And for a hundred visions and revisions,
Before the taking of a toast and tea.

35   In the room the women come and go
Talking of Michelangelo.

    And indeed there will be time
To wonder, "Do I dare?" and, "Do I dare?"
Time to turn back and descend the stair,
40 With a bald spot in the middle of my hair—
[They will say: "How his hair is growing thin!"]
My morning coat, my collar mounting firmly to the chin,
My necktie rich and modest, but asserted by a simple pin—
[They will say: "But how his arms and legs are thin!"]
45 Do I dare
Disturb the universe?
In a minute there is time
For decisions and revisions which a minute will reverse.

    For I have known them all already, known them all:—
50 Have known the evenings, mornings, afternoons,
I have measured out my life with coffee spoons;
I know the voices dying with a dying fall

29/*works and days*: The Works and Days *of the Greek poet Hesiod (eighth century* B.C.*) stresses the need for doing the strenuous work of farming at the proper times.*

52/*a dying fall*: Cf. *the opening of* Twelfth Night: *"If music be the food of love, play on;/ Give me excess of it . . . / That strain again! It had a dying fall. . . ." A dying fall is a cadence in music that seems to languish or fall away.*

Beneath the music from a farther room.
    So how should I presume?

55   And I have known the eyes already, known them all:—
The eyes that fix you in a formulated phrase,
And when I am formulated, sprawling on a pin,
When I am pinned and wriggling on the wall,
Then how should I begin
60 To spit out all the butt-ends of my days and ways?
    And how should I presume?

      And I have known the arms already, known them all—
Arms that are braceleted and white and bare
[But in the lamplight, downed with light brown hair!]
65 Is it perfume from a dress
That makes me so digress?
Arms that lie along a table, or wrap about a shawl.
    And should I then presume?
    And how should I begin?

      • • •

70 Shall I say, I have gone at dusk through narrow streets
And watched the smoke that rises from the pipes
Of lonely men in shirt-sleeves, leaning out of windows? . . .

      • • •

    I should have been a pair of ragged claws
Scuttling across the floors of silent seas.

75 And the afternoon, the evening, sleeps so peacefully!
Smoothed by long fingers,
Asleep . . . tired . . . or it malingers,
Stretched on the floor, here beside you and me.
Should I, after tea and cakes and ices,
80 Have the strength to force the moment to its crisis?
But though I have wept and fasted, wept and prayed,
Though I have seen my head [grown slightly bald] brought in upon a
    platter,
I am no prophet—and here's no great matter;
I have seen the moment of my greatness flicker,
85 And I have seen the eternal Footman hold my coat, and snicker,
And in short, I was afraid.

    And would it have been worth it, after all,
After the cups, the marmalade, the tea,

---

[82]/**my head . . . brought in upon a platter:** *The reference is to Saint John the Baptist, beheaded by order of Herod at the request of Salome, whose dancing had pleased the king. Saint John's head was brought to the girl on a platter. As generally depicted in art, the severed head has magnificent locks.*

Among the porcelain, among some talk of you and me,
90 Would it have been worth while,
To have bitten off the matter with a smile,
To have squeezed the universe into a ball
To roll it toward some overwhelming question,
To say: "I am Lazarus, come from the dead,
95 Come back to tell you all, I shall tell you all"—
If one, settling a pillow by her head,
    Should say: "That is not what I meant at all.
    That is not it, at all."

    And would it have been worth it, after all,
100 Would it have been worth while,
After the sunsets and the dooryards and the sprinkled streets,
After the novels, after the teacups, after the skirts that trail along the
    floor—
And this, and so much more?—
It is impossible to say just what I mean!
105 But as if a magic lantern threw the nerves in patterns on a screen:
Would it have been worth while
If one, settling a pillow or throwing off a shawl,
And turning toward the window, should say:
    "That is not it at all,
110   That is not what I meant, at all."

        • • •

No! I am not Prince Hamlet, nor was meant to be;
Am an attendant lord, one that will do
To swell a progress, start a scene or two,
Advise the prince; no doubt, an easy tool,
115 Deferential, glad to be of use,
Politic, cautious, and meticulous;
Full of high sentence, but a bit obtuse;
At times, indeed, almost ridiculous—
Almost, at times, the Fool.

120   I grow old . . . I grow old . . .
I shall wear the bottoms of my trousers rolled.

    Shall I part my hair behind? Do I dare to eat a peach?
I shall wear white flannel trousers, and walk upon the beach.
I have heard the mermaids singing, each to each.

89/**some talk of you and me:** *Cf.*
"The Rubáiyát of Omar Khayyám,"
XXXII (p. 410).
92/**squeezed . . . into a ball:** *Cf.*
Marvell, "To His Coy Mistress," lines
41–44, (p. 391).
94/**"I am Lazarus . . .":** *Lazarus*
was the brother of Martha and Mary,

raised from the dead by Jesus according to
John 11:1–44.
117/**full of high sentence:** *the speech*
of the "Clerk . . . of Oxenford" (Oxford
scholar) in the Prologue to Chaucer's
Canterbury Tales is described as "ful
of hy sentence"—wise maxims.
121/**rolled:** *turned up, with cuffs*

125   I do not think that they will sing to me.

I have seen them riding seaward on the waves
Combing the white hair of the waves blown back
When the wind blows the water white and black.

We have lingered in the chambers of the sea
130   By sea-girls wreathed with seaweed red and brown
Till human voices wake us, and we drown.   [1917]

ARCHIBALD MACLEISH (1892–1982)

Ars Poetica

A poem should be palpable and mute
As a globed fruit,

Dumb
As old medallions to the thumb,

5   Silent as the sleeve-worn stone
Of casement ledges where the moss has grown—

A poem should be wordless
As the flight of birds.

       • • •

A poem should be motionless in time
10   As the moon climbs,

Leaving, as the moon releases
Twig by twig the night-entangled trees,

Leaving, as the moon behind the winter leaves,
Memory by memory the mind—

15   A poem should be motionless in time
As the moon climbs.

       • • •

A poem should be equal to:
Not true.

For all the history of grief
20   An empty doorway and a maple leaf.

For love
The leaning grasses and two lights above the sea—

A poem should not mean
But be.   [1926]

The title means "The art of poetry."

EDNA ST. VINCENT MILLAY (1892–1950)

I Shall Forget You Presently, My Dear

I shall forget you presently, my dear,
So make the most of this, your little day,
Your little month, your little half a year,
Ere I forget, or die, or move away,
5   And we are done forever; by and by
I shall forget you, as I said, but now,
If you entreat me with your loveliest lie
I will protest you with my favorite vow.
I would indeed that love were longer-lived,
10   And oaths were not so brittle as they are,
But so it is, and nature has contrived
To struggle on without a break thus far—
Whether or not we find what we are seeking
Is idle, biologically speaking.   [1920]

E. E. CUMMINGS (1894–1962)

anyone lived in a pretty how town

anyone lived in a pretty how town
(with up so floating many bells down)
spring summer autumn winter
he sang his didn't he danced his did.

5   Women and men(both little and small)
cared for anyone not at all
they sowed their isn't they reaped their same
sun moon stars rain

children guessed(but only a few
10   and down they forgot as up they grew
autumn winter spring summer)
that noone loved him more by more

when by now and tree by leaf
she laughed his joy she cried his grief
15   bird by snow and stir by still
anyone's any was all to her

someones married their everyones
laughed their cryings and did their dance
(sleep wake hope and then)they
20   said their nevers they slept their dream

stars rain sun moon
(and only the snow can begin to explain
how children are apt to forget to remember
with up so floating many bells down)

25 one day anyone died i guess
(and noone stopped to kiss his face)
busy folk buried them side by side
little by little and was by was

all by all and deep by deep
30 and more by more they dream their sleep
noone and anyone earth by april
wish by spirit and if by yes.

Women and men(both dong and ding)
summer autumn winter spring
35 reaped their sowing and went their came
sun moon stars rain   [1940]

JEAN TOOMER (1894–1967)

Reapers

Black reapers with the sound of steel on stones
Are sharpening scythes. I see them place the hones
In their hip-pockets as a thing that's done,
And start their silent swinging, one by one.
5 Black horses drive a mower through the weeds,
And there, a field rat, startled, squealing bleeds,
His belly close to ground. I see the blade,
Blood-stained, continue cutting weeds and shade.   [1923]

LOUISE BOGAN (1897–1970)

Women

Women have no wilderness in them,
They are provident instead,
Content in the tight hot cell of their hearts
To eat dusty bread.

5 They do not see cattle cropping red winter grass,
They do not hear
Snow water going down under culverts
Shallow and clear.

They wait, when they should turn to journeys,
10 They stiffen, when they should bend.
They use against themselves that benevolence
To which no man is friend.

They cannot think of so many crops to a field
Or of clean wood cleft by an axe.
15 Their love is an eager meaninglessness
Too tense, or too lax.

They hear in every whisper that speaks to them
A shout and a cry.
As like as not, when they take life over their door-sills
20 They should led it go by.   [1923]

HART CRANE (1899–1932)

My Grandmother's Love Letters

There are no stars tonight
But those of memory.
Yet how much room for memory there is
In the loose girdle of soft rain.

5 There is even room enough
For the letters of my mother's mother,
Elizabeth,
That have been pressed so long
Into a corner of the roof
10 That they are brown and soft,
And liable to melt as snow.

Over the greatness of such space
Steps must be gentle.
It is all hung by an invisible white hair.
15 It trembles as birch limbs webbing the air.

And I ask myself:

"Are your fingers long enough to play
Old keys that are but echoes:
Is the silence strong enough
20 To carry back the music to its source
And back to you again
As though to her?"

Yet I would lead my grandmother by the hand
Through much of what she would not understand;
25 And so I stumble. And the rain continues on the roof
With such a sound of gently pitying laughter.   [1926]

ROBERT FRANCIS (1901–1987)

Pitcher

His art is eccentricity, his aim
How not to hit the mark he seems to aim at,

His passion how to avoid the obvious,
His technique how to vary the avoidance.

5 The others throw to be comprehended. He
   Throws to be a moment misunderstood

   Yet not too much. Not errant, arrant, wild,
   But every seeming aberration willed.

   Not to, yet still, still to communicate
10 Making the batter understand too late.   [1960]

Swimmer

I

   Observe how he negotiates his way
   With trust and the least violence, making
   The stranger friend, the enemy ally.
   The depth that could destroy gently supports him.
5 With water he defends himself from water.
   Danger he leans on, rests in. The drowning sea
   Is all he has between himself and drowning.

II

   What lover ever lay more mutually
   With his beloved, his always-reaching arms
10 Stroking in smooth and powerful caresses?
   Some drown in love as in dark water, and some
   By love are strongly held as the green sea
   Now holds the swimmer. Indolently he turns
   To float.—The swimmer floats, the lover sleeps.   [1960]

KENNETH FEARING (1902–1961)

Love, 20¢ the First Quarter Mile

   All right, I may have lied to you, and about you, and made a few
     pronouncements a bit too sweeping, perhaps, and possibly forgotten
     to tag the bases here or there,
   And damned your extravagance, and maligned your tastes, and libeled
     your relatives, and slandered a few of your friends,
   O.K.,
   Nevertheless, come back.

5 Come home. I will agree to forget the statements that you issued so
     copiously to the neighbors and the press,
   And you will forget that figment of your imagination, the blonde from
     Detroit;
   I will agree that your lady friend who lives above us is not crazy, bats,
     nutty as they come, but on the contrary rather bright,
   And you will concede that poor old Steinberg is neither a drunk, nor a
     swindler, but simply a guy, on the eccentric side, trying to get along.
   (Are you listening, you bitch, and have you got this straight?)

10   Because I forgive you, yes, for everything,
I forgive you for being beautiful and generous and wise,
I forgive you, to put it simply, for being alive, and pardon you, in short,
for being you.

Because tonight you are in my hair and eyes,
And every street light that our taxi passes shows me you again, still
you,
15   And because tonight all other nights are black, all other hours are cold
and far away, and now, this minute, the stars are very near and bright.

Come back. We will have a celebration to end all celebrations.
We will invite the undertaker who lives beneath us, and a couple of the
boys from the office, and some other friends,
And Steinberg, who is off the wagon, by the way, and that insane
woman who lives upstairs, and a few reporters, if anything should
break.   [1940]

LANGSTON HUGHES (1902–1967)

Dream Variations

To fling my arms wide
In some place of the sun,
To whirl and to dance
Till the white day is done.
5   Then rest at cool evening
Beneath a tall tree
While night comes on gently,
Dark like me—
That is my dream!

10   To fling my arms wide
In the face of the sun,
Dance! Whirl! Whirl!
Till the quick day is done.
Rest at pale evening . . .
15   A tall, slim tree . . .
Night coming tenderly
Black like me.   [1926]

The Negro Speaks of Rivers

I've known rivers:
I've known rivers ancient as the world and older than the flow of
human blood in human veins.

My soul has grown deep like the rivers.

I bathed in the Euphrates when dawns were young.
5   I built my hut near the Congo and it lulled me to sleep.
I looked upon the Nile and raised the pyramids above it.

I heard the singing of the Mississippi when Abe Lincoln went down to
    New Orleans, and I've seen its muddy bosom turn all golden in the
    sunset.

I've known rivers:
Ancient, dusky rivers.

10   My soul has grown deep like the rivers.   [1926]

OGDEN NASH (1902–1971)

Very Like a Whale

One thing that literature would be greatly the better for
Would be a more restricted employment by authors of simile and
    metaphor.
Authors of all races, be they Greeks, Romans, Teutons or Celts,
Can't seem just to say that anything is the thing it is but have to go out
    of their way to say that it is like something else.
5   What does it mean when we are told
That the Assyrian came down like a wolf on the fold?
In the first place, George Gordon Byron had had enough experience
To know that it probably wasn't just one Assyrian, it was a lot of
    Assyrians.
However, as too many arguments are apt to induce apoplexy and thus
    hinder longevity,
10 We'll let it pass as one Assyrian for the sake of brevity.
Now then, this particular Assyrian, the one whose cohorts were
    gleaming in purple and gold,
Just what does the poet mean when he says he came down like a wolf
    on the fold?
In heaven and earth more than is dreamed of in our philosophy there
    are a great many things,
But I don't imagine that among them there is a wolf with purple and
    gold cohorts or purple and gold anythings.
15 No, no, Lord Byron, before I'll believe that this Assyrian was actually
    like a wolf I must have some kind of proof;
Did he run on all fours and did he have a hairy tail and a big red
    mouth and big white teeth and did he say Woof woof woof?
Frankly I think it very unlikely, and all you were entitled to say, at the
    very most,
Was that the Assyrian cohorts came down like a lot of Assyrian cohorts
    about to destroy the Hebrew host.
But that wasn't fancy enough for Lord Byron, oh dear me no, he had
    to invent a lot of figures of speech and then interpolate them.
20 With the result that whenever you mention Old Testament soldiers to
    people they say Oh yes, they're the ones that a lot of wolves dressed
    up in gold and purple ate them.
That's the kind of thing that's being done all the time by poets, from
    Homer to Tennyson;

They're always comparing ladies to lilies and veal to venison,
And they always say things like that the snow is a white blanket after a
    winter storm.
Oh it is, is it, all right then, you sleep under a six-inch blanket of snow
    and I'll sleep under a half-inch blanket of unpoetical blanket material
    and we'll see which one keeps warm,
25   And after that maybe you'll begin to comprehend dimly
What I mean by too much metaphor and simile.   [1935]

For the title, see Hamlet, *III, ii, 384–389.*

STEVIE SMITH (1902–1971)

Not Waving but Drowning

Nobody heard him, the dead man,
But still he lay moaning:
I was much further out than you thought
And not waving but drowning.

5   Poor chap, he always loved larking
And now he's dead
It must have been too cold for him his heart gave way,
They said.

Oh, no no no, it was too cold always
10 (Still the dead one lay moaning)
I was much too far out all my life
And not waving but drowning.   [1957]

STANLEY KUNITZ (*b.* 1905)

The Abduction

Some things I do not profess
to understand, perhaps
not wanting to, including
whatever it was they did
5   with you or you with them
that timeless summer day
when you stumbled out of the wood,
distracted, with your white blouse torn
and a bloodstain on your skirt.
10 "Do you believe?" you asked.
Between us, through the years,
from bits, from broken clues,
we pieced enough together

to make the story real:
15 how you encountered on the path
a pack of sleek, grey hounds,
trailed by a dumbshow retinue
in leather shrouds; and how
you were led, through leafy ways,
20 into the presence of a royal stag,
flaming in his chestnut coat,
who kneeled on a swale of moss
before you; and how you were borne
aloft in triumph through the green,
25 stretched on his rack of budding horn,
till suddenly you found yourself alone
in a trampled clearing.

That was a long time ago,
almost another age, but even now,
30 when I hold you in my arms,
I wonder where you are.
Sometimes I wake to hear
the engines of the night thrumming
outside the east bay window
35 on the lawn spreading to the rose garden.
You lie beside me in elegant repose,
a hint of transport hovering on your lips,
indifferent to the harsh green flares
that swivel through the room,
40 searchlights controlled by unseen hands.
Out there is childhood country,
bleached faces peering in
with coals for eyes.
Our lives are spinning out
45 from world to world;
the shapes of things
are shifting in the wind.
What do we know
beyond the rapture and the dread?   [1985]

W. H. AUDEN (1907–1973)

Lullaby

Lay your sleeping head, my love,
Human on my faithless arm;
Time and fevers burn away
Individual beauty from
5 Thoughtful children, and the grave

Proves the child ephemeral:
But in my arms till break of day
Let the living creature lie,
Mortal, guilty, but to me
10   The entirely beautiful.

Soul and body have no bounds:
To lovers as they lie upon
Her tolerant enchanted slope
In their ordinary swoon,
15   Grave the vision Venus sends
Of supernatural sympathy,
Universal love and hope;
While an abstract insight wakes
Among the glaciers and the rocks
20   The hermit's carnal ecstasy.

Certainty, fidelity
On the stroke of midnight pass
Like vibrations of a bell
And fashionable madmen raise
25   Their pedantic boring cry:
Every farthing of the cost,
All the dreaded cards foretell,
Shall be paid, but from this night
Not a whisper, not a thought,
30   Not a kiss nor look be lost.

Beauty, midnight, vision dies:
Let the winds of dawn that blow
Softly round your dreaming head
Such a day of welcome show
35   Eye and knocking heart may bless,
Find our mortal world enough;
Noons of dryness find you fed
By the involuntary powers,
Nights of insult let you pass
40   Watched by every human love.   [1940]

In Memory of W. B. Yeats

(d. Jan. 1939)

I

He disappeared in the dead of winter:
The brooks were frozen, the airports almost deserted,
And snow disfigured the public statues;
The mercury sank in the mouth of the dying day.
5   What instruments we have agree
The day of his death was a dark cold day.

Far from his illness
The wolves ran on through the evergreen forests,
The peasant river was untempted by the fashionable quays;
10   By mourning tongues
The death of the poet was kept from his poems.

But for him it was his last afternoon as himself,
An afternoon of nurses and rumours;
The provinces of his body revolted,
15   The squares of his mind were empty,
Silence invaded the suburbs,
The current of his feeling failed; he became his admirers.

Now he is scattered among a hundred cities
And wholly given over to unfamiliar affections,
20   To find his happiness in another kind of wood
And be punished under a foreign code of conscience.
The words of a dead man
Are modified in the guts of the living.

But in the importance and noise of to-morrow
25   When the brokers are roaring like beasts on the floor of the Bourse,
And the poor have the sufferings to which they are fairly accustomed,
And each in the cell of himself is almost convinced of his freedom,
A few thousand will think of this day
As one thinks of a day when one did something slightly unusual.

30   What instruments we have agree
The day of his death was a dark cold day.

II

You were silly like us; your gift survived it all:
The parish of rich women, physical decay,
Yourself. Mad Ireland hurt you into poetry.
35   Now Ireland has her madness and her weather still,
For poetry makes nothing happen: it survives
In the valley of its making where executives
Would never want to tamper, flows on south
From ranches of isolation and the busy griefs,
40   Raw towns that we believe and die in; it survives,
A way of happening, a mouth.

III

Earth, receive an honoured guest:
William Yeats is laid to rest.
Let the Irish vessel lie
45   Emptied of its poetry.

²⁵/**the Bourse:** *the stock exchange*

Time that is intolerant
Of the brave and innocent,
And indifferent in a week
To a beautiful physique,

50 Worships language and forgives
Everyone by whom it lives;
Pardons cowardice, conceit,
Lays its honours at their feet.

Time that with this strange excuse
55 Pardoned Kipling and his views,
And will pardon Paul Claudel,
Pardons him for writing well.

In the nightmare of the dark
All the dogs of Europe bark,
60 And the living nations wait,
Each sequestered in its hate;

Intellectual disgrace
Stares from every human face,
And the seas of pity lie
65 Locked and frozen in each eye.

Follow, poet, follow right
To the bottom of the night,
With your unconstraining voice
Still persuade us to rejoice;

70 With the farming of a verse
Make a vineyard of the curse,
Sing of human unsuccess
In a rapture of distress;

In the deserts of the heart
75 Let the healing fountain start,
In the prison of his days
Teach the free man how to praise.   [1940]

46–57/*Included in the 1939 version of the poem. Auden later chose to omit these lines.*

56/***Paul Claudel:*** *French Catholic diplomat, poet, and dramatist (1868–1955)*

LOUIS MACNEICE (1907–1963)

Snow

The room was suddenly rich and the great bay-window was
Spawning snow and pink roses against it
Soundlessly collateral and incompatible:
World is suddener than we fancy it.

5 World is crazier and more of it than we think,
Incorrigibly plural. I peel and portion
A tangerine and spit the pips and feel
The drunkenness of things being various.

And the fire flames with a bubbling sound for world
10 Is more spiteful and gay than one supposes—
On the tongue on the eyes on the ears in the palms of one's hands—
There is more than glass between the snow and the huge roses.   [1935]

The Sunlight on the Garden

The sunlight on the garden
Hardens and grows cold,
We cannot cage the minute
Within its nets of gold,
5 When all is told
We cannot beg for pardon.

Our freedom as free lances
Advances towards its end;
The earth compels, upon it
10 Sonnets and birds descend;
And soon, my friend,
We shall have no time for dances.

The sky was good for flying
Defying the church bells
15 And every evil iron
Siren and what it tells:
The earth compels,
We are dying, Egypt, dying

And not expecting pardon,
20 Hardened in heart anew,
But glad to have sat under
Thunder and rain with you,
And grateful too
For sunlight on the garden.   [1937]

THEODORE ROETHKE (1908–1963)

Root Cellar

Nothing would sleep in that cellar, dank as a ditch,
Bulbs broke out of boxes hunting for chinks in the dark,
Shoots dangled and drooped,
Lolling obscenely from mildewed crates,
5 Hung down long yellow evil necks, like tropical snakes.
And what a congress of stinks!—

Roots ripe as old bait,
Pulpy stems, rank, silo-rich,
Leaf-mold, manure, lime piled against slippery planks.
10 Nothing would give up life:
Even the dirt kept breathing a small breath.   [1948]

Forcing House

Vines tougher than wrists
And rubbery shoots.
Scums, mildews, smuts along stems,
Great cannas or delicate cyclmen tips,—
5 All pulse with the knocking pipes
That drip and sweat,
Sweat and drip,
Swelling the roots and steam and stench,
Shooting up lime and dung and ground bones,—
10 Fifty summers in motion at once,
As the live heat billows from pipes and pots.   [1948]

Elegy for Jane

My Student, Thrown by a Horse

I remember the neckcurls, limp and damp as tendrils;
And her quick look, a sidelong pickerel smile;
And how, once startled into talk, the light syllables leaped for her,
And she balanced in the delight of her thought,
5 A wren, happy, tail into the wind,
Her song trembling the twigs and small branches.
The shade sang with her;
The leaves, their whispers turned to kissing;
And the mold sang in the bleached valleys under the rose.

10 Oh, when she was sad, she cast herself down into such a pure depth,
Even a father could not find her:
Scraping her cheek against straw;
Stirring the clearest water.

My sparrow, you are not here,
15 Waiting like a fern, making a spiny shadow.
The sides of wet stones cannot console me,
Nor the moss, wound with the last light.

If only I could nudge you from this sleep,
My maimed darling, my skittery pigeon.
20 Over this damp grave I speak the words of my love:
I, with no rights in this matter,
Neither father nor lover.   [1953]

The Waking

I wake to sleep, and take my waking slow.
I feel my fate in what I cannot fear.
I learn by going where I have to go.

We think by feeling. What is there to know?
5   I hear my being dance from ear to ear.
I wake to sleep, and take my waking slow.

Of those so close beside me, which are you?
God bless the Ground! I shall walk softly there,
And learn by going where I have to go.

10 Light takes the Tree; but who can tell us how?
The lowly worm climbs up a winding stair;
I wake to sleep, and take my waking slow.

Great Nature has another thing to do
To you and me; so take the lively air,
15 And, lovely, learn by going where to go.

This shaking keeps me steady. I should know.
What falls away is always. And is near.
I wake to sleep, and take my waking slow.
I learn by going where I have to go.

[1953]

ROBERT FITZGERALD (1910–1985)

Cobb Would Have Caught It

In sunburnt parks where Sundays lie,
Or the wide wastes beyond the cities,
Teams in grey deploy through sunlight.

Talk it up, boys, a little practice.
5   Coming in stubby and fast, the baseman
Gathers a grounder in fat green grass,
Picks it stinging and clipped as wit
Into the leather: a swinging step
Wings it deadeye down to first.
10 Smack. Oh, attaboy, attyoldboy.

Catcher reverses his cap, pulls down
Sweaty casque, and squats in the dust:
Pitcher rubs new ball on his pants,
Chewing, puts a jet behind him;
15 Nods past batter, taking his time.
Batter settles, tugs at his cap:
A spinning ball: step and swing to it,
Caught like a cheek before it ducks
By shivery hickory: socko, baby:
20 Cleats dig into dust. Outfielder,

On his way, looking over shoulder,
Makes it a triple. A long peg home.

Innings and afternoons. Fly lost in sunset.
Throwing arm gone bad. There's your old ball game.
25   Cool reek of the field. Reek of companions.   [1943]

ELIZABETH BISHOP (1911–1979)

The Fish

I caught a tremendous fish
and held him beside the boat
half out of water, with my hook
fast in a corner of his mouth.
5   He didn't fight.
He hadn't fought at all.
He hung a grunting weight,
battered and venerable
and homely. Here and there
10   his brown skin hung in strips
like ancient wallpaper,
and its pattern of darker brown
was like wallpaper:
shapes like full-blown roses
15   stained and lost through age.
He was speckled with barnacles,
fine rosettes of lime,
and infested
with tiny white sea-lice,
20   and underneath two or three
rags of green weed hung down.
While his gills were breathing in
the terrible oxygen
—the frightening gills,
25   fresh and crisp with blood,
that can cut so badly—
I thought of the coarse white flesh
packed in like feathers,
the big bones and the little bones,
30   the dramatic reds and blacks
of his shiny entrails,
and the pink swim-bladder
like a big peony.
I looked into his eyes
35   which were far larger than mine
but shallower, and yellowed,
the irises backed and packed
with tarnished tinfoil
seen through the lenses

40 of old scratched isinglass.
They shifted a little, but not
to return my stare.
—It was more like the tipping
of an object toward the light.
45 I admired his sullen face,
the mechanism of his jaw,
and then I saw
that from his lower lip
—if you could call it a lip—
50 grim, wet, and weaponlike,
hung five old pieces of fish-line,
or four and a wire leader
with the swivel still attached,
with all their five big hooks
55 grown firmly in his mouth.
A green line, frayed at the end
where he broke it, two heavier lines,
and a fine black thread
still crimped from the strain and snap
60 when it broke and he got away.
Like medals with their ribbons
frayed and wavering,
a five-haired beard of wisdom
trailing from his aching jaw.
65 I stared and stared
and victory filled up
the little rented boat,
from the pool of bilge
where oil had spread a rainbow
70 around the rusted engine
to the bailer rusted orange,
the sun-cracked thwarts,
the oarlocks on their strings,
the gunnels—until everything
75 was rainbow, rainbow, rainbow!
And I let the fish go.

[1946]

Sandpiper

The roaring alongside he takes for granted,
and that every so often the world is bound to shake.
He runs, he runs to the south, finical, awkward,
in a state of controlled panic, a student of Blake.

5 The beach hisses like fat. On his left, a sheet
of interrupting water comes and goes
and glazes over his dark and brittle feet.
He runs, he runs straight through it, watching his toes.

4/William Blake's "Auguries of Innocence" begins: "To see a World in a Grain of Sand . . ."

—Watching, rather, the spaces of sand between them,
10   where (no detail too small) the Atlantic drains
rapidly backwards and downwards. As he runs,
he stares at the dragging grains.

The world is a mist. And then the world is
minute and vast and clear. The tide
15   is higher or lower. He couldn't tell you which.
His beak is focussed; he is preoccupied,

looking for something, something, something.
Poor bird, he is obsessed!
The millions of grains are black, white, tan, and gray,
20   mixed with quartz grains, rose and amethyst.   [1965]

One Art

The art of losing isn't hard to master;
so many things seem filled with the intent
to be lost that their loss is no disaster.

Lose something every day. Accept the fluster
5   of lost door keys, the hour badly spent.
The art of losing isn't hard to master.

Then practice losing farther, losing faster:
places, and names, and where it was you meant
to travel. None of these will bring disaster.

10   I lost my mother's watch. And look! my last, or
next-to-last, of three loved houses went.
The art of losing isn't hard to master.

I lost two cities, lovely ones. And, vaster,
some realms I owned, two rivers, a continent.
15   I miss them, but it wasn't a disaster.

—Even losing you (the joking voice, a gesture
I love) I shan't have lied. It's evident
the art of losing's not too hard to master
though it may look like (*Write* it!) like disaster.   [1976]

ROBERT HAYDEN (1913–1980)

Those Winter Sundays

Sundays too my father got up early
and put his clothes on in the blueblack cold,
then with cracked hands that ached
from labor in the weekday weather made
5   banked fires blaze. No one ever thanked him.

I'd wake and hear the cold splintering, breaking.
When the rooms were warm, he'd call,
and slowly I would rise and dress,
fearing the chronic angers of that house,

10 Speaking indifferently to him,
who had driven out the cold
and polished my good shoes as well.
What did I know, what did I know
of love's austere and lonely offices?   [1962]

JOHN FREDERICK NIMS (1913–1999)

Love Poem

My clumsiest dear, whose hands shipwreck vases,
At whose quick touch all glasses chip and ring,
Whose palms are bulls in china, burs in linen,
And have no cunning with any soft thing

5 Except all ill-at-ease fidgeting people:
The refugee uncertain at the door
You make at home; deftly you steady
The drunk clambering on his undulant floor.

Unpredictable dear, the taxi drivers' terror,
10 Shrinking from far headlights pale as a dime
Yet leaping before red apoplectic streetcars—
Misfit in any space. And never on time.

A wrench in clocks and the solar system. Only
With words and people and love you move at ease;
15 In traffic of wit expertly manoeuvre
And keep us, all devotion, at your knees,

Forgetting your coffee spreading on our flannel,
Your lipstick grinning on our coat,
So gayly in love's unbreakable heaven
20 Our souls on glory of spilt bourbon float.

Be with me, darling, early and late. Smash glasses—
I will study wry music for your sake.
For should your hands drop white and empty
All the toys of the world would break.   [1947]

MURIEL RUKEYSER (1913–1980)

Effort at Speech between Two People

Speak to me.   Take my hand.   What are you now?
I will tell you all.   I will conceal nothing.

When I was three, a little child read a story about a rabbit
who died, in the story, and I crawled under a chair:
5   a pink rabbit: it was my birthday, and a candle
burnt a sore spot on my finger, and I was told to be happy.

Oh, grow to know me.   I am not happy.   I will be open:
Now I am thinking of white sails against a sky like music,
like glad horns blowing, and birds tilting, and an arm about me.
10   There was one I loved, who wanted to live, sailing.
Speak to me.   Take my hand.   What are you now?
When I was nine, I was fruitily sentimental,
fluid: and my widowed aunt played Chopin,
and I bent my head on the painted woodwork, and wept.

15   I want now to be close to you.   I would
link the minutes of my days close, somehow, to your days.

I am not happy.   I will be open.
I have liked lamps in evening corners, and quiet poems.
There has been fear in my life.   Sometimes I speculate
20   On what a tragedy his life was, really.

Take my hand.   Fist my mind in your hand.   What are you now?
When I was fourteen, I had dreams of suicide,
and I stood at a steep window, at sunset, hoping toward death:
if the light had not melted clouds and plains to beauty,
25   if light had not transformed that day, I would have leapt,
I am unhappy.   I am lonely.   Speak to me.
I will be open.   I think he never loved me:
he loved the bright beaches, the little lips of foam
that ride small waves, he loved the veer of gulls:
30   he said with a gay mouth: I love you.   Grow to know me.

What are you now?   If we could touch one another,
if these our separate entities could come to grips,
clenched like a Chinese puzzle. . . . yesterday
I stood in a crowded street that was live with people,
35   and no one spoke a word, and the morning shone.
Everyone silent, moving. . . . Take my hand.   Speak to me.   [1935]

JOHN BERRYMAN (1914–1972)

Dream Songs

4

Filling her compact & delicious body
with chicken páprika, she glanced at me
twice.
Fainting with interest, I hungered back
5   and only the fact of her husband & four other people
kept me from springing on her

or falling at her little feet and crying
'You are the hottest one for years of night
Henry's dazed eyes
10   have enjoyed, Brilliance.' I advanced upon
(despairing) my spumoni.—Sir Bones: is stuffed,
de world, wif feeding girls.

    —Black hair, complexion Latin, jewelled eyes
downcast . . . The slob beside her   feasts . . . What wonders is
15   she sitting on, over there?
The restaurant buzzes. She might as well be on Mars.
Where did it all go wrong? There ought to be a law against Henry.
—Mr. Bones: there is.   [1964]

22

of 1826

I am the little man who smokes & smokes.
I am the girl who does know better but.
I am the king of the pool.
I am so wise I had my mouth sewn shut.
5   I am a government official & a goddamned fool.
I am a lady who takes jokes.

I am the enemy of the mind.
I am the auto salesman and lóve you.
I am a teenage cancer, with a plan.
10   I am the blackt-out man.
I am the woman powerful as a zoo.
I am two eyes screwed to my set, whose blind—

It is the Fourth of July.
Collect: while the dying man,
15   forgone by you creator, who forgives,
is gasping 'Thomas Jefferson still lives'
in vain, in vain, in vain.
I am Henry Pussy-cat! My whiskers fly.   [1964]

For some explanatory remarks about "22," see the discussion in the text (p. 286).

RANDALL JARRELL (1914–1965)

Next Day

Moving from Cheer to Joy, from Joy to All,
I take a box
And add it to my wild rice, my Cornish game hens.
The slacked or shorted, basketed, identical
5   Food-gathering flocks
Are selves I overlook. Wisdom, said William James,

Is learning what to overlook. And I am wise
If that is wisdom.
Yet somehow, as I buy All from these shelves
10 And the boy takes it to my station wagon,
What I've become
Troubles me even if I shut my eyes.

When I was young and miserable and pretty
And poor, I'd wish
15 What all girls wish: to have a husband,
A house and children. Now that I'm old, my wish
Is womanish:
That the boy putting groceries in my car

See me. It bewilders me he doesn't see me.
20 For so many years
I was good enough to eat: the world looked at me
And its mouth watered. How often they have undressed me,
The eyes of strangers!
And, holding their flesh within my flesh, their vile

25 Imaginings within my imagining,
I too have taken
The chance of life. Now the boy pats my dog
And we start home. Now I am good.
The last mistaken,
30 Ecstatic, accidental bliss, the blind

Happiness that, bursting, leaves upon the palm
Some soap and water—
It was so long ago, back in some Gay
Twenties, Nineties, I don't know . . . Today I miss
35 My lovely daughter
Away at school, my sons away at school,

My husband away at work—I wish for them.
The dog, the maid,
And I go through the sure unvarying days
40 At home in them. As I look at my life,
I am afraid
Only that it will change, as I am changing:

I am afraid, this morning, of my face.
It looks at me
45 From the rear-view mirror, with the eyes I hate,
The smile I hate. Its plain, lined look
Of gray discovery
Repeats to me: "You're old." That's all, I'm old.

And yet I'm afraid, as I was at the funeral
50 I went to yesterday.
My friend's cold made-up face, granite among its flowers,

Her undressed, operated-on, dressed body
Were my face and body.
As I think of her I hear her telling me

55 How young I seem; I *am* exceptional;
I think of all I have.
But really no one is exceptional,
No one has anything, I'm anybody,
I stand beside my grave
60 Confused with my life, that is commonplace and solitary.   [1965]

DYLAN THOMAS (1914–1953)

Fern Hill

Now as I was young and easy under the apple boughs
About the lilting house and happy as the grass was green,
        The night above the dingle starry,
            Time let me hail and climb
5   Golden in the heydays of his eyes,
And honoured among wagons I was prince of the apple towns
And once below a time I lordly had the trees and leaves
            Trail with daisies and barley
        Down the rivers of the windfall light.

10 And as I was green and carefree, famous among the barns
About the happy yard and singing as the farm was home,
        In the sun that is young once only,
            Time let me play and be
        Golden in the mercy of his means,
15 And green and golden I was huntsman and herdsman, the calves
Sang to my horn, the foxes on the hills barked clear and cold,
            And the sabbath rang slowly
        In the pebbles of the holy streams.

All the sun long it was running, it was lovely, the hay
20 Fields high as the house, the tunes from the chimneys, it was air
        And playing, lovely and watery
            And fire green as grass.
        And nightly under the simple stars
As I rode to sleep the owls were bearing the farm away,
25 All the moon long I heard, blessed among stables, the nightjars
        Flying with the ricks, and the horses
            Flashing into the dark.

And then to awake, and the farm, like a wanderer white
With the dew, come back, the cock on his shoulder: it was all
30   Shining, it was Adam and maiden,

[3]/*dingle: deep hollow or valley*   [25]/*nightjars: nocturnal birds (European)
rather like our nighthawk*

The sky gathered again
And the sun grew round that very day.
So it must have been after the birth of the simple light
In the first, spinning place, the spellbound horses walking warm
35   Out of the whinnying green stable
On to the fields of praise.

And honoured among foxes and pheasants by the gay house
Under the new made clouds and happy as the heart was long,
In the sun born over and over,
40   I ran my heedless ways,
My wishes raced through the house high hay
And nothing I cared, at my sky blue trades, that time allows
In all his tuneful turning so few and such morning songs
Before the children green and golden
45   Follow him out of grace.

Nothing I cared, in the lamb white days, that time would take me
Up to the swallow thronged loft by the shadow of my hand,
In the moon that is always rising,
Nor that riding to sleep
50   I should hear him fly with the high fields
And wake to the farm forever fled from the childless land.
Oh as I was young and easy in the mercy of his means,
Time held me green and dying
Though I sang in my chains like the sea.   [1946]

JOHN CIARDI (1916–1986)

Faces

Once in Canandaigua, hitchhiking from Ann Arbor
to Boston in the middle of December, and just
as dark came full on a stone-cracking
drill of wind that shot a grit of snow,
5 I was picked up outside an all-night diner
by a voice in a Buick. "Jump in," it said. "It's cold."

Four, five miles out, in the dead winter of nowhere
and black as the insides of a pig, we stopped.
"I turn off here."
10   I looked around at nothing.
"The drive's up there," he said.
                        But when I was out,
he headed on, turned round, drove back, and stopped.

"You haven't thanked me for the ride," he said.

15 "Thanks," I said, shuffling to find a rock
I might kick loose and grab for just in case.
But he wasn't that kind of crazy. He just waved:

"You're welcome, brother. Keep the rest for change."
Then he pulled in his head and drove away—
20 back toward Canandaigua.
                                    I thought about him
a good deal, you might say, out there in the sandblast
till a truck lit like a liner picked me up
one blue-black inch from frostbite.
25 And off and on for something like twenty years
I've found him in my mind, whoever he was,
whoever he is—I never saw his face,
only its shadow—but for twenty years
I've been finding faces that might do for his.
30 The Army was especially full of possibles,
but not to the point of monopoly. Any party
can spring one through a doorway. "How do you do?"
you say and the face opens and there you are
back in the winter blast.
35   But why tell you?
It's anybody's world for the living in it:
You know as much about that face as I do.   [1961]

GWENDOLYN BROOKS (*b.* 1917)

The Bean Eaters

They eat beans mostly, this old yellow pair.
Dinner is a casual affair.
Plain chipware on a plain and creaking wood,
Tin flatware.

5 Two who are Mostly Good.
Two who have lived their day,
But keep on putting on their clothes
And putting things away.

And remembering . . .
10 Remembering, with twinklings and twinges,
As they lean over the beans in their rented back room
    that is full of beads and receipts and dolls and cloths,
    tobacco crumbs, vases and fringes.   [1960]

ROBERT LOWELL (1917–1977)

Skunk Hour

(For Elizabeth Bishop)

Nautilus Island's hermit
heiress still lives through winter in her Spartan cottage;

The setting is around Castine, Maine.

her sheep still graze above the sea.
Her son's a bishop. Her farmer
5   is first selectman in our village,
she's in her dotage.

Thirsting for
the hierarchic privacy
of Queen Victoria's century,
10 she buys up all
the eyesores facing her shore,
and lets them fall.

The season's ill—
we've lost our summer millionaire,
15 who seemed to leap from an L. L. Bean
catalogue. His nine-knot yawl
was auctioned off to lobstermen.
A red fox stain covers Blue Hill.

And now our fairy
20 decorator brightens his shop for fall;
his fishnet's filled with orange cork,
orange, his cobbler's bench and awl;
there is no money in his work,
he'd rather marry.

25 One dark night,
my Tudor Ford climbed the hill's skull;
I watched for love-cars. Lights turned down,
they lay together, hull to hull,
where the graveyard shelves on the town. . . .
30 My mind's not right.

A car radio bleats,
"Love, O careless Love . . ." I hear
my ill-spirit sob in each blood cell,
as if my hand were at its throat. . . .
35 I myself am hell;
nobody's here—

only skunks, that search
in the moonlight for a bite to eat.
They march on their soles up Main Street:
40 white stripes, moonstruck eyes' red fire
under the chalk-dry and spar spire
of the Trinitarian Church.

I stand on top
of our back steps and breathe the rich air—

[15]/**L. L. Bean:** *a store and mail-order house in Maine, specializing in sportswear and camping equipment*

[25]/**one dark night:** *an allusion to "The Dark Night" of Saint John of the Cross* (p. 55)

45 a mother skunk with her column of kittens swills the garbage pail.
She jabs her wedge-head in a cup
of sour cream, drops her ostrich tail,
and will not scare.   [1959]

For the Union Dead

"Relinquunt Omnia Servare Rem Publicam."

The old South Boston Aquarium stands
in a Sahara of snow now. Its broken windows are boarded.
The bronze weathervane cod has lost half its scales.
The airy tanks are dry.

5 Once my nose crawled like a snail on the glass;
my hand tingled
to burst the bubbles
drifting from the noses of the cowed, compliant fish.

My hand draws back. I often sigh still
10 for the dark downward and vegetating kingdom
of the fish and reptile. One morning last March,
I pressed against the new barbed and galvanized

fence on the Boston Common. Behind their cage,
yellow dinosaur steamshovels were grunting
15 as they cropped up tons of mush and grass
to gouge their underworld garage.

Parking spaces luxuriate like civic
sandpiles in the heart of Boston.
A girdle of orange, Puritan-pumpkin colored girders
20 braces the tingling Statehouse,

shaking over the excavations, as it faces Colonel Shaw
and his bell-cheeked Negro infantry
on St. Gauden's shaking Civil War relief,
propped by a plank splint against the garage's earthquake.

25 Two months after marching through Boston,
half the regiment was dead;
at the dedication,
William James could almost hear the bronze Negroes breathe.

Their monument sticks like a fishbone
30 in the city's throat.

"Relinquunt . . . Publicam":
"They Gave up Everything to
Preserve the Republic"
[21]/**Colonel Shaw:** *Robert Gould*
Shaw was commander of the first
all-black regiment in the Union Army
during the Civil War. A bronze memorial
to him and his men, made by the sculptor
Saint-Gaudens in 1897, faces the State
House on Boston Common. The 1989
movie Glory *is the story of Shaw and his*
men.

Its Colonel is as lean
as a compass-needle.

He has an angry wrenlike vigilance,
a greyhound's gentle tautness;
35 he seems to wince at pleasure,
and suffocate for privacy.

He is out of bounds now. He rejoices in man's lovely,
peculiar power to choose life and die—
when he leads his black soldiers to death,
40 he cannot bend his back.

On a thousand small town New England greens,
the old white churches hold their air
of sparse, sincere rebellion; frayed flags
quilt the graveyards of the Grand Army of the Republic.

45 The stone statues of the abstract Union Soldier
grow slimmer and younger each year—
wasp-waisted, they doze over muskets
and muse through their sideburns . . .

Shaw's father wanted no monument
50 except the ditch,
where his son's body was thrown
and lost with his "niggers."

The ditch is nearer.
There are no statues for the last war here;
55 on Boylston Street, a commercial photograph
shows Hiroshima boiling

over a Mosler Safe, the "Rock of Ages"
that survived the blast. Space is nearer.
When I crouch to my television set,
60 the drained faces of Negro school-children rise like balloons.

Colonel Shaw
is riding on his bubble,
he waits
for the blessèd break.

65 The Aquarium is gone. Everywhere,
giant finned cars nose forward like fish;
a savage servility
slides by on grease.   [1960]

44/**Grand Army** . . . : *Union soldiers*
52/*Among the many verses written in the
North in praise of Shaw and his brave
soldiers, nearly half of whom were killed
with Shaw in attacking a fort near
Charleston, one had the commander of
the fort denying Shaw the honorable*
*burial to which his rank entitled him,
ordering him instead to be thrown "with his
niggers" into a common ditch. Shaw's father
refused to have the body moved, declaring
that his most honorable grave.*
60/**drained faces:** *in news reports of
integration disorders*

MAY SWENSON (1919–1989)

Stripping and Putting On

I always felt like a bird blown through the world.
I never felt like a tree.

I never wanted a patch of this earth to stand in,
that would stick to me.

5 I wanted to move by whatever throb my muscles
sent to me.

I never cared for cars, that crawled on land or
air or sea.

If I rode, I'd rather another animal: horse, camel,
10 or shrewd donkey.

Never needed a nest, unless for the night, or when
winter overtook me.

Never wanted an extra skin between mine and the sun,
for vanity or modesty.

15 Would rather not have parents, had no yen for a child,
and never felt brotherly.

But I'd borrow or lend love of friend. Let friend be
not stronger or weaker than me.

Never hankered for Heaven, or shied from a Hell,
20 or played with the puppets Devil and Deity.

I never felt proud as one of the crowd under
the flag of a country.

Or felt that my genes were worth more or less than beans,
by accident of ancestry.

25 Never wished to buy or sell. I would just as well
not touch money.

Never wanted to own a thing that I wasn't born with.
Or to act by a fact not discovered by me.

I always felt like a bird blown through the world.
30 But I would like to lay

the egg of a world in a nest of calm beyond
this world's storm and decay.

I would like to own such wings as light speeds on,
far from this globule of night and day.

35 I would like to be able to put on, like clothes,
the bodies of all those

creatures and things hatched under the wings
of that world.

[1994]

HOWARD NEMEROV (1920–1991)

Because You Asked about the Line between Prose and Poetry

Sparrows were feeding in a freezing drizzle
That while you watched turned into pieces of snow
Riding a gradient invisible
From silver aslant to random, white, and slow.

5   There came a moment that you couldn't tell.
And then they clearly flew instead of fell.   [1980]

RICHARD WILBUR (*b.* 1921)

The Catch

From the dress-box's plashing tis-
Sue paper she pulls out her prize,
Dangling it to one side before my eyes
Like a weird sort of fish

5   That she has somehow hooked and gaffed
And on the dock-end holds in air—
Limp, corrugated, lank, a catch too rare
Not to be photographed.

I, in my chair, make shift to say
10   Some bright, discerning thing, and fail,
Proving once more the blindness of the male.
Annoyed, she stalks away

And then is back in half a minute,
Consulting, now, not me at all
15   But the long mirror, mirror on the wall.
The dress, now that she's in it,

Has changed appreciably, and gains
By lacy shoes, a light perfume
Whose subtle field electrifies the room,
20   And two slim golden chains.

With a fierce frown and hard-pursed lips
She twists a little on her stem
To test the even swirling of the hem,
Smooths down the waist and hips,

25   Plucks at the shoulder-straps a bit,
Then turns around and looks behind,
Her face transfigured now by peace of mind.
There is no question—it

Is wholly charming, it is she,
30   As I belatedly remark,
And may be hung now in the fragrant dark
Of her soft armory.   [1987]

Hamlen Brook

At the alder-darkened brink
Where the stream slows to a lucid jet
I lean to the water, dinting its top with sweat,
And see, before I can drink,

5 A startled inchling trout
Of spotted near-transparency,
Trawling a shadow solider than he.
He swerves now, darting out

To where, in a flicked slew
10 Of sparks and glittering silt, he weaves
Through stream-bed rocks, disturbing foundered leaves,
And butts then out of view

Beneath a sliding glass
Crazed by the skimming of a brace
15 Of burnished dragon-flies across its face,
In which deep cloudlets pass

And a white precipice
Of mirrored birch-trees plunges down
Toward where the azures of the zenith drown.
20 How shall I drink all this?

Joy's trick is to supply
Dry lips with what can cool and slake,
Leaving them dumbstruck also with an ache
Nothing can satisfy.   [1987]

PHILIP LARKIN (1922–1985)

At Grass

The eye can hardly pick them out
From the cold shade they shelter in,
Till wind distresses tail and mane;
Then one crops grass, and moves about
5 —The other seeming to look on—
And stands anonymous again.

Yet fifteen years ago, perhaps
Two dozen distances sufficed
To fable them: faint afternoons
10 Of Cups and Stakes and Handicaps,
Whereby their names were artificed
To inlay faded, classic Junes—

Silks at the start: against the sky
Numbers and parasols: outside,

9/*fable: make fabulous or legendary*

₁₅   Squadrons of empty cars, and heat,
And littered grass: then the long cry
Hanging unhushed till it subside
To stop-press columns on the street.

Do memories plague their ears like flies?
₂₀   They shake their heads. Dusk brims the shadows.
Summer by summer all stole away,
The starting-gates, the crowds and cries—
All but the unmolesting meadows.
Almanacked, their names live; they

₂₅   Have slipped their names, and stand at ease,
Or gallop for what must be joy,
And not a fieldglass sees them home,
Or curious stop-watch prophesies:
Only the groom, and the groom's boy,
₃₀   With bridles in the evening come.   [1951]

---

[18]/**stop-press:** *news (of the races) sensational enough to "stop the presses"*

The Explosion

On the day of the explosion
Shadows pointed towards the pithead:
In the sun the slagheap slept.

Down the lane came men in pitboots
₅   Coughing oath-edged talk and pipe-smoke,
Shouldering off the freshened silence.

One chased after rabbits; lost them;
Came back with a nest of lark's eggs;
Showed them; lodged them in the grasses.

₁₀   So they passed in beards and moleskins,
Fathers, brothers, nicknames, laughter,
Through the tall gates standing open.

At noon, there came a tremor; cows
Stopped chewing for a second; sun,
₁₅   Scarfed as in a heat-haze, dimmed.

The dead go on before, they
Are sitting in God's house in comfort,
We shall see them face to face—

Plain as lettering in the chapels
₂₀   It was said, and for a second
Wives saw men of the explosion

---

[2]/**pithead:** *the top of a mine shaft*

Larger than in life they managed—
Gold as on a coin, or walking
Somehow from the sun towards them,

25 One showing the eggs unbroken.   [1974]

Aubade

I work all day, and get half-drunk at night.
Waking at four to soundless dark, I stare.
In time the curtain-edges will grow light.
Till then I see what's really always there:
5 Unresting death, a whole day nearer now,
Making all thought impossible but how
And where and when I shall myself die.
Arid interrogation: yet the dread
Of dying, and being dead,
10 Flashes afresh to hold and horrify.

The mind blanks at the glare. Not in remorse
—The good not done, the love not given, time
Torn off unused—nor wretchedly because
An only life can take so long to climb
15 Clear of its wrong beginnings, and may never;
But at the total emptiness for ever,
The sure extinction that we travel to
And shall be lost in always. Not to be here,
Not to be anywhere,
20 And soon; nothing more terrible, nothing more true.

This is a special way of being afraid
No trick dispels. Religion used to try,
That vast moth-eaten musical brocade
Created to pretend we never die,
25 And specious stuff that says *No rational being*
Can fear a thing it will not feel, not seeing
That this is what we fear—no sight, no sound,
No touch or taste or smell, nothing to think with,
Nothing to love or link with,
30 The anaesthetic from which none come round.

And so it stays just on the edge of vision,
A small unfocused blur, a standing chill
That slows each impulse down to indecision.
Most things may never happen: this one will,
35 And realisation of it rages out
In furnace-fear when we are caught without
People or drink. Courage is no good:
It means not scaring others. Being brave
Lets no one off the grave.
40 Death is no different whined at than withstood.

Slowly light strengthens, and the room takes shape.
It stands plain as a wardrobe, what we know,
Have always known, know that we can't escape,
Yet can't accept. One side will have to go.
45   Meanwhile telephones crouch, getting ready to ring
In locked-up offices, and all the uncaring
Intricate rented world begins to rouse.
The sky is white as clay, with no sun.
Work has to be done.
50   Postmen like doctors go from house to house.   [1988]

JAMES DICKEY (1923–1997)

Cherrylog Road

Off Highway 106
At Cherrylog Road I entered
The '34 Ford without wheels,
Smothered in kudzu,
5   With a seat pulled out to run
Corn whiskey down from the hills,

And then from the other side
Crept into an Essex
With a rumble seat of red leather
10   And then out again, aboard
A blue Chevrolet, releasing
The rust from its other color,

Reared up on three building blocks.
None had the same body heat;
15   I changed with them inward, toward
The weedy heart of the junkyard,
For I knew that Doris Holbrook
Would escape from her father at noon

And would come from the farm
20   To seek parts owned by the sun
Among the abandoned chassis,
Sitting in each in turn
As I did, leaning forward
As in a wild stock-car race

25   In the parking lot of the dead.
Time after time, I climbed in
And out the other side, like
An envoy or movie star
Met at the station by crickets.
30   A radiator cap raised its head,

---

⁴/**kudzu:** *a vine from the Orient that spreads rapidly in much of the South*

Become a real toad or a kingsnake
As I neared the hub of the yard,
Passing through many states,
Many lives, to reach
35 Some grandmother's long Pierce-Arrow
Sending platters of blindness forth

From its nickel hubcaps
And spilling its tender upholstery
On sleepy roaches,
40 The glass panel in between
Lady and colored driver
Not all the way broken out,

The back-seat phone
Still on its hook.
45 I got in as though to exclaim,
"Let us go to the orphan asylum,
John; I have some old toys
For children who say their prayers."

I popped with sweat as I thought
50 I heard Doris Holbrook scrape
Like a mouse in the southern-state sun
That was eating the paint in blisters
From a hundred car tops and hoods.
She was tapping like code,

55 Loosening the screws,
Carrying off headlights,
Sparkplugs, bumpers,
Cracked mirrors and gear-knobs,
Getting ready, already,
60 To go back with something to show

Other than her lips' new trembling
I would hold to me soon, soon,
Where I sat in the ripped back seat
Talking over the interphone,
65 Praying for Doris Holbrook
To come from her father's farm

And to get back there
With no trace of me on her face
To be seen by her red-haired father
70 Who would change, in the squalling barn,
Her back's pale skin with a strop,
Then lay for me

In a bootlegger's roasting car
With a string-triggered 12-gauge shotgun
75 To blast the breath from the air.

Not cut by the jagged windshields,
Through the acres of wrecks she came
With a wrench in her hand,

Through dust where the blacksnake dies
80 Of boredom, and the beetle knows
The compost has no more life.
Someone outside would have seen
The oldest car's door inexplicably
Close from within:

85 I held her and held her and held her,
Convoyed at terrific speed
By the stalled, dreaming traffic around us,
So the blacksnake, stiff
With inaction, curved back
90 Into life, and hunted the mouse

With deadly overexcitement,
The beetles reclaimed their field
As we clung, glued together,
With the hooks of the seat springs
95 Working through to catch us red-handed
Amidst the gray breathless batting

That burst from the seat at our backs.
We left by separate doors
Into the changed, other bodies
100 Of cars, she down Cherrylog Road
And I to my motorcycle
Parked like the soul of the junkyard

Restored, a bicycle fleshed
With power, and tore off
105 Up Highway 106, continually
Drunk on the wind in my mouth,
Wringing the handlebar for speed,
Wild to be wreckage forever.   [1964]

ANTHONY HECHT (1923–2004)

The Dover Bitch

A Criticism of Life
for Andrews Wanning

So there stood Matthew Arnold and this girl
With the cliffs of England crumbling away behind them,
And he said to her, "Try to be true to me,
And I'll do the same for you, for things are bad
5 All over, etc., etc."

Well now, I knew this girl. It's true she had read
Sophocles in a fairly good translation
And caught that bitter allusion to the sea,
But all the time he was talking she had in mind
10 The notion of what his whiskers would feel like
On the back of her neck. She told me later on
That after a while she got to looking out
At the lights across the channel, and really felt sad,
Thinking of all the wine and enormous beds
15 And blandishments in French and the perfumes.
And then she got really angry. To have been brought
All the way down from London, and then be addressed
As a sort of mournful cosmic last resort
Is really tough on a girl, and she was pretty.
20 Anyway, she watched him pace the room
And finger his watch-chain and seem to sweat a bit,
And then she said one or two unprintable things.
But you mustn't judge her by that. What I mean to say is,
She's really all right. I still see her once in a while
25 And she always treats me right. We have a drink
And I give her a good time, and perhaps it's a year
Before I see her again, but there she is,
Running to fat, but dependable as they come.
And sometimes I bring her a bottle of *Nuit d'Amour*.   [1967]

The Book of Yolek

> *Wir haben ein Gesetz,*
> *Und nach dem Gesetz soll er sterben.*

The dowsed coals fume and hiss after your meal
Of grilled brook trout, and you saunter off for a walk
Down the fern trail, it doesn't matter where to,
Just so you're weeks and worlds away from home,
5 And among midsummer hills have set up camp
In the deep bronze glories of declining day.

You remember, peacefully, an earlier day
In childhood, remember a quite specific meal:
A corn roast and bonfire in summer camp.
10 That summer you got lost on a Nature Walk;
More than you dared admit, you thought of home;
No one else knows where the mind wanders to.

The epigraph, which the poet has called "the text of a stirring chorus in Bach's
'St. John Passion,'" is the German translation of John 19:7, which the King James
version gives as "We have a law, and by our law he ought to die." The words are
spoken of Jesus when he is accused before Pilate; the irony of their being in German
suggests that the Nazis might have used these very words in regard to Yolek.

The fifth of August, 1942.
It was morning and very hot. It was the day
15 They came at dawn with rifles to The Home
For Jewish Children, cutting short the meal
Of bread and soup, lining them up to walk
In close formation off to a special camp.

How often you have thought about that camp,
20 As though in some strange way you were driven to,
And about the children, and how they were made to walk,
Yolek who had bad lungs, who wasn't a day
Over five years old, commanded to leave his meal
And shamble between armed guards to his long home.

25 We're approaching August again. It will drive home
The regulation torments of that camp
Yolek was sent to, his small, unfinished meal,
The electric fences, the numeral tattoo,
The quite extraordinary heat of the day
30 They all were forced to take that terrible walk.

Whether on a silent, solitary walk
Or among crowds, far off or safe at home,
You will remember, helplessly, that day,
And the smell of smoke, and the loudspeakers of the camp.
35 Wherever you are, Yolek will be there, too.
His unuttered name will interrupt your meal.

Prepare to receive him in your home some day.
Though they killed him in the camp they sent him to,
He will walk in as you're sitting down to a meal.   [1990]

DONALD JUSTICE (1925–2004)

Variations on a Text by Vallejo

Me moriré en Paris con aguacero . . .

I will die in Miami in the sun,
On a day when the sun is very bright,
A day like the days I remember, a day like other days,
A day that nobody knows or remembers yet,
5 And the sun will be bright then on the dark glasses of strangers
And in the eyes of a few friends from my childhood
And of the surviving cousins by the graveside,
While the diggers, standing apart, in the still shade of the palms,
Rest on their shovels, and smoke,
10 Speaking in Spanish softly, out of respect.

*Cesar Vallejo: Peruvian poet (1895–1938), who once wrote that he would die in Paris
on a rainy day.*

I think it will be on a Sunday like today,
Except that the sun will be out, the rain will have stopped,
And the wind that today made all the little shrubs kneel down;
And I think it will be Sunday because today,
15 When I took out this paper and began to write,
Never before had anything looked so blank,
My life, these words, the paper, the gray Sunday;
And my dog, quivering under a table because of the storm,
Looked up at me, not understanding,
20 And my son read on without speaking, and my wife slept.

Donald Justice is dead. One Sunday the sun came out,
It shone on the bay, it shone on the white buildings,
The cars moved down the street slowly as always, so many,
Some with their headlights on in spite of the sun,
25 And after awhile the diggers with their shovels
Walked back to the graveside through the sunlight,
And one of them put his blade into the earth
To lift a few clods of dirt, the black marl of Miami,
And scattered the dirt, and spat,
30 Turning away abruptly, out of respect.   [1973]

Psalm and Lament

Hialeah, Florida
in memory of my mother (1897–1974)

The clocks are sorry, the clocks are very sad.
One stops, one goes on striking the wrong hours.

And the grass burns terribly in the sun,
The grass turns yellow secretly at the roots.

5 Now suddenly the yard chairs look empty, the sky looks empty,
The sky looks vast and empty.

Out on Red Road the traffic continues; everything continues.
Nor does memory sleep; it goes on.

Out spring the butterflies of recollection,
10 And I think that for the first time I understand

The beautiful ordinary light of this patio
And even perhaps the dark rich earth of a heart.

(The bedclothes, they say, had been pulled down.
I will not describe it. I do not want to describe it.

15 No, but the sheets were drenched and twisted.
They were the very handkerchiefs of grief.)

Let summer come now with its schoolboy trumpets and fountains.
But the years are gone, the years are finally over.

And there is only
20   This long desolation of flower-bordered sidewalks

That runs to the corner, turns, and goes on,
That disappears and goes on

Into the black oblivion of a neighborhood and a world
Without billboards or yesterdays.

25   Sometimes a sad moon comes and waters the roof tiles.
But the years are gone. There are no more years.   [1987]

MAXINE KUMIN (*b.* 1925)

The Retrieval System

It begins with my dog, now dead, who all his long life
carried about in his head the brown eyes of my father,
keen, loving, accepting, sorrowful, whatever;
they were Daddy's all right, handed on, except
5   for their phosphorescent gleam tunneling the night
which I have to concede was a separate gift.

Uncannily when I'm alone these features
come up to link my lost people
with the patient domestic beasts of my life. For example,
10   the wethered goat who runs free in pasture and stable
with his flecked, agate eyes and his minus-sign pupils
blats in the tiny voice of my former piano teacher

whose bones beat time in my dreams and whose terrible breath
soured *Country Gardens, Humoresque,* and unplayable Bach.
15   My elderly aunts, wearing the heads of willful
intelligent ponies, stand at the fence begging apples.
The sister who died at three has my cat's faint chin,
my cat's inscrutable squint, and cried catlike in pain.

I remember the funeral. *The Lord is my shepherd,*
20   we said. I don't want to brood. Fact: it is people who fade,
it is animals that retrieve them. A boy
I loved once keeps coming back as my yearling colt,
cocksure at the gallop, racing his shadow
for the hell of it. He runs merely to be.
25   A boy who was lost in the war thirty years ago
and buried at sea.

Here, it's forty degrees and raining. The weatherman
who looks like my resident owl, the one who goes out and in
by the open haymow, appears on the TV screen.
30   With his heart-shaped face, he is also my late dentist's double,
donnish, bifocaled, kind. Going a little gray,

advising this wisdom tooth will have to come out someday,
meanwhile filling it as a favor. Another save.
It outlasted him. The forecast is nothing but trouble.
35 It will snow fiercely enough to fill all these open graves.   [1970]

GERALD STERN (*b.* 1925)

The Dog

What I was doing with my white teeth exposed
like that on the side of the road I don't know,
and I don't know why I lay beside the sewer
so that lover of dead things could come back
5   with his pencil sharpened and his piece of white paper.
I was there for a good two hours whistling
dirges, shrieking a little, terrifying
hearts with my whimpering cries before I died
by pulling the one leg up and stiffening.
10 There is a look we have with the hair of the chin
curled in mid-air, there is a look with the belly
stopped in the midst of its greed. The lover of dead things
stoops to feel me, his hand is shaking. I know
his mouth is open and his glasses are slipping.
15 I think his pencil must be jerking and the terror
of smell—and sight—is overtaking him;
I know he has that terrified faraway look
that death brings—he is contemplating. I want him
to touch my forehead once and rub my muzzle
20 before he lifts me up and throws me into
that little valley. I hope he doesn't use
his shoe for fear of touching me; I know,
or used to know, the grasses down there; I think
I knew a hundred smells. I hope the dog's way
25 doesn't overtake him, one quick push,
barely that, and the mind freed, something else,
some other thing, to take its place. Great heart,
great human heart, keep loving me as you lift me,
give me your tears, great loving stranger, remember
30 the death of dogs, forgive the yapping, forgive
the shitting, let there be pity, give me your pity.
How could there be enough? I have given
my life for this, emotion has ruined me, oh lover,
I have exchanged my wildness—little tricks
35 with the mouth and feet, with the tail, my tongue is a parrot's,
I am a rampant horse, I am a lion,
I wait for the cookie, I snap my teeth—
as you have taught me, oh distant and brilliant and lonely.   [1986]

A. R. AMMONS (1926–2001)

The Constant

When leaving the primrose, bayberry dunes, seaward
I discovered the universe this morning,
        I was in no
mood
5   for wonder,
        the naked mass of so much miracle
already beyond the vision
of my grasp:

along a rise of beach, a hundred feet from the surf,
10   a row of clam shells
        four to ten feet wide
        lay sinuous as far as sight:

in one shell—though in the abundance
        there were others like it—upturned,
15   four or five inches across the wing,
a lake
three to four inches long and two inches wide,
all dimensions rounded,
        indescribable in curve:

20   and on the lake a turning galaxy, a film of sand,
co-ordinated, nearly circular (no real perfections),
        an inch in diameter, turning:
turning:
counterclockwise, the wind hardly perceptible from 11 o'clock
25   with noon at sea:
        the galaxy rotating,
        but also,
at a distance from the shell lip,
revolving
30   round and round the shell:

        a gull's toe could spill the universe:
two more hours of sun could dry it up:
a higher wind could rock it out:

the tide will rise, engulf it, wash it loose:
35   utterly:

the terns, their
        young somewhere hidden in clumps of grass or weed,
were diving *sshik sshik* at me,
        then pealing upward for another round and dive:

40   I have had too much of this inexhaustible miracle:
miracle, this massive, drab constant of experience.

                                            [1966]

Cut the Grass

The wonderful workings of the world: wonderful,
wonderful: I'm surprised half the time:
ground up fine, I puff if a pebble stirs:

I'm nervous: my morality's intricate: if
5   a squash blossom dies, I feel withered as a stained
zucchini and blame my nature: and

when grassblades flop to the little red-ant
queens burring around trying to get aloft, I blame
my not keeping the grass short, stubble

10   firm: well, I learn a lot of useless stuff, meant
to be ignored: like when the sun sinking in the
west glares a plane invisible, I think how much

revelation concealment necessitates: and then I
think of the ocean, multiple to a blinding
15   oneness and realize that only total expression

expresses hiding: I'll have to say everything
to take on the roundness and withdrawal of the deep dark:
less than total is a bucketful of radiant toys.   [1971]

[8]/**burring:** *bustling, fumbling, hurrying*

ALLEN GINSBERG (1926–1997)

A Supermarket in California

What thoughts I have of you tonight, Walt Whitman, for I walked
    down the sidestreets under the trees with a headache self-
    conscious looking at the full moon.
In my hungry fatigue, and shopping for images, I went into the
    neon fruit supermarket, dreaming of your enumerations!
What peaches and what penumbras! Whole families shopping at
    night! Aisles full of husbands! Wives in the avocados, babies in
    the tomatoes!—and you, Garcia Lorca, what were you doing
    down by the watermelons?

I saw you, Walt Whitman, childless, lonely old grubber, poking
    among the meats in the refrigerator and eyeing the grocery boys.
5   I heard you asking questions of each: Who killed the pork chops?
    What price bananas? Are you my Angel?
I wandered in and out of the brilliant stacks of cans following you,
    and followed in my imagination by the store detective.

[3]/**Garcia Lorca:** *Federico García Lorca, Spanish poet and dramatist (1899–1936).*
Ginsberg suggests we look at García Lorca's "Ode to Walt Whitman."

We strode down the open corridors together in our solitary fancy
tasting artichokes, possessing every frozen delicacy, and never
passing the cashier.

Where are we going, Walt Whitman? The doors close in an hour.
Which way does your beard point tonight?
(I touch your book and dream of our odyssey in the supermarket
and feel absurd.)
10 Will we walk all night through solitary streets? The trees add shade
to shade, lights out in the houses, we'll both be lonely.
Will we stroll dreaming of the lost America of love past blue
automobiles in driveways, home to our silent cottage?
Ah, dear father, graybeard, lonely old courage-teacher, what
America did you have when Charon quit poling his ferry and
you got out on a smoking bank and stood watching the boat
disappear on the black waters of Lethe?

[(*Berkeley* 1955) 1956]

12/*Charon: in classical mythology, the ferryman who carried the dead across an
underworld river called the Styx. Lethe is a different river whose waters caused
forgetfulness in the drinker.*

JAMES MERRILL (1926–1996)

Charles on Fire

Another evening we sprawled about discussing
Appearances. And it was the consensus
That while uncommon physical good looks
Continued to launch one, as before, in life
5 (Among its vaporous eddies and false calms),
Still, as one of us said into his beard,
"Without your intellectual and spiritual
Values, man, you are sunk." No one but squared
The shoulders of his own unloveliness.
10 Long-suffering Charles, having cooked and served the meal,
Now brought out little tumblers finely etched
He filled with amber liquor and then passed.
"Say," said the same young man, "in Paris, France,
They do it this way"—bounding to his feet
15 And touching a lit match to our host's full glass.
A blue flame, gentle, beautiful, came, went
Above the surface. In a hush that fell
We heard the vessel crack. The contents drained
As who should step down from a crystal coach.
20 Steward of spirits, Charles's glistening hand
All at once gloved itself in eeriness.
The moment passed. He made two quick sweeps and
Was flesh again. "It couldn't matter less,"
He said, but with a shocked, unconscious glance

25 Into the mirror. Finding nothing changed,
    He filled a fresh glass and sank down among us.   [1966]

The Blue Grotto

for Mona Van Duyn

    The boatman rowed into
    That often-sung impasse.
    Each visitor foreknew
    A floor of lilting glass,
5   A vault of rock, lit blue.

    But here we faced the fact.
    As misty expectations
    Dispersed, and wavelets thwacked
    In something like impatience,
10 The point was to react.

    Alas for characteristics!
    Diane fingered the water.
    Don tested the acoustics
    With a paragraph from Pater.
15 Jon shut his eyes—these mystics—

    Thinking his mantra. Jack
    Came out with a one-liner,
    While claustrophobiac
    Janet fought off a minor
20 Anxiety attack.

    Then from our gnarled (his name?)
    Boatman (Gennaro!) burst
    Some local, vocal gem
    Ten times a day rehearsed.
25 It put us all to shame:

    The astute sob, the kiss
    Blown in sheer routine
    Unselfconsciousness
    Before one left the scene . . .
30 Years passed, and I wrote this.   [1985]

The grotto of the title, a famous tourist attraction on the island of Capri in the Bay of Naples, is "lit blue" by sunbeams refracted through its flooded entrance from the sea. The boatman Gennaro is named for the saint most venerated in Naples.

W. D. SNODGRASS (b. 1926)

Leaving the Motel

    Outside, the last kids holler
    Near the pool: they'll stay the night.

Pick up the towels; fold your collar
Out of sight.

5   Check: is the second bed
Unrumpled, as agreed?
Landlords have to think ahead
In case of need,

Too. Keep things straight: don't take
10   The matches, the wrong keyrings—
We've nowhere we could keep a keepsake—
Ashtrays, combs, things

That sooner or later others
Would accidentally find.
15   Check: take nothing of one another's
And leave behind

Your license number only,
Which they won't care to trace;
We've paid. Still, should such things get lonely,
20   Leave in their vase

An aspirin to preserve
Our lilacs, the wayside flowers
We've gathered and must leave to serve
A few more hours;

25   That's all. We can't tell when
We'll come back, can't press claims;
We would no doubt have other rooms then,
Or other names.

                                                           [1967]

DAVID WAGONER (b. 1926)

For a Man Dancing by Himself in a Tavern

In the hallway between the Ladies' and Gentlemen's
The man in the overcoat with the lost lining
Has started dancing. He is slow at first
To lift his sleeves with his arms, having almost nowhere
5   To put his brimful glass but his own lips,
But now he toasts the ceiling with one hand,
Presses his belly like the small of a back,

And waltzes to rock and roll, his tongueless shoes
Sliding on open tiptoes, dividing three
10   By four with abrupt rubatos, with dizzy changes
Of signature and runs of accidentals,
His face suffused with the gold light bathing him
By courtesy of the Miller Brewing Company
And eyelids like shut petals of rosebuds.

15 He is so wonderfully and completely happy
Holding her in his arms, so sure of the pleasure
She takes in his sweet nothings, so unaware
Of the comings and goings of insignificant
Others, so filled with her, his follower,
20 His drinking partner lighter than Lite beer
And more fulfilling, what else could he wish for?

Revolving slowly like the overhead fans
And the room, and down and around to a bent knee,
He doffs his baseball cap to the wallflowers
25 And shakes hands with himself. His hands shaking,
He takes himself by the elbows. The bartender
Takes him too, still bowing and still glowing,
Toward the door and out into the dark.   [1999]

JOHN ASHBERY (b. 1927)

Mixed Feelings

A pleasant smell of frying sausages
Attacks the sense, along with an old, mostly invisible
Photograph of what seems to be girls lounging around
An old fighter bomber, circa 1942 vintage.
5 How to explain to these girls, if indeed that's what they are,
These Ruths, Lindas, Pats and Sheilas
About the vast change that's taken place
In the fabric of our society, altering the texture
Of all things in it? And yet
10 They somehow look as if they knew, except
That it's so hard to see them, it's hard to figure out
Exactly what kind of expressions they're wearing.
What are your hobbies, girls? Aw nerts,
One of them might say, this guy's too much for me.
15 Let's go on and out, somewhere
Through the canyons of the garment center
To a small café and have a cup of coffee.
I am not offended that these creatures (that's the word)
Of my imagination seem to hold me in such light esteem,
20 Pay so little heed to me. It's part of a complicated
Flirtation routine, anyhow, no doubt. But this talk of
The garment center? Surely that's California sunlight
Belaboring them and the old crate on which they
Have draped themselves, fading its Donald Duck insignia
25 To the extreme point of legibility.
Maybe they were lying but more likely their
Tiny intelligences cannot retain much information.
Not even one fact, perhaps. That's why
They think they're in New York. I like the way

30 They look and act and feel. I wonder
How they got that way, but am not going to
Waste any more time thinking about them.
I have already forgotten them
Until some day in the not too distant future
35 When we meet possibly in the lounge of a modern airport,
They looking as astonishingly young and fresh as when this picture
    was made
But full of contradictory ideas, stupid ones as well as
Worthwhile ones, but all flooding the surface of our minds
As we babble about the sky and the weather and the forests of change.

[1975]

W. S. MERWIN (*b.* 1927)

For the Anniversary of My Death

Every year without knowing it I have passed the day
When the last first will wave to me
And the silence will set out
Tireless traveller
5 Like the beam of a lightless star

Then I will no longer
Find myself in life as in a strange garment
Surprised at the earth
And the love of one woman
10 And the shamelessness of men
As today writing after three days of rain
Hearing the wren sing and the falling cease
And bowing not knowing to what

[1977]

On the Old Way

After twelve years and a death
returning in August to see the end of summer
French skies and stacked roofs the same grays
silent train sliding south through the veiled morning
5 once more the stuccoed walls the sore
pavilions of the suburbs glimpses
of rivers known from other summers leaves
still green with chestnuts forming for their
only fall out of old dark branches and again
10 the nude hills come back and the sleepless
night travels along through the day as it
once did over and over for this was the way
almost home almost certain that it was
there almost believing that it could be
15 everything in spite of everything

[1992]

JAMES WRIGHT (1927–1980)

Autumn Begins in Martins Ferry, Ohio

In the Shreve High football stadium,
I think of Polacks nursing long beers in Tiltonsville,
And gray faces of Negroes in the blast furnace at Benwood,
And the ruptured night watchman of Wheeling Steel,
5   Dreaming of heroes.

All the proud fathers are ashamed to go home.
Their women cluck like starved pullets,
Dying for love.

Therefore,
10   Their sons grow suicidally beautiful
At the beginning of October,
And gallop terribly against each other's bodies.   [1963]

A Blessing

Just off the highway to Rochester, Minnesota,
Twilight bounds softly forth of the grass.
And the eyes of those two Indian ponies
Darken with kindness.
5   They have come gladly out of the willows
To welcome my friend and me.
We step over the barbed wire into the pasture
Where they have been grazing all day, alone.
They ripple tensely, they can hardly contain their happiness
10   That we have come.
They bow shyly as wet swans. They love each other.
There is no loneliness like theirs.
At home once more,
They begin munching the young tufts of spring in the darkness.
15   I would like to hold the slenderer one in my arms,
For she has walked over to me
And nuzzled my left hand.
She is black and white,
Her mane falls wild on her forehead,
20   And the light breeze moves me to caress her long ear
That is delicate as the skin over a girl's wrist.
Suddenly I realize
That if I stepped out of my body I would break
Into blossom.   [1963]

PHILIP LEVINE (b. 1928)

Keep Talking

If it ain't simply this, what is it?
he wanted to know, and she answered,

"If it ain't just this it ain't nothing,"
and they turned off the light, locked
the door, and went downstairs and out
of the hotel and started looking around
for a bar that would stay open all night.
In the first one she said, "When do
you close?" The bartender said, "What's
yours?" Then he got mad, her man,
because she'd asked politely, and so
he shouted, "Please answer the question."
Then he said, "How late are you open?"
"Until the law says we gotta close."
They went out into the early summer
which was still light even though
kids were probably already in bed.
The wind stood out against the sails
on the Sound, and the last small boats
were coming in on the blackening waters.
After a while he said, "Maybe we could
just eat and take a long walk or sit
somewhere for a while and say things."
She didn't answer. The wind had picked
up and just might have blown his words
into nothing. "Why don't we talk?"
he said. She turned and stared right
into his eyes, which were light blue
and seemed to be bulging out with tears.
He was unshaven and wore a wool cap
which he'd removed. "I've been here
before," he said, "as a boy I wanted
to talk about things, but there was no
one to talk to." "Talk to me," she said.
"I don't know what to say. I didn't
know then." "When?" she said. "When
I was a boy." So she explained that
being a kid was not knowing what to say
but that now he was a grown man. The lights
of the city were coming on, the high
ones in the tall buildings repeated
themselves in the still waters now as dark
as the night would ever be. He thought
about what she'd said and was sure
it had been different, that other kids
spoke about who they were or walked
with each other and said all the things
that jumbled in his head then and now.
He sat down on the curb and pressed
his face into his knees. She just stood
looking down at the shaven white back

of his neck, thin and childish, and she
thought, If it ain't this what is it?

ADRIENNE RICH (*b.* 1929)

From Twenty-one Love Poems

VI

Your small hands, precisely equal to my own—
only the thumb is larger, longer—in these hands
I could trust the world, or in many hands like these,
handling power-tools or steering-wheel
5   or touching a human face. . . . Such hands could turn
the unborn child rightways in the birth canal
or pilot the exploratory rescue-ship
through icebergs, or piece together
the fine, needle-like sherds of a great krater-cup
10   bearing on its sides
figures of ecstatic women striding
to the sibyl's den or the Eleusinian cave—
such hands might carry out an unavoidable violence
with such restraint, with such a grasp
15   of the range and limits of violence
that violence ever after would be obsolete.

XVI

Across a city from you, I'm with you,
just as an August night
moony, inlet-warm, seabathed, I watched you sleep,
the scrubbed, sheenless wood of the dressing-table
5   cluttered with our brushes, books, vials in the moonlight—
or a salt-mist orchard, lying at your side
watching red sunset through the screendoor of the cabin,
G minor Mozart on the tape-recorder,
falling asleep to the music of the sea.
10   This island of Manhattan is wide enough
for both of us, and narrow:
I can hear your breath tonight, I know how your face
lies upturned, the halflight tracing
your generous, delicate mouth
15   where grief and laughter sleep together.

XVIII

Rain on the West Side Highway,
red light at Riverside:
*the more I live the more I think
two people together is a miracle.*
5   You're telling the story of your life

for once, a tremor breaks the surface of your words.
The story of our lives becomes our lives.
Now you're in fugue across what some I'm sure
Victorian poet called the *salt estranging sea.*
10 Those are the words that come to mind.
I feel estrangement, yes. As I've felt dawn
pushing toward daybreak. Something: a cleft of light—?
Close between grief and anger, a space opens
where I am Adrienne alone. And growing colder.   [1978]

⁹/*salt estranging sea:* *refers to "The unplumb'd salt, estranging sea" in Matthew*
Arnold's "To Marguerite—Continued."

The Slides

Three dozen squares of light-inflicted glass
lie in a quarter-century's dust
under the skylight. I can show you this:
also a sprung couch spewing
5 desiccated mouse-havens, a revolving bookstand
rusted on its pivot, leaning
with books of an era: *Roosevelt vs Recovery*
The Mystery & Lure of Perfume   My Brother Was Mozart
I've had this attic in mind for years
10   Now you
who keep a lookout for
places like this, make your living
off things like this: You see, the books are rotting,
sunbleached, unfashionable
15 the furniture neglected past waste
but the lantern-slides—their story
could be sold, they could be a prize

                                   I want to see
your face when you start to sort them. You want
20 cloched hats of the Thirties, engagement portraits
with marcelled hair, maillots daring the waves,
my family album:
                         This is the razing of the spinal cord
by the polio virus
25 this, the lung-tissue kissed by the tubercle bacillus
this with the hooked shape is
the cell that leaks anemia to the next generation
Enlarged on a screen
they won't be quaint; they go on working; they still kill.   [1987]

What Kind of Times Are These

There's a place between two stands of trees where the grass grows uphill
and the old revolutionary road breaks off into shadows

near a meeting-house abandoned by the persecuted
who disappeared into those shadows.

5   I've walked there picking mushrooms at the edge of dread, but don't
      be fooled,
this isn't a Russian poem, this is not somewhere else but here,
our country moving closer to its own truth and dread,
its own ways of making people disappear.

I won't tell you where the place is, the dark mesh of the woods
10   meeting the unmarked strip of light—
ghost-ridden crossroads, leafmold paradise:
I know already who wants to buy it, sell it, make it disappear.

And I won't tell you where it is, so why do I tell you
anything? Because you still listen, because in times like these
15   to have you listen at all, it's necessary
to talk about trees.   [1991]

Author's note: The title is from Bertolt Brecht's poem "An Die Nachgeborenen" ("For Those Born Later"): What kind of times are these / When it's almost a crime to talk about trees / Because it means keeping still about so many evil deeds?

GARY SNYDER (*b.* 1930)

Why Log Truck Drivers Rise Earlier Than Students of Zen

In the high seat, before-dawn dark,
Polished hubs gleam
And the shiny diesel stack
Warms and flutters
5   Up the Tyler Road grade
To the logging on Poorman creek.
Thirty miles of dust.

There is no other life.   [1974]

Axe Handles

One afternoon the last week in April
Showing Kai how to throw a hatchet
One-half turn and it sticks in a stump.
He recalls the hatchet-head
5   Without a handle, in the shop
And go gets it, and wants it for his own.
A broken-off axe handle behind the door
Is long enough for a hatchet,
We cut it to length and take it
10 With the hatchet head
And working hatchet, to the wood block.

There I begin to shape the old handle
With the hatchet, and the phrase
First learned from Ezra Pound
15 Rings in my ears!
"When making an axe handle
        the pattern is not far off."
And I say this to Kai
"Look: We'll shape the handle
20 By checking the handle
Of the axe we cut with—"
And he sees. And I hear it again:
It's in Lu Ji's *Wên Fu,* fourth century
A.D. "Essay on Literature"—in the
25 Preface: "In making the handle
Of an axe
By cutting wood with an axe
The model is indeed near at hand."
My teacher Shih-hsiang Chen
30 Translated that and taught it years ago
And I see: Pound was an axe,
Chen was an axe, I am an axe
And my son a handle, soon
To be shaping again, model
35 And tool, craft of culture,
How we go on.   [1983]

DEREK WALCOTT (*b.* 1930)

Sea Grapes

That sail which leans on light,
tired of islands,
a schooner beating up the Caribbean

for home, could be Odysseus,
5 home-bound on the Aegean;
that father and husband's

longing, under gnarled sour grapes, is
like the adulterer hearing Nausicaa's name
in every gull's outcry.

10 This brings nobody peace. The ancient war
between obsession and responsibility
will never finish and has been the same

for the sea-wanderer or the one on shore
now wriggling on his sandals to walk home,
since Troy sighed its last flame,

and the blind giant's boulder heaved the trough
from whose ground-swell the great hexameters come
to the conclusions of exhausted surf.

The classics can console. But not enough. [1976]

Note: For a discussion of the backgrounds of this poem, see Appendix C, pp. 614–615.

SYLVIA PLATH (1932–1963)

Tulips

The tulips are too excitable, it is winter here.
Look how white everything is, how quiet, how snowed-in.
I am learning peacefulness, lying by myself quietly
As the light lies on these white walls, this bed, these hands.
5   I am nobody; I have nothing to do with explosions.
I have given my name and my day-clothes up to the nurses
And my history to the anaesthetist and my body to surgeons.

They have propped my head between the pillow and the sheet-cuff
Like an eye between two white lids that will not shut.
10 Stupid pupil, it has to take everything in.
The nurses pass and pass, they are no trouble,
They pass the way gulls pass inland in their white caps,
Doing things with their hands, one just the same as another,
So it is impossible to tell how many there are.

15 My body is a pebble to them, they tend it as water
Tends to the pebbles it must run over, smoothing them gently.
They bring me numbness in their bright needles, they bring me sleep.
Now I have lost myself I am sick of baggage—
My patent leather overnight case like a black pillbox,
20 My husband and child smiling out of the family photo;
Their smiles catch onto my skin, little smiling hooks.

I have let things slip, a thirty-year-old cargo boat
Stubbornly hanging on to my name and address.
They have swabbed me clear of my loving associations.
25 Scared and bare on the green plastic-pillowed trolley
I watched my tea-set, my bureaus of linen, my books
Sink out of sight, and the water went over my head.
I am a nun now, I have never been so pure.

I didn't want any flowers, I only wanted
30 To lie with my hands turned up and be utterly empty.
How free it is, you have no idea how free—
The peacefulness is so big it dazes you,
And it asks nothing, a name tag, a few trinkets.
It is what the dead close on, finally; I imagine them
35 Shutting their mouths on it, like a Communion tablet.

The tulips are too red in the first place, they hurt me.
Even through the gift paper I could hear them breathe
Lightly, through their white swaddlings, like an awful baby.
Their redness talks to my wound, it corresponds.
40 They are subtle: they seem to float, though they weigh me down,
Upsetting me with their sudden tongues and their colour,
A dozen red lead sinkers round my neck.

Nobody watched me before, now I am watched.
The tulips turn to me, and the window behind me
45 Where once a day the light slowly widens and slowly thins,
And I see myself, flat, ridiculous, a cut-paper shadow
Between the eye of the sun and the eyes of the tulips,
And I have no face, I have wanted to efface myself.
The vivid tulips eat my oxygen.

50 Before they came the air was calm enough,
Coming and going, breath by breath, without any fuss.
Then the tulips filled it up like a loud noise.
Now the air snags and eddies round them the way a river
Snags and eddies round a sunken rust-red engine.
55 They concentrate my attention, that was happy
Playing and resting without committing itself.

The walls, also, seem to be warming themselves.
The tulips should be behind bars like dangerous animals;
They are opening like the mouth of some great African cat,
60 And I am aware of my heart: it opens and closes
Its bowl of red blooms out of sheer love of me.
The water I taste is warm and salt, like the sea,
And comes from a country far away as health.   [1965]

Blackberrying

Nobody in the lane, and nothing, nothing but blackberries,
Blackberries on either side, though on the right mainly,
A blackberry alley, going down in hooks, and a sea
Somewhere at the end of it, heaving. Blackberries
5 Big as the ball of my thumb, and dumb as eyes
Ebon in the hedges, fat
With blue-red juices. These they squander on my fingers.
I had not asked for such a blood sisterhood; they must love me.
They accommodate themselves to my milkbottle, flattening their sides.

10 Overhead go the choughs in black, cacophonous flocks—
Bits of burnt paper wheeling in a blown sky.
Theirs is the only voice, protesting, protesting.
I do not think the sea will appear at all.
The high, green meadows are glowing, as if lit from within.
15 I come to one bush of berries so ripe it is a bush of flies,
Hanging their bluegreen bellies and their wing panes in a Chinese screen.

The honey-feast of the berries has stunned them; they believe in heaven.
One more hook, and the berries and bushes end.

The only thing to come now is the sea.
20 From between two hills a sudden wind funnels at me,
Slapping its phantom laundry in my face.
These hills are too green and sweet to have tasted salt.
I follow the sheep path between them. A last hook brings me
To the hills' northern face, and the face is orange rock
25 That looks out on nothing, nothing but a great space
Of white and pewter lights, and a din like silversmiths
Beating and beating at an intractable metal.   [1971]

Mirror

I am silver and exact. I have no preconceptions.
Whatever I see I swallow immediately
Just as it is, unmisted by love or dislike.
I am not cruel, only truthful—
5 The eye of a little god, four-cornered.
Most of the time I meditate on the opposite wall.
It is pink, with speckles. I have looked at it so long
I think it is a part of my heart. But it flickers.
Faces and darkness separate us over and over.

10 Now I am a lake. A woman bends over me,
Searching my reaches for what she really is.
Then she turns to those liars, the candles or the moon.
I see her back, and reflect it faithfully.
She rewards me with tears and an agitation of hands.
15 I am important to her. She comes and goes.
Each morning it is her face that replaces the darkness.
In me she has drowned a young girl, and in me an old woman
Rises toward her day after day, like a terrible fish.   [1971]

VERN RUTSALA (*b.* 1934)

Words

We had more than
we could use.
They embarrassed us,
our talk fuller than our
5 rooms. They named
nothing we could see—
dining room, study,
mantel piece, lobster
thermidor. They named
10 things you only

saw in movies—
the thin flicker Friday
nights that made us
feel empty in the cold
15 as we walked home
through our only great
abundance, snow.
This is why we said "ain't"
and "he don't."
20 We wanted words to fit
our cold linoleum,
our oil lamps, our
outhouse. We knew
better but it was wrong
25 to use a language
that named ghosts,
nothing you could touch.
We left such words at school
locked in books
30 where they belonged.
It was the vocabulary
of our lives that was
so thin. We knew this
and grew to hate
35 all the words that named
the vacancy of our rooms—
looking here we said
studio couch and saw cot;
looking there we said
40 *venetian blinds* and saw only the yard;
brick meant tarpaper,
fireplace meant wood stove.
And this is why we came to love
the double negative.   [1981]

MARK STRAND (b. 1934)

The Tunnel

A man has been standing
in front of my house
for days. I peek at him
from the living room
5 window and at night,
unable to sleep,
I shine my flashlight
down on the lawn.
He is always there.

10 After a while
I open the front door
just a crack and order
him out of my yard.
He narrows his eyes
15 and moans. I slam
the door and dash back
to the kitchen, then up
to the bedroom, then down.

I weep like a schoolgirl
20 and make obscene gestures
through the window. I
write large suicide notes
and place them so he
can read them easily.
25 I destroy the living
room furniture to prove
I own nothing of value.

When he seems unmoved
I decide to dig a tunnel
30 to a neighboring yard.
I seal the basement off
from the upstairs with
a brick wall. I dig hard
and in no time the tunnel
35 is done. Leaving my pick
and shovel below,

I come out in front of a house
and stand there too tired to
move or even speak, hoping
40 someone will help me.
I feel I'm being watched
and sometimes I hear
a man's voice,
but nothing is done
45 and I have been waiting for days.   [1964]

MARY OLIVER (*b.* 1935)

Shadows

Everyone knows the great energies running amok cast
terrible shadows, that each of the so-called
senseless acts has its thread looping
back through the world and into a human heart.
5   And meanwhile

the gold-trimmed thunder
wanders the sky; the river
may be filling the cellars of the sleeping town.
Cyclone, fire, and their merry cousins
10   bring us to grief—but these are the hours
with the old wooden-god faces;
we lift them to our shoulders like so many
black coffins, we continue walking
into the future. I don't mean
15   there are no bodies in the river,
or bones broken by the wind. I mean
everyone who has heard the lethal train-roar
of the tornado swears there was no mention ever
of any person, or reason—I mean
20   the waters rise without any plot upon
history, or even geography. Whatever
power of the earth rampages, we turn to it
dazed but anonymous eyes; whatever
the name of the catastrophe, it is never
25   the opposite of love.   [1986]

The Storm

Now through the white orchard my little dog
        romps, breaking the new snow
        with wild feet.
Running here running there, excited,
5   hardly able to stop, he leaps, he spins
until the white snow is written upon
        in large, exuberant letters,
a long sentence, expressing
        the pleasures of the body in this world.

10   Oh, I could not have said it better
        myself.   [1999]

LUCILLE CLIFTON (b. 1936)

homage to my hips

these hips are big hips.
they need space to
move around in.
they don't fit into little
5   petty places. these hips
are free hips.
they don't like to be held back.
these hips have never been enslaved,
they go where they want to go

10   they do what they want to do.
these hips are mighty hips.
these hips are magic hips.
i have known them
to put a spell on a man and
15   spin him like a top!   [1980]

C. K. WILLIAMS (b. 1936)

Tar

The first morning of Three Mile Island: those first disquieting,
   uncertain, mystifying hours.
All morning a crew of workmen have been tearing the old decrepit
   roof off our building,
and all morning, trying to distract myself, I've been wandering out
   to watch them
as they hack away the leaden layers of asbestos paper and disassemble
   the disintegrating drains.
5   After half a night of listening to the news, wondering how to know
   a hundred miles downwind
if and when to make a run for it and where, then a coming bolt awake
   at seven
when the roofers we've been waiting for since winter sent their ladders
   shrieking up our wall,
we still know less than nothing: the utility company continues making
   little of the accident,
the slick federal spokesmen still have their evasions in some semblance
   of order.
10   Surely we suspect now we're being lied to, but in the meantime,
   there are the roofers,
setting winch-frames, sledging rounds of tar apart, and there I am, on
   the curb across, gawking.

I never realized what brutal work it is, how matter-of-factly and
   harrowingly dangerous.
The ladders flex and quiver, things skid from the edge, the materials
   are bulky and recalcitrant.
When the rusty, antique nails are levered out, their heads pull off; the
   under-roofing crumbles.
15   Even the battered little furnace, roaring along as patient as a donkey,
   chokes and clogs,
a dense, malignant smoke shoots up, and someone has to fiddle with a
   cock, then hammer it,

*On March 28, 1979, a nuclear accident at the Three Mile Island reactor at
Middletown, Pennsylvania, caused widespread alarm.*

before the gush and stench will deintensify, the dark, Dantean broth
wearily subside.
In its crucible, the stuff looks bland, like licorice, spill it, though, on
your boots or coveralls,
it sears, and everything is permeated with it, the furnace gunked with
burst and half-burst bubbles,

20   the men themselves so completely slashed and mucked they seem
almost from another realm, like trolls.
When they take their break, they leave their brooms standing at
attention in the asphalt pails,
work gloves clinging like Brer Rabbit to the bitten shafts, and they
slouch along the precipitous lip,
the enormous sky behind them, the heavy noontime air alive with
shimmers and mirages.

Sometime in the afternoon I had to go inside: the advent of our vigil
was upon us.
25   However much we didn't want to, however little we would do
about it, we'd understood:
we were going to perish of all this, if not now, then soon, if not soon,
then someday.
Someday, some final generation, hysterically aswarm beneath an
atmosphere as unrelenting as rock,
would rue us all, anathematize our earthly comforts, curse our surfeits
and submissions.
I think I know, though I might rather not, why my roofers stay so clear
to me and why the rest,
30   the terror of that time, the reflexive disbelief and distancing, all we
should hold on to, dims so.
I remember the president in his absurd protective booties, looking
absolutely unafraid, the fool.
I remember a woman on the front page glaring across the misty
Susquehanna at those looming stacks.
But, more vividly, the men, silvered with glitter from the shingles,
clinging like starlings beneath the eaves.
Even the leftover carats of tar in the gutter, so black they seemed to
suck the light out of the air.
35   By nightfall kids had come across them: every sidewalk on the
block was scribbled with obscenities and hearts.   [1983]

CHARLES SIMIC (*b.* 1938)

Fear

Fear passes from man to man
Unknowing,
As one leaf passes its shudder
To another.

⁵ All at once the whole tree is trembling
and there is no sign of the wind.   [1967]

Fork

This strange thing must have crept
Right out of hell.
It resembles a bird's foot
Worn around the cannibal's neck.
⁵ As you hold it in your hand,
As you stab with it into a piece of meat,
It is possible to imagine the rest of the bird:
Its head which like your fist
Is large, bald, beakless and blind.   [1969]

Classic Ballroom Dances

Grandmothers who wring the necks
Of chickens; old nuns
With names like Theresa, Marianne,
Who pull schoolboys by the ear;

⁵ The intricate steps of pickpockets
Working the crowd of the curious
At the scene of an accident; the slow shuffle
Of the evangelist with a sandwich-board;

The hesitation of the early morning customer
¹⁰ Peeking through the window-grille
Of a pawnshop; the weave of a little kid
Who is walking to school with eyes closed;

And the ancient lovers, cheek to cheek,
On the dancefloor of the Union Hall,
¹⁵ Where they also hold charity raffles
On rainy Monday nights of an eternal November.   [1980]

Slaughterhouse Flies

Evenings, they ran their bloody feet
Over the pages of my schoolbooks.
With eyes closed, I can still hear
The trees on our street
⁵ Saying a moody farewell to summer,

And someone, under our window, recalling
The silly old cows hesitating,
Growing suddenly suspicious
Just as the blade drops down on them.   [1996]

MARGARET ATWOOD (*b.* 1939)

Siren Song

This is the one song everyone
would like to learn: the song
that is irresistible:

the song that forces men
5   to leap overboard in squadrons
even though they see the beached skulls

the song nobody knows
because anyone who has heard it
is dead, and the others can't remember.

10   Shall I tell you the secret
and if I do, will you get me
out of this bird suit?

I don't enjoy it here
squatting on this island
15   looking picturesque and mythical

with these two feathery maniacs,
I don't enjoy singing
this trio, fatal and valuable.

I will tell the secret to you,
20   to you, only to you.
Come closer. This song

is a cry for help: Help me!
Only you, only you can,
you are unique

25   at last. Alas
it is a boring song
but it works every time.   [1976]

Half women, half birds, the three Sirens are described by Homer in the Odyssey as living on an island where they sing so enchantingly that they lure mariners to their destruction.

STEPHEN DUNN (*b.* 1939)

At the Smithville Methodist Church

It was supposed to be Arts & Crafts for a week,
but when she came home
with the "Jesus Saves" button, we knew what art
was up, what ancient craft.

5   She liked her little friends. She liked the songs
    they sang when they weren't
    twisting and folding paper into dolls.
    What could be so bad?

    Jesus had been a good man, and putting faith
10 in good men was what
    we had to do to stay this side of cynicism,
    that other sadness.

    O.K., we said. One week. But when she came home
    singing "Jesus loves me,
15 the Bible tells me so," it was time to talk.
    Could we say Jesus

    doesn't love you? Could I tell her the Bible
    is a great book certain people use
    to make you feel bad? We sent her back
20 without a word.

    It had been so long since we believed, so long
    since we needed Jesus
    as our nemesis and friend, that we thought he was
    sufficiently dead,

25 that our children would think of him like Lincoln
    or Thomas Jefferson.
    Soon it became clear to us: you can't teach disbelief
    to a child,

    only wonderful stories, and we hadn't a story
30 nearly as good.
    On parents' night there were the Arts & Crafts
    all spread out

    like appetizers. Then we took our seats
    in the church
35 and the children sang a song about the Ark,
    and Hallelujah

    and one in which they had to jump up and down
    for Jesus.
    I can't remember ever feeling so uncertain
40 about what's comic, what's serious.

    Evolution is magical but devoid of heroes.
    You can't say to your child
    "Evolution loves you." The story stinks
    of extinction and nothing

45 exciting happens for centuries. I didn't have
    a wonderful story for my child
    and she was beaming. All the way home in the car
    she sang the songs,

occasionally standing up for Jesus.
50   There was nothing to do
but drive, ride it out, sing along
in silence.   [1986]

SEAMUS HEANEY (*b.* 1939)

Death of a Naturalist

All year the flax-dam festered in the heart
Of the townland; green and heavy headed
Flax had rotted there, weighted down by huge sods.
Daily it sweltered in the punishing sun.
5   Bubbles gargled delicately, bluebottles
Wove a strong gauze of sound around the smell.
There were dragon-flies, spotted butterflies,
But best of all was the warm thick slobber
Of frogspawn that grew like clotted water
10   In the shade of the banks. Here, every spring
I would fill jampotfuls of the jellied
Specks to range on window-sills at home,
On shelves at school, and wait and watch until
The fattening dots burst into nimble-
15   Swimming tadpoles. Miss Walls would tell us how
The daddy frog was called a bullfrog
And how he croaked and how the mammy frog
Laid hundreds of little eggs and this was
Frogspawn. You could tell the weather by frogs too
20   For they were yellow in the sun and brown
In rain.

     Then one hot day when fields were rank
With cowdung in the grass the angry frogs
Invaded the flax-dam; I ducked through hedges
25   To a coarse croaking that I had not heard
Before. The air was thick with a bass chorus.
Right down the dam gross-bellied frogs were cocked
On sods; their loose necks pulsed like sails. Some hopped:
The slap and plop were obscene threats. Some sat
30   Poised like mud grenades, their blunt heads farting.
I sickened, turned, and ran. The great slime kings
Were gathered there for vengeance and I knew
That if I dipped my hand the spawn would clutch it.   [1966]

Follower

My father worked with a horse-plough,
His shoulders globed like a full sail strung
Between the shafts and the furrow.
The horses strained at his clicking tongue.

5   An expert. He would set the wing
And fit the bright steel-pointed sock.
The sod rolled over without breaking.
At the headrig, with a single pluck

Of reins, the sweating team turned round
10   And back into the land. His eye
Narrowed and angled at the ground,
Mapping the furrow exactly.

I stumbled in his hobnailed wake,
Fell sometimes on the polished sod;
15   Sometimes he rode me on his back
Dipping and rising to his plod.

I wanted to grow up and plough,
To close one eye, stiffen my arm.
All I ever did was follow
20   In his broad shadow round the farm.

I was a nuisance, tripping, falling,
Yapping always. But today
It is my father who keeps stumbling
Behind me, and will not go away.   [1966]

Damson

Gules and cement dust. A matte tacky blood
On the bricklayer's knuckles, like the damson stain
That seeped through his packed lunch.
                            A full hod stood
5   Against the mortared wall, his big bright trowel
In his left hand (for once) was pointing down
As he marvelled at his right, held high and raw:
King of the castle, scaffold-stepper, shown
Bleeding to the world.
10   Wound that I saw
In glutinous colour fifty years ago—
Damson as omen, weird, a dream to read—
Is weeping with the held-at-arm's-length dead
From everywhere and nowhere, here and now.

                •

15   Over and over, the slur, the scrape and mix
As he trowelled and retrowelled and laid down
Courses of glum mortar. Then the bricks
Jiggled and settled, tocked and tapped in line.
I loved especially the trowel's shine,
20   Its edge and apex always coming clean
And brightening itself by mucking in.
It looked light but felt heavy as a weapon,
Yet when he lifted it there was no strain.

It was all point and skim and float and glisten
25 Until he washed and lapped it tight in sacking
Like a cult blade that had to be kept hidden.

•

Ghosts with their tongues out for a lick of blood
Are crowding up the ladder, all unhealed,
And some of them still rigged in bloody gear.
30 Drive them back to the doorstep or the road
Where they lay in their own blood once, in the hot
Nausea and last gasp of dear life.
Trowel-wielder, woundie, drive them off
Like Odysseus in Hades lashing out
35 With his sword that dug the trench and cut the throat
Of the sacrificial lamb.
                              But not like him—
Builder, not sacker, your shield the mortar board—
Drive them back to the wine-dark taste of home,
40 The smell of damsons simmering in a pot,
Jam ladled thick and steaming down the sunlight.   [1996]

TED KOOSER (*b.* 1939)

Abandoned Farmhouse

He was a big man, says the size of his shoes
on a pile of broken dishes by the house;
a tall man too, says the length of the bed
in an upstairs room; and a good, God-fearing man,
5 says the Bible with a broken back
on the floor below the window, dusty with sun;
but not a man for farming, say the fields
cluttered with boulders and the leaky barn.

A woman lived with him, says the bedroom wall
10 papered with lilacs and the kitchen shelves
covered with oilcloth, and they had a child,
says the sandbox made from a tractor tire.
Money was scarce, say the jars of plum preserves
and canned tomatoes sealed in the cellar hole.
15 And the winters cold, say the rags in the window frames.
It was lonely here, says the narrow country road.

Something went wrong, says the empty house
in the weed-choked yard. Stones in the fields
say he was not a farmer; the still-sealed jars
20 in the cellar say she left in a nervous haste.
And the child? Its toys are strewn in the yard
like branches after a storm—a rubber cow,

a rusty tractor with a broken plow,
a doll in overalls. Something went wrong, they say.   [1980]

That Was I

I was that older man you saw sitting
in a confetti of yellow light and falling leaves
on a bench at the empty horseshoe courts
in Thayer, Nebraska—brown jacketed, soft cap,
5   wiping my glasses. I had noticed, of course,
that the rows of sunken horseshoe pits
with their rusty stakes, grown over with grass,
were like old graves, but I was not letting
my thoughts go there. Instead I was looking
10 with hope to a grapevine draped over
a fence in a neighborhood yard, and knowing
that I could hold on. Yes, that was I.

And that was I, the round-shouldered man
you saw that afternoon in Rising City
15 as you drove past the abandoned Mini Golf,
fists deep in my pockets, nose dripping,
my cap pulled down against the wind
as I walked the miniature Main Street
peering into the child-sized plywood store,
20 the poor red school, the faded barn, thinking
that not even in such an abbreviated world
with no more than its little events—the snap
of a grasshopper's wing against a paper cup—
could a person control this life. Yes, that was I.

25 And that was I you spotted that evening
just before dark, in a weedy cemetery
west of Staplehurst, down on one knee
as if trying to make out the name on a stone,
some lonely old man, you thought, come there
30 to pity himself in the reliable sadness
of grass among graves, but that was not so.
Instead I had found in its perfect web
a handsome black and yellow spider
pumping its legs to try to shake my footing
35 as if I were a gift, an enormous moth
that it could snare and eat. Yes, that was I.   [2004]

ROBERT PINSKY (b. 1940)

A Woman

Thirty years ago: gulls keen in the blue,
Pigeons mumble on the sidewalk, and an old, fearful woman
Takes a child on a long walk, stopping at the market

To order a chicken, the child forming a sharp memory
Of sawdust, small curls of droppings, the imbecile
Panic of the chickens, their affronted glare.

They walk in the wind along the ocean: at first,
Past cold zinc railings and booths and arcades
Still shuttered in March; then, along high bluffs

In the sun, the coarse grass combed steadily
By a gusting wind that draws a line of tears
Toward the boy's temples as he looks downward,

At the loud combers booming over the jetties,
Rushing and in measured rhythm receding on the beach.
He leans over. Everything that the woman says is a warning,

Or a superstition; even the scant landmarks are like
Tokens of risk or rash judgment—drowning,
Sexual assault, fatal or crippling diseases:

The monotonous surf; wooden houses mostly boarded up;
Fishermen with heavy lines cast in the surf;
Bright tidal pools stirred to flashing

From among the jetties by the tireless salty wind.
She dreams frequently of horror and catastrophe—
Mourners, hospitals, and once, a whole family

Sitting in chairs in her own room, corpse-gray,
With throats cut; who were they? Vivid,
The awful lips of the wounds in the exposed necks,

Herself helpless in the dream, desperate,
At a loss what to do next, pots seething
And boiling over onto their burners, in her kitchen.

They have walked all the way out past the last bluffs,
As far as Port-Au-Peck—the name a misapprehension
Of something Indian that might mean "mouth"

Or "flat" or "bluefish," or all three: Ocean
On the right, and the brackish wide inlet
Of the river on the left; and in between,

Houses and landings and the one low road
With its ineffectual sea-wall of rocks
That the child walks, and that hurricanes

Send waves crashing over the top of, river
And ocean coming violently together
In a house-cracking exhilaration of water.

In Port-Au-Peck the old woman has a prescription filled,
And buys him a milk-shake. Pouring the last froth
From the steel shaker into his glass, he happens

To think about the previous Halloween:
Holding her hand, watching the parade
In his chaps, boots, guns and sombrero.

A hay-wagon of older children in cowboy gear
50   Trundled by, the strangers inviting him up
To ride along for the six blocks to the beach—

Her holding him back with both arms, crying herself,
Frightened at his force, and he vowing never,
Never to forgive her, not as long as he lived.   [1984]

BILLY COLLINS (*b.* 1941)

Embrace

You know the parlor trick.
Wrap your arms around your own body
and from the back it looks like
someone is embracing you,
5   her hands grasping your shirt,
her fingernails teasing your neck.

From the front it is another story.
You never looked so alone,
your crossed elbows and screwy grin.
10   You could be waiting for a tailor
to fit you for a straitjacket,
one that would hold you really tight.   [1988]

The Dead

The dead are always looking down on us, they say,
while we are putting on our shoes or making a sandwich,
they are looking down through the glass-bottom boats of heaven
as they row themselves slowly through eternity.

5   They watch the tops of our heads moving below on earth,
and when we lie down in a field or on a couch,
drugged perhaps by the hum of a warm afternoon,
they think we are looking back at them,

which makes them lift their oars and fall silent
10   and wait, like parents, for us close our eyes.   [1991]

WILLIAM MATTHEWS (1942–1997)

Mood Indigo

From the porch; from the hayrick where her prickled
brothers hid and chortled and slurped into their young pink
lungs the ash-blond dusty air that lay above the bales

like low clouds; and from the squeak and suck
5   of the well-pump and from the glove of rust it implied
on her hand; from the dress parade of clothes

in her mothproofed closet; from her tiny Philco
with its cracked speaker and Sunday litany
(Nick Carter, The Shadow, The Green Hornet, Sky King);

10   from the loosening bud of her body; from hunger,
as they say, and from reading; from the finger
she used to dial her own number; from the dark

loam of the harrowed fields and from the very sky;
it came from everywhere. Which is to say it was
15   always there, and that it came from nowhere.

It evaporated with the dew, and at dusk when dark
spread in the sky like water in a blotter, it spread, too,
but it came back and curdled with milk and stung

with nettles. It was in the bleat of the lamb, the way
20   a clapper is in a bell, and in the raucous, scratchy
gossip of the crows. It walked with her to school and lay

with her to sleep and at last she was well pleased.
If she were to sew, she would prick her finger with it.
If she were to bake, it would linger in the kitchen

25   like an odor snarled in the deepest folds of childhood.
It became her dead pet, her lost love, the baby sister
blue and dead at birth, the chill headwaters of the river

that purled and meandered and ran and ran until
it issued into her, as into a sea, and then she was its
30   and it was wholly hers. She kept to her room, as we

learned to say, but now and then she'd come down
and pass through the kitchen, and the screen door
would close behind her with no more sound than

an envelope being sealed, and she'd walk for hours
35   in the fields like a lithe blue rain, and end up
in the barn, and one of us would go and bring her in.   [1989]

SHARON OLDS (*b.* 1942)

The Death of Marilyn Monroe

The ambulance men touched her cold
body, lifted it, heavy as iron,
onto the stretcher, tried to close the
mouth, closed the eyes, tied the
5   arms to the sides, moved a caught

strand of hair, as if it mattered,
saw the shape of her breasts, flattened by
gravity, under the sheet,
carried her, as if it were she,
down the steps.

These men were never the same. They went out
afterwards, as they always did,
for a drink or two, but they could not meet
each other's eyes.
                        Their lives took
a turn—one had nightmares, strange
pains, impotence, depression. One did not
like his work, his wife looked
different, his kids. Even death
seemed different to him—a place where she
would be waiting,

and one found himself standing at night
in the doorway to a room of sleep, listening to a
woman breathing, just an ordinary
woman
breathing.   [1983]

Physics

Her first puzzle had three pieces,
she'd take the last piece, and turn it,
and lower it in, like a sewer-lid,
flush with the street. The bases of the frames
were like wooden fur, guard-hairs sticking out of the
pelt. I'd set one on the floor and spread
the pieces out around it. It makes me
groan to think of Red Riding Hood's hood
a single, scarlet, pointed piece, how
long since I have seen her. Later, panthers,
500 pieces, and an Annunciation,
1000 pieces, we would gaze, on our elbows,
into its gaps. Now she tells me
that if I were sitting in a twenty-foot barn,
with the doors open at either end,
and a fifty-foot ladder hurtled through the barn
at the speed of light, there would be a moment
—after the last rung was inside the barn
and before the first rung came out the other end—
when the whole fifty-foot ladder would be
inside the twenty-foot barn, and I believe her,
I have thought her life was inside my life
like that. When she reads the college catalogues, I
look away and hum. I have not grown up

25 yet, I have lived as my daughter's mother
the way I had lived as my mother's daughter,
inside her life. I have not been born yet.   [1996]

LOUISE GLÜCK (b. 1943)

The School Children

The children go forward with their little satchels.
And all morning the mothers have labored
to gather the late apples, red and gold,
like words of another language.

5 And on the other shore
are those who wait behind great desks
to receive these offerings.

How orderly they are—the nails
on which the children hang
10 their overcoats of blue or yellow wool.

And the teachers shall instruct them in silence
and the mothers shall scour the orchards for a way out,
drawing to themselves the gray limbs of the fruit trees
bearing so little ammunition.   [1975]

Mock Orange

It is not the moon, I tell you.
It is these flowers
lighting the yard

I hate them.
5 I hate them as I hate sex,
the man's mouth
sealing my mouth, the man's
paralyzing body—

and the cry that always escapes,
10 the low, humiliating
premise of union—

In my mind tonight
I hear the question and pursuing answer
fused in one sound
15 that mourns and mounts and then
is split into the old selves,
the tired antagonisms. Do you see?
We are made fools of.
And the scent of mock orange
20 drifts through the window.

How can I rest?
How can I be content
where there is still
that odor in the world.   [1985]

ELLEN BRYANT VOIGT (b. 1943)

The Starveling

Hunger is a stone in her belly
against which she sharpens her angular body.
Lithe in the fourth month of fasting,
she rises from bed to the full-length mirror;
5 nude, examines every betrayal—
a palmful of breast,
a softening at the hips or collarbones.

Her father sits in the study sick with rage.
Before him, the exposed lawn unfolds
10 like an album: there, elf-child with dog;
langorous under the beech in peau-de-soie;
their sly games of tag and wrestle.

It is summer. In the other wing of the house
her mother is crooning, is wielding
15 ratatouille with its thick juice and odor.   [1978]

MARGARET BENBOW (b. 1944)

Crazy Arms: Earlene Remembers

Though I grew up to marry a snowman,
though I look like a glass of milk,

once I was the queen of consuming passions:
and in my mind distant hotbeds
5 buck and bloom with big-bear hugs, pink
tulip skin, and the edible wild plants
of lips and ears. Oh, Dave may have been
just a lord of the streets,
but he was Baby Child to me.
10 He would rub his harsh curls
against my neck, and tug with excellent teeth
at the peach chemise made for big tomatoes.
I breathed beastly suggestions
in his marvelously ready ear . . .
15 How happy I was, in his clutches!
Words failed us, we fell into broken English

and then to the searing nubs of vowels,
Ahh, ee, I, ohh, you.

A night lush with stars.
20 "Look at me, baby."
I kissed him so hard my nose bled,
and he said: "Welcome to rock and roll."

[1997]

JEANNE MURRAY WALKER (*b*. 1944)

Studying Physics with My Daughter

For years now I have heard the cracking of
my memory, reluctantly falling apart like an
ancient building. At first a little cement dust,

then portions of the wall—The Natural Resources
5 Of Brazil, the Shape Of Utah—nothing,
in the beginning, that left me structurally unsound,

but it grew to a steady pouring—Co-efficients,
Participles, and Tammany Hall—lying in
the chilly basement of my mind mixed up together.

10 This went on for years, no matter how much
I paid bricklayers an hour, the slow habits of love
like shadows sliding across the yard each day,

and putting children to bed every night like
the relentless caress of wind on the foundation.
15 They wore me down to vague certainties.

That's why, when Molly came in her blue flannel
shirt and baggy jeans, holding her physics book,
I was surprised. I hardly recognized my child

rolling up her sleeves in the sharp daylight,
20 hauling enormous words into the sun
slapping them together with new mortar

so fast I could barely get the idea. Do you know,
she asks, why water climbs a paper napkin?
She says water and the napkin both have Partial Charges.

25 She says the word *Cohesion* and the word *Adhesion*.
Her words fall into the rubble in my poor memory.
I tell her I used to believe in physics.

But experience has taught me what makes water
climb a paper napkin. The water loves the napkin
30 and longs for it. My daughter turns her brilliant eyes

on me. She is the only teacher who can save me.
She goes to work, digging in the rubble.

[1990]

WENDY COPE (*b.* 1945)

Some More Light Verse

You have to try. You see a shrink.
You learn a lot. You read. You think.
Your struggle to improve your looks.
You meet some men. You write some books.
5 You eat good food. You give up junk.
You do not smoke. You don't get drunk.
You take up yoga, walk and swim.
And nothing works. The outlook's grim.
You don't know what to do. You cry.
10 You're running out of things to try.

You blow your nose. You see the shrink.
You walk. You give up food and drink.
You fall in love. You make a plan.
You struggle to improve your man.
15 And nothing works. The outlook's grim.
You go to yoga, cry, and swim.
You eat and drink. You give up looks.
You struggle to improve your books.
You cannot see the point. You sigh.
20 You do not smoke. You have to try.

                 [1992]

B. H. FAIRCHILD (*b.* 1945)

Brazil

This is for Elton Wayne Showalter, redneck surrealist
who, drunk, one Friday night, tried to hold up the local 7-Eleven
with a caulking gun, and who, when Melinda Bozell boasted
that she would never let a boy touch her "down there," said
5 "Down there? You mean, like Brazil?"
           Oh, Elton Wayne,
with your silver-toed turquoise-on-black boots and Ford Fairlane
dragging, in a ribbon of sparks, its tailpipe down Main Street
Saturday nights, you dreamed of Brazil and other verdant lands,
but the southern hemisphere remained for all those desert years
10 a vast mirage shimmering on the horizon of what one might call
your mind, following that one ugly night at the Snack Shack
when, drunk again, you peed on your steaming radiator
to cool it down and awoke at the hospital, groin empurpled
from electric shock and your pathetic maleness swollen
15 like a bruised tomato. You dumb bastard, betting a week's wages
on the trifecta at Raton, then in ecstasy tossing the winning ticket
into the air and watching it float on an ascending breeze
with the lightness and supple dip and rise of a Bach passacaglia
out over the New Mexico landscape forever and beyond: gone.

20 The tears came down, but the spirit rose late on Sunday night
on a stepladder knocking the middle letters from FREEMAN GLASS
to announce unlimited sexual opportunities in purple neon
for all your friends driving Kansas Avenue as we did each night
lonely and boredom-racked and hungering for someone like you,
25 Elton Wayne, brilliantly at war in that flat, treeless country
against maturity, right-thinking, and indeed intelligence
in all its bland, local guises, so that reading the announcement
in the hometown paper of your late marriage to Melinda Bozell
with a brief honeymoon at the Best Western in Junction City,
30 I know that you have finally arrived, in Brazil, and the Kansas
that surrounds you is an endless sea of possiblility, genius, love.   [2003]

KAY RYAN (*b.* 1945)

Blandeur

If it please God,
let less happen.
Even out Earth's
rondure, flatten
5 Eiger, blanden
the Grand Canyon.
Make valleys
slightly higher,
widen fissures
10 to arable land,
remand your
terrible glaciers
and silence
their calving,
15 halving or doubling
all geographical features
toward the mean.
Unlean against our hearts.
Withdraw your grandeur
20 from these parts.   [2000]

THOMAS LUX (*b.* 1946)

Cellar Stairs

It's rickety down to the dark.
Old skates, long-bladed, hang by leather laces
on your left and want to slash your throat,
but they can't, they can't, being only skates.

5   On a shelf above, tools: shears,
three-pronged weed hacker, ice pick,
poison—rats and bugs—and on the landing,
halfway down, a keg of roofing nails
you don't want to fall face first into,

10   no, you don't. To your right,
a fuse box with its side-switch—a slot machine,
on a good day, or the one the warden pulls,
on a bad. Against the wall,
on nearly every stair, one boot, no two
15   together, no pair, as if the dead
went off, short-legged or long, to where they go,
which is down these steps,
at the bottom of which is a swollen,

humming, huge white freezer
20   big enough for many bodies—
of children, at least. And this
is where you're sent each night
for the frozen bag of beans
or peas or broccoli
25   that lies beside the slab
of meat you'll eat for dinner,
each countless childhood meal your last.

[1990]

MARILYN NELSON (b. 1946)

Epithalamium and Shivaree

for Linda and Debbie

All Cana was abuzz next day with stories:
Some said it had a sad aftertaste; some said
its sweetness made them ache with thirst.
Years later those who had been there
5   spoke of it with closed eyes, and swayed
like the last slow-dance of the prom.
The village children poked each other's ribs
when they reeled past, still drunk at eighty.

Lovers know what that drunkenness is:
10   It makes a festive sacrament of praise
for the One who loans us each other
and this too-brief time.
One sip of the wine of Cana
and lovers become fools. And fools lovers.
15   *The willows are drunk tralala; they shimmy*
in the silly wind of Spring,

lovers sing noisily. With a little pink parasol
a lover pedals out to the halfway point on the wire.
Below, a silver thread of river. She waves, blows kisses,
20   wavers, and oops,
her unicycle disappears into mystery.
Her face mimes our gasp.
We hear an unseen, slide-whistle chorus.
She sings: *Tralala, the willows are drunk;*

25   *they shimmy in the silly April wind.*
And I'm just a kitten in catnip, a pup
rollin' in some ambrosial doggie cologne.
Why settle for less than rapture?
Your pulse against my lips, your solitude
30   *snoring next to mine. The wine we drink from each other.*
She leaps. And now there are two of them out there,
jitterbugging on shimmering air.   [1986]

How I Discovered Poetry

It was like soul-kissing, the way the words
filled my mouth as Mrs. Purdy read from her desk.
All the other kids zoned an hour ahead to 3:15,
but Mrs. Purdy and I wandered lonely as clouds borne
5   by a breeze off Mount Parnassus. She must have seen
the darkest eyes in the room brim: The next day
she gave me a poem she'd chosen especially for me
to read to the all except for me white class.
She smiled when she told me to read it, smiled harder,
10   said oh yes I could. She smiled harder and harder
until I stood and opened my mouth to banjo playing
darkies, pickaninnies, disses and dats. When I finished
my classmates stared at the floor. We walked silent
to the buses, awed by the power of words.   [1990]

LAWRENCE RAAB (*b.* 1946)

Learning How to Write

The whole thing looks like things that
would show up anywhere around here.
                    —*Derek, Grade 5*

It's cold outside, or it's dark.
It's raining, or it could be.
Why not begin with that?
In the bright sun the trees
5   are perfectly still,
which only a moment ago thrashed about

in the storm. Similar things
happen elsewhere. The sky
is a sheet of blue paper, which may lead
10 to an ocean, or sorrow.
There are streets and pathways,
and people stroll along them.
Or just yourself. Or your father.
It's years ago and he's happy
15 having learned he's becoming your father.
You see how easy it is. Things
show up, and you gather them together,
things that look like anything
that might be around here.
20 Now you're walking home from school,
the day the dog chased you
into the street and the car
almost hit you. And it's possible now
to see the funeral, your small coffin
25 (because, in fact, you were hit)
the way they lower it so carefully,
the way they don't start
shoveling the dirt on top of you
until the family has left.
30 It's cold outside, and it's dark.
But you can follow them home, you can be
a ghost in the corner of your own room,
and at night you can listen, and find out
how much they really miss you.
35 And after you've heard enough
you might decide to be back
in your body, waiting on the corner
by the curb, so when the dog comes out
you turn on him with the stick
40 you've given yourself, except
this time maybe it should be raining,
not hard but steadily, and all the cars
are moving very slowly and very carefully
since at any moment and for no reason
45 someone might run out there.

[1993]

YUSEF KOMUNYAKAA (b. 1947)

Facing It

My black face fades,
hiding inside the black granite.
I said I wouldn't,
dammit: No tears.

5   My stone. I'm flesh.
My clouded reflection eyes me
like a bird of prey, the profile of night
slanted against morning. I turn
this way—the stone lets me go.
10   I turn that way—I'm inside
the Vietnam Veterans Memorial
again, depending on the light
to make a difference.
I go down the 58,022 names,
15   half-expecting to find
my own in letters like smoke.
I touch the name Andrew Johnson;
I see the booby trap's white flash.
Names shimmer on a woman's blouse
20   but when she walks away
the names stay on the wall.
Brushstrokes flash, a red bird's
wings cutting across my stare.
The sky. A plane in the sky.
25   A white vet's image floats
closer to me, then his pale eyes
look through mine. I'm a window.
He's lost his right arm
inside the stone. In the black mirror
30   a woman's trying to erase names:
No, she's brushing a boy's hair.

                                                             [1988]

ROBERT B. SHAW (b. 1947)

Shut In

Like many of us, born too late,
(like all of us, fenced in by fate),
    the late October fly
    will fondly live and die

5   insensible of the allure
of carrion or cow manure.
    Withindoors day and night,
    propelled by appetite,

he circles with approving hums
10   a morning's manna-fall of crumbs
    hoping to find a smear
    of jelly somewhere near.

In such an easeful habitat
while autumn wanes he waxes fat

15   and langorous, but not
      enough to let the swat

      of hasty, rolled-up magazine
      eliminate him from the scene.
            Outside, the air is chill.
20   Inside, he's hard to kill.

      Patrolling with adhesive feet
      the ceiling under which we eat,
            he captures at a glance
            the slightest threat or chance,

25   and flaunts the facets of his eyes
      that make him prince of household spies.
            And as he watches, we,
            if we look up, will see

      a life of limits, like our own,
30   enclosed within a temperate zone,
            not harsh, not insecure,
            no challenge to endure,

      but yet, with every buzz of need,
      by trifles running out of speed.
35   One day he will be gone
            Then the real cold comes on.   [1994]

AMY UYEMATSU (b. 1947)

Deliberate

      So by sixteen we move in packs
      learn to strut and slide
      in deliberate lowdown rhythm
      talk in a syn/co/pa/ted beat
5   because we want so bad
      to be cool, never to be mistaken
      for white, even when we leave
      these rowdier L.A. streets—
      remember how we paint our eyes
10   like gangsters
      flash our legs in nylons
      sassy black high heels
      or two inch zippered boots
      stack them by the door at night
15   next to Daddy's muddy gardening shoes.   [1992]

R. S. GWYNN (*b.* 1948)

Body Bags

I

Let's hear it for Dwayne Coburn, who was small
And mean without a single saving grace
Except for stealing—home from second base
Or out of teammates' lockers, it was all
5   The same to Dwayne. The Pep Club candy sale,
However, proved his downfall. He was held
Briefly on various charges, then expelled
And given a choice: enlist or go or jail.

He finished basic and came home from Bragg
10 For Christmas on his reassignment leave
With one prize in his pack he thought unique,
Which went off prematurely New Year's Eve.
The student body got the folded flag
And flew it in his memory for a week.

II

15 Good pulling guards were scarce in high school ball.
The ones who had the weight were usually slow
As lumber trucks. A scaled-down wild man, though,
Like Dennis "Wampus" Peterson, could haul
His ass around right end for me to slip
20 Behind his blocks. Played college ball a year—
Red-shirted when they yanked his scholarship
Because he majored, so he claimed, in Beer.

I saw him one last time. He'd added weight
Around the neck, used words like "grunt" and "slope,"
25 And said he'd swap his Harley and his dope
And both balls for a 4-F knee like mine.
This happened in the spring of '68.
He hanged himself in 1969.

III

Jay Swinney did a great Roy Orbison
30 Impersonation once at Lyn Rock Park,
Lip-synching to "It's Over" in his dark
Glasses beside the jukebox. He was one
Who'd want no better for an epitaph
Than he was good with girls and charmed them by
35 Opening his billfold to a photograph:
Big brother. The Marine. Who didn't die.

He comes to mind, years from that summer night,
In class for no good reason while I talk
About Thoreau's remark that one injustice

40   Makes prisoners of us all. The piece of chalk
Splinters and flakes in fragments as I write,
To settle in the tray, where all the dust is.   [1990]

LESLIE MARMON SILKO (*b.* 1948)

Prayer to the Pacific

I traveled to the ocean
                    distant
                            from my southwest land of sandrock
                            to the moving blue water.
5   Big as the myth of origin.

Pale
pale water in the yellow-white light of
                    sun   floating west
                        to China
10   where ocean herself was born.
Clouds that blow across the sand are wet.

Squat in the wet sand and speak to the Ocean:
                I return to you   turquoise   the red coral you sent us,
                    sister spirit of Earth.
15   Four round stones in my pocket.   I carry back the ocean
                        to suck and to taste.

Thirty thousand years ago
                    Indians came riding across the ocean
                    carried by giant sea turtles.

20   Waves were high that day
                great sea turtles waded   slowly out
                            from the gray sundown sea.

Grandfather Turtle rolled in the sand   four times
                    and disappeared
25   swimming into the sun.

And so   from that time
            immemorial,
                        as the old people say,
rain clouds drift from the west
30   gift from the ocean.

Green leaves in the wind
Wet earth on my feet
            swallowing raindrops
                        clear from China.   [1981]

AUGUST KLEINZAHLER (*b.* 1949)

Watching Dogwood Blossoms Fall
in a Parking Lot off Route 46

Dogwood blossoms drift down at evening
    as semis pound past Phoenix Seafood

and the Savarin plant, west to the Turnpike,
    Paterson or hills beyond.

5   The adulterated, pearly light and bleak perfume
    of benzene and exhaust

make this solitary tree and the last of its bloom
    as stirring somehow after another day

at the hospital with Mother and the ashen old ladies
10   lost to TV reruns flickering overhead

as that shower of peach blossoms Tu Fu watched
    fall on the riverbank

from the shadows of the Jade Pavilion,
    while ghosts and the music

15   of yellow orioles found out the seam of him
    and slowly cut along it.   [1996]

JULIA ALVAREZ (*b.* 1950)

Old Heroines

Where do heroines go when their novels are over?
If she's not married off, she gets on a train
and rides to the city to see her old lover—
though it's clear from the ending he has broken things off.
5   And as she is racing through Russia or Iowa
she looks out the window, the dark fields rolling by,
or maybe the night sky grainy with stars. . . .
She sees her reflection, a face still dramatic,
pale and young in that afterward light.
10   She wonders, how long must I still play this part?

Outside in those farmhouses bathed in pale porchlight,
the unstoried women who formed the mere backdrop
to her beauty, betrayals, drift off to sleep
in the arms of their husbands, dreaming themselves
15   in elegant furs racing towards Moscow, Chicago,
some heady excitement! They wake with a start,
turning on lights to make sure of their status—
brief lights she beholds from her jailhouse train
as she rides on forever in the haze of bright dreams
20   which her sorrows inspire in these happier women.   [1984]

CAROLYN FORCHÉ (*b.* 1950)

For the Stranger

Although you mention Venice
keeping it on your tongue like a fruit pit
and I say yes, perhaps Bucharest, neither of us
really knows. There is only this train
5   slipping through pastures of snow,
a sleigh reaching down
to touch its buried runners.
We meet on the shaking platform,
the wind's broken teeth sinking into us.
10   You unwrap your dark bread
and share with me the coffee
sloshing into your gloves.
Telegraph posts chop the winter fields
into white blocks, in each window
15   the crude painting of a small farm.
We listen to mothers scolding
children in English as if
we do not understand a word of it—
sit still, sit still.

20   There are few clues as to where
we are: the baled wheat scattered
everywhere like missing coffins.
The distant yellow kitchen lights
wiped with oil.
25   Everywhere the black dipping wires
stretching messages from one side
of a country to the other.
The men who stand on every border
waving to us.

30   Wiping ovals of breath from the windows
in order to see ourselves, you touch
the glass tenderly wherever it holds my face.
Days later, you are showing me
photographs of a woman and children
35   smiling from the windows of your wallet.

Each time the train slows, a man
with our faces in the gold buttons
of his coat passes through the cars
muttering the name of a city. Each time
40   we lose people. Each time I find you
again between the cars, holding out
a scrap of bread for me, something
hot to drink, until there are
no more cities and you pull me
45   toward you, sliding your hands

into my coat, telling me
your name over and over, hurrying
your mouth into mine.
We have, each of us, nothing.
50 We will give it to each other.   [1978]

The Garden Shukkei-en

By way of a vanished bridge we cross this river
as a cloud of lifted snow would ascend a mountain.

She has always been afraid to come here.

It is the river she most
5 remembers, the living
and the dead both crying for help.

A world that allowed neither tears nor lamentation.

The *matsu* trees brush her hair as she passes
beneath them, as do the shining strands of barbed wire.

10 Where this lake is, there was a lake,
where these black pine grow, there grew black pine.

Where there is no teahouse I see a wooden teahouse
and the corpses of those who slept in it.

On the opposite bank of the Ota, a weeping willow
15 etches its memory of their faces into the water.

Where light touches the face, the character for heart is written.

She strokes a burnt trunk wrapped in straw:
I was weak and my skin hung from my fingertips like cloth

Do you think for a moment we were human beings to them?

20 She comes to the stone angel holding paper cranes.
Not an angel, but a woman where she once had been,

who walks through the garden Shukkei-en
calling the carp to the surface by clapping her hands.

Do Americans think of us?

25 So she began as we squatted over the toilets:
If you want, I'll tell you, but nothing I say will be enough.

We tried to dress our burns with vegetable oil.

Her hair is the white froth of rice rising up kettlesides, her mind also.
In the postwar years she thought deeply about how to live.

*Shukkei-en is an ornamental garden in Hiroshima. It has been restored. The Ota is
one of the rivers of Hiroshima.*

8/*matsu: any of several Japanese pine trees, including the black pine*

30   The common greeting *dozo-yiroshku* is please take care of me.
      All *hibakusha* still alive were children then.

      A cemetery seen from the air is a child's city.

      I don't like this particular red flower because
      it reminds me of a woman's brain crushed under a roof.

35   Perhaps my language is too precise, and therefore difficult to understand?

      We have not, all these years, felt what you call happiness.
      But at times, with good fortune, we experience something close.
      As our life resembles life, and this garden the garden.
      And in the silence surrounding what happened to us

40   it is the bell to awaken God that we've heard ringing.   [1994]

³¹/*hibakusha: literally, "suffer-explosion-people"; survivors of an atomic explosion,
especially those at Hiroshima and Nagasaki in 1945*

DANA GIOIA (*b.* 1950)

Planting a Sequoia

      All afternoon my brothers and I have worked in the orchard,
      Digging this hole, laying you into it, carefully packing the soil.
      Rain blackened the horizon, but cold winds kept it over the Pacific,
      And the sky above us stayed the dull gray
5   Of an old year coming to an end.

      In Sicily a father plants a tree to celebrate his first son's birth—
      An olive or a fig tree—a sign that the earth has one more life to bear.
      I would have done the same, proudly laying new stock into my father's
          orchard,
      A green sapling rising among the twisted apple boughs,
10   A promise of new fruit in other autumns.

      But today we kneel in the cold planting you, our native giant,
      Defying the practical custom of our fathers,
      Wrapping in your roots a lock of hair, a piece of an infant's birth cord,
      All that remains above earth of a first-born son,
15   A few stray atoms brought back to the elements.

      We will give you what we can—our labor and our soil,
      Water drawn from the earth when the skies fail,
      Nights scented with the ocean fog, days softened by the circuit of bees.
      We plant you in the corner of the grove, bathed in western light,
20   A slender shoot against the sunset.

      And when our family is no more, all of his unborn brothers dead,
      Every niece and nephew scattered, the house torn down,
      His mother's beauty ashes in the air,
      I want you to stand among strangers, all young and ephemeral to you,
25   Silently keeping the secret of your birth.   [1991]

RODNEY JONES (*b.* 1950)

A Blasphemy

A girl attacked me once with a number 2 Eagle pencil
for a whiny lisping impression of a radio preacher
she must have loved more than sophistication or peace,
for she took the pencil in a whitened knuckle
5   and drove the point with all her weight behind it
through a thick pair of jeans, jogging it at the end
and twisting it, so the lead broke off under the skin,
an act undertaken so suddenly and dramatically
it was as though I had awakened in a strange hotel
10 with sirens going off and half-dressed women rushing
in every direction with kids tucked under their arms;
as though the Moslems had retaken Jerusalem for
the twelfth time, the crusaders were riding south,
and the Jews in Cadiz and Granada were packing
15 their bags, mapping the snowy ghettos of the north.
But where we were, it was still Tuscaloosa, late
summer, and the heat in her sparsely decorated room
we had come to together after work was so miserable
and intense the wallpaper was crimping at each seam,
20 the posters of daisies and horses she had pasted up
were fallen all over the floor. Whatever I thought
would happen was not going to happen. Nothing
was going to happen with any of the three billion women
of the world forever. The time it would take
25 for the first kindness was the wait for a Campbellite
to accept Darwin and Galileo or for all Arkansas
to embrace a black Messiah. The time it would take
for even a hand to shyly, unambiguously brush my own
was the years Bertrand Russell waited for humanism,
30 disarmament, and neutrality. And then she was
there, her cloth daubing at the darkly jellying wound.
In contrition, she bowed with tweezers to pick the grit.
With alcohol, she cleansed the rubbery petals.
She unspooled the white gauze and spread the balm of mercy.
35 Because she loved Christ, she forgave me. And what
was that all about? I wondered, walking home
through the familiar streets, the steeple of each church
raised like a beneficent weapon, the mark of the heretic
on my thigh, and mockery was still the unforgivable sin.   [1989]

---

[25]/**Campbellite:** *a member of the Disciples of Christ, a fundamentalist denomination*

JOY HARJO (*b.* 1951)

Eagle Poem

To pray you open your whole self
To sky, to earth, to sun, to moon
To one whole voice that is you.
And know there is more
5 That you can't see, can't hear,
Can't know except in moments
Steadily growing, and in languages
That aren't always sound but other
Circles of motion.
10 Like eagle that Sunday morning
Over Salt River. Circled in blue sky
In wind, swept our hearts clean
With sacred wings.
We see you, see ourselves and know
15 That we must take the utmost care
And kindness in all things.
Breathe in, knowing we are made of
All this, and breathe, knowing
We are truly blessed because we
20 Were born, and die soon within a
True circle of motion,
Like eagle rounding out the morning
Inside us.
We pray that it will be done
25 In beauty.
In beauty.

[1990]

ANDREW HUDGINS (*b.* 1951)

The Persistence of Nature in Our Lives

You find them in the darker woods
occasionally—those swollen lumps
of fungus, twisted, moist, and yellow—
but when they show up on the lawn
5 it's like they've tracked me home. In spring
the persistence of nature in our lives
rises from below, drifts from above.
The pollen settles on my skin
and waits for me to bloom, trying
10 to work green magic on my flesh.
They're indiscriminate, these firs.
They'll mate with anything. A great
green-yellow cloud of pollen sifts
across the house. The waste of it

15 leaves nothing out—not even men.
The pollen doesn't care I'm not
a tree. The golden storm descends.
Wind lifts it from the branches, lofts
it in descending arches of need
20 and search, a grainy yellow haze
that settles over everything
as if it's all the same. I love
the utter waste of pollen, a scum
of it on every pond and puddle.
25 It rides the ripples and, when they dry,
remains, a line of yellow dust
zigzagging in the shape of waves.
One night, perhaps a little drunk,
I stretched out on the porch, watching
30 the Milky Way. At dawn I woke
to find a man-shape on the hard
wood floor, outlined in pollen—a sharp
spread-eagle figure drawn there like
the body at a murder scene.
35 Except for that spot, the whole damn house
glittered, green-gold. I wandered out
across the lawn, my bare feet damp
with dew, the wet ground soft, forgiving,
beneath my step. I understood
40 I am, as much as anyone,
the golden beast who staggers home,
in June, beneath the yearning trees.   [1985]

BRIGIT PEGEEN KELLY (b. 1951)

Song

Listen: there was a goat's head hanging by ropes in a tree.
All night it hung there and sang. And those who heard it
Felt a hurt in their hearts and thought they were hearing
The song of a night bird. They sat up in their beds, and then
5 They lay back down again. In the night wind, the goat's head
Swayed back and forth, and from far off it shone faintly
The way the moonlight shone on the train track miles away
Beside which the goat's headless body lay. Some boys
Had hacked its head off. It was harder work than they had imagined.
10 The goat cried like a man and struggled hard. But they
Finished the job. They hung the bleeding head by the school
And then ran off into the darkness that seems to hide everything.
The head hung in the tree. The body lay by the tracks.
The head called to the body. The body to the head.
15 They missed each other. The missing grew large between them,

Until it pulled the heart right out of the body, until
The drawn heart flew toward the head, flew as a bird flies
Back to its cage and the familiar perch from which it trills.
Then the heart sang in the head, softly at first and then louder,
20 Sang long and low until the morning light came up over
The school and over the tree, and then the singing stopped. . . .
The goat had belonged to a small girl. She named
The goat Broken Thorn Sweet Blackberry, named it after
The night's bush of stars, because the goat's silky hair
25 Was dark as well water, because it had eyes like wild fruit.
The girl lived near a high railroad track. At night
She heard the trains passing, the sweet sound of the train's horn
Pouring softly over her bed, and each morning she woke
To give the bleating goat his pail of warm milk. She sang
30 Him songs about girls with ropes and cooks in boats.
She brushed him with a stiff brush. She dreamed daily
That he grew bigger, and he did. She thought her dreaming
Made it so. But one night the girl didn't hear the train's horn,
And the next morning she woke to an empty yard. The goat
35 Was gone. Everything looked strange. It was as if a storm
Had passed through while she slept, wind and stones, rain
Stripping the branches of fruit. She knew that someone
Had stolen the goat and that he had come to harm. She called
To him. All morning and into the afternoon, she called
40 And called. She walked and walked. In her chest a bad feeling
Like the feeling of the stones gouging the soft undersides
Of her bare feet. Then somebody found the goat's body
By the high tracks, the flies already filling their soft bottles
At the goat's torn neck. Then somebody found the head
45 Hanging in a tree by the school. They hurried to take
These things away so that the girl would not see them.
They hurried to raise money to buy the girl another goat.
They hurried to find the boys who had done this, to hear
Them say it was a joke, a joke, it was nothing but a joke. . . .
50 But listen: here is the point. The boys thought to have
Their fun and be done with it. It was harder work than they
Had imagined, this silly sacrifice, but they finished the job,
Whistling as they washed their large hands in the dark.
What they didn't know was that the goat's head was already
55 Singing behind them in the tree. What they didn't know
Was that the goat's head would go on singing, just for them,
Long after the ropes were down, and that they would learn to listen,
Pail after pail, stroke after patient stroke. They would
Wake in the night thinking they heard the wind in the trees
60 Or a night bird, but their hearts beating harder. There
Would be a whistle, a hum, a high murmur, and, at last, a song,
The low song a lost boy sings remembering his mother's call.
Not a cruel song, no, no, not cruel at all. This song
Is sweet. It is sweet. The heart dies of this sweetness.   [1995]

JUDITH ORTIZ COFER (*b.* 1952)

Quinceañera

My dolls have been put away like dead
children in a chest I will carry
with me when I marry.
I reach under my skirt to feel
5 a satin slip bought for this day. It is soft
as the inside of my thighs. My hair
has been nailed back with my mother's
black hairpins to my skull. Her hands
stretched my eyes open as she twisted
10 braids into a tight circle at the nape
of my neck. I am to wash my own clothes
and sheets from this day on, as if
the fluids of my body were poison, as if
the little trickle of blood I believe
15 travels from my heart to the world were
shameful. Is not the blood of saints and
men in battle beautiful? Do Christ's hands
not bleed into your eyes from His cross?
At night I hear myself growing and wake
20 to find my hands drifting of their own will
to soothe skin stretched tight
over my bones.
I am wound like the guts of a clock,
waiting for each hour to release me.   [1987]

Quinceañera: "coming out" party for a fifteen-year-old girl

RITA DOVE (*b.* 1952)

Ö

Shape the lips to an *o*, say *a*.
That's *island*.

One word of Swedish has changed the whole neighborhood.
When I look up, the yellow house on the corner
5 is a galleon stranded in flowers. Around it

the wind. Even the high roar of a leaf-mulcher
could be the horn-blast from a ship
as it skirts the misted shoals.

*The Swedish word for "island" is ö—itself like a little island with, the poet has
remarked, two birds flying over it.*

We don't need much more to keep things going.
10   Families complete themselves
and refuse to budge from the present,
the present extends its glass forehead to sea
(backyard breezes, scattered cardinals)

and if, one evening, the house on the corner
15   took off over the marshland,
neither I nor my neighbor
would be amazed. Sometimes

a word is found so right it trembles
at the slightest explanation.
20   You start out with one thing, end
up with another, and nothing's
like it used to be, not even the future.   [1980]

ALICE FULTON (*b.* 1952)

News of the Occluded Cyclone

Night usually computes itself in stars,
cryptic as a punchcard, but now the sky is blurry
as a turp-soaked rag.

At the siren we flip through frequencies
5   for the latest in tornado
warnings. We lose power and light

candles, their mild spices
comforting as cookies baking.
Thunder comes, galumphing its important

10   gavels. I wish it could call the storm
to an order arbitrary and dependable
as the ABCs. Instead, blackboards

embellished with unsteady
Y's are where
15   the windows used to be.

The sky is strung with lightning
like the lines of fighting
kites or tined with royal

racks that leave afterimages
20   of antlers on our sight.
We cling to each other

in the dead center of the living
room, as if the least space we can displace
is the one zoned for oasis, sensing as much

25 as seeing the dowsing
sticks above us. And it storms
till the candles form bright

putties in glass saucers, till the messy,
soft-edged dawn comes on
30 in rebuttal, and a voice disembodied

as God's proclaims the warning
over. There's a welcome
sense of excavation in the full-

frontal rush of morning, the horizon's
35 hierarchy under calm free-
falls of sun: it's deliverance

at a designated hour, this propriety
of day, this reliable frame
that lets color be

40 color and light light.   [1986]

MARK JARMAN (*b.* 1952)

From Unholy Sonnets

13

Drunk on the Umbrian hills at dusk and drunk
On one pink cloud that stood beside the moon,
Drunk on the moon, a marble smile, and drunk,
Two young Americans, on one another,
5 Far from home and wanting this forever—
Who needed God? We had our bodies, bread,
And glasses of a raw, green, local wine,
And watched our Godless perfect darkness breed
Enormous softly burning ancient stars.
10 Who needed God? And why do I ask now?
Because I'm older and I think God stirs
In details that keep bringing back that time,
Details that are just as vivid now—
Our bodies, bread, a sharp Umbrian wine.   [1997]

Ground Swell

Is nothing real but when I was fifteen,
Going on sixteen, like a corny song?
I see myself so clearly then, and painfully—
Knees bleeding through my usher's uniform
5 Behind the candy counter in the theater

After a morning's surfing; paddling frantically
To top the brisk outsiders coming to wreck me,
Trundle me clumsily along the beach floor's
Gravel and sand; my knees aching with salt.
10 Is that all that I have to write about?
You write about the life that's vividest.
And if that is your own, that is your subject.
And if the years before and after sixteen
Are colorless as salt and taste like sand—
15 Return to those remembered chilly mornings,
The light spreading like a great skin on the water,
And the blue water scalloped with wind-ridges,
And—what was it exactly?—that slow waiting
When, to invigorate yourself, you peed
20 Inside your bathing suit and felt the warmth
Crawl all around your hips and thighs,
And the first set rolled in and the water level
Rose in expectancy, and the sun struck
The water surface like a brassy palm,
25 Flat and gonglike, and the wave face formed.
Yes. But that was a summer so removed
In time, so specially peculiar to my life,
Why would I want to write about it again?
There was a day or two when, paddling out,
30 An older boy who had just graduated
And grown a great blonde moustache, like a walrus,
Skimmed past me like a smooth machine on the water,
And said my name. I was so much younger,
To be identified by one like him—
35 The easy deference of a kind of god
Who also went to church where I did—made me
Reconsider my worth. I had been noticed.
He soon was a small figure crossing waves,
The shawling crest surrounding him with spray,
40 Whiter than gull feathers. He had said my name
Without scorn, just with a bit of surprise
To notice me among those tryng the big waves
Of the morning break. His name is carved now
On the black wall in Washington, the frozen wave
45 That grievers cross to find a name or names.
I knew him as I say I knew him, then,
Which wasn't very well. My father preached
His funeral. He came home in a bag
That may have mixed in pieces of his squad.
50 Yes, I can write about a lot of things
Besides the summer that I turned sixteen.
But that's my ground swell. I must start
Where things began to happen and I knew it.

[1997]

DAVID MURA (*b.* 1952)

The Natives

Several months after we lost our way,
they began to appear, their quiet eyes
assuring us, their small painted legs
scurrying beside us. By then our radio
5   had been gutted by fungus, our captain's cheek
stunned by a single bullet; our ammo vanished
the first night we discovered our maps were useless,
our compasses a lie. (The sun and stars
seemed to reel above us.) The second week
10 forced us on snakes, monkeys, lizards, and toads;
we ate them raw over wet smoking fires.
Waking one morning we found a river boat
loaded with bodies hanging in trees
like an ox on a sling, marking the stages
15 of flood. One of us thought he heard the whirr
of a chopper, but it was only the monsoon
drumming the leaves, soaking our skin so damp
you felt you could peel it back to scratch
the bones of your ankle. Gradually our names
20 fell from our mouths, never heard again.
Nights, faces glowing, we told stories of wolves,
and the jungle seemed colder, more a home.
And then we glimpsed them, like ghosts of children
darting through the trees, the curtain of rain;
25 we told each other nothing, hoping they'd vanish.
But one evening the leaves parted. Slowly
they emerged and took our hands, their striped
faces dripping, looking up in wonder
at our grizzled cheeks. Stumbling like gods
30 without powers, we carried on our backs
what they could not carry, the rusted grenades,
the ammoless rifles, barrels clotted with flies.
They waited years before they brought us
to their village, led us in circles till
35 time disappeared. Now, stone still, our feet
tangled with vines, we stand by their doorway
like soft-eyed virgins in the drilling rain:
the hair on our shoulders dangles and shines.   [1989]

See comment (p. 36)

NAOMI SHIHAB NYE (*b.* 1952)

Famous

The river is famous to the fish.

The loud voice is famous to silence,
which knew it would inherit the earth
before anybody said so.

5   The cat sleeping on the fence is famous to the birds
watching him from the birdhouse.

The tear is famous, briefly, to the cheek.

The idea you carry close to your bosom
is famous to your bosom.

10   The boot is famous to the earth,
more famous than the dress shoe,
which is famous only to floors.

The bent photograph is famous to the one who carries it
and not at all famous to the one who is pictured.

15   I want to be famous to shuffling men
who smile while crossing streets,
sticky children in grocery lines,
famous as the one who smiled back.

I want to be famous in the way a pulley is famous,
20   or a buttonhole, not because it did anything spectacular,
but because it never forgot what it could do.   [1982]

JIM SIMMERMAN (*b.* 1952)

Child's Grave, Hale County, Alabama

Someone drove a two-by-four
through the heart of this hard land
that even in a good year
will notch a plow blade worthless,
5   snap the head off a shovel,
or bow a stubborn back.
He'd have had to steal
the wood from a local mill
or steal, by starlight, across
10   his landlord's farm, to worry
a fencepost out of its well
and lug it the three miles home.
He'd have had to leave his wife
asleep on a cornshuck mat,
15   leave his broken brogans

by the stove, to slip outside,
lullaby soft, with the child
bundled in a burlap sack.
What a thing to have to do
20   on a cold night in December,
1936, alone
but for a raspy wind
and the red, rock-ridden dirt
things come down to in the end.
25   Whoever it was pounded
this shabby half-cross
into the ground must have toiled
all night to root it so:
five feet buried with the child
30   for the foot of it that shows.
And as there are no words
carved here, it's likely that
the man was illiterate,
or addled with fatigue,
35   or wrenched simple-minded
by the one simple fact.
Or else the unscored lumber
driven deep into the land
and the hump of busted rock
40   spoke too plainly of his grief:
forty years layed by and still
there are no words for this.   [1989]

GARY SOTO (b. 1952)

Oranges

The first time I walked
With a girl, I was twelve,
Cold, and weighted down
With two oranges in my jacket.
5   December. Frost cracking
Beneath my steps, my breath
Before me, then gone,
As I walked toward
Her house, the one whose
10   Porch light burned yellow
Night and day, in any weather.
A dog barked at me, until
She came out pulling
At her gloves, face bright
15   With rouge. I smiled,
Touched her shoulder, and led
Her down the street, across

A used car lot and a line
Of newly planted trees,
20 Until we were breathing
Before a drugstore. We
Entered, the tiny bell
Bringing a saleslady
Down a narrow aisle of goods.
25 I turned to the candies
Tiered like bleachers,
And asked what she wanted—
Light in her eyes, a smile
Starting at the corners
30 Of her mouth. I fingered
A nickel in my pocket,
And when she lifted a chocolate
That cost a dime,
I didn't say anything.
35 I took the nickel from
My pocket, then an orange,
And set them quietly on
The counter. When I looked up,
The lady's eyes met mine,
40 And held them, knowing
Very well what it was all
About.
        Outside,
A few cars hissing past,
45 Fog hanging like old
Coats between the trees.
I took my girl's hand
In mine for two blocks,
Then released it to let
50 Her unwrap the chocolate.
I peeled my orange
That was so bright against
The gray of December
That, from some distance,
55 Someone might have thought
I was making a fire in my hands.   [1985]

MARK IRWIN (b. 1953)

The Irises

The irises were so beautiful I had trouble
leaving. One day, one day it will be lonely
when people go. I wanted to linger a bit
longer among irises. Some white, some purple,
5 some pale blue. What can one say among

irises. One's speech grows dumb as they touch
the air. I wanted to linger a bit longer
among irises. The moment moves. Are you
ready? I think the body's a mansion
10   with two doors, one luminescent and open,
one dark and closed. I wanted to linger
a bit longer among irises. I felt something
opening into the room among our tangled
arms. One day, one day it will be lonely. Petals,
15   paper doors, walls, clouds. I wanted to,
you wanted to. That your desire may spill
into eternity, an impatience whose lingering is all.   [2003]

GJERTRUD SCHNACKENBERG (b. 1953)

Walking Home

Walking home from school one afternoon,
Slightly abstracted, what were you thinking of?
Turks in Vienna? Luther on Christian love?
Or were you with Van Gogh beneath the moon
5   With candles in his hatband, painting stars
Like singed hairs spinning in a candle flame?
Or giant maps where men take, lose, reclaim
Whole continents with pins? Or burning cars
And watchtowers and army-censored news
10   In Chile, in the Philippines, in Greece,
Colonels running the universities,
Assassinations, executions, coups—

You walked, and overhead some pipsqueak bird
Flew by and dropped a lot of something that
15   Splattered, right on the good professor, splat.
Now, on the ancient Rhine, so Herod heard,
The old Germanic chieftains always read
Such droppings as good luck: opening the door,
You bowed to improve my view of what you wore,
20   So luckily, there on the center of your head.

Man is not a god, that's what you said
After your heart gave out, to comfort me
Who came to comfort you but sobbed to see
Your heartbeat zigzagging on a TV overhead.
25   You knew the world was in a mess, and so,
By God, were you; and yet I never knew
A man who loved the world as much as you,
And that love was the last thing to let go.   [1982]

*This is the third of a twelve-poem sequence written in memory of the poet's father,
a professor of history.*

BENJAMIN ALIRE SÁENZ (b. 1954)

To the Desert

I came to you one rainless August night.
You taught me how to live without the rain.
You are the thirst and thirst is all I know.
You are sand, wind, sun, and burning sky,
5   The hottest blue. You blow a breeze and brand
Your breath into my mouth. You reach—then *bend*
Your force, to break, blow, burn, and make me new
You wrap your name tight around my ribs
And keep me warm. I was born for you
10   Above, below, by you, by you surrounded.
I wake to you at dawn. Never break your
Knot. Reach, rise, blow, *Sálvame, mi dios,*
Trágame, mi tierra. Salva, traga, Break me,
I am bread. I will be the water for your thirst.   [1995]

6–7/lines quoted from John Donne's
14th Holy Sonnet, "Batter My Heart,
Three-Personed God."

12–13/(Spanish) "Save me, my God /
Swallow me, my earth. Save, swallow."

MARY JO SALTER (b. 1954)

Boulevard du Montparnasse

Once, in a doorway in Paris, I saw
the most beautiful couple in the world.
They were each the single most beautiful thing in the world.
She would have been sixteen, perhaps; he twenty.
5   Their skin was the same shade of black: like a shiny Steinway.
And they stood there like the four-legged instrument
of a passion so grand one could barely imagine them
ever working, or eating, or reading a magazine.
Even they could hardly believe it.
10   Her hands gripped his belt loops, as they found each other's eyes,
because beauty like this must be held onto,
could easily run away on the power
of his long, lean thighs; or the tiny feet of her laughter.
I thought: now I will write a poem,
15   set in a doorway on the Boulevard du Montparnasse,
in which the brutishness of time
rates only a mention; I will say simply
that if either one should ever love another,
a greater beauty shall not be the cause.   [1994]

MARK DOTY (*b.* 1955)

Brilliance

Maggie's taking care of a man
who's dying; he's attended to everything,
said goodbye to his parents,

paid off his credit card.
5   She says *Why don't you just
run it up to the limit?*

but he wants everything
squared away, no balance owed,
though he misses the pets

10   he's already found a home for
—he can't be around dogs or cats,
too much risk. He says,

I can't have anything.
She says, *A bowl of goldfish?*
15   He says he doesn't want to start

with anything and then describes
the kind he'd maybe like,
how their tails would fan

to a gold flaring. They talk
20   about hot jewel tones,
gold lacquer, say maybe

they'll go pick some out
though he can't go much of anywhere and then
abruptly he says *I can't love*

25   *anything I can't finish.*
He says it like he's had enough
of the whole scintillant world,

though what he means is
he'll never be satisfied and therefore
30   has established this discipline,

a kind of severe rehearsal.
That's where they leave it,
him looking out the window,

her knitting as she does because
35   she needs to do something.
Later he leaves a message:

Yes to the bowl of goldfish.
Meaning: let me go, if I have to,
in brilliance. In a story I read,

40 a Zen master who'd perfected
his detachment from the things of the world
remembered, at the moment of dying,

a deer he used to feed in the park,
and wondered who might care for it,
45 and at that instant was reborn

in the stunned flesh of a fawn.
So, Maggie's friend—
is he going out

into the last loved object
50 of his attention?
Fanning the veined translucence

of an opulent tail,
undulant in some uncapturable curve,
is he bronze chrysanthemums,

55 copper leaf, hurried darting,
doubloons, icon-colored fins
troubling the water?   [1993]

LOUISE ERDRICH (*b.* 1955)

Jacklight

The same Chippewa word is used both for flirting and hunting game,
while another Chippewa word connotes both using force in intercourse
and also killing a bear with one's bare hands.
                    —R. W. DUNNING, *Social and Economic*
                    Change Among the Northern Ojibwa (1959)

We have come to the edge of the woods,
out of brown grass where we slept, unseen,
out of knotted twigs, out of leaves creaked shut,
out of hiding.

5 At first the light wavered, glancing over us.
Then it clenched to a fist of light that pointed,
searched out, divided us.
Each took the beams like direct blows the heart answers.
Each of us moved forward alone.

10 We have come to the edge of the woods,
drawn out of ourselves by this night sun,
this battery of polarized acids,
that outshines the moon.

Jacklight: a portable light for hunting or fishing at night

We smell them behind it
15   but they are faceless, invisible.
We smell the raw steel of their gun barrels,
mink oil on leather, their tongues of sour barley.
We smell their mothers buried chin-deep in wet dirt.
We smell their fathers with scoured knuckles,
20   teeth cracked from hot marrow.
We smell their sisters of crushed dogwood, bruised apples,
of fractured cups and concussions of burnt hooks.

We smell their breath steaming lightly behind the jacklight.
We smell the itch underneath the caked guts on their clothes.
25   We smell their minds like silver hammers
cocked back, held in readiness
for the first of us to step into the open.

We have come to the edge of the woods,
out of brown grass where we slept, unseen,
30   out of leaves creaked shut, out of our hiding.
We have come here too long.

It is their turn now,
their turn to follow us. Listen,
they put down their equipment.
35   It is useless in the tall brush.
And now they take the first steps, not knowing
how deep the woods are and lightless.
How deep the woods are.   [1984]

CAROL MOLDAW (b. 1956)

Beads of Rain

Each day I've looked
into the beveled mirror
on this desk, vainly
asking it questions
5   reflection cannot answer.

Outside, fog and frost
and silver olive leaves.
I can see at most
a half field's depth,
10   then the trees are lost
in the gauzy mist
like thin unbraceleted arms
swallowed by billowing sleeves.

I'd like to face
15   that stringent looking glass
transparent to myself

as beads of rain
pooled on a green leaf.

But ever self-composed
20 in self-regard,
and my eyes opaque,
as a dancer's leotard,
to see straight through myself
I need what love supplies:
25 its dark arrows, dear,
not its white lies.

[1998]

LI-YOUNG LEE (*b.* 1957)

Eating Alone

I've pulled the last of the year's young onions.
The garden is bare now. The ground is cold,
brown and old. What is left of the day flames
in the maples at the corner of my
5 eye. I turn, a cardinal vanishes.
By the cellar door, I wash the onions,
then drink from the icy metal spigot.

Once, years back, I walked beside my father
among the windfall pears. I can't recall
10 our words. We may have strolled in silence. But
I still see him bend that way—left hand braced
on knee, creaky—to lift and hold to my
eye a rotten pear. In it, a hornet
spun crazily, glazed in slow, glistening juice.

15 It was my father I saw this morning
waving to me from the trees. I almost
called to him, until I came close enough
to see the shovel, leaning where I had
left it, in the flickering, deep green shade.

20 White rice steaming, almost done. Sweet green peas
fried in onions. Shrimp braised in sesame
oil and garlic. And my own loneliness.
What more could I, a young man, want.

[1986]

JANE HILBERRY (*b.* 1958)

The Moment

In those days, Betty Crocker
always called for sifted flour, and so

in homes across America, women sifted.
When my mother's mother turned
5 the wobbly red knob, hulls and stones
jumped in the wire basket,
but by my mother's time,
the flour was fine—
now women sifted to achieve
10 precision, purity, perfection.
It made the white flour whiter.
Then flour came in bags,
already sifted. Then women stopped
making their own cakes and bread,
15 and didn't have time anyway
for sifting. But for a flicker
of history, my mother stood
staring down into the cylinder,
watching the moment shuttered into tiny parts,
20 slowed by the fanning blunt blades,
a moment of nothing else to do
but watch the perfection of time, sifted,
into the waiting bowl.

[2005]

KATE LIGHT (*b.* 1960)

There Comes the Strangest Moment

There comes the strangest moment in your life,
when everything you thought before breaks free—
what you relied upon, as ground-rule and as rite
looks upside down from how it used to be.

5 Skin's gone pale, your brain is shedding cells;
you question every tenet you set down;
obedient thoughts have turned to infidels
and every verb desires to be a noun.

I want—my want. I love—my love. I'll stay
10 *with you. I thought transitions were the best*
but I want what's here to never go away.
I'll make my peace, my bed, and kiss this breast . . .

Your heart's in retrograde. You simply have no choice.
Things people told you turn out to be true.
15 You have to hold that body, hear that voice.
You'd have sworn no one knew you more than you.

How many people thought you'd never change?
But here you have. It's beautiful. It's strange.

[2003]

JOE BOLTON (1961–1990)

Adult Situations

These moves we make
To do and un-
Do each other
Must be lovely
5 From a distance.

Such a music,
Such a twilight,
A surfacing,
A sense of style.
10 No end to it.

The white hotels
We check into
Keep standing. They
Survive each blond
15 Who comes and goes.

Cities go on.
The lights go on
In cities. Cars
Go to the sea.
20 The Sea goes on.

What's left of us
Lasts in what is
Least us: in cars,
In the twilight
25 Of white cities,

In our houses,
In our closets—
Clothes we put on
In the hope of
30 Taking them off.

[1999]

APRIL LINDNER (b. 1962)

Girl

Plug her in, she's yours, twenty-four/seven,
the girl who glows and beckons from your screen.
Unfurling like a one-armed bandit's jackpot,
her body parts skirl past, bathed in blue light,
5 as lush as plums or cherries or split melon.
They airy tits of one girl float like clouds
above another's mega-legs, an ass

spliced from yet a third, these random fragments
assembled into woman by your eye,
10 real as a model airplane. If she speaks,
her come-on lines are scripted. If she's wrapped,
she's easy to unwrap; between her skin
and your parched lips nothing by convex glass.
Smiling is her job. She knows you want her
15 because who wouldn't? Hell, I want her too
or want to be her, sometimes, in the buzz
after I've stared too long, my flesh exhausted
by its own weight, my skin's dull tendency
to slough off into dust, the daily tug
20 toward obsolescence. I would hone my legs down—
they're all wrong—inject my lips with honey,
and paint my smile white as the Parthenon.
Beauty is truth, truth beauty—that is all?

No, beauty is the lie we'd carve and starve for.
25 We'd suck it till the juice ran down our arms,
or live inside it like a suit of armor—
if only that were possible. Instead
we lie here, shipwrecked by her ceaseless motion.
Reaching for her prow, we catch her wake.   [2002]

RAFAEL CAMPO (*b.* 1964)

What the Body Told

Not long ago, I studied medicine.
It was terrible, what the body told.
I'd look inside another person's mouth
And see the desolation of the world.
5   I'd see his genitals and think of sin.

Because my body speaks the stranger's language,
I've never understood those nods and stares.
My parents held me in their arms, and still
I think I've disappointed them; they care
10 And stare, they nod, they make their pilgrimage

To somewhere distant in my heart, they cry.
I look inside their other-person's mouths
And see the sleek interior of souls.
It's warm and red in there—like love, with teeth.
15 I've studied medicine until I cried

All night. Through certain books, a truth unfolds.
Anatomy and physiology,
The tiny sensing organs of the tongue—
Each nameless cell contributing its needs.
20 It was fabulous, what the body told.   [1996]

SHERMAN ALEXIE (*b.* 1966)

The Powwow at the End of the World

I am told by many of you that I must forgive and so I shall
after an Indian woman puts her shoulder to the Grand Coulee Dam
and topples it. I am told by many of you that I must forgive
and so I shall after the floodwaters burst each successive dam
5   downriver from the Grand Coulee. I am told by many of you
that I must forgive and so I shall after the floodwaters find
their way to the mouth of the Columbia River as it enters the Pacific
and causes all of it to rise. I am told by many of you that I must forgive
and so I shall after the first drop of floodwater is swallowed by that
    salmon
10   waiting in the Pacific. I am told by many of you that I must forgive and
    so I shall
after that salmon swims upstream, through the mouth of the Columbia
and then past the flooded cities, broken dams and abandoned reactors
of Hanford. I am told by many of you that I must forgive and so I shall
after that salmon swims through the mouth of the Spokane River
15   as it meets the Columbia, then upstream, until it arrives
in the shallows of a secret bay on the reservation where I wait alone.
I am told by many of you that I must forgive and so I shall after
that salmon leaps into the night air above the water, throws
a lightning bolt at the brush near my feet, and starts the fire
20   which will lead all of the lost Indians home. I am told
by many of you that I must forgive and so I shall
after we Indians have gathered around the fire with that salmon
who has three stories it must tell before sunrise: one story will teach us
how to pray; another story will make us laugh for hours;
25   the third story will give us reason to dance. I am told by many
of you that I must forgive and so I shall when I am dancing
with my tribe during the powwow at the end of the world.   [1996]

DIANE THIEL (*b.* 1967)

The Minefield

He was running with his friend from town to town,
They were somewhere between Prague and Dresden.
He was fourteen. His friend was faster
and knew a shortcut through the fields they could take.
5   He said there was lettuce growing in one of them,
and they hadn't eaten all day. His friend ran a few lengths ahead,
like a wild rabbit across the grass,
turned his head, looked back once,
and his body was scattered across the field.

10   My father told us this, one night,
and then continued eating dinner.

He brought them with him—the minefields.
He carried them underneath his good intentions.
He gave them to us—in the volume of his anger,
15 in the bruises we covered up with sleeves.
In the way he threw anything against the wall—
a radio, that wasn't even ours,
a melon, once, opened like a head.
In the way we still expect, years later and continents away,
20 that anything might explode at any time,
and we would have to run on alone
with a vision like that
only seconds behind.

[2000]

KEVIN YOUNG (*b.* 1970)

Quivira City Limits

For Thomas Fox Averill

Pull over. Your car with its slow
breathing. Somewhere outside Topeka

it suddenly all matters again,
those tractors blooming rust

5 in the fields only need a good coat
of paint. Red. You had to see

for yourself, didn't you; see that the world
never turned small, transportation

just got better; to learn
10 we can't say a town or a baseball

team without breathing in
a dead Indian. To discover why Coronado

pushed up here, following the guide
who said he knew fields of gold,

15 north, who led them past these plains,
past buffaloes dark as he was. Look.

Nothing but the wheat, waving them
sick, a sea. While they strangle

him blue as the sky above you
20 The Moor must also wonder

When will all this ever be enough?
this wide open they call discovery,

disappointment, this place my
thousand bones carry, now call home.

[1995]

APPENDIXES

POETICS

Perhaps you've heard good carpenters talk about their work, and have discovered that craftsmen can be very philosophical. On the one hand, carpenters might talk about the craft itself: when to use double studs in a wall for extra strength, how a roof ought to be sloped for adequate drainage, and so on. But the same carpenters might also talk about the pleasures of their work, the feel of good lumber, the graceful way to do a job, or the way to do it with the least damage to the environment. Any human task has its aesthetic side. Doctors might talk about beautiful surgical work, lawyers about pleasure in seeing some justice done, athletes about graceful moves on a field. People who have labored long at anything will argue that some ways of working are better than others.

When poets ruminate philosophically upon their art, they enter the realm of **poetics,** theories about the forms and purposes of poetry. When we ask what poetry is, we discover that no one has ever satisfactorily answered the question once and for all, just as no one can tell us with utter certainty the ultimate meaning of life. One common reaction to the difficulty we have in defining poetry is to assume that "everything is relative" and that aesthetic distinctions cannot be made. "Poetry is whatever I say it is," students sometimes argue. Despite its solipsism, there is perhaps some truth in this challenge to authority. We do, in fact, need to argue about our assumptions, and not take everything our teachers say on faith. It would be a shame if we all gave up, like Charlie Brown in the cartoon below, and let other people define our tastes.

Good theories are worth arguing about. What is poetry? What does it mean to be a poet? Can anyone appreciate the art, or must you be a

PEANUTS reprinted by permission of United Feature Syndicate, Inc.

professional reader—a professor, critic, or poet—to participate? These are questions that have fascinated philosophers and other thinkers for a long time.

What follows is a miniature anthology of statements about poetry and poets, each of which contains assumptions about the art that you may or may not agree with. Some of these writers express beliefs that clearly contradict the beliefs of others. Do you notice any patterns of thinking that would allow you to group some of these writers together and pit them against others in a debate? Notice that some rely on metaphysical contexts to make sense of their ideas, whereas others believe that art and nature are in utterly separate camps. Remember that these statements are taken out of context. If you want to use them in an essay of your own, it would be a good idea to look up the originals and follow the whole arguments in which they appear.

PLATO (427?–347 B.C.E.)

Just so the Muse. She first makes men inspired, and then through these inspired ones others share in the enthusiasm, and a chain is formed, for the epic poets, all the good ones, have their excellence, not from art, but are inspired, possessed, and thus they utter all these admirable poems. So it is also with the good lyric poets; as the worshipping Corybantes are not in their senses when they dance, so the lyric poets are not in their senses when they make these lovely lyric poems. No, when they launch into harmony and rhythm, they are seized with the Bacchic transport, and are possessed—as the bacchants, when possessed, draw milk and honey from the rivers, but not when in their senses. So the spirit of the lyric works, according to their own report. For the poets tell us, don't they, that the melodies they bring us are gathered from rills that run with honey, out of glens and gardens of the Muses, and they bring them as bees do honey, flying like the bees? And what they say is true, for a poet is a light and winged thing, and holy, and never able to compose until he has become inspired, and is beside himself, and reason is no longer in him. So long as he has this in his possession, no man is able to make poetry or chant in prophecy. Therefore, since their making is not by art, when they utter many things and fine about the deeds of men, . . . but is by lot divine—therefore each is able to do well only that to which the Muse has impelled him—one to make dithyrambs, another panegyric odes, another choral songs, another epic poems, another iambs.

From "Ion," translated by Lane Cooper, in The Collected Dialogues of Plato. *Edith Hamilton and Huntington Cairns, eds. Princeton University Press, 1961.*

ARISTOTLE (384–322 B.C.E.)

In composing plots and working them out so far as verbal expression goes, the poet should, more than anything else, put things before his eyes, as he then sees the events most vividly as if he were actually present, and can therefore find what is appropriate and be aware of the opposite. . . . For given the same natural endowment, people who actually feel passion are the most convincing; that is, the person who most realistically expresses distress is the person in distress and the same is true of a person in a temper. That is why poetry is the work of a genius rather than of a madman; for the genius is by nature adaptable, while the madman is degenerate.

From "Poetics," translated by M. E. Hubbard, in Classical Literary Criticism. *D. A. Russell and M. Winterbottom, eds. Oxford University Press, 1989.*

LONGINUS (C.E. 213–273)

Some people think it is a complete mistake to reduce things like this to technical rules. Greatness, the argument runs, is a natural product, and does not come by teaching. The only art is to be born like that. They believe moreover that natural products are very much weakened by being reduced to the bare bones of a textbook.

In my view, these arguments can be refuted by considering three points:

(i) Though nature is on the whole a law unto herself in matters of emotion and elevation, she is not a random force and does not work altogether without method.

(ii) She is herself in every instance a first and primary element of creation, but it is method that is competent to provide and contribute quantities and appropriate occasions for everything, as well as perfect correctness in training and application.

(iii) Grandeur is particularly dangerous when left on its own, unaccompanied by knowledge, unsteadied, unballasted, abandoned to mere impulse and ignorant temerity. It often needs the curb as well as the spur.

What Demosthenes said of life in general is also true of literature: good fortune is the greatest of blessings, but good counsel comes next, and the lack of it destroys the other also. In literature, nature occupies the place of good fortune, and art that of good counsel. Most important of all, the very fact that some things in literature depend on nature alone can itself be learned only from art.

From "On Sublimity," translated by M. Winterbottom, in Classical Literary Criticism. *D. A. Russell and M. Winterbottom, eds. Oxford University Press, 1989.*

LU CHI (261–303)

Learn to recite the classics;
   sing in the clear virtue
   of ancient masters.

Explore the treasures of the classics
   where form and content are born.

Thus moved, I lay aside my books
   and take writing brush in hand
   to compose this poem.

From Wen Fu: The Art of Writing, *translated*
by Sam Hamill, Milkweed, 2000.

SIR PHILIP SIDNEY (1554–1586)

Only the poet, . . . lifted up with the vigor of his own invention, doth grow, in effect, into another nature, in making things either better than nature bringeth forth, or, quite anew, forms such as never were in nature, as the heroes, demigods, cyclops, chimeras, furies, and such like; so as he goeth hand in hand with nature, not enclosed within the narrow warrant of her gifts, but freely ranging within the zodiac of his own wit. Nature never set forth the earth in so rich tapestry as divers poets have done; neither with pleasant rivers, fruitful trees, sweet-smelling flowers, nor whatsoever else may make the too-much-loved earth more lovely; her world is brazen, the poets only deliver a golden.

From "An Apology for Poetry," in Selected Poetry and Prose.
David Kalstone, ed. Signet, 1970.

SAMUEL JOHNSON (1709–1784)

Poetry is the art of uniting pleasure with truth, by calling imagination to the help of reason. Epic poetry undertakes to teach the most important truths by the most pleasing precepts, and therefore relates some great event in the most affecting manner. History must supply the writer with the rudiments of narration, which he must improve and exalt by a nobler art, must animate by dramatic energy, and diversify by retrospection and anticipation; morality must teach him the exact bounds and different shades of vice and virtue; from policy and the practice of life he has to learn the discriminations of character and the tendency of the passions, either single or combined; and physiology must supply him with illustrations and images. To put these materials to poetical use is required an imagination capable of painting nature and realizing fiction. Nor is he yet a poet till he has attained the whole extension of his language, distinguished all the delicacies of phrase, and all the colors of words, and learned to adjust their different sounds to all the varieties of metrical modulation.

From The Lives of the Most Eminent English Poets,
vol. I, "Milton." Methuen, 1896.

WILLIAM BLAKE (1757–1827)

When this Verse was first dictated to me I consider'd a Monotonous Cadence like that used by Milton & Shakespeare & all writers of English Blank Verse, derived from the modern bondage of Rhyming; to be a necessary and indispensable part of Verse. But I soon found that in the mouth of a true Orator such monotony was not only awkward, but as much a bondage as rhyme itself. I therefore have produced a variety in every line, both of cadences & number of syllables. Every word and every letter is studied and put into its fit place: the terrific numbers are reserved for the terrific parts—the mild & gentle for the mild & gentle parts, and the prosaic, for inferior parts: all are necessary to each other. Poetry Fetter'd Fetters the Human Race! Nations are Destroy'd, or Flourish, in proportion as Their Poetry Painting and Music, are Destroy'd or Flourish! The Primeval State of Man, was Wisdom, Art and Science.

From "To The Public," a preface to "Jerusalem," in The Complete Poetry and Prose. *David V. Erdman, ed. Anchor Books, 1982.*

WILLIAM WORDSWORTH (1770–1850)

Taking up the subject, then, upon general grounds, let me ask, what is meant by the word Poet? What is a Poet? To whom does he address himself? And what language is to be expected from him?—He is a man speaking to men: a man, it is true, endowed with more lively sensibility, more enthusiasm and tenderness, who has greater knowledge of human nature, and a more comprehensive soul, than are supposed to be common among mankind; a man pleased with his own passions and volitions, and who rejoices more than other men in the spirit of life that is in him; delighting to contemplate similar volitions and passions as manifested in the goings-on of the universe, and habitually impelled to create them where he does not find them.

From "Preface to the Second Edition of Lyrical Ballads," *in* The Oxford Authors: William Wordsworth. *Stephen Gill, ed. Oxford University Press, 1984.*

PERCY BYSSHE SHELLEY (1792–1822)

It is impossible to read the compositions of the most celebrated writers of the present day without being startled with the electric life which burns within their words. They measure the circumference and sound the depths of human nature with a comprehensive and all-penetrating spirit, and they are themselves perhaps the most sincerely astonished at its manifestations, for it is less their spirit than the spirit of the age. Poets are the hierophants of an unapprehended inspiration, the mirrors of the gigantic shadows which futurity casts upon the present, the words which express what they understand not; the trumpets which sing to battle, and feel not what they inspire: the influence which is moved not, but moves. Poets are the unacknowledged legislators of the World.

From "A Defence of Poetry," in Shelley's Critical Prose. *Bruce R. McElderry, ed. University of Nebraska Press, 1967.*

JOHN KEATS (1795–1821)

As to the poetical Character itself, (I mean that sort of which, if I am any thing, I am a Member; that sort distinguished from the wordsworthian or egotistical sublime; which is a thing per se and stands alone) it is not itself—it has no self—it is every thing and nothing—It has no character—it enjoys light and shade; it lives in gusto, be it foul or fair, high or low, rich or poor, mean or elevated—It has as much delight in conceiving an Iago as an Imogen. What shocks the virtuous philosopher, delights the camelion Poet. It does no harm from its relish of the dark side of things any more than from its taste for the bright one; because they both end in speculation. A Poet is the most unpoetical of any thing in existence; because he has no Identity—he is continually in for—and filling some other Body—The Sun, the Moon, the Sea and Men and Women who are creatures of impulse are poetical and have about them an unchangeable attribute—the poet has none; no identity—he is certainly the most unpoetical of all God's Creatures.

From a letter to Richard Woodhouse, 27 October 1818, in Letters of John Keats: A Selection. *Robert Gittings, ed. Oxford University Press, 1970.*

RALPH WALDO EMERSON (1803–1882)

For it is not metres, but a metre-making argument that makes a poem—a thought so passionate and alive that like the spirit of a plant or an animal it has an architecture of its own, and adorns nature with a new thing. The thought and the form are equal in the order of time, but in the order of genesis the thought is prior to the form. The poet has a new thought; he has a whole new experience to unfold; he will tell us how it was with him, and all men will be the richer in his fortune. For the experience of a new age requires a new confession, and the world seems always waiting for its poet.

From "The Poet," in Selections from Ralph Waldo Emerson. *Stephen Whichler, ed. Riverside Editions, 1960.*

EDGAR ALLAN POE (1809–1849)

I need scarcely observe that a poem deserves its title only inasmuch as it excites, by elevating the soul. The value of the poem is the ratio of this elevating excitement. But all excitements are, through a psychal necessity, transient. That degree of excitement which would entitle a poem to be so called at all, cannot be sustained throughout a composition of any great length. At the lapse of half an hour, at the very utmost, it flags—fails—a revulsion ensues—and then the poem is, in effect, and in fact, no longer such.

From "The Poetic Principle," in Selected Prose, Poetry and Eureka. *W. H. Auden, ed. Holt, Rinehart, and Winston, 1950.*

WILLIAM BUTLER YEATS (1865–1939)

I tried to make the language of poetry coincide with that of passionate, normal speech. I wanted to write in whatever language comes most naturally when we soliloquise, as I do all day long, upon the events of our own lives or of any life where we can see ourselves for the moment.

From "A General Introduction for My Work," in Essays and Introductions. *Collier Books, 1968.*

WILLIAM CARLOS WILLIAMS (1883–1963)

If the inventive imagination must look, as I think, in the field of art for its richest discoveries today it will best make its way by compass and follow no path.

But before any material progress can be accomplished there must be someone to draw a discriminating line between true and false values.

The true value is that peculiarity which gives an object a character by itself. The associational or sentimental value is the false. Its imposition is due to lack of imagination, to an easy lateral sliding.

From "Prologue to Kora in Hell," *in* Selected Essays. *New Directions, 1969.*

T. S. ELIOT (1888–1965)

There is a great deal, in the writing of poetry, which must be conscious and deliberate. In fact, the bad poet is usually unconscious where he ought to be conscious, and conscious where he ought to be unconscious. Both errors tend to make him "personal." Poetry is not a turning loose of emotion, but an escape from emotion; it is not the expression of personality, but an escape from personality. But, of course, only those who have personality and emotions know what it means to want to escape from these things.

From "Tradition and the Individual Talent," in The Sacred Wood. *Methuen, 1920.*

LOUISE BOGAN (1897–1970)

"Verse as speech" and "verse as song": these are the two attitudes toward formal poetry—or rather in formal poetry—that die out first, and perennially need to be renewed. Formal poetry should continually remain in contact with the speech and the life around it, but this it does not do, and this division is made easier by the fact that poetry has for centuries been encased—one might almost say embalmed—in print. The technique becomes rigidified, and poets begin to write by the rules that scholars have deduced from this or that poetic canon. Poets become frightened of emotion and of the Sublime. . . . In this situation, we have the keepers of the canon, and we have the breakers of the canon.

From "The Pleasures of Formal Poetry," in The Poet's Work. *Reginald Gibbons, ed. Houghton Mifflin, 1979.*

RANDALL JARRELL (1914–1965)

Modernist poetry exerted its attraction because it was carrying the tendencies of romanticism to their necessary conclusions; now most of those conclusions have been arrived at; and how can the poet go any further? How can poems be written that are more violent? more disorganized? more obscure? more—the adjectives throng to me—than those that have already been written? And the poets, at the ends of their processes of specialization, are more or less conscious of what has happened. Some of them have tried to make their poetry conform to their critical principles, spoiling their poetry in the process.

From "A Note on Poetry," in Kipling, Auden and Co.
Farrar, Straus, and Giroux, 1980.

DENISE LEVERTOV (1923–1998)

For me, back of the idea of organic form is the concept that there is a form in all things (and in our experience) which the poet can discover and reveal. There are, no doubt, temperamental differences between poets who use prescribed forms and those who look for new ones—people who need a tight schedule to get anything done, and people who have to have a free hand— but the difference in their conception of "content" or "reality" is functionally more important. On the one hand is the idea that content, reality, experience, is essentially fluid and must be given form; on the other, this sense of seeking out inherent, though not immediately apparent form.

From "Some Notes on Organic Form," in New and Selected Essays.
New Directions, 1992.

LISEL MUELLER (*b.* 1924)

Still, love is the impulse from which poetry springs. Even dark poems. Especially dark poems. To know the worst and write in spite of that, that must be love. To celebrate what's on the other side of the darkness. Surely great poetry has always sprung from love-in-spite-of, like love for a deeply flawed person.

And if it's true, as Williams wrote, that people die from the lack of what is found in poems, then poetry must not be trivial, peripheral, ivory-towerish, as it is often accused of being; then we have a responsibility to speak to and for others. Certainly that means acknowledging suffering. But it also means to heal, to bring delight and hope. It implies consolation. How to console without being false, shallow or sentimental: I find that the hardest challenge.

From The Poet's Notebook. *Stephen Kuusisto, Deborah Tall,*
and David Weiss, eds. Norton, 1995.

LOUISE GLÜCK (*b.* 1943)

To recapitulate: the source of art is experience, the end product truth, and the artist, surveying the actual, constantly intervenes and manages, lies and deletes, all in the service of truth.

From Proofs and Theories, *Ecco Press, 1994.*

DANA GIOIA (*b*. 1950)

I have read poetry as long as I have been able to read. Before that, my mother, a woman of no advanced education, read or recited it to me from memory. Consequently, I have never considered poetry an intrinsically difficult art whose mysteries can be appreciated only by a trained intellectual elite. Poetry is an art—like painting or jazz, opera or drama—whose pleasures are generally open to any intelligent person with the inclination to savor them. Critics, justly obsessed with the difficulty of interpreting poetical texts, often forget the sheer immediacy of the medium's appeal. Study may deepen and training refine one's taste for poetry, but the appetite itself is not an especially sophisticated thing.

From Can Poetry Matter? *Graywolf Press, 1992.*

EMILY GROSHOLZ (*b*. 1950)

A poem is compelling and preserved because it is beautiful. The aesthetic appeal of a poem itself has a moral dimension, allying it to an ethic of gratification. Reading a poem should provide the joys of aesthetic satisfaction. It should refine our ability to hear and see, our delight in a particular language, in the sensual presence of life in a particular locale. And thus it persuades us of the pleasures and intrinsic value of this world. . . . Eloquence can be abused, but the cure for that abuse is not silence and deformity but more eloquence and more beauty.

From "Milosz and the Moral Authority of Poetry,"
Hudson Review, *Summer 1986.*

ALICE FULTON (*b*. 1952)

Poems are linguistic models of the world's working. Now our knowledge of form includes the new concept of manageable chaos, along with the ancient categories of order and chaos. If order is represented by the simple Euclidean shapes of nature and by metered verse, chaos might be analogous to failed free verse and gibberish. (It's somehow reassuring that chaos is still with us, evident in natural forms that show no underlying pattern.) And manageable chaos or fractal form might find its corollary in harmonious structures that surround and delight us, the body electric, where geography ends and pebbles begin.

From "Of Formal, Free and Fractal Verse: Singing the Body Electric,"
in Conversant Essays: Contemporary Poets on Poetry.
James McCorkle, ed. Wayne State University Press, 1990.

JANE HIRSCHFIELD (*b*. 1953)

The story of poetry has many beginnings. One is Mnemosyne—Remembrance— earliest-born of the Greek goddesses, mother of the Muses and also of the poem. Hesiod calls her the goddess of the first hour, as it would have to be: at the moment that time appears in the world, change appears in the world, and change alone, lacking memory's steadying counterweight, would mean Chaos. . . . Through Mnemosyne, the knowable world continues from moment to moment, and through the poetry she engendered, words at first learned to transcend time.

From Nine Gates: Entering the Mind of Poetry,
HarperCollins, 1997.

APPENDIX B

WRITING ABOUT POETRY

In college classes we tend to divide writing into separate disciplines. Some professors use *Western Wind* in creative writing classes and expect their students to write poems rather than essays. Others focus on reading critically and expect essays that reflect upon such reading. This textbook is designed for both possibilities, and assumes that they are not mutually exclusive. Why shouldn't students of literature also attempt to write poems, whether or not they intend to become poets? And why shouldn't "creative" writers learn to write essays? As the previous appendix illustrates, good poets are very often good critics as well. We might add that good critics frequently have a touch of the poet.

If your professor assigns you an essay topic, no doubt you will assume that you are writing to please that particular professor. "What kind of essay does Jones like?" students may ask, often feeling anxiety about just what is expected of them. Perhaps you've noticed the sort of game that often gets played in which students try to get the word on professors who seem to make confusing and contradictory demands. Before writing any essay, you will be faced with several questions; no matter how long you labor in this field, the same questions arise, and you will not always be confident that you have answered them. All writers live with some degree of uncertainty and doubt; nevertheless, the following approaches might be helpful.

What will I write about?
The teacher may settle this for you by assigning a particular poem or poems as your topic. If you are free to choose the poems you write about, however, your first task will be to pay close attention to what you read. Choose poems

to which you have strong reactions, either of love or dislike. Read them carefully several times. Read them aloud to yourself or to friends. Talk about them; mull them over. If possible, even memorize them, taking the poems into your nervous system. If a poem gets under your skin, as it were, chances are you will have a lot to say about it. Be honest. Admit what you like and dislike, but ask yourself why. Admit what you do not know or understand, and ask yourself whether you need to do further reading before you write. If you take any notes, be sure to keep track of the books or articles they come from, taking down any information you might need later and quoting accurately.

What will I say?

Readers of essays don't want to waste time any more than writers do, so they will want you to have a point, or thesis. They will want to know where you stand in relation to your subject. Chances are, when you begin your essay, you will not be entirely sure what you believe. That is why revision is usually necessary—to clarify exactly what it is you mean to say.

One approach is to write the first draft of your essay without having entirely made up your mind what your point will be. Simply respond to the poem, following its apparent logic (or lack thereof) and paying close attention to its strategies, using any skills that come to hand. Once you have a draft done, let it sit, even if only for a few hours. Go shoot some hoops or eat dinner or talk with a friend or listen to James Brown or Mozart. If you want some help later on, it's not a crime to ask your friends to read or listen to what you have written; hopefully they will be honest enough to tell you whether you have been clear.

Go back and interrogate your essay. Try to enunciate clearly and simply just what it is you want to say about this poem. Are you making a point about its technique? About its relevance to some social or historical event? About its moral value? About a particular kind of pleasure you get from it? About its relation to other poems by the same author or by others? Are your ideas fully developed, and illustrated with images, examples or quotations? When readers finish your essay, they ought to know what you believe about some aspect of life and art. Try to avoid writing a conclusion that merely repeats your opening in a formulaic fashion. Instead, ask yourself why anyone should care about what you are trying to say, and respond with as much passion and insight as you can muster.

Who am I writing for?

The best critics give us clear, incisive ideas in lively prose, choosing words for accuracy as well as rhythm, often using active verbs to charge the language the way a poet might. To do this, you will have to imagine your readers, just as professional writers do. Professors may be able to follow a lot of technical jargon, and such language can be useful, but you might be better off imagining your readers as people outside of class, even far away from the campus—intelligent, interested people who happen to like reading about poetry. These readers might be familiar with your subject, but you might still give background and context for your essay, just to put things clearly on track.

At some point, all writers learn by imitating models left by other good writers. One of the best ways for an essayist to do this is to read magazines and journals that publish good current criticism. Even reading movie or music reviews written by good critics will help you get a feel for the shape of the essay, because reviewers should have strong opinions and write lively prose. We hope you can read these magazines and journals in your library. Ask your professor to recommend some—especially those journals that publish articles intended for the educated common reader.

Seeing examples of good student writing can also be very helpful, and we offer two examples below. The first paper is by Kathleen M. Romero, who wrote her essay after discovering two poems back to back in the Anthology (pp. 542–544) that both used train motifs.

ALL ABOARD?
The Use of the Train by Alvarez and Forché

In the anthology section of *Western Wind*, two poems by two different poets appear one after the other by coincidence—though not actually by coincidence, but rather most likely in chronological order by the poets' birthdates, then by alphabetical order. Yet reading these two poems, placed together by an editorial rule, can reveal fascinating parallels. Both Julia Alvarez's "Old Heroines" and Carolyn Forché's "For the Stranger" use a train as a symbol for a false dream world that allows its passengers to remove themselves from reality and view it through the frame of a window, as if life were merely a display in a moving museum or a painting we could examine without entering and participating in it. The train is, however, fleeting and transitory, leaving its inhabitants only temporarily suspended in its dream world while reality passes by often ignored, with no regard to the consequences of such neglect. This image of the train works in different ways in each poem: for Forché, the train's suspended reality is shown positively and is encouraged by metaphorical language that seems itself to escape mundane reality, while for Alvarez this same image is seen as a "jailhouse" that entraps its passenger in perpetual discontent. Each utilizes inherent aspects of the train to create a world between realities, but ultimately reveals something different about this world through their language.

The two poems are strikingly similar in many ways. Both describe a vague landscape filled with farmhouses and faint lights engulfed in a sea of endless fields rolling by as passengers watch from their windows. This element of looking out is accompanied by moments of reflection in each poem, as the characters see themselves in the panes of glass instead of clearly seeing the world beyond it. This introspection is found in both poems, but in contrast to the reality passing by them outside the window. This leads to the overall similarity between the two poems, which is the way that the train symbolizes a type of dream world in which reality is suspended. The nature of the train is as a vehicle that does not necessarily escape reality (like a plane, for instance, defying gravity), but instead passes through it. Those inside the train can pass through reality in a state of suspension, where anything can happen without consequence or acknowledgement of the world outside. The train allows for the unique experience of watching the world go by from an observatory rather than a participatory viewpoint—off the roads to which cars are limited and through real peoples' backyards and lives. Both poets use all these aspects of the train. Each poet ultimately, however, uses this image for a different purpose. Forché advocates this dream world and clings to it with metaphorical language that almost seeks to suspend reality, and Alvarez uses the train to show how damaging this dream world can be.

While Alvarez uses fairly basic language in "Heroines," Forché tends to use more figurative language in her poem. She scatters metaphors, personification, and various other devices throughout "Stranger." In the first few lines, Forché uses a simile to illustrate the tense interaction, seemingly mundane but charged with meaning, between the speaker and the stranger, whose simple utterance lingers "like a fruit pit" (2) on his tongue. Forché then moves right into a comparison of the train to a sleigh, "reaching down / to touch its buried runners" (6–7) and racing along as the only reality for these passengers, free of geographical locations and boundaries. "There is only this train . . . ," she states (4), for these passengers. As they meet on the platform, Forché personifies the wind as having "broken teeth" (9) that sink into them, giving the reader a sharp sensual image. She then personifies the telegraph post as chopping the snowy fields "into white blocks" (14), as fields usually do appear from the windows of a train. One of the most significant poetic devices Forché uses in this poem occurs in lines 14–15 when she states that also in each window there is "the crude painting of a small farm." This direct comparison of the world outside the train windows to paintings illustrates the way in which the poet evokes her uncertain reality. The fact that this "painting" seems "crude" only underlies the detachment one can achieve from reality—a detachment sought by the passengers in "Stranger." All of this metaphorical language seems to illustrate this sense of detachment, as if she can escape ordinary language or reality with this kind of imagery. Perhaps she uses these metaphors and other poetic devices to transfer the core reality of the language to other meanings and images, and consequently create that sense of being above the commonplace or out of the ordinary.

This is further illustrated by the following lines, in which the passengers in "Stranger" continue to seek detachment from reality by purposely ignoring that very commonplace language just discussed—the simple diction of mothers scolding their children. This couple continues to relish their place outside reality; watching it from windows and pretending that they are in another realm, in which ordinary words and concrete locations cease to exist. They halfheartedly try to ascertain their location, but end up describing the same ambiguous landscapes:

> There are few clues as to where
> we are: the baled wheat scattered
> everywhere like missing coffins.
> The distant yellow kitchen lights
> wiped with oil.
> Everywhere the black dipping wires
> stretching messages from one side of a country to another. (20–27)

The landscapes are in this case, however, compared dismally to "missing coffins" and the kitchen lights of farmhouses are "distant" and "wiped with oil," as if the reality that exists within those homes is obscure and indiscernible.

In later lines of this poem the passengers wipe off the foggy window, but not to look out to this bleak landscape of reality; instead, they do this "in order to see ourselves" (31). In the following lines, perhaps the most poignant moment of the poem, the stranger shows the speaker photos of his wife and children. This is the one moment in which the passengers acknowledge the reality of their lives—and yet they still view it "from the windows of [a] wallet" (35), as if it too can be watched from afar, detached. This is a moment of bittersweet recognition that follows a tender exchange between the lovers in the preceding lines as a sinking sense of the inevitable fact that this ride might end sets in. The speaker becomes more desperate, longing to hold onto these dreamlike tender moments as they slip by with each city they pass. Their faces are reflected "in the gold buttons" of the porter (37), as if they are literally faced with the fact that the alternate time-space in which they have traveled is being counted down by this porter "each time the train slows" (36). The two lovers cling to each other, frantically wanting this ride to last, and when "there are / no more cities" left (43–44), Forché uses verbs of desperation to illustrate the urgency of these final moments before the passengers have to face reality: *holding, pulling, sliding,* finally *hurrying* their mouths together in one final kiss (47). The end of the poem implies that the lovers decide to attempt to forgo the reality of their lives even after the ride is over, but technically the ride never ends in this poem. The reader will never know what happens to them.

In her "Heroines" Alvarez seeks to destroy this dream-world mentality. She places her character on a train in a mockery of the type of fantasy world produced by novels or the literature of romance. "If she's not married off, she gets on a train," Alvarez states of this old heroine (2). Though it is clear that her lover "has broken things off" (4), the heroine still follows him on a train to unknown destinations. This statement exemplifies a story in which the heroine is placed in an unrealistic situation, reason and common sense dismissed along with reality. Alvarez says that this heroine could be "racing through Russia or Iowa" (5), mocking the tendency in the accused literature to use exotic locales, such as the Venice or Bucharest in Forché's poem (implying the route of that very mysterious and glamorous Orient Express), by the addition of Iowa. The heroine could be looking out at this nondescript landscape, or this other nondescript landscape, but eventually catches her own reflection in the glass, tragic and dramatic. In contrast to the Forché poem, this self-reflection brings a pang of reality to the character rather than a prolonged delusion. "How long must I still play this part?" the heroine asks herself (10) before Alvarez hits home in the following stanza.

The next stanza take the reader outside the moving train, straight into the reality of the ambiguous houses watched absently by train passengers. Alvarez introduces us to "the unstoried women" who occupy those farmhouses and form deep contrasts to the fantasy heroines of novels (12). The heroine would not exist without these women, for they are the reality against which the heroine is created—the "mere back-drop" for her. The heroine is false, unrealistic, living in a dream world, just like the speaker in "Stranger." The dream world plays to a human desire to transcend the everyday reality of life and enter an exotic realm in which they can do whatever they wish without consequence. It appeals to these women in farmhouses, who dream of whisking away in a train to said exotic locations and leaving their commonplace exis-tences for "some heady excitement" (16). But when these women awaken, they realize the security and true contentment with their place, and snuggle back into theirs husbands' arms.

Alvarez brilliantly transports us back and forth between these two realms—that of reality and that of the dream-world of the heroine—as the farm women turn on their lights in reassurance of their place in the world, and the heroine catches a faint glimpse of these lights as she glides by on the train. Here Alvarez refers to the train as a "jailhouse," as if this dream-world had trapped the heroine in a suffocating fiction she cannot escape. While our society, or Forché's poem, glorify this dream-world, Alvarez sees it as a damaging deception. Her heroine will "ride on forever" (19), entrapped in unhappiness and dissatisfaction. While many women seek such glamour after reading about it, their own reality of farmhouse kitchens might be what matters.

Both heroines in these poems will ride on for eternity, and to what end? Forché and Alvarez seem to use their poetry to convey different messages about this end. While Forché uses figurative language to convey this intimate, fleeting dream-world that perhaps she herself entered at one time, Alvarez uses more direct language and irony to convey a message of her own against this romantic fantasy. It's up to the readers to decide if they wish to hop on a train and see what kind of ride is in store for them.

The second paper is by William M. Fischer, who wrote about Frost's "Mending Wall" (Anthology, p. 438). Notice his interesting title and complex stance toward his subject.

TEARING DOWN FROST'S "MENDING WALL"

Robert Frost's poem "Mending Wall" is often read as a simple argument against civilization and its need to construct arbitrary boundaries, or "walls." The narrator of the poem, for example, champions the force of nature—that "something" which tears walls down—and argues that walls are unnecessary and that we would be better off without them. The narrator's neighbor is read as a "civilized" man who, by building the walls he believes support civilization, actually degenerates into savagery. And, indeed, this sort of reading may be exactly what Frost intended in the poem. To interpret the work so simply, however, is to do it a disservice, for there is another argument running through the poem, one in which Frost concedes that the building of walls is potentially a positive activity. Rather than simply arguing for or against walls, Frost actually takes both sides, suggesting that the tension between nature and civilization will never be resolved. In fact, it is this very tension—the continual tearing down and rebuilding of the wall—that gives Frost's poem its power and saves it from being a shallow, simplistic attack against civilization and its "walls."

Frost establishes this tension in the first line of "Mending Wall": "Something there is that doesn't love a wall [. . .] ." The narrator of the poem knows that walls, when left unattended, have a tendency to fall apart. He is reluctant, however, to define exactly what this force is that tears down walls, and only calls it "something." If Frost had simply said that "nature" doesn't love a wall, the meaning of this line would have been more definite. At the same time, such a statement might have diminished the intensity of the poem, as it would have been far too simplistic. Rather than stating unquestionable axioms, Frost allows for uncertainty. Later in the line, for example, the narrator refuses to say that nature "hates" walls, or even "dislikes" them. The tone is much more ambiguous—the most he can say is that nature "doesn't love" a wall. True, the narrator will later say that nature "wants [walls] down" (line 36), but for now Frost is not nearly so direct. Rather, he is content simply to create uncertainty. Frost suggests that nature tears down walls, but does not say so openly in order to heighten the tension of the piece.

Frost employs a similar strategy in lines 5 through 9. Throughout the poem, he suggests that walls are human structures, and that nature works against them by sending "the frozen-ground-swell under [them]," spilling "the upper boulders in the sun" and making "gaps even two can pass abreast" (2–4). He admits, however, that hunters can tear down walls as well, leaving "not one stone on a stone" (7). Thus, the tearing down of walls is not the exclusive domain of nature—

humans can do it too. Later, when the narrator contemplates telling his neighbor that "Elves" destroy their wall, Frost again suggests that the force which tears down walls cannot be simply defined. Rather than telling his neighbor that "nature" ruins the wall, the narrator instead resorts to fictitious creatures to describe that "something" which actually destroys it. While it seems that Frost is constructing a clear-cut division between humankind and nature, he allows that the conflict is much more complicated.

How Frost feels about the wall itself is uncertain. For example, even though he suggests that mending the wall is an act of separation—"We keep the wall between us as we go" (15)—his description of the process is not entirely negative. Mending the wall seems almost play-ful; it's "just another kind of outdoor game," the narrator says (21). One senses that, although they "wear [their] fingers rough with han-dling" the stones (20), the narrator and his neighbor are also having fun rebuilding the wall. The two men have returned to their childhood, playing, pretending, and speaking to the rocks with which they work as if they were alive: "Stay where you are until our backs are turned!" (19). While in a literal sense this process separates the men, symbolically it has also brought them together. The work is a ritual, and Frost speaks of it in a suitably reverent tone. When "spring mending-time" comes, the narrator lets his "neighbor know beyond the hill; / And on a day [they] meet to walk the line / And set the wall between [them] once again" (11–14). Mending the wall is an annual tradition, one in which both men participate. Although the narrator and his neighbor are rebuilding the very wall which separates them, they have never-theless been brought together in doing so. The wall connects as well as separates.

Frost does, of course, make a strong argument against the build-ing of walls in the next section of the poem. "He is all pine," the nar-rator claims, "and I am apple orchard. / My apple trees will never get across / And eat the cones under his pines [. . .] " (24–26). There is no reason to separate the land, and yet the wall remains. His neighbor's rebuttal—"Good fences make good neighbors" (27)—is catchy, but spe-cious. Ultimately, the wall dividing the two men is illogical. Fences are useful only when they divide property, but here that is not necessary—as the narrator muses: "Why do [fences] make good neighbors? Isn't it / Where there are cows? But here there are no cows" (30–31). Because of his insistence on maintaining the unnecessary wall, the neighbor seems a primitive caveman, "[b]ringing a stone grasped firmly by the top / In each hand, like an old-stone savage armed" (39–40). Even though the building of walls is supposedly a "civilized" act, the neighbor is portrayed as a crude, almost barbarous person. While he would no doubt consider himself an enlightened man, the neighbor in fact "moves in darkness" (41), content to rebuild the wall merely because his father did before him: "He will not go behind his father's saying, / And he likes having thought of it so well / He says again, 'Good fences make good neighbors'" (43–45). Like a parrot, the neighbor can repeat what he has been told, but cannot think on his own. In contrast to this man, the narrator seems much more respectable, and thus his argument is the more convincing one.

Yet, one cannot help leaving the poem with a lingering sense of ambiguity. *Do* good fences make good neighbors? Frost has admitted that in some cases they do, and has depicted the mending itself in a positive light. While the overall argument of the poem seems to be against walls, Frost has allowed another side to the debate. He begins the poem with his basic argument, and later repeats it—"Something there is that doesn't love a wall, / That wants it down" (35–36)— suggesting that he is adamant in his belief that the wall is unnecessary. However, he also repeats the opposing argument—"Good fences make good neighbors"—placing it in the final line and thus granting it some status in the poem. While one may lean toward one argument or the other, neither will ultimately win. Rather, Frost suggests that what goes on between two arguments—the substance of the poem itself, the continual process of building, tearing down, and building up again—is the only constant upon which one can rely.

It is not unusual to find in the poems of Robert Frost themes or motifs set in opposition to one another, so that out of the conflict of opposites arises a tension which, rather than undermining the unity of the work, instead strengthens it. Refusing simply to advocate one side of an issue or another, Frost allows ideas to battle against one another and uses this energy to fuel his work. We may at first wish to find clear-cut answers in the poem, but it is important to recognize that Frost does not simply argue for or against walls. Though the narrator of "Mending Wall" supports the side of nature and suggests that walls are a contrivance of civilization we could do better without, Frost himself portrays the conflict between nature and civilization as ultimately more important than its final outcome.

WORK CITED

Frost, Robert. "Mending Wall." <u>The Poetry of Robert Frost: The Collected Poems, Complete and Unabridged.</u> Ed. Edward Connery Lathem. New York: Holt, 1969. 156–157.

Another student, Molly Williams, wrote her short paper on Yeats's "Leda and the Swan" (see Chapter 2, p. 40), but makes use of other Yeats poems as well. Because she is writing about more than one poem, she cites page numbers in Yeats's *Collected Poems*.

PASSION OR CONQUEST: THE BIRD IMAGE IN YEATS'S "LEDA AND THE SWAN"

William Butler Yeats's "Leda and the Swan" is, of course, a poem about an event from Greek mythology: Zeus comes to the mortal Leda in the form of a swan, and from their union are born Helen, the beauty for whom the Trojan War is fought, and Clytemnestra, who has her husband, Agamemnon, murdered. It is an exciting mythological moment told in vivid language in the form of a sonnet, and the poem may be read on this level alone. But there is a completely separate aspect to this poem, one entirely distinct from the myth, and just as devastating, if not more so. This second aspect hinges on the image of the swan as representing ideal love, or at least the possibility of ideal love, established by Yeats in earlier poems. When this representation is kept in mind, the poem becomes a question about whether or not a human is capable of obtaining or even understanding such eternal, perfect love. The question is left unanswered, but in such a way that we cannot help feeling the answer would be *no*.

In Greek mythology, Zeus is notorious for his extramarital affairs with mortals, and for many of these affairs he would take on an earthly shape. It cannot be overlooked that Yeats chose for his poem the particular myth in which Zeus becomes a *swan*, rather than a bull or a shower of gold or some other avatar. The swan is important because in earlier poems Yeats has already established this bird as an image resonating with questions about the human soul and ideal love, and this imagery is carried over to "Leda."

In "Nineteen Hundred and Nineteen," Yeats writes that "Some moralist or mythological poet / Compares the solitary soul to a swan; / I am satisfied with that [. . .]" (208). The poet of whom he writes may well be himself, and the poem to which he refers could be

"The Wild Swans at Coole." In this poem, Yeats uses the fact that swans mate for life to create of the birds an image of ideal, requited, eternal love:

> Unwearied still, lover by lover,
> They paddle in the cold
> Companionable streams or climb the air;
> Their hearts have not grown old;
> Passion or conquest, wander where they will,
> Attend upon them still. (131)

Swans mate for life, but there are "nine and fifty swans" in the poem, meaning that one of them is without a mate, and the poet himself stands alone by the side of the pond, watching the birds. Yeats' unrequited love for Maud Gonne being common knowledge, it is natural to identify Yeats with the lone swan, though whether the swan represents Yeats himself, or the lover he wishes to have but cannot, is arguable. Nevertheless, "The Wild Swans at Coole" connects the image of swans firmly to the ideas of perfect, ideal love and the possibility of such love, as yet unrequited.

But how does such imagery relate to "Leda," in which the couple consists of a swan and a human, and the relationship is violent and confused? It does seem that there is some connection between the two poems, for "Leda" in some places echoes the earlier poem. For instance, in the beginning of "Leda" we have "the great wings beating still / Above the staggering girl" (214), and in "Wild Swans" the poet describes "The bell-beat of their wings above my head" (131). This puts both Yeats and Leda beneath the level of the swans. Symbolically, it places them in sight of perfect love, but not connected to it or part of it. Leda is, after all, apparently being raped. Also, Yeats asks of Leda, "And how can body, laid in that white rush, / But feel the strange heart beating where it lies?" (214). He has written of the hearts of swans before in "Wild Swans": "Their hearts have not grown old; / Passion or conquest, wander where they will, / Attend upon them still" (131). A heart that does not grow old might indeed be called "strange," for growing old is a most common thing for humans. Also, in the final lines of "Wild Swans," the poet asks, "Among what rushes will they build, / By what lake's edge or pool / Delight men's eyes when I awake some day / To find that they have flown away?" (132). He writes that the swans will be found in "rushes," and we find Leda in the "white rush" that is the bird; though in the later poem the word "rush" connotes motion more than reeds, the word is the same. And finally, in "Wild Swans" the reason that the loving hearts of the birds are not old is that "Passion or conquest / [. . .] / Attend upon them still." They are like gods in this, outside human griefs.

The echoes of "Wild Swans" in "Leda" may be somewhat faint, barely enough even to be called allusions, but there are enough of them to be called more than coincidence and certainly too many to be ignored. A definite connection is drawn between the two poems, and the idea of swans as solitary souls capable of perfect, eternal love is carried over to "Leda."

But how does the swan image function in the latter poem? We have a swan, a creature which now encompasses for us the possibility of ideal love, and a human girl, who begins the poem in a position of complete subjugation. And in "Leda" we have actual contact between the human and the bird; the interaction is a striking, ultimately confusing blend of violence and sensuality.

The most obvious language in the poem is the language of violence which renders Leda subordinate; she is "staggering," "caught," "terrified," "helpless" and "mastered by the brute blood of the air" (214–15). This language suggests domination rather than outright cruelty, yet the words and phrases are violent enough to describe a rape. The poem probably would, in fact, demand to be read as a rape situation if only these words were used. But Yeats uses subtle, less shocking language in describing Leda's reactions as well. For instance, he writes that the bird holds the girl's "breast upon his breast," a phrase strikingly similar to those he has used in "The Heart of a Woman" and "He Hears the Cry of the Sedge" to describe the possibility of peaceful, fulfilled love, although in the latter poem such love is unattained. Also, though Leda's fingers are "terrified," they are also "vague," suggesting that she is not entirely sure what she wishes to do with them. Her "thighs" are "caressed / By the dark webs," and they are "loosening," though whether this is because they are forced to do so or because she wishes to loosen them is left for us to ponder. The image of her feeling "the strange heart beating where it lies" is not at all violent, but rather intimate. In addition, Yeats writes of "A shudder in the loins," not only "A shudder in *his* loins," which would fit the meter just as well. Though the language of sensuality is more subtle and ambiguous than that of violence, it is undeniably present.

This mixture of violence and sensuality creates the effect that Leda is not quite certain how she feels or what she wants, and the reader is left wondering just what the encounter between the girl and the bird *is*. It is a problem left unresolved, for the poem itself ends with a question: "Did she put on his knowledge with his power / Before the indifferent beak could let her drop?" Just what is "his knowledge"? It is the knowledge of what will come to pass in Greece and Troy, and the poem asks if Leda has any inkling of these coming events, or idea of what this moment will "engender." But also, if the swan is a creature with the capability of perfect love, the poem asks if Leda, even for a moment, understood this kind of knowledge. Did a mere mortal feel, however briefly, what a creature of "feathered glory" and "strange heart" is capable of feeling—what a god is capable of knowing?

The question is not answered, and we are left with the image of "the indifferent beak" letting "her drop." We are not told why the beak is "indifferent"; perhaps it was so all along, or perhaps it became so when it found that she could not "put on his knowledge with his power." The poem leaves us with a feeling of desolation, of inevitable destruction, and we are reminded that however beautiful Leda is, she is a mere mortal, and the swan is a god, a "perfect" lover, a creature by its very nature ranked above and beyond human beings. This fact perhaps necessitates the violent language of domination in the poem, for what other words would be strong enough to describe the *power* of this creature, this image of a type of love beyond human comprehension? The poem ends with a question, because it is a question we do not wish to answer: Leda cannot have the "knowledge" of a perfect love; a human cannot mate for life with a swan or comprehend the lofty indifference of the gods.

WORK CITED

Yeats, William Butler. The Collected Poems. 2nd rev. ed. Ed. Richard J. Finneran New York: Scribner, 1996.

In both essays, the MLA method of documentation is used. Documentation is especially important if you are writing research papers. "MLA" stands for the Modern Language Association, a body of academics that has a very large influence upon current discussions of literature and criticism. Almost any good handbook of rhetoric and composition will give you full details about MLA forms of documentation: how to cite articles from various kinds of books and periodicals, music CDs, movies, and even material taken from the Internet. These guidebooks may also offer alternative methods of documentation, such as the method described in *The Chicago Manual of Style* or the APA (American Psychological Association) method, which is more commonly used in the social sciences. The MLA method is in many ways the simplest method yet devised.

Citations at the end of a paper should usually be given in alphabetical order by author. The following are examples of common MLA citations you might find at the end of an essay:

- **A book by a single author:**
  Format:
  Author's name. Book Title. City: Publisher, Date.
  Example:
  Gwynn, R. S. No Word of Farewell: Selected Poems 1970–2000. Ashland, OR: Story Line, 2001.

- **An article in an edited book:**
  Format:
  Author. "Title of Article." Title of Book. Editor's name. City: Publisher, Date. Pages.
  Example:
  Hadas, Rachel. "Word by Word, Page by Page." Unrelenting Readers: The New Poet-Critics. Ed. Paul M. Hedeen and D. G. Myers. Ashland, OR: Story Line, 2004. 235–59.

- **An article in a journal:**
  Format:
  Author Name. "Article Title." Journal Volume (Date): Pages.
  Example:
  Bell, Millicent. "Rilke's Duino Elegies." Sewanee Review CXI (2003): 631–42.

- **A work cited from a website:**
  Format:
  Author's Name. "Title." Name of website Date of access <web address>
  Example:
  Foley, Jack. "David Mason, the Poetry of Life and the Life of Poetry." The Alsop Review 22 June 2004 <www.alsopreview.com/foley/jfdmason.html>

SOME TECHNICAL MATTERS

If you take writing seriously, you will learn to think like a professional writer, not only imagining that "educated general reader" out there, but producing an error-free typescript. Never turn in an essay that you haven't carefully proofread. Computers make the correction of technical errors far easier than it used to be, and it is now time for you to take full responsibility for everything you write. Look up every word you don't know how to spell. Don't be duped by computer spell-checks; they do not distinguish between words like *there, they're,* and *their,* so you can easily be fooled into thinking you have chosen the correct one. Also, correct grammar and punctuation. If you are unsure whether you have written a coherent sentence and don't know how to fix it, scratch it out and write another one, or several, to take its place. Think of the process this way: The more you save your professors from having to mark technical errors, the more favorably they might look upon your ideas.

Learn to use quotations with absolute accuracy. Notice in the student papers above that there are two methods of quotation: the block quote, with its extra margins instead of quotation marks, and the quote given within your paragraph margins. The former is best used when quoting longer passages, say, four lines or more. When quoting verse, always remember to stack the lines exactly as they are in the text; poets care deeply about the arrangement of their lines. If you quote a short passage within your paragraph margins, you can denote line breaks with a slash mark (/) as follows:

> In "Stopping By Woods on a Snowy Evening," Frost writes that "The woods are lovely, dark and deep, / But I have promises to keep / And miles to go before I sleep [. . .]."

Not only are line breaks properly marked in this passage, but bracketed ellipsis points ([. . .]) are used at the end of the quotation to designate that the author is leaving out the last part of Frost's sentence. The ellipsis points are followed by a period before the quotation mark.

Give credit where credit is due. When you use someone else's words, put the words in quotation marks and acknowledge their source. Stealing someone else's words is called *plagiarism,* and must be avoided at all costs. There is a difference between asking a friend for helpful criticism of your paper and using any part of your friend's paper in writing for which you expect to receive credit. Stealing so much as a phrase from an article on the Internet is just as serious an offense. Besides, plagiarism goes against the whole purpose of writing essays, which is to command your own ideas rather than let yourself be commanded by the ideas of others.

Finally, learn to take pleasure in writing and revising. Sure, you've got assignments and deadlines to worry about, but try to meet them on your own terms when you can. Invest your writing with the kind of color and precision you find in the best poetry. The essay is a good place to learn what you really believe about what you read and how it relates to life. Ideas can be conveyed with gusto and grace; as a writer, your job is to be both interesting and accurate. Ideally, you would be making "fresh sense" (in Delmore Schwartz's phrase) out of the world and the word. All of us find this difficult, but it is supremely important that we try.

APPENDIX C

LITERARY CRITICISM

In the twentieth century a funny thing happened to poetry: It became more a subject for the classroom than a popular art form. This may now be changing as we observe new performance and publication strategies, including the Slam scene and electronic media, but it remains an important fact that schools of literary criticism have carried a great deal of cultural weight in the last century. They have also offered us ways of reading that we can extend to other aspects of our lives, often liberating us from static patterns of thought. The following brief essays are intended to introduce you to eight of these important "schools." You may wish to apply one or more of them in your own essays.

NEW CRITICISM

The term New Criticism has been around at least since 1941, when poet John Crowe Ransom published a book of essays under that title. Also called "formalist criticism," the New Criticism was characterized chiefly by its close, careful reading of canonical texts—and such close reading remains a very important skill. New Critics were often themselves poets, less interested, perhaps, in the social place of poetry than in the inner workings of the art. But it is not true that they read poems entirely without concern for historical contexts. Their chief contribution was to keep alive the distinctions that separate poetry from prose. In a preface to their highly-influential textbook, *Understanding Poetry*,

Cleanth Brooks and Robert Penn Warren suggested three rules for teachers:

1. Emphasis should be kept on the poem as a poem.
2. The treatment should be concrete and inductive.
3. A poem should always be treated as an organic system of relationships, and the poetic quality should never be understood as inhering in one or more factors taken in isolation. (ix)

These are reasonable, if limited, guidelines; Brooks and Warren went on to offer many examples of the close reading of poems. In the following passage they read an old Scots ballad, "The Wife of Usher's Well," which you can find in the Anthology (p. 369).

What is the intention of this poem? And, judged in the light of the intention, in what ways is the poem superior to the prose paraphrase? If one considers the poem carefully, he notices that the poem, like so many ballads, breaks up into a number of little pictures, and that some of the detail (otherwise irrelevant) becomes justified when we realize that it has been employed to make the scenes vivid for us. The poem is not content merely to state certain things *abstractly*: we must see the pictures. For example, consider the pictures given us in the sixth and seventh stanzas. The sixth conveys some sense of the bustling excitement with which the woman puts her maids to work when her sons unexpectedly arrive; the seventh conveys with a great deal of intensity the joy with which the mother receives her long-lost sons. She is anxious to make them comfortable; she has prepared the beds carefully for them. But she cannot tear herself away from them, even to let them go to sleep, and having thrown a shawl around her shoulders to keep warm as she sits up in the late chill night air, lingers for a little while by their beds. The poem does not *tell* us of her joy and relief at seeing them home again; it conveys a sense of this to us by showing the mother's joyful activity. In preferring the concrete form of statement to the abstract, "The Wife of Usher's Well" is typical of poetry in general. Consider also the last four stanzas. The poet might have merely stated that the sons regretted having to leave their home and having to go back to the grave. He wishes to do more than communicate the idea, however: he wishes us to share in their feeling of dread as well as to know that they had such a feeling. Which is the better means of doing this: to say, they dreaded leaving "very much," or "a great deal," or "bitterly,"—use whatever adverb you will; or to describe the scene itself? The latter method, the concrete method, is very properly the one chosen.

The crowing of the cocks announcing day is described, and the brief conversation between the brothers is given. Notice that the poem does not use words of great intensity in giving the conversation, but *understatement*. The eldest brother merely says, " 'Tis time we were away"; the youngest brother, "Brother, we must awa." There is no shrieking of terror. And yet in this case the brief understatement conveys perhaps more of a feeling of horror and grief than exaggerated outcries would have conveyed. We can readily see why this use of understatement is particularly effective here. The poet has refrained throughout from making comments on the situation or from hinting to us what we ought to feel. The poem is *objective;* the poet stands aside, and lets the poem do its work on us in its own way.

Notice too that this poem, like the previous ones considered, makes use of suggestion. People prefer suggestion to explicit statement in these matters—if for no other reason than that the person who feels the suggestion participates fully and immediately—he feels that he has made a discovery for himself, which is quite another thing than having some one tell him what he ought to feel. Moreover, suggestion is rich in that, the reader's own imagination, aroused, goes on to enrich the whole subject with feeling. We have an excellent example of this power in the last stanza. After the dialogue between the brothers to the effect that they must go back to the grave, the youngest brother says,

> "Fare ye well, my mother dear!
>   Farewell to barn and byre!
> And fare ye well, the bonny lass
>   That kindles my mother's fire."

Was the youngest brother in love with the bonny lass before his death? We have received no earlier hint that he was. Perhaps he has been. But it is not necessary for an appreciation of the poem to read this interpretation into the passage. The stanza gives us all we need to have if we see the bonny lass as representing the warm, beautiful life of flesh and blood which the dead men have lost and which they now must leave. If the girl does stand for this, then one may perhaps find the reason for the effect which the last line gives—

> "That kindles my mother's fire."

The description in its effect on us is not merely an identification of the girl; the association of the girl with the fire makes us think of her particularly in her contrast with the cold and desolate grave to which the dead brothers must return.

One may raise the question at this point as to whether the average reader will feel that the line means this. Is the average reader expected to be able to make this interpretation? The answer must be, no; most readers do not make this interpretation consciously; and it is not necessary for them to make it consciously is order to enjoy the poem. Many of the details of poetry affect us *unconsciously*. We can not explain just how the effect was made. But if we are to enjoy poetry to its fullest we must be alert and sensitive to such details as this. . . .

We have seen that this poem differs from the prose paraphrase in being concrete where the prose is abstract, in concerning itself with feelings as well as with mere ideas, and in making use of suggestions rather than depending merely on explicit statement. One more point may be worth making. The *structure* of the poem is based on an appeal to the reader's feelings. It is not merely logical or chronological. The poem takes advantage of a reader's natural curiosity. It employs suspense. (Though the end is foreshadowed when we are told where the birch grew which adorns the dead men's hats, we are not told that they are dead—only that the wife was told that she would never see them. The solution is held up to the end.) Furthermore, the poem builds to a climax. That climax lies in the contrast between the horrors of the grave and the warmth and friendliness of life. The channering worm is contrasted with the bonny lass in the last two stanzas, and the final crowing of the cock has been so prepared for that we feel it as a gruesome summons—we feel it as the dead men feel it. Moreover, the effectiveness is increased by an ironic contrast in the crowing itself. The scene is a farm-scene. The atmosphere of warmth and life has been developed in terms of the farmhouse setting. But the crowing of the birds, which have an integral part in this friendly setting—the crowing which is only one of the friendly noises associated with the boys' home—itself becomes the signal for departure from this comfortable and human world to the monstrous world to which the dead men must return. (42–45)

WORK CITED
Brooks, Cleanth and Robert Penn Warren. <u>Understanding Poetry</u>. New York: Holt, 1938.

FROM STRUCTURALISM TO DECONSTRUCTION

If New Criticism implied a stable canon of texts that could be read for their layers of irony and ambiguity, modern philosophy often undermined such notions of stability. Building on the field of cultural anthropology, Claude Lévi-Strauss and others developed the study of patterns of social custom and thought while removing such patterns from hierarchies of value. In the work of Roland Barthes one finds multiple readings of a given text, each playing with patterns or "codes." A later writer, Roberto Calasso, would reassemble mythologies of ancient Greece and India according to narrative structures he observed.

This approach is called Structuralism, but while it is fundamentally relativistic in approach, it does not deny the existence or validity of the text in question. It merely points out the multiple possibilities of our "readings" by positing language as signification rather than as a concrete referent.

Paul de Man, writing in his transitional book called *Blindness and Insight: Essays in the Rhetoric of Criticism*, points out that Structuralist readings like those of Barthes were often indistinguishable from formalist criticism done by such figures as I. A. Richards, and inconsistent with the profound skepticism of modern philosophy. In the following passage, de Man finds what is, for him, a more satisfying example in William Empson. Empson is reading one of Shakespeare's sonnets, number 73 (Anthology, p. 374), and it may be significant that here we have a critic reading a critic reading a poem, rather than a critic "directly" reading a poem.

But what happens when one studies poetry a little closer following these instructions? A surprising answer is to be found in the work of William Empson, a brilliant student of Richards. Empson, a poet in his own right, and, moreover, a reader of great acuity, applied Richards's principles faithfully to a set of texts drawn mainly, though not exclusively, from Shakespeare and the metaphysical poets of the seventeenth century. From the very first example studied in *Seven Types of Ambiguity*, the results are troubling. It is a line from one of Shakespeare's sonnets. To evoke old age, the poet thinks of winter, more precisely a forest in winter, which, he says, is like:

Bare ruined choirs, where late the sweet birds sang.

The thought is stated in a metaphor whose perfection is immediately felt. But if it is asked what is the common experience awakened by the forest and the ruined choir, one does not discover just one but an indefinite number. Empson lists a dozen of them and there are many others; it would be impossible to tell which was dominant in the poet's mind or at which we should stop. What the metaphor does is actually the opposite: instead of setting up an adequation between two experiences, and thereby fixing the mind on the repose of an established equation, it deploys the initial experience into an infinity of associated experiences that spring from it. In the manner of a vibration spreading in infinitude from its center, metaphor is endowed with the capacity to situate the experience at the heart of a universe that it generates. It provides the ground rather than the frame, a limitless anteriority that permits the limiting of a specific entity. Experience sheds its uniqueness and leads instead to a dizziness of the mind. Far from referring back to an object that would be its cause, the poetic sign sets in motion an imaging activity that refers to no object in particular. The "meaning" of the metaphor is that it does not "mean" in any definite manner.

This is obviously problematic. For if a simple metaphor suffices to suggest an infinity of initial experiences and, therefore, an infinity of valid readings, how can we live up to Richards's injunction to bring the reader's experience in line with the typical experience ascribed to the author? Can we still speak of communication here, when the text's effect is to transform a perfectly well-defined unity into a multiplicity whose actual number must remain undetermined? Empson's argument, as it proceeds from simple to increasingly complex examples, becomes apparent: a fundamental ambiguity is constitutive of all poetry. The correspondence between the initial experience and the reader's own remains forever problematic because poetry sets particular beings in a world yet to be constituted, as a task to fulfill. (235–236)

Here de Man is becoming a Deconstructive or Post-Structuralist critic. That is, all issues of ontology in the text itself, as well as in the world that "surrounds" it, have now become problematic. The leading philosopher of Deconstruction, Jacques Derrida, appears at times to assert the absolute arbitrariness of our readings, while at other times arguing the importance of our political and social positions. What has been removed is the stability of the text being read as well as the person reading it, and de Man's essay includes a critique of what he calls "naïve" readers—those who wish for an immediate ontological connection between word and experience.

It remains for us to define the attitude we called naïve, which rests on the belief that poetry is capable of effecting reconciliation because it provides an immediate contract with substance through its own sensible form. In a famous letter, Keats had already cried out: "O for a life of sensation not of thought," but he had sense enough to speak of sensation as something one desires but cannot have. A contemporary American poet is far less prudent when he writes: "[the poet] searches for meanings in terms of the senses. The intelligence of art is a sensory intelligence, the meaning of art is a sensory meaning. . . . There is no such thing as a good work of art which is not immediately apprehensible in the senses."[27] There is no doubt that there is a sensory dimension, as intention, in all poetry, but to assert

27. Karl Shapiro, Beyond Criticism (Lincoln: University of Nebraska Press, 1953), pp. 43, 45 [de Man's note].

its exclusive and immediate presence is to ignore the origin of all creative and imaging consciousness. The distinction, so often formulated, that the experience of the object is not the experience of the consciousness of the object, remains basic and valid. In a way, if it were not for the fact that substance is problematic and absent, there would not be art. (244)

Ultimately, the importance of Structuralism and Deconstruction may well have been two-fold: They demolished the hierarchy of stable canons, making it possible for literature to be opened to all sorts of new (and old) writing; and they fostered a sort of backlash in which critics of many stripes desired—perhaps less naively than before—to assert social values for the arts. Many of the critical approaches that follow straddle the issues of problematic reading and social relevance.

NEW HISTORICISM

Historicism "is the belief that past events can best be understood not in universal terms but in terms of the particular contexts in which they occurred," Stephen Bonnycastle suggests in his guide to literary theory, *In Search of Authority* (Bonnycastle 163). New historicism, in turn, is historicism influenced by structuralism and ultimately reimagined through the lens of deconstruction. Both approaches may prove fruitful for reading literary texts. However, as Lee Patterson observes, new historicism includes the understanding that "the literary text is an object that can never be *explained* as the effect of local historical causes but only *interpreted* as a bearer of cultural significance" (Patterson 254). Historicist criticism usually focuses on either determining the meaning a work had when its author was alive or on recreating the original audience for a specific literary work or object d'art. In contrast, New Historicism is grounded in Michel Foucault's understanding that what we value as knowledge differs from century to century. In assessing the past, new historicists focus on how nondominant cultures or ideologies respond to received tradition, how they express themselves in the face of prevailing cultural norms. For the New Historicist, the literary past is available through a spectrum of contemporary discourses—religious, legal, medical, philosophical, social—but is not transparent. As Bonnycastle emphasizes, these cultural frames "do not simply give access, like a window, to a reality which exists beyond them" (Bonnycastle 166). They require interpretation with an eye to how art functions ideologically as a reflection of the social environment in which it is created.

Upon a first reading, the poem "Western Wind" seems resistant to this theoretical approach. It's a lovely poem—small (four short lines); carefully and deliberately crafted into two halves; densely packed with the prosodic, rhetorical, and affective markers of the lyric as a genre. Continuous alliteration in the first half of the poem sets the tone. Repetition of "w" in the opening line recreates, through onomatopoeia, the whisper of a soft spring wind and registers for readers the desire of the lyrical "I"—a profound wish for an end to rough winter weather and the resulting separation from the lover. The assonance of open vowels in line two and the scattershot use of initial consonants similarly mimic the longed-for "small rain" that will signal the end of a harsh season plagued by rutted, muddied roads and seemingly impossible passage (whether by land or sea). The speaker's focus in the final two lines is much more intimate. There the expression of his (her?) desire to be home and in bed again with his lover clearly borders on the kind of transcendent, universal experience that non-historical readers love to claim for poetry. What this non-historical reading can't account for, however, is the packed resonance of what can be called the "turn" of the poem—the articulated pause between the rather sweeping opening two lines and the intimate closing lines where the lover imagines himself in bed again with his beloved. The poet achieves this shift in focus through a simple exclamation—"Christ." For readers in our culture, where profanity has become so common that it's trite to assign any value to swear words, this little outcry slips by almost unnoticed. However, it raises all kinds of questions if we understand this deeply visceral oath as grounded in contemporary struggles about the nature of Christ's body and the efficacy of swearing by that body. First, there's the immediate indeterminacy of "Christ" as a swear word. This could, on the one hand, be a curse—a simple expression of frustration with God for creating seasonal miserable weather that interferes with the reunion of lovers. Or it might be read as an oath of allegiance of sorts—a promise to swear by Christ if Christ will deliver the beloved. Either resonance reflects the deep seriousness with which swearing was entered into during the sixteenth century when "Western Wind" was written. In western Europe, book curses were used throughout the Middle Ages and well into the 1500s to safeguard precious volumes from thieves. With startling consistency these oaths wish on prospective book thieves some kind of visceral, horribly enfleshed retribution (*Anathema* 87–89). With *contrapasso*-like force Geoffrey Chaucer, in this tradition, wishes a scaly skin disease on a scribe whose miscopying forces Chaucer to scrape and rub the fleshy vellum of his manuscripts to repair the scribal error that results in the "rape" of his work. The following fierce poetic curse from the same time period as "Western Wind" indicates that such retribution would be vindicated by God, himself:

> Thomas Hyllbrond owe this book,
> Whosoever will yt tooke,
> Whoso stellyt shall be hangyd,
> By ayre, by water, or by lande.
> With a hempen bande.
> God is where he was. (*Anathema* 108).

Cursing/swearing, then, takes for granted that the linguistic space between signifier and signified must collapse. It grounds its power in the central Christian mystery of the Word made flesh. With a delightfully ironic twist, that kind of collapse is precisely what the lover-narrator longs for when he swears by/at/to "Christ": that his poetic words will be capable of morphing into the real enfleshed experience of the beloved's presence.

To further complicate the resonance of swearing by "Christ," it's also worthwhile to recall that this poem was written during the century in which England became most deeply involved in a religious schism that called into question the literal presence of Christ's body in the Eucharist. Luther posted his ninety-five theses which led to the Reformation in 1517. England's Henry VIII convened the Reformation Parliament in the following decade (1529); in the subsequent seven years this parliament passed 137 statutes which led to the definitive separation of the Church of England from Roman Catholicism. That separation entailed, as its most distinctive characteristic, a change in attitude towards the doctrine of Transubstantiation. Reformation Protestants no longer held that the bread and wine offered up at Mass had its substance changed to that of the body, blood, soul and divinity of Jesus Christ.

Which side of the debate is the narrator hailing from and why does it matter to a reading of this poem? As a Protestant exclamation, we might understand the "Christ" curse to underscore the lover's despair that no words, poetic or otherwise, can conjure the presence of his beloved in the flesh. If informed by Catholic convictions about the transubstantive nature of Christ's body, then perhaps the lover is reiterating his conviction that the desired reunion with the beloved is destined to take place, in time if not in the immediate now. Obviously, the poem is accessible without this historical context for the "Christ" oath. However, once we explore some of the possible resonances of swearing on Christ's body during the sixteenth century, then the connection between otherwise disparate halves of the poem becomes self-evident. The longing for the return of spring expressed in the opening lines parallels the longing for Christ's embodied return which, somewhat shockingly, correlates with the lover's desire for reunion with his beloved.

WORKS CITED

Bonnycastle, Stephen. An Introductory Guide to Literary Theory. New York: Broadview Press, 1998.

Drogin, Mark. Anathema: Medieval Scribes and the History of Book Curses. New Jersey: Allanheld & Schram, 1983.

Patterson, Lee, "Literary History." Critical Terms for Literary Study. Ed. Frank Lentricchia and Thomas McLaughlin. Chicago: U of Chicago Press, 1995.

The New Catholic Encyclopedia (online edition). http://www.newadvent.org/cathen/.

READER-RESPONSE CRITICISM

Reader-response criticism is commonly defined as the pursuit of meaning in the process of reading a text, rather than in the text itself. It is an intuitively plausible premise: One of the great pleasures of re-reading a poem later in life is the recognition that one is really reading the poem again for the first time, that its meaning has changed along with the changing perspective of the reader. In literary criticism, however, the shift of emphasis from poem to reader can be a bold and sometimes controversial move. How can we talk about meaning at all if it is a purely subjective construct? If there is no objective meaning to explore, then what is the special task of the critic? The reader-response approach can represent a philosophical threat to the very foundations of text-centered criticism. But at its best, reader-response criticism rejects *both* extremes, exploring aspects of a text's meaning that can only be approached once the sharp theoretical boundaries between author, reader, and text have been dissolved. This critical paradigm shift has led to some fascinating new per-spectives on long-standing critical debates. Generations of Milton schol-ars have argued over the exceptionally vivid portrayal of Lucifer in *Paradise Lost*—whether Milton intended his readers to sympathize with this hero-ically defiant character, or whether the poet was simply carried away in his characterization and upset the aesthetic balance of the poem as a whole. Stanley Fish, in one of the seminal books of reader-response criticism,* argued that the way a reader responds to the character of Lucifer in the poem is part of the way the poem works—that the indeterminacy of the poem's meaning (with respect to Lucifer, at least) is *part* of the poem's meaning. One species of reader-response criticism invokes a rhetorical model that is particularly helpful in the analysis of certain poems. The dramatic monologues of Robert Browning, for example, produce their effect through a complex triangular relationship: The reader must sym-pathize with the speaking voice to some extent, and at the same time dis-tinguish that unreliable narrator's voice from the "voice" of the author—a distinction between what the rhetorical critic would call the *author* and the *implied author*.

Elizabeth Bishop's descriptive poems do not tend to raise questions about the reliability of the voice doing the describing. In "The Fish," for example, there is little to discourage the reader from identifying the poem's first-person voice with Bishop herself (or at least with someone who shares the values and sensibility of the poet). Bishop's descriptive mode may seem straightforward, almost artless at times. A reader-response critic, however, would emphasize Bishop's own subtle emphasis in her poems on the *process* of describing, rather than the object described. The reader-response perspective does seem to account for the peculiar experience of reading a poem like "The Fish": The poem's crescendo of close description seduces the reader in its drive toward aesthetic "possession" of a beautiful object, and the effect of the sudden letting go in the final line of the poem depends on how we, as readers, have arrived at that point in the poem. The poem itself is best described as a process, rather than a fixed "thing" with fixed meaning. In a later poem of Bishop's, "The Filling Station," this process-centered aesthetic is pursued further and made more complex by a Browningesque unreliable voice. The first voice we hear in the poem expresses contempt for what is being described: "Oh, but it is

Surprised by Sin. Cambridge: Harvard University Press, 1967.

dirty!" What begins as a biased description of various objects at the filling station—the comic books, the doily, the begonia—gradually dissolves into curiosity about their function and their meaning:

> Why the extraneous plant?
> Why the taboret?
> Why, oh why, the doily?
> (Embroidered in daisy stitch
> with marguerites, I think,
> and heavy with gay crochet.)

The speaker's distance from the objects she describes, and her uncertainty about their meaning, not only undermine her authority as speaker—they also create an indeterminacy of meaning in the poem itself (a process that distinguishes Bishop's poem from the relatively simple irony of Browning's monologues). A reader-response critic would see meaning in this indeterminacy of meaning, an "open" text rather than an obscure text. In the concluding stanza of "The Filling Station," it is not even clear who—or what—is speaking. The final cadence arrives at a final statement whose meaning, at this point, is entirely ambiguous: "Somebody loves us all." Is this the voice of the original speaker? Do the cans of oil "softly say" this about themselves? Or should we think of this epiphany (is it an epiphany?) as a function of the process by which an individual reader arrives at the line?

FEMINIST CRITICISM

Feminist criticism takes a multitude of forms, but to open a text to a feminist reading sometimes requires nothing more than a change in point of view. What happens if we adopt the perspective of a woman figure within a work and look around at the imaginative landscape through her eyes, even if the text is not constructed from her point of view? Andrew Marvell's "To His Coy Mistress" exemplifies how a simple shift in perspective can radically alter the interpretation of a poem.

For generations critics celebrated "To His Coy Mistress" as a classic example of the "carpe diem" tradition: the speaker urges his reluctant lover to "seize the day," to make love now, rather than allow her "long preserved virginity" to become the province of worms. Students of the poem admired Marvell's technical brilliance. The couplets are so elegantly handled that even in a relatively short tetrameter line, the exact rhymes do not distract the ear. Polysyllabic words seem to melt into the tetrameter: *virginity* and *vegetable love*. And the immediacy of the voice—"I think," "if you please"—makes the highly controlled verse sound relaxed and natural.

The poem is a rhetorical tour de force. In the first part of the argument, the speaker appropriates the blazon form, which praises each part of the lover's body, in order to acknowledge that the woman deserves centuries of adoration. He validates her position—if they had "world enough, and time," she would be right to prolong their wooing. In the second section of the poem ("But at my back . . ."), he presents the counterargument: they *don't* have unlimited time, and if they don't hurry, they will die before they enjoy the fruits of wooing. He evokes images of the grave to lend urgency to his point. In the third and concluding section, beginning "Now, therefore," he closes his argument with what would seem to be the inevitable conclusion: "Now let us sport us while we may. . . ." For centuries, the speaker's argument has left readers inspired to go out and seize the day.

But what if we stop for a moment and consider the perspective of the woman being courted? First, a little historical context is useful. In the Renaissance, a woman's honor was equated with her chastity. If an unmarried woman lost her virginity, she, not her lover, would suffer the social consequences. She would be unmarriageable—and a Renaissance woman could not simply go out and make a living for herself. She also, of course, risked pregnancy.

So there were compelling social reasons for a Renaissance woman to defend her chastity. But the progression of images in the poem itself might also give a woman pause. The verbs in the first section, detailing the woman's wishes, are celebratory: The speaker imagines how he would "gaze," "adore," "praise." Here the images associated with courtship suggest abundance: rubies, empires, long love's day. By contrast, the images of the second stanza excite fear: worms, ashes, dust. The speaker evokes a graphic image of the woman's decomposing dead body: "Then worms shall try / That long preserved virginity." The third stanza, finally, does not present images of contented consummated love, or reciprocal passion, or transcendent joy, as one might expect in a poem of seduction, but images of violence and coercion. The lovers will "devour" time, "tear" their pleasures "with rough strife," and force the sun to run. The tenderness posited in the first section is gone, and the woman, spurred by fearsome images of her own dead body, is urged to engage in lovemaking that sounds vaguely violent.

We don't, of course, know how Marvell's "Coy Mistress" responded; her perspective—and any articulation of her resistance—drops out after the first section of the poem. This lack of response itself is problematic for a feminist reader: The would-be lover, whose objections are at least addressed in the first section, is never heard from again. In the past, critics seemed to accept the woman's constructed silence as consent. As feminists, however, we may choose a strategy of resistant reading. We can still take pleasure in the poem's linguistic brilliance—without being seduced by it.

PSYCHOLOGICAL CRITICISM

Psychological criticism was, at one time, virtually synonymous with *Freudian* criticism and its application of now-familiar psychoanalytic concepts to the interpretation of literature—concepts such as the *id, ego,* and *superego,* the more general distinction between the conscious and the subconscious, and the connection between neurosis and creativity. Sigmund Freud's theories were clearly indebted to examples offered by literature; the critic Harold Bloom has even gone so far as to assert that Freud is essentially Shakespeare in prose. Indeed, it is often difficult to distinguish between the explicit influence of Freud on much of twentieth-century literature (*The Interpretation of Dreams* was published in 1900) and the more subtle manifestations of Freudian concepts in literature not directly influenced by Freud (or written before 1900). One of the original projects of psychoanalytic criticism, its analysis of the psychology of the creative process, is closely related to what we would call biographical criticism. Another branch of psychological criticism is more interested in the finished work and what is represented there—the real versus the apparent motives of a character in a novel or play, for example, or the psychological dynamics behind the modulations of voice in a lyric poem. The term psychological criticism, in fact, covers a wide range of interpretive approaches, and not all of the working premises derive directly from Freud. The French psychologist Jacques Lacan, for example, has revised some of the insights of psychoanalytic criticism and pursued them in a poststructuralist context more concerned with the apprehension of the world through language and symbols.

For many years, the poems of Sylvia Plath were read as personal documents in the so-called "confessional" mode established by Robert

Lowell, Anne Sexton, John Berryman, and other poets of Plath's generation. More recently, however, critics have begun to read Plath's
poems, and particularly her later poems, as an implicit critique of the
confessional aesthetic with which she has long been associated. The
relationship between the poems and Plath's own psychological states
now seems much more complex than it once did, and there has been
a gradual shift away from a biographical mode of inquiry to a consideration of the poems as independent explorations of psychological
themes. Plath's "Mirror," for example, explores the theme of the
divided self that may be found in Plath's earliest work. But according
to some critics, the mature poem "Mirror" is less a reflection of Plath's
own state of mind in 1961 (the year the poem was written) than it is
about the way a subject—a female subject—constructs a self-image.
The poem may, in other words, lend itself more to psychological interpretation of a non-biographical kind. A bit of biographical is nevertheless relevant to this alternate reading. Plath is known to have read an
essay by the German psychologist Otto Rank on the concept of "The
Double as Immortal Self," in which Rank claimed that a constructed
self-image—an artist's self-portrait, for example—signifies an energetic denial of the power of death. Rank warned, however, that the
simple mirroring of one's self or of one's personal experience would
ultimately prove inadequate and lead to a crisis of self-realization.
Plath's "Mirror" examines a crisis similar to the one Rank identified.
Significantly, the poem offers the point of view of the mirror—an
object—rather than the point of view of the woman who looks in the
mirror. On one reading, then, it is the aesthetic aspect of the crisis that
seems to have interested Plath the most—the difficulties of mirroring
one's self in a work of art as an attempt to define and preserve the self.
The poem reflects upon itself as much as it mirrors the mental state of
the poet, and it questions the aesthetic goal of "confessional" poetry
as perhaps partly an act of psychological self-delusion.

INTERTEXTUAL CRITICISM

Intertextual criticism is interested in language in its social aspect, in
the way meaning derives from a text's relationship to other texts and
other utterances within a shared language. We have already seen how
poems incorporate other texts by way of simple allusion. "No, I am not
Prince Hamlet!" declares the speaker in Eliot's "Love Song of J. Alfred

Prufrock," and the analogy to Shakespeare's characters lends a comic poignancy to Prufrock's musings about his own character. But consider a far more radical instance of intertextual association in the closing lines of Eliot's later, longer poem, *The Waste Land*:

London Bridge is falling down falling down falling down

Poi s'ascose nel foco che gli affina
Quando fiam ceu chelidon—O swallow swallow
Le Prince d'Aquitaine à la tour abolie
These fragments I have shored against my ruins
Why then Ile fit you. Hieronymo's mad againe.
Datta. Dayadhvam. Damyata.

    Shantih shantih shantih

What is *this* "about"? The passage is quoted out of context, and the context is a notoriously complex poem, but it should be clear that whatever poignancy these lines contain comes about through means quite different from Prufrock's allusion to Shakespeare. Here, texts are quoted and juxtaposed in the way of a collage, rather than simply alluded to by an identifiable speaker. The fragments are literally the material of the poem—representing, in the space of only eight lines, no fewer than four different genres in four different languages (and we might well consider the antiquated form of English in "Why then Ile fit you" a virtual *fifth language*). *The Waste Land* is an extreme example of poetic intertextuality, but Eliot's method highlights what intertextual critics emphasize as the essential quality of all poetic discourse: Poems are always—to some extent—"about" other poems, just as the meaning of fragments within a language is a function of their use and re-use. Language can be the material of a poem, and not simply its medium. These critical insights prove particularly useful in the analysis of much twentieth-century poetry,* but they are also a key to understanding much of what we would more broadly characterize as "postmodern" art—from the pastiche methods of hip-hop music to Quentin Tarantino's "movies about movies."

Intertextual criticism is also concerned with another important kind of allusion—with the ways in which a poem derives its meaning

---

*There are a number of poems written in the twentieth century that pursue an aesthetic similar to that of *The Waste Land*: see, for example, Marianne Moore's extensive use of quotation in "Marriage" and "An Octopus" and Ezra Pound's use of collage in the *Cantos*.

from the exploitation of established poetic forms and conventions. W. H. Auden adopted the conventions of the English pastoral elegy for his poem "In Memory of W. B. Yeats," but the poem was written at a moment in history (1939) when the world-view underlying those conventions seemed inadequate to the subject matter of modem life. Auden's choice of this form thus sets up a chain of associations with earlier pastoral elegies: Milton's "Lycidas," Shelley's "Adonais," the elegiac poems of A. E. Housman's *A Shropshire Lad*, and the elegies of the ancient Greek poet Theocritus from which Milton drew his inspiration. In the traditional pastoral elegy, a personified Nature mourns for the deceased subject of the poem:

> Thee shepherd, thee the woods and desert caves,
> With wild thyme and the gadding vine o'ergrown,
> And all their echoes mourn . . .
> (Milton, *Lycidas*)

"In Memory of W. B. Yeats" describes a nature that is indifferent to death and suffering, a nature described from the peculiarly alienated point of view of a twentieth-century speaker: "O all the instruments agree / The day of his death was a dark cold day." What we have instead is the poet's death represented in urban, geopolitical terms:

> The provinces of his body revolted,
> The squares of his mind were empty,
> Silence invaded the suburbs,
> The current of his feeling failed . . .

Auden works within the established parameters of the pastoral, but the content of the poem has little to do with nature and its woods and wild thyme. It is a poem written on the bitter eve of World War II, and it is a poem that is about more than the passing of W. B. Yeats. This dissonance between form and content reflects one of the poem's central themes. "To write poetry after Auschwitz is barbaric," critic Theodor Adorno famously wrote in 1949. Auden's 1939 elegy does not parody and reject the pastoral mode, nor does it reject poetry itself as irrelevant in the twentieth century; the poem suggests, rather, that conventions like those of the pastoral elegy must be adapted in a new context, where the familiar maneuvers can assume a different meaning. Auden's "elegy about elegies" has, in fact, taken its place alongside Milton's and Shelley's as one of the great elegies in the language.

POSTCOLONIAL CRITICISM

Postcolonial criticism is a relatively new critical perspective. Most of its theoretical ideas were formulated only within the past three or four decades, but the theory's range of application is extraordinarily wide and its impact has already been profound. Thanks to postcolonial criticism, we no longer read Joyce's *Ulysses* in quite the same way; what now seems a fairly prominent feature of Joyce's novel—its complex dialogue between the discourses of Irish nationalism, British imperialism, and the Roman Catholic church—was not so obvious to readers two decades ago. Postcolonial criticism is essentially concerned with the dynamics of competing discourses, with the clash of world-views and its manifestation as a clash between *languages*. Postcolonial critics study how individual writers living in formerly colonized cultures struggle with the issue of cultural identity. Does an Irish poet's decision to write in the language of Shakespeare constitute a political act of submission to a dominant power? (An American poet writing in 2004, rather than 1776, would not think of Shakespeare in quite the same way.) To what extent is it possible to recover one's "true" cultural identity, to speak in one's own untainted vernacular? Postcolonial critics can cite extreme cases: Joyce made a point of quoting dialogue in the French manner (set off by dashes) rather than using the quotation marks of English; Kenyan writer Ngugi Wa Thiongo defiantly wrote novels in his native language of Kikiyu (expecting only a handful of readers) and only later translated the novels into English. More typical, however, is a phenomenon that postcolonial critics refer to as "hybridity"— the negotiation and mutual compromise between co-existing discourses. Postcolonial criticism may be thought of as a branch of cultural criticism, but one of its strengths—even in its infancy—is that it is able to analyze hybrid discourses with a refined subtlety that owes much to poststructural theories of language (Derrida, Foucault, et al.). Postcolonial critics treat culture as language, language as culture.

West Indian poet and playwright Derek Walcott, who has spent much of his life in Trinidad, describes himself as a "mulatto of style." Much of his poetry deals with a peculiarly postcolonial variant of the theme of alienation, with the feeling of being caught between two cultures and of having to partake of two incompatible discourses. Walcott employs what might be characterized as a "postcolonial mythic method"—that is to say, his poems invoke the archetypal characters and stories of Western literature and adapt them in a contemporary context where the tension between two discourses can be explored (comparable to what Joyce did with the Homeric parallels in *Ulysses*). The long poem *Omeros* (1990) is Walcott's retelling of *The Iliad* and *The Odyssey* in a Caribbean setting. An earlier poem, "Sea Grapes," is a foray on a smaller scale. Homer's tale of Odysseus' voyage home to Ithaca provides what may seem the perfect parallel to a contemporary feeling of postcolonial alienation. In "Sea Grapes," Walcott might easily have explored this parallel with the "hero" of Homer's tale, just as Alfred Lord Tennyson, writing in Victorian England, invoked Odysseus and invited readers to identify with another of his heroic qualities:

> One equal temper of heroic hearts,
> Made weak by time and fate, but strong in will
> To strive, to seek, to find, and not to yield.
> (Tennyson, "Ulysses")

But these parallels do not quite work in a postcolonial context, where the original myth is likely to be read from a different perspective. Walcott assumes this alternate perspective in "Sea Grapes," the perspective of a native inhabitant of one of the islands that Odysseus visited and has left behind on his voyage home. In the climax of the poem, we are asked to identify not with Odysseus, but with Polyphemus—the Cyclops in Homer's story whose island is colonized by Odysseus and his crew, and who is then blinded by Odysseus as he engineers an escape from the giant's cave:

> And the blind giant's boulder heaved the trough
> From whose groundswell the great hexameters come
> To the conclusions of exhausted surf.

The Homeric myths represent a complicated heritage for a writer like Derek Walcott. The "great hexameters" of Homer supply the material and the inspiration for Walcott's poetry, as they did for Tennyson; but Walcott is not of "one equal temper" with the values embodied by this tradition or this discourse. A colonial subject is perhaps more likely to identify with Polyphemus than with Odysseus, more likely to sympathize with the enslaved Caliban of Shakespeare's *The Tempest* than with the imperialist Prospero. Postcolonial criticism, like much of the literature that deals with postcolonial themes, is often more interested in the lens through which we read stories handed down to us than in the stories themselves.

PERMISSIONS ACKNOWLEDGMENTS

Alice Fulton. "What I Like" by Alice Fulton from *Dance Script with Electric Ballerina: Poems.* Copyright 1983 by Alice Fulton; "News of the Occluded Cyclone" by Alice Fulton from *Palladium: Poems.* Copyright © 1987 by Alice Fulton. All of the above are used with permission of the poet and the University of Illinois Press.

Brewster Ghiselin. "Rattler Alert" from *Windrose: Poems 1929–1979* by Brewster Ghiselin. Copyright © 1941 and renewed 1969 by Brewster Ghiselin. Reprinted by permission of the University of Utah Press.

Allen Ginsberg. "A Supermarket in California." All lines from "A Supermarket in California" from *Collected Poems 1947–1980* by Allen Ginsberg. Copyright © 1955 by Allen Ginsberg. Reprinted by permission of HarperCollins Publishers, Inc.

Dana Gioia. "Planting a Sequoia" by Dana Gioia. © 1991 by Dana Gioia. Reprinted from *The Gods of Winter,* published by Graywolf Press.

Louise Glück. "The School Children" and "Mock Orange" from *The First Four Books of Poems* by Louise Glück. Copyright 1968, 1971, 1972, 1973, 1974, 1975, 1976, 1977, 1978, 1979, 1980, 1985, 1995 by Louise Glück. Reprinted by permission of HarperCollins Publishers, Inc.

Jorie Graham. "San Sepolcro" from *Erosion,* © 1983 Princeton University Press. Reprinted by permission of Princeton University Press.

Robert Graves. "The Face in the Mirror," "Spoils," "The Persian Version," "Counting the Beats," and Lines from "Rocky Acres" from *The Collected Poems 1975* by Robert Graves. Copyright 1988 by Robert Graves. All of the above are used by permission of Carcanet Press Limited.

Emily Grosholz. "Remembering the Ardeche" by Emily Grosholz. © Emily R. Grosholz. First published in *The River Painter,* University of Illinois Press, 1984. Used by permission.

R. S. Gwynn. "Black Helicopters" and "Body Bags" from *No Word of Farewell,* 2000, by R. S. Gwynn. Reprinted with permission of the author and Story Line Press. www.storylinepress.com

Jenn Habel. "Another Poem About the Heart" by Jenn Habel. First published in the *Pittsburgh Post-Gazette,* 10 Oct. 2002. Used by permission.

Marilyn Hacker. Excerpt from *Love, Death, and the Changing of the Seasons* by Marilyn Hacker. Copyright © 1986, 1995 by Marilyn Hacker. Reprinted by permission of the author.

Joy Harjo. "Eagle Poem" from *In Mad Love and War* © 1990 by Joy Harjo and reprinted by permission of Wesleyan University Press.

Robert Hass. "A Story About the Body" from *Human Wishes* by Robert Hass. Copyright © 1989 by Robert Hass. Reprinted by permission of HarperCollins Publishers, Inc.

Robert Hayden. "Those Winter Sundays." Copyright © by Robert Hayden from *Collected Poems of Robert Hayden* by Robert Hayden, edited by Frederick Glaysher. Used by permission of Liveright Publishing Corporation.

Seamus Heaney. "Damson," "Follower," and "Death of a Naturalist" from *Opened Ground: Selected Poems 1966–1996* by Seamus Heaney. Copyright © 1998 by Seamus Heaney. All of the above are reprinted by permission of Farrar, Straus and Giroux, LLC. Also used with permission of Faber and Faber, Ltd.

Anthony Hecht. "The End of the Weekend" and "The Dover Bitch" from *Collected Earlier Poems* by Anthony Hecht. Copyright © 1990 by Anthony E. Hecht; "The Book of Yolek" from *The Transparent Man* by Anthony Hecht. All of the above are used by permission of Alfred A. Knopf, a division of Random House, Inc.

Jane Hilberry. "The Moment" by Jane Hilberry. First appeared in *The Hudson Review,* Autumn 2003, and is used by permission of the author.

Jan D. Hodge. "Carousel" by Jan D. Hodge. © Jan D. Hodge 1995. Used by permission of the author.

John Hollander. From "The Night Mirror," Macmillan, 1971.

Marie Howe. "Part of Eve's Discussion" from *The Good Thief* by Marie Howe. Copyright © 1988 by Marie Howe. Reprinted by permission of Persea Books, Inc. (New York).

Andrew Hudgins. "The Persistence of Nature in Our Lives" from *Saints and Strangers: Poems by Andrew Hudgins.* Copyright © 1985 by Andrew Hudgins. Reprinted by permission of Houghton Mifflin Company. All rights reserved.

Langston Hughes. "Dream Variations" and "The Negro Speaks of Rivers" from *The Collected Poems of Langston Hughes* by Langston Hughes. Copyright © 1994 by The Estate of Langston Hughes. Used by permission of Alfred A. Knopf, a division of Random House, Inc.

Mark Irwin. "X" by Mark Irwin from *White City.* Copyright © 2000 by Mark Irwin. Reprinted with the permission of BOA Editions, Ltd. www.BOAEditions.org; "The Irises." Originally appeared in *The New Republic,* March 10, 2003. Used with permission.

Mark Jarmon. From "Unholy Sonnets" and "Ground Swell" in *Questions for Ecclesiastes* by Mark Jarman, 1997. Reprinted with permission of the author and Story Line Press. www.storylinepress.com

Stevie Smith. "Out Bog is Dood," "Not Waving But Drowning" by Stevie Smith from *Collected Poems of Stevie Smith.* Copyright © 1972 by Stevie Smith. Reprinted by permission of New Directions Publishing Corp.

W. D. Snodgrass. "Leaving the Motel" by W. D. Snodgrass from *After Experience.* Reprinted by permission of the author.

Gary Snyder. "Oil" and "Four Poems for Robin" (brief excerpt) by Gary Snyder from *The Back Country.* Copyright © 1968 by Gary Snyder; "Why Log Truck Drivers Rise Earlier than Students of Zen" by Gary Snyder from *Turtle Island.* Copyright © 1974 by Gary Snyder. All of the above are reprinted by permission of New Directions Publishing Corp. "Bubbs Creek Haircut" from *Mountains and Rivers Without End* by Gary Snyder. Copyright © 1996 by Gary Snyder. Reprinted by permission of Counterpoint Press, a member of Perseus Books, L.L.C. "Axe Handles" by Gary Snyder from *Axe Handles,* copyright by Gary Snyder, 1983. Reprinted by arrangement with Shoemaker & Hoard.

Jason Sommer. "For Whoever Reads My Book in Solitude" by Jason Sommer from *Other People's Troubles,* University of Chicago Press. Reprinted by permission of the author.

Gary Soto. "Oranges" from *New and Selected Poems.* © 1995 by Gary Soto. Used with permission of Chronicle Books LLC, San Francisco. Visit ChronicleBooks.com.

Stephen Spender. Four lines from "The Landscape Near an Aerodrome." Copyright 1934 and renewed 1962 by Stephen Spender, from *Collected Poems 1928–1985* by Stephen Spender. Used by permission of Random House, Inc., and Ed Victor Ltd.

William Stafford. "Godiva County, Montana" and "Traveling Through the Dark" by William Stafford. Copyright 1962, 1998 by the Estate of William Stafford. Reprinted from *The Way It Is: New & Selected Poems* with the permission of Graywolf Press, Saint Paul, Minnesota.

A. E. Stallings. "Sine Qua non" by A. E. Stallings. "Sine Qua Non" first published in *Poetry* Oct.-Nov. 2002. Reprinted by permission of the author.

Timothy Steele. "Sapphics Against Anger" by Timothy Steele. Reprinted by permission of the University of Arkansas Press. Copyright 1995 by Timothy Steele.

Gerald Stern. "The Dog" by Gerald Stern as appeared in *The Breadloaf Anthology of Contemporary American Poetry,* 1986. Reprinted by permission of the author.

Wallace Stevens. "Sunday Morning," "The Snow Man," and "The Sense of the Sleight-of-Hand Man" from *The Collected Poems of Wallace Stevens.* Copyright 1954 by Wallace Stevens and renewed 1982 by permission of Alfred A. Knopf, a division of Random House, Inc.

Anne Stevenson. "Making Poetry" by Anne Stevenson from *Collected Poems.* Courtesy of Anne Stevenson and Bloodaxe Books, U.K.

Mark Strand. "The Tunnel" from *Reasons for Moving: Darker; The Sargentville Notebook* by Mark Strand. Copyright © 1973 by Mark Strand. Used by permission of Alfred A. Knopf, a division of Random House, Inc.

Terese Svoboda. "Old God" from *Treason,* Zoo Press, 2002. Reprinted with permission from the author.

May Swenson. "Cat & the Weather" by May Swenson from *New and Selected Things Taking Place,* 1964; "Question" by May Swenson; excerpt from "Half Sun Half Sleep" by May Swenson; and six lines from "Robert Frost at Breadloaf: His Hand Against a Tree" from *A Cage of Spines,* 1958. All of the above are used with the permission of The Literary Estate of May Swenson; "Stripping and Putting On" from *Nature* by May Swenson. Copyright © 1994 by The Literary Estate of May Swenson. Reprinted by permission of Houghton Mifflin Company. All rights reserved.

George Szirtes. "Like a Black Bird" by George Szirtes. First published in *Poetry* June/July 2004. Reprinted by permission of the author.

James Tate. "Miss Cho Composes in the Cafeteria" by James Tate. Reprinted by permission of the author.

Diane Thiel. "The Mine Field" from *Ecolocations* by Diane Thiel. Reprinted with permission of the author and Story Line Press, 2000. www.storylinepress.com

Dylan Thomas. "Do Not Go Gentle Into That Good Night" by Dylan Thomas from *The Poems of Dylan Thomas.* Copyright © 1952 by Dylan Thomas; "In My Craft or Sullen Art" by Dylan Thomas from *The Poems of Dylan Thomas.* Copyright © 1946 by New Directions Publishing Corp.; "Fern Hill" by Dylan Thomas from *The Poems of Dylan Thomas.* Copyright © 1945 by The Trustees for the Copyrights of Dylan Thomas. All of the above are reprinted by permission of New Directions Publishing Corp. and David Higham Associates.

Jean Toomer. "Reapers" from *Cane* by Jean Toomer. Copyright © 1923 by Boni & Liveright, renewed 1951 by Jean Toomer. Used by permission of Liveright Publishing Corporation.

Gail Tremblay. "Not Sense" by Gail Tremblay. Published by permission of the publisher from *Indian Singing.* © 1998 by Gail Tremblay. (Calyx Books, 1998).

Catherine Tufariello. "The Child" from *Keeping My Name* by Catherine Tufariello. Copyright © 2003 Catherine Tufariello. Texas Tech University Press, 800.832.4042.

John Updike. "Player Piano" from *The Carpentered Hen and Other Tame Creatures* by John Updike. Copyright © 1982 by John Updike; Four lines from *Midpoint and Other Poems* by John Updike. Copyright © 1969 and renewed 1997 by John Updike. All of the above are used by permission of Alfred A. Knopf, a division of Random House, Inc.

Amy Uyematsu. "Deliberate" from *30 Miles from J-Town* by Amy Uyematsu, 1992. Reprinted by permission of the author and Story Line Press. www.storylinepress.com

Peter Viereck. "To Helen of Troy (N.Y.): from *Tide & Continuities* by Peter Viereck. University of Arkansas Press, 1996. Reprinted by permission of the author.

Ellen Bryant Voigt. "The Starveling" by Ellen Bryant Voigt. Copyright © Ellen Bryant Voigt. First published in *Poetry*, May 1978. Copyright © 1978 by The Modern Poetry Association. Reprinted by permission of the editor of *Poetry* and the author.

David Wagoner. "For a Man Dancing by Himself in a Tavern" by David Wagoner from *Good Morning and Good Night*. Copyright 2005 by David Wagoner. Used with permission of the poet and University of Illinois Press.

Derek Walcott. "Sea Grapes" from *Collected Poems 1948–1984* by Derek Walcott. Copyright © 1986 by Derek Walcott. Reprinted by permission of Farrar, Straus and Giroux, LLC.

Jeanne Murray Walker. "Studying Physics with My Daughter" by Jeanne Murray Walker from *Coming Into History*. Copyright © 1990 by Jeanne Murray Walker. Reprinted by permission of the author.

Richard Wilbur. "The Pardon" from *Ceremony and Other Poems*. Copyright 1950 and renewed 1979 by Richard Wilbur "Junk" from *Advice to a Prophet and Other Poems*, copyright © 1989 by Richard Wilbur; "Sleepless at Crown Point" from *The Mind-Reader*. Copyright © 1973 and renewed 2001 by Richard Wilbur; "The Catch" and "Hamlen Brook" from *New and Collected Poems*. Copyright © 1988 by Richard Wilbur. All of the above reprinted by permission of Harcourt, Inc.; Quatrain by Richard Wilbur, "If a sheepdog ate a cantaloupe, . . ."; Used by permission of the author.

C. K. Williams. "Tar" from *Poems 1963–1983* by C. K. Williams. Copyright © 1988 by C. Williams. Reprinted by permission of Farrar, Straus and Giroux, LLC.

Emmett Williams. "Like Attracts Like" (1958) from *An Anthology of Concrete Poetry* edited by Emmett Williams, Something Else Press, New York, 1967. Used by permission of the author.

Miller Williams. "A Poem for Emily" reprinted by permission of Louisiana State University Press from *The Private Life* by Lisel Mueller. Copyright © 1986 by Lisel Mueller.

William Carlos Williams. "Nantucket" and "The Red Wheelbarrow" by William Carlos Williams from *Collected Poems: 1909–1939, Volume I*. Copyright © 1938 by New Directions Publishing Corp.; "The Descent" and "Iris" by William Carlos Williams from *Collected Poems 1939–1962, Volume II*. Copyright © 1948, 1962 by William Carlos Williams; "The Dance (In Brueghel's)" by William Carlos Williams from *Collected Poems 1939–1962, Volume II*. Copyright © 1944 by William Carlos Williams. All of the above are reprinted by permission of New Directions Publishing Corp.

James Wright. "A Song for the Middle of the Night," Autumn Begins in Martins Ferry, Ohio," and "A Blessing" from *Above the River: The Complete Poems*, © 1990 by Anne Wright and reprinted by permission of Wesleyan University Press.

William Butler Yeats. "Leda and the Swan," "Sailing to Byzantium," and "Among School Children." Reprinted with the permission of Scribner, an imprint of Simon & Schuster Adult Publishing Group, from *The Collected Works of W. B. Yeats, Volume I: The Poems, Revised*, edited by Richard J. Finneran. Copyright © 1928 by The Macmillan Company. Copyright renewed © 1956 by Georgie Yeats; "The Spur." Reprinted with the permission of Scribner, an imprint of Simon & Schuster Adult Publishing Group from *The Collected Works of W. B. Yeats, Volume I: The Poems, Revised*, edited by Richard J. Finneran. Copyright © 1949 by Georgie Yeats. Copyright renewed © 1968 by Bertha Yeats, and Anne Yeats; "The Statues." Reprinted with the permission of Scribner, an imprint of Simon & Schuster Adult Publishing Group, from *The Collected Works of W. Yeats, Volume I: The Poems, Revised*, edited by Richard J. Finneran. Copyright © 1940 by Georgie Yeats. Copyright renewed © 1968 by Bertha Georgie Yeats, Michael Butler Yeats, and Anne Yeats; "A Last Confession." Reprinted with the permission of Scribner, an imprint of Simon & Schuster Adult Publishing Group, from *The Collected Works of W. Yeats, Volume I: The Poems, Revised*, edited by Richard J. Finneran. Copyright © 1933 by The Macmillan Company. Copyright renewed © 1961 by Bertha Georgie Yeats.

Al Young. "Up Vernon's Alley" from *The Sound of Dreams Remembered*, Creative Arts Book Co., 2001. Reprinted with permission from the author.

Kevin Young. "Quivira City Limits" from *Most Way Home* by Kevin Young/Fisted Pick Productions. Reprinted by permission of HarperCollins Publishers, Inc.

Louis Zukovsky. Four lines from *Complete Short Poetry*, p. 325. © 1997 Louis Zukovsky. Reprinted with permission of The Johns Hopkins University Press.

PHOTO CREDITS

p. 21, Courtesy of David Mason p. 51, Edwin Gross; p. 74, © AP/Wide World Photos; p. 141, Albrecht Durer. The Knight, Death and the Devil, 1513. Engraving, 24.4 × 18.8 cm. The Art Institute of Chicago, Clarence Buckingham Collection, 1938. 1449. Photograph © 1999 The Art Institute of Chicago. All rights reserved.; p. 155, Charles Darwin, The Expression of Emotions of Man and Animals, Plate V. The University of Chicago Library; p. 161, Charles Darwin, The Expression of Emotions of Man and Animals, Plate IV. The University of Chicago Library; p. 168, Courtesy Department of Library Services, American Museum of Natural History, Neg. #16227. Photo by T. Bierwert; p. 179, Pascal Rioult Dance Company. "Harvest." Photo © 1998 Johan Elbers, New York; p. 204, Photo © Scala/Art Resource. © 2005 Artists Rights Society (ARS), New York/ADAGP, Paris; p. 232, © Bettmann/Corbis; p. 296, © Robert A. Ross/Color-Pic, Inc.; p. 298, Statue of Diadoumenos, Roman copy of Greek original. Pentelic marble. The Metropolitan Museum of Art, Fletcher Fund, 1925 (25.78.56); p. 303, W.A. Bentley & W.J. Humphreys, Snow Crystals, 1931/1963. Dover Publications, Inc.; p. 350, John Keats, "Eve of St. Agnes," Ms. Keats 2.21, by permission of the Houghton Library, Harvard University; p. 354, E.E. Cummings, "Rosetree, rosetree." © E.E. Cummings, copyright renewed by permission of George J. Firmage, Literary Agent, c/o Liveright Publishers, New York and London; p. 358, 359, William Blake, "The Tyger," manuscripts division, The British Library; p. 362, Verlag Berninger & Pampaluchi, Zurich, Switzerland Color Plates Color Plate 1, Paolo Uccello. Saint George and the Dragon. Oil on canvas, 56.5 × 74 cm. The National Gallery, London. Photo © National Gallery Picture Library; Color Plate 3, © Scala/Art Resource, NY; Color Plates 4, 6, © Erich Lessing/Art Resource, NY; Color Plate 8, Paul Delvaux. The Village of the Mermaids, 1942. Oil on panel, 104.3 × 124.1 cm. Gift of Mr. and Mrs. Maurice E. Culberg, 1951.73. Photograph © The Art Institute of Chicago, All rights reserved. © Artists Rights Society (ARS), New York/SABAM, Brussels

INDEX OF NAMES AND TITLES

INDEX OF FIRST LINES

INDEX OF PRINCIPAL TERMS AND TOPICS